SAMS Teach Yourself

Windows® XP
Computer Basics

Greg Perry
Jill T. Freeze
Galen A. Grimes
Matt Hayden
Ned Snell

SAMS *201 West 103rd St., Indianapolis, Indiana, 46290 USA*

Sams Teach Yourself Windows XP Computer Basics All in One
Copyright © 2003 by Sams Publishing

International Standard Book Number: 0-672-32535-7

Library of Congress Catalog Card Number: 2003102941

Printed in the United States of America

First Printing: May 2003

06   05   04   03   4   3   2

Trademarks

All terms mentioned in this book that are known to be trademarks or service marks have been appropriately capitalized. Sams Publishing cannot attest to the accuracy of this information. Use of a term in this book should not be regarded as affecting the validity of any trademark or service mark.

Warning and Disclaimer

Every effort has been made to make this book as complete and as accurate as possible, but no warranty or fitness is implied. The information provided is on an "as is" basis. The author and the publisher shall have neither liability nor responsibility to any person or entity with respect to any loss or damages arising from the information contained in this book.

Bulk Sales

Sams Publishing offers excellent discounts on this book when ordered in quantity for bulk purchases or special sales. For more information, please contact:

U.S. Corporate and Government Sales
1-800-382-3419
corpsales@pearsontechgroup.com

For sales outside of the U.S., please contact:

International Sales
+1-317-581-3793
international@pearsontechgroup.com

ACQUISITIONS EDITOR
Betsy Brown

DEVELOPMENT EDITOR
Damon Jordan

MANAGING EDITOR
Charlotte Clapp

PROJECT EDITOR
Matthew Purcell

INDEXER
Heather McNeil

PROOFREADERS
Juli Cook
Jessica McCarty

TEAM COORDINATOR
Vanessa Evans

DESIGNER
Gary Adair

PAGE LAYOUT
Bronkella Publishing
Susan Geiselman

GRAPHICS
Tammy Graham

Contents at a Glance

Contents

PART 2: Making Things Happen with Your PC   47

4 It's All About the Software   49

5 Enjoying Multimedia   61

PART 6: Seeing What the Internet Is Really About 239

17 Exploring the Internet's Technology 241

PART 13: Upgrading Your Communications and Peripherals 627

44 Upgrading Your Modem 629

45 Upgrading Your Keyboard, Mouse, and Other Input Devices 645

Lead Author

Greg Perry is a speaker and a writer on both the programming and the application sides of computing. He is known for his skills at bringing advanced computer topics to the novice's level. Perry has been a programmer and a trainer since the early 1980s, teaching at computer conferences and at the college level. He received his first degree in computer science and a master's degree in corporate finance. Perry has sold more than 2 million computer books, including such titles as *Sams Teach Yourself Windows XP in 24 Hours*, *Sams Teach Yourself Visual Basic 6 in 21 Days*, and *Sams Teach Yourself Microsoft Office XP in 24 Hours*. He also writes about rental property management and loves to travel. His favorite place to be when away from home is either at New York's Patsy's or in Italy, because he enjoys only the best pasta!

Acknowledgments

I want to send special thanks to Betsy Brown and Damon Jordan for putting up with me on this project. They were the driving force behind the work. They kept me on schedule, and what a schedule it was! Fortunately, with Sams Publishing, the people behind the books keep things flowing smoothly even when the authors don't.

This book is a compendium of information from many sources. I had the able help of numerous other authors who helped with the fundamental material within this book. My fiercely sincere gratitude goes to the following masters of writing: Jill T. Freeze, Galen A. Grimes, Matt Hayden, and Ned Snell.

In addition, the other staff and editors on this project, namely Matt Purcell, Heather McNeil, Juli Cook, Jessica McCarty, Tim Osborn and Susan Geiselman made this book better than it otherwise could be.

My lovely and gracious bride stands by my side night and day. Thank you once again. You, precious Jayne, are everything that matters to me on earth. The best parents in the world, Glen and Bettye Perry, continue to encourage and support me in every way. I am who I am because of both of them.

—Greg Perry

We Want to Hear from You!

As the reader of this book, *you* are our most important critic and commentator. We value your opinion and want to know what we're doing right, what we could do better, what areas you'd like to see us publish in, and any other words of wisdom you're willing to pass our way.

You can email or write me directly to let me know what you did or didn't like about this book—as well as what we can do to make our books stronger.

Please note that I cannot help you with technical problems related to the topic of this book, and that due to the high volume of mail I receive, I might not be able to reply to every message.

When you write, please be sure to include this book's title and author as well as your name and phone or email address. I will carefully review your comments and share them with the author and editors who worked on the book.

Email: consumer@samspublishing.com

Mail: Mark Taber
        Associate Publisher
        Sams Publishing
        201 West 103rd Street
        Indianapolis, IN 46290 USA

Reader Services

For more information about this book or others from Sams Publishing, visit our Web site at www.samspublishing.com. Type the ISBN (excluding hyphens) or the title of the book in the Search box to find the book you're looking for.

Introduction

Have you ever wished you had just one book, a truly complete reference that tells you what you need to know about your new or upgraded computer? Have you wanted one that's written in plain talk, one that tells you what you need to know to get started, and one that takes you to the next level without being too techie? Have you wanted a book that could talk to your level without talking down to you?

You are holding such a book. *Sams Teach Yourself Windows XP Computer Basics All in One* is one massive title out of the team of tomes in the *All in One* series.

The goal of this book is to provide you with all the information you need, and no more, to understand these topics:

- Windows XP
- Computer Hardware Basics
- Computer Software Basics
- Microsoft Office
- Upgrades and Computer Fixes
- Networking Issues

The expert teachers, trainers, and technical writers who put this book together all understand precisely what computer problems you face and they know how to provide the solutions. For example, if you've bought your first computer and have no idea how to start a program, the answer is here. If you want to create a network computer system for an organization and provide security and reliability, the answer is here.

Who Should Read This Book?

This book is for everyday computer users who want one single book that helps make them better computer users. In addition, this text takes most users to a higher level of mastery.

Don't buy five or more books when this one takes you to where you want to be.

What This Book Does for You

Although this book is not a complicated reference book, you learn something about almost every aspect of computers from a typical user's point of view. As you progress through the book, your skills will increase.

Those of you who are tired of the plethora of quick-fix computer titles cluttering today's shelves will find a welcome reprieve here. This book presents both the background and descriptions that a Windows XP-based computer user needs. In addition to the background, this book is practical and provides hundreds and hundreds of step-by-step walk-throughs that you can work through to gain practical hands-on experience. These tasks guide you through all the common actions you need to make your Windows XP computer work for you.

Conventions Used in This Book

This book uses several common conventions to help teach its topics most effectively. Here is a summary of those typographical conventions:

- Commands, computer output, and words you type appear in a special `monospaced computer font`.
- To type a shortcut key, such as Alt+F, press and hold the first key, and then press the second key before releasing both keys.
- If a task requires you to select from a menu, the book separates menu commands with a comma. For example, File, Save As is used to select the Save As option from the File menu.

In addition to typographical conventions, the following special elements are included to set off different types of information to make them easily recognizable:

Special notes augment the material you read in each chapter. These notes clarify concepts and procedures.

You find numerous tips that offer shortcuts and solutions to common problems.

The cautions are about pitfalls. Reading them saves you time and trouble.

Sidebars

Take some time out of your training to sit back and enjoy a more in-depth look at a particular feature. The sidebars are useful for exploring unusual features and show you additional ways to utilize the chapter material.

PART I

Understanding Computer Fundamentals

Chapter

CHAPTER 1

Beyond the On Switch...

Now you're ready to start computing. You've lugged the boxes into your home or office and have managed to piece together all the cables, cords, and system components. At last, it's time to start setting up the machine and getting it to work for you.

Go ahead—flip the switch, press the button, or do whatever your computer's manufacturer tells you to do to get the thing up and running. Did you hear that? That sound was Windows revving into action. If you bought your computer recently, the tones you heard were most likely those of Microsoft Windows XP, Home Edition (the operating system we'll focus on in this book). If you use an earlier operating system, you're not left in the cold though because so much of the underlying computer basics work the same under all operating systems and environments.

What Is an Operating System?

Now that you've joined the ranks of proud computer owners everywhere, you'll need to adjust your definition of windows. Rather than being a mere clear pane of glass that separates you from rain, snow, bitter cold, and sweltering heat, it also now is Windows with a capital *W*.

Even if you're entering the world of computers for the first time, you've undoubtedly heard about Microsoft Windows. It's that revolutionary, controversial operating system that caused such a stir over its inclusion of the Microsoft Internet Explorer web browser. Court battles went on for ages until eventually Microsoft allowed computer manufacturers like Gateway and Dell to remove Internet Explorer or include non-Microsoft software.

Operating system? Web browser? First things first. We all know how air traffic controllers monitor airport comings and goings to make sure everything runs smoothly, right? Well that's basically what an operating system does on your computer. It tells various pieces of software what to do when. The operating system is the brain of the PC because it has to do all the thinking. Windows helps your PC prioritize its workload in much the same way corporate managers need to prioritize and re-prioritize depending on the projects or crises at hand.

A PC without an operating system is like a flashlight without batteries—pretty much useless. Given that, the operating system is the first piece of software to be installed on your machine. In virtually every case, the operating system is preinstalled on your new computer so that when you hook up the machine and turn it on for the first time, you'll be greeted by what's known as the Windows desktop (see Figure 1.1). Your Windows desktop may differ by displaying a different background picture or more items on top of the picture than Figure 1.1 shows.

FIGURE 1.1
The modernized look of the Windows XP Home Edition Desktop is the first thing you'll see once your computer finishes booting.

Once an operating system has been successfully installed however, you can do all sorts of neat things with your new investment. You can install a word processor to generate a professional-looking resume. You can get a spreadsheet application and perform all kinds of complex calculations. You can play the hottest computer games. And with Windows XP, you can effortlessly publish family photos to the Web, "burn" a music CD containing all your favorite tunes, and even create a funky music video. And these ideas only scratch the surface of what you can do with your PC!

So What's Behind the Name "Windows"?

Windows is much more than just a product name. In fact, its introduction represented a new way of computing (that is, it's "new" when you compare it to how things were done in the early years of personal computing). Way back in the old days of personal computing, machines were run by an operating system called *DOS*. With DOS, you could do only one thing at a time. If you were writing a letter and needed to reference a specific number in a spreadsheet, for example, you would have to shut down the word processing program, open the spreadsheet application to get the information you needed, shut down the spreadsheet program, and finally reopen the word processor to continue drafting your letter—a major hassle to say the least.

After much research and development time, the folks at Microsoft came up with an operating system that allowed users to do two things at once (known as *multitasking*). That operating system was known as *Microsoft Windows* because it literally created a separate window for each application or task you had running. That enabled you to easily hop from your word processor to the spreadsheet and back again with a few simple mouse clicks—a major improvement over the cumbersome, text-based DOS.

Windows offered other advantages besides multitasking, however. At the time Windows was created, Macintosh computers were reputedly the most user-friendly because they relied heavily on graphics rather than esoteric keyboard commands in order to complete various tasks. For example, to print a document, you would click on a picture of a printer rather than typing in the Print command, pressing Ctrl+P, etc. With Windows, you can still use those shortcuts, but new users also have a more foolproof method of learning how to use their PC's pictures (also known as *icons*).

> Those gooey graphics... When a program depends on the user clicking icons in order to run, the collection of graphics and resulting commands are referred to as a graphical user interface (or GUI, as in "My daughter Samantha just loves chewy, gooey brownies, fresh from the oven.").

Microsoft tried to emulate Mac's ease of use in Windows. It took a few revisions of the software to produce a viable product, but it has evolved and improved over time to become the operating system you have on your computer today: Windows XP, Home Edition.

How Can I Tell If I Have Windows XP?

Many of the leading computer manufacturers, such as Gateway, Dell, and so on, started shipping their systems with Windows XP, Home Edition in late October 2001. The same goes for machines sold in stores across the country.

If the version of Windows you have isn't clearly identified in the printed documentation included with your computer, then turn on your machine and watch it boot (start up).

When Windows is ready to launch, you'll see the logo for the operating system you have installed on your machine. If you miss it in passing, the default grassland wallpaper (which is actually referred to as Bliss in some more advanced Windows options) and bright green Start button in the lower-left corner of the screen is a dead giveaway that you're running Microsoft Windows XP, Home Edition.

Even if you don't have Windows XP, you'll still be able to learn a great deal from this book. In fact, the differences between various versions of Windows are minimal in many ways with the exception of a few new bells and whistles, which you'll read about later this chapter.

These differences typically appear in subtle things, such as in changes in the graphics as opposed to more radical variations of how tasks are done. After you've spent some time behind the keyboard with Windows XP, everything you may have learned or experienced in an earlier version of Windows will come rushing back to you.

Looking at Windows XP

If your computer runs Windows XP, here is a small sampling of how your operating system differs from others (we'll dive into the details of some of these features in the chapters that follow):

- **Easy PC sharing**—If you like your icons big, and your spouse likes them small, you're both in luck! Windows XP lets you save your personal preferences into separate accounts that you can now move to and from with ease.
- **New Task-Focused design**—Rather than presenting users with an often esoteric assortment of words and phrases from which to choose an option, Windows now

"asks" you what you'd like to do based on your current activity on the machine. For example, opening the My Documents folder from the Start menu will present you with the following possibilities: Make a new folder, and Publish this folder to the Web. It may not sound like much now, but compared with the old maze of menus, it is truly a big deal.

- **See Your Photo Data**—When browsing your folders full of documents, Windows XP can show you a thumbnail picture of the selected document. That way you can verify you have the material you want before you launch the necessary program and open the wrong file.

- **Photo-friendly**—Connecting a digital camera to your PC is easier than ever with Windows XP, and once the photos are on your hard drive, you can effortlessly create a slide show, print them, publish them to the Web, email them to a friend, or even order professional quality prints from one of Microsoft's Internet partners.

- **A Gamer's delight**—With XP's new Compatibility Mode, running older computer games is a snap. No more fretting over whether your favorite game will run on the new operating system.

- **Get remote assistance**—For those who don't have an in-house computer expert: It's called *Remote Assistance*. That's right, you can now email your favorite computer nerd an invitation to come and fix your computer. That person can take control of your machine from another location entirely (with your permission of course)!

- **Make movies like a pro**—If you've ever fantasized about being the next pop star, then you're in for a treat. Microsoft has spruced up Windows movie-making tools to bring you a simple moviemaker. It's easier than ever to send videos via email, publish them to the Web, make music videos, and add special effects and voiceovers to your movies.

Some operating system version releases are little more than bug fixes, but Windows XP's major overhaul and facelift may very well sport enough funky new features to make upgrading worthwhile to current computer owners who have not yet made the move.

What's What on the Windows Desktop

As you read earlier, after your computer boots, you'll see a screen similar to the one shown in Figure 1.1. This view is known as the Windows *Desktop*. In Figure 1.2, study the desktop elements.

This desktop is meant to resemble your desk at work or in your den in that it keeps the most regularly used items close at hand. In the case of Windows, however, those items include shortcut icons and task buttons rather than pens, note paper, scissors, and tape.

FIGURE **1.2**

These are the crucial parts of the Windows Desktop.

Desktop ———

Start button ———

Task/Window button   Taskbar   Shortcut icon   Notification area

The more time you spend on your computer, the more these technical terms will become second nature to you. When you think about it, many of the terms are self-explanatory anyway.

The Windows Desktop: Just Another Pretty Face

Like your desktop at work, the Windows desktop is the surface you can actually see when the desktop is clean of application windows (in other words, the word processor, email program, Web browser, and so on are all closed). Instead of wood grain Formica however, the Windows desktop is adorned with a colorful image of grassland that you can easily change, as you will learn in the next chapter.

The sole purpose of the Windows desktop is to hold all those important program buttons and icons. Believe it or not, it can get just as cluttered as your desk if you're not careful!

Taking Shortcuts

The little pictures you see dotting your Windows desktop are called *icons*. Microsoft ships Windows with a lone Recycle Bin icon in the lower right corner of the screen, but chances are your PC manufacturer loaded your desktop with goodies when they pre-installed all that free software for you.

Each icon is a graphical representative of your word processing program, your Internet connection, or some other application. When you double-click an icon, the corresponding program (or document or Web site) launches.

Don't fret over how to double-click the icons properly; I'll bring you up to speed on working with your mouse in a moment.

You also should be aware that you could put your own shortcuts on the desktop. This gives you immediate access to the resources you use most. I'll show you how to create your own shortcuts in the next lesson.

Getting a Good Start in Computing

As you'll quickly discover, the Windows Start button is where it all begins. By clicking it, you open lists of everything on your computer. These lists are called *menus* because you can make a selection from the items presented to you.

Try clicking the bright green Start button. If you've ever used Windows before, you'll notice a striking difference—the Start menu has become larger, more colorful, and customizable.

The menu appears in two columns. The white part on the left is where Windows displays your most frequently used applications. (I'll show you how to modify this number in your next chapter.) The blue part on the right is reserved for shortcuts to predefined Windows folders, the Control Panel, and the Search and Help tools.

FIGURE 1.3
Windows XP, Home Edition keeps your most frequently used programs close at hand.

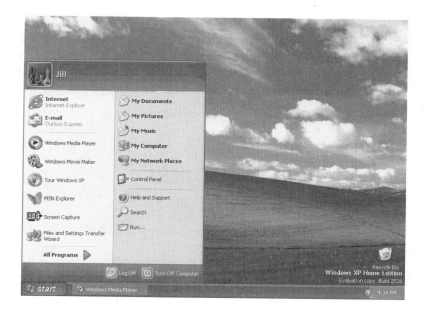

Dealing with the Tasks at Hand

At the bottom of your screen is a narrow, bright blue band known as the taskbar. This is where you'll find a button for each application you have running (or, as is the case with Microsoft Word and Excel, each document you have open). Simply click the desired button, and the corresponding item appears at the front of your display.

The Windows taskbar is without a doubt the simplest way to move from one task to another. And in Windows XP, it's become a lot less cluttered. In previous versions of Windows, there would be a task button for each Word document open. Now Word has a single button, which, when clicked, displays a list of all open Word documents from which you can choose (see Figure 1.4).

FIGURE 1.4

Consolidated taskbar buttons keep clutter under control.

Presenting the Windows Notification Area

As was illustrated in Figure 1.2, the Notification Area is in the lower right corner of the Windows desktop. At bare minimum, it holds the system's clock and icons for MSN Messenger Service if you use Messenger, as well as alerts for available Windows updates.

Other tools you may find there, depending on the software you have installed and the type of machine you're using, might include an icon to access your antivirus program; your RealPlayer program that plays sounds and movies on the Web; and, in the case of laptops, an icon showing whether the computer is powered by electricity or its battery.

We'll revisit some of these tools in greater depth as you progress through the lessons in this book.

Making (Mouse) Tracks

Working with Windows requires using a mouse—that sometimes-corded, sometimes-wireless two-or-more button thing that sits next to your keyboard (see Figure 1.5), or a similar pointing device such as a touch pad or trackball.

FIGURE 1.5

This little rodent will help you get all your work done in a snap.

Mice components can get clogged with dust and lint, making them more frustrating than useful. Likewise, trackballs can tire your wrists or fingers. To spare you the agony, consider an optical wheel mouse. Such a mouse is comfortable in your hand; navigation by the optical light eliminates the skipping and jumpiness commonly associated with standard mice; the wheel makes scrolling up and down Web pages and Word documents trivial; and the two side buttons act as Back and Forward buttons on your Web browser. With special software installed, you can do even more with these mice.

To make getting used to your mouse easier, you can walk through a fun and educational exercise in a moment that will help you get used to moving the pointer where you want it.

Some mice are not mice. If you have a laptop, you may be using a touch pad instead of a mouse. Or maybe you tried a trackball at your friend's house and decided to use one of those rather than a mouse. In any case, you can still follow the steps below even if you're not working with a mouse. Rather than dragging the mouse in the direction indicated, touch pad users will move their index finger in the same direction across the touch pad. Likewise, trackball users will roll the little ball as indicated. No matter what type of pointing device you use, it's imperative that you grow comfortable with it.

Learning All the Moves

Perform the following steps to start getting acquainted with your pointing device of choice:

1. If you've not already done so, turn on your computer.
2. After you see a screen similar to the one shown in Figure 1.1, jiggle your mouse around to help you find the pointer. You're looking for a small, white arrow.

3. When the arrow is in sight, try to drag it in the direction of the Start button.

4. With the arrow resting over the top of the Start button, press the left mouse button. You'll see a Start menu similar to the one shown in Figure 1.6.

FIGURE 1.6

The Start menu is the first step in locating what has been installed on your computer.

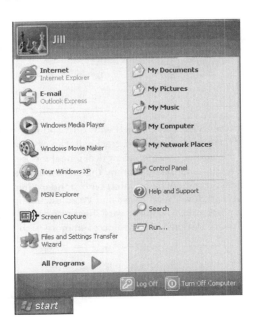

5. Hover the mouse pointer over the green More Programs arrow. An expanded Programs menu pops out. A black arrow to the right of a word means another menu will appear if that option is selected.

6. From the resulting menu, point to Games and then click Solitaire. The window shown in Figure 1.7 appears.

7. That's right, a game actually helps you master mouse-eye coordination! Look at the cards that are face up and see if there are any valid moves.

Not sure what you're doing? For those of you who aren't familiar with the rules of Solitaire, here's an oversimplification. The object is to get all the aces up top and build them up, one-by-one, according to suit. You reveal additional cards by arranging them in descending order, alternating red and black suits as you go. Don't knock yourself out trying to become a Solitaire pro; the point here is to get comfortable using Windows. Be warned that Solitaire can be very addicting; it may be hard to stop playing once you start!

FIGURE 1.7

Solitaire is a fun way to learn how to control your mouse.

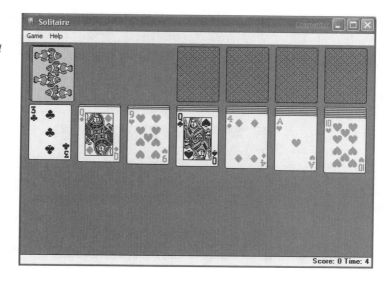

8. If there are any aces at the front of any of the lines of cards, simply double-click them (press the left mouse button twice in rapid succession), and they will automatically move up to one of the four slots at the top of the screen.

9. To move a card from one row to another, click on it and, with the button still pressed, drag the card to the desired location and release the button to drop it. This maneuver is referred to as *drag-and-drop*.

10. After you make all possible moves, click the pile of cards on the upper left to draw a card and place it like you did the others. If it doesn't fit anywhere, draw again.

11. Keep playing until you've made all possible moves and have run out of cards in the draw pile.

12. Hooked and want to play again? Click the word "Game" at the left end of the gray bar at the top of the Solitaire window to reveal a menu. Choose Deal to play another round, or Exit to end the game and close the window.

The more you play, the more at ease you should feel working with Windows and your mouse. Who said learning couldn't be fun?

That's All, Folks!

You need to understand how to safely shut the computer down. Don't just flip the switch; that could stress your machine and make the next start up a long, agonizing process as Windows attempts to repair itself.

To make life more pleasant for you and your computer, do the following when you're ready to shut down the machine for the day:

1. Click the bright green Start button.

2. Click the red Turn Off Computer button. The Turn Off Computer screen shown in Figure 1.8 appears.

FIGURE 1.8

From here, you can put your PC on standby, turn it off, reboot it, or cancel the entire process.

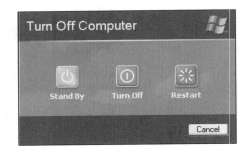

3. Click Turn Off, and the PC will safely power down on its own.

Summary

In this chapter, you learned how to find your way around the Windows desktop. As you'll continue to discover in subsequent lessons, comfort with Windows is vital to your success with PCs. By now, you also should feel a lot better about using a mouse. From this point on, it only gets easier! If you're a new computer user, understand that sometimes newcomers find that progress is hampered by the ability to use a mouse effectively. The old adage, "Practice makes perfect," applies to mouse use as well. After a few hands of Solitaire you'll be a pro!

CHAPTER 2

Diving into Windows

No two people are alike, so why should your Windows desktop look (and sound) like everyone else's? Whether you're an animal lover and want your PC to reflect that, or you simply can't stand the thought of staring at that blissful grassy knoll background another day, you'll be happy to know you can change all that and more. Once this chapter presents an overview of Windows, you'll have enough understanding to work with your computer for a while before returning in Chapter 6 to master more Windows tricks.

Rearranging the Desktop Icons

If you want to move a certain shortcut icon from one location to another, simply click it and drag it into position, just as you dragged the Solitaire cards in the last chapter.

For more global changes in the icon layout, right-click on a clean spot of the desktop (any part of your background picture that has no icons or text) and select Arrange Icons By from the resulting shortcut menu (see Figure 2.1).

This produces a menu of choices for arranging the icons including by Name, Type, Size, or Date Modified. Just click the desired option to rearrange your desktop in the specified order. By default, the icons are auto arranged, which means Windows automatically places them in the most space-efficient, aesthetically appealing layout.

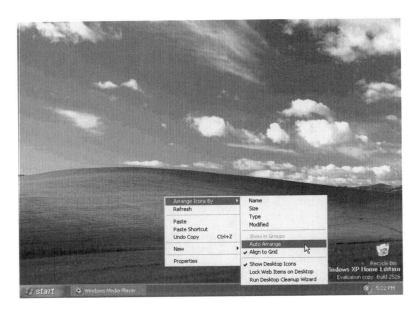

When you're working with a dozen open windows at once, it takes a long time to minimize each window individually. To minimize all application windows at one time, simply right-click the taskbar and click Show the Desktop from the menu. That clears the desktop in a flash, leaving the respective task buttons available on the taskbar so you can get back to work in an instant.

Enlarging Your Desktop Icons

Small detailed icons can be difficult to see depending on your monitor, eyesight, and lighting. Fortunately, Windows makes it easy to enlarge the icons without affecting the way your programs run.

To make your desktop icons larger, just follow these steps:

1. If you can't see a piece of your Windows desktop, right-click the taskbar and click Show the Desktop from the resulting shortcut menu.

2. Right-click over the desktop to reveal the same shortcut menu you accessed to arrange your icons (see Figure 2.1).

3. Select the Properties item from the menu to open the Display Properties *dialog box*.

Although the term dialog box may sound a bit intimidating, the concept is quite simple. A dialog box basically is a window that opens and prompts you to provide information or answer a question.

4. The Display Properties dialog box contains a series of tabs that you can open to change various settings. Access the Appearance tab and then click the Effects button to see the options in Figure 2.2.

FIGURE 2.2
The Effects dialog box.

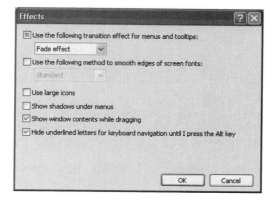

5. Next, click the Use Large Icons check box.

6. Click the OK button to exit the dialog box and click OK again to clear the Display Properties dialog box. In a few moments, the icons will be larger.

To return the icons to their normal size, just repeat the preceding steps. The option check box is like a toggle button—clicking it turns the option to the opposite state you found it in (that is, clicking an enabled option turns it off; clicking it a second time turns it on again, and so on).

Maximize Screen Size by Hiding the Taskbar

Depending on your work style, the taskbar can occasionally take up valuable real estate onscreen that could be better allocated to your work.

If this situation describes you, then you may want to consider hiding your taskbar. When hidden, the taskbar stays out of sight until you hover the mouse pointer over the taskbar area. At that point it pops up, letting you work with it as usual.

While it increases the amount of viewing area onscreen, it has the drawback of being a royal pain when working on the bottom portion of a program window. That may not seem like a problem at first glance, but many popular programs have buttons in that area you need to get to on a regular basis. You may be trying to use the scroll bars to navigate your document and find the taskbar popping up at seemingly random intervals.

If the hiding taskbar gets in the way of your work, there's another possibility that may let you have your cake and eat it too, so to speak. Consider moving the taskbar to one side of the screen. That way you can gain the onscreen real estate without making yourself crazy. To move the taskbar, you'll first have to unlock it. To do this, just right-click the taskbar and click the Lock the Taskbar option to remove the checkmark. Then click the taskbar and drag it toward the desired edge of the screen while holding the left mouse button down. An outline of the taskbar's footprint appears in the specified location. If you like what you see, release the button to drop the taskbar into place.

To make your taskbar disappear until you need it again, simply do the following:

1. Make sure part of your taskbar is empty. This is crucial to getting the menu you'll need.
2. Right-click over the taskbar to open its corresponding shortcut menu.
3. Select the Properties item to launch the Taskbar Properties dialog box.
4. Select the Taskbar tab of the Taskbar and Start Menu Properties dialog box as shown in Figure 2.3.
5. Click the Auto-hide the taskbar check box to enable the option, and then click OK to exit the dialog box.

You can repeat the process to restore the taskbar to its previous state.

Figure 2.3

The Taskbar tab of the Taskbar Properties dialog box is where you'll find the setting to hide your taskbar.

Banishing the Desktop Blues

You might want to change your desktop's appearance either because you get bored with the default background or you want to put pictures of your family, pets, or a corporate logo on the background.

Changing the Background Texture Using Files Provided

The simplest way to make a switch is to change the display's background using one of the files provided by Microsoft with Windows.

To do this, you'll need to perform the following steps:

1. Right-click over an uncovered portion of the desktop to open the now-familiar shortcut menu.

2. Choose the Properties item to launch the Display Properties dialog box.

3. Select the Desktop tab shown in Figure 2.4.

4. In the Background section of the tab, select the name of the file you want to use by clicking it. You'll see a preview of what it will look like in the monitor at the top of the tab.

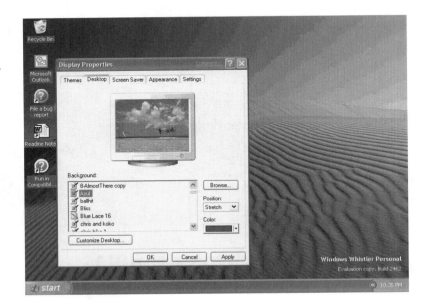

5. If you like what you see, click OK to apply the design to your desktop. If it doesn't quite suit you, keep choosing from the designs available until you find the right one. You can also use the Color drop-down box (the arrow button) to select a solid color background for your desktop.

Put Your Own Pictures on Your Desktop

If you get a scanner or digital camera someday, you might be interested to know that you can even use those images for your background. Just follow the preceding steps, except rather than choosing the name of a background file, click the Browse button and surf over to the desired file. The only gotcha is the file needs to be in .bmp or .jpg format. Not only can you use a personal image, but you can click the black arrow next to the Display options box in the Background tab to choose an effect for the image. As the following figures illustrate, you can stretch, center, or tile the image.

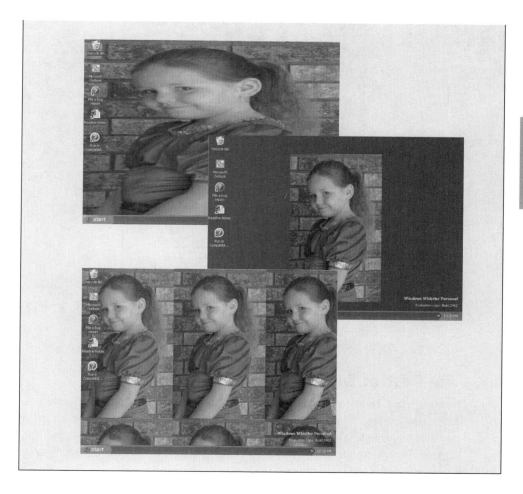

Coming Up with a New Scheme

Microsoft has taken the facelift thing even further by enabling you to choose a totally new color scheme for Windows as a whole. Not only can you change the desktop color, but you also can change the colors of other Windows elements, such as dialog boxes.

To apply a new color scheme, just follow these simple steps:

1. Find a clear area of your desktop and right-click it to access the shortcut menu.

2. Click the Properties menu item to open the familiar Display Properties dialog box.

3. Click the Themes tab and use the drop-down box (click the arrow button) to choose a new theme for your desktop, as shown in Figure 2.5.

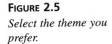

FIGURE 2.5

Select the theme you prefer.

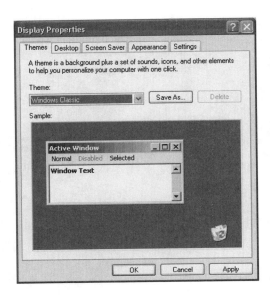

4. After you click the name of the chosen color scheme, you can preview it at the bottom of the tab.

5. Click OK to apply your selected color scheme and exit the dialog box.

The Best of Desktop Decorating

Not only can you add special images to your desktop, but you can install entire desktop themes containing a wide range of sounds and animations as well. You can turn your PC into a virtual jungle complete with monkey noises, among other possibilities! Some desktop themes even include customized animated mouse pointers that change, depending on where the mouse is hovering.

While you may not have many themes at your disposal now (you have to admit it would take a bit more than a Windows Classic theme to cause a stir), just wait until you become skilled with using the Internet! If you surf over to www.themeworld.com, you will find hundreds of desktop themes devoted to TV shows, cars, rock stars, cartoons, you name it.

Web sites with their own themes available for free download will have their own downloading and installation instructions, so be sure to read them thoroughly before you attempt to download and install them. If you're not careful, you could end up stuck with honking geese for new email alert sounds and car crashes for Windows shutdown sounds permanently!

Defining Your Own Desktop Shortcuts

The best way to define a shortcut for easy access depends on the type of file you're dealing with. If the item is a document or Web page, you can simply click on its icon and drag it to a clear space on your desktop.

When you attempt to drag-and-drop an icon, one of two things will happen. Either it appears on your desktop on the spot, or Windows launches a dialog box saying it can't move the selected item in that manner. If Windows is unable to create the shortcut on the spot, it asks you if you really intended to make a shortcut. Click the Yes button, and Windows does what it needs to build the shortcut.

2

So where do you find a file's icon? Click the Start button followed by the My Computer link and then click your way to the desired file. This will make more sense to you after you've worked more with Windows and completed a few more chapters of this text. In the case of Web pages, surf to the Web page you want; then drag its icon from the Internet Explorer Address Bar to your desktop. (The location of the Address Bar will be covered in Chapter 19, "Browsing Basics.")

Customizing the Windows XP Start Menu

One of the draws of Windows XP is its ability to offer customized Start menus. You can tell Windows what you do and do not want it to display, you can tell it how you want the information displayed, or you can even have it serve up frequently opened documents or spreadsheets.

Changing the Look of Your Start Menu

Windows XP not only lets you change the size of the icons displayed on your Start menu, but you can also tell it how many of your most recently used applications you want it to show at any given time.

To make these adjustments, just follow these steps:

1. Right-click the Start button and select Properties from the menu. (Gee, you've done that a time or two before, haven't you?)
2. Open the Start Menu tab of the Taskbar and Start Menu dialog box.
3. Next, click the Customize button. The Customize Start Menu dialog box shown in Figure 2.6 pops up with the General tab displayed by default.

FIGURE 2.6

The power of customized Start menus starts here.

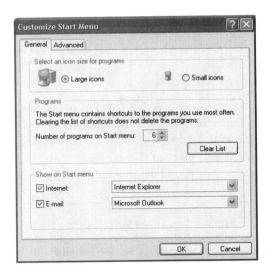

4. In the first section of the dialog box, you can choose whether you want the Start menu icons to be large or small by clicking the respective button. (Large icons are displayed by default.)

5. The middle section of the dialog box is where you will specify how many recently used programs you want Windows to give you instant access to. The default number is 6; however, you can adjust this number as desired by clicking the arrow button and clicking the number you want. Your choices range from a low of zero, to a high of nine.

In time, you may find your Start menu cluttered with all kinds of programs you may not want or need anymore. You can clear this list of program shortcuts by clicking the Clear List button. Of course, this doesn't remove the programs from your machine; it simply clears the list of most recently used programs so only the most heavily used (your default Internet and email programs in Microsoft's opinion) remain.

6. Finally, in the bottom section of the dialog box, you can decide whether or not you want Windows to include your Internet or email programs on the list. Just check the option (or options) you want; then use the arrow buttons to select the specific Internet and email program you want it to display. Typically, Internet Explorer and Outlook Express will appear by default.

7. When the settings meet with your approval, click OK to dismiss the Customize Start Menu dialog box. You'll need to click OK again to close the Taskbar and Start Menu dialog box.

Summary

In this chapter, you learned many ways to personalize your Windows desktop. From reorganizing the icons to modifying the background's appearance and creating your own special shortcuts, it's all here. In many cases, tinkering with these settings is as much a necessity as it is fun. Visually impaired individuals can benefit immensely from larger icons or high contrast desktop color schemes. It can even enhance your productivity by keeping frequently used programs and documents close at hand.

In the next chapter, "Keeping Your PC Healthy," you will be introduced to a number of tools you can use to keep your computer in tip-top shape.

2

CHAPTER 3

Health Care for PCs

The more software you install or uninstall and the more files you add or delete, the more pertinent it becomes to perform maintenance on your system. Whether you are trying to accomplish an advanced task or you are trying to figure out why your computer is acting up, you will find the troubleshooting tips and tricks in this chapter helpful.

Just when you think you have the hang of controlling this hunk of machinery, the unexpected happens. Maybe your monitor doesn't flicker into action when you boot your machine, or perhaps your computer doesn't seem to recognize the new CD you just put into the CD drive.

Archiving Your Files

To protect your valuable data, it's best to make an extra copy of it. The easiest way to do so is to back up your files onto a diskette, recordable CD, or a Zip drive cartridge. Then, if something happens to the original file (or worse yet, to your hard drive), you can restore the backup copy onto your hard drive.

Choosing Your Backup Media

With today's computers, data files are typically backed up onto diskette, CD, or Zip drive. Owners of older PCs also had the option of using Jaz drive media and tape backup units, but the limited storage capability, high price of storage media, and lack of market share made these options all but disappear in the light of affordable CD recording capabilities.

With all these options, deciding what to use when may get a bit confusing. There are basically three factors that should be considered in making your decision: (1) what devices you have available to you, (2) what type of data you want to back up, and (3) your intended use of the backup media.

Do You Have Drive?

Almost every machine has a floppy drive, but other devices or drives are often optional. Obviously, the type of backup method you use will depend on your computer's components. If you have a recordable/read writable CD drive and/or a Zip drive, you will also need to take the following factor into account when making your decision.

So That's What You Want to Put on That Disk!

If your goal is to back up word processing documents or spreadsheets, just about any of the backup media options will do. However, when it comes to graphic-intensive documents, photographs, and audio and video files, you will need to take into account the storage capacity of each type of media. Table 3.1 shows you just how much material you can fit onto each type of storage media.

TABLE 3.1   Storage capacity of various types of media.

Media	Data capacity
High-density diskette	1.44MB
Zip disk	100MB or 250MB
CD-ROM	650MB

You can fit more than 300,000 pages of text on a single CD-ROM. That's more than 400 copies of this book on one CD, excluding graphics!

With that in mind, it should come as no real surprise that in order to deal with the large files such as photographs, video files, or music files, you will need to work with CD-ROMs or Zip disks or other large capacity media that you find at the computer store.

Music files can also get large in a hurry. A standard 3- to 4-minute song can easily reach 3MB when converted to the popular MP3 format. The larger and more numerous your file collection gets, the more important backing up your data becomes.

CD-Rs versus CD-RWs

When you go shopping for blank CDs, you will notice that there are two kinds: CD-R (recordable) and CD-RW (read writable). The newest drives will record on either, but check your documentation because some older drives will accept only one type.

CD-Rs can only be written to once. You can always add data to the unused parts of the disk with the right software, but you can't overwrite the data recorded on the disk; once it's there, it's there for good. This makes it a fine alternative for creating music CDs and virtual photo albums but perhaps a waste for data backup, since you would probably want to overwrite your data backups periodically to reflect any changes.

CD-RWs are sort of like overgrown diskettes; you can write over them again and again, making them good data backup candidates. However, CD-RWs can only be read by other CD-RW drives. If the plan is to make a CD to play in your car or at a friend's party, you will definitely need to go with CD-Rs.

3

What Are Your Plans for the Disk?

When deciding which type of backup media to use, make sure that the intended recipient can work with it. Also, think back to the earlier caution about the differences in blank CDs.

Defragmenting Your Hard Drive

When a file is stored to a hard drive, it is broken into tiny chunks, and each piece is stored in the first available sector of the hard drive. After the drive starts getting full and files are deleted (creating certain random sectors available here and there on the hard drive), file parts are no longer saved in adjacent sectors.

Thus a file may be scattered (or *fragmented*) all over the drive, which can slow down its retrieval. To improve the speed of your PC, you should defragment your hard drive. Defragmenting reorganizes the parts of each file so that they are once again adjacent to each other on the hard drive, eliminating excess search time.

Analyze Before You Defragment

Defragmenting a drive can take seemingly ages, especially with the huge hard drives installed in new computers these days. Windows XP gives you the opportunity to analyze the hard drive before committing to a full defragmentation. The analysis takes almost no time at all, and it will tell you whether a full defragmentation is warranted.

Follow these steps to see whether it is time to defrag your hard drive:

1. Click the Start button; then point to All Programs, Accessories, System Tools, and click the Disk Fragmenter option. The Disk Fragmenter program window opens (see Figure 3.1).

FIGURE 3.1

Any hard drives you have installed in your computer will appear in the Volume display window.

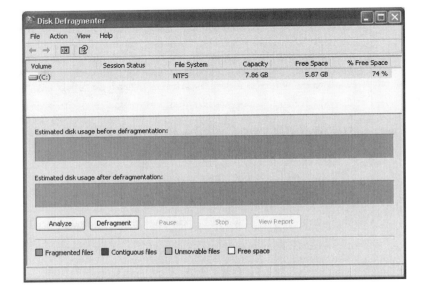

2. By default, your primary hard drive should already be highlighted. Verify that this is the case and then click the Analyze button on the lower left part of the window.

3. After the Disk Fragmenter has finished its analysis, you will see a report that shows the defragmentation analysis. You are given three options: View Report, Defragment, and Close. If the utility recommends that you defrag your hard drive and you have the time, go ahead and click the Defragment button. Otherwise, click Close and return to the task later. If the drive appears to be in good shape, simply click Close.

4. Close Disk Defragmenter by clicking the red x button in the upper right corner of the window.

> If you look in the Analysis display in the center of the screen, you see a color-keyed representation of the state of your hard drive. Red marks space containing fragmented files, blue marks space occupied by files in a single location, green marks space housing files that cannot be moved, and finally white denotes free disk space. The more white and blue you see, the better it is. A lot of red means a disk defragmentation is definitely in order.

Running the Defragmenter

If you opted to run Disk Defragmenter at a later date, simply launch the program as you did previously, only this time, click the Defragment button instead of the Analyze button. The utility will work its way through the hard drive, making any repairs it can.

Generally, defragging a cluttered, fragmented hard drive helps Windows run a bit more smoothly.

Cleaning Your Disk

Another tool that can help you recover chewed-up space on your hard drive is the Disk Cleanup utility. It analyzes the specified disk, comes back with a list of "safe" files to delete, and lets you select which ones you want removed.

The amount of space you can recover using this tool varies from a fraction of a megabyte to tens of megabytes, so the results will vary, depending on the way you use your machine (or perhaps the way you have used your machine in the past).

Here are the steps you will want to take to reclaim some of your disk space:

1. To begin the Disk Cleanup process, click Start and then choose All Programs, Accessories, System Tools, and click Disk Cleanup.

2. After a bit of behind-the-scenes work, the Disk Cleanup tab shown in Figure 3.2 opens, showing you which files you can safely delete and how much disk space you would regain by making the selected deletions.

3. Click a file type's name to see a description of what it is and how deleting it would affect your system. Place a checkmark in the checkboxes of file types you want to remove from your system. Should you change your mind about deleting a file type, simply click the checkbox a second time to remove the check.

4. When you are ready to start deleting the files, click OK. The utility will ask you if you are sure about the deletion. Click Yes or No as appropriate. A status bar

appears, displaying the progress of the job. When the files have been successfully deleted, the application shuts itself down.

FIGURE 3.2

You might be surprised by just how much disk space you can get back.

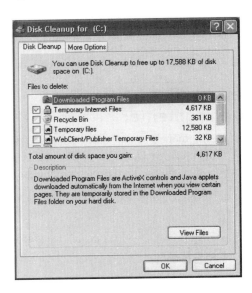

Protecting Yourself Against Computer Viruses

Much like humans can catch a bug from unsuspecting carriers, computers can catch a virus. With a thorough understanding of viruses, how they are transmitted, what their symptoms are, and how you can protect yourself, your PC can lead a long, healthy life.

Antivirus Programs: Vitamin C for Your PC

The best bet for safe computing is getting, installing, running, and most importantly, updating, a good antivirus program. The two most popular antivirus manufacturers are Norton and McAfee.

There is a good chance your computer's manufacturer may have preinstalled one on your system before you bought it. It would be worth your while to poke around your computer's files a bit to see if such a treasure exists. If it does, spend a few minutes getting acquainted with the program. Learn how to turn it on and off, register it for regular updates, and even give it a test run on your hard drive in order to get comfortable with it.

From that moment on, keep the program running in the background so that it scans every file you come in contact with. If that drags down your system's performance too much, scan for viruses manually by following these steps:

1. Click the Start button and then click My Computer.

2. Next, click the name of the hard drive, floppy drive, or removable device you want to scan for viruses.

3. In the Tasks pane on the left side of the screen, you will see a Scan for viruses command (if an antivirus program is installed on your PC). Click that link to initiate the scan. The length of time required to complete the scan will depend on how large (or how small) the item is you're scanning.

4. Check your antivirus program's documentation for further instructions.

When Bad Things Happen to Good Systems: Using System Restore

"I downloaded a screensaver from the Internet and installed it on my computer. My PC hasn't been the same since!"

Something as simple as installing a computer game can alter files on your system and unintentionally create all kinds of problems for you. Sadly, in the past the only solution seemed to be to reformat the machine's hard drive and reinstall everything from scratch.

With Windows XP's new System Restore feature, you can literally take your computer back in time to when it worked its best, and most importantly, all your data files will remain perfectly intact.

To restore your system to a previous working state, follow these steps:

1. Launch System Restore by clicking the Start button; then choose All Programs, Accessories, System Tools, System Restore. The System Restore welcome screen appears (see Figure 3.3).

2. Next, click the Restore my computer to an earlier time button and press the Next button.

3. A calendar like the one shown in Figure 3.4 opens, asking you to click a date and time to which you'd like to restore your computer.

4. After you have chosen a date and time that you recall the PC working its best, click the Next button.

FIGURE 3.3

A brief explanation of what System Restore does appears on the left side of the screen.

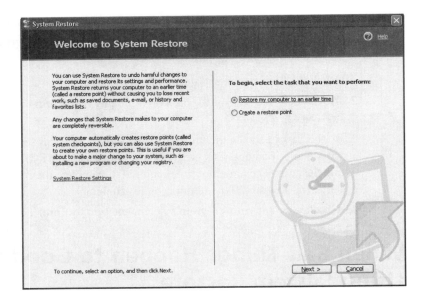

FIGURE 3.4

Pick your day to go back in time.

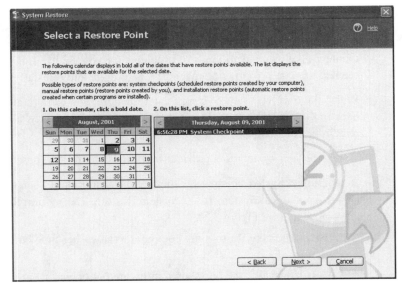

5. You are then asked to verify the date and time you chose. System Restore then urges you to save and close all other documents and applications because Windows

will need to reboot your system to make the desired changes. If everything appears correct onscreen, click Next.

6. Windows restores your files and settings and then reboots itself so that all of the modifications can be made.

Computer Chaos

Some problem solutions may seem overly obvious, but they are things you should always double-check. With children, pets, and other distractions, you may miss the warning signs of a computer acting up.

Likewise, you should understand that you can treat this section as a reference that you can flip back to at a later date. Perhaps some of the topics should have been reserved for later if you've not yet had a chance to get fully up and running on a new computer, but we want to give you the ammunition you need to solve any problems that may come up early on.

My Computer Won't Turn On!

Before you panic, a number of things can remedy the problem. Ask yourself any of the following first:

1. Are all other electronics in the area working? If not, you could have a blown fuse, or you may have a general power failure on your hands.

2. Are the monitor and the console (the big box with the power switch and disk drives in it) plugged in and turned on? They both have power switches, so it is possible the console is spinning up; you just can't tell because the monitor may be turned off.

3. Is your power strip in the ON position? A pet can easily switch them off, as can a falling object from your desk, so it is worth a peek.

4. Is the power to your PC driven by a light switch? If so, verify that it is in the ON position.

5. Still nothing? Then double-check to make sure all of the cables are securely in place.

6. If you still get no response, try unplugging the computer and plugging something else into the power strip. If the other item works, you can assume the power strip is fine, but there may be a problem with the PC's power supply. That warrants a call to your PC's technical support because a blown power supply isn't repairable by an untrained person.

My Computer Froze! What Now?

Nothing's more unnerving than your computer freezing on you. No matter what you do, nothing happens; even Ctrl+Alt+Del (the keyboard shortcut to restart your computer) may fail. Before you start inventing new curse words as you yell at your PC, try the following:

1. If at all humanly possible, try to get into any open word processing documents or spreadsheets to save your work. The next steps you take may result in data loss if you don't. Of course, if your system is entirely frozen, you may not be able to get anywhere. (You did back up your hard drive recently, didn't you?)

2. Next try pressing Ctrl+Alt+Del, but do it only once! (If you do it twice, the system resets without giving you the chance to save anything.) The Windows Task Manager dialog box shown in Figure 3.5 appears, listing all open applications. If an open application is causing the problem, you will see the words Not Responding next to the application's name. Click the name of the problem application and then click the End Task button.

FIGURE 3.5
The Status column lets you see where the problem lies.

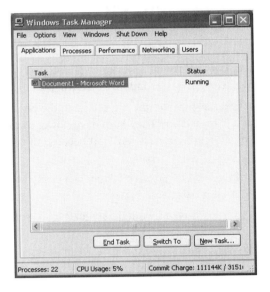

Hopefully, the problem application wasn't one containing unsaved data. (Usually, it is a Web browser with a memory leak or some other innocuous problem.) If it was an application like your word processor or spreadsheet program, there may be no way to recover your work. Office XP programs boast an AutoRecover feature which should, in theory, attempt to recover the active document during the crash when you relaunch the application in question but don't count on this too heavily since it seems to fail as often as it works.

3. If there is still a problem, repeat step 2 to see whether a second application is not responding.

4. Still frozen? Rebooting may be the only answer. On the Windows Task Manager toolbar, click Shutdown, Restart. Hopefully, Windows will shut itself down smoothly. If it doesn't, you will have to turn the PC off, wait a few minutes, and then turn it on again. In cases like this, the system restart may take a bit longer than normal as Windows tries to repair itself.

5. If you get repeated system lockups with a certain application, check the Internet to see if a patch or update to the program is available that may solve the problem. An update or upgrade can often cure what ails your computer.

6. Have you checked for computer viruses, as directed earlier in the chapter?

7. When repeated system lockups occur and you can't trace them to a specific application, there may be an underlying hardware problem. It may be worth a call to your PC's technical support department to see whether they can offer additional guidance.

Disk and Drive Dilemmas

Nothing lasts forever, and that includes disk drives. That's why people are paranoid about backing up files. Disk drive failures don't happen often, but when they do, they can be catastrophic if you are not prepared. Likewise, you may be deceived into thinking your disk drive has failed when there is really a simple solution to the problem.

The Floppy That Won't Fit

Here again, there are several things you can try in order to isolate the problem.

1. Verify that the disk you are trying to insert is the same size as the drive into which you are trying to insert it. An ancient 5.25-inch disk stands no chance of fitting into today's standard floppy drive, and diskettes can't fit into a CD drive.

2. Is the disk in the right position? A disk that is upside down or sideways will not fit into the drive. In the case of CDs, even if an upside-down disk fits, it can't run using the wrong side of the CD.

3. Make sure you are really trying to insert the disk into a disk drive and not a vent in the system unit.

4. Examine the disk for any abnormalities such as warping, sticky spots, and other things because any of these could potentially cause a problem for you.

5. If there is still a problem, you may want to have a qualified person check out the drive itself. Under no circumstances should you ever stick an object other than a disk into the disk drive, especially when the machine is plugged in.

The Unrecognizable CD

CD-ROMs can be very finicky, depending on the sensitivity of your drive. If you run into a glitch, try the following:

1. Open the CD drive, take out the disk, and blow any dust off of it. Blow any dust out of the drive too. Examine the disk for any scratches, since they can also cause problems. Replace the CD and see if the computer recognizes it now.

2. A more thorough cleaning may be in order. Cleaning methods vary depending on whom you ask. There are plenty of commercial cleaning products on the market from which to choose. However, if you want to try cleaning a CD using things around the house, start by finding a soft cotton rag. I use an old cloth diaper that was used during infant feedings. It has been washed a million times and is softer than just about anything else around. Next, take out the CD and breathe hot air onto the bottom of the disk. Finally, wipe the CD gently from the inside of the disk to the outside in a straight line and retry it in the drive.

3. If that doesn't cure the problem, try putting another CD in the drive. If everything goes smoothly, you can attribute the problem to the CD itself. If it still doesn't work, you might want to try a third CD (perhaps a music CD, if the problem CD was a data CD, or vice versa) before calling technical support.

Monitor Messes

A computer is useless without a monitor or display. It is completely understandable to panic when the monitor starts acting up but you can troubleshoot many of the common problems.

All Powered Up and Nothing to See

If your computer is on but there is nothing to see, don't write off the monitor yet. Try the following things first:

1. If the monitor was on when it "died," check to see whether it is in Power Saver mode by moving your mouse or pressing a key. If it comes to life, you may want to

consider either disabling or at least adjusting the Power Saver setting. Do this by clicking the Start button on the Windows taskbar and then clicking Control Panel. Click the Performance and Maintenance link near the bottom of the screen. On the bottom right corner of the Performance and Maintenance screen, you will see a link to Power Options; click that. The Power Schemes tab of the Power Options Properties dialog box shown in Figure 3.6 opens. Use the drop-down arrow buttons to make any desired changes and then click OK to save your settings.

FIGURE 3.6

Using the Power Schemes drop-down box, you can optimize your computer's power for use as a laptop or home PC.

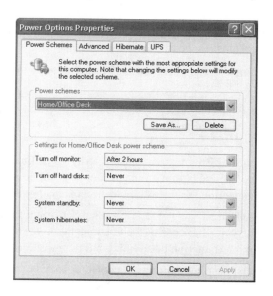

2. Verify that the monitor was not shut off manually, as opposed to with the rest of the computer via the power strip.

3. If that doesn't do it, check the monitor's connection to the console and make sure that the monitor is plugged in.

4. Still in the dark? If the monitor's LED power light is on, you might want to try tweaking the brightness and contrast on your monitor. Because the location of these controls can vary depending on your monitor's manufacturer, consult the documentation that came with your system.

5. If it is still dead, it may be time to call your friendly technical support people. Be sure you have any warranty information with you when you call, along with the information you wrote on the tear card at the front of this book.

Printing Problems

It usually happens when you are more pressed for time than normal. You send a document to the printer, go over to pick it up, and find nothing. What can you do?

Assuming that your printer has been properly installed with the necessary drivers, there are tons of other quirky things that can happen to make life with your printer miserable. Here's a bit of guidance to help keep you sane.

Where's My Document?

When you send a document to the printer and nothing comes out, consider the following:

1. Is the printer turned on and plugged in? Furthermore, is the printer securely attached to your PC?

2. Make sure that the printer has enough paper to complete the job. This is especially true in the case of shared printers, since you may not know who has printed what when.

3. Is the printer online? Printers may unexpectedly go offline, which requires you to press the Online/Offline button on the printer to generate output. (Consult your printer's documentation for the exact location of this button.)

4. Check the printer's LED screen to see if it's given you a specific error message. You'll most likely need to consult the documentation or the printer manufacturer's Web site for an interpretation of anything but the most basic problems.

5. If the print request is routed through a server, as may be the case with a computer attached to a network, contact the server's administrator (or the house nerd in the case of a home network) to verify that the request actually made it. If it didn't, there could be a loose network connection.

6. If there is output, although blotchy, disfigured, or completely black, it may be time to change the toner/ink cartridge.

7. If everything listed here fails to remedy the problem, it is time to call a professional. Keep in mind that unless you purchased the printer from the company that manufactured and/or sold your PC, you will most likely need to call a different technical support number.

Partial Printing

Sometimes print jobs are not complete. This typically happens due to one of the following reasons:

1. Obviously, if your printer runs out of paper halfway through the print job, you will end up with an unfinished product.

2. Go into the application's Print dialog box and make sure that the All Pages option is checked. (You will find this by clicking File, Print in most any Windows application.)

3. Did you exit the application before the entire document could be downloaded to the printer's memory? Some older applications will abort a print job in this situation.

4. If the document was a frame-based Web page, you may not have gotten the frame you intended to print. Go into the Web browser's Print dialog box, select the applicable frame, and then resubmit the job.

5. Could there have been a power surge that interfered with the process? If so, simply resubmitting the job may be all you need to do.

Internet Irks

With something as massive as the Internet, complications can occur at any number of points. In fact, it may take significant amounts of time to isolate an Internet-related problem for that very reason.

Slow Connections

If your Internet connection is crawling at a snail's pace, several things could be going on, including any of the following:

1. If you are surfing during the day and find Web pages loading at an excruciatingly slow pace, chances are, the Internet is bogged down with traffic. Given the time differences across the United States, along with the millions of leisure surfers who log on from home, the Internet may very well be clogged at all hours of the day. The only thing you can do is surf at odd hours, invest in a high-speed Internet connection for your home, or simply tolerate the sluggishness.

2. For those of you who have the opportunity to take advantage of DSL or cable modem service, go for it. You get super speed, and you don't even have to tie up a telephone line! If you plan to do much surfing and there is anything less than a 56K modem in your computer, then you should seriously consider upgrading.

3. If things are crawling along into the wee hours of the night, there may be a cut cable somewhere along the line. Unfortunately, there is nothing you can do about it, since it is more than likely halfway across the country. In such a situation, you will certainly feel the effects of masses of rerouted Internet traffic.

4. Perhaps your connections are continually hit or miss. It could mean your Internet service provider (ISP) doesn't have a high-speed link to the Internet. If they don't plan on upgrading soon, you may want to shop around for better service.

Dropped Connections

If you keep getting those pesky "Do you want to reconnect?" messages, look into the following:

1. Pick up your phone and listen to the dial tone. Is it crisp and clear, or do you hear crackles and static? A bad phone line can often kill a connection. If the weather is stormy and windy, check the lines again when things settle down. If you have always had problems with your phone lines, there may not be much anyone can do about it until the phone company decides to upgrade or service its underground cables.

2. Sometimes older Windows 98 machines are almost hypersensitive to incoming calls if you have call waiting or even subscribe to some voice mail through your local phone company. Therefore, if the phone rings and the line is busy or goes unanswered, the call is forwarded to a mailbox at a phone company substation. Interestingly, when a call came in and was forwarded to voicemail, I would often get booted off the Internet. The hassle may not be worth giving up voicemail, but such a situation can occur. Luckily, Windows XP seems a bit better behaved in that regard.

3. Check your modem's configuration. Many machines are set up to drop an Internet connection if it remains idle for a given amount of time. To learn whether this is the case for you, click the Start button on the Windows taskbar and then click the Control Panel. Click the Network and Internet Connections link and then click Phone and Modem Options in the See Also pane at the upper left part of the page. Open the Modems tab and look for an option under Call preferences that reads: "Disconnect a call if idle for more than ___ min." If this option is checked, you can either disable it by clicking it or adjust the time as desired by clicking inside the text box and entering a new number.

4. If the disconnects persist even in the absence of either situation mentioned previously, check with your ISP to see whether others have reported a similar problem. A flaky modem at its end can cause plenty of grief on your end. After you have the

answer to this question, you should have a pretty good idea of whether the problem potentially lies with your modem or your ISP.

Busy Internet Connections

If you keep getting busy signals when you try to connect, here are some suggestions.

1. Get additional dialup numbers from your ISP to try in a pinch. A high number of customers dialing in at once can clog lines in no time.

2. If that doesn't remedy the problem, call your ISP and inquire about the user-to-modem ratio. Some say that a 7-to-1 is ideal, so if it is significantly higher than that, you may want to explore alternatives or pressure them to add more modems.

3. For night owls, surfing in the middle of the night may be all that is needed.

4. Here again, cable, DSL, or ISDN access from home will eliminate the problem entirely. Certainly, it will cost you, but for those who need the Internet to work, there is nothing better, especially when you factor in the benefit of increased file transfer speed as well.

3

Summary

By now, you should be familiar with all the tools to help keep your computer in shape for years to come. Not only do you know how to call on the utilities when you need them, but you also learned how to protect yourself against nasty computer viruses. In addition, you now understand how to troubleshoot and repair common problems.

PART II

Making Things Happen with Your PC

Chapter

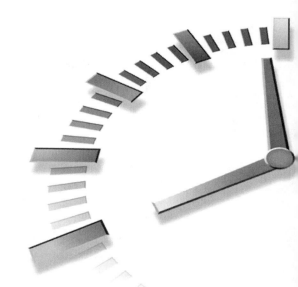

CHAPTER 4

It's All About the Software

Windows acts as the controlling brain for your computer and the other types of software on your PC do the jobs you want your computer to perform. A computer loaded with plenty of productivity software suggests that someone who gets down to business and stays on task uses that machine. At the other extreme is the system with a screaming video card, sound system complete with subwoofer, a big monitor, and a sizeable hard drive, chockfull of the latest and greatest games. If that computer doesn't belong to a kid, it most certainly belongs to a kid at heart. This will be your introduction to various types of software.

Software Defined

To perform a certain type of task using your computer, such as typing a letter, you need an application or program for that task. When you purchase a new PC, you might receive some applications as part of the purchase. In fact, many of the most reasonably priced systems today are shipped with some flavor of Microsoft Office (or at the very least, Microsoft Word, which you will learn throughout the seventh part of this book). As you may have noticed while exploring your new machine, Windows also includes some applications such as a paint program, a calculator, and an ever-popular Solitaire card game.

As time passes, you will form your own preferences for the types of software you want to use. Software can get expensive so spend time with an application before you pay a lot for it. The Internet often provides a way for you to try demonstrations, or just *demos* of software, so that you can "try before you buy."

After you get comfortable using your new system, you will want to purchase additional applications. Software generally falls into one of the categories described in the following sections.

It might seem simpler to borrow a friend's disks rather than wait for a lengthy download over the Internet, but as long as a friend has registered the software and is still using it on a computer, sharing the software breaks the law. The practice of installing the single-licensed software on multiple computers at once is referred to as *software piracy*. The same copyright laws that protect books, music, and other works are also applicable to software.

You will hear the terms program, application, or some combination thereof used interchangeably. They all mean basically the same thing.

Word Processors

The most common type of application is word processing software. You can use this type of program to create documents such as letters, memos, reports, resumes, manuscripts, and so on. If there is something you would have once done on a typewriter, you can now use a word processing program for the task.

Word processing programs are much more than just a fancy typewriter. They offer many editing and formatting features so that you have a great deal of control over the content and look of your document. Here is a quick list of some of the things you can do with this type of program:

- Easily edit text. You can move text from one page to another and even from one document to another. You can also copy or delete text with just a few keystrokes or mouse clicks.

- Format text. Formatting means changing the appearance of text. You can make text bold, change the font, use a different color, and so on.

- Format paragraphs and pages. In addition to simple text changes, you can also format paragraphs (indent, add bullets, or add a border) and pages (change the margins, add page numbers, or insert a header).

- Check accuracy. Most programs include a spell-check tool for checking the spelling. Some programs also include a mini-application, or applet, for checking grammar.

Word processing programs can differ in terms of what features they offer. If your needs are simple, you might do just fine with the simple word processing program included with Windows. This program, called WordPad, includes basic editing and formatting features.

If you plan to create a lot of documents and want a stunning professional appearance, you may want to purchase a more robust program. One of the most popular programs is Microsoft Word, shown in Figure 4.1. You will learn a lot about this powerful tool in this text. Word includes all the preceding features, as well as desktop publishing features for setting up columns, inserting tables, adding graphics, and so on. Word also includes features for sending faxes, creating Web documents, and much more.

FIGURE 4.1

Microsoft Word, a part of the Microsoft Office suite, is the most popular word processing program.

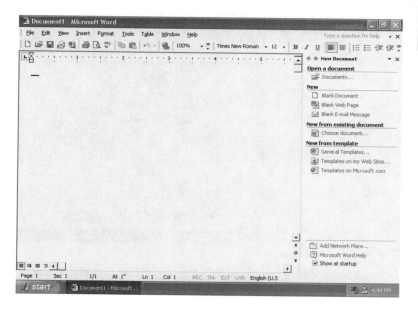

To produce the highest quality newsletters, brochures, catalogs, and other items, you may want a desktop publishing program. These programs provide even more control of the layout of the page. Microsoft Publisher, which is technically part of the Office family but no longer included in the various suite packages, is a fairly simple desktop publishing program, yet it provides numerous templates to achieve quick, professional-looking results. Adobe PageMaker is a more powerful package; however, it may take more time to master the subtleties, not to mention the cost which is about four times more than Publisher and other competitors.

Spreadsheets (aka Worksheets)

If numbers are your game, you will most likely work with a spreadsheet application. Spreadsheet programs enable you to enter and manipulate all kinds of financial information such as budgets, sales statistics, income, expenses, and so on. You enter these figures into a grid of columns and rows known as a worksheet or spreadsheet (see Figure 4.2). The intersection of a row and column is called a cell, and you enter text, numbers, or formulas into the cells to create a worksheet.

FIGURE 4.2

Use a spreadsheet program for any type of numerical data you want to calculate or track.

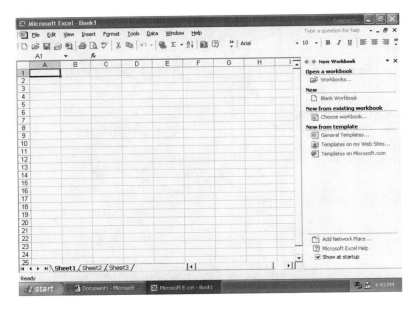

The benefit of a spreadsheet program is that you have so many options for working with the data you enter. You can do any of the following:

- Perform simple-to-complex calculations. You can total a column of numbers, calculate a percentage, figure the amortization of a loan, and more.

- Format the data. You can make changes to how text and numbers appear in the worksheet. You can also adjust the column width, add borders, change the alignment of entries, and more.

- Chart the data. You can create different types of charts to visually represent the data. For example, you can add a line chart to a report to illustrate a sales trend.

- Manage data lists. Most spreadsheets also include features for managing simple data lists. You can enter, sort, and query simple data lists using the grid structure of a worksheet.

Microsoft Excel and Lotus 1-2-3 are popular spreadsheet programs, but today Excel leads the race in being used by far more people than Lotus and other competitors.

In addition to spreadsheet programs, you can also use other types of financial programs. For example, you can purchase a program to keep track of your check register. Some of the most popular check management programs are Quicken and Microsoft Money. You can also find programs for calculating your income tax (TurboTax), managing your small business (QuickBooks), handling major accounting tasks (PeachTree Accounting), and others.

Databases

If word processing and spreadsheets rank first and second in application popularity, databases and other productivity applications come in a close third. You can use a database program to track and manage any set of data such as clients, inventory, orders, events, or personal collections. Database programs vary from simple list managers to complex programs you can use to manage linked systems of information residing on huge mainframe computers at major corporations and educational institutions.

Databases offer a lot of advantages when you are working with large amounts of information. First, you can easily search for and find a particular piece of information. You can also sort the data into different orders as needed, a client list alphabetically for a phone list, or a mailing list by ZIP code. You can even work with subsets of the data: all clients in South Dakota, all clients that ordered more than $1,000 worth of products, Beanie Babies purchased for more than $10, and so on.

Some popular database programs include Microsoft Access, and Corel Paradox. As you saw in the previous section on spreadsheets, you can even experiment with lightweight databases by modifying a spreadsheet application.

Graphics and Presentation Programs

Even if you aren't artistic, you can use your PC and the right software program to create graphics. Depending on your needs and skills, you can consider any of the three types of programs in this category:

- Simple drawing programs. You can use a simple drawing program, such as Paint, which is included with Windows, to create simple illustrations. In addition, larger applications like Word include applets like WordArt and AutoShapes that let you dabble in the visual arts, regardless of whether or not you have artistic talent.

- Complex drawing programs. You can also find more sophisticated programs for drawing and working with images. Adobe Illustrator and Adobe Photoshop are two such packages. For more technical renderings, you might consider Visio, a fairly recent acquisition of Microsoft. This product will undoubtedly go through some major revisions and enhanced Microsoft Office integration in the near future, but even older versions of Visio can easily be imported into Word documents.

- Presentation programs. If you ever have to give a presentation, you might want to use a program designed just for creating presentations. You can use this program to create slides, handouts, and notes—a great tool for educators, executives, or sales people. Microsoft PowerPoint (see Figure 4.3), Corel Presentations, and Freelance Graphics are popular presentation programs.

FIGURE 4.3

PowerPoint's TriPane interface makes it simple to create colorful presentations.

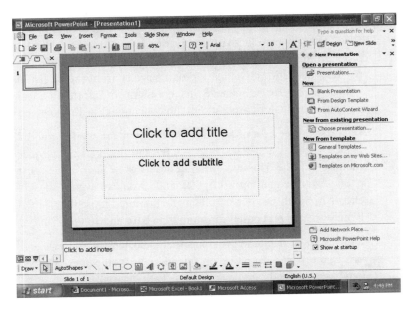

Personal Information Managers

Most people have several things to track: people, events, appointments, places, and so on. Personal information managers (PIMs) store names and addresses, maintain your schedule, keep notes, and perform many other tasks. You can think of this type of program as an electronic planner. Microsoft Outlook (not to be confused with its little brother, Outlook Express, which comes free with Internet Explorer) acts as a PIM in addition to being an email program.

Games

When you go into a store that sells computer software, you will probably see more games than anything else. Within this broad category, you will find several classifications of the programs. Take a look at the following list to see what titles you might find in each category:

- **Puzzle/Arcade:** Just about anything you ever played in an arcade in college can be found on store shelves. Centipede, Pac-Man, and many other favorites, along with a slew of pinball machine programs can be found. You will even find familiar board games like Boggle and Clue. Even electronic versions of your favorite televised game shows are represented, such as *Who Wants to be a Millionaire?*, *The Weakest Link*, and *Wheel of Fortune*.

- **Strategy:** Among the classic games making up this category are Battleship, Mastermind, Scrabble, the best selling SimCity series, Microsoft's Ages of Empire series, Sid Meier's Alpha Centauri, The Sims, Sim Theme Park, and Railroad Tycoon. Newer popular releases in this category include Black & White, Startopia, Zoo Tycoon, and Tropico.

- **Action:** If you like action-packed games, you might enjoy some of these titles: Duke Nuke'em, Quake, Earthworm Jim, the Half-Life series, Descent, Tom Clancy's Rainbow Six, and Delta Force. Beware that many of these are gory primary shooter games that are not suitable for young players.

- **Adventure:** Harry Potter and the Sorcerer's Stone, Tomb Raider, Final Fantasy, Star Trek, and Star Wars, as well as series like Alone in the Dark, Myst, and King's Quest, fall into this category.

- **Driving:** Whether you want to be behind the wheel of an exotic sports car, a motorcycle, or even a pod racer, you are bound to find something that strikes your fancy among these titles: eRacer; Star Wars Racer; NASCAR Racing; the Test Drive and Need for Speed series; Viper Racing; Lego Racer; Grand Theft Auto; Carmageddon (for those with a strong stomach); Destruction Derby; Moto Racer; and one of my favorites, Microsoft's Midtown Madness.

4

- **Simulations:** Simulations are a lot of fun. You can fly an old warplane, drive a tank on the frontlines, pilot a helicopter over a city you built in SimCity, even run a hospital or theme park. Simulations you might want to take a peek at include Microsoft Flight Simulator, Microsoft Train Simulator, Comanche, SimCopter, X-Wing Vs. Tie Fighter, Theme Hospital, and Independence War.

- **Sports:** No matter what sport you prefer, you will find a game that makes you want to be a part of the team. Some of the more popular sports titles include FIFA Major League Soccer, Madden NFL, Tony Hawk's Pro Skater, NHL, NBA Live, Links, Dave Mirra Freestyle BMX, and Cycling Manager.

- **Reference/Educational:** Titles found in this category include Compton's Encyclopedia, Microsoft Encarta, Mavis Beacon Typing, home designing software, family tree makers, as well as a wide range of college test preparation software and programs to help you learn a new language.

- **Edutainment:** Geared toward kids, this hybrid of educational and entertainment software is designed to help kids have fun at learning. Popular programs in this category include the JumpStart series, Reader Rabbit titles, and the Magic School Bus offerings. These programs really do give kids a head start. My own children are reading three grade levels ahead of their age thanks to a great school and a terrific collection of edutainment CDs at home.

- **Miscellaneous:** This includes everything that fits nowhere else! You will find titles like The Electric Quilt and Quilt Pro (for quilt designing), Microsoft Streets Plus for trip planning, and collectibles cataloging software like Beanie Baby Collector. You can even find pregnancy and wedding planning software, astronomy programs, greeting card makers, photo editors, and other highly specialized titles.

Get the full scoop. Before buying a game, you may want to visit
http://www.gamespot.com. From there, you can view descriptions, previews,
and reviews of computer games before you invest in them. In many cases,
you can even see screen shots of the game in action, watch videos, or download playable demos.

Internet Programs

If you want to use your computer to hook up to the Internet, you need a Web browser. The two most popular are Netscape and Microsoft's Internet Explorer, which I will cover in more detail throughout this book. These programs are actually suites of smaller Internet applications as well. For example, Internet Explorer also contains Outlook Express as an email client, and Netscape has Netscape Mail.

Other Internet programs you might come across in your travels are Eudora (email), Opera (comparable to Netscape and Internet Explorer), and AOL's Internet access software. There is also an ever-growing assortment of instant messaging applications like MSN Messenger, AOL's Instant Messenger, and others.

Utility Programs

When you want to fine-tune your computer, you may want to investigate some of the utility programs available. These programs add capabilities to your system such as virus checking or file backup. Norton Utilities is an example of this type of application. Other utilities include WinZip, which handles file compression; Partition Magic, which helps you subdivide your hard drive; and Norton and McAfee antivirus programs.

Purchasing a New Program

Although your computer more than likely came with a number of preinstalled applications, you may eventually want to make some changes. You may want to upgrade an existing program to the newest version or purchase an entirely new program.

You can find software in some retail stores, at online stores and auctions, in computer stores, and through mail-order outlets. Scan through any computer magazine to get an idea of what programs are available and how much they cost. You can also use the Internet as a resource for researching and finding programs. For example, ZDNet at http://www.zdnet.com nearly always has reviews posted for both software and hardware.

4

When you are looking for a new program to purchase, be sure that you can run that program on your system. Each program has a set of system requirements—that is, the type of microprocessor, amount of memory, hard disk space, video card, and any other required equipment needed to run the software. You can usually find these requirements printed on the side of the software box. Check the requirements before purchasing anything to be sure your PC is capable of running the software. It might even be a good idea to test a demo of the software on your machine when one is available. You can find many of demos at http://www.download.com and http://www.gamespot.com.

The most popular software out there will be compatible with Windows XP and any later versions of Windows that post-dates XP.

As a final precaution, check to see if the software is distributed on diskettes, a CD-ROM, or a DVD-ROM. If you have both a floppy drive and DVD-ROM drive, you are safe, but if you don't have a DVD-ROM drive, be sure to get the version on standard CD or diskettes. CD-ROMs have become the most popular and least expensive method for distributing programs, especially large programs, so you might not even be able to find a version on diskette anymore.

Where to Buy Software

If you are in no hurry, some of the best prices can be had from online stores where competition is fierce. Although you must often pay postage, the absence of sales tax, along with a lower retail price, still make it worthwhile to buy online. Always research shipping costs and terms before you commit to buy. Many online retailers offer low prices but pad shipping costs to make up for the discount.

If you are in a hurry, you can seldom beat Wal-Mart, your local wholesale clubs, or the Sunday circulars for good prices. Most popular computer games and productivity applications are pretty easy to find, but if you can't find what you want in those places, it's time to visit your local Best Buy, CompUSA, Fry's Electronics, or Computer MicroCenter.

Registering Your Software

When you purchase a piece of software, you will often find a postcard in the box requesting your name, address, email address, location where the software was purchased, when it was purchased, and other points. This registration card enables software manufacturers to contact you if a bug fix becomes available over the Internet or when they simply want to inform you that an updated version of your purchase is now available.

Typically, manufacturers allow you to register their products online. When you install the program, it will ask you if you want to go online now and register the software or do it later; the choice is yours.

So, if you are wondering if you should bother registering software, yes, you should! Not only does registering it keep you up-to-date on the latest news about a given program, but it also leads to money-saving offers for program upgrades or add-ons. That alone could be worth dealing with the occasional junk mail.

Along a similar line, Microsoft now requires you to activate many of its products online before you use them for any length of time. Activation may seem tedious when you first do it but activation can potentially lead to extra support and good offers down the road. In addition, when you pay for software you do not actually own the software but you own the right to use the software (called a *software license*). Registering and activation entitles you to the license you bought.

Upgrading Software

When should you upgrade your software? Software is expensive to be continually purchasing newer versions, especially when you may not really need it. Much like with hardware upgrades, it is important to think about whether the computer or software does what you want and need it to do. If it does, then don't waste your money. You should wait until the need or a real desire for it is there.

This is especially true for productivity software like Word, Excel, and others. Enhancements are often targeted toward corporate or power users, offering no real value to the average consumer. Of course, an upgrade is warranted if there are file compatibility issues between your home and work machines, but even many of those can be resolved without costly software upgrades.

Games are a different matter, however. Technological advances, the desire to have new levels or playing arenas, and optimized performance might very well make upgrading a game desirable, especially if you really liked the game the first time around. Again, though, use extreme caution to make sure your machine can drive the latest and greatest offering.

Summary

You now know more about the types of software you can get, along with some guidelines for purchasing and upgrading your chosen software. You even got a feel for what kinds of titles you can find in each category of software.

CHAPTER 5

Enjoying Multimedia

Did you know that in addition to being an Internet surfing machine, a word processor, a spreadsheet compiler, and a computer game playing device, your PC has the potential to become a compact disc (CD) player, radio tuner, sound recorder, digital video disc (DVD) player, and television too? Surely you have heard about some of the possibilities, but a few may surprise you, especially when you learn how little it takes to get up and running. Although you may still be new to computers, so many people want to utilize multimedia that this chapter leaps into the multimedia foray and introduces you to hardware and fundamental software that will get you started. Later in the book, you'll discover additional ways to use your computer for audio and video entertainment and software enjoyment.

The Computers Are Alive, with the Sound of Music!

Windows Media Player comes with Windows. Windows Media Player started out as just an audio playing program with simple video playback but has evolved into a full-functioning multimedia center. Playing audio CDs using Windows Media Player is a real treat. Much like with stereo components, you can program Windows Media Player to play only the tracks you want, to repeat the current disc until you stop it, or to play selected tracks at random (often known as shuffling).

Beginning with the basics, playing an audio CD, seems to be the best place to start enjoying your computer for its multimedia capabilities. When you insert an audio CD into your computer's CD-ROM drive, the Windows Media Player typically launches on its own. If it doesn't, you can call it into action by clicking the Start button on the Windows taskbar and then choosing All Programs, Accessories, Entertainment, Windows Media Player.

The CD begins to play automatically while the Windows Media Player attempts to download CD information from the Internet. If an active Internet connection is available, the names of the artist, album, and individual tracks will appear in the Windows Media Player Window. If no connection is found, the text will be filled in with generic information such as Unknown Artist, Unknown Album, and Track 1.

If you dial up to the Internet after the CD has started playing, you can tell the Windows Media Player to go out and download album information. To do this, click the CD Audio button on the left side of the Windows Media Player window and then click the Get Name button. Within seconds, full album information will be downloaded for you. You'll be surprised at how accurate the online database can be, even for CDs recorded from albums many years ago.

You can control the CD by using the buttons on the Windows Media Player panel, as shown in Figure 5.1.

Although most of the buttons pictured in Figure 5.1 are self-explanatory, a few could benefit from more detailed coverage. For example, if a CD is playing, the big round Play button becomes a Pause button. Likewise, when the CD is stopped, the big round button becomes a Play button.

The Volume button is essentially a slider lever. Click it and drag it to the right to make the music louder or drag it to the left to make it softer. Also fairly new to the Windows Media Player is the Mute button, which silences the music the instant you click it.

You will also notice a big window full of all kinds of colorful animations. When not displaying videos, this window produces all kinds of funky visualizations for your viewing pleasure. This visualization window can be customized, too, but I'm sure you would rather learn how to burn music CDs, play DVD movies, find radio stations and police scanners on the Internet and other cool stuff like that than fiddle with the look of your Windows Media Player.

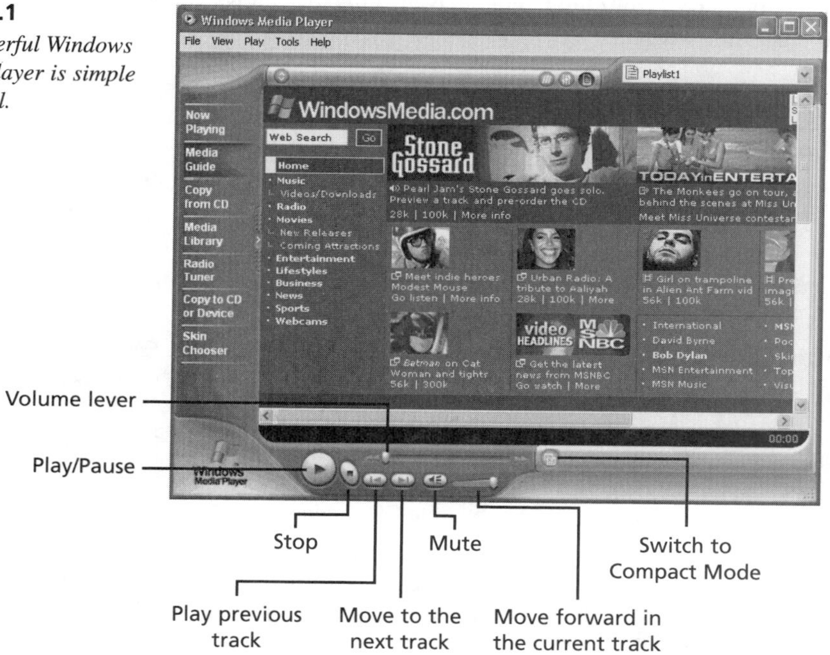

FIGURE 5.1

The powerful Windows Media Player is simple to control.

Volume lever

Play/Pause

Stop

Mute

Switch to Compact Mode

Play previous track

Move to the next track

Move forward in the current track

Setting CD Playback Options

By default, the CD Player will play the current disc once through and then stop. However, a number of additional playback options are available to you, too, all of which can be set with little more than a couple of mouse clicks.

To set them, click the Play menu on the Windows Media Player with the desired CD playing and then click either of the following options. Note that clicking the selected option a second time will remove the check mark, thus deselecting the chosen option.

- **Shuffle**—Instructs the Windows Media Player to play tracks on the selected disc at random. This option is a great way to refresh the predictability of an overplayed CD.

- **Repeat**—Click this playback option to have Windows Media player repeat the selected CD until you tell it to stop.

More Facts About the CD in the Hot Seat

If you poke around Windows Media Player a bit, you will discover a lot of interesting tidbits about the CD currently being played. Table 5.1 shows you what bits of information you will find where.

TABLE 5.1   Gathering Information About the CD

To Discover This...	...Look Here
Artist's name	In Now Playing mode, the top line of text above the visualization window. This data also appears in the Copy from CD window.
Song title	Look just below the artist's name. This information also appears in the Copy from CD window.
List of songs on album	On the right side of the window is a pane reserved for the list of songs on the currently playing CD. This data also appears in the Copy from CD window.
Length of each song in minutes	Immediately to the right of each song is its length expressed in minutes and seconds. This information also appears in the Copy from CD window.
Copy status	In the Copy from CD window, you can learn whether a CD has been copied to your Media Library (the place where all your personally copied music files are stored), in the process of being copied, or in the copy queue.
Genre	Windows Media Player assigns a music style to the CDs it can identify. This information is in the Copy from CD window.
Style	The music style of the CD also appears in the Copy from CD section.
Artist biography	From the Copy from CD window, click the Album Details button. A picture of the CD's cover and list of tracks appears along with a link to an artist biography. This information is not available for all artists, however.
Album review	Click the Album Details link to locate links to any available album reviews.

Selecting CD Tracks to Play

Do you own CDs containing only two or three tracks you like because you have to take the good music along with the bad?

Windows Media Player has a simple solution for you. By disabling unwanted tracks, you can play only the songs on the CD you want to hear. You will, of course, need to do this while the CD is playing. Using the default Now Playing view shown in Figure 5.1, right-click the songs you don't want to hear; then choose Disable Selected Tracks from the shortcut menu. The songs you disabled are grayed out, leaving the ones you want to hear with their usual bright print. Believe it or not, Windows Media Player remembers this information regardless of how many times you remove the CD, play others, and then return to it.

To enable the songs again, simply right-click them and choose Enable Selected Tracks from the shortcut menu.

Burning Music CDs

If you have a recordable CD drive, then you have the makings of your own personal recording studio. If you like Herb Alpert, Kansas, The Dixie Chicks, Gary Chapman, Donna Summer, Norah Jones, and John Tesh, you can have them all on one CD (as scary as that may sound).

> Obviously, these CDs should be created for personal use and not sold for commercial use. Reproducing music for resale without permission is a blatant violation of copyright laws. It should also be noted that borrowing a friend's CD to make a copy is also a copyright violation. That's true whether you want to copy the whole CD or a single song.

5

Three major steps are involved in burning your own CDs. First, you must record the music to the Media Library on your hard drive. This makes duplication quicker, simpler, and more flexible in terms of track choice. Second, you will need to create a playlist for the CD, which basically tells the Windows Media Player which songs you want on the CD. The actual burning of the CD is your last step.

Copying Music Files to Your Media Library

Copying files to your Media Library is not only the first step required to burn a music CD, but it also enables you to play favorite tunes directly from your hard drive. Fragile CDs can stay nice and safe in their jewel cases, and people who travel with laptops, personal PCs, or other portable devices can now "take with them" dozens of CDs from their home music libraries.

You will need to follow these steps in order to copy music from your audio CDs to your Media Library:

1. Put the CD you want to record in your CD-ROM drive and give Windows Media Player enough time to download album information. This makes it easier for you to decide which tracks you want to record versus those you want to leave behind.

2. Next, access the CD Audio window by clicking the Copy from CD button on the left side of the screen. As shown in Figure 5.2, this window displays all pertinent information about the album in your CD-ROM drive.

FIGURE 5.2

It is easy to be selective about the songs you copy.

3. By default, all tracks of a CD are selected for reproduction. You can remove specific songs by clicking inside their check box to remove the check mark. Only songs with a check mark will be copied to your Media Library.

4. To begin copying the files, click the round, red Copy Music button. The Copy Status column will keep you apprised of the job's progress.

You can even listen to the CD while the job is running. Simply click the Play button to play the CD. Your computer will continue copying the specified files in the background.

Building a Playlist from Files in Your Media Library

Creating a playlist enables you to select only the songs you want and burn a CD or maintain on your hard drive that simple list alone. You can create a party mix for a shindig in your home, or you can compile a playlist of your favorite songs of all time and listen to them repeatedly while working at your computer or using your portable music device. However, to be included in a playlist, a song must first be copied to the Media Library, as directed in the previous section.

Saving Space

Copying a single song much less an entire CD can take tens of megabytes of disk space if done using the MP3 sound file format. With Windows Media Player's Audio 8 format, you can get the quality of MP3 for around a third of the disk space.

By default, Windows Media Player copies your files at near CD quality. (You can bump up the quality by clicking Tools, Options, opening the Copy Music tab, and moving the Copy music at this quality lever to the right.) With this default file size, an average music CD will take up 28 megabytes of disk space. The highest quality files take a whopping 86 megabytes of storage.

Given the large size of most disk drives these days, you may not encounter any problems with storing your files, but you should be aware of the sound file sizes just the same.

To build your own Windows Media Player playlist, follow these steps:

1. Click the Media Library button down the left side of the screen. This takes you to the Media Library window shown in Figure 5.3.

FIGURE 5.3
The Media Library is where you will create playlists and organize your media collection.

5

2. Next, click the New playlist button at the left end of the Media Library button bar. Windows Media Player asks you to name the playlist you are about to define.

3. Type in a name that accurately describes the list and then click OK. Your new playlist will be added to the My Playlists collection on the left side of the window.

4. Now you will need to add songs to the playlist. In the left pane of the Medial Library window, you will see a list of all the CDs you have stored in your library. Under the Album section, click the name of a CD containing a track you want to include in the playlist. The album's track listing appears in the right half of the window.

> The contents of your Media Library can also be viewed by artist or genre if you prefer. Just click the plus (+) sign next to the preferred method of organization to see the contents displayed in the chosen manner.

5. Click the name of a track you want to include and then hit the Add to Playlist button. Remember, you can select multiple tracks by holding down the Ctrl key while you click.

6. Keep adding sound files until all the songs you want have been added. If the playlist is going to be accessed on your PC only, then the playlist can be as long as you want. If it is destined for a CD or portable device, then you may want to be a bit more judicious in your selections, since not all of it is likely to fit.

Making Your Own CD

Now that you have invested all that time and energy into making a good playlist, it is time to turn it into an audio CD.

Start by verifying that your recordable CD drive is properly connected to your computer. Then make sure you have a blank CD in the drive that's ready to record.

Just follow these steps to make a CD:

1. Launch Windows Media Player and access the Media Library.

2. Once there, click the name of the playlist you want to record on the blank CD.

3. Now click the Copy to CD or Device button on the left side of the Windows Media Player. The tracks on the chosen playlist appear onscreen with checkboxes next to each one.

You may not have the Copy to CD option; this feature may not have been installed with Windows Media Player. You can either get your CD containing Windows Media Player and install the add-in from there, or you can download it from the Web using Windows Media's Help, Check for Player Upgrades command.

4. Make sure that the tracks you want to include in your CD or device are checked, and then click the little red Record button in the upper right corner of the Media Player window.

If your device (writable CD drive or portable music device) is not always connected to your computer, Windows Media Player may prompt you to connect it and then hit the F5 key.

Music and Videos on the Web

One great thing about Windows Media Player is that it is equipped to handle just about any kind of audio or video it finds on the Net. Simply click the sound or video link, and Windows Media Player fires up with its familiar, easy-to-use controls. As you surf the Net, you will find you can use Windows Media Player to watch movie trailers, see video game footage, or listen to sound clips of a soon-to-be-released single.

Go ahead, give it a test drive. Launch Windows Media Player with a live connection to the Internet and then click the Media Guide button. From there, you can jump to Movies, Music, Business, Webcams, or Sports, to name just a few topics. Try one video and an audio clip. It is just like playing a regular CD.

5

Tuning into the Radio Online

You want to try something really interesting like go browsing for radio stations around the world? Seriously, from peppy contemporary music stations in Denmark to rap from Chicago, it is all out there. Listen to local news from Jamaica or hear a top-rated morning show from the East Coast.

Radio advertisers and their respective talent protested the broadcasting of their ads online by "regular" radio stations, so many stations have disabled their live audio streams for the time being. Others have found creative workarounds. Be prepared to hit a few roadblocks as you search for your favorite radio station online. To learn more about this dispute and one company's solution, point your Web browser to: http://www.internetnews.com/IAR/article/0,,12_786891,00.html.

Although you can access radio stations from a variety of points across the Net, the best place to start is Windows Media Player's Radio Tuner. Just launch Windows Media Player, click the Radio Tuner button on the left side of the screen, and you are at your starting point, as shown in Figure 5.4.

FIGURE 5.4

Get a jumpstart to your favorite radio stations or just ones you listened to most recently.

You will see links to several featured stations on the left side of the window, along with links for types of music in the upper right section. If nothing strikes you there, click the Find More Stations link. From there, you can search by ZIP code or tune in to some editors' choice stations by clicking their links.

You may not know the postal code for an elusive city across the world (or for that matter if there even is a postal code). What you really need is the Advanced Search (click the Use Advanced Search link underneath the ZIP code text box). The Advanced Search lets you look for stations based on genre, language, country, state, link speed, band (AM, FM, or Internet only, not Genesis or Cheap Trick), or a keyword of your choice.

Once you have performed your search, the results appear in the right half of the screen. Simply click the link of interest and choose Play to hear the radio station's broadcast (see Figure 5.5).

FIGURE 5.5

When you click the link of an interesting station, you are faced with three choices.

In addition to playing a station whose link you clicked, you can also click the Add to My Stations link to add it to your My Stations list, which will make it easier to find the next time around, or Visit Website (to learn more about the selected station).

For the Record

With a microphone and Windows XP, Home Edition, you can record the voices of friends and family for use in e-mail and on Web pages. The quality isn't professional caliber, but hey, it doesn't cost much, so who can complain?

To begin working with the Windows Sound Recorder, click the Start button on the Windows taskbar and then select All Programs, Accessories, Entertainment, Sound Recorder. The Sound Recorder window shown in Figure 5.6 appears.

Next, verify that your microphone is properly connected to the back of your PC. If it is, you should be able to click the Record button and begin recording instantly. No more hitting Play and Record to set the recorder in motion! Use the other buttons just as you would those on any tape recorder you have used in the past.

5

FIGURE 5.6
This recorder is even easier to use than the cassette recorders of yesteryear.

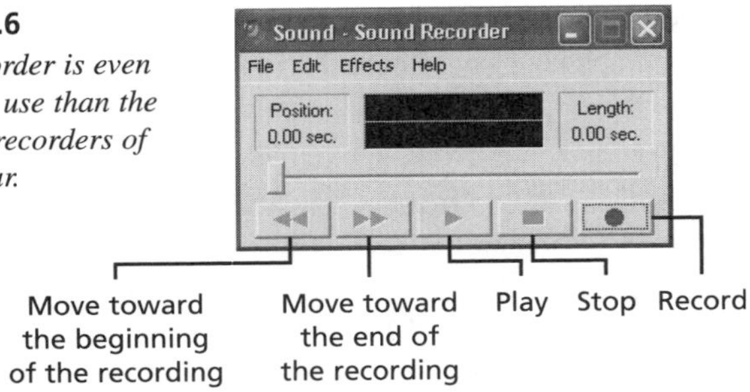

Move toward   Move toward   Play   Stop   Record
the beginning   the end of
of the recording   the recording

To save your recording, go to the Sound Recorder's menu bar and click File, Save on; give the file a meaningful name; and then click the Save button. You will now be able to access the file from any software application that enables you to insert or embed .wav files.

> Although you can only record 60 seconds worth of audio, you should know that the files are huge! It will take what seems like an eternity to mail, open, or download them onto a Web page, so use them sparingly.

DVD Is Here to Stay

You can find DVD players in a variety of price ranges and forms, and even the Xbox and Sony PlayStation 2 game consoles include DVD capabilities. Video discs can be found by the binful at wholesale clubs/membership warehouses.

DVD is the next generation of optical disc storage. Not only can DVDs hold more data and run faster than other optical storage devices, but they can also hold video, sound, and computer data. Furthermore, DVD broadcasts at twice the resolution of VHS videos and Dolby sound. Some of the technology's biggest supporters believe DVD may eventually replace audio CDs, videocassettes, laser discs, CD-ROMS, and perhaps even game cartridges. In fact, the technology has gained the support of major electronics companies, computer software manufacturers, and a near majority of movie and music studios.

It is important, however, to understand the difference between DVD and DVD-ROM players. A DVD player refers to the video players you connect to TVs. These players play only video discs like those you rent at your local video store. DVD-ROM players, on the other hand, can be found in newly manufactured computers. DVD-ROM drives not only read video discs, but they also can read audio and data CDs.

Even if your computer didn't come with a DVD-ROM drive, you can always upgrade later by either swapping out your old CD-ROM for a DVD-ROM or adding the DVD-ROM to your machine as an additional drive.

I Want My DVD!

You can do lots of things to maximize the value of the DVD-ROM drive you choose. Here are some important considerations:

- **Your current processor speed.** If the computer into which you wish to put a DVD drive has anything slower than a 133MHz Pentium processor, DVD performance may suffer.

- **The availability of titles you want to view.** Although there aren't many computer software titles that take full advantage of DVD technology yet, remember that a DVD-ROM can play DVD movies and any audio CD. Also, if you are not convinced that there are many DVD videos out yet either, surf over to the DVD Review at http://www.dvdreview.com and take a look around; that should change your mind in a hurry!

- **Durability.** Do you have children who repeatedly watch the same movie? I know my kids are like that, often wearing out a poor VHS tape within weeks. At least DVDs are more durable, and they don't disintegrate over time like videotapes do. However, you do have to consider potential smudging and scratching of the DVD's delicate surface.

- **The best in DVD.** To get the most out of DVD video, try to get a setup that includes a hardware decoder board. This essentially maximizes DVD performance while minimizing the strain on your computer's processor. Obviously, it is more technical than that, but this gives you more than enough information to make the best purchasing decision.

5

> If you do not have a DVD player, you may want to check Chapter 42, "Replacing, Upgrading, or Adding a CD/DVD Drive."

- **Hardware versus software decoding.** If your computer is slower than a 300MHz Pentium II, it is a good idea to invest the extra money into a hardware decoding board. Faster processors, however, may be able to handle the demands.

- **The rest of the setup.** To get the most pleasure out of DVD videos, you may want a 17-inch monitor or larger; good multimedia speakers, complete with subwoofers; and a high-quality sound card. You can get by with less than this, but these three items comprise the optimum setup for DVD video enjoyment.

Playing a DVD Movie

Playing a DVD will now seem so simple to you. To play a DVD using Windows Media Player, put the DVD in the DVD drive and wait for Windows Media Player to launch itself and start the movie.

The button you used to skim forward through a CD's current track is the counterpart to a VCR's fast forward button. Likewise, the Next track/Previous track buttons move you backward or forward through chapters on the DVD movie.

 DVD-formatted movies are divided up into bookmarked scenes called *chapters*. They help you navigate to particular points within a movie.

The one DVD-centered command you will most likely want to know is how to run the movie the whole size of the screen, since many DVD videos display in letterbox format (to look more like you are "at the movies"). To do this, click View, Full Screen. The movie-viewing window expands to cover the entire monitor surface.

Summary

Playing sights and sounds on your computer were the focus for this chapter. You saw how similar it is to use your PC to play an audio CD, the radio, and a DVD movie. You also learned how to record sound bites, and you even walked through the process of burning your own CD.

PART III

Getting Started with Windows

Chapter

CHAPTER 6

Managing the Windows Interface

The taskbar and the Start button are closely related. Most people use the Start button to display the Start menu and then execute their programs. When a program begins running, the taskbar displays a button with an icon, along with a description that represents the running program. The taskbar, the Start button, and the Start menu are the most fundamental components in Windows XP. The taskbar is the cornerstone of Windows XP. This chapter explains how to customize the taskbar to best suit your computing style.

A Quick Taskbar and Start Button Review

Starting with Chapter 2, "Diving into Windows," as well as throughout Chapters 3 through 5, you have used Windows by clicking the Start button and working within the Windows environment. In this chapter you will learn more details and go deeper into the Windows desktop so you can better manage your Windows-based computer.

To review, clicking the taskbar's Start button produces the Start menu.

The Start menu does all these things and more:

- It makes itself available to you no matter what else you are doing in Windows XP.
- It displays a list of programs and windows on your system using the Start menu's cascading system.
- It provides easy access to recently-used data documents that you can view or edit.
- It provides a search engine that navigates through all your files looking for the one you need.
- It activates the Windows XP help engine, which provides online help for working within Windows XP.

The next few sections explain how you can customize the taskbar and its associated Start menu so that the Start menu acts and looks the way you expect.

Sometimes the Start button temporarily disappears (when you're working in a full-screen command prompt session, for example). When this occurs, you can press Ctrl+Esc to display the Start menu when it disappears. If your keyboard contains a key with the Windows logo, that key also displays the Start menu.

Moving the Taskbar

The taskbar does not have to stay at the bottom of your screen. You can move the taskbar to either side of your monitor or even to the top of your screen. The taskbar placement is easy to change. Some people prefer their taskbar at the top of the screen or attached to the left or right edge of the screen.

Figure 6.1 shows that the taskbar does not have the width necessary to display lengthy descriptions when you place it on the side of the screen. When you place the taskbar at the bottom or top of the screen, the taskbar has more room for longer descriptions.

If you place the taskbar at the top of the screen, the Start menu falls from the Start button, whereas the Start menu pops up from the Start button when you place the taskbar at the bottom of the screen.

The newly placed taskbar

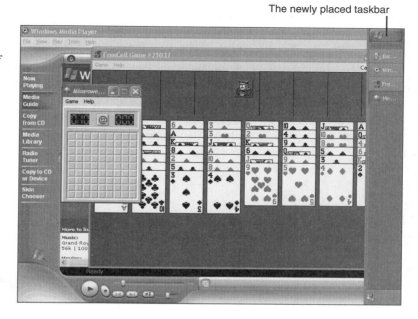

When working on a wide spreadsheet or document, you might want as much screen width as you can get. You then want the taskbar at the bottom or top of your screen. When working with graphics, you usually need more vertical screen space, so you can move the taskbar to either side of the screen.

Moving the taskbar to any of the four edges of your screen is easy. Simply drag the taskbar to the new location as the following steps demonstrate.

1. Find a blank spot on your taskbar and point to the spot with the mouse cursor. Be sure that you are pointing within the taskbar and not over a button.

2. Drag the taskbar to another edge of the screen. As you drag the mouse, the taskbar moves with the mouse and appears at the edge of the screen where you release the mouse.

3. Release the mouse button to anchor the taskbar at its new position.

6

The Taskbar Menu

A right mouse button click often displays a *pop-up menu* (sometimes called a *context-sensitive menu*) of options available to you. Windows XP looks at what you are doing when you right-click. Depending on the context, Windows displays commands appropriate to that task. The taskbar is one such location where the right mouse button brings up a helpful menu. You can use it to change the appearance and performance of the taskbar and the windows controlled by the taskbar. After finding a blank spot on your taskbar, right-clicking brings up the taskbar's pop-up menu shown in Figure 6.2.

The taskbar's pop-up menu

FIGURE 6.2

A right-click on a blank space of the taskbar displays a pop-up menu.

The taskbar menu is not necessarily a menu you want to display often. Most users play around with different taskbar and window settings for a while until they find preferences that suit them best. Thereafter, those users might rarely use the taskbar properties menu.

The taskbar actually displays several menus, depending on where you right-click and how you've configured the taskbar. For example, if you right-click over the notification area, the area at the far right (assuming your taskbar's on the bottom of the screen), several more options appear that don't otherwise show.

The Taskbar Properties Menu

When you select Properties from the taskbar menu, the Taskbar and Properties dialog box appears as shown in Figure 6.3.

If you have too many windows open to locate a blank spot on your taskbar to right-click upon, you can display the Taskbar and Start Menu Properties dialog box by selecting Appearance and Themes from the Control Panel and then selecting Taskbar and Start Menu.

FIGURE 6.3

Adjust your taskbar and Start menu settings from this properties dialog box.

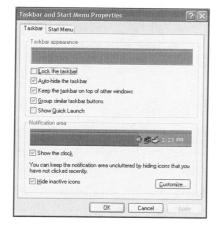

In Chapter 9, "Improving Your Desktop Experience," you'll learn how to use the Taskbar and Start Menu Properties dialog box to change the contents of the Start menu.

The Taskbar and Start Menu Properties dialog box accepts information that controls the way the taskbar appears on the screen. You can allow (or disallow) windows to overlap the taskbar if those windows are large enough to do so, you can eliminate the clock from the taskbar, and you can even minimize the taskbar so that it does not appear until you need it.

The following steps enable you to practice changing some of the taskbar's properties.

To Do: Working with Taskbar Properties

▼ To Do

1. Display the Taskbar and Start Menu properties dialog box by right-clicking over the Start button and selecting Properties.

2. Click the first option, Lock the taskbar. This option enables you to lock the taskbar so you cannot move it to another edge of the screen.

3. Check the option labeled Auto-hide the taskbar. When you click the Apply button, the taskbar disappears. The taskbar hasn't gone far—point the mouse cursor to the bottom of the screen and the taskbar will reappear. You can now have your taskbar and hide it, too! (When you click a dialog box's Apply command button, Windows XP implements your selected options immediately without closing the dialog box. You then can make further changes or click OK to close the dialog box.)

▲

6

If you display the Taskbar and Start Menu Properties dialog box but decide that you don't want to make any changes after all, click the Cancel command button.

Remaining Taskbar Properties

The Taskbar and Start Menu Properties dialog box ensures that the Taskbar always stays on top of whatever might appear on your window below it. When you uncheck this option, a window could overlap the taskbar and hide some or all of it.

The fourth option is labeled Group similar taskbar buttons. Microsoft Word users will appreciate this option which is checked by default. Windows XP watches how you open windows and, if checked and if the taskbar is already full of buttons, Windows ensures that only one taskbar button appears for all files you open with the same application. In other words, you can open three documents in Microsoft Word and all three buttons will appear next to each other on the taskbar even if you opened another program before you opened all three documents. In addition, if the taskbar cannot comfortably show all three buttons, Windows XP combines the buttons into one button, thus saving room on your taskbar.

The notification area contains the time of day if you've checked the option labeled Show the clock. The other icons that you find on the notification area represent special notices such as the new mail icon that alerts you that you have unread mail. To save taskbar space, only those notification icons that you've clicked recently appear if you check the last option labeled Hide inactive icons.

Toolbars on your Taskbar

Right-click over the toolbar and select Toolbars to see an array of choices. Table 6.1 explains each kind of element you can place on the taskbar from this menu.

TABLE 6.1   You Can Add These Toolbar Elements to Your Windows XP Taskbar

Toolbar Element	Description
Address	Displays a drop-down list box on your taskbar where you can enter a Web address to open that Web page from your Windows XP desktop.
Links	Displays popular Web links that you can quickly return to with the click of a button. You can modify the list of links.
Desktop	Displays an icon bar that matches those on your Windows XP desktop. You can click one of the icons to start that icon's program or open that icon's window instead of having to return to your desktop to locate the icon.

TABLE 6.1 continued

Toolbar Element	Description
Quick Launch	Adds Internet access control buttons so that you can quickly get on the Web. In addition, the Show Desktop icon appears in the Quick Launch section so that you can minimize all open windows with a single taskbar click.
New Toolbar	Enables you to select a disk drive, folder, or Web location whose contents appear as a secondary toolbar slider control on the taskbar. Subsequently, the taskbar's right-click menu contains the new toolbar that you can deselect to hide once again.

The Quick Launch toolbar is extremely helpful, especially due to its Show Desktop button. The following steps show how to display and use the Quick Launch toolbar.

1. Right-click over a blank area on your taskbar to display the pop-up menu.
2. Select Toolbars to display the list of available toolbars.
3. Select Quick Launch to place the Quick Launch toolbar on your taskbar. Although the Quick Launch toolbar consumes some taskbar space, it contains one-button access to popular programs such as your Internet Web browser and email. If you don't yet have an email program installed, the email program's icon will appear in the Quick Launch area when you install the email program. You can also drag any program icon from your my Computer window to the Quick Launch area. Figure 6.4 shows the Quick Launch toolbar with icons available for you to click.

Quick Launch toolbar

FIGURE 6.4

The Quick Launch toolbar puts your favorite programs right on your taskbar.

Show Desktop icon

6

4. Open your My Computer window and the Control Panel.
5. Click the Quick Launch toolbar's Show Desktop button. Immediately, your desktop appears. Windows XP did not close the windows but only minimized them. The Show Desktop button is handy when you need to return to your desktop without closing any programs you have open.

You can easily remove icons from the Quick Launch toolbar. Right-click on an icon and select Delete from the pop-up menu. Windows XP removes the icon but does not remove the associated program from your computer. You can add more programs to the Quick Launch toolbar by dragging their icons from the Start menu to the Quick Launch area. You can even place your favorite Web pages on the Quick Launch toolbar by dragging the Web page's icon that appears to the left of its address in your Web browser to your Quick Launch toolbar. When you subsequently click that Web page's icon, Windows XP will display that Web page, starting your Internet Web browser if needed first.

When you want to return to all the windows that you had open before clicking Show Desktop, right-click your taskbar to display the taskbar's pop-up menu and select Undo Minimize All.

Adjusting Your System Clock and Date

You can change your computer's date and time by double-clicking your notification area's clock. The Date/Time Properties dialog box shown in Figure 6.5 will appear.

FIGURE 6.5

You can change your PC's date and time.

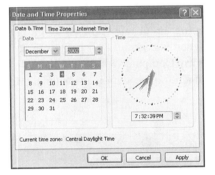

Managing Multiple Windows with the Taskbar

The taskbar's pop-up menu includes menu options that help you work with more than one open window at the same time. These menu options offer three ways of arranging your open windows so that they are more manageable. If you open two or more windows at once, all those windows can be difficult to manage individually. You could maximize each window and display only one window at a time. There are many reasons, however, to keep more than one window open and displayed at the same time, such as when you want to copy data from one window to another. (Chapter 8, "Navigating with Windows Explorer," explains how to copy between windows.)

Tiling Windows

When you want to see more than one open window at a time, the taskbar properties menu gives you tools that provide quick management of those windows so that you do not have to size and place each window individually. Figure 6.6 shows how too many windows open at the same time can be confusing.

FIGURE 6.6

Too many open windows can quickly cause disorganization.

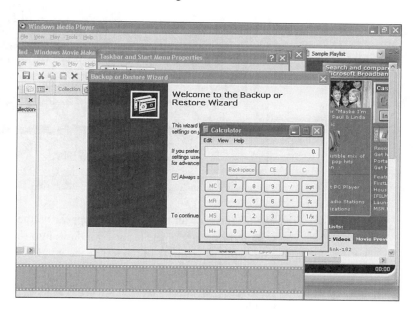

Three ways exist to organize several windows that are open at once: You can cascade them, horizontally tile them, or vertically tile them. The following steps demonstrate the cascade option.

1. From a clean desktop without any open windows, open your My Computer window. If My Computer opens maximized, click the Restore button to shrink the window down in size.

2. Open the Control Panel.

3. Open the Help and Support window. These open windows are open just to put some things on your desktop to work with for this task.

4. Now that you've opened three windows, ask Windows XP to organize those windows for you. Display the taskbar's properties menu by right-clicking after pointing to a blank spot on the taskbar.

5. Select the menu item labeled Cascade Windows. Windows XP instantly organizes your windows into the cascaded series of windows shown in Figure 6.7.

6

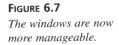

FIGURE 6.7

The windows are now more manageable.

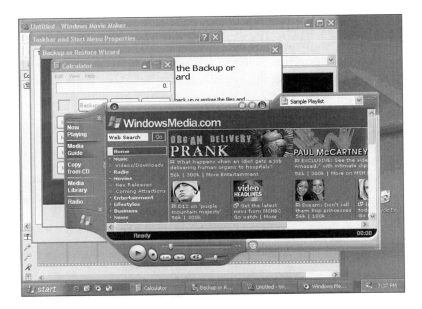

Notice that the title bars of all open windows appear on the Windows desktop area. When you want to bring any of the hidden windows into focus, click that window's title bar and the window will rise to the top of the window stack. The cascading effect always gives you the ability to switch between windows. As long as any part of a hidden window is peeking out from under another, you can click the title bar to bring that hidden window into focus.

6. Sometimes, you need to see the contents of two or more windows at the same time. Windows enables you to *tile* the open windows so that you can see the actual body of each open window. Windows supports two kinds of tiling methods: horizontal tiling and vertical tiling. Display the taskbar's properties menu and select Tile Windows Horizontally. Windows will properly resize each of the three open windows, as shown in Figure 6.8. (If a window's title bar is hidden but another part of the window is visible, you can bring that window into focus by clicking the part of the window that is visible.)

At first glance, the tiling might seem too limiting to you. After all, to fit those three open windows on the screen at the same time, Windows cannot show you a lot of any one of the windows. Keep in mind that you can move any window by dragging its title bar with your mouse as long as the window is not maximized to your full screen size. You can also point to an edge of a window and drag the edge to resize that window. Once you've tiled several open windows, you can still use the moving and resizing feature of the individual windows to arrange your desktop. Therefore, you can move the Help window toward the top of the screen, after tiling the windows, if you want to see more of that window. (Scrollbars automatically appear in tiled windows if the contents of the window consume more space than can be displayed at once. Click the arrows at each end of the scrollbar to move window contents into view.)

FIGURE 6.8

The windows are now tiled horizontally.

7. The vertical tiling method produces side-by-side windows that are fairly thin but offer yet another kind of open window display. Select Tile Windows Vertically and Windows reformats the screen again. Now that you've vertically tiled the open windows, you can restore the original placement of the windows by selecting Undo Tile. (The Undo option appears only after you've selected the Cascade, Tile, or Minimize option.)

8. The Minimize All Windows taskbar properties menu option attempts to minimize all open windows at the same time. The problem with the Minimize All Windows option is that not all windows can be minimized. Therefore, the option minimizes only those windows that have a minimize button (most do). The Show Desktop icon does minimize all open windows.

9. Close all open windows.

6

No matter how you tile or cascade the windows, each window's Minimize, Maximize, and Restore buttons work as usual. Therefore, you can maximize any cascaded window at any time by clicking that window's Maximize button.

Sizing the Taskbar

What happens if you open a number of windows by starting several programs? The single-line taskbar fills up very quickly with buttons and icons and descriptions that represent those open windows. The taskbar can become extremely full if you display multiple toolbars on the taskbar. Figure 6.9 shows such a taskbar.

Click here to see
more buttons

FIGURE 6.9

*This taskbar needs
more room.*

Two programs on one button

You can click the up and down arrows that Windows XP places on the toolbar to the right of your program buttons to see additional buttons. Windows cycles through all the taskbar buttons that are active.

Just as you can resize a window, you also can resize the taskbar. Simply point to the top edge of the taskbar (or the inside edge if you've moved the taskbar to an edge or top of the screen) and drag the edge toward the center of the screen. The taskbar enlarges as you drag your mouse. Figure 3.10 shows a wider version of the taskbar in Figure 6.9. Notice how all the taskbar buttons are more readable and have room to be noticed.

FIGURE 6.10

*This taskbar now has
breathing room—at
the expense of screen
space.*

When you enlarge the taskbar, it can more comfortably hold several buttons for open windows, and the descriptions on those buttons can be longer. Use the pop-up ToolTips if you need a reminder of the purpose of the taskbar buttons, such as the Show Desktop button. Of course, the larger taskbar means that you don't have as much screen space as you might need for your programs.

Starting Programs with the Start Menu

The Start menu offers an extremely simple way for you to start the programs on your computer. Two or three clicks start virtually any program on your disk drive. When you install new programs on your computer, those programs add themselves to your Start menu. (Chapter 11, "Installing Programs with Windows," explains how to install programs on your computer.)

As you open programs and use your computer, Windows XP keeps track of your most recent programs and places them in a handy position on the Start menu as Figure 6.11 shows.

FIGURE 6.11

The Start menu keeps track of the programs you've used recently.

Recently run programs ——

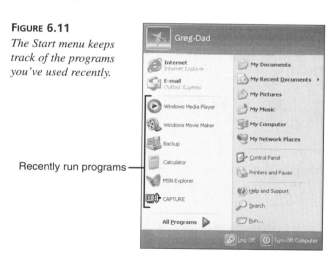

The More Programs command on the Start menu enables you to launch any program on your disk. To start a program, you display the menu that contains that program and then click the program's name or icon.

6

Using the Run Command

In addition to the Start menu's Programs command, you can use another method to start programs that aren't set up on the Programs' cascade of menus. The Run command on the Start menu provides a way for you to execute specific programs.

Reaching Your Files

A *pathname* is the exact computer system location of a file. The document and folder concept in Windows makes working with paths much easier than before Windows. Most often, you specify pathnames visually by clicking folder icons instead of typing long pathnames, as you had to do before Windows.

The folders in Windows used to be called *directories*. A directory is just a collection of files and other directories. In file listings, Windows often displays a folder icon with a name to represent a directory that holds other files. Folders can hold subfolders, so the location of a file, the file's path, might be deep within several nested folders on a disk or CD-ROM drive.

A full pathname begins with a disk drive name followed by a colon (:) followed by a backslash (\). If the file resides in the disk drive's top folder (called the *root directory*), you then type the filename. If, however, the file resides in another folder, you must list the folder after the backslash. If the file resides in several nested folders, you must list each folder in order, from the outermost to the innermost, and separate each folder name with a backslash. Both of the following are full pathnames to specific files:

```
c:\autoexec.bat
```

```
d:\Sherry\WordProc\Home\Insure\Fire and Casualty
```

The first filename is `autoexec.bat` located in the root directory. The second filename is `Fire and Casualty` located within a series of nested directories.

The Start menu's Run command offers a tedious way to execute any program on your computer. If you want to run a program that would not properly set up in Windows (perhaps the program is an old MS-DOS–based program), you have to execute the program using Run.

To run a program from the Run menu option, display the Start menu and select the Run command. Windows displays the Run dialog box.

There might or might not be text next to the Open prompt. Windows XP needs to know the exact name and path of the program you want to open (and run).

Almost all users install Windows XP on drive C. If your Windows XP system is installed on another drive, substitute your drive name for the `c:` and type the following exactly as you see it (using either uppercase or lowercase letters): `c:\WINDOWS\SOL` and press Enter.

The Solitaire game is normally installed on the Windows directory on drive C. The name of the program is `SOL.EXE`. To execute any program with an `.EXE` filename extension, you need to type only the first part of the filename, such as `SOL`. If Solitaire does not start, you might have typed the line incorrectly. Try again and be sure that you use backslashes and not forward slashes.

You might be one of the lucky few who never needs the Run command. Nevertheless, there are many programs on the market that Windows cannot execute in its environment. Using Run, you can execute any program on your computer as long as you know the program's pathname and filename.

> Windows supports a strong data document concept. It is data-driven more than program-driven. If you type a data file (such as a Microsoft Word document) instead of a program name with the Run command, Windows automatically starts the program needed to work with that data file and loads the data file for you. Therefore, you worry less about your programs, and you can concentrate more on your data. In addition, you can type an Internet address (often called a uniform resource locator, or, URL) at Run and Windows XP automatically starts your Internet browser and takes you to the Web site you entered.

Summary

This chapter concentrated mostly on the taskbar. The taskbar gives you a play-by-play status of the open windows on your system. As you open and close windows, the taskbar updates with new buttons to show what's happening at all times. If you start more than one program, you can switch between those programs as easily as you switch between cable TV shows: Click a button on the taskbar.

The taskbar works along with the Start menu to start and control the programs running on your system. Use the Programs command on the Start menu to start programs with a total of two or three mouse clicks. Although you can use the Run command to start programs, the Programs menu is easier to use as long as the program is set up properly in Windows XP.

6

CHAPTER 7

Working with the My Computer Window

The My Computer icon opens to a window, as you learned in the previous chapter, "Managing the Windows Interface," and contains information that relates to your computer's hardware and software. You will often open the My Computer window when you add or remove both hardware and software. The My Computer window provides access to many different areas of your computer.

Many computer beginners and advanced users ignore the My Computer window more than they should. The My Computer window, which always appears on your Windows desktop, enables you to access every hardware device on your system in a uniform fashion. In this chapter, you will also begin using the Control Panel window to change the behavior of your mouse and also to modify the screen background that you see. You must look at the desktop often, so changing the graphics behind the desktop can break the monotony that you might otherwise face with a dull Windows XP desktop screen. People often spend the first few sessions with any new operating environment getting to know the environment and modifying the appearance to suit their preferences.

Looking at My Computer

Your computer system is comprised of hardware (the system unit, monitor, keyboard, CD-ROM, networked components, and so on), firmware (the internal memory), and software (for example, Windows XP and its auxiliary programs such as the Windows Media Player, word processors, spreadsheets, and games). There are several ways to access your computer's hardware and software through different areas of Windows XP. The My Computer window contains one of the most helpful hardware and software management resources available in Windows XP.

Open your My Computer window now by selecting its entry from the Start menu. Windows XP displays the My Computer window like the one shown in Figure 7.1. The My Computer window contains icons for your computer's primary components such as the disk drives. The computer in Figure 7.1 is fairly comprehensive and your My Computer window might contain fewer or more devices. In addition, your My Computer window's format might be set up to look slightly different from the one in the figure.

FIGURE 7.1
The My Computer window displays your computer's storage hardware.

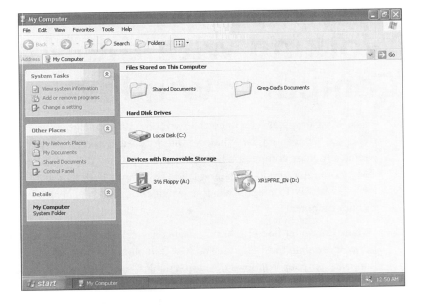

The Tasks and Other Places sections enable you to jump to other Windows system windows to perform other tasks. You can get to these other areas from the Start menu and from other program windows as well. Windows almost always gives you multiple avenues to its various areas.

Working in the My Computer Window

People's needs for the My Computer window differ greatly, depending on which hardware they use to run Windows XP. For example, a network user probably displays the My Computer window more often than a single user working primarily on a spreadsheet program. The network user might have more reason to check the properties of a shared folder or disk drive.

Before looking at a sample My Computer window work session, you should understand that there are several ways to view the My Computer window, as well as most other Windows XP windows:

- In the tiled view shown in the previous section in Figure 7.1 with the links to other places on the left and icons for each hardware component on the right
- In the icon view so that more icons can be seen if your computer has many shared folders and drives
- In the detail view that shows disk drive sizes and free space

The tiled view is the default view that is set when you install Windows XP. The next chapter, "Navigating with Windows Explorer," explains how to move files from one disk drive to another by dragging a file to the disk icon in which you want to put that file instead of typing a disk drive name, as computer users of older operating systems have to do.

As you progress, you might prefer to switch to a detail view to view more information about the items inside My Computer. Select View, Details from the menu to change to the detailed view. Although small icons still appear next to most of the items in a list view of the My Computer window, the icons are extremely small.

Figure 7.2 shows the detailed view. The detailed view becomes even more important if you display additional information in a window. The detailed list view shows the filename, size in bytes, file type, and the most recent date modified. You will learn in the next section how to display additional information inside My Computer and the detailed view shows more information than the tiled view can show.

As you add hardware and as you traverse additional windows from within the My Computer window, your current view might no longer be adequate to display the data. For example, for only a few icons, the tiled view works well to show an overview of your machine.

7

FIGURE 7.2

The My Computer window shown in a detailed list view.

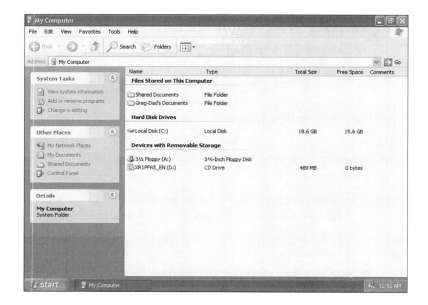

Working with My Computer

The best way to begin learning about the My Computer window is to work within it. Follow the several steps to see some of the things that are possible with My Computer and, therefore, with all windows that you need to manage.

1. Open the My Computer window if you don't have it open already.

2. From the menu bar, select View, List. The view instantly changes to the list view.

3. Select View, Details. The list view expands to tell you more about each item, such as free space and total space on the disk and CD-ROM drives.

4. Go back to the tiled view.

5. If not maximized already, maximize your My Computer window by clicking the Maximize button or by double-clicking the title bar.

6. Click the C disk drive icon once to select it. The Details section shows the disk's size.

7. Now double-click the C disk drive icon. When you do, you should see a window of folders and other icons. Each folder represents a folder on your disk drive named C. A folder is a list of files (and subfolders) stored together in one group. The folder name appears under each folder icon. If you also see a hand holding the folder, the folder is known as a *shared folder* available to others on the network you're working on.

You might see some grayed-out icons in the list. These are hidden system files that you generally do not need access to and you generally shouldn't change or delete. To protect these from view, if you can see them, you can select Tools, Folder Options and click the View tab to designate whether you want to see all hidden files and folders (in which case Windows XP grays out the system and normally hidden files and folders), all files except the hidden ones, or all files except both the hidden and system files. You generally won't work with system or hidden files, and by turning off their display, you clean up your file listings considerably. Click OK to save your changes.

Folders enable you to group similar files together so that you can work with the entire group at once instead of having to work with individual files. For example, you can keep all your personal correspondence in a single folder so that you can copy it easier to a disk when you want to back up that set of files.

The icons that look like pieces of paper are document icons that represent individual files, including programs and text files, on your system's C drive. You find other kinds of icons as well. If you see the list view when you display the C disk drive, select View, Tiles to see the icons.

8. To look at the contents of a file folder, double-click the file folder. When you do, yet another window will open up, or possibly the current window will change to reflect the new file folder depending on the options set in your Tools, Options menu.

If you have lots of files on drive C, and most people do, you might have to use the scrollbars to see all the window's contents. As you open additional windows by opening new folders, you can always return to the previous folder window by clicking the toolbar's Back button.

9. Click the Back button to return to a previous view.

10. Every time you change the window contents from the My Computer window by double-clicking an icon such as the C drive icon, a new set of window contents appears. You can traverse right back through all the windows you visited and return to the My Computer window contents by pressing the Back button on the toolbar, just as you do to traverse back through Web pages you might have traveled.

7

Click the arrow next to the My Computer toolbar's Views button. A view list drops down from which you can quickly select Thumbnails, Tiles, Icons, List, and Details. *Thumbnails* are small pictures that represent the contents of your file, unlike icons that only represent the file type.

Other Start Menu Windows

You will master other Start menu windows besides the My Computer window as you learn more about Windows XP. The previous three lessons began describing many of these windows, such as the My Pictures, My Music, and the Control Panel window.

Here are two Start menu windows that you're not yet familiar with:

- **My Documents**—Contains a list of data files for many of your application programs.
- **My Network Places**—Contains a list of computers that are networked to yours (although you might not see this option if you do not use a network).

All the windows view commands you've learned so far work throughout the Windows XP environment. Therefore, you can now change views for all windows you work with using the same View menu commands you learned about earlier in the My Computer window section.

Accessing the Control Panel

The Control Panel enables you to adjust and manage the way hardware devices are attached to and respond to your computer. Open the Control Panel from the Start menu and you'll see a window like the one in Figure 7.3.

Notice the option on the left pane of the Control Panel labeled Switch to Classic View. When you click this option, Windows XP changes your Control Panel's view to the *classic view* used in previous Windows versions. The classic view, as opposed to the *category view* that you saw previously, groups all available icons located in your Control Panel window by function. Figure 7.4 shows the Control Panel classic view.

The Control Panel's toolbar and menus work in a similar manner to those of the My Computer window. When you master windows basics for one kind of window, you can apply that talent to all other windows. From the Control Panel, you can change or modify system and hardware settings.

FIGURE 7.3

Modify the system settings from within the Control Panel.

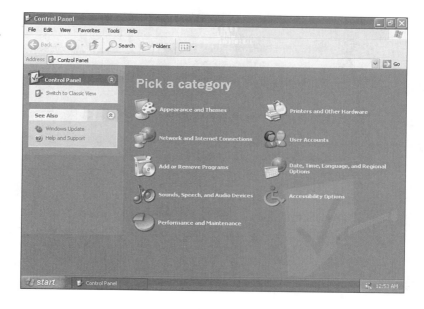

FIGURE 7.4

You can see all the Control Panel's icons from the classic view.

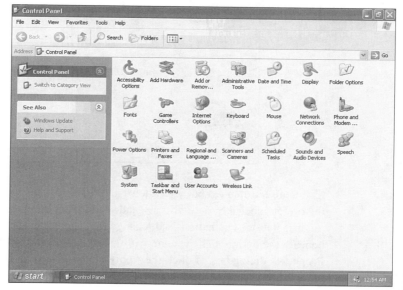

7

Be very sure that you know what to change before modifying values within the Control Panel. You could change a required setting that might be difficult to reverse later.

Modifying the Mouse Properties

Some operations inside the Control Panel are complex and could violate your system's setup. Many tasks are safe inside the Control Panel, however. Follow these steps to learn how to modify the way your mouse behaves.

1. Open the Control Panel window if you have not yet done so.

2. Select the Mouse icon. The icon indicates that the mouse settings are found here. You see the Mouse Properties dialog box appear, as shown in Figure 7.5.

FIGURE 7.5

You can change the behavior of the mouse.

3. If you are left-handed but your mouse is set for a right-handed user, you can select the option labeled Switch primary and secondary buttons to change the mouse button orientation. The buttons will change their functionality as described in the text beneath the option. (The change will not take effect until you close the Mouse Properties dialog box or click the Apply button.) You can change the button back to its original state by clicking the option once again.

4. Click the tab marked Pointers at the top of the Mouse Properties dialog box. From the Pointer portion of the dialog box, you can change the default appearance of the mouse. A scrolling list of mouse shapes indicates all the kinds of cursor shapes that appear when certain Windows XP events take place.

5. To change the default mouse pointer (called the Normal Select shape), double-click the row with the Normal Select text. Windows XP displays another screen, shown in Figure 7.6, with different mouse pointers you can use. The mouse pointers are stored in files on your system. Some pointers (those whose filenames end with the .ani filename extension) are animated cursors that move when you select them and use the mouse.

FIGURE 7.6

Select a mouse cursor shape file.

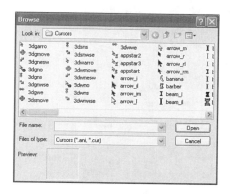

6. Windows XP can change the *theme*, or overall look of all your mouse pointers, to make them uniform. Just for grins, click the down arrow next to (None) inside the Scheme area and point to 3D-Bronze in the list. Windows changes all your mouse pointers to three-dimensional bronze shapes.

7. Before leaving the Mouse Properties window, click the Use Default button to return the standard mouse cursor to its default pointer shape unless you want to keep another selection.

8. Click OK to close the Control Panel.

Different Wallpaper

Wallpaper is the name for the background you see on the screen when you start Windows XP and work within its windows. You can change that wallpaper to a different picture or eliminate the wallpaper altogether by following these steps:

1. Open your Control Panel window.

2. Select the Appearance and Themes category. Here, you can change several desktop elements such as the wallpaper background and your *desktop themes*. Desktop themes are predesigned icons and colors and desktop settings, combined in a single collection, so that you can easily change the overall look of your desktop and other windows elements. Instead of modifying the entire look of Windows XP, you

7

should probably keep most of the default settings as they are until you learn how to navigate the default Windows XP theme. For this To Do item, you will change only your desktop wallpaper's background.

3. Select the option labeled Change the desktop background to display the Display Properties dialog box shown in Figure 7.7.

FIGURE 7.7

You can change your desktop's appearance.

4. The Background list of choices determines the wallpaper pattern you might want to use for your desktop's background. Scroll through the list of choices looking for an interesting name, such as Azul, and click on that selection. Windows models the new wallpaper style in the small screen to give you a preview of it. You can go with that selection or choose another.

5. When you are happy with your selection, click the OK button, and presto, you've hung new wallpaper without messy cutting or gluing!

You can change your wallpaper without first displaying the Control Panel. Simply right-click over a blank spot on your desktop, select Properties, and click the Desktop tab.

When surfing the Internet, you can quickly set any image you find on a Web page as wallpaper. Just right-click over a Web page's picture, select Set as Wallpaper, and Windows XP transfers the picture to your desktop immediately, replacing whatever wallpaper you had there before.

Adding Handy Desktop Icons

You already know that the taskbar's Show Desktop icon quickly minimizes all open windows and returns you to the desktop. Some Windows users prefer to place program icons on their desktop so that they can keep common windows and routine programs handy. When you place an icon on your desktop that represents a window such as the My Computer window, you only need to double-click that icon, while at your desktop, to see the window or start the program.

The following steps explain how to place programs on your desktop:

1. Click the Show Desktop Quick Launch toolbar button to minimize any windows you may have open.
2. Locate the program in your Start menu that you want to represent with a desktop icon. You may have to open a few cascading Start menu folders to locate the program.
3. Click and hold your right mouse button and drag the program's icon from its Start menu location to your desktop and release the mouse button.
4. Select Copy Here from the pop-up menu that appears and Windows XP places the icon on your desktop. You now only need to double-click this icon from the desktop to start the program.

You can also place icons that take you to specific Web pages on your desktop. When viewing a Web page in your Internet browser, drag the icon to the left of the Web page's address to your desktop. The next time you double-click that desktop icon, the Web page appears, dialing your Internet connection first if needed.

Summary

This chapter taught you how to use the My Computer window. Don't be dismayed that this hour just skimmed the surface of what's available in the My Computer window because the My Computer icon provides a launching point for many powerful hardware and software interactions that sometimes take a while to master. The typical Windows XP user does not have to know all the details of the My Computer window to use Windows XP effectively.

7

CHAPTER 8

Navigating with Windows Explorer

Windows includes a comprehensive program that you might use every time you turn on your computer, the *Windows Explorer* program, which graphically displays your entire computer system, including all its files, in a hierarchical tree structure. With Explorer, you have access to everything inside your computer (and outside if you are part of a network or on the Internet).

This chapter demonstrates the Windows Explorer, a program that enables you to manipulate all of your computer's program and data files. After you've learned about Explorer, the chapter concludes by showing you some time- and disk-saving features of Windows XP.

Introducing the Windows Explorer

Often, Windows users call the Windows Explorer program just *Explorer*. You'll find Explorer listed on the Start menu system. Click the Start button to display the Start menu. Select More Programs, Accessories, and then select Windows Explorer. (Do not select Internet Explorer as that's your

Internet browser.) The Windows Explorer window opens to look like the one shown in Figure 8.1. By default, Explorer opens to your My Documents folder located on your Windows disk drive. Your Explorer window might look somewhat different from the one in the figure. As Figure 8.1 shows, you can make Explorer point to any drive and folder, including a My Documents folder on a non-Windows drive if one exists. Simply type the location you wish to view in the Address bar.

FIGURE 8.1

Explorer's opening window shows folders and files.

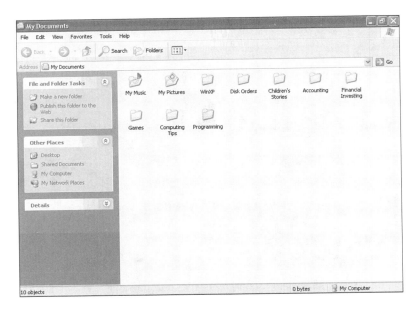

 You'll see how to customize your Explorer screen throughout this section.

Although the figure shows the Explorer screen fully maximized, you can run Explorer in a smaller window if you want something else to appear on your screen as well. In addition, your Explorer screen might differ slightly from the figures depending on your computer's files, disks, and theme.

 You can quickly start Explorer by right-clicking over the Start menu and selecting Explore from the pop-up menu that appears. Even faster, locate your Windows key, the one with the flying Windows logo on it, and press Windows+E to start Explorer.

You can replace the task area of your Explorer screen with a hierarchical overview of your computer system by selecting View, Explorer Bar, Folders. You will recognize many of the icon entries from your My Computer window. If a vertical scrollbar appears on the left window, scroll to see the rest of the hierarchical system tree. You can replace the task area once again by selecting View, Explorer Bar, Folders so that common tasks are available to you.

If a folder icon appears in the Explorer bar with a plus sign to the left of it, that folder contains additional folders and files. Folder icons without the plus sign contain only data files (called *documents* throughout Windows XP) but not additional folders. When you open a folder and display its contents, the plus sign changes to a minus sign, as you'll see at the end of this section.

The right side of the Explorer window contains a pictorial overview of the contents of whichever device or folder you select in the left window. The overview might contain large or small icons or a list view, depending on the view you select.

As with the My Computer window, you can display a thumbnail view that shows a small version of any Web page or graphic file that appears in the Windows Explorer window. As you select different items (by clicking to open folders or by selecting from a displayed Explorer bar), the right window changes to reflect your changes. The task area contains tasks you'll often perform inside the Explorer window as well as quick links to other places you may need to see such as the My Computer window or your desktop.

The following steps guide you through an initial exploration of Explorer.

1. Start Windows Explorer.

2. Select View, Explorer Bar, Folders to display your computer disk drive hierarchy.

3. Scroll through the Explorer bar's hierarchy until you see the icon for the C: drive in the window.

4. If you see a plus sign next to your C: icon in the left window (you might have to scroll the window's scrollbar to see the C: icon), click the plus sign to display the contents of the C: drive. The plus becomes a minus sign, and the left window opens the C: icon showing the list of folders and documents on the C: drive. Click the drive's minus sign again to close the window. Click once more to turn the plus to a minus and watch the right window. As you change between these two views of the C: drive (detailed and overview), watch the right window.

> Notice that the right window does not change as you click the C: icon in the left window. The reason is that the right window always displays the contents of whatever you highlight in the left window. Whether the C: icon is open (with a minus sign) or closed (with a plus sign), the C: icon is highlighted. If you were to click one of those documents on the C: drive, the right window would then update to show the contents of that folder (don't click a folder just yet).

5. Click the highest level in the left window, labeled Desktop, and Windows XP displays the contents of your desktop in the right window.

6. Click the C: icon to display the contents of the C: drive. Depending on the contents and size of your C: drive, the right window can contain a few or many document files.

7. Press Alt+V to open the View menu on the menu bar. Select Toolbar to display a list of tools you can display on your toolbar. Whatever you know about other windows applies to the Explorer window. For example, you can add text labels to the toolbar icons if you right-click the toolbar and select Customize.

8. Type a Web address inside the Address Bar's textbox to replace the contents of your Explorer window with a Web page. Press Back to return to the Explorer window. As you can see, Windows XP attempts to blur the distinction between your computer and the online world. Whether data is on your hard disk or on the disk of a computer across the globe, Explorer gives you quick access.

9. Select View, Details. Windows XP Explorer displays the items in a detailed format that describes the name, type, and modified date of each item. Actually, given the detail that you normally have by using Explorer, you will almost always want to display the right window in this detailed list view. When you work with files, you will often need to know their size, type, or last modified date.

   Click Name, the title of the first detailed column in the right window. Watch the window's contents change as you then click Modified. Explorer sorts the display to appear in date order (earliest first). Click Modified again and Explorer displays the items in reverse date order from the oldest to the most recent. If you click any column twice in a row, Windows sorts the column in reverse order. You can always sort columns in order or reverse order by clicking the column's name when working in a columnar Windows window.

10. If you want to see more of one of Explorer's windows, you can drag the edge of the left window pane (the pane marked Folders) left or right. For example, if you

8

want the left window to be smaller to make room for more large icons, drag the right edge of the Folders pane to the left and release the mouse when the left window is as small as you want it. (Remember that the mouse cursor changes shape when you place it at the proper position on the dividing column.) Figure 8.2 shows the Explorer screen with the Explorer bar and no task window. Perhaps you'll prefer this configuration over the Task pane appearing. You'll learn which window configuration works best for you as you gain more experience with Explorer.

FIGURE 8.2

Make more room by closing the Folders window pane and changing the view.

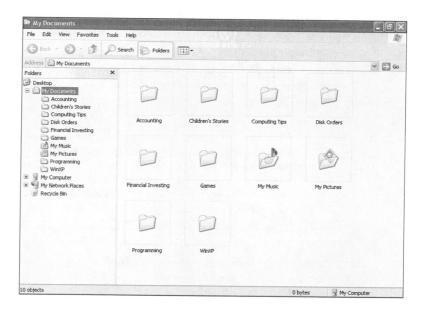

11. Click the toolbar's Folders button to see the Folders pane once again. As you can see, the Folders button quickly changes between the Explorer bar and your Task pane.

Explorer does not update the display every time you resize a window or change the size of the Folders pane. Therefore, if you enlarge the right window while in an icon view, Explorer does not automatically rearrange the right window's icons to fill up the newly enlarged space. You will almost always want to select View, Refresh after modifying Explorer's window sizes because Refresh analyzes any changes you've made to your disk while inside Explorer and updates the Explorer window. Perform Refresh when you open Explorer in a window and then add or delete files from another window.

If you make the left or right window too small, Windows XP adds a horizontal scrollbar to the small window so that you can scroll its contents back and forth to see what's highlighted or to select another item.

12. The Explorer environment is always updating itself to reflect your current actions. Therefore, the right-click menu commands change, depending on whether you select a text document, folder, sound document, graphics document, disk drive, or network drive. Click a folder and right-click to see the menu that appears. Now, right-click over a document file to see a slightly different menu. The actions you might want to perform on a document are often different from the actions you might want to perform on a folder, and the menu reflects those differences. The right-click's pop-up menus are context-sensitive, so they contain only the options you can use at the time.

Open a folder by double-clicking it, and then return to the previous (parent) folder by clicking the Up icon on the Explorer's toolbar. Use the Up toolbar button to return to your previous Explorer window's contents. You can return to the previous folder you opened (which is not necessarily the parent folder) by clicking the toolbar's Back button instead of Up.

13. Many Explorer users copy files to and from disk drives and other kinds of drives, such as networked drives.

You can use Explorer to copy and move individual files or multiple files at once. Often, you want to put one or more files from work on a diskette to use on your home computer for weekend overtime. (Sure, you want to do that a lot!)

To select a Windows file (called a document, remember), click that document. To select more than one document at a time, hold down the Ctrl key while clicking each document that you want to select. You can select folders, as well as documents. When you select a folder and other document files to copy to a disk, for example, Windows XP copies all the document files within the folder, as well as the other document files you've selected, to the disk. Figure 8.3 shows an Explorer screen with several document files and a folder selected. The File, Send To command (from the right-click pop-up menu) is about to send those files to the disk in the A: drive. The Send To command is useful for sending copies of selected files and folders to a disk, a fax recipient, or one of several other destinations you've set up.

FIGURE 8.3

Select multiple documents and folders if you need to copy several at a time.

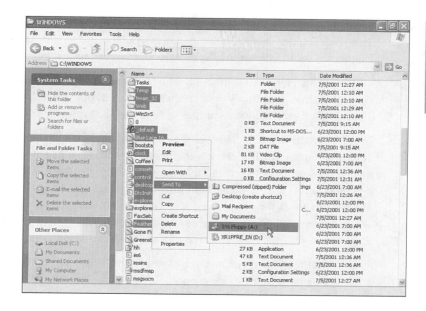

14. When you want to move or copy a file to another location (the Send To command works only for diskettes and other nonhard disk devices), select the file (or select a group of files) in the right window and drag while holding down the *right* mouse button to the folder or disk where you want to move or copy the file. Windows opens a pop-up menu when you release the files from which you can select a move or copy operation.

15. Rename files and folders if you need to by selecting the file or folder and pressing the F2 shortcut key. (F2 is the shortcut for the File, Rename menu command.) Windows XP highlights the name, so you can edit or enter a new name. When you press Enter, Windows XP saves the new name.

The strength of Explorer is that your entire computer system appears in the left window at all times. When you want to drag a document or folder to a different directory on a completely different drive (or even to another computer on the network if you are connected to a network), the target disk drive always appears in the left window. As long as you've clicked the disk drive's plus sign to display that disk's directories, you can drop a file into that directory from elsewhere in the system.

The Explorer Options

Explorer supports various display options for the items inside its windows. Files have filename *extensions*, a file suffix three or more letters long that appears after a filename.

A filename might be MyPayments.TXT or All Accounts.act (filenames can contain spaces). The Tools, Folder Options command displays tabbed dialog boxes that enable you to control the way Explorer displays items.

Different users require different screens from the Explorer program. There are types of documents that you simply don't need to display during normal work inside Explorer. The system files are good examples of files that the typical user does not need to see.

In addition, the actual location of the file—its pathname—does not always match the system of embedded folders. In other words, a document might be located inside two embedded folders shown with the Explorer display, but the actual file might be embedded three levels deep on your hard disk. The system of folders—usually but not always—matches the system of directories on your disk. If you need to know exactly where folders and documents are located on your disk drive, you can request that Explorer display the full pathname of those folders and documents using these steps:

1. Select the Tools, Folder Options command to display the Folder Options tabbed dialog box shown in Figure 8.4.

FIGURE 8.4

The Folder Options dialog box determines the appearance of Explorer.

2. Click the View tab to see the folder display options.

3. If you click the option labeled Display the full path in title bar, Explorer displays a full pathname of selected documents in the title bar every time you select one of the items in the left window.

4. Another option, Hide file extensions for known file types, determines how Windows responds to known file types. Windows comes installed with several types of files already *registered*, and you might not ever need to register additional

types. Registered files are files that Windows recognizes by their filename extensions. When you install a program whose data file is not registered, the installation program registers the file type with Windows.

The file type's registration tells Windows the required program needed to process files with that extension. Once registered, when you double-click that file's icon, Windows starts the program you've associated with that file. For example, when you double-click a file with a .cda extension, Windows starts the CD Player application because CD Player is the application associated to all files that end with the .cda extension.

5. Look through the remaining items to see the other folder options that Windows provides. Click OK to finish your selection.

If you are familiar with MS-DOS and filenames, you might feel more comfortable if you display the file extensions on the Explorer screen documents. Hiding the extensions reduces clutter in the right window, but with the extension, you can determine the exact name of the file when you need the exact name. Fortunately, with or without the extensions, the icons next to the filenames help remind you of the file's type.

If you hide filename extensions in Explorer, Windows hides those extensions in almost every other file listing. For example, if you hide Explorer's extension display, you will no longer see extensions in WordPad's Open dialog boxes. You won't even see them in applications that you purchase in addition to Windows applications, such as Microsoft Excel.

Managing Documents with a Right Mouse Click

After you display the Explorer (or any other file list in Windows), you can point to any folder or document and click the right mouse button to perform several actions on the document. Here's what you can do with documents:

- Select documents by clicking them to highlight them
- Play sound or video files and view graphics
- Print selected documents
- Copy selected files to a disk

- Cut or copy selected text to the *Windows Clipboard* (an area of memory that holds data that you copy there until you replace the Clipboard's contents with something else or log off Windows)
- Create a shortcut access to the file so that you can later open the file without using the Open dialog box
- Delete documents
- Rename documents
- Change documents' system attributes

Right-clicking a folder's name produces a menu that enables you to perform these actions.

The following steps walk you through many of these right-click actions:

1. Inside an Explorer window, point to a text file on your C: drive. Text files use a spiral notepad icon. Open your Windows folder if you see no text files in your C: drive's root folder. Point to the file and right-click. A pop-up menu opens to the right of the document, as shown in Figure 8.5.

FIGURE 8.5

A right-click displays a pop-up menu.

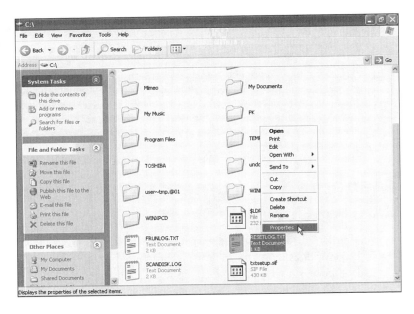

The Open command always attempts to examine the document's native format and open the document with an appropriate program such as the Windows's Notepad program. Although the first command is Open for text files, the command is Play if you right-clicked a sound file. For now, don't select Open.

2. Find a blank formatted diskette. Insert the diskette in the A: drive. Right-click over the text document and select the Send To command. The disk drive appears in the list that appears when you select Send To. When you select the disk drive, Windows XP begins sending an exact copy of the text file to the disk. Windows graphically displays the sending of the document to the A: drive with a flying document going from one folder to another.

3. Point to the text file once again and right-click. Select Delete. Windows displays the message box shown in Figure 8.6. Don't choose Yes because you need to keep the text file where it is.

FIGURE 8.6

The Recycle Bin holds deleted documents for a while.

The *Recycle Bin* is a special location inside Windows that holds the documents you delete. The Recycle Bin's icon appears on your Windows desktop. Windows gives you one last chance to recover deleted documents. When you delete a document file of any type, Windows sends that file to the Recycle Bin. The documents are then out of your way but not deleted permanently until you empty the Recycle Bin. Remember that you can delete documents directly from any Open dialog box.

4. Click No because you should not delete the text file now.

5. It's extremely easy to rename a document. Right-click to display the document's pop-up menu and select Rename. Windows highlights the name, and you can edit or completely change the name to something else. Change the filename now to XYZ. Press Enter to keep the new name. (If you want to cancel a rename operation you've started, press Esc.)

Do not supply an extension when you rename the file unless you've turned on the filename extension display. For example, if you renamed a Readme document (that is really named Readme.txt) to NewName.txt, the document would actually be named NewName.txt.txt! Fortunately, Windows XP warns you if you change a file's extension, so you can accept or reject the change before it becomes permanent.

6. Try this: Move the mouse pointer to an area of the Explorer's right pane where no icon appears and right-click. A new menu appears.

   The Undo Rename command reverses the previous renaming of the document. Select Undo Rename, and the XYZ text file you just renamed reverts to its original name.

You now understand the most important commands in the Explorer's primary right-click pop-up menus. These menus differ slightly depending on the kind of document you click (folder, video, sound, graphic, program, text, word processor document, and so on), but the fundamental menu of commands stays the same and works the way this section describes. If you want to make copies of files on the hard disk or move the file to a different location, you should master the techniques described in the next section.

Right-Click to Copy and Move Documents

A file icon's right-click menu offers advanced copying and moving of files. You'll use the Windows Clipboard as the go-between for all Windows copy, cut, paste, and move operations. When you want to copy a file from one place to another, you can place a copy of the file on the Windows Clipboard. When you do, the file is on the Clipboard and out of your way, until you go to where you want the file copied. You'll then paste the file to the new location, in effect copying from the Clipboard to the new location. When you copy a file to another location, the file remains in its original location and a copy is made elsewhere.

> The Clipboard holds one item at a time. If you copy a document to the Clipboard, a subsequent copy overwrites the first copy.

When you move a file from one location to another, Windows XP first performs a cut operation. This means that Windows XP deletes the file from its current location and sends the file to the Clipboard (overwriting whatever was on the Clipboard). When you find the location to which you want to move the file, Windows XP copies the Clipboard's contents to the new location (such as a different folder or disk drive).

About the Clipboard

In a way, the Clipboard is like a short-term Recycle Bin, which holds all deleted files until you are ready to remove them permanently. The

8

Clipboard holds deleted (or copied) documents and pieces of documents, but only until you send something else to the Clipboard or exit Windows XP and log off Windows XP.

1. Right-click a text file's icon.

2. Select the Copy command. Windows sends a complete copy of the document to the Clipboard. The Clipboard keeps the document until you replace the Clipboard's contents with something else or until you exit Windows. Therefore, you can send the Clipboard document to several subsequent locations.

3. Right-click a folder in Explorer's right window. The menu appears with the Paste command. Windows knows that something is on the Clipboard (a copy of the text file), and you can send the file's copy to the folder by clicking Paste. Don't paste the file now, however, unless you then open the folder and remove the file. There is no need to have two copies of the text file on your disk.

4. Right-click once again over the text file. This time, select Cut instead of Copy. Windows erases the document file from the Windows folder and places the file on the Clipboard.

Windows keeps the name of the document in place until you paste the document elsewhere. The name is misleading because it makes you think the document is still in the Windows folder. A ghost outline of an icon appears where the document's icon originally appeared. As long as the name still appears in the Windows folder, you can open the file and do things with it, but as soon as you paste the Clipboard contents elsewhere, the file permanently disappears from the Windows folder.

5. Right-click a folder. If you select Paste, the text document leaves its original location and goes to the folder. Don't paste now but press Esc twice (the first Esc keypress removes the right-click menu, and the second restores the cut file).

6. Windows lets you change your mind. If you change your mind after a copy or cut operation, you can always reverse the operation! Right-click the icon area and the pop-up menu contains an Undo command that reverses the most recent copy or cut.

Here's a much faster way to move a document to another folder listed in the Explorer windows: Drag the document to the folder! Try it by dragging a test file over to another hard disk or to another folder on the same disk. An outline of the document travels with the mouse cursor during the drag. When you release the mouse button, the file anchors into its new position. Want to restore the item? Right-click the mouse and select Undo Move or Undo Copy. Windows always enables you to undo copies and moves, no matter how you perform the move, through menus or with the mouse.

If you want to use the drag-and-drop shortcut method for copying documents, hold down the Ctrl key while dragging the document to the other folder. (The key combination is easy if you remember that both copy and Ctrl begin with the same letter.) As you drag an item, Windows displays a plus sign at the bottom of the icon to indicate that you are copying and not moving. To cancel a copy you've started, drag the item back to its original location before releasing your mouse button or press Esc before releasing your mouse button. In addition, if you drag the item while holding the right mouse button, Windows XP displays a pop-up menu, enabling you to specify that you want to move or copy the document.

7. Sometimes, you might need a document for a program outside of the program in which you're currently working. You can place a document on the Windows desktop. Select a text file and copy the document to the Clipboard by right-clicking and selecting Copy. (You also can use drag-and-drop if you want. Hold down Ctrl and drag the document out of the Explorer window, if you've resized Explorer so that you can see part of the desktop, and continue with Step 8.)

8. Move the cursor on the Windows desktop to an area of the wallpaper that has no icon on it. Right-click to display a menu and select Paste. The document's file will now have an icon on your desktop along with the other icons already there.

   To copy or move the wallpaper document, use the right-click menu or drag the document with the mouse, as explained earlier in this chapter.

Placing Documents on the Desktop

The items you place on the desktop, whether by copying or by moving, stay on the desktop until you remove them from the desktop. Even after shutting down Windows XP and turning off your computer, a desktop item will be there when you return.

Although you shouldn't clutter your desktop with too many documents, you might want to work with a document in several different programs over a period of a few days. By putting the document on the desktop, it is always easily available to any application that's running. Of course, if you run an application in a maximized window, you must shrink the window to some degree to retrieve the document because you have to see the desktop to copy and move the items on it. Also, you can even drag Web pages to your desktop.

8

Using the Explorer's Task Pane

A mastery of the previous section is critical to using your computer to its fullest. The file-related copy, cut, and move operations, using the right-click pop-up menus and your mouse for dragging are skills that all Windows users should understand. So many programs support these file operations that their mastery is critical.

Having said that, throughout the previous section, you may have noticed that the Task pane of the Explorer window changed as you selected files. As Figure 8.7 shows, when you select a text file, the Task pane offers to rename, move, copy, publish to the Web (assuming you have the rights to post to an Internet site), send the file as an email, print the file on your printer, or send the file to the recycle bin. For these common file operations, clicking the task is often easier than right-clicking and selecting from the pop-up menu. (Remember, if your Task pane is not showing, click the toolbar's Folders button to display it.)

Tasks you can perform

FIGURE 8.7

The Explorer Task pane simplifies common file operations.

Where Do the Deleted Files Go?

When you delete files by using dialog boxes or Explorer, you now know that those files go to the Recycle Bin. While in the Recycle Bin, those files are out of your way and deleted in every respect except one: They are not really deleted. Those files are not in their original locations, but they stay in the Recycle Bin until you empty it.

Periodically, you will want to check the Recycle Bin for files that you can erase completely from your hard disk. The following steps demonstrate the Recycle Bin in more detail.

> The Recycle Bin icon changes from an overflowing bin to an empty one when you empty the Recycle Bin, enabling you to tell at a glance whether your Recycle Bin is empty.

1. Display your desktop by minimizing any open windows you might have on the screen.

2. Double-click the Recycle Bin icon. The Recycle Bin window opens.

3. If you've deleted at least one file, you should have one or two files already in the Recycle Bin. There might be many more, depending on what has taken place on your system. You will recognize the format of the Recycle Bin's column headings; you can adjust the width of the columns by dragging the column separators with your mouse.

4. Most of the Recycle Bin dialog box's menu bar commands and toolbar are identical to the ones in Explorer and other windows. When you select an item (or more than one item by using Ctrl+click), your commands apply to that selected item.

5. Right-click any Recycle Bin item to display a Properties dialog box for that item. The box tells you additional information about the deleted item, such as the date you created and deleted the item. Click OK to close the dialog box.

6. Perhaps the most important menu command is Empty the Recycle Bin in the left pane. This command empties the entire Recycle Bin. Select this command now, if there is nothing in your Recycle Bin that you think you will need later.

7. Select File, Close to close the Recycle Bin dialog box.

Although the Recycle Bin adds a level of safety to your work so that you have a second chance to recover files that you delete, if you hold the Shift key when you highlight a file and press Delete (from Explorer or any other window), Windows XP bypasses the Recycle Bin and deletes the files from your system immediately.

Making Windows XP Easier to Use

There are numerous ways to make Windows easier for your day-to-day work. Three time-saving techniques are as follows:

- Changing the Start menu
- Adding single-key access to programs
- Shortcuts

After you create single-key access to a program or a shortcut or you change the Start menu, those time-savers stay in effect, making work inside Windows XP much more efficient.

These time-savers might not help everyone, but they often help users of Windows XP. You have to experiment with the techniques until you find the ones that help you the most. Practice using the time-savers by following these steps:

1. You can add programs to the top of the Start menu by dragging a program from Explorer or My Computer to the Start button. Open Windows Explorer.

2. Click the Windows folder. The folder's contents appear in the right window.

Before adding programs to the Start menu, you must know the location of the program you are adding. If you do not know the path to the program, you can use the Find commands described in the next chapter.

3. Scroll down the window to locate a game called FreeCell (the extension is .exe). FreeCell is a solitaire card game.

4. Drag the FreeCell icon to your Start button. The icon stays in place, but an outline of the icon moves with your dragged mouse cursor.

5. Release the icon over the Start button. You've just added the FreeCell game to the top of your Start menu.

6. Close Explorer and click your Start button. Your Start menu now includes the FreeCell game, located directly beneath your user account name, as shown in Figure 8.8. You can now start FreeCell without traversing several Start menu layers for those times when the boss is away for a short while. (Other recently used programs will be there with FreeCell and they are all as close as your Start menu.)

FIGURE 8.8

Your Start menu now includes the FreeCell game.

Windows XP offers a great way to rearrange and modify your Start menu without going through the windows and buttons of the Settings, Taskbar and Start Menu option. Any time you want to move one of the Start menu's entries from one location to another, display that item on the Start menu and drag that item to another location on the menu. (Don't click the item and release the mouse; be sure that you click and hold your mouse button.) If you right-click over any Start menu item, a pop-up menu appears, enabling you to rename or delete that item.

7. Remove FreeCell from the Start menu (you can add it later if you really want it there) by right-clicking on the menu entry and selecting Unpin from the Start menu.

8. Select More Programs and then open the Accessories menu folder to view the contents of the Accessories group. The Calculator program's icon appears in this folder group.

9. Right-click the Calculator icon to display a pop-up menu.

10. Select Properties to display the Calculator program's Properties tabbed dialog box.

11. Press Alt+K to move the cursor to the Shortcut key text prompt. Type c at the prompt. Windows XP changes the C to Ctrl + Alt + C on the screen. Ctrl+Alt+C is now the shortcut for the Calculator program. If you run a program that uses a shortcut key you've added to Windows XP, the program's shortcut key takes precedence over the Windows XP shortcut key.

12. Click OK to close the dialog box.

13. Select File, Close to exit Explorer and then close the Taskbar and Start Menu Properties dialog box.

Whenever you now press Ctrl+Alt+C, Windows starts its Calculator program. This single-key shortcut (actually a simultaneous three-key shortcut) enables you to start programs instantly, from virtually anywhere in the Windows system, without having to locate the program's menu or icon.

Shortcuts

A subfolder resides in your Windows folder called Start Menu. The Start Menu's folder contains all the items that appear on your Start menu, including the items you drag to the Start menu as you did in the previous task. If you display the contents of the Start menu in Explorer, you'll see small arrows at the bottom of the icons there. The arrows indicate shortcuts to the file.

The name shortcut has a double meaning in Windows XP—one of the reasons that this section's timesavers can become confusing.

A shortcut is actually better termed an *alias file*. When you create a shortcut, such as on the Start menu, Windows does not make a copy of the program in every location where you place the icon. Windows actually creates a link to that program, called a shortcut, that points to the program on your disk wherever its location might be.

If you right-click a document or folder in Explorer's right window, you see the Create Shortcut command that creates a shortcut to the document or folder to which you are pointing. Windows creates a new icon and title (the title begins with Shortcut too) but does not actually create a copy of the item. Instead, Windows creates a link to that item. The link reduces disk space taken up by multiple copies of the same files. The shortcut pointer takes much less space than a copy of the actual file would.

Summary

This chapter showed you how to use the Explorer to manage your documents and folders. Copying and moving among folders and documents are painless functions when you use Explorer. You can display the item to be moved in the right window and drag that item to any device listed in the left window. Inside Explorer, you can associate file types to programs, so you can click a document and run the appropriate program that works with a document.

Three shortcuts exist that help you access your programs. You can add a shortcut to the desktop, to the Start menu system, and even to the keyboard to start programs quickly.

CHAPTER 9

Improving Your Desktop Experience

This chapter contains a potpourri of desktop-management tips and procedures that improve the way you use the Windows environment. You can activate your desktop with the Windows Active Desktop feature. Place Web pages and other files directly on your desktop to customize your Windows wallpaper. Windows comes with several screensaver designs, and you can purchase and download additional screensavers. Screensavers not only provide something for your computer to do while it is idle, but they also offer security features. This chapter also offers a collection of tips that help you customize Windows to suit your preferences.

Activate Your Desktop

Windows includes an *active desktop* feature that allows you to place Web page content directly on your desktop. The Web page acts like part of your wallpaper. The Active Desktop is Windows' way of more seamlessly integrating your Windows desktop into the online Internet world.

Web pages are the result of their underlying language, *HTML*, which defines the colors, pictures, embedded *applets* (small programs that activate Web pages by using yet another language called Java), and information that appears on those pages. HTML stands for *Hypertext Markup Language*.

HTML documents end with the .html filename extension and use a Web page icon in Windows Explorer views. Some document names still follow the pre–Windows 95 file-name limitations that require a maximum three-letter extension; therefore, some HTML documents end with a filename extension of .htm.

You can learn about the active desktop by following these steps:

1. Right-click over your Windows wallpaper to display the pop-up menu.

2. Select Properties and click the Desktop tab. The Display Properties dialog box appears, as shown in Figure 9.1. (As with most of Windows, you can access the Display Properties dialog box from other locations, such as from the Control Panel's Appearance and Themes category.) The Desktop page enables you to set up a wallpaper file. You can select one of the supplied wallpaper files by scrolling and selecting from the list box.

FIGURE 9.1

You can control your desktop's settings from the Display Properties dialog box.

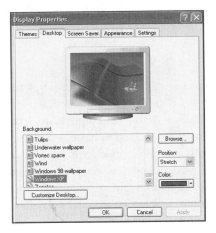

3. If you've stored a Web page on your disk, you can click the Browse button to search for any HTML file to use as your wallpaper. When you locate the HTML file you want as your wallpaper, click the Open button to select the file. The file and its pathname now appear in the Wallpaper list for subsequent selections.

4. Instead of a stored Web page, you can place an online Web page on your desktop. Click the Customize Desktop button to display the Desktop Items dialog box.

5. Click the Web tab and select from the list of Web pages in the list (initially, your default home page will be listed) or click New to type a new Web page address. When you click OK to close each of the open dialog boxes, the Web page will be part of your desktop, such as the one in Figure 9.2.

The Web page appears here

FIGURE 9.2

You can set wallpaper to any HTML or graphics file.

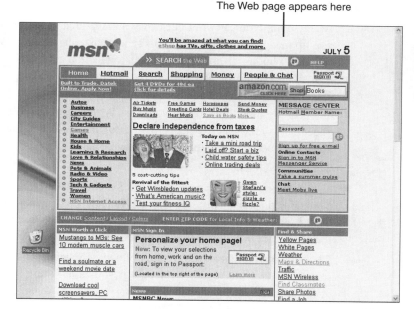

You can resize and move the desktop Web page (assuming you did not choose the option labeled Lock Desktop Items when you placed the Web page on your desktop). As Figure 9.2 shows, the Web page will not show with a title bar that includes the Minimize, Maximize, Restore, or Close buttons. However, if you point to the top of the Web page, Windows will add the title bar and the buttons so that you can move, resize, and close the Web page when you want to do so.

Synchronizing Your Web Page Desktop

The advantage of placing a Web page on your desktop is that, unlike regular wallpaper, the Web page content can frequently change. The Web page will not change on its own after you place the page on your desktop. Windows stores the page in an *offline format*, meaning that the Web page contains whatever it contained when you first placed it on your desktop. You can close your Internet connection after placing the Web page on your desktop because the Web page content will already be on your computer's hard drive, as a snapshot of what it contained when you placed the page.

If you want the Web page to be updated regularly, you must tell Windows XP to *synchronize* the page, or go to the Internet and update the page at specified time intervals.

The following steps explain how to synchronize your Web page.

1. At any point, you can right-click over a blank area of the Web page to display a pop-up menu and select Refresh to synchronize the desktop Web page to its current Internet. Windows starts your Internet connection automatically if needed to refresh the page. Instead of manually synchronizing the page, you can request that Windows do so automatically as the remaining steps show.

2. To specify a time interval that you want Windows to use to synchronize the Web page, display the Display Properties dialog box and click the Customize Desktop button to open the Desktop Items dialog box.

3. Click the Web tab.

4. To synchronize immediately, click the Synchronize button. Doing so performs the same action as manually selecting the Refresh pop-up menu option as described in Step 1. To set up a synchronization schedule for automatic synchronization, click the Properties button and then click the Schedule tab to display the Schedule page.

5. Click the option labeled Using the Following Schedule(s) and click the Add button to display the New Schedule dialog box shown in Figure 9.3.

FIGURE 9.3

Tell Windows XP how often to synchronize the Web content.

6. Select a time when you want Windows XP to synchronize your desktop Web page's content and choose how often to synchronize. Click the check box at the bottom if you don't have an always-on Internet connection (such as a T-1, DSL, or cable modem line).

7. Click OK and close all the open dialog boxes. At the time you scheduled, Windows XP will handle the synchronization automatically so that you can keep a fresh Web page on your desktop.

Active Content

Instead of putting a Web page on your desktop and having Windows synchronize it every once in a while, you can have extremely active content, such as a moving stock ticker or weather and news ticker flying across your desktop. The following steps explain how.

1. Display the Display Properties dialog box and click the Customize Desktop button to open the Desktop Items dialog box.
2. Click the Web tab.
3. Click the New button.
4. Click the Visit Gallery button. A Web page appears that shows the Microsoft Desktop Gallery Web page, such as the one shown in Figure 9.4. The Desktop Gallery contains a stock ticker, news service, weather service, and several other items that you can place on your desktop. As long as your Internet connection is active, the items update. Therefore, during market hours, you will be able to see the price of a stock, news, or other information updated regularly.

FIGURE 9.4

Locate the content you want to place on your desktop.

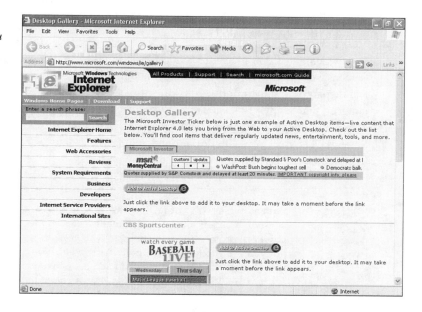

5. Click the Add to Active Desktop button next to the feature that you want on your desktop. Depending on the kind of gallery item you select, Windows will ask you to customize the content, perhaps by providing the stock symbols you want to track or the area of the country in which you live so you can get the local weather. When you return to your desktop, the content will be active.

SOS—Save Our Screens!

Almost everyone has heard of screensavers. Computer software stores contain shelf after shelf of screensaver programs that display pictures of your favorite television characters, cartoons, and geometric and 3D designs. Microsoft designed Windows to include several screensavers, so you don't have to buy one.

Want to know an insider's computer industry secret? Here it is: Screensavers really don't save many screens these days. In the past, computer monitors, especially the mono-chrome green-letters-on-black kind, would *burn in* characters when left on too long without being used. In other words, if you left the monitor on for a long time and did not type anything, the characters on the monitor would begin to leave character trails that stayed on the monitor even after you turned it off.

To combat character burn-in, programmers began to write *screensavers* that blanked the screen or displayed moving characters and pictures. The blank screens had no burn-in problems, and the moving text never stayed in one place long enough to burn into the monitor. The screensavers kicked into effect after a predetermined length of nonuse. When you wanted to start work again, you could press any key to restore the computer screen to the state in which you left it.

Today's monitors don't have the kind of burn-in problem that previous monitors had. Screensavers aren't typically needed. Although a color monitor that is turned on all day and displays the same information will still get the burn-in effect, the effect is less pronounced than a few years ago. Why, during an age when they are not needed, are screensavers more popular than ever before? The answer is simple: Screensavers are fun! Screensavers greet you with designs and animated cartoons when you would otherwise look at a boring screen. It's *cool* to use a screensaver.

Screensavers aren't just for fun and games. Windows screensavers offer an additional benefit over entertainment: The Windows screensavers provide password protection. If you need to walk away from your screen for a while but you want to leave your computer running, you can select a password for the screensaver. Although you can add a password to your Windows XP account and log off before you leave your computer, you might not always remember to do this. After the screensaver begins, a user has to enter the correct password to use your computer. This ensures that payroll and other departments can safely leave their computers without fear of disclosing confidential information. Often, computer stores display their PCs with password-protected screensavers to keep customers from tampering with the systems.

Setting Up a Screensaver

Windows contains several screensavers from which you can choose. Through the Screensaver dialog box, you can set up a blank screensaver or one that moves text and graphics on the screen. You control the length of time the monitor is idle before the screensaver begins. The following steps explain how to implement a screensaver.

1. Open the Display Properties dialog box and click the Screen Saver tab. (You can also open the Control Panel window, select Appearance and Themes, and then select the option labeled Choose a Screen Saver to display the same Screen Saver page.) Windows displays the page shown in Figure 9.5.

FIGURE 9.5

The Screen Saver tab controls the screen-saver's timing and selection.

If your monitor is designed to be *Energy Star–compliant*, meaning that your monitor supports energy-efficiency options, the lower dialog box settings will be available to you. You can adjust these options to save electricity costs. The Energy Star controls work independently and override any screensaver settings you might use.

2. The drop-down list box—directly below the Screen Saver prompt—that you display when you click the down arrow contains a list of Windows screensavers. Click the box now to see the list. When (None) is selected, no screensaver will be active on your system.

3. If you select Blank Screen, Windows uses a blank screen for the screensaver. When the screensaver activates, the screen goes blank, and a keypress (or password if you set up a password) returns the screen to its previous state.

   The remaining screensavers are generally more fun than a blank screensaver. If you want to see the other screensavers, click any one of the remaining screensavers in the list (such as 3D Flying Objects or 3D Maze), and Windows will display a preview of it on the little monitor inside the dialog box, as shown in Figure 9.6.

FIGURE 9.6

You can preview any of the screensavers.

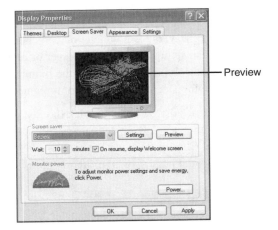

Preview

4. The animated screensavers can move fairly fast. To adjust their speed, click the Settings button. In some cases, you can also adjust the number of animated items that appear on the screensaver screen. Click OK when done.

5. The Preview button enables you to view the screensaver full-screen if you want a better preview than the small screen inside the dialog box provides. Click Preview to see the actual screensaver in action. Press any key or move the mouse to terminate the screensaver preview and return to the dialog box.

6. The Wait prompt determines how many minutes your computer must remain idle for the screensaver to activate itself. By pressing Alt+W (the shortcut key combination for the Wait prompt), you can enter a new minute value or click the up and down arrow keys to change to a new minute value.

7. When you click the OK command button at the bottom of the dialog box, Windows activates the screensaver program. The screensaver remains active in all future Windows sessions until you change it again by using the Screen Saver dialog box.

8. The screensaver operates in the background but never shows itself, even on the taskbar of program buttons, until your computer sits idle for the specified time value. If you keep your hands off the keyboard and mouse for the waiting time period, you'll see the screensaver go into action. Press any key (or move the mouse) to return to the desktop.

Windows enables you to create your own screensaver! Store pictures in the following folder: c:\Documents and Settings*yourLogonName*\
My Documents\My Pictures. You can capture these pictures from a digital camera or scan the pictures with an attached scanner. Select the My Pictures

> Slideshow and Windows randomly displays your pictures on the screen when the screensaver begins its work. You can adjust settings such as the length of time each picture appears by clicking the Settings button after you select the My Pictures Screensaver option from the Screen Saver tabbed page.

If you click the option labeled Return to the Welcome Screen, Windows returns to the account logon screen. There, you or another user will have to log on once again (and possibly enter a password if your account is password-protected) to use the computer after pressing a key to stop the screensaver.

Paint Windows XP

Windows offers several color schemes for you to select. Microsoft designed multiple color schemes that work well together. Depending on your taste, you can choose from conservative to very wild colors.

The color schemes that you can select have nothing to do with the colors of icons, wallpaper, or screensavers on your system. The color schemes determine the color for various systemwide items such as screen title bars, window backgrounds, and dialog box controls.

By selecting from various color schemes, you can determine the colors that Windows XP uses for common system-level items such as window controls. You'll use the Display Properties dialog box to change the color of your Windows XP environment as the following steps show:

1. Right-click over a blank area of your desktop and select Properties. The now-familiar Display Properties tabbed dialog box appears.

2. Click the Appearance tab to display the Appearance page, shown in Figure 9.7.

3. If you want to take the time, you can change the color of every item on the Windows screen including dialog boxes, window borders, and title bars. However, it's much easier to pick a color scheme from the list of the many choices that Microsoft supplies.

   On the top half of the Appearance page, you see the currently selected color scheme. If you select a different color scheme, you will see that scheme's color appear at the top of the dialog box.

4. The color scheme of your Windows installation does not instantly change. You're still in the process of selecting colors at this point. If you don't like your selected color scheme, try another. As a matter of fact, try *all* of them to find one you really like.

FIGURE 9.7

Change system colors in the Appearance page of the Display Properties dialog box.

 High contrast color schemes work well for times when you take your Windows laptop outdoors.

5. Click the Effects button to display the Effects dialog box shown in Figure 9.8. Use the Effects settings to determine how menus and ToolTips appear and disappear, whether large icons appear for Windows XP items such as menus, whether a shadow appears under menus, and other special effects that transpire as you use Windows XP.

FIGURE 9.8

Select from several screen effects.

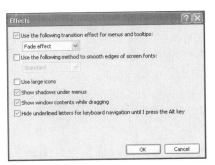

6. When you find a color scheme that you really like, click the OK button to close the dialog box and change the color scheme to your selected colors. You can now begin working with the new color scheme. As soon as you open a window, you'll see the difference.

As you change your color scheme, feel free to change the Windows display font as well. From the Appearance dialog box, you can select a different font for almost every kind of text Windows XP displays.

Summary

You now have a collection of tips and desktop-management tools that can help you work with Windows more effectively. After completing the first few chapters, you now have a good understanding of the tools that are available to you as a Windows user.

9

CHAPTER **10**

Calling for Help

This chapter shows you how to help yourself! That is—how to help yourself find help when using Windows. Although this book is *really* all you'll ever need to use your computer effectively (self-promotion was never one of our weak points), when you get confused, Windows offers a good set of online tools that you can access to find out how to accomplish a specific task. If you've recently upgraded to Windows XP from a previous version, you will notice that Microsoft has added a lot to the Windows XP entire help system.

Introducing the Help and Support Center (HSC)

Even Windows XP experts need help now and then with Windows. Windows is simply too vast, despite its simple appearance and clean desktop, for users to know everything about the system. Windows includes a powerful built-in help system. The help system connects to the Internet when needed so that help is on your disk and up-to-the-minute help is available from Microsoft's Web site. Help is available whenever you need it. For example, if you are working with the My Computer window and have a question, just search the online help system for the words *My Computer*, and Windows gives advice about using the My Computer window.

Microsoft calls the Windows XP help screens the *Help and Support Center* (the *HSC*). The help system goes far beyond the standard online help you may be used to in other applications and previous versions of Windows.

There are a number of ways you can request help while working in Windows XP. There are also numerous places from which you can get help. This chapter focuses on the most common ways that you can use online help and also offers tips along the way.

To use every help feature available to you in Windows, you need Internet access. Microsoft keeps up-to-date advice on the Web, such as bug reports and add-on programs to Windows that you can download to improve your use of Windows.

The taskbar is always available to you no matter what else you are doing in Windows XP. Even if you've hidden the taskbar behind a running program, the taskbar is available as soon as you press your Windows key to display the taskbar and Start menu. The HSC's command is located on the taskbar's Start menu. Selecting the Help and Support Center option displays the online help's opening screen by using a Web browser format. To get started, the next few steps show you how to access the online HSC.

1. Click the Start button to display the Start menu.
2. Select Help and Support to view the online help window. After a brief pause, you see Windows XP's HSC window shown in Figure 10.1.

The HSC window offers two kinds of help: local help that searches your PC's Windows XP help files for answers to your questions and Web help resources that connect to your Internet provider and access Microsoft's huge online help resource.

The Help and Support window contains a toolbar that works like a Web-browsing toolbar.

Therefore, when you need help, you aren't limited to your own system help files. Although you can get many answers from your PC's local help files, Microsoft's online Help window makes it easy for you to contact the large online help databases Microsoft stores on the Web.

FIGURE 10.1

The Help and Support Center window offers all kinds of help.

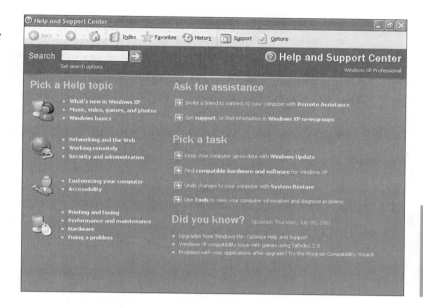

10

The HSC window resides on your disk as an HTML file, which is the format behind all Web pages. Web pages can be local or on the Internet—your PC reacts to both in the same manner. Therefore, the HSC window acts like a Web page. When you rest your mouse cursor over a *hot spot* (a link to another location, also called a *hyperlink*), the mouse cursor changes to a pointing hand to let you know that if you click that hot spot, another page will appear. As with all help pages, you can traverse backward through your help screen travels by clicking the toolbar's Back button.

Any time you click the HSC's History button at the top of the HSC screen, the HSC displays a window that includes every link you've visited recently within the HSC. You can quickly return to any HSC item you've viewed recently by clicking its link in the History window pane.

Getting Topical Help

If you have a question about Windows XP or about a certain utility program that comes with Windows, just ask for help and Windows will supply it. Although the Windows XP help extends to the Web for more complete help topics, you'll find most answers to common Windows questions on your own system and searching your local disk is generally quicker than waiting on a Web search, as the following steps demonstrate:

1. Open the Help and Support Center window if it is no longer open from the previous section.

2. After a brief pause, the HSC screen that you saw in Figure 10.1 appears.

   The initial Help and Support Center window offers a summary of the help items available to you in an Explorer-like format. Click an item to read more about that topic. When you click a topic, more details emerge from which you can select.

3. Click the entry labeled Music, video, games and photos. Several topics appear in the left window pane for which you can get more detailed help by clicking on one of the topics.

4. Click the Music and sounds topic to open that topic and see the related help topics. An overview of the topic appears in the right pane.

5. Click the Playing and copying music topic to see the help tasks shown in Figure 10.2.

FIGURE 10.2

The Help and Support Center helps you get started with playing and recording music.

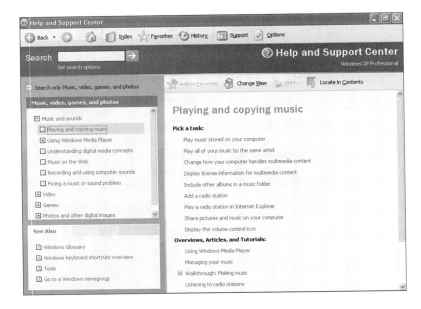

6. Click the toolbar's Back button to see the HSC screen before you displayed the detail. As with any Web page, you can click the Back button to return to the previous help screen. If you view several topics in succession, you sometimes want to return to a previous topic. Return to the detail page once again. You can also return to pages you've backed up from by clicking the Forward button.

You can click the Home link at the top of the Help and Support Center to return to the initial HSC page.

Obtaining Support

The Support area of the HSC contains several topics that provide you with third-party assistance and Internet-based information that can help you get past problems.

Contacting Remote Assistance

When you have a problem with your computer, wouldn't it be nice to ask an expert to come look over your shoulder and explain what's going on? In a way, Windows XP does just that.

The HSC's Support link provides the following kinds of assistance:

- Provides links to Microsoft-based Web sites and other online areas (such as chats and by email) that contain advanced troubleshooting information for Windows XP.

- Provides links to your own computer's system tools, such as the Advanced System Information utility that lists all hardware and software settings currently set for your computer.

- Provides *remote assistance*, a system that allows others connected to your computer via the Internet or local network to temporarily take over your computer remotely, looking at your screens and applications, to determine where problems are occurring.

The remote assistance is the most innovative feature inside Windows XP because previous operating systems did not offer such support. When you choose Remove Assistance, you'll see the Remove Assistance screen shown in Figure 10.3 that explains what will occur when you make a connection with a remote user.

During the remote session, the remote user will be able to look at the same screen you are. Your computer will receive the remote user's keystrokes in a manner that makes the computer believe it is you doing the typing. The remote user will then be able to reproduce the problems you are having and, after seeing your system the same way that you see it, will hopefully be able to suggest solutions.

During the remote session, you and the remote user will be able to chat back and forth in a pop-up chat window. You'll use the chat window to explain what is happening and to answer questions the remote user may have.

10

FIGURE 10.3

Another user can connect directly to your computer and run your programs remotely to locate problems.

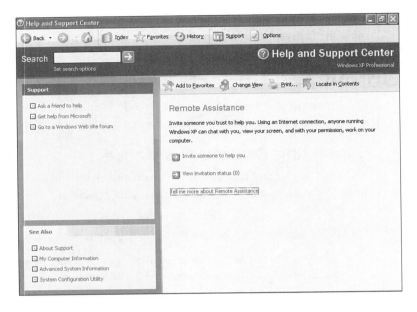

Your remote user must be using Windows XP (any version) and must have Internet access or access to your computer through a local area network. Some networks have *firewalls* attached that add security from unauthorized break-in attempts. Such firewalls sometimes wreak havoc with the Remote Assistance and your network's System Administrator will have to help ensure that the firewall allows for remote access before you can be connected to such a user.

So many variations of equipment and connections exist that it would be virtually impossible to walk you through steps that would work in all readers' cases. Nevertheless, the general steps that you must take to connect to a remote user are fairly common. Here are the general steps you'll go through when using the Remote Assistance:

1. Display the Help and Support Center window.
2. Click the Remote Assistance link beneath the first topic in the Support area.
3. Click the link labeled Invite someone to help you. Before connecting to a remote user, you need to send that user an invitation to connect to your system. As Figure 10.4 shows, you can send the invitation by email, by the *MSN Messenger* service (provided by Microsoft), or save the invitation in a file that your remote user can retrieve.

FIGURE 10.4

The HSC offers three ways to send an invitation to your remote user.

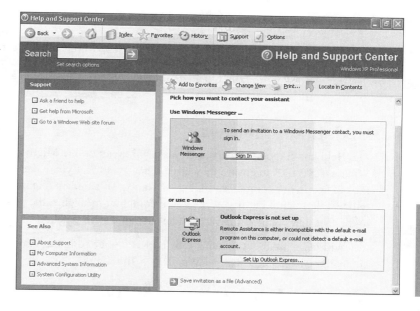

You'll learn in Chapter 21, "Chatting with Instant Messaging," how to sign up for Microsoft's free MSN Messenger, an online service that provides free email, chat sessions, phone calls, and other features.

If you send an email or save your request as a file, the email or file-based invitation will expire at the time you designate. After all, if you need help in the next two hours but your remote user happens to be on vacation, you don't want your remote user getting back in a week and trying to respond to the invitation long after you no longer need the response. If you use the MSN Messenger service, your remote user must be logged on to respond immediately but you can also send an email to the user through the MSN Messenger system so the user learns of your invitation the moment that user logs into the Internet.

4. After your remote user responds to your invitation and agrees by clicking the appropriate link on the remote computer, Windows will connect your machine to your remote user and give control over to the user. You will still be able to control your computer as well and you can communicate with the remote user during the session using the pop-up chat window.

Don't send an invitation to a remote user you don't trust. Obviously, the ability to access your computer's resources is not a gift you'd offer to someone you don't know. Some software and hardware firms will surely be offering to provide remote assistance through XP's Remote Assistance service. Generally, if you initiate the support request to a company you trust, and you'll be at your computer watching the session, your files should be fine. You can terminate the Remote Assistance session any time you want to.

Updating Windows

The Help and Support Center provides a link to an online Microsoft site that checks your Windows XP files to ensure they are the latest and that you have all the needed system files to keep your computer running smoothly. This update feature is not actually an online help feature but if you're having computer problems, the problems may be related to the fact that you don't have the latest Windows XP patch.

You will learn all about this link labeled Keep your computer up-to-date with Windows Update in Chapter 15, "Giving Windows a Tune-Up."

Checking Hardware and Software

If you suspect that a graphics adapter or other hardware device is having problems working with Windows, or if a program does not behave the way you expect, you can click the link labeled Find compatible hardware and software for Windows XP to see if the item in question is approved to work within Windows XP. You must have an Internet connection available to use this HSC feature.

When you click the Find compatible hardware and software for Windows XP link, the HSC provides a Product Search dialog box that you can type the name and model of your hardware device or the name and version of the software you're having trouble with. When you click Search, the HSC goes to Microsoft's Web site and checks to see if the hardware or software program is compatible with Windows XP. If not, you may have to upgrade your hardware or program. If so, then you know the problem you might be having is not a compatibility issue.

Staying Current with *Did You Know?*

The section labeled Did you know? is a section of the HSC that changes periodically. As you use the Internet, the HSC will often download new topics for the Did you know? section. These topics are generally guides about using Windows XP features and information about upgrading to newer versions as they become available.

When you go to the HSC for help, you might want to glance at the Did you know? section to see if something interests you there. Click any of the links to learn more about that link's topic.

Searching the Index

As good and complete as the HSC is, you may have difficulty locating exact help on a specific topic that you need help with. The times that you are not sure where to look, check the HSC's Index link. The Index link helps you zero in to a specific item for which you need help.

Follow these steps to use the Index link.

1. Click the Index link at the top of the Help and Support Center window. An alphabetical list of all items within the help system appears in a scrollable window pane, as Figure 10.5 shows.

Your selected item's detail will appear here

10

FIGURE 10.5

The Index enables you to find details quickly.

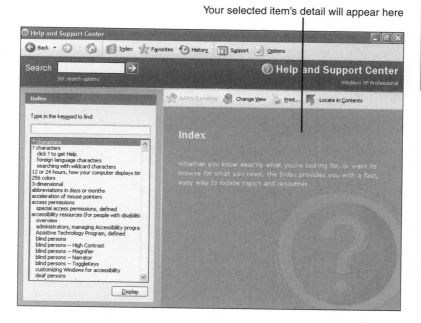

2. To find something in the index, scroll the indexed list to the item you want to find. You can quickly move to an item by clicking the text box and typing your requested entry. As you type, the index item that matches your typed letters begins to appear.

3. Scroll through the entries, looking at the various index items.

4. Locate the indexed entry, direct cable connections, and double-click the overview entry below the main topic. A detailed overview window opens in the right window pane. A hot spot appears in the right window labeled Related Topics. The help

pages are often cross-referenced to other related help pages and Windows acces-
sory programs, so you can read all the information related to the topic in which
you are interested and start that topic's program when needed. You can move to
other topics by clicking on the Index pane's items or by selecting hot spots in the
right pane. As you move to various hot spots, the Back button always returns you
to the previous help page, so you can always get back from where you came in the
Help system.

5. Every once in a while, an indexed topic requires additional information. Sometimes
the Help system narrows a search to a more specific item. For example, if you
click the indexed item labeled overview, located beneath the entry named accessi-
bility resources (for people with disabilities), a Topics Found dialog box appears
like the one in Figure 10.6. When you select one of the dialog box's topics and
click the Display button, that topic's Detail page appears.

FIGURE **10.6**
*Help needs you to be
more specific.*

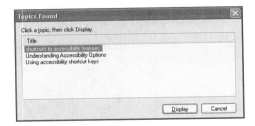

6. Click Home to return to the main Help and Support Center window.

If you know with which specific Windows element you need help, you can often locate
the help quicker by selecting from the Index page instead of the more general Contents
pages that first appears when you request help.

The Search box at the top of the Help and Support Center screen allows you
to type an entry and search your computer's help files for any topic.
Surprisingly, the Search box doesn't always produce an extremely helpful list
of topics (this is true of the early versions of Windows XP at least), but you'll
sometimes find exactly what you need. If a quick search doesn't produce
good results, you can use one of the other methods discussed in this chapter
to locate exactly the help you need.

Other Forms of Help

The help you obtain in Windows XP does not always come from the help system itself but from auxiliary help systems that add support to the tasks and programs you work with.

Using Application Help

When you use a Windows XP program, you often need help with the program rather than Windows. Almost every Windows application's menu bar includes a Help option you can click for help with that program.

For example, if you select Help, Help Topics from the Windows XP Calculator program, a Help dialog box appears with tabs at the top of the window that list helpful help divisions such as Contents, Index, and Search. The Contents pages offer a general overview of the program. You're already familiar with the Index page because it mimics the Index page in the Help and Support Center window described in the previous section. Figure 10.7 shows the Calculator's Index page.

10

FIGURE 10.7

Most applications provide indexed help topics.

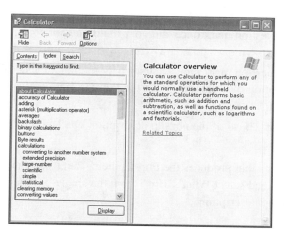

The Search tab on many applications' help screen makes looking for a particular topic not indexed on the Index tab easier. To search for a topic, click the Search tab, enter a topic, and then click the command button labeled List Topics. If the help engine locates your search candidate, a list of all help pages that include your search topic appears, and you can open that help page to view its details in the right pane by clicking the Display button.

Using Pop-Up Help

Sometimes, you'll be in the middle of a dialog box working inside Windows when you spot a command button or other control that you do not understand. Look in the upper-right corner of the window for a question mark on one of the command buttons. If you find such a question mark, you've found the Windows *Pop-Up Help* command button and cursor (sometimes called *Roving Help*).

The Pop-Up Help enables you to narrow the focus and request help on a specific screen item. Not all dialog boxes or screens inside Windows contain the Pop-Up Help feature, so look for the question mark command button, which is to the left of the window mini-mizing and resizing buttons.

As long as the dialog box contains the Pop-Up Help button, you can request Pop-Up Help for any item on the dialog box as the following steps demonstrate.

1. Right-click on the Start button to display the Taskbar and Start Menu Properties dialog box (you can also access this dialog box from the Control Panel). The dialog box displays the Pop-Up help button with the question mark in the upper-right corner.

2. Click the question mark once and your mouse cursor changes to a question mark that follows the mouse pointer as you move the mouse.

3. Point the question mark mouse cursor over the link labeled Show the clock and click the option. Windows displays the Pop-Up Help message box shown in Figure 10.8.

4. Press Esc to get rid of the pop-up description box and return to the regular mouse cursor shape.

Another way exists that produces the Pop-Up help. Point your mouse cursor over an item. Right-click and select What's This? from the single-option menu that appears to display the pop-up description.

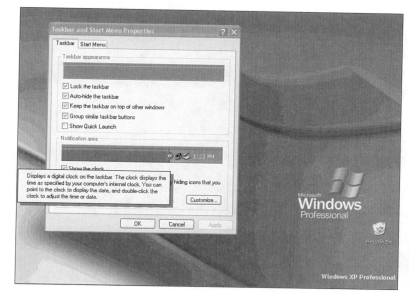

FIGURE 10.8

The Pop-Up Help helps you when you point to a place on the screen.

10

Summary

This chapter showed you how to access the powerful Help features in Windows XP. When you have a question about Windows XP, you can ask Windows XP for help. There are several ways to access the helpful dialog boxes about a variety of topics. The most common method of getting detailed help is to select the Help and Support command from the Start menu. You can access your local PC's help files, search the Internet for the answers you need, or ask a remote user to take a look. Most Windows XP programs contain a Help command that displays a tabbed dialog box containing different kinds of help search screens.

PART IV

Working with Files, Folders and the Desktop

Chapter

CHAPTER 11

Installing Programs with Windows

By itself, Windows doesn't help you directly with your work. Your application programs do the work. You use application programs to write documents, create graphics, explore the Internet, manage database files, and play games. Somehow you have to get application programs onto your PC. Programs come on CD-ROMs or are downloadable from the Internet. You must run new programs through an *installation routine* so that Windows XP properly recognizes them.

Some application programs require their own unique, one-of-a-kind installation routines, although, fortunately, you'll install most of today's programs using a uniform method. This chapter looks at Windows's support for adding programs, discusses unique installation problems you might encounter, explains how to make older programs run, and reviews how to remove programs that you've installed and no longer need.

Using the Add or Remove Programs Window

Before Windows, you could add a program to your computer simply by copying a file
from the disk you purchased to your hard disk. To remove the program, you only had to
delete the file. Things got messier with Windows, however, because Windows expected a
lot from application programs. Programs are no longer simple to add or remove unless
you familiarize yourself with the proper techniques.

> If you don't follow the proper program-installation techniques, your applica-
> tion probably won't run correctly. Even worse, with the Windows integrated
> set of files, a program you add to your PC incorrectly might make other pro-
> grams fail.

The Windows Control Panel contains an entry that you'll frequently visit to manage the
programs on your PC. This icon is labeled Add or Remove Programs. When you open
this icon, the tabbed dialog box shown in Figure 11.1 appears. Depending on the number
of your PC's installed applications, you'll probably see different applications listed in the
lower half of your PC's Add or Remove Programs window.

FIGURE 11.1

*You manage your
installed programs
from the Add or
Remove Programs
dialog box.*

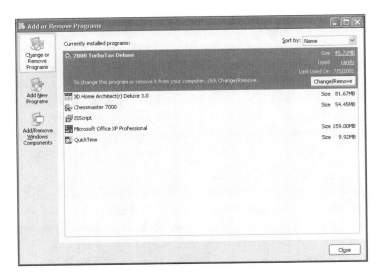

To the left of the dialog box is an Add New Programs button that you can click to install
new software. Surprisingly, you'll rarely, if ever, use this button when installing
Windows XP programs because most programs install automatically, as explained later

in this chapter. The dialog box's lower half contains a list of many application programs on your PC. Not every program on your PC will appear in the list. The list contains programs that you can *uninstall* from your system. If you uninstall using the Add or Remove Programs dialog box, you can be assured that the application will completely disappear.

Although you can uninstall most Windows applications, occasionally an application will share a support or system file with another application. Even more common, sometimes the uninstallation routine detects *incorrectly* that the file is shared by another program. Therefore, during some uninstallation routines, you might see a dialog box message asking if you want the routine to remove one of the shared files. Generally, it's difficult to know what to do. The safest advice is to keep the file by responding as such to the dialog box if it appears. Although in many cases retaining the file simply wastes disk space, you'll avoid possible trouble with other applications that might use the file.

If you make a system backup before uninstalling an application, you can safely remove the file and then keep the backup handy until you're convinced that the system is stable. Again, it's often simpler just to keep the file in question when the uninstallation program prompts you about it. These orphaned files often make for heated discussions among the PC community—and rightly so. Windows and uninstallation routines should be written so that they work together more accurately without requiring the user to make such ambiguous file-deletion decisions.

Sometimes you'll rerun an application program's installation routine to change installation settings. The Add or Remove Programs window contains a button labeled Change or Remove Programs that many applications utilize to let you change program options or remove the program altogether.

If a program stops working properly, you might have to reinstall it completely. Although you can rerun the installation again in some cases, you're probably better off uninstalling the program first to remove all traces of it and then running the installation from scratch again. (Be sure to back up your data files before you do that.)

Customizing Windows

After you've opened the Control Panel's Add or Remove Programs dialog box, click the Add/Remove Windows Components button to display the Windows Components Wizard page shown in Figure 11.2. A Windows XP *Wizard* is a step-by-step procedure that guides you through some process, such as installing a program. Unlike your applications, you'll never remove Windows XP because you would be removing the operating system that controls your PC. (You wouldn't sit on the same tree branch you're sawing off, would you?) When you update to a future version of Windows, the new version will remove Windows XP, but you can worry about that later. For now, the Windows Components Wizard lets you add and remove various Windows XP options.

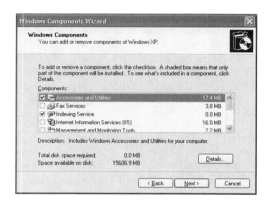

FIGURE 11.2

Change Windows options from the Windows Components Wizard dialog box.

When you make a change to a Windows setting, that setting might not show until you restart Windows.

The following steps show you how to change Windows installation settings. Although the various Properties menu options you find throughout Windows XP let you change settings that affect Windows's performance, appearance, and operation, the Windows Components Wizard lets you add or remove pieces of Windows's functionality.

Some manufacturers store the Windows XP system on your computer's hard disk instead of supplying a separate CD-ROM. You'll want to keep your system backed up completely in case you need to reconfigure your computer. Other users get Windows from a purchased CD-ROM. If you obtained Windows on CD-ROM, you might need your Windows CD-ROM to change Windows options, so locate it. If prompted for the CD-ROM, the Windows XP banner will automatically appear when you insert the CD-ROM. Just close the window if this occurs. Some systems come with the Windows XP operating system stored on the hard disk, so don't worry about locating the Windows CD-ROM unless prompted for it.

1. Select Add/Remove Windows Components to run the Windows Components Wizard. The Components scrolling list box shows which groups of Windows XP options you've installed. An empty check box means that none of those options is installed to run. A grayed-out check mark means that some of the options in that group are installed. A regular check mark means that the entire group is installed. If you didn't install Windows XP, or if you installed Windows XP using all the default options, you might not be completely familiar with all the groups that appear. As you work through this text, you'll learn more about the various options available for Windows XP.

2. Click the title for Accessories and Utilities. (If you click the check mark and not the title, you'll change the setting.) Then click the Details button, and a new list appears that shows entries for Accessories and Games.

3. Click Accessories to select the item.

4. Click the Details button to see the details of the Accessories group of programs. You'll see a scrollable list of Accessories programs like those shown in Figure 11.3. Accessories are most of the programs that appear when you select the Start menu's More Programs, Accessories option.

FIGURE 11.3

See which Accessories options are installed.

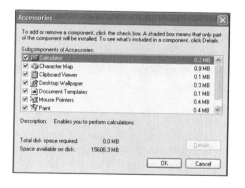

5. Uncheck the Clipboard Viewer. Rarely will you need this leftover from Windows 3.1 days. Unchecking it requests that Windows XP remove it from your system. (You can repeat this task afterward to put it back.)

6. Click OK twice to return to the Windows Components Wizard.

7. Click Next and Windows XP begins the process of removing the Clipboard Viewer from your system. This update can take a while if you have just added or removed several Windows XP components.

8. Click Finish to close the Windows Components Wizard and return to Windows.

Installed Applications

Almost every time you purchase a new application program to install on your PC, you'll insert its CD into the drive, close the drive door, and see an installation screen such as the one shown in Figure 11.4.

FIGURE 11.4

An application program is about to install.

In most cases, such an application checks your PC to see if the program is already installed. If it isn't, the program gives you an installation screen such as the one shown in Figure 11.4. The software authors know that you probably wouldn't be inserting the CD into the drive if you didn't want to install the program.

> If the program is already installed, the program often, but not always, begins executing (without the installation prompt) after you close the CD-ROM drive door. This is mostly true of some games that require that you insert the actual CD-ROM into your CD-ROM drive any time you want to play the game.

If the application doesn't start, or if you have *AutoPlay* disabled (AutoPlay is a feature of Windows XP that starts reading your CD as soon as you place a CD-ROM in the drive) and you want to leave it that way, you can choose Run from the Start menu and type *d*:\Setup. Replace the *d* with the letter of your CD-ROM drive.

Not many programs still come on floppy disk; however, if you're installing from a floppy disk, you'll have to insert the first installation disk into the disk drive, choose Run from the Start menu, and type `a:\Setup`.

If you get an error message, choose the Start menu's Run command to make sure that you've entered the drive, backslash, and Setup command properly. If you get an error message again, your program might require a different command. Replace `Setup` with `Install` to see what happens. If the Run command still fails, check the program's owner's manual to locate the correct command.

Each application's setup is different. Nevertheless, the following list provides guidelines that almost every installation follows:

- You can often read installation notes (usually called a *Readme* file) by clicking an appropriate selection in the installation window.

- Sometimes multiple installation options are available. Check the manual for the installation that suits you if you can't determine from the opening window which one to use.

- When you start the installation, an installation wizard usually guides you step-by-step through the process.

- You can often accept all installation defaults if you're unsure whether to install an option during the wizard's performance. The wizard asks questions such as which disk drive and folder you want to install to.

- If you don't have adequate disk space, the installation program will tell you. You'll have to remove other files, get more disk space, reduce the installation options, or do without the program if you don't have space for it.

- At the end of the installation, you will probably have to restart Windows for all the installation options to go into effect. If you're asked whether you want to restart Windows, you can answer No, but don't run the installed program until you restart Windows.

Uninstallation Procedures

Most application programs written for Windows XP include a standard uninstallation routine that removes the application from Windows and from your PC. Remember that an application program is often made up of several files. The program's installation routine stores those files in several different locations. Therefore, without an uninstallation routine, removing the application is a tedious task.

11

Before displaying the Control Panel's Add or Remove Programs window to uninstall a program you've installed, check the Start menu group where the program resides. Sometimes, in a program's menu group, the installation routine sets up the uninstallation routine that you can run from that group. For example, if you installed a game called Side-to-Side, you might start the game by selecting from a series of Start menu options that look like this: More Programs, Side Game, Play Side-to-Side. Look on the same menu and see if you can select an uninstall option, such as More Programs, Side Game, Uninstall Side-to-Side. When you begin the uninstallation process, a wizard steps you through the program's removal.

If no menu option exists for the uninstallation, go to the Control Panel's Add or Remove Programs window. Scroll through the list of items in the lower part of the window to see if the program you want to remove appears in the list. If it does, select that entry and click the Change or Remove Programs button to begin the uninstall wizard.

If no entry appears, you are running out of options! Insert the program's CD once again and see if the opening window contains an uninstall option. If it doesn't, look through the Readme file to see if you can get help. Also, look in the program's owner's manual. Lacking an uninstall routine, try one more place if you have access: the Web. See if you can find the company's Web page somewhere in the Readme file or owner's manual. If you can't find it, try going to the Web address `http://www.companyname.com/` and see if something comes up. Replace *companyname.com* with the name of the company that manufactured the application you want to uninstall.

A Last Resort

If your search for an uninstall procedure comes up empty, you are forced to do one of two things:

- Leave the program on your system if you have ample disk space
- Manually remove as much of the program as you can

That last option can get messy because it requires searching for the program files. In the next chapter, you'll learn how to search for files, so you might want to browse Chapter 12, "Finding Information," before attempting to manually remove the application. After you've removed the program's files and the folder where the application resides, you need to remove the Start menu entry.

Deleting Start menu entries is simple, but keep in mind that you're only removing items from a menu and not deleting files from your disk. Simply open your Start menu and locate the item you want to delete. Right-click the item and select Delete from the pop-up menu. Confirm the prompt and Windows XP removes the entry. You can remove a program group from the menu, instead of just individual items, the same way.

Summary

This chapter described how to install and uninstall application programs on your PC. Before Windows XP came along, program installation and removal was simple because programs rarely resided in more than one file on your disk. Today's Windows XP programs, however, install with multiple files in multiple locations, and their removal can become tedious.

The next chapter describes how to use Windows's file-searching capabilities to locate files on your computer. You might need to search for a file if you manually need to remove a program from Windows, as described in the last section.

11

CHAPTER 12

Finding Information

Hard disks are getting bigger, more information appears on the Internet by the minute, and you've got to find things fast! Fortunately, Windows comes to your rescue with powerful searching tools. Windows can quickly find files and folders that you need. You can search by filename, date, and location. In addition, Windows includes several Internet searching tools that enable you to find people and Web sites that match the exact specifications you want to match.

Introducing Search

Click the Start menu to select the Search option. When you select Search, Windows XP uses the *Search Companion*, an animated screen character that can help you form your searches, to walk you through searching. You can turn off Search Companion by selecting the option labeled Turn off animated character. If you elect to use the Search Companion, Windows XP displays the Search Companion pane shown in Figure 12.1.

FIGURE 12.1

The Search Companion helps you form your searches.

 Click the option labeled Change Preferences if you want to choose a different Search Companion character or search without the character altogether.

Whether you elect to use a Search Companion, the Search window lets you search for many different things as Table 12.1 describes.

TABLE 12.1 Using Search to Locate Information

Target	Description
Pictures, music, or video	Looks for files and folders that are registered as media files.
Documents (word processing, spreadsheet, and so forth)	Looks for nonapplication documents, such as data files and word processor documents.
All files and folders	Looks for any type of file.
Computers or people	Looks for computers networked to yours and people who might be logged onto your network. Each computer on a network has a unique name.
Information in Help and Support Center	Takes you to the HSC to locate what you need.

You should master the Start menu's Search command because you'll search for information quite often. Today's computers have extremely large disk drives, and locating a file that you worked on previously is not always a trivial task without some help. Using

Search, you won't have to wade through disks, folders, and subfolders looking for an older document. Let Windows XP do the work for you.

> You can quickly display the Search Files and Folders window by right-clicking the Start menu and selecting the Search option or by pressing the Windows key on your keyboard and then pressing F for Find before releasing both keys.

Searching for Pictures, Music, or Video

When you select the Pictures, music, or video option, Windows XP asks you for the type of file for which you want to search such as a picture, a music file, or a file containing video, as well as for a filename. These kinds of multimedia files can take on many different filename extensions; therefore, knowing the exact filename extension is not always easy. Fortunately, by telling Windows XP the file type (picture, music, or video), you don't have to know or care what kind of extension is on your file because Windows XP recognizes most file extensions related to the type of file for which you want to search.

After you select one or more file types, type the name of the file to search. You can type just a few letters of the name including letters from the middle or end of the file and Windows will search for all files that contain those letters in their names. The list of files, if any matches are found that meets your search type and name, are listed in the right window pane.

Searching for Data Documents

Searching for data is similar to searching for multimedia files. Windows looks for files with filename extensions that are commonly used for data documents in Windows applications.

Instead of selecting a file type, you must tell the Search window when you last modified the document. Fortunately, you don't have to know for sure. The Search window gives you these choices:

- You don't remember when you last modified the file.
- You last modified the file sometime last week.
- You last modified the file sometime last month.
- You modified the file within the past year.

12

In addition to the modification date, you also must enter the filename or the part of the filename before clicking the Search button to let Windows locate the file or multiple files that match your search criteria.

Searching for Any File

When you search for a file of any type, including program and system files, the Search window provides more search options than the previous kinds of searches provide. The Search window gives you the ability to search based on these criteria:

- Part or all of the filename
- Letters, a word, or a phrase in the file; this works best for data document files
- The drive or drives that Windows XP is to search
- The date you last modified the file
- The approximate size of the file
- Advanced search options you'll learn about later in this chapter in the section, "Improving Your Searches."

> The Windows Explorer's toolbar's Search button opens a Search pane with the same searching capabilities as the Start menu's Search command. Therefore, after you master the Search command, you'll also know how to look for information from inside Windows Explorer and other windows.

Searching Files and Folders

You'll probably use the Start menu's Search command to search for files and folders on your PC. Search gives you access to many different search criteria. You can search for files in a specific folder, on a disk, or on your entire computer system, including networked drives if you have any.

If you know a partial filename, you can find all files that contain that partial filename. If you want to search for a file you changed two days ago, you can find all files with modification dates that fall on that day. You can even save searches that you perform often so that you don't have to create the search criteria each time you need to search, as discussed in the next section.

You can search for a computer connected to your network by selecting the option labeled Computers or people and then selecting A computer on the network. After you enter the name or a few characters from the computer's name, the Search window begins looking over your network of computers. If found, a computer icon appears in the results window pane. You can double-click that icon to search the computer for files, assuming you have the proper network permission to search that computer.

If you select the option labeled People in your address book, the Search window searches for people located in your Windows *address book*, a list of names and addresses that you'll automatically have if you use Outlook Express or Microsoft Outlook for your email and address list. (Other contact applications may act as your address book if you use them.) When you click the option labeled People in your address book, the Search window displays the Find People dialog box shown in Figure 12.2.

FIGURE 12.2

You can locate people stored in your address book and elsewhere.

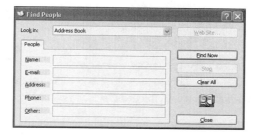

You can search for people not only stored in your address book files, but also anybody listed on one of several people-finding Internet search engines. Simply click the down arrow on the drop-down list box labeled Look in and select the type of online service you want to use for your search.

If you click the option labeled Search the Internet, either from the initial Search Companion pane or from the Computers or people window pane, the Search window displays the Internet search pane shown in Figure 12.3. Type a word or phrase for which you want to search, click the Search button, and the right Search window pane fills up with a Web page full of Internet search results that match your request. A list of further options you can use to narrow your search will appear if you don't see what you are looking for in the right pane.

12

FIGURE 12.3

*Enter your search
query and Windows XP
will search the Internet
to fulfill your request.*

Improving Your Searches

You can use *wildcard characters* to narrow your search results. A wildcard character stands for one or more groups of characters, just as a joker often functions as a wildcard in card games. Search supports two wildcard characters: * and ?.

* acts as a wildcard for zero, one, or more characters. For example, if you want to see all files that end with the .txt extension, you can specify *.txt as your search criteria. The asterisk wildcard tells Search to locate every file that ends in .txt, no matter what appears before the file extension. The criteria ABC*.* represents all files that begin with the letters ABC, no matter what follows the letters and no matter what extension the file has. (ABC*.* even locates files that begin with ABC and have no extension.)

The question mark wildcard replaces single characters within a criteria. Therefore, ACCT??.DAT finds all files that begin with ACCT, have two more characters, and end in the .DAT extension. The following files would successfully match that criteria: ACCT02.DAT, ACCT03.DAT, and ACCT04.DAT. However, neither ACCT.DAT nor ACCTjun03.DAT would match because the two question marks specify that only two characters must replace the wildcards in those positions.

The following steps walk you through a search session that uses wildcard characters.

1. Display the Search window.
2. Click the option labeled All files and folders. The Search Companion's window pane appears, as shown in Figure 12.4. Your screen might differ slightly if your Search window's toolbar is displayed.

FIGURE 12.4

Search searches across drives for specific documents and folders.

3. Type `winmine.*` at the prompt labeled Part or all of the file name. This wildcard specification looks for all files and folders that begin with the letters `winmine`. It turns out that you can just type `winmine` to achieve the same result, except that without the wildcard, the Search window will locate all files with the letters `winmine` anywhere in the name, not just at the beginning.

4. Leave the defaults in the other fields and click Search. Windows automatically searches your disks and subdirectory folders, although you can click the option labeled More advanced options to limit the search to top-level, root-folder directories only.

   After a brief pause, your dialog box should resemble the one shown in Figure 12.5, although you may show more or fewer results. The list contains not only the document's filename, but also the folder in which the document resides, the size of the document, the type of file, and the date and time that the file was last modified. (You might need to use the horizontal scrollbar at the bottom of the results window pane to see the file sizes and dates.)

> If you don't see filename extensions but you want to, select the window's Tools, Folder Options, click the View tab, and uncheck the option labeled Hide file extensions for known file types.

You can drag the edge of any result's column left or right to expand or shrink the width of that column.

12

Search results appear here

FIGURE 12.5

Search locates your files.

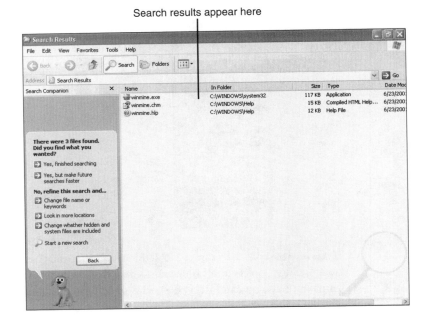

If you click any of the result window pane's column title, Search sorts the found information in alphabetical, numerical, or date and time order.

At least four files should appear, and they'll appear in your Windows folder. One of these files has an .exe extension, meaning that you can run that file.

If your filename extensions are turned off, the executable file is the file with the land mine icon to the left of its Name entry. Now that Windows XP has located the executable file, you can run the program directly from the Search window.

When Search finishes, the left Search window pane offers you several choices. You can click the option labeled Yes, finished searching to close the left window pane and display the list of results in a wider right window pane so you can see all the details. (You can click the toolbar's Search button to initiate a new search.) The option labeled Change file name or keywords returns you to the initial search window pane so you can modify the search options. The Look in more locations option enables you to change the disk drives you are searching to see if the file resides somewhere you were not expecting.

5. Double-click the winmine.exe entry, and a Windows game named Minesweeper appears. Start clicking away on the squares, but be very careful!

   Windows is smart. If the file you click isn't an executable file, Windows attempts to open the file using other resources. For example, if you click a Microsoft Word document, Windows automatically looks for the Microsoft Word program on your PC and opens the document using Word (assuming that you have Word). If you select a help file, Search opens a help window with that file displayed. If you select an email message file, Search locates your email reader and displays the message there. As long as the file is registered (explained in Chapter 8, "Navigating with Windows Explorer"), Windows can associate the file's parent program and display the file.

6. After you've played Minesweeper for a while, close its window and then close the Search window.

If your search is taking too long, you may have entered too general a search so that too many files are being found. Perhaps you entered too many drives to search. If a search takes too long, click the Stop button. You then can continue the search if you want by clicking the option labeled Yes, finished searching or refine your search by changing the search drives or locations being searched.

Summary

This chapter helped you find information you need on both your own PC and the Internet. Get in the habit of using Search for your PC, network, and Internet files when you need to locate information. You can search for the file you want to find and then select the file to open it and begin working with it.

Internet search engines help convert the Internet's information overload to a manageable repository of information. You can search Web sites that fit your exact criteria, as well as look for people's names and addresses.

12

PART V

Interfacing Windows and Hardware

Chapter

CHAPTER 13

Exploring Your Hardware Interface

Microsoft designed Windows so that you could take advantage of the latest hardware advances. Windows recognizes most devices currently in use and is designed with future devices and expandability in mind. This chapter shows how the Windows interface utilizes your hardware. Windows supports *Plug and Play*, a term that describes automatic installation of new hardware you add to your PC. Prior to Plug and Play, you had to set jumper switches and make operating system settings. Often, hardware and software conflicts would occur, creating many hours of debugging headaches. With Plug and Play, you simply plug new hardware components such as memory, disk drives, CD-ROM drives, and expansion boards into your computer, and Windows immediately recognizes the change and sets up everything properly. In addition to plug-and-play devices, many external peripherals such as external hard drives, keyboards, and mice, now connect to USB and FireWire connections which make adding such peripheral equipment even simpler than Plug and Play allows.

Plug and Play requires almost no thought when installing new hardware to your system. At least that's the theory. In reality, you might still encounter problems, as this chapter demonstrates. If Plug and Play does not perform as expected, Windows provides a hardware setup wizard that you can use to walk you through the new hardware's proper installation.

Plug and Play

Despite the industry hype over Plug and Play, it does not always work. If you attempt to install an older board into your computer, Windows might not recognize the board, and you could have all kinds of hardware problems that take time to correct. Generally, devices currently billed as Plug and Play are fairly stable and install well.

USB (*USB* stands for *Universal Serial Bus* and is also known as USB-1), *USB-2* (faster than USB and backward compatible), and FireWire, also called *IEEE 1394*, hardware generally works better than the plug-and-play installations described here. The advantage to USB and FireWire is that you don't have to power-off your computer to install new devices. Simply plug the device's connector into your computer's USB or FireWire port and Windows recognizes the device, prompts you for installation software if any is required, and you are ready to use the device. In spite of the advantages to these connections, plug-and-play devices are still needed, such as graphics adapters that must plug directly into your computer's motherboard.

 Windows prior to Windows XP did not support FireWire or USB well. USB-2 and FireWire connections provide high-speed transfer of video and audio data. Many digital cameras, audio, and video devices now connect to computers through a FireWire or USB port.

Using USB and FireWire connections are so simple in most cases that a long discussion of them is not even justified here. You'll run into more potential problems inserting video cards, internal modems, and other non-USB and non-FireWire devices into your computer so the concept of Plug and Play is still a timely issue and one that computer users still should understand today. Ultimately, it's hoped that all hardware connects to your computer, including internal devices such as hard disks and video cards, as easily and effortlessly as USB and FireWire connections.

Things do not always go as planned when installing non–plug-and-play hardware. New hardware that supports Plug and Play often has a seal with *PnP* on the box indicating its compatibility. You often have to set certain hardware switches correctly. You might also have to move certain jumpers so that electrical lines on your new hardware flow properly to work with your specific computer. The new hardware can conflict with existing hardware in your machine. Most hardware devices, such as video and sound boards, often require new software support contained in small files called drivers that you must install and test.

> Hardware designed before the invention of plug-and-play specifications is called *legacy hardware*.

Before Plug and Play can work in Windows, these two plug-and-play items must be in place:

- A Basic Input Output System called the *BIOS* in your computer's system unit that is compatible with Plug and Play. The computer manual's technical specifications or technical support should tell you whether the BIOS is compatible with Plug and Play. Fortunately, virtually all PCs sold since early 1996 have supported Plug and Play.
- A device to install that is compatible with Plug and Play.

You are running Windows XP, which is compatible with Plug and Play. If you do not have the Plug and Play BIOS inside your computer (most computers made before 1994 have no form of Plug and Play compatibility at all), you have to help Windows with the installation process by answering some questions posed by a new hardware setup wizard.

> One key in knowing whether the hardware is designed for Plug and Play is to make sure that the Windows logo appears on the new hardware's box or instructions. Before a hardware vendor can sell a product with the Windows logo, that product must offer some level of plug-and-play compatibility. If you have older hardware already installed under a version of Windows when you install Windows, you will not have to reinstall this hardware.

13

If you run Windows, own a computer with a Plug and Play BIOS, and purchase only plug-and-play hardware, the most you usually have to do is turn off the computer, install the hardware, and turn the computer back on. Everything should work fine after that.

Although most hardware sold today supports Plug and Play, some notable exceptions do not. For example, some backup devices require several non–plug-and-play steps that you must go through to install these devices. When possible, purchase USB or FireWire versions of products such as these. However, if you already have an inventory of such devices, you can certainly make them work with Windows XP in almost every case.

Plug and Play works both for newly installed hardware and for removed hardware. If you remove a sound card that you no longer want, or remove memory and replace that memory with a higher capacity memory, Plug and Play should recognize the removal and reconfigure the computer and operating system automatically. Again, Plug and Play is not always perfect and does not always operate as expected, but as long as you run a Plug-and-Play BIOS and install plug-and-play hardware, you should have little trouble with installation.

Windows Offers Hardware Help

If you install hardware and find that Windows does not properly recognize the change, double-click the Add Hardware icon in the Control Panel window. You might have to click the option labeled Switch to Classic View to see the Add Hardware icon. Windows starts the Add Hardware Wizard, shown in Figure 13.1, which helps walk you through the installation process.

FIGURE 13.1
The Add Hardware Wizard helps you install non–plug-and-play hardware.

The wizard goes through a series of tests and attempts to detect the newly added hardware. Remember that Windows recognizes most plug-and-play hardware; that is, when you install a new graphics card, for example, and then restart Windows, Windows often recognizes the graphics card and configures itself for use with your new card. Nevertheless, Windows cannot automatically recognize all plug-and-play hardware.

After the Add Hardware Wizard searches for plug-and-play hardware, you can have it search for non–plug-and-play hardware, or you can select the hardware from the list of vendors and products that Windows offers. Of course, if your hardware is newer than Windows, Windows will not list your specific hardware.

> You can let the Add Hardware Wizard search for the new hardware, and if the wizard does not recognize the hardware, you can select from the list of devices.

Be sure to read your new hardware's installation documentation thoroughly before you begin the installation. Often the new hardware comes with updated drivers that fix minor bugs and add features to drivers that Windows already includes. Therefore, instead of letting the wizard search for the new device, and instead of selecting from the list of supported devices shown in Figure 13.2, you use a disk or CD-ROM that comes with the new hardware to add the latest hardware support for the device to Windows. Therefore, you have to click the dialog box's Have Disk button and select the hardware's disk or CD-ROM location to complete the installation.

FIGURE 13.2

Select from the list of known hardware or use your hardware's own installation disk.

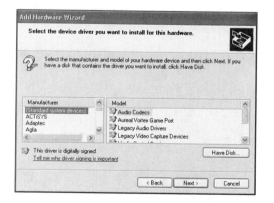

13

> If you add a new modem to a serial port or a printer to a parallel port, you should not run the Add Hardware Wizard. The wizard works only for hardware you physically connect to the system unit, such as a disk drive or graphics card. If you plug a modem into an existing serial port, that serial port will

already be installed, so you don't need to run Add Hardware. You will, however, have to double-click the Control Panel's Modems icon and select your
modem from the list of modems displayed if the modem does not automatically install.

If you have a laptop or desktop with a PC card (PC cards are sometimes called *PCMCIA
cards*), you can plug it directly into the laptop, changing a PC card hard disk to a PC
card modem, and Windows will adjust itself automatically.

Additional Hardware Support

Windows uses a Registry and hardware tree to keep track of the current and changeable
hardware configuration. The Registry is a central repository of all possible hardware
information for your computer. The hardware tree is a collection of hardware configurations, taken from part or the entire Registry, for your computer. In addition, your Registry
holds software settings.

Luckily, you don't have to know anything about the Registry because Windows keeps
track of the details for you. If, however, you want to look at the hardware tree currently
in place on your computer, you can display the Control Panel, double-click the System
icon, and click the Device Manager button on the Hardware page to display the Device
Manager page shown in Figure 13.3. This hardware tree shows the devices currently in
use.

FIGURE 13.3

*Analyze and change
your computer's hard-
ware settings from the
Device Manager
window.*

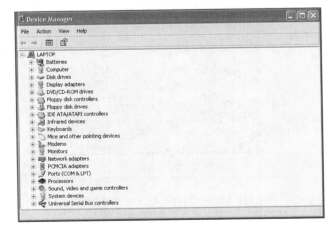

Setting Up a Second PC

When you purchase a second PC, such as a laptop or a second home PC, you'll probably want to transfer files from your current PC to the new one. For example, you might have data files on the current PC that you want to place on the new one. The best way to transfer files is through a network. Part 9, "Learning How to Network Computers," explains how to put together and configure a network. Nevertheless, some people do not want to install networking hardware simply to transfer a lot of files from one computer to another for just one time. Perhaps you're setting up a new laptop and don't want to purchase a network card for the laptop.

Windows supports a feature called *direct cable connection* that lets you transfer files between computers without the need of a network and without moving data between the PCs via disk. The cable must be a *DirectParallel cable*, a special cable that connects one PC's parallel port to another's, or a *null modem cable* connected between the two computer serial ports. If both computers have an infrared eye, as most laptops have, you don't even need a cable; the infrared links serve as the "cable" between the two machines.

If you attach such a cable between two computers, or if they both have infrared ports, those computers can share files and printer resources with one another. This is a simple replacement for a more expensive and extensive network system. The direct cable connection is useful if you have the need only for two computers to share resources.

You'll access the direct cable connection option from your Network Connections window even if you don't have an existing network of any kind connected to your computer. When you double-click the link called Create a new connection, the Network Connection Wizard initiates, as shown in Figure 13.4. After answering the wizard's prompts, your two computers will be linked as the next steps explain.

1. Connect your two computers' parallel or serial ports with the cable. If both computers have infrared ports, point one infrared port to the other.
2. Select the Network Connection Wizard.
3. Click Next to select the connection type. Choose the last option labeled Set up an advanced connection to let the wizard know that you want to connect your computer to another by a direct cable connection.
4. Click Next and select the option labeled Connect directly to another computer.
5. Click Next. You will select one PC as the *host* and one as the *guest* by clicking the appropriate options on the wizard's screen. The host is the PC from which you'll transfer the file or files, and the guest receives those files. After you designate a host and guest, you cannot send information in the other direction without restarting the wizard on both computers.

13

FIGURE 13.4

The Network Connection Wizard helps you connect two computers via a cable or infrared port.

6. Click the Next button to select the port on which you've connected the computers from the dialog box that appears in Figure 13.5. You'll have to select the port used on each PC.

FIGURE 13.5

Tell the wizard to which port the cable connects.

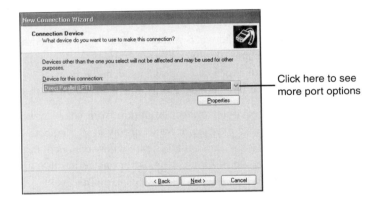

Click here to see more port options

7. Click Next to display the permission screen where you designate which of the computer's users can connect to the computer through the direct cable connection. The permissions determine whether the connecting user must have a password to connect to your computer.

8. Click Next to assign a name to the direct cable connection so that the other computer will recognize the connection option by its name. You can set up multiple direct cable connections, each with its own name and with different user permissions.

9. Click Finish to make the connection. After you've followed the wizard on the connecting PC, the two should be able to communicate with each other. If they do not

both recognize the connection, you might have to check cable connections and rerun the wizard to ensure that all the options are set correctly. For example, you'll want to make sure that both PCs are not set as host or both as guest.

The guest's Windows Explorer or My Computer window now holds an icon for the host PC, and you can transfer files from the host as easily as you can transfer from one of your disks to another. In addition, the guest's application programs can now print to the host printer because the host printer will be available from all File, Print dialog boxes.

The direct cable connection provides a way for you to connect two computers to use the files and printer on one (the host) by the other (the guest). The direct cable connection enables the guest computer to share the host's file and printer resources without requiring expensive and elaborate networking hardware and software.

 After you set up a host or guest PC, your subsequent use of the direct cable connection is easier. You then have to specify the dialog box settings only if you change computers or if you decide to change directions and switch between the host and guest when transferring files.

Summary

This chapter got fairly technical during the discussion of hardware. An operating system must run through several operations before it can recognize and work with new hardware. Fortunately, the plug-and-play process makes such work slightly easier and sometimes trouble free.

If you do not use 100% plug-and-play or USB or FireWire hardware, the Add Hardware Wizard will walk you through each installation and make the hardware easier to install. Suppose, for example, you add an internal modem, but you cannot communicate with it. The Add Hardware Wizard might realize that you have a new internal modem after running through its series of tests, but might not be able to determine exactly what kind of internal modem you have. You and the wizard together should be able to determine the proper configuration.

The direct cable connection wizard means that you'll be connecting more computers than ever before. You'll be able to transfer files and share printers easily from one to the other by attaching a cable between the parallel ports of each machine.

13

CHAPTER 14

Understanding Printing and Fonts

This chapter explains the printing options available to you as a Windows user. The printer is one of those devices that you don't want to think much about; you want to print a document and a few moments later, grab the resulting printed output from the printer. You can better manage your printer's output with this chapter's information. When you work with documents, the availability of fonts is important so that you have the richness that fonts provide. You'll see here how to work with fonts inside Windows. With ample fonts, you can view more documents accurately.

Introduction to Spooled Printing

When you print documents, Windows automatically starts the printer *subsystem*, a program within Windows that handles printing requests. The printer subsystem controls all printing from within Windows. Windows *spools* output through the printer subsystem. When spooled, the print job first goes to a disk file, managed by the printer subsystem, before being sent directly to the printer.

By routing printed output to a spooled disk file instead of sending the output directly to the printer, you can intercept it before that output goes to paper. That gives you more control over how the output appears on the printer. You also can select which printer receives the output in case more than one printer is connected to your computer.

Setting Up a Printer

If you add a printer to your system, remove a printer from your system, or set up Windows to use a printer for the first time, you'll have to inform Windows. But that's not always a problem because Windows supports Plug and Play as well as gives you the Add Printer Wizard to help you each step of the way.

Turn off your PC before you plug a new printer into your PC's parallel printer port. If you have a USB-based printer, you usually don't have to do this. After plugging in the printer and Windows XP restarting, Windows will often recognize, through Plug and Play, that you've added a new printer and perform one of the following tasks:

- Automatically recognize the printer and install the drivers for you
- Recognize that you've changed the hardware and start the Add Printer Wizard so that you can select the new printer
- Not realize that you added a printer, requiring you to run the Add Printer Wizard yourself

A special Printers and Other Hardware category appears on the Start menu's Control Panel. This category provides information about your computer's printer hardware. If you haven't set up your printer, and Plug and Play failed to install it, you will have to open the Printers and Other Hardware category window and walk through the Add Printer Wizard so that Windows knows exactly which printer to use.

Windows needs to know how to format the printed output that you want. Almost every printer supports different combinations of print functions, and almost every printer requires unique *print codes* that determine how the printer interprets specific characters and character-formatting options. The Add Printer Wizard configures the necessary details and asks you appropriate questions that determine how printed output eventually appears. The next few steps walk you through the process of adding a new printer to your computer system.

If you use a network and you need to set up a network printer in Windows, use the Network and Internet Connections category in the Control Panel window to open the network printer; you can browse the network to find

> the printer. Then set up the printer following the instructions that appear onscreen.

1. Connect your printer to your computer using a printer cable. Most printers connect to the computer's parallel port or USB port.

2. Click the Start button to display the Start menu.

3. Select Control Panel, Printers and Other Hardware, and then click the option labeled View installed printers or fax printers. The Printers and Faxes window shown in Figure 14.1 opens.

FIGURE 14.1

The Printers and Faxes window controls the setup and operation of printers and any online faxing software you might have.

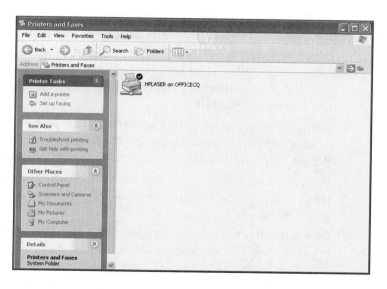

 If you have not set up a printer, you will see only the Add Printer icon in the Printers and Faxes window.

The Printers and Faxes window provides access to all your printer subsystem capabilities. It is from the Printers window that you can manage and rearrange print jobs you've started from Windows applications.

4. Click the link labeled, Add a printer, to start the Add Printer Wizard. If you haven't set up a printer, select the Add Printer icon now. When you select it, you will see the first screen of the Add Printer Wizard shown in Figure 14.2.

14

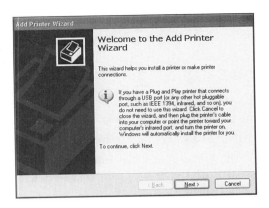

FIGURE 14.2

The Add Printer Wizard walks you through the setup of a new printer.

5. Click the Next command button to start the Add Printer Wizard's operation. Select either the Local printer or the Network printer option. (If you want to set up your computer to print to a printer attached to another PC on your network, select the option labeled Printer Connection before clicking Next.) The wizard will look for a plug-and-play printer and install it if possible. If no plug-and-play printer exists, you'll proceed to the next step.

6. The Add Printer Wizard will ask how you connect your printer to your computer. If you use a parallel printer, you'll select the default option, LPT1:. Doing so informs Windows XP that the printer is connected to your PC's printer port.

7. A list of printer manufacturers appears in the left scrolling window. When you choose a manufacturer, such as *Epson* or *HP*, that manufacturer's printer models appear in the right scrolling window.

   Over time, printer manufacturers update their printers and offer new models. There is no way that Microsoft can predict what a printer manufacturer will do next. Therefore, you might buy a printer that's made after Windows was written. If so, the printer should come with a disk that you can use to add the printer to Windows. If this is the case, click the Have Disk button and follow the instructions on the screen.

   If your printer *is* in the list, find your printer's model on the right, highlight the model, and click the Next button.

8. When you see the screen shown in Figure 14.3, you can enter the name you want to use for the printer when selecting among printers within Windows. If you like the default name, don't change it. If you want a different name, such as Joe's Printer (in case you're setting up a network printer that others will use), type the new name. If this is the only printer you are setting up, select Yes when the wizard asks about this being the default printer. (If this is the first printer you've installed,

Windows makes it the default printer.) Windows will then use the printer automatically every time you print something. If you are setting up a secondary printer, select No.

FIGURE 14.3

You must tell Windows how to refer to the printer.

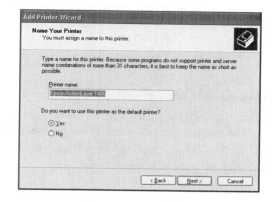

9. Click the Next command button to move to the next wizard screen. If you are going to allow others to use this computer over the network, indicate that you want to share this printer. Click Next.

10. Use the Location and Comment fields that appear to enter a brief description of the printer's location and, optionally, a comment about its use (such as a note telling the users to check the printer's ink weekly). On a large network, such descriptions help ensure that users route printing to the proper printer.

11. If you click Yes on the next wizard screen, Windows will print a test page on the printer. (Be sure that your printer is turned on and that it has paper.) By printing a test page, you ensure that Windows properly recognizes the printer. Click the Finish command button to complete the wizard.

12. After Windows completes the printer setup, a new icon with your printer's name appears in the Printers window.

When running the Add Printer Wizard, you specify which printer Windows should use for the default printer. (The default printer might appear with a check mark next to it in the Printers and Faxes window.) Of course, any time you print documents, you can select a printer that differs from the default printer if you want the output to go to a secondary printer source. You can also change the default printer by right-clicking over the printer you want to set as the default printer and selecting the Set As Default command from the menu.

14

If you use your computer for accounting or personal finance, you might
have a laser printer for reports and a color ink-jet printer for color banners.
The default printer should be the printer that you print to most often. If
your laser printer is the default printer, you'll have to route output, using
the Print dialog box explained in the next section, back to the default check
printer when you want to print checks.

The Print Dialog Box

When you print from an application such as WordPad, you'll see the Print dialog box
shown in Figure 14.4. The Print dialog box contains several options from which you can
choose. Most of the time, the default option values are appropriate, so you'll simply
press Enter to select the OK command button when printing.

FIGURE 14.4
*The Print dialog box
controls the way a
print job is routed.*

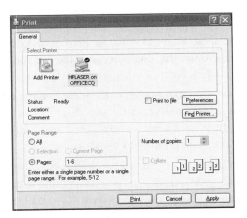

The Print dialog box contains a drop-down list box of every printer you've added to
Windows. The default printer will be the printer you've chosen using the Add Printer
Wizard's final screen. To change the default printer to another printer so that Windows
automatically routes output to it when you print (unless you select another printer at
printing time), right-click the printer's icon from within the Printers dialog box in My
Computer and choose Set as Default.

You can route the printer's output to a file by clicking the Print-to-File
option. If you want output to go to a physical printer as soon as possible, as
is most often the case, leave this option unchecked. By printing to the file,
you can print the file at a later time.

The Print range will be All if you want to print all pages. For example, if you are printing 20 pages from a word processor, the All option sends all 20 pages to the printer. If you select the Pages option, you can enter a starting page number and ending page number to print only a portion of the document.

The Copies section determines how many copies you want to print. The default is one copy, but you can request an additional number of copies. If you enter a number greater than 1, check the Collate option if you want the pages collated (you usually do). If you highlight part of the text before beginning the print process, you can click the Selection option button to print only the selected text.

For special print jobs, you can click the Properties command button to display a printer Properties dialog box. Each printer model supports a different set of options so each printer's Properties dialog box contains different options. In the Properties dialog box, you specify the type of paper in the printer's paper tray, the *orientation* (the direction the printed output appears on the paper), and the printer resolution (the higher the printer resolution, the better your output looks, but the longer the printer takes to print a single page), among other options that your printer might support.

Keep in mind that the output goes to the print spooler and *not* directly to the printer. The next section explains how you can manage the print spooler.

Some print jobs take a while to send their output to the spool file and, subsequently, to the printer. The taskbar displays a printer icon to the left of the clock during the printing process. If you rest the cursor over the printer icon, Windows displays a roving help box that describes how many jobs are in line to print. If you open the print icon, Windows displays the list of all print jobs (the next section describes the window of print jobs). If you right-click over the icon, Windows gives you the choice of displaying a window containing a list of all print jobs or the print jobs for specific printers that are queued up waiting for printed output.

Explorer and Open dialog boxes all display documents, as you've seen throughout this book. If you want to print a document, such as a bitmap graphics document file, a text document file, or a word processing document file, the right-click menu contains a Print command that automatically prints the selected document (or documents) that you right-click over. The right-click does *not* produce the Print dialog box described in this section; rather, Windows automatically and instantly prints one copy of the document on the primary default printer.

14

There's one more way to print documents that works well in some situations. If you have the My Computer window open or if you are using Windows Explorer, you can print any printable document by dragging it to any printer icon inside the Printers window. Windows automatically begins printing the document that you drag to the printer icon.

Managing Print Jobs

When you print documents, Windows formats the output into the format required by the default printer and then sends that output to a spool file. When the output completes, the printer subsystem routes the output to the actual printer, as long as it is connected and turned on.

Suppose that you want to print several documents to your printer in succession. Although today's printers are fairly fast, the computer's disk drives and memory are much faster than the relative speed of printers. Therefore, you can end up sending several documents to the printer before the first document even finishes printing on paper.

After printing one or more documents, open your Printers and Faxes window and double-click the Printer icon that represents the printer you printed to. A scrolling list of print jobs, such as the one shown in Figure 14.5, appears inside the window.

FIGURE 14.5

You can see all the print jobs spooled up, waiting to print.

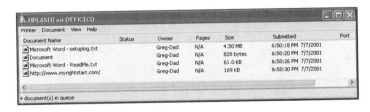

Each line in the window describes one print job. If you've printed three documents, all three documents appear inside the window. The Progress column shows how far along your print job is by telling you how many pages of the print job have completed. The remaining print jobs on the list are awaiting their turn to print.

If you want to change the order of the print jobs in the *queue* (another name for the list of print jobs), you can drag a print job to the top or bottom. Dragging a print job around in the list changes priority for that print job. For example, your boss might be waiting over your shoulder for a report. If you had several jobs you had sent to print before your boss showed up, you could move the boss's print job to the top of the list so that it would print next.

Right-clicking over a print job gives you the option of pausing a print job (putting it on hold until you resume the job) or canceling the print job altogether.

Deferred Printing

Sometimes you'll print documents but *not* want those documents to appear on a printer. Often people carry a laptop with them but not a printer. Even if you don't have a printer with you, you might create expense reports and other documents that you want to print as soon as you get back to your office.

Instead of keeping track of each document you want to print later, you can go ahead and issue a *deferred printing* request. When you do this, Windows spools the document or documents to a file on your disk drive. The printer subsystem will not attempt to send the spooled data to a printer just yet. When you later attach a printer to your PC, you can release the deferred printing request and Windows begins printing the saved print jobs.

Ordinarily, if you were to print a document to a printer but you had no printer attached to your computer, Windows would issue a taskbar error message, shown in Figure 14.6. Although Windows can spool the output properly and set up a print job for the output, Windows cannot finish the job because of a lack of a printer. The dialog box lets you know about the problem.

FIGURE 14.6

Windows cannot print if a printer is not attached to your PC.

If you do have a printer attached to your computer but you get the error dialog box shown in Figure 14.6, you probably forgot to turn on the printer or put the printer *online* so that it can accept output. You can correct the problem and click Retry to restart the printing. If you do not click Retry, Windows will automatically retry printing every five seconds.

If you want to defer printing for another time, open the Printers folder and right-click over the icon that matches the printer for which you want to store print jobs. After you right-click, select Use Printer Offline. When you return to your office or plug a printer into the printer port, you can repeat this process to deselect the Use Printer Offline option. As soon as you set the printer icon back to its normal online status, Windows XP will begin printing to that printer.

14

Fonts Have Style

Because of the design of documents, the way that Windows displays documents is critical to your viewing of them. The documents must be easy to read. If Windows doesn't automatically display a document in a format that is easy to read, you'll have to change the way the document appears. Perhaps the simplest way to make a document easier to read, no matter what tool you use to view those documents, is by changing the document's font. A font is the typeface Windows uses to display a character. If you see two letter A's on the screen and one is larger, more slanted, bolder, fancier, or more scripted, you are looking at two different fonts.

Fonts from the same *font family* contain the same typeface (they look alike), but they come in standard formatting versions such as italicized, boldfaced, and underlined text. Therefore, an italicized font named *Courier* and a boldfaced font named *Courier* both belong to the same font family, even though they look different because of the italicized version of the one and the boldface version of the other. A font named *Algerian* and a font named *Symbol*, however, would belong to two different font families; not only do they look different, but they also come in various styles.

Fonts and Typefaces

Before computers were invented, printer experts stored collections of typefaces in their shops. Each typeface contained every letter, number, and special character the printer would need for printed documents. Therefore, the printer might have 50 typefaces in his inventory with each of those typefaces containing the same letters, numbers, and special characters but each having a different appearance or size.

Windows also contains a collection of typefaces, and those typefaces are stored as fonts on the hard disk. If you want to use a special typeface for a title, you must make sure that Windows contains the typeface in its font collection. If not, you will have to purchase the font and add that font to your system. Software dealers sell numerous font collections. Several fonts come with Windows and with the programs that you use, so you might not even need additional fonts.

The Control Panel's classic view (available when you select Switch to Classic View from the Control Panel window) contains an icon labeled Fonts from which you can manage, add, and delete fonts from Windows XP's collection. When you open the Control Panel window's Fonts icon, Windows opens the Fonts window shown in Figure 14.7. The following steps explain how to manage fonts from the Fonts window.

FIGURE 14.7

The Fonts window displays your fonts.

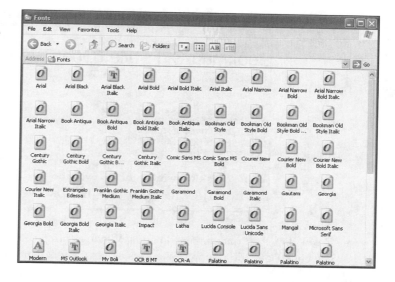

1. Open the Control Panel window.
2. Click Switch to Classic View if you see the Control Panel categories listed.
3. Open the Fonts icon. Windows opens the Fonts window.

    Each icon inside the Fonts window contains information about one specific font on your system. Some fonts are *scaleable*, which means that Windows can display the fonts in one of several different sizes.

 Font sizes are measured in *points*. A font that is 12 points high is 1/6 inch high, and a font that is 72 points is one inch high.

4. Open any of the icons inside the Fonts window, and Windows immediately displays a preview of that font, as shown in Figure 14.8. When you want to create a special letter or flier with a fancy font, you can preview all of the fonts by opening each one until you find one you like. When you find a font, you can select it from your word processor to enter the text using that font.

 Many fancy fonts are available to you. Don't go overboard, though. Your message is always more important than the font you use. Make your font's style fit the message, and don't mix more than two or three fonts on a single page. Too many different fonts on a single page make the page look cluttered.

14

FIGURE 14.8

Get a preview before selecting a font.

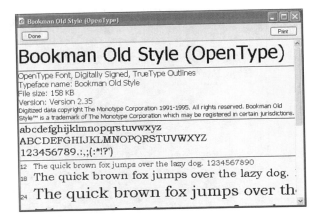

5. If you click the Print command button, Windows prints the preview of the font. If you click Done (do so now), Windows closes the font's preview window.

6. Another way to gather information about certain kinds of fonts is to right-click over a font and select Properties from the menu that appears. The Font Properties dialog box will appear.

   The font icons with a green, rounded *O* symbol are *TrueType* fonts (you can verify that a font is a TrueType font from its Properties window. A TrueType font is a scaleable font that Windows prints using 32-bit technology so it will look as close to typeset characters as possible. The remaining fonts, with the letter A or another icon, refer to screen and printer fonts of more limited size ranges than TrueType fonts normally can provide.

Some users prefer to work only with TrueType fonts because of their rich look and scalability. If you want to view only TrueType fonts in the Fonts window, select View, Options and click the TrueType tab. Click the screen's option to display only TrueType fonts.

7. Click the Similarity toolbar button. Windows searches through your fonts looking for all other fonts that are similar to the font you choose from the drop-down list box and displays the result of that search.

8. Click Large Icons to return to the icon view.

9. Check or uncheck View, Hide Variations (Bold, Italic, and so on) depending on whether you want to see variations within font families. If the box is unchecked, Windows displays a different icon for each font variation within the same family.

10. When you purchase new fonts, you cannot simply copy those fonts to a directory and expect Windows to know that the fonts are there. When you want to add fonts, you'll probably obtain those fonts on a CD, disk, or from the Internet. Insert the disk or CD (or make sure that you know where the file is located on your hard disk if you downloaded it from the Internet) and select File, Install New Font. Windows displays the Add Fonts dialog box.

    Select the drive with the new fonts inside the Drives list box, and Windows displays a list of fonts from that drive in the upper window. Click on the font you want to install (hold Ctrl and click more than one font if you want to install several fonts) and click the OK command button to install the font to the Windows folder named Fonts.

11. Close the Fonts window.

After you install fonts, they will immediately be available to all your Windows applications.

Windows provides a single location, the Fonts window, where you can view and manage all the fonts on your system. Because of the graphical and document-centered design of Windows, your collection and selection of fonts is vital to making your documents as easy to read as possible.

Removing Fonts

Fonts take up a lot of disk space and slow down the startup of Windows. If your disk space is a premium and if you have lots of fonts you rarely or never use, you can follow the steps next to remove some of them. Often, today's word processing and desktop publishing programs add more fonts to your system than you'll ever use.

1. Open the Control Panel window.
2. Open the Fonts icon.
3. Scroll to the font you want to delete.
4. Click the font you want to delete; Windows highlights the font. If you hold the Ctrl key while you click, you can select more than one font to delete. By selecting several at once, you can remove the fonts with one task instead of removing each one individually.
5. Right-click over any highlighted font to display the menu.

14

6. Select Delete.

7. Click the Yes button to confirm the removal.

Remove unwanted fonts if you want to save disk space and make your fonts more manageable. The Control Panel window's Fonts entry lets you easily select and remove fonts.

Summary

This chapter explored the printer options you have with Windows. Before using a printer for the first time, you must set up the printer using the Add Printer Wizard available inside the Printers folder. Windows supports several hundred makes and models of printers, so you stand a good chance of finding your printer on the list. The Fonts window contains a centralized location from which you can manage all the fonts used by Windows. When you purchase new fonts, you'll add those fonts using the Fonts window.

CHAPTER **15**

Giving Windows a Tune-Up

This chapter shows you how Windows checks and updates itself. If you have Web access, you don't need to wait for a disk mailing or go to the store to get the latest Windows drivers and updates. You only click a menu option and Windows updates itself. Not only can you be assured that you have the latest Windows support files, but you can also make sure that any new computer you purchase looks and acts just as your current computer does. A wizard helps you transfer all your data and system settings to a new computer when you purchase one.

Updating Windows

As long as you have Internet access, you can request that Windows XP check the Microsoft Internet sites and update any Windows files that have changed, have been added, or have had bugs which have been corrected. The update site gives you full control over the update. You can

- View a list of files that are needed by your system to run the latest versions
- Read a description of each update to help you decide whether you need the update
- Submit problem reports that you experience
- Keep track of the updates you apply to your system

The Windows Update program updates your Windows XP operating system files to ensure that you have the latest system files available. Windows Update can be automatic; you don't have to initiate Windows Update although you can if you want.

If you have an always-on Internet connection, you'll probably want to set up the Windows automatic update routine so your version of Windows XP stays as current as possible. The following steps explain how to set up the automatic Windows Update feature.

1. Open your Control Panel window.
2. Click the Switch to Classic View link to see all Control Panel items.
3. Double-click the System icon.
4. Click the Automatic Update tab to display the Automatic Update page shown in Figure 15.1.

FIGURE 15.1

Set up Windows automatic update so your operating system remains current.

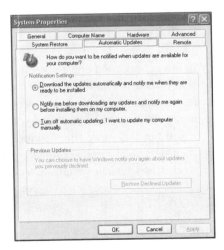

You have three ways to respond to automatic Windows updates. You can request that Windows automatically download any operating system updates when they become available, assuming you haven't already downloaded them, and notify you by a pop-up message from the taskbar's notification area when the update is downloaded to your PC and ready to be installed. You can also request that Windows XP notify you, via a message in your taskbar's notification area, before an update is downloaded to your PC. You can read about the update by clicking the notification area's message and decide if you want to take the time to make the update or ignore it for now. Finally, you have the option to turn off automatic updates so that you only update your Windows when you specifically select Windows Update from the Start menu.

5. Make your selection and click OK.

Instead of installing an update that's available, you can click the Remind Me Later button that appears in your notification area when an update is available. You can select the time frame from the list, such as Tomorrow, when you want to be reminded to install the update.

How the Updates Work

Where do the updates come from? You got a hint of that from the previous steps if you followed along. When you log on to the Internet, Windows, in the background, goes to the Microsoft Web site and looks to see if any updates are required for your particular combination of operating system components. If an update is available, Windows either downloads the update at that time and signals you with the taskbar's notification area message, or Windows tells you that the updates are available and asks if you want to install them. Windows notifies you in one of these two ways depending on how you set up Windows Update, not unlike the way you changed the settings in the previous steps.

Updating Windows Yourself

If you don't want Windows to do any updating or file-retrieval automatically in preparation for an update, you can request that Windows XP not update itself until you take the action that directs Windows to locate updates that might be needed.

If you select the third option of the Automatic Updates dialog box, as you could have done at the end of the previous steps, Windows waits until you select the Start menu's Windows Update option. Until then, Windows will not update your computer or download updates until you request them.

If you select the Windows Update option from the Start menu, Windows always goes to the Internet to see if a current update is available, even if an update has been recently downloaded but has not been installed.

If you want to trigger your own Windows Update and forego the automatic update process as you'll want to do if you use a slower, dial-up modem, select Windows Update from the Start menu. Figure 15.2 shows the Windows Update screen that will appear.

FIGURE 15.2

Select your own time for updating Windows.

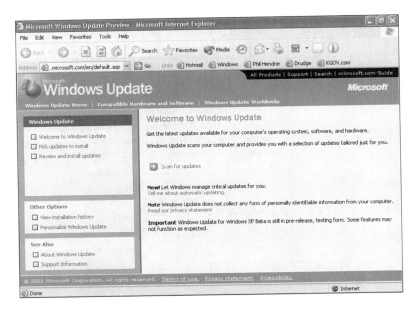

When you click the Scan for Updates option, Windows Update scans your system and compares what it finds to the updates available online. The available updates then appear and you can determine which, if any, you want to apply.

Windows Update attempts to locate these three types of updates:

- Critical Updates: These updates are important for bug fixes or security holes that Microsoft deems critical.
- Windows XP: These updates are new options and utilities that might be available for Windows XP but are not deemed critical or urgent.
- Driver Updates: Updates to specific hardware *drivers* (internal programs that enable your specific computer devices to work with Windows) to fix bugs or make your hardware work better with Windows.

To view the updates you've applied in the past, click the option labeled View Installation History. Windows XP displays the updates you've applied in the past, along with the dates on which you applied each of those updates.

Often, Windows must restart your computer to complete the update process. You should close all program windows before submitting to the system restart.

 If you've elected not to use Windows XP's automatic Windows Update feature, be sure to perform the update routinely to ensure that you have the latest and most correct system files possible.

Transferring Settings from One Computer to Another

When you purchase a new computer, one of the most time-consuming and difficult tasks in the past was transferring all your old computer's settings and files to the new one. You might have Windows set up a particular way, specific features set in Outlook Express, or perhaps have tasks that you've scheduled for automatic execution, such as a daily backup.

Windows XP supports a new feature called the Files and Settings Transfer Wizard that helps you mirror and transfer the settings from your current computer to a new one that you purchase.

Here are just some of the things the Files and Settings Transfer Wizard transfers to a new computer:

- Display property settings
- Dial-up settings
- Desktop settings such as colors and wallpaper
- Data files such as My Documents, My Pictures, and your shared documents
- Email settings
- Mouse and keyboard settings
- Regional settings, such as the time zone and country
- Sounds and other multimedia options
- Folder and taskbar options
- Internet Explorer browser settings

15

The following steps show you how to use the Files and Settings Transfer Wizard.

1. Select the Start menu's All Programs, Accessories, System Tools, Files and Settings Transfer Wizard to open the introductory wizard window shown in Figure 15.3.

FIGURE 15.3

The first Files and Settings Transfer Wizard window describes the wizard's operation.

2. Click Next to move to the next window in the wizard. You must tell the wizard whether you're moving your settings *from* the current computer or *to* the current computer. In other words, the wizard must know whether the computer you are on is receiving settings from another computer or is sending settings to another computer.

3. If you're working from the existing computer, when you click Next, Windows XP takes a few moments to analyze the current system to see what can be transferred to the machine.

4. Click Next to display the transfer method window shown in Figure 15.4. You must tell the wizard how you are going to get the settings from the existing computer to the new one. You can transfer the settings by disk or by network. If you are transferring via a networked drive, you must tell the wizard the location of the drive by specifying the pathname in the text box labeled Folder or drive.

If you transfer data files along with your system settings, you'll need to transfer using a medium larger than a floppy disk. The easiest and fastest way to transfer is over a network connection if both your old computer and your new one are connected to the same network.

FIGURE 15.4

Specify how you want to transfer the settings.

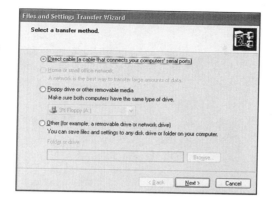

FIGURE 15.5

Specify what you want to transfer.

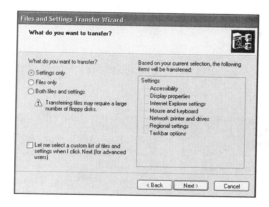

5. Click Next to display Figure 15.5's window where you specify exactly which files and settings you want to transfer.

You must tell the wizard whether you want to transfer data files, settings, or both files and settings, from the older computer to the new one. Once you select your choice, Windows XP might take several minutes to gather the information and complete the process.

As the wizard gathers the information to transfer, you'll be able to monitor the progress on the collection window shown in Figure 15.6.

6. After you complete the collection phase of the old computer, you now must start your new computer and run the Transfer Files and Settings Wizard on that computer. When you tell the wizard that you're on the new computer, the wizard will prompt you for the location of the other computer's settings and files, and you can make the transfer.

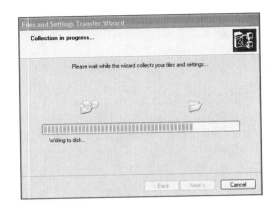

FIGURE 15.6

The wizard is storing your current system's information and preparing to make the transfer.

What's in Your System

Periodically, you might need to know specifics about your system, such as what hardware, memory, disk space, or other detail currently exists in case you want to upgrade your computer.

Windows XP supports a System Information window that displays all the details about your system. Figure 15.7 shows the results of running System Information on one computer.

FIGURE 15.7

Run System Information to learn about your computer's contents.

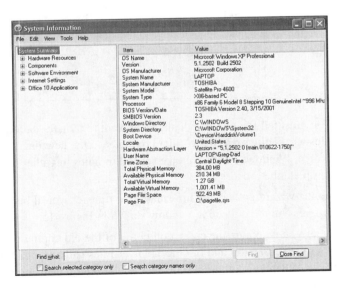

Run System Information from your Start menu's Accessories, System Tools folder. Not only does the opening screen, shown in Figure 15.7, show the details of your system, but you can get more specific information by selecting from the menus. For example, the Tools menu enables you to learn the specifics about your network connections.

Almost all the details from the System Information window are available elsewhere. For example, you can get network connection information from the Control Panel window. The System Information is the primary repository, however, of your system's every detail.

Much is available from the System Information window. You might want to look through the menu options to learn what is available. Perhaps the most important thing you can do right now is print a copy of your system information and save the printout in case you need to restore your system at a later time after a hardware failure of some kind. For example, if you later need to replace a faulty disk drive, you'll be glad you printed a copy of your system information so you can set up your replacement disk drives with the same system settings as the previous drive.

The System Information screen keeps track of the following details of your computer system:

- Your hardware and the internal resources each device uses
- Components such as the status of your USB ports and modem
- Software such as drivers and startup programs that automatically execute when Windows XP first starts
- Internet Explorer settings
- Office application settings (if you have installed Microsoft Office)

To print the system information, select File, Print and select All in the Print range field. Be warned, though, that this list can consume quite a lot of paper.

Whenever you change or add hardware, be sure to print a fresh copy of your system information so you'll always have an up-to-date copy.

Summary

This chapter described how you can keep Windows in top condition. The Windows Update manager makes sure that you have the latest Windows files on your system. To guard against possible application conflicts that sometimes occur with new Windows components, Windows Update enables you to restore from previous updates you made that might now be causing problems with older software you run. When you have the latest Windows files, you can transfer your settings to a new computer with the Files and Settings Transfer Wizard. To make sure you can restore your system if a hardware failure occurs, keep a fresh copy of your system information on hand at all times.

CHAPTER 16

Using Windows with Multimedia

You saw how to work with the Windows Media Player in Chapter 5, "Enjoying Multimedia," and this chapter dives deeper into multimedia but more from a hardware standpoint. You'll learn about digital images which is vital in today's digital camera–filled world. In addition, you will see how Windows supports the creation and editing of movies from your video files. If you don't yet have digital equipment, you're fortunate because this chapter will help you decide on a scanner and camera purchase if either or both are in your near future.

Not only can you transfer home videos to your PC, but once they are there, you can also do so much with them. In this chapter you will learn all about the Windows Movie Maker.

Selecting a Scanner

Like computers, scanners come in all shapes, sizes, and price points. Choosing the right one for you involves a lot more thought than simply choosing a brand within your budget. Scanners are available for around $100, but many may not be capable of doing what you want at the level of quality you desire. You do often get what you pay for.

What Scanners Can Do for You

Scanners are one of those peripherals that are equally useful for work and play. A scanner can convert a paper document into a word processing document, produce high-quality images for a corporate Web page, or even scan the merchandise you sell at online auctions. You can also scan old photos to preserve them for the long term and maybe even touch them up a bit. You can put your children's pictures on special transfer media for creating personalized T-shirts and memory quilts. You can also put current photos on special-theme CDs for long-term storage or sharing.

How Do Scanners Work?

Scanners work by moving a row of silicon cells from the top to the bottom of the scanner's bed. These cells basically bounce light off of and through the object on the scanner bed. The results are then translated into color waves that eventually become the photo-realistic image you see onscreen.

Which Scanner Is Right for Me?

You'll find good scanners today for under $100. Why pay hundreds of dollars for a scanner when one for well under $100 does the trick? If you eventually become a professional graphic artist or Web page designer, then you can go out and pay the big bucks; but for now, your money would be better spent on a less expensive scanner. That way, you can afford to pick up some good photo editing software if you don't receive any with the scanner.

If you do have the money and hope to enlarge and print out photos on your color inkjet printer, here are some things to look for when shopping for a scanner. With scanners, there are fewer features to consider and compare than you may think. First, check the number of levels of color a scanner can replicate. This information is often expressed in bits, and the general rule of thumb is the bigger, the better. The more bits at which a scanner operates, the more authentic are the coloring and details of the image. However, as you may also expect, there are always exceptions to this rule. Some manufacturers soup up their scanners to deliver better performance than their counterparts with the same specifications. In any case, the minimum quality you should consider is 24 bits.

Another specification, or spec, is the scanner's optical resolution. Although 600 dpi is best for reproducing fine art, line drawings, and detailed photos, 300 dpi is sufficient for the needs of many.

DPI actually stands for dots per inch. The more dots per inch, the tinier the dots are that make up an image. And the tinier the dots are, the better the image quality since small dots (technically called *pixels* from the words *picture elements*) can form neatly rounded edges or sharp corners more effectively than their larger counterparts.

16

You will also see mention of parallel and USB scanners. You will need your hardware and software specs to determine whether you need a parallel or USB scanner. Parallel scanners can work with just about any current PC no matter what version of Windows you are running. Some parallel scanners will even let you pass through to your printer, but make sure the printer you have will be happy with the scanner you are considering, or neither may work properly.

USB scanners are much faster than parallel scanners and you can and should consider USB scanners as long as you use Windows XP or later.

The World of Digital Cameras

Do you have dozens of rolls of exposed film lying around just waiting to be developed? Are you tired of spending $15 for film and developing of 24 exposures, only to find three or four of them acceptable and even fewer that are actually good? Have you ever wished you could keep only the good pictures and just throw out the bad? Now you can, thanks to digital cameras.

Choosing a Digital Camera

Choosing a digital camera is a bit more complicated than selecting a scanner. When it comes to selecting a good one, there is lots to consider, and in this case, the average user will be able to see the difference.

The price of digital cameras varies widely, ranging from $50 (for low-resolution models marketed at youth) to several thousand for professional models. Let me help you decide which features are worth paying for and which may not be worth your investment.

Price Does Matter

Unfortunately, price is still a dominating factor for most of us. Although you can get inexpensive digital cameras, be leery of them. They are a great and economical way to teach children basic photography skills, but you can't rely on them for photo-realistic output in all lighting conditions.

Expect to pay $300 or more for a digital camera that truly rivals 35mm quality. Although that may seem like a lot of money, just think of how much you will save over time on film and film processing! There are intangible benefits to a good digital camera—you can take pictures whenever you want without having to worry about the cost or wait involved with developing them. Think about it; how many times have you wasted the end of a roll of film shooting useless stuff just to get to the prized pictures you shot somewhere in the middle of the roll?

Higher Resolution: An Investment Worth Making

Regardless, don't settle for a camera with anything less than 640×480 resolution. Even then, don't expect crystal-clear results.

When you scan an image or shoot a digital picture, the result needs to be enlarged to be of any real use. If it weren't enlarged, you would have a tiny image about the size of a postage stamp. The downside to this, however, is that when you make a low-resolution image bigger, it can become grainy or pixilated. That means the resulting image will not be sharp to the eye.

Given that, take a look at Table 16.1 to see a list of image resolutions and their corresponding results.

TABLE 16.1 Camera Resolutions and Image Production Results

Image Resolution	Product
640×480	Produces a 3 ½×5 printout at best
1024×768 (1 megapixel)	Produces an acceptable 5×7 photo-quality image
1280×1024 (1.3 megapixels)	Produces prints up to 8×10 in size
1.6 megapixels and up	The higher the resolution, the greater the image detail and the bigger the high-quality image produced

Also keep in mind that even if you don't anticipate generating large images, the higher resolution may also enhance the quality of smaller images, and it will certainly give you higher-quality results on the Web.

CMOS Versus CCD

CMOS and CCD describe the types of light sensors in the digital camera. Although CMOS sensors generally cost less and have a longer battery life than their CCD counterparts, CCD cameras are more responsive to various lighting conditions. Thus it is possible that a higher resolution CMOS camera may actually generate inferior results when compared with a slightly lower resolution CCD camera.

Printed Output Versus Online Output

If you plan to use a digitized image on a Web page, you can generally get by with a lower resolution. However, if you are hoping to print your own photos from digital camera output, you will want to go with the highest digital camera resolution you can afford, as well as the best color printer you can get your hands on.

> You may not get what you pay for. Where printers are concerned, paying more doesn't necessarily give you better print quality. Many times the higher price tag can be attributed to increased printing speed or commercial-rated durability. Take your time and choose wisely.

16

Give Me Light!

Digital cameras in any price range will shoot reasonably good pictures in sunlight, but if you hope to make use of the camera inside, having a flash is a must. Some fancier models even have red-eye reduction, which is a plus when photographing people.

The good news is that although you won't find flash capabilities on the least expensive models, it is becoming a standard feature on higher-end models.

Putting Things Into Focus

Focus features are similar to those found on traditional 35mm cameras. With fixed focus, one size fits all, so-to-speak. Autofocus automatically focuses on a specific object or person, although the subject's surroundings often become somewhat fuzzy. Manual focus with f-stops and various other settings enables you to tweak your view, like with professional 35mm cameras.

In general, the low-end digital cameras use fixed focus because it is the most reasonably priced option. Autofocus is available on midpriced cameras because it offers some artistic freedom without the headaches of knowing about f-stops and other complex features. Available to professional photographers are the $1,000-plus cameras that give them the freedom and quality to which they have grown accustomed.

As always, these general rules of thumb are subject to exceptions and change. As more technical features become less expensive to incorporate, you will start seeing them on lower-priced models because all the manufacturers will be competing heavily for your business.

More Power to You!

Digital cameras can eat batteries almost as quickly as I can put away a plate of fresh, hot, and gooey chocolate chip cookies, especially a camera with a liquid crystal display (LCD) and flash capability.

Although lithium batteries provide the longest life, they can often be so pricey that they offset any savings you may see by switching from a standard camera to a digital camera. I have read that Rayovac's rechargeable alkaline batteries typically last longer than NiCads and may actually save you money in the long run, but your mileage may vary. To complicate matters further, prices of batteries and other power sources are constantly fluctuating, so what may be true as this is written may no longer be true when you read this.

Finally, if you often take pictures indoors and have access to an electrical outlet, you may want to buy the manufacturer's optional A/C adapter to save energy.

Use the A/C adapter when downloading images to your PC. That way, you can shoot the photos without being tied down by the device's power cord in the nearest electrical outlet, and you won't burn up batteries while performing maintenance tasks.

Zooming In on the Subject

Fixed focus cameras may do just fine for shooting scenery or group pictures of your son's swim team, but you will be much happier with a model that gives you at least a 2× zoom. That way, you can tighten the shot to capture a special moment or a silly smile.

However, when it comes to zoom lenses, read the fine print. You will want to be sure you are getting optical zoom instead of digital zoom. The optical zoom resets the resolution of the image you zoom in on to the highest level possible, whereas digital zoom merely crops the image without considering the resolution. This makes digitally zoomed images appear grainier than their optical counterparts.

Even if you don't read the fine print, the price and zoom factor should be a dead give-away. Cameras touting noticeably higher zoom factors than the norm are most likely employing digital zooms. Likewise, if the price is obviously lower than an equivalent camera, that may be a clue that this is digital and not optical technology.

Getting Connected

At the time of this writing, there are two primary ways a digital camera can be connected to your PC for image download: FireWire and USB (both USB-1 and USB-2) and both work well as long as your computer has a FireWire or one of the USB ports.

Buying Your Virtual Film

Like traditional cameras need film to store images, digital cameras need SmartCards, floppy disks, or other specialized media. The average camera comes with 4 to 8 megabytes (MB) of storage, but you can purchase media that will hold as much as 90MB or more before you need to dump it onto your computer.

Some storage media can fit right into your computer's floppy drive with a special adapter, whereas others, like Sony's Mavica, store images on a standard PC floppy disk making it a breeze to use. Although the Mavica has won many over with its standardized storage media, you can only fit up to five high-resolution images on a single floppy. That can be bothersome, especially when all your spare floppies fly out of your pockets while on a roller coaster ride during your theme park vacation!

Having It All!

The majority of cameras, except for the extreme low-end models, come with an LCD that gives you a glance at the picture you just took—a great way to kill, on the spot, those shots that aren't perfect.

Unfortunately, these tiny displays are huge battery hogs. Make sure you get a camera with an optical viewfinder and an LCD so that you can save your batteries for what really counts—more pictures.

Some argue that LCDs give you more authentic "what-you-see-is-what-you-get" results when it comes to composing a picture, but although that may be true, remember that we are dealing with computerized images here. With a photo editing program, you can get exactly what you want regardless of what actually ended up inside the camera.

You Oughta Be in Pictures!

Although you can email your images to family and friends, post them on a Web site, or print them out on your color printer, how do you share images with noncomputer users?

16

Some digital cameras come with a TV-OUT outlet that lets you connect the camera to any TV from which you can either give your slide show manually or program the camera to cycle through the images one-by-one. Of course, this implies that the images are still on your camera's storage media, which may not be practical.

Speak to Me!

Many digital cameras give you the opportunity to record 30-second sound bytes for each picture. Although this is a wonderful way to preserve that special Mother's Day program in which your son performed or that speech your sister gave at a local rally, it does soak up precious space on your storage media. You decide if sound is important to you or not. Also, just because your camera supports sound doesn't mean you have to use it; it can be turned off and on, giving you the opportunity to take advantage of the feature on demand.

Still Versus Video

You can also get digital camcorders from which you can create movies and still shots using the software provided. With digital camcorders, the storage media is the tape on which you record the video, so there is no pricey storage media to purchase.

If you decide to go with a digital camcorder, expect to pay between $800 and $1,000. Also, if you travel a lot, you will want to factor in the camcorder's bulkier shell, which could be a real pain to lug around.

Your Scanner or Digital Camera and Windows XP

Consult your PC and scanner or digital camera documentation to install everything correctly. Once you are all connected, turn on the device.

After a few fleeting moments of disk drive activity, Windows XP announces the presence of new hardware via a text balloon over the right end of the Windows taskbar. Seconds later, a dialog box similar to the one in Figure 16.1 appears.

The digital camera or scanner is literally all set up, ready to go to work for you.

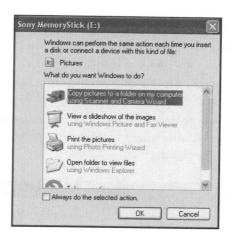

FIGURE 16.1

Because Windows sees my Sony CyberShot camera as a removable disk drive, the dialog box's title bar reads Sony MemoryStick (E:). Your title bar will most likely say something different.

16

From Digital Camera to...

You may have also noticed in Figure 16.1 that several digital camera operations are available to you without having to scour the Start menu for them. They are as follows:

- **Copy pictures to a folder on my computer using Scanner and Camera Wizard.** This moves the pictures from your digital camera to your computer.

- **View a slideshow of the images using Windows Picture and Fax Viewer.** This lets you quickly browse the contents of your digital camera without having to move the pictures to a hard drive.

- **Print the pictures using Photo Printing Wizard.** This enables you to immediately print selected photos on a printer to share with others.

- **Open folder to view files using Windows Explorer.** This allows you to see images already stored on your computer.

- **Take no action.** This closes the dialog box and leaves the images in place on your camera.

Acquiring Pictures with the Scanner and Camera Wizard

To move images from your digital camera to your computer's hard drive, you will have the help of the Windows XP Scanner and Camera Wizard.

You can transfer the pictures by following these steps.

1. Plug the camera into your Windows XP computer and turn it on. In seconds, you will see the dialog box shown back in Figure 16.1.

2. Click the Copy pictures to a folder on my computer option and then click the OK button. This launches the Scanner and Camera Wizard Welcome Screen.

3. Click the Next button to begin importing the images onto your hard drive. The wizard displays a dialog box displaying a preview of all photos on your digital camera's storage media (see Figure 16.2).

FIGURE 16.2

The wizard makes it easy for you to decide which images to keep and which to toss out.

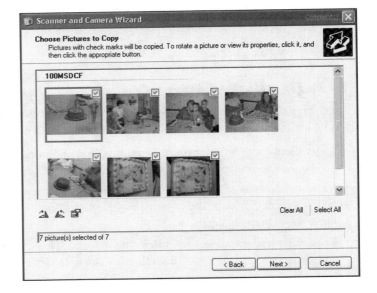

4. By default, all images will be moved to the hard drive. However, you can easily eliminate certain pictures by clicking the green check mark in the upper-right corner of the unwanted image. Once the images you want are marked for big move, click Next.

5. The Select a Picture Name and Destination dialog box shown in Figure 16.3 opens, presenting you with four important decisions to make. First, you will need to pick a name for the selected set of pictures. The more descriptive it is, the easier your life will be down the road. Manhattan 2004 for your summer vacation or Samantha 7 for your daughter's seventh birthday are good options. Type the chosen name into Step 1 of the dialog box. Each of the pictures in the set will reside in that directory with a unique number to identify it.

FIGURE 16.3

This is where you will tell the wizard how you want your pictures stored.

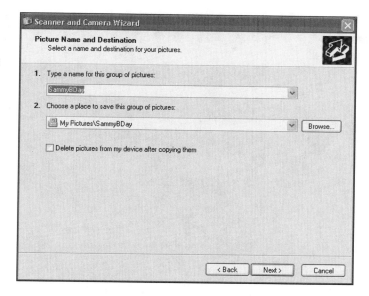

6. Next, you will be asked to name the folder in which you would like to store the images. By default, the folder will be given the name you selected in the previous step, and it will appear in the My Pictures hierarchy. I strongly recommend you leave it there so that all your images are in one central location.

7. Finally, by checking the box at the bottom of the dialog box, you can instruct the wizard to delete the images from your camera once they have been moved to your computer. They will stay on your camera by default, so if you want to eliminate the step of manually deleting them from the camera, go ahead and check the box. Click Next to proceed.

8. The wizard relocates each image to your hard drive one-by-one, as you can see in Figure 16.4. When the job is finished, the wizard reports the successful transfer of your pictures to the hard drive and presents some additional options for actions you can take on the images. You can opt to publish the photos to a Web site, order prints from a photo printing Web site, or do nothing more with them (the default). Click the Next button to continue.

9. The wizard reports how many pictures were copied to your hard drive and presents a link you can click to view them. Click Finish to exit the wizard. When the wizard closes, the relocated pictures appear onscreen in the newly defined My Pictures directory. I will show you how to work with them later in the chapter in the section called, "Managing Your Images from the My Pictures Folder."

FIGURE **16.4**

The Scanner and Camera Wizard gives you an ongoing status report of the file transfers.

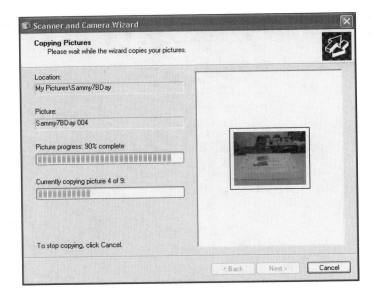

Viewing a Slideshow of the Images on Your Camera

This is a wonderful way to browse images on your camera, especially when you are away from your own computer. If you have a friend or relative with a Windows XP machine and the proper cables, you can share the photos right there on the spot. Just plug in the camera, turn it on, and follow these steps to conduct a slideshow:

1. Plug the camera into the proper cable, turn it on, click the View a slideshow of the images option, and then click OK. After a few moments, a slideshow loads (see Figure 16.5).

2. The slideshow commences with each photo being displayed for a few seconds. If for some reason it doesn't start on its own (or if you need to restart the slideshow after pausing it), simply click the first button, the green Start Slideshow button.

3. To pause the slideshow, click the second button. The current image stays onscreen until you restart the slideshow or move to another image.

4. The next two buttons let you move through the pictures one-by-one. The first button takes you backward, and the second takes you forward.

5. To close the slideshow, click the red Close button at the right end of the button bar.

Printing the Images Residing on Your Camera

Windows XP makes it easy to print images directly from your digital camera. Simply plug the camera into your computer, turn it on, and then follow these steps:

Pause slide   Next
show   Picture

Start slide   Previous   Close this
show   Picture   window

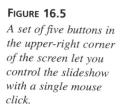

FIGURE 16.5

A set of five buttons in the upper-right corner of the screen let you control the slideshow with a single mouse click.

16

1. To get started, click the Print the pictures option, and then click OK. This launches the Photo Printing Wizard. Click Next to begin working with the wizard.

2. Previews of the photos residing on your digital camera appear inside the wizard's dialog box. (It is nearly identical to the dialog box shown back in Figure 16.2.) By default, all will be printed, but you can pick and choose the ones you want by clicking their check marks to toggle them on and off. When you are happy with your selection, click Next.

3. The next step requires you to define the printer you want to use. If there is only one printer connected to your computer, you are all set. Otherwise, use the drop-down arrow box to choose the one you want to use.

4. If you merely want a plain paper copy of the picture in normal quality, you can click Next to move on. Otherwise, click the Printing Preferences button. From there, you can choose paper type, print quality, and so on. The placement of these options will vary depending on the type of printer you are using. With the desired printer options set, click OK to dismiss the dialog box and then Next to continue with the wizard.

5. Now it's time to choose the layout of your prints (see Figure 16.6). You can print out a single large image, a sheet of 3 ½×5-inch prints, wallet prints, and so on. In fact, they do look much like those professional photo sheets from photographers. Click the layout/size you want and then click Next.

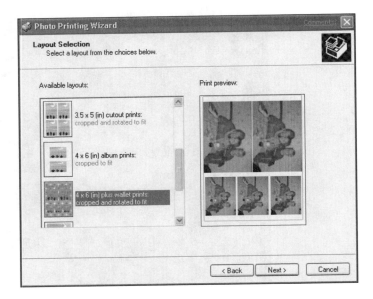

6. The Photo Printing Wizard sends the job to your printer, and within minutes, you have a set of photos just like you ordered.

Opening the Folder to View Files

This option takes you directly to the files on your camera using the My Pictures folder interface. See "Managing Your Images from the My Pictures Folder" for a detailed explanation of how to work with this interface.

Scanning Images into Word

When you plug in your scanner and turn it on, Windows XP attempts to auto-detect it (determine what is the make, model, and manufacturer). After it determines the type of scanner, it launches a Word insert picture window like the one shown in Figure 16.7.

FIGURE 16.7

Your scanner is now ready to pull an image into Word.

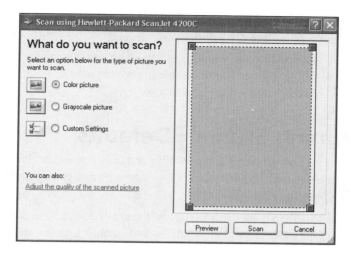

Perform the following steps to run the scan:

1. Put the photo or drawing you want to scan on the scanner bed and close the lid.

2. Next, tell Word whether it is a color or grayscale image by clicking the applicable radio button.

3. Click the Preview button to see how the scan would look.

4. At this point, you can click any of the hash mark borders and drag them in or out to crop the image as desired (see Figure 16.8).

FIGURE 16.8

Take as much or as little of a picture as you want by clicking and dragging its borders.

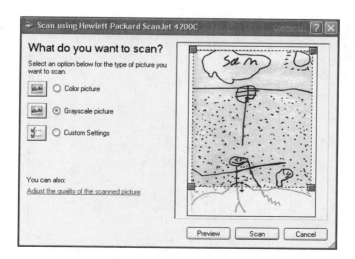

5. Are you happy with what you see? Click the Scan button. The full-size image appears in your Word document in seconds.

6. When you save the Word document, the scanned image will be saved as part of a Word file. If you want to be able to save the scan as a .jpg image file for use on the Web, read on to the next section.

Redefining Scanner Defaults

Scanning an image directly into Word is certainly convenient, but what if you want to put it on the Web, print it out, or modify it using a picture editing tool? Being able to save it as an image file would be helpful.

By resetting the scanner's properties, you can tell it to call the Scanner and Camera Wizard into action instead of Word. To do this, hook up your scanner to your PC, turn it on, and then follow these steps:

1. Click the Start button on the Windows taskbar and then choose Control Panel. From there, click the Printers and Other Hardware link, followed by the Scanners and Cameras link.

2. Right-click over the scanner's icon and choose Properties from the shortcut menu.

3. Open the Events tab seen in Figure 16.9. In the Action section, use the Start this program drop-down box to select the Scanner and Camera Wizard as your new default.

FIGURE 16.9

Choose the program you want to fire automatically or have Windows XP ask you each time the scanner is started.

4. If you can't decide which program you would use most often, choose the Prompt for which program to run option. Now you are prepared for anything.

5. Click the OK button to save the new default settings.

Safely Removing the Hardware from Your Computer

16

Although Windows XP can recover successfully from less-than-optimal system shut-downs, it is always good to take the time to properly shut down the system. The same holds true for unplugging your scanner or digital camera from your computer.

To safely remove the hardware from your system, double-click the Safely remove hardware icon shown at the right end of the taskbar in Figure 16.10 and then click the single menu item that appears to confirm it.

FIGURE 16.10

A single menu item leaves you no doubt about what needs to be selected.

Create taskbar with
single menu item

Managing Your Images from the My Pictures Folder

Whether you want to email a photo to a friend, compress images for inclusion on a photo CD, or publish a directory of photos to the Web, this is the perfect starting point. To get there, click the Start button on the Windows taskbar and then select the My Pictures link.

Setting Up the My Pictures Slide Show

Once inside My Pictures, you can set up a custom slideshow by clicking the pictures or folders to include in the show and then clicking the View as a slideshow link.

If zero or one image is selected, the entire directory will be included in the slide show. If two or more photos are selected, only the selected photos will be included in the show.

Don't forget your shortcuts for selecting multiple files. Either hold down the Ctrl key while clicking random files, or to grab several files in a row, click the first files, press the Shift key and while holding it down, click the last file you want to include.

Emailing Photos to Friends and Family

To send a photo via email, you will need to follow these steps:

1. From the My Pictures directory, click the picture you want to share and then click the Email this file link in the File and Folder Tasks section of the Task pane.

2. Windows XP displays a Send Pictures via Email dialog box saying it can Make all my pictures smaller so that it not only downloads quicker from the Internet but it can also fit it on the recipient's screen. You can also choose to Keep the original sizes, which may increase download time and make it harder for the recipient to view. Click the Make all my pictures smaller option shown in Figure 16.11.

FIGURE 16.11

An optimized message travels the Internet faster than the original.

3. Once the file is compressed, an Outlook Express New Message screen opens, bearing the name of the image file as the note's subject line. The image file is also already attached to the message, so before sending it on, just address it and add a personal note to the body of the message.

4. Click the Send button to send the message and attached image on its way.

Creating a Photo CD

There is no real mystery to burning a photo CD. Just open Windows Explorer, select the files, and then copy them to their new CD-based location.

Ordering Photo Prints from the Internet

Just because you don't have a photo-quality color printer doesn't mean you can't have printouts of your digital images.

Microsoft has forged a partnership with a company that can generate printed output for you and then send it to you via snail mail.

To take advantage of this service, enter the My Pictures directory, select the images you want to have printed, and then click the Order pictures online link. You will need to follow these steps in order to complete the process:

1. The preceding actions launch the Microsoft Online Print Ordering Wizard. Click the Next button to begin working your way through the wizard.

2. All the images you selected are displayed onscreen, giving you another chance to pick and choose the photos you want printed. Make your selections and then click Next.

3. Microsoft gives you multiple photo printing companies to choose from. Click one and then click Next.

4. Since the steps required at the providers will vary, simply follow the onscreen prompts to select and order your photos.

Publishing Photos to the Web

Here again, Microsoft employs a wizard to make the task easier. To publish photos to the Web, visit the My Pictures directory, select the files you want to publish to the Web, and then click the Publish the selected items to the Web link. This launches the Web Publishing Wizard. Click Next to continue.

You are given a second chance to select the images you want included on your Web page. Make your choices and then click Next. Microsoft gives you a few choices for the location of the upload: some online storage services and any other network location you specify.

Again, since the steps needed for each of the selections may vary widely, you will need to follow the prompts onscreen for best results.

Viewing Your Virtual Filmstrip

The default thumbnail view of the My Pictures directory makes it a snap to find what you are looking for, but there is an even better option: viewing the images as a filmstrip (see Figure 16.12).

To move to this view, click View, Filmstrip on the Menu bar. When you click a photo in the filmstrip at the bottom of the screen, it appears in the large viewing window. Using the buttons provided, you can do the following from left to right:

- **Previous Image (Left).** This button puts the photo immediately to the left of the currently viewed photo in the primary viewing area.

- **Next Image (Right).** To look at the next picture to the right of the currently selected image, click this button.

- **Rotate Clockwise.** This button can be used to turn an image taken sideways into its proper position.

- **Rotate Counterclockwise.** This button can also be used to reposition an image.

FIGURE 16.12
Filmstrips make it fun and easy to browse through your photos.

Making Movies with the Windows Movie Maker

Aside from cutting-edge game playing, video production can be one of the most demanding tasks for your computer. Just because your computer meets the minimum requirements for running Windows XP doesn't necessarily mean it will be amenable when working with videos.

Here is a quick rundown of necessary items to get started as an amateur movie maker with Windows XP Movie Maker:

- A 300MHz Pentium II class or faster machine. "Or faster" is the key phrase here. The faster the machine, the better your performance is.

Do you have a digital camcorder at your disposal? If you have invested in a fancy digital camcorder, you will see even better results than those working with "regular" camcorders or VCRs. However, improved performance comes with a cost. You will need a 600MHz system at bare minimum plus 128MB of RAM (memory). Again, the further you go beyond those specs, the better is your capability.

- According to Microsoft, you will also need at least 64MB of RAM, but I am not sure I would even try it with less than 128MB of RAM. I mean you can try it, of course, but the results may be less than optimal.

- You will also need a minimum of 2GB of free disk space to get started. You will need plenty more if you intend to make or save a lot of movies. Of course, disk space is cheap these days, so you can always add more if necessary (see Chapter 40, "Replacing, Upgrading, or Adding a Hard Disk Drive," for more information on adding memory).

- An audio capture device like a microphone will come in handy for recording voice narratives for your movies.

- Of course, you will also need a video capture device like a camcorder, digital camera with video capabilities, or something similar. You can use the high-end digital video camcorders, or you can use an older analog camcorder or VCR.

- For true digital video captures from a digital video device, you will need an IEEE 1394 DV (digital video) capture card to hook the device to your computer. IEEE 1394 is a FireWire connector, so you can cable from your camera directly to your computer's FireWire port. Likewise, you will need a special video adapter or capture card for your analog device. Consult your computer and camcorder documentation, as well as the ZDNet (http://www.zdnet.com) Web site for guidelines for making the best choice under your particular circumstances.

Planning for a Great Video

The right hardware goes a long way in making a great video, but a little planning never hurts either. You can do a lot to boost the quality of your movie before you even pick up the camera. Obviously, you can't plan spontaneous videos, but if you are out to make one, then you may find some of these tips helpful.

Keep the Background in the Background

One thing that makes a video sluggish is something called a low framerate. As you know, videos are made up of lots of pictures "pasted" together. When the pictures are very similar from one frame to another, the computer has to do very little work to refresh the screen and move to the next frame, thus speeding up the framerate.

If, on the other hand, you do a lot of panning (moving from one side to the other) across a wide area or shoot with a "busy" or moving background, then video performance is bound to suffer.

Choose solid or static backgrounds whenever possible. If that isn't possible, try focusing the camera on your primary subject by bringing him or her closer to the lens or using a telephoto lens to zoom in on him or her. This reduces the depth of field, making the background fuzzy and less distracting.

Light Up Your Life

It goes without saying that your video subject should appear in adequate lighting conditions. What kind of lighting is best? Soft, diffuse, and—most importantly—consistent lighting will give you the best results. Harsh lighting like direct sunlight may cause shadows or silhouettes to appear instead of your subject.

It may be worth taking some sample shots before you go into production to maximize your results and minimize the time commitment of the subjects.

It's What You Wear That Counts

Believe it or not, the clothes your video subject wears can dramatically affect the quality of your video. Bright colors can "bleed" onto the subject's face and other surroundings, and stripes can cause distracting moiré patterns (video artifacts that make the lines look like they are crawling or moving onscreen).

The best advice is to stick with something that closely resembles your subject's coloring yet stands out from the background.

Presenting Windows Movie Maker

Before you begin working with Movie Maker, it is a good idea to know your way around its workspace. Figure 16.13 illustrates the parts of the Movie Maker screen.

Here is a bit more detail about each element so that you will know your way around when we get rolling:

- **Menu bar/toolbars**—These elements perform similar functions to their counterparts in other Windows applications. You can open and save files, change views, and gain single-click access to unique Movie Maker tasks. You can also move, show, and hide Movie Maker toolbars like other toolbars you have worked with previously.

- **Collections Area**—In the left pane, you will see a list of the video collections and files you are working with in the current project. In the right pane, you will see shortcuts to clips contained within the selected file or movie in your collection. Movie Maker automatically creates a new clip whenever the entire makeup of the frame changes suddenly.

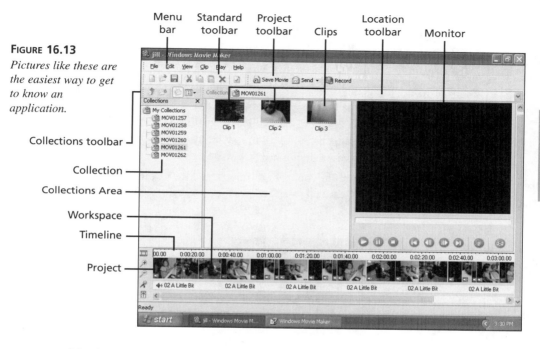

FIGURE 16.13

Pictures like these are the easiest way to get to know an application.

- **Monitor**—Drag a clip into the monitor to view it or play a whole project by clicking Play, Play Entire Storyboard/Timeline. Use the buttons underneath to control video play much like you did in Media Player. The seek bar above the buttons lets you know how much of the clip or movie has been viewed or has yet to be viewed.

- **Workspace**—This is the proper term for the strip of workspace near the bottom of the window. This is where you will drag all your clips to make a movie. You can view your project in two ways: Storyboard or Timeline (as shown in Figure 16.13).

Getting Video for the Movie

Although Movie Maker lets you record video while being hooked up to the computer, you have video somewhere you want to work with and you must transfer it to your computer. Maybe it is currently on a videocassette, in your camcorder, or on your digital camera with video clip capabilities. Regardless, you will have to do the following to make the movie (or movies) and their associated clips available for use in Movie Maker:

1. With your video device securely attached to your PC, copy the files to your hard drive. If your device is perceived as an added disk drive, as with my Sony CyberShot digital camera, then you can use Windows Explorer to move the files.

Otherwise, you may need to use the software that came with your video device or the capture adapter or card (in the case of older analog devices). Your mission here is simply to get the content onto your PC's hard drive. For simplicity sake, you may want to put the files in the My Videos folder.

2. Next, you will need to import the files into Movie Maker. With Movie Maker up and running (click the Start button; then point to All Programs, Accessories, and click Windows Movie Maker), click File, Import from the Menu bar. A Select File to Import dialog box opens. You will immediately notice it looks a lot like any standard Open or Save As dialog box.

3. Click your way to the file you want to import and then double-click its name when you find it. Movie Maker takes a few moments to scan the file and create clips as needed (see Figure 16.14).

FIGURE 16.14
MovieMaker creates clips as needed.

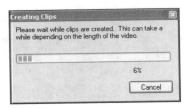

4. The selected file then appears by name in the My Collections window. You can view any clips Movie Maker generated by clicking the file's name. Images representing the resulting clips appear in the right Collections Area pane.

The movie and clips are now available for use in your current project. Repeat the preceding steps until all the video images you want to use can be viewed in the Collections area.

Pasting Clips Together

You can view the movie files as they exist on your hard drive, but you could have a whole lot of fun pasting clips together to make a real movie.

To get started, click View, Storyboard on the Menu bar. The Movie Maker workspace view now resembles a film where each clip you place eventually becomes an image on that film. This is the best way to see which clips are where in the movie you are piecing together.

Now, to move a clip into the project, click the applicable filename, click the image of the clip you want in the Collections area, and then drag it into the desired position on the

Storyboard (the filmstrip-looking thingy). Don't forget: You can certainly use a clip more than once if you want.

> By default, Movie Maker divides a movie file into clips when the majority of the video's background changes in a single frame. This can be helpful for longer videos, but for shorter ones, it can be a nuisance. To disable this feature, click View, Options on the Menu bar, and then clear the Automatically create clips option. Clicking OK dismisses the dialog.

If the file you want to use in your project is a single clip, simply click its filename in the My Collections pane and drag it onto the desired position on the Storyboard.

Trimming the Clips

You can shorten a clip by using Movie Maker's Timeline view. This is a great way to cut unwanted parts out of your clips. You should also know that any changes made to the clips are saved in the project files. The source files are not modified in any way.

To trim your clips, follow these steps:

1. First, you will need to click View, Timeline to change the workspace view.

2. Next, click the clip you want to shorten. You will see that the clip's image is outlined in blue, its duration on the project timeline is shaded, and two gray trim handles appear at either end of the clip's timeline (see Figure 16.15).

Trim Handles

FIGURE 16.15
Trim your clips as desired using the trim handles.

3. To begin trimming, run your mouse over one of the trim handles until it becomes an east/west double-headed arrow. (Obviously, you will click the left handle to trim from the front of the clip or the right handle to trim from the end of the clip.) This ensures that you are in the right position to grab the trim handle. To make the trim, click and drag the handle in the desired direction and then release it in place. You can use the elapsed time as a guide or keep an eye on the monitor that displays the frames you are dealing with as you drag the trim handle.

Click the Play button in the Monitor. Only the selected clip will play.

Repeat as necessary to get all your clips to the desired length.

Rearranging the Clips

As you work with the project, you may discover that you want to move a clip from one spot to another. That is what makes working with a computer so great—you can move it with ease.

To relocate a clip, you will first need to enter Storyboard view by clicking View, Storyboard. Next, click the image of the clip you want to move and drag it across the filmstrip. See the dark line that moves as you drag the clip? This is where the click will be placed when you release the mouse button.

Adding Cross-Fade Transitions

Real movies fade out of one scene and gradually fade into another. You can do that, too. Movie Maker gives you the ability to fade out of and into adjoining clips by entering the Trimline view and then clicking and dragging the second clip so it overlaps the first clip.

You can overlap the two clips as much as you want, but keep in mind that the audio tracks will be overlapped as well, potentially making it confusing and just plain noisy if it is not done effectively.

After the desired transitions are in place, click Play, Play Entire Storyboard/Timeline to view the whole sequence of clips in the monitor.

Saving Your Work

The two kinds of saves you will need to perform in Movie Maker are Save Project and Save Movie.

Saving a project means that the files you have chosen to work with for the current project will stay intact as will the edits you have made to them (trims, fades, and so on). When you click File, Save Project, you will have the opportunity to save these elements so you can go back and work with them at any point.

Saving a Movie, however, splices all your work together to create a final product. When you click File, Save Movie, you will see a dialog box similar to the one shown in Figure 16.16.

FIGURE 16.16

You can add a title or description to your video.

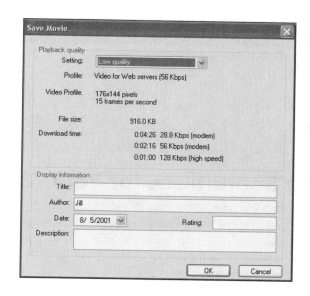

At the top of the dialog box, you will see a drop-down box from which you can choose the quality of your movie. You can choose a low-quality version for play on a Web server or a high-quality version for playing on your PC. The estimated download times at various Internet connection speeds appear halfway down the dialog box.

You will notice that Movie Maker filled in the author and date for you, but you can also title the movie, describe it, or give it a rating.

When you are finished filling out the box, click OK. You will be taken to a standard Save As–like dialog box where you will give the movie a filename. Movie Maker will attempt to provide one for you, which you can keep or type in an appropriate one, and then click the Save button. Movie Maker displays a status box like the one in Figure 16.17 to let you know your movie is indeed being made.

FIGURE 16.17

It may take a while to pull everything together, but soon you will be able to enjoy the fruits of your labor.

The higher the quality of video you are making, the longer it will take Movie Maker to pull it all together.

When the job is done, Movie Maker asks you if you want to watch the movie you just made. Click Yes or No as desired. If you click Yes, Windows Media Play opens and plays the movie.

Creating a Soundtrack for Your Movie

You can add a special soundtrack to your movie, too. Maybe you want to narrate your son's Little League game or make a music video of your daughter dancing to the latest Britney Spears track. Perhaps you want to create an anniversary movie for a special couple containing wedding video footage with "their song" playing as the soundtrack. The possibilities are almost endless.

Movie Maker makes it a piece of cake to do any of these things.

Recording a Narrative

If you have a microphone that connects to your PC, you are in business. The good news is just about any microphone will do, since computers have a standard-size mic jack.

To begin recording a voice narrative track for your movie, just follow these steps:

1. Launch Movie Maker with your work in progress and plug in your microphone.

2. Enter Timeline view by clicking View, Timeline.

3. To the left end of the Timeline workspace, you will see a tiny button with a microphone on it. Click it to open the Record Narration Track dialog box shown in Figure 16.18.

FIGURE 16.18

You can monitor the elapsed time of your recording on this dialog box.

4. You should see the words "Mic Volume" next to the Line: item. If those words don't appear, you will need to click the Change button and select Mic Volume from the Input Line drop-down box; then click OK.

5. When you are ready to begin recording, click the Mute Video Soundtrack option and then click the Record button. You will see the elapsed counter work its way up, and the video plays on the Movie Maker monitor so you can see what you are narrating.

6. To end the recording, click the Stop button. You will be prompted to give the recording a filename and to save it. Do as instructed and then click Save. The narrative will appear in the Collections area with its own special sound icon.

7. Move the narrative to your project's soundtrack by clicking and dragging the narrative's icon into the Soundtrack workspace (the thin white area just beneath the images on the project's Timeline).

8. You can tweak the balance of sound by clicking the Set Audio Levels button, which resides just below the microphone button. Just click and drag the lever button toward more audio or more video sound as desired and then click the Close (x) button.

Remember to save your project. At this point, you can even save the movie as described previously if you are happy with it.

Adding Tunes to Your Movie

Believe it or not, adding music to your video is even easier. Just record the song as you would in Windows Media Player and then in Movie Maker, click File, Import. Navigate to the sound file you want and then double-click its name or icon.

The file and sound icon appear in the Collections area. To add it to your movie, click and drag it down to the Soundtrack bar (the thin white bar just below the Timeline images). Remember to set the audio levels by clicking the bottom button on the left side of the Timeline. Click and drag the lever to favor video audio or your chosen audio soundtrack. Save your project; then save the actual movie when you like what you see.

Summary

This chapter described the basics of digital imaging and gave you enough information to get up and running. You should now have a better idea of what to look for in a digital camera or scanner. You should also be prepared to do some basic image browsing, sharing, and printing.

16

Working with images, sounds, and movies on your PC can be a tremendous amount of fun. It is also a great way to preserve videos that might otherwise fade or wear out over time. Imagine a CD of your wedding video, and if you have a DVD recorder, you can even record your own DVDs.

PART VI

Seeing What the Internet Is Really About

Chapter

CHAPTER 17

Exploring the Internet's Technology

You probably think you already know what the Internet (also called the *Net*) is. And you're probably 90% right, for all practical purposes. But by developing just a little better understanding of what the Net's all about, you'll find learning to use it much easier.

You don't need to know exactly how the Net works to use it, any more than you need to know the mechanics of an engine to drive. This chapter is not about the tiny, techie details of how the Net works. Rather, this chapter is designed to give you some helpful background—and perhaps dispel a few myths and misconceptions—so you can jump confidently into the material coming up in later chapters.

Understanding the Net (Easy Version)

No doubt you've heard of a computer network, a group of computers that are wired together so that they can communicate with one another. When computers are hooked together in a network, users of those computers can send each other messages and share computer files and programs.

Computer networks today can be as small as two PCs hooked together in an office. They can be as big as thousands of computers of all different types spread all over the world and connected to one another not just by wires, but through telephone lines and even through the air via satellite.

To build a really big network, you build lots of little networks and then hook the networks to each other, creating an internetwork. That's all the Internet really is: the world's largest internetwork (hence its name). In homes, businesses, schools, and government offices all over the world, millions of computers of all different types—PCs, Macintoshes, big corporate mainframes, and others—are connected together in networks, and those networks are connected to one another to form the Internet. Because everything's connected, any computer on the Internet can communicate with any other computer on the Internet (see Figure 17.1).

A Little History Lesson

The successful launch of Sputnik by the Soviets in 1957 may have triggered the space race, but it also helped bring about the Internet (although somewhat indirectly). In part because of Sputnik, the Advanced Research Projects Agency (ARPA) was formed as part of the U.S. Department of Defense, also in 1957.

Among other things, ARPA created research centers at a number of universities across the country. It soon became clear that these research centers needed to be able to communicate with each other through some type of infrastructure. The first four sites to be connected were at the University of California-Los Angeles (UCLA), the Stanford Research Institute, the University of California-Santa Barbara (UCSB), and the University of Utah.

Because this first network was military-oriented, the distribution of information through it was highly secretive. A system of splitting data into tiny "packets" that took different routes to the same destination was developed to make it more difficult to "eavesdrop" on these transmissions. It is this method of "packet switching" that allows the Internet to function as it does today: Large numbers of computers can go down, and data can still be transferred.

By 1969, new research into networking was being conducted. Standard systems of networking were needed in order for computers to be able to communicate with each other. Over time a system known as *TCP/IP* was developed; it became the standard protocol for internetworking in 1982.

TCP/IP is an abbreviation for the Internet's fundamental communications system. It stands for Transmission Control Protocol/Internet Protocol, but you don't need to know that unless you think it will impress your friends. (Pronounce it "tee see pee eye pee," and say it real fast.)

FIGURE 17.1

The Internet is a global internetwork, a huge collection of computers and networks interconnected so they can exchange information.

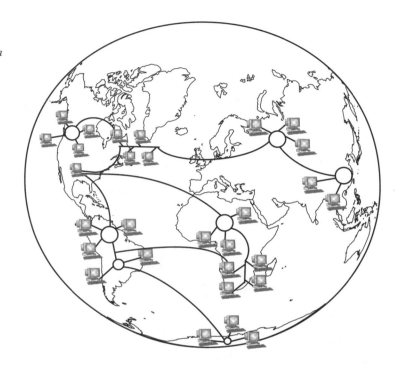

17

Because all these internetworks communicated in the same way, they could communicate with one another, too. The government, defense contractors, and scientists often needed to communicate with one another and share information, so they hooked all of their computers and networks into one big TCP/IP internetwork. And that fat internetwork was the infant Internet.

When you use a computer that's connected to the Internet, you can communicate with any other computer on the Internet.

But that doesn't mean you can access everything that's stored on the other computers. Obviously, the government, university, and corporate computers on the Net have the capability to make certain kinds of information on their computers accessible through the Internet, and to restrict access to other information so that only authorized people can see it.

Similarly, when you're on the Net, any other computer on the Net can communicate with yours. However, that does not mean that someone can reach through the Net into your computer and steal your résumé and recipes.

What It Became

The first great thing about the Internet's design is that it's open to all types of computers. Virtually any computer—from a palmtop PC to a supercomputer—can be equipped with TCP/IP so it can get on the Net. And even when a computer doesn't use TCP/IP, it can access information on the Net using other technologies, "back doors" to the Net, so to speak.

The other important thing about the Net is that it allows the use of a wide range of communications media—ways computers can communicate. The "wires" that interconnect the millions of computers on the Internet include the wires that hook together the small networks in offices, private data lines, local telephone lines, national telephone networks (which carry signals via wire, microwave, and satellite), and international telephone carriers.

It is this wide range of hardware and communications options, and the universal availability of TCP/IP, that has enabled the Internet to grow so large so quickly. That's also why you can get online from your home or office, right through the same telephone line you use to call out for pizza. Heck, you can even get online from the neighborhood park using wireless technology. It's a crazy world.

When your computer has a live, open connection to the Internet that you can use to do something, you and your computer are said to be *online*. When the Internet connection is closed, you're *offline*.

Making the Net Work: Clients and Servers

The key to doing anything on the Net is understanding two little words: "client" and "server." Figure 17.2 illustrates the relationship between clients and servers.

Most of the information you will access through the Internet is stored on computers called servers. A server can be any type of computer; what makes it a server is the role it plays: It stores information for use by clients.

A client is a computer—or, more accurately, a particular computer program—that knows how to communicate with a particular type of server to use the information stored on that server (or to put information there). For example, when you surf the Web, you use a client program called a *Web browser* to communicate with a computer where Web pages are stored—a Web server.

In general, each type of Internet activity involves a different type of client and server: To use the Web, you need a Web client program to communicate with Web servers. To use email, you need an email client program to communicate with email servers.

This client/server business shows what the Internet really is—just a communications medium, a virtual wire through which computers communicate. It's the different kinds of clients and servers—not the Net itself—that enable you to perform various activities. And because new kinds of clients and servers can be invented, new types of activities can be added to the Internet at any time.

FIGURE 17.2

From your computer, you use a set of client programs, each of which accesses a different type of server computer on the Net.

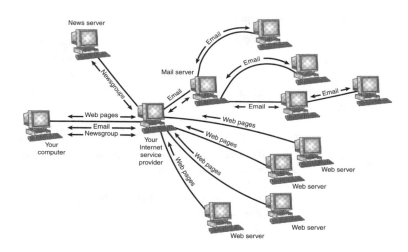

17

What Can You Do Through the Net?

I've known people who have gone out and bought a PC, signed up for an Internet account, and then called me to say, "Okay, so I'm on the Internet. Now what am I supposed to do there?"

That's backward. I think the marketers and the press have pushed so hard that some folks simply think they must be on the Net, without knowing why, sort of the way everybody thinks they need a cell phone. But unless there's something on the Net you want or need to use, you don't need the Net. You shouldn't buy a rice steamer unless you like rice. You don't need a cell phone if you never leave the house. Don't let Madison Avenue and Microsoft push you around.

So here's a good place to get a feel for what you can actually do on the Net. If nothing here looks like something you want to do, please give this book to a friend or to your local library. You can check out the Net again in a year or two, to see whether it offers anything new.

A great place to try out the Internet without having to spend a bunch of money up front is your local library. Usually, you can get online for free there, and see what's available.

Browse the Web

It's very likely that your interest in the Internet was sparked by the World Wide Web, even if you don't know it. When you see news stories about the Internet showing someone looking at a cool, colorful screen full of things to see and do, that person is looking at the World Wide Web, most commonly referred to as "the Web" or occasionally as "WWW."

The term "the Web" is used so often by the media to describe and illustrate the Internet, many folks think the Web is the Internet. But it's not; it's just a part of the Net, or rather one of many Internet-based activities. The Web gets the most attention because it's the fastest-growing, easiest-to-use part of the Net.

All those funky-looking Internet addresses you see in ads today—www.pepsi.com and so forth—are the addresses you need to visit those companies on the Web. With an Internet connection and a Web browser on your computer, you can type an address to visit a particular *Web site* and read the *Web pages* stored there. (Figure 17.3 shows a Web page, viewed through a Web browser.)

These terms are used flexibly, but, in general, a Web site is a particular Web server, or a part of a Web server, where a collection of Web pages about a particular organization or subject is stored.

When you use your Web browser to contact a Web site, the information on the server is displayed on your computer screen. The particular screenful of information you view is described as one Web page.

For example, the site shown in Figure 17.3 is one Web page from www.pepsi.com. All the pages that Pepsi has put up for you to see make up Pepsi's Web site.

By browsing the Web, you can do a staggering number of different things, including all the activities described in the following sections—and much, much more.

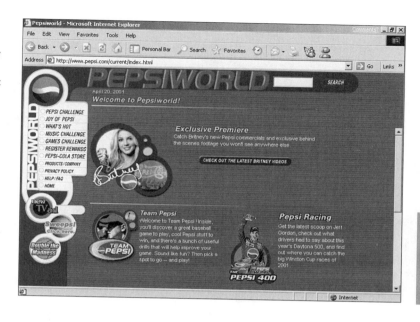

FIGURE 17.3

Seen through a Web browser, a Web page is a file of information stored on a Web server.

Visit Companies, Governments, Museums, Schools...

Just about any large organization has its own Web site these days. Many smaller organizations have their own sites, too, or are covered in pages stored on others' sites. You can visit these sites to learn more about products you want to buy, school or government policies, and much more.

For example, I belong to an HMO for medical coverage. I can visit my HMO's Web site to find and choose a new doctor, review policy restrictions, and much more. I can do this any day, any time, without waiting on hold for the "next available operator."

Just as easily, I can check out tax rules or order forms on the Internal Revenue Service Web site. Or view paintings in museums all over the world. Or find out when the next Parent's Night is at the local elementary school.

Read the News

CNN has its own Web site (see Figure 17.4), as do the *New York Times*, the *Wall Street Journal*, and dozens of other media outlets, ranging from major print magazines and fly-by-night rags spreading rumors, to small sites featuring news about any imaginable topic. You'll also find a number of great news sources that have no print or broadcast counterpart—they're exclusive to the Web.

Whatever kind of news you dig, you can find it on the Web. And often, the news online is more up-to-the-minute than any print counterpart because unlike broadcast news, you can look at it any time you find convenient. Best of all, after you read a news story on the Web, no one ever says, "Thanks for that report, Carla. What a terrible tragedy."

FIGURE 17.4

CNN is among the up-to-the-minute news sources available on the Web.

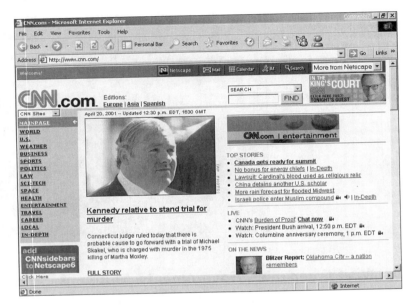

Explore Libraries

Increasingly, libraries large and small are making their catalogs available online. That means I can find out which of the dozen libraries I use has the book I need, without spending a day driving to each. Some libraries even let you borrow online; you choose a book from the catalog of a library across the state, and in a few days you can pick it up at a library closer to you, or right from your mailbox.

Often, entire collections of works, scholarly papers, entire texts of books, research works, and more are available through libraries online.

Read

Books are published on the Web, including classics (Shakespeare, Dickens) and new works. You can read them right on your screen, or print them out to read later on the bus. (Please don't read while you drive. I hate that.) The Web has even initiated its own kind of literature, collaborative fiction, in which visitors to a Web site can read—and contribute to—a story in progress.

Get Software

Because computer software can travel through the Internet, you can actually get software right through the Web and use it on your PC. Some of the software is free; some isn't.

But it's all there, whenever you need it—no box, no disc, no pushy guy at the electronics store saying, "Ya want a cell phone with that? Huh? C'mon!"

Shop

One of the fastest-growing, and perhaps most controversial, Web activities is shopping (see Figure 17.5). Right on the Web, you can browse an online catalog, choose merchandise, type in a credit card number and shipping address, and receive your merchandise in a few days, postage paid. Besides merchandise, you can buy just about anything else on the Web: stocks, legal services, you name it. Everything but surgery, and I'm sure that's only a matter of time. One of the hottest trends in online shopping continues to be the online auction house, a Web site where you can bid on all kinds of items, new and old, from odds and ends to *objets d'art*.

The controversy arises from the fact that sending your credit card number and other private information through the Internet exposes you to abuse of that information by anyone clever enough to cull it from the din of Web traffic. But that risk factor is rapidly shrinking as the Web develops improved security. And while shopping from your PC, you can't get mugged in the mall parking lot.

17

FIGURE 17.5

Shopping may be the fastest-growing online activity.

Watch TV and Listen to CD-Quality Music and Radio Broadcasts

Through your Internet connection, you can actually watch live TV broadcasts and listen to radio programs. The sound and picture quality won't always be as good as you get from a real TV or radio. But the Net gives you access to programs you can't get on your own TV or radio, such as shows not offered in your area or special programs broadcast only to the Internet. With music, however, there's no compromise. Right from the Internet, you can copy high-quality music files that you can listen to anytime, even when you're not on the Internet.

> You can not only listen to CD-quality music online, but also buy it by downloading it to your computer and playing it there, or copying it to a portable player.

Play Games, Get a College Degree, Waste Time...

Have I left anything out? There's too much on the Web to cover succinctly. But I hope you get the idea. The Web is where it's at. In fact, there are many folks on the Internet who use the Web and nothing else to get and disperse information. But those folks are missing out. Read on.

> There's one more thing you can do on the Web: publish. Just as you can access any Web server, you can publish your own Web pages on a Web server, so that anyone on the Internet with a Web browser can read them.
>
> You can publish Web pages to promote your business or cause, to tell others about a project or hobby that's your passion, or just to let the world know you're you.

Exchange Messages

As you know, using Internet email, you can type a message on your computer and send it to anyone else on the Internet (see Figure 17.6).

Each user on the Internet has a unique email address; if your email address is suzyq@netknow.com, you're the only person in the world with that email address. So if anyone, anywhere in the world, sends a message to that address, it reaches you and you alone. As mentioned earlier, to use email, you need an email client program, which interacts with the email servers that store and send email around the world.

Email is great for simple messages, but these days, it can do more. You can attach computer files to email messages to send them to others, broadcast a message to two or a hundred recipients at once, and even create cool, colorful messages with graphics and sound.

FIGURE 17.6

Email is a great way to keep in contact with people, especially those who live far away.

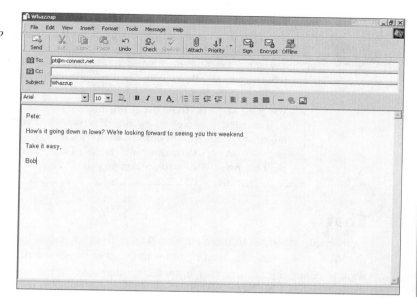

17

Most email is sent and received through a program called an email client. But some folks send and receive email directly from a Web page, using their Web browsers. Still others can send and receive Internet email through their digital cell phones, pagers, and palmtop computers.

Have a Discussion

Using your email program, you can join mailing lists related to topics that interest you. Members of a mailing list automatically receive news and other information—in the form of email messages—related to the list's topic. Often, members can send their own news and comments to the list, and those messages are passed on to all members.

One of the Internet's principal discussion venues is the newsgroup, a sort of public bulletin board. There are thousands of newsgroups, each centering on a particular topic—everything from music to politics, from addiction recovery to TV shows.

Visitors to a newsgroup post messages that any other visitor can read. When reading a message, any visitor can quickly compose and post a reply to that message, to add information to the message, or to argue with it (usually to argue—you know how folks are). As the replies are followed by replies to the replies, a sort of free-form discussion evolves.

You may have heard that you can pick up a lot of unreliable information on the Internet, and, indeed, that's true. As when absorbing information from any communications medium—print, broadcast, Internet, water cooler, back fence—you must always consider the source, and take much of what you learn with a grain of salt.

You must also trust that, just as the Internet offers a forum to nutballs with axes to grind, it also offers an incredible wealth of authoritative, accurate information that's often difficult to find elsewhere. It's just like TV: You can watch *FoxNews*, or you can watch tabloid TV. If you choose the latter, you can't blame the TV for misinforming you.

Chat

Exchanging messages through email and newsgroups is great, but it's not very interactive. You type a message, send it, and wait hours or days for a reply. Sometimes, you want to communicate in a more immediate, interactive, "live" way. That's where Internet Relay Chat—a.k.a. "IRC" or just "Chat"—comes in.

Using chat client programs, folks from all over the world contact chat servers and join one another in live discussions. Each discussion takes place in a separate chat "room" "channel" reserved for discussion of a particular topic. The discussion is carried out through a series of typed messages; each participant types his or her contributions, and anything anyone in the room types shows up on the screen of everyone else in the room.

Run Programs on Other Computers

Not everything on the Internet sits on a Web server, email server, news server, or chat server. There are other kinds of computers and servers connected to the Net—ones you can use, if you know how, through an Internet technology called Telnet. When you use a distant computer through Telnet, you can run programs on it and access its data as if you were there.

There's so much on Web and news servers these days that you may never want or need to journey beyond them. But for the adventurous, Telnet offers access to information you can't get any other way.

Summary

The Internet is a huge, and growing, internetwork that nobody really planned but that happened anyway. Your job is not really to understand it, but to enjoy it and to use it in whatever way you find valuable or entertaining. The value and entertainment are stored all over the world on a vast array of servers; to tap the benefits of the Net, you deploy a family of client programs that know how to talk to the servers. In a way, most of this book is really about choosing and using client programs to make the most of the Internet's servers.

17

CHAPTER 18

Connecting to the Internet

If you have a mailing address, you probably know about Internet providers, because they're the people who keep cramming free signup CD-ROMs and disks in your mailbox and begging you to join. Heck, you don't even need an address—you get free signup disks today in magazines, cereal boxes, and bundled along with any new computer.

In this chapter, you'll discover the full range of different ways to get signed up for the Internet, so you can choose the provider that best matches your needs and bank account. You'll also learn the basics of making that connection, so we can get you on your way.

Types of Internet Accounts

When you sign up with—subscribe to—an Internet service, you get what's called an *Internet account*.

With an Internet account, you get the right to use the provider's Internet service, your very own email address (so you can send and receive email), and all of the other information you need to set up your computer for accessing the Internet through the service.

Dial-Up Accounts

Most Internet accounts are called "dial-up" accounts because you use them by "dialing up" the Internet provider through your modem and telephone line. These are sometimes also described as "IP" accounts because they require your computer to communicate through TCP/IP. Dial-up IP accounts are the principal, general-purpose accounts offered by most Internet providers.

Dial-up accounts generally come as what's called a *PPP account*. With a PPP account, you have access to the full range of Internet activities, and can use any client programs you want to.

An account with an online service like America Online is also a "dial-up" account, but it's not the same thing as a regular Internet PPP or SLIP account. An online service account requires a different kind of communications software (supplied by the service) for accessing the service and its non-Internet content.

When you access the Internet through an online service, the service may temporarily switch you over to a PPP account, or it may funnel you to the Internet using a different communications scenario.

This is why online services often limit you to one or two different Web browsers and other clients, instead of letting you choose the one you want. Any client software used through the service must be specially configured for the service's unique communications system.

Cable Internet and DSL (Broadband)?

In the last few years, a new category of personal Internet account has emerged, sometimes described as *broadband* because it sends and receives information so much faster than a regular dial-up account—as if the information were moving through a nice, fat, "broad" pipe instead of a slow, skinny pipe.

Depending on what's available to you, you have your choice between two different kinds of broadband Internet access, described in the next sections: "Cable Internet" and "DSL." (There are other broadband options, used mostly in business environments. But these two are the popular options for personal users.)

The two options are different from each other, but have seven characteristics in common:

- They are much, much faster than a 56K dial-up account.

- Their speed enables them to carry Internet activities that are simply impractical over a dial-up connection, such as watching a movie online, high-quality videoconferencing, or using a computer somewhere out on the Net as a storage facility for your own files or backups.

- They allow you to use your phone line for telephone calls, faxing, or anything else while you are online.

- They can be set up so that you are always online. You don't have to do anything to get online each time you use the Net (as you must with a dial-up account); you just sit down and get to business.

- They are more expensive, on a monthly basis.

- They require more expensive communications hardware for your computer, rather than relying on the inexpensive modems included in nearly all computers today.

- Once you're online, actually using a broadband account—opening Web pages, exchanging email, and so on—takes the same steps you use on a regular dial-up account, the steps described throughout this book.

Broadband services are not yet available everywhere. There are many neighborhoods today that cannot get any type of broadband service, even though they may have regular phone and cable service. The hardware in local phone and cable systems must be upgraded in order to support broadband Internet. Phone and cable companies are furiously making these upgrades in order to begin selling broadband service, but it will still take a few years to get broadband availability to everyone.

As more and more neighborhoods gain access to both broadband technologies, the monthly cost should drop as the phone and cable companies compete for those customers.

Cable Internet

Supplied by your local cable TV company, cable Internet enters your house through the same cable that TV signals travel through. Cable Internet can support speeds up to 4,096K—more than 70 times as fast as a 56K dial-up connection. Figure 18.1 shows a Web site describing Road Runner, a cable Internet service offered by Time Warner Cable in some (but not all) of the neighborhoods it serves.

FIGURE 18.1

The Web site of Road Runner, a cable Internet service offered by Time Warner Cable to some of its subscribers.

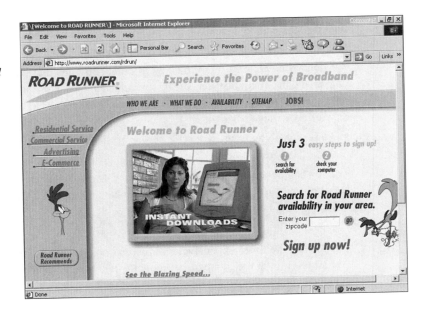

To use cable Internet, you must have

- A cable Internet account, offered only by the cable TV company that serves your neighborhood.
- A cable modem installed in, or connected to, your PC. A cable modem is not really a modem, but a specialized network adapter. You can usually rent your cable modem from the cable company, which also makes it easy for the cable company to set up your computer for you. You can also purchase cable modems, which run more than $100—but, before buying, be sure to talk first to your cable company to determine the specific hardware required.
- An *Ethernet card* installed in your computer (or other network adapter). This allows the modem to talk to your computer. Many computer manufacturers are now preinstalling Ethernet cards in their computers.

At this writing, a cable Internet account costs from about $40 to $50 per month—twice the cost of a regular dial-up account. To learn whether cable Internet is available at your home, call your cable TV company.

There are two potential minuses to cable Internet that are worth considering before you take the plunge.

First, the "always-on" nature of a cable Internet connection has been found to make computers using cable connections somewhat more vulnerable to computer hackers than those on regular dial-up lines. You can protect your-self from hackers with a "personal firewall" program such as *Black Ice* or *ZoneAlarm*. And, as with any Internet connection, users of a cable Internet connection need to use a good antivirus program.

Second, cable Internet connections have been shown to become dramati-cally slower when many people within a neighborhood are using cable Internet simultaneously. At such times, cable would still remain much faster than a dial-up connection. But you might be disappointed by the times when you felt you were not getting all the speed you paid for.

DSL

Used through your regular phone line, a *Digital Subscriber Line* (*DSL*; also known by various other abbreviations such as *ADSL* or *xDSL*) account is supplied by, or in cooper-ation with, your local telephone company. The fastest broadband option, DSL can sup-port speeds up to 7,270K.

Oddly, DSL can be faster than cable Internet when you are receiving infor-mation—such as opening a Web site or video clip. But it is usually slower than cable when you are sending information, such as sending email.

18

Note that although DSL uses your regular phone line, it transforms that line into a carrier of multiple services; with DSL, you can use the Internet and talk on the phone at the same time.

Like cable Internet, DSL requires a special modem, typically called a DSL modem, which can cost substantially more than a cable modem. The monthly cost of a DSL account, however, is roughly the same as for a cable Internet account, around $40 to $50.

To find out whether you can get DSL where you live, contact your local phone company, or contact an Internet Service Provider that serves your neighborhood and offers DSL service.

Email-Only Accounts

With an email-only account, you get full access to Internet email, and nothing else—no Web, no newsgroups, no chat, no shoes, no shirt, no service. You will have access to mailing lists, however, which enable you to get through email much of the same discus-sion content you'd see in newsgroups.

Email accounts can be run from the lowliest of computers, and cost next to nothing. In fact, a few companies now offer you an email account free of charge, in exchange for the right to send you targeted advertisements.

Where Can I Get Dial-Up Access?

You can get your Internet account from any of three main sources:

- A national Internet Service Provider (ISP)
- A local ISP, one that's headquartered in your city or town
- A commercial online service, such as AOL or CompuServe

Each of these options is explained next.

Commercial Online Services

You've no doubt heard of at least one of the major online services, such as America Online (AOL; see Figure 18.2) or CompuServe (CSi). These services promote themselves as Internet providers, and they are—but with a difference.

In addition to Internet access, these services also offer unique activities and content not accessible to the rest of the Internet community. These services have their own chat rooms, newsgroup-like message boards (usually called "forums"), online stores, and reference sources that only subscribers to the service can use. Setup for an online service is usually very easy: You install the free software the company provides, follow the onscreen instructions, and you're connected.

The principal drawback to online services is flexibility. You often cannot choose and use any client software you want; you must use a single client environment supplied by the service, or one program from among a limited set of options. When new, enhanced releases of client programs come out, ISP users can install and use them right away, whereas most online service users must wait until the online service publishes its customized version.

On the plus side, for Web browsing, most online services do supply a version of either Navigator, Internet Explorer, or both (specially customized for compatibility with the service), making the look and feel of the Web through an online service essentially identical to that of an ISP.

Online services used to be dramatically more expensive than ISPs. Lately, they've adopted pricing policies that are generally competitive with the local and national ISPs, although you can still usually get a slightly better deal from a regular ISP than from any online service. For example, America Online offers a respectable flat rate of around $20 per month; if you shop around, you can get a flat rate from an ISP for as little as $15.

Figure 18.2

Online services such as America Online (AOL) offer Internet access as well as other services available only to their own subscribers.

America Online (AOL)

Voice Number: 800-827-6364

America Online is the biggest of the online services (and also, therefore, the single largest Internet provider in the world), largely because of aggressive marketing and the initial convenience of setting up an account from a CD-ROM that came in junk mail. The non-Internet content is indeed the easiest to use of all services. AOL's Internet access, however, is notoriously slow, and busy signals continue to be a problem. AOL offers a wide range of pricing plans, including a flat rate, an annual rate, and several different pay-as-you-go plans.

CompuServe (CSi)

Voice Number: 800-848-8199

CompuServe (see Figure 18.3) wasn't the first online service, but it's the oldest still in operation, and it was once the undisputed king. That legacy leaves CompuServe with an unbeatable range of local access numbers. CompuServe is owned by America Online, but still operates as an independent service.

Functionally, CompuServe is similar to America Online in most respects, and it still offers some non-Internet content, exclusively to its own subscribers. Its reputation for providing fast and reliable Internet service is somewhat better than America Online's; its reputation for non-Internet ease-of-use, slightly worse. However, CompuServe can support almost any computer in the world, whereas AOL is essentially limited to popular personals: PCs and Macs.

Figure 18.3

The Web home page of CompuServe, an online service.

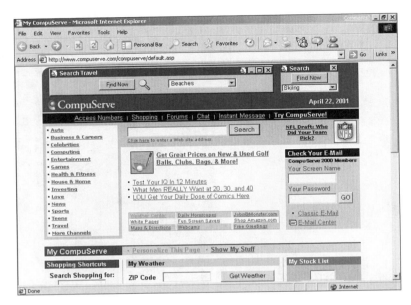

Microsoft Network (MSN)

Voice Number: 800-FREE-MSN

Microsoft Network started out in 1995 as a service very much like AOL, as the first foray in Bill Gates's ongoing effort to own the Internet. MSN has since evolved away from the online service model, to the point where it is now more or less a regular national (actually international) ISP, although it still supplies some content accessible only to its subscribers. MSN offers true PPP access, so you can use any browser you want to. (Although, not surprisingly, MSN works best through Microsoft's own browser, Internet Explorer or the dedicated MSN browser.) The service offers a variety of reasonable flat-rate and pay-as-you-go plans.

Internet Service Providers (ISPs)

Unlike an online service, an Internet Service Provider, or ISP, does not offer its subscribers special content that's not accessible to the rest of the Net. You get Internet access, period.

ISPs offer greater flexibility than online services, providing dial-up IP, shell, and email accounts (and often DSL, as well). Through IP accounts, they can enable you to use virtually any client software you want and to add or change that software whenever you feel like it. ISPs also might offer more attractive rates and better service than the online services, although that's not always the case.

There are many large, national ISPs that provide local access numbers all over the United States (and often across North America). Table 18.1 lists a few of the major national ISPs and their voice telephone numbers, so you can call to learn more about the service and also find out whether the service offers a local access number in your area. Just in case you have access to the Net through a computer at school, work, or the local library, the table also shows the address of a Web page where you can learn more about each service.

TABLE 18.1   A More-or-Less Random Selection of National ISPs

Company	Voice Number	Web Page Address
Earthlink	800-395-8425	http://www.earthlink.net
AT&T WorldNet	800-967-5363	http://www.att.com/worldnet
Prodigy	800-213-0992	http://www.prodigy.com
US Internet	888-873-4959	http://www.usinternet.com

18

Free Internet!

You may have heard that you can get a completely free Internet account, and that's a fact. In exchange for the right to show you a steady stream of advertising whenever you are online, some companies supply you with free access to the most popular Internet activities: the Web and email.

Free Internet services abounded a year or so ago, but like so many dotcom businesses, these companies fell on hard times and began to charge for access. One of those that still offers free access, NetZero (see Figure 18.4), only allows 40 hours per month for free (this limit can change). It also now offers a low-cost unlimited-access service with no banner ads to clog up your screen.

There are a few others still out there, and it's a great idea, and worth a try. The benefit is obvious: You'll have an extra $20 a month for sandwiches. Here's the potential downside:

- At this writing, the free accounts are somewhat notorious for poor performance and a complete lack of customer service.
- It's difficult to sign up for these accounts unless you are already online and already know how to use the Web, because signing up requires access to the company's Web site. So they make a nice money-saver for those who already know their way around, but may befuddle newcomers to the Internet.

- The ads may grow tiresome.
- You may prefer the features and flexibility of using a real email program instead of the Web-based email the free accounts require.

Figure 18.4

While it still offers free access at this writing, even NetZero is offering a for-pay service.

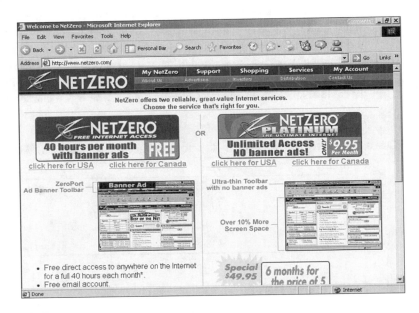

Finding a Local ISP

Besides the national ISPs, there are thousands of local ISPs in cities and towns all over the United States and Canada. Typically, a local ISP cannot offer access numbers beyond a small, local service area of a few cities, towns, or counties. But it can provide reliable Internet access, personal service, and often the best rates you can get. If you're having a problem, it can be a terrific help to be able to stop by your Internet provider's office and chat face-to-face. Local providers also play a vital role in keeping the big national providers honest; the continual reduction of rates by the big providers was spurred in large part by competition from even lower-priced local ISPs.

Unlike online services and national ISPs, local ISPs don't have the marketing muscle to advertise heavily or send out free disks. That's what makes them harder to find, but it's also why they're often cheaper. Finding a local ISP is getting easier all the time. Friends, coworkers, and local computer newsletters are all good sources for finding a local ISP. You can also check the Yellow Pages for ISPs: Look first under Internet, and then try Computers—Internet Services. The folks at your nearest computer store may also know of a good local ISP or two.

How Do I Choose a Dial-Up Internet Plan?

Of all the options that are available to you, a dial-up account is still the most popular type of home Internet connection, by a long shot. So, how do you go about picking a dial-up provider and plan?

If there were one reliable way to choose the best Internet provider, we would all be using the same one. But different people have different priorities: For some, it's price. For others, it's a range of access numbers; for others, it's speed. Some people have a particular need to use content that's available only through a particular online service; most people don't. You have to check out how each of your available ISP options addresses your own priorities.

Obviously, if you have friends who use the Internet, find out which services they use, and ask whether they're happy. It's always a good idea to use a friend's Internet account to test the service the friend uses, and to explore your other options. Magazine reviews can help, but they rarely cover more than the online services and the largest national ISPs. To judge a local ISP, you need to listen to the word of mouth.

For what it's worth, here's a quick look at a few things to consider:

> The only caveat to switching services is that your email address changes any time you switch. But many services will forward your email to your new service for a few months after you quit, and you can always get in touch with all your email partners and let them know your new address.
>
> Of course, switching services also provides an excellent opportunity to not tell some folks your new email address, if those folks have been getting on your e-nerves.

18

- **Plans and Rates**—Most providers offer a range of different pricing plans. The kinds of plans you'll see most often, however, are unlimited access (or flat rate) and pay-as-you-go. Flat-rate plans are the most common, because they allow unlimited access for a flat monthly fee. Pay-as-you-go plans charge a low base rate for a small number of hours (such as $10 for the first 20 hours), then an hourly rate after that. I generally recommend that new users first choose a flat rate plan with no long-term commitment, and to keep track of their monthly hours for six months or so. If you do that, you'll know whether you're getting your money's worth at the flat rate or should switch to a per-hour plan.

- **Billing Options**—Most providers will bill your monthly charges automatically to any major credit card. Some local ISPs can bill you by mail, and some others can actually add your monthly Internet charges to your regular monthly telephone bill (itemized separately from your calls to Grandma, of course). All other things being equal, you may lean toward the provider that will bill you in the way that's most convenient for you.

- **Access Numbers**—Obviously, you want a provider that offers a local access number in the area where your computer resides. But what if you need to use your account from both home and work, using two different computers or bringing a portable back and forth? Does the provider offer local access numbers that work from both locations? What if you want to be able to use the Internet when you travel? Does the provider offer local access everywhere you and your computer might go?

- **Software**—The online services require that you use a software package they supply for setting up your connection, using their non-Internet content, and often for using the Internet, too. Most ISPs can also supply you with any communications or client software you require, although using the ISP's software package is optional. If you need software to get started, you may want to consider what each ISP offers as a software bundle.

- **Web Server Space**—If you think you might want to publish your own Web pages, you'll need space on a Web server to do so. Many ISPs and most online services offer an amount of Web server space free to all customers; others charge an additional monthly fee.

- **Newsgroup Access**—Be aware that there are tens of thousands of newsgroups, and that not all providers give you access to all of them. Some exclude "racy" ones, while others only offer those specifically requested by users.

Getting Connected

So you've chosen an ISP for dial-up access to the Internet. Whether that's an online service like AOL or a local or national ISP, your next step is to actually connect to them.

In most cases, the company you've chosen is going to make this as easy as possible for you. They'll either supply you with the software you need—which is often preinstalled on your computer, if you choose a national service—or they'll give you some type of brochure that walks you through the process, step-by-step.

Since the provider usually takes care of that type of thing and there are so many different ways of getting started, we're not going to spend much time on that type of stuff here. Instead, we'll just concentrate on the basics—things that you'll need to understand regardless of which provider you use.

Number, Username, and Password

No matter how you set up your account and computer, you'll wind up with three pieces of information that are essential to getting online:

- **Local access number**—The telephone number your modem dials to connect to your Internet provider.

- **Username**—To prevent just anybody from using its service, your Internet provider requires each subscriber to use a unique name, called a username (or sometimes user name, user ID, or userID), to connect.

- **Password**—To prevent an unauthorized user from using another's username to sneak into the system, each subscriber must also have his or her own secret password.

Entering your username and password to go online is called "logging on" (or sometimes "logging in" or "signing in") and the name used to describe that activity is "logon" (or "login," or "sign-in"). If you use a signup program to set up your Internet account and computer as described next, you'll choose your username and password while running the program. If you set up your computer without a signup disk (as described later in this chapter), you'll choose a username and password while on the phone with your provider to open your account.

Every user of a particular Internet provider must have a different username. If you choose a large provider, there's a good chance that your first choice of username is already taken by another subscriber. In such cases, your provider will instruct you to choose another username, or to append a number to the name to make it unique. For example, if the provider already has a user named *CameronDiaz*, you can be *CameronDiaz2*.

18

The rules for a username and password vary by provider, but, in general, your username and password must each be a single word (no spaces or punctuation) of five or more letters and/or numerals. Nonsense words, like *FunnyDad* or *MonkeyMary*, are fine as usernames. For a password, avoid using easy-to-guess items such as your birthday or kids' names. Total nonsense—like *xkah667a*—makes the most effective password, as long as you can remember it.

Your username often doubles as the first part of your email address; if your username is Stinky, your email address might be something like *Stinky@serveco.com*. Before choosing a username, consider whether you also like it as an email address, which your friends and associates will see and use.

Some systems are case-sensitive; that is, they pay attention to the pattern of upper- and lowercase letters. On a case-sensitive system, if your username is *SallyBu*, you must type *SallyBu* to log on—*sallybu* or *SALLYBU* won't work.

Using Supplied Software

As pointed out earlier in this chapter, a special signup program is required for each online service provider, and many ISPs can also supply you with a signup program for your computer. I highly recommend using signup programs whenever they're available, even when they're optional. You can get free signup disks by mail from the providers, just by calling them on the telephone. Also, signup programs often come preinstalled on new computers, and in computer magazines and junk mail. If you choose to go with a local ISP, you can usually pick up a signup CD or disks just by stopping by the provider's office.

Why Use a Signup Program?

Why? Well, first, the signup programs kill two birds at once: They sign you up with a provider and configure your computer to access that provider. The program automatically takes care of all the communications configuration required in your computer, some of which can be tricky for inexperienced computer users.

Depending on the provider you select, the signup program might or might not set up all your client software.

Running a Typical Signup Program

Before running a signup program, make sure your modem is connected to a telephone line, because the signup software usually dials the provider at least once during the signup process. Also, make sure you have a major credit card handy; you'll need to enter its number and expiration date to set up payment.

Signup programs are almost always designed to set up credit card payments for your Internet service. If you do not want to pay by credit card, you may not be able to use the signup program. (Actually, you may not even be able to use a particular provider; some accept payment solely by credit card.)

You'll find instructions for starting the program on a page or card that accompanies it, or printed right on the CD or disk.

After you start the program, just follow its lead. The program will prompt you to type in your name, address, phone number, and credit card information, and to choose a logon username and password, email address, and email password. The program may also present you with a list of payment plans from which to choose (see Figure 18.5).

Once or twice during the signup process, the program uses your modem to contact the provider. It does this to verify your payment information, find the best local access number for you, check that your selected username is not already taken, and ultimately to send all of the information it collected to the provider to open your account.

When the program closes, your computer and account are ready to go online and explore.

FIGURE 18.5

A typical signup program prompts you for all the info required for setting up your account, such as choosing a payment method.

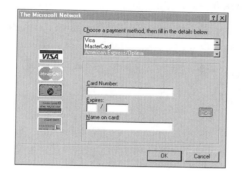

Using the Connection Wizard on Your Own

18

Setting up your computer without a signup program is a little more difficult, but well within anybody's capabilities. Often your ISP will provide you with all the instructions you need on a brochure or instruction sheet.

When you don't use a signup disk, you must set up your account with your selected Internet provider over the telephone first, then configure your computer. While setting up your account, your provider will tell you all of the communications settings required for the service, and will work with you to select your local access number, username, and password.

It's important that you make careful notes of everything your provider tells you. You'll use all of that information when setting up. In addition to your access number and logon username and password, you'll probably come out of the conversation with the following information:

- One or more IP addresses—a string of numbers separated by periods—that may be required for communicating with the provider.
- The addresses of the provider's email and news servers. You'll need these addresses to configure your email program and newsreader. Email server addresses may be described as SMTP and POP3 servers, and news servers may be described as NNTP servers. You don't need to know what the abbreviations mean; just know that if your provider mentions an NNTP server, he's talking about a news server.

- Your own email address, the one others can use to send email to you.
- Your email username and password, required for retrieving email people have sent to you. These may be different from your logon username and password.
- The telephone number and hours of the provider's customer service or technical support departments.
- Any other special communications steps or settings the particular provider requires.

No matter how you go about it, setting up your computer for the Internet is a simple matter of entering this information in your communications software. Once that's done, you can go online.

Running the Connection Wizard

Short of using a signup program, the next easiest way to set up an ISP account on a PC running Windows 95 or 98 is to set up Internet Explorer and run its Connection Wizard. Internet Explorer is included in every copy of Windows 98, Me, and XP, and is often included with Windows 95.

The Connection Wizard leads you through each step of the process, prompting you for all of the required information, such as IP addresses. That's almost as easy as using a signup disk, except that the Connection Wizard doesn't sign you up with your ISP—you must take care of that first—and it prompts you for your IP address and other setup information, which a signup program can supply for itself.

To launch the Connection Wizard, simply right-click the Internet Explorer icon on your desktop, choose the Connections tab, and click the Setup button. You'll see a screen like in Figure 18.6. From there, you follow the prompts, filling in the appropriate information. The wizard walks you through the process quite succinctly.

FIGURE 18.6

The Connection Wizard offers easy-to-follow instructions for getting connected to your ISP.

Connecting at Last

When it's done, you'll end up with an icon on your desktop for your connection to your provider. When you want to connect to use the Internet, just double-click that icon. You'll get a dialog box (see Figure 18.7) with your username already included. Just type your password, click Connect, and off you go. Now, you're ready to browse the Web, a topic that (conveniently enough) is covered in the next chapter.

FIGURE 18.7

After opening your connection program, you supply your password to log on to the Internet.

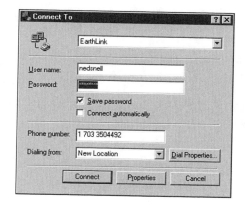

Summary

You now know what the Internet is, what hardware and software you need to get on the Internet, how to find and choose your Internet provider, and how to get connected. It's time to begin your browsing experience in the next chapter.

18

CHAPTER 19

Browsing Basics

With this chapter, you begin to get into the meat of why you wanted to get on the Internet in the first place—browsing the World Wide Web. The Web is one of the two biggest reasons that the average person hops online; the other is email.

Over the last few years, the Web has exploded. In this chapter, you'll pick up the basics of getting all around the Web. You'll learn specific information for different browsers.

About Your "Home Page"

Most Web browsers are configured to go automatically to a particular Web page as soon as you open them and connect to the Internet. This page is generally referred to as the browser's *home page*.

Note that home page has two meanings in Web parlance: It also describes a Web page that serves as the main information resource for a particular person or organization. For example, www.toyota.com may be described as Toyota's home page.

For example, if you get Internet Explorer directly from Microsoft, it opens at the Microsoft Network's home page at http://www.msn.com (see Figure 19.1). If you get Netscape Navigator directly from Netscape, it opens automatically to a similar startup page at Netscape.

However, if you get your software from your Internet provider, your browser may have been reconfigured with a new home page, one that's set up by your provider as a starting point for its subscribers. This home page also serves as a source of news and information about the provider and its services.

A few specific Web sites are used as home pages by a very high proportion of Web users because these pages offer a convenient set of links to the things many folks like to do as soon as they go online: Search for something, check out the latest news, weather, or sports scores, or other common activities.

Some folks call these sites *Web portals* because they function as an everyday point of entry to the Web. Popular portals include such search pages as Yahoo!, Excite, and Lycos, and other sites such as Netscape's Netcenter.

FIGURE 19.1

Your browser goes automatically to its "home page." The home page may have been selected by the browser maker or by your Internet provider.

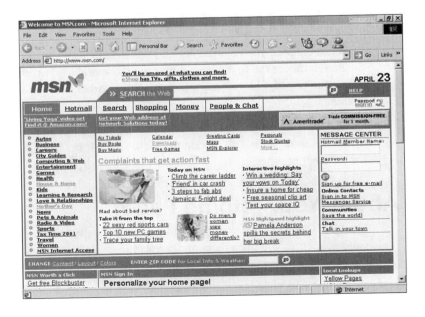

You don't have to do anything with your home page. You can just ignore it, and jump from it to anywhere on the Web you want. But some home pages provide valuable resources, especially for newcomers.

Often, you'll find a great selection of *links* on your home page to other fun or useful pages. If your home page happens to be one set up by your local ISP, the page may even contain local news, weather, and links to other pages with information about your community. Now and then, before striking out onto the Web, be sure to give your home page a glance to check out what it has to offer.

Understanding Web Page Addresses

Using the Web is easy—that's why it's so popular. But if there's one thing about Web surfing that trips up newcomers, it's using Web page addresses effectively. So here and now, I'll set you straight on Web page addresses so that you can leap online with confidence.

For the most part, you'll deal with only two kinds of addresses for most Internet activities:

- **Email addresses**—These are easy to spot because they always contain the "at" symbol (@).

- **Web addresses**—These never contain the @ symbol. Web page addresses are expressed as a series of letters separated by periods (.) and sometimes forward slashes (/), for example, `www.microsoft.com/index/contents.htm`. A Web address is sometimes referred to as a *URL*.

Although most URLs are Web page addresses, other types of URLs may be used in a Web browser for accessing other types of Internet resources.

If you keep your eyes open, you'll see Web page and site addresses everywhere these days. By typing an address in your Web browser (as you learn to do shortly), you can go straight to that page, the page the address points to. Just to give you a taste of the possibilities, and to get you accustomed to the look and feel of a Web site address, Table 19.1 shows the addresses of some fun and/or interesting Web sites.

As Table 19.1 shows, many addresses begin with the letters "www". But not all do, so don't assume.

TABLE 19.1 A Few Out of the Millions of Fun and Interesting Web Sites

Address	Description
www.foxnews.com	The most popular cable news network
www.ebay.com	eBay, an online auction house

19

TABLE 19.1 continued

Address	Description
www.epicurious.com	A trove of recipes
www.scifi.com	The SciFi Channel
www.carprices.com	A site where you can learn all about buying a new or used auto
www.uncf.org	The United Negro College Fund
www.rockhall.com	Cleveland's Rock & Roll Hall of Fame Museum
www.nyse.com	The New York Stock Exchange
college-solutions.com	A guide to choosing a college
www.sleepnet.com	Help for insomniacs
www.nasa.gov	The space agency's site
www.adn.com	The Anchorage, Alaska, Daily News
www.twinsmagazine.com	Advice for parents of multiples
imdb.com	The Internet Movie Database, everything about every film ever made
www.amazon.com	Amazon.com, a popular online bookshop
www.nfl.com	The National Football League

Anatomy of a Web Address

The address of a Web site is made up of several different parts. Each part is separated from those that follow it by a single, forward slash (/).

The first part of the address—everything up to the first single slash—is the Internet address of a Web server. Everything following that first slash is a directory path and/or filename of a particular page on the server. For example, consider the following fictitious URL:

www.dairyqueen.com/icecream/sundaes/fudge.htm

The filename of the actual Web page is fudge.htm. (Web page files often use a filename extension of .htm or .html.) That file is stored in a directory or folder called sundaes, which is itself stored in the icecream directory. These directories are stored on a Web server whose Internet address is www.dairyqueen.com.

Sometimes, an address will show just a server address, and no Web page filename. That's okay—many Web servers are set up to show a particular file to anyone who accesses the server (or a particular server directory) without specifying a Web page filename.

For example, if you go to the address of Microsoft's Web server, www.microsoft.com, the server automatically shows you an all-purpose Web page you can use for finding and jumping to other Microsoft pages. Such pages are often referred to as "top" or "index" pages, and often even use index.htm as their filename. The extension at the end of a filename (such as .htm) will vary based on the program that created it. You'll see lots of .cfm, .jsp, and .asp extensions along with the .htm and .html ones.

Technically, every Web page address begins with http:// or https://, particularly when described as a URL, the technical designation for the address format you use when working in a Web browser.

But the latest releases of Netscape Navigator and Internet Explorer no longer require you to type that first part. For example, using either of those browsers, you can surf to the URL http://www.sams.com just by typing

www.sams.com

(In fact, you don't even need to type the www part—if it's required, these browsers will fill it in for you.) Because of this change, Web page addresses often appear in advertising, books, and magazines with the http:// part left off.

Follow these steps to help understand Web addresses better:

1. Connect to the Internet and open your Web browser. After a few moments, your home page (whatever it may be) appears (see Figure 19.2).

2. Examine your browser's toolbar area. The address you see there is the address of your home page (see Figure 19.3).

3. Make a mental note of the spot where you saw the home page address. That's where you'll always see the address of whatever page you're currently viewing. That's usually also the place where you'll type addresses to navigate the Web, as described next.

19

FIGURE **19.2**
Open your browser to
your home page.

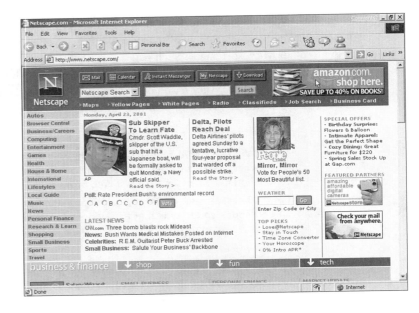

Address of home page   Toolbar area

FIGURE **19.3**
Find the address of
your home page.

Going Straight to Any Web Address

Before you can jump to a page by entering its address, you must find the place in your
browser provided for typing addresses. The term used to describe this area varies from
browser to browser, but to keep things simple, I'll just call it the *address box*. Figure 19.4
shows the toolbar area of Internet Explorer, with the address box containing an address.

In both Internet Explorer and Netscape Navigator, you'll see the address box as a
long text box somewhere in the toolbar area, showing the address of the page you're currently viewing. If you don't see it, the toolbar that contains the address box might be
switched off.

Address box showing URL of current page

FIGURE 19.4

In most graphical browsers, you'll see an address box in the toolbar area where you type an address to go to a particular Web page or site.

To switch on the toolbar that contains the address box:

- In Internet Explorer, choose View, Toolbars, and make sure a check mark appears next to Address Bar in the menu that appears. If not, click Address Bar. If you still don't see an address box, try dragging each toolbar to the bottom of the stack, so that all toolbars are visible, and none overlap.

- In Netscape, choose View, Show, Location Toolbar. If you still don't see it, it's there, but collapsed so it's not visible. Click at the far-left end of each line in the toolbar area, and it should appear.

If you use a browser other than the Big Two (Internet Explorer or Netscape Navigator), you may see an address box in the toolbar area, or at the bottom of the browser window. In some browsers, you may have to choose a menu item to display a dialog that contains the address box. Look for a menu item with a name like "Enter URL" or "Jump to New Location."

Entering and Editing URLs

After you've found the address box, you can go to a particular address by typing the address you want to visit in the box and pressing Enter. When the address box is in a toolbar, you usually must click in it first, then type the address, and press Enter.

19

Before you type an address in the address box, the address of the current page already appears there. In most Windows and Mac browsers, if you click once in the address box, the whole address there is highlighted, meaning that whatever you type next will replace that address.

If you click twice in the address box, the edit cursor appears there so that you can edit the address. That's a handy feature when you discover that you made a typo when first entering the address.

Note that when you type an address to go somewhere, your starting point doesn't matter—you can be at your home page or on any other page.

When typing the address, be careful of the following:

- Spell and punctuate the address exactly as shown, and do not use any spaces.

- Match the exact pattern of upper- and lowercase letters you see. Some Web servers are case-sensitive, and will not show you the page if you don't get the capitalization in the address just right.

- Some addresses end in a final slash (/), and some don't. But servers can be quirky about slashes, and many print sources where you see addresses listed mistakenly omit a required final slash, or add one that doesn't belong. Always type the address exactly as shown. But if that doesn't work, and the address appears not to end in a filename, try adding or removing the final slash.

- If you do not use a recent version of Internet Explorer or Netscape Navigator, you may be required to include the `http://` prefix at the beginning of the URL. For example, when you see an address listed as `www.ebay.com`, you must enter it in your address box as

`http://www.ebay.com`

What happens if you type an address wrong? Nothing bad—you just don't go where you want to go. Usually, your browser displays an error message, reporting that the browser could not find the address you requested. Check that you spelled, punctuated, and capitalized the address correctly. If you discover a mistake, edit (or retype) the address and press Enter to try again.

Note that Web servers and their pages are not permanent. From time to time, an address will fail not because you made a mistake, but just because the page or server to which it points is no longer online, either temporarily (because of a system glitch) or permanently.

Looking at the Sams Publishing Web Site

Web pages come and go. Most Web site URLs for large organizations work fine for years. But addresses can change, and Web pages and sites do disappear from time to time.

These steps take you to the Sams Publishing Web site, a site that will still be around when you read this.

1. Connect to the Internet and open your Web browser (see Figure 19.5).

FIGURE **19.5**

Open your Web browser.

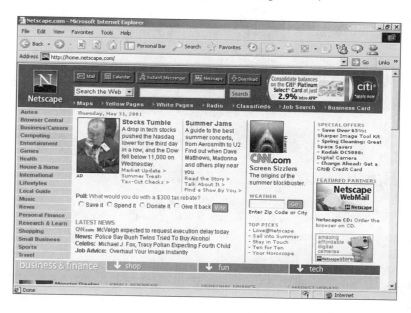

2. Find the address box, and click in it once.
3. Type the URL (see Figure 19.6).

    www.samspublishing.com

    (If you are using an older browser, you may have to add the `http://` prefix.)

FIGURE **19.6**

Type in the URL
`http://www.`
`samspublishing.com.`

4. Press Enter. Sams's Web site appears (see Figure 19.7).

19

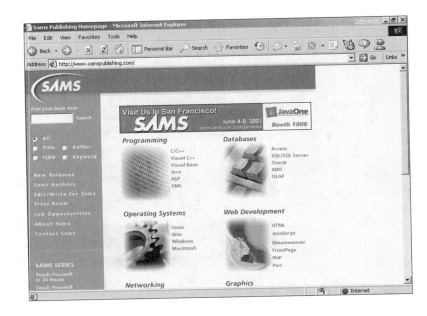

FIGURE 19.7

Press Enter to see the Sams Publishing Web site.

Basic Jumping Around

Many—even most—of the times you jump from page to page, you won't type an address. All you'll do is click a link or button. URLs are like cars—they take you directly to a particular place. Links are like the bus: They often take you just to the right neighborhood.

Some Web pages take a long time to appear, even if you have a fast modem and Internet connection. If some pages do seem terribly slow, don't worry that there's something wrong with your computer, modem, or connection. The problem is probably that the page you're accessing is very complex.

Each time you display a particular Web page, the whole page must travel through the Internet to your computer to appear on your screen. A page that's mostly text appears quickly, because text pages contain little data, and thus travel quickly through the Net. Pictures, multimedia, and Java programs balloon the number and size of the files that make up the Web page, and thus take much longer to appear.

Reclicking the link to a page over and over again is only going to slow down the process, and may cause your computer to freeze.

Finding and Using Links

Activating a link in most browsers is simple: Point to the link and click it; your browser takes you wherever the link leads.

Most links lead to another Web page, or to another part of a long Web page you're viewing. However, links can do much more. For example, some links, when activated, may start the download of a software file or play a multimedia file.

It's not using links that can be tricky, but finding them in Web pages that aren't designed well enough to make the links obvious. Links appear in a Web page in any of three ways:

- **As text.** You'll notice text in Web pages that appears to be formatted differently from the rest. The formatting differs depending upon your browser, but text that serves as a link is usually underlined (see Figure 19.8) and displayed in a different color than any other text in the page.

- **As pictures.** Any picture you see in a Web page may be a link. For example, a company logo may be a link leading to a page containing information about that company.

- **As imagemaps.** An imagemap is a single picture that contains not just one link, but several. Clicking on different parts of the picture activates different links (see Figure 19.9).

Text links are usually easy to spot because of their color and underlining (see Figure 19.8). Picture and imagemap links can be harder to spot at a glance.

But most browsers provide a simple way to determine what is and is not a link. Whenever the mouse pointer is on a link, it changes from the regular pointer to a special pointer that always indicates links.

19

Using Navigation Buttons: Back, Forward, Home, and Stop

In most browsers for Windows and the Mac, you'll see a whole raft of toolbar buttons, many of which you'll examine as this book progresses. But by far, the most important are the Big Four: Back, Forward, Home, and Stop (see Figure 19.10). These buttons help you move easily back and forth among any pages you've already visited in the current online session, and to conveniently deal with the unexpected.

For example, when exploring a particular Web site, you often begin at a sort of "top" page that branches out to others. After branching out a few steps from the top to explore particular pages, you'll often want to work your way back to the top again, to start off in a new direction. The Big Four buttons make that kind of Web navigation simple and typing-free.

Links

FIGURE 19.8

*Often, links are indi-
cated by underlined
text.*

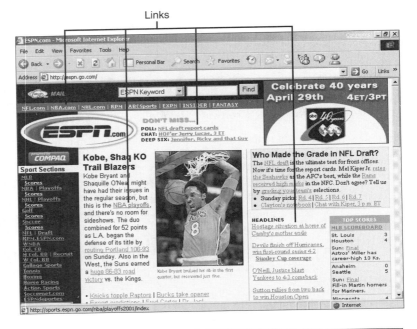

FIGURE 19.9

*Each part of this
imagemap is a differ-
ent link. In this case,
clicking on any of the
signs these people are
holding will take you
to a different page.*

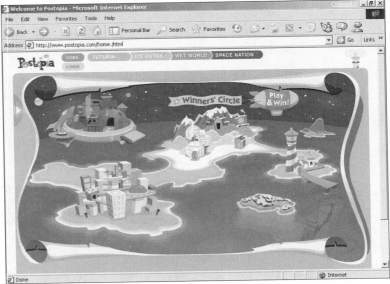

FIGURE 19.10

The main toolbars in Internet Explorer (shown here) and Netscape Navigator prominently feature the invaluable Back, Forward, Stop, and Home buttons.

Here's how you can use each of these buttons:

- **Back** retraces your steps, taking you one step backward in your browsing each time you click it. For example, if you move from Page A to Page B, clicking the Back button takes you back to A. If you go from A to B to C, pressing Back twice returns you to A. When you reach the first page you visited in the current online session, the Back button is disabled; there's nowhere left to go back to.

- **Forward** reverses the action of Back. If you've used Back to go backward from Page B to A, Forward takes you forward to B. If you click Back three times—going from D to C to B to A—clicking Forward three times takes you to D again. When you reach the page on which Back was first clicked, the Forward button is disabled because you can only move Forward to pages you've come "Back" from.

- **Home** takes you from anywhere on the Web directly to the page configured in your browser as "home," described at the start of this chapter. Going Home is a great way to reorient yourself if you lose your way and need to get back to a reliable starting point.

- **Stop** immediately stops whatever the browser is doing. If you click Stop while a page is materializing on your screen, the browser stops getting the page from the server, leaves the half-finished page on your screen, and awaits your next instruction.

19

> Back, Forward, and Home do not care how you got where you are. In other words, no matter what techniques you've used to browse through a series of pages—entering URLs, clicking links, using buttons, or any combination of these—Back takes you back through them, Forward undoes Back, and Home takes you home.

Back and Stop are particularly useful for undoing mistakes. For example, if you click on a link that downloads a file, and while the file is downloading you decide you don't want it, you can click Stop to halt the download but stay on the current page. Click Back to halt the download and return to the preceding page.

Practicing with Links and Buttons

1. Go to the ESPN Web site at `espn.go.com`, find any interesting-looking link, and click it (see Figure 19.11).

2. A new page opens, the one the link you clicked points to (see Figure 19.12). Click Back to return to the top ESPN page.

3. Click another link on the top ESPN page (see Figure 19.13). On the page that appears, find and click yet another link (see Figure 19.14). (If you see no links, click Back to return to the top ESPN page, and try another route.)

4. Click Back twice (see Figure 19.15) to return to the top ESPN page.

5. Click Forward twice. You go ahead to where you just came back from (see Figure 19.16).

FIGURE 19.11

Go to `espn.go.com` *and click on a link.*

Link

Back button

FIGURE 19.12
Click the Back button.

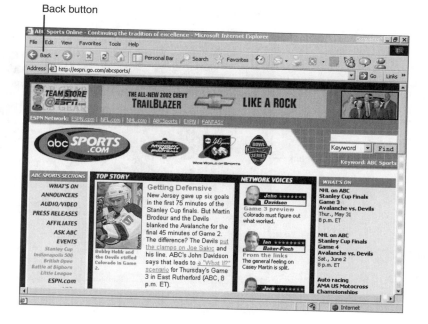

FIGURE 19.13
Click on another link.

Another link

19

FIGURE 19.14
Click on yet another link.

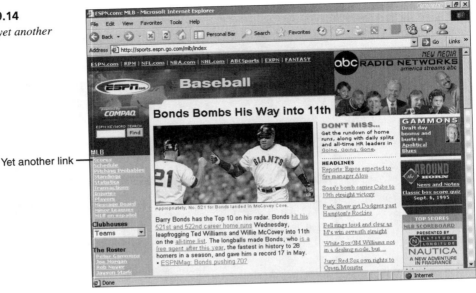

Yet another link ─────

FIGURE 19.15
Click Back twice.

Back button

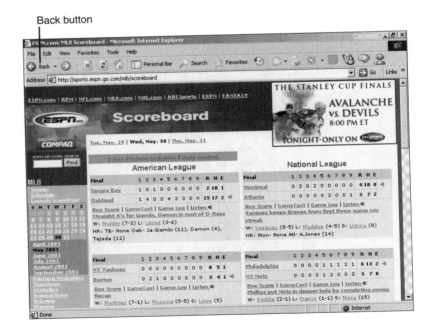

Forward button

FIGURE 19.16
Click Forward twice.

6. Try a new URL: Enter www.akc.org for the American Kennel Club (see Figure 19.17).

FIGURE 19.17
Enter a new URL.

19

7. From the AKC page (see Figure 19.18), click Back once. You return to a page at ESPN.

8. Click home, and you'll return to your home page, as you see in Figure 19.19.

FIGURE 19.18

Click Back once.

FIGURE 19.19

Click home.

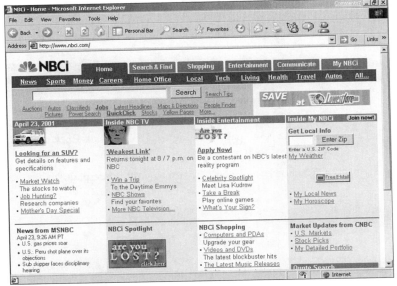

Fussing with Frames

You'll find that some pages are split into frames, two or more separate panes (see Figure 19.20).

In effect, each pane in a frames page contains its own, separate little Web page. That enables each pane to operate independently of the others; for example, clicking a link in one pane can change the contents of another.

Some folks get all boxed up by frames, but using a frames-based page doesn't have to be tricky. Just remember the following tips:

- All links within panes are active all the time.
- Some panes have their own scrollbars. When you see scrollbars on a pane, use them to scroll more of the pane's contents into view. If you want to use your keyboard's Up and Down arrows to scroll within a pane, you need to click within the appropriate pane first.
- While you're on a frames page, the Back and Forward buttons take you back and forth among the panes you've used in the current frames page, not among pages. Sometimes, it can be tough to use Back to "back out" of a frames page to the page you saw before it; at such times, it's often easier to enter a new URL or click Home to break free of the frames, then go from there.

FIGURE 19.20

A frames page can show two or more separate documents at once, each in its own pane.

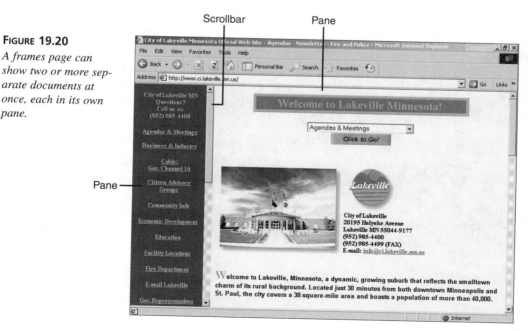

- Some pages use "borderless" frames, and so do not appear at first glance to be frames pages. But after a little experience, you'll quickly learn to identify any frames page when it appears, even when the frames are implemented subtly.

> Internet Explorer, Netscape Navigator, and a few other major browsers support frames, but some others do not.
>
> For this reason, many frames pages are preceded by a non-frames page that provides two links: One for displaying a frames page, and another for displaying the same content in a no-frames version.
>
> If your browser can't handle frames—or if your browser can handle them but you can't—just choose the no-frames version.

Summary

That's all there is to basic browsing. Just by entering URLs, clicking links, and using buttons like Back and Home, you can explore near and far. Little bumps like frames add a little complexity to the mix, but nothing you can't handle.

Part VII
Talking to the World

Chapter

CHAPTER 20

Using Email

Internet email enables you to exchange messages easily with anyone else on the Internet. An email message typically reaches its addressee within minutes (or at most, within an hour or so), even on the opposite side of the globe. It's faster than paper mail, easier than faxing, and sometimes just plain fun.

Types of Email Programs

Not everybody has Outlook, and even some with Outlook do not use Outlook for email. If you do not, or if you were waiting for a more broad overview of the email process, this chapter will help you out.

Email can be as complicated or as basic as you want it to be. There are a wide variety of different email programs—some that you have to buy as part of a huge suite of applications, some you get automatically with a browser, and some you can use right over the Web, without installing anything.

Making matters more confusing is the fact that both Microsoft and Netscape, the two companies who hold all the cards when it comes to using the Web, offer a wide variety of choices. Both offer a free program as part of their browser suite, but both also offer free Web-based email (Microsoft has *Hotmail*, Netscape has Netscape *Webmail*). Web-based email allows you to read messages right off a Web page, just like you are browsing. It is covered later in this chapter.

Understanding Email Addresses

The only piece of information you need to send email to someone is that person's Internet email address. An email address is easy to spot: It always has that at symbol (@) in the middle of it. For example, you know at a glance that

`sammy@fishbait.com`

is an email address. In most email addresses, everything following the @ symbol is the domain address of a company, Internet Service Provider, educational institution, or other organization.

Each online service has its own domain, too: For example, America Online's is `aol.com`, and Microsoft Network's is `msn.com`. So you can tell that the email address

`neddyboy@aol.com`

is that of the America Online user named `neddyboy`.

Setting Up Your Email Program

There are many different email programs out there. Internet suites such as Internet Explorer and Netscape Communicator include an email program—but you must take care when installing these programs not to optionally omit the email component of the suite. Choosing the "full" installation option when setting up a suite ensures that you include all the suite's client programs.

In the suites, the email programs are called

- Messenger, in Netscape Communicator. You can open Messenger from within the Navigator browser by choosing Communicator, Messenger (see Figure 20.1).
- Outlook Express, in Internet Explorer. You can open Outlook Express from within the Internet Explorer browser by clicking the Mail button on the toolbar and choosing Read Mail from the menu that appears (see Figure 20.2).

Configuring Email

After installing an email program, you need to configure it before you can use it. All email programs have a configuration dialog of some kind (or a series of dialog boxes) in which you can enter the information required for exchanging email. You'll find the configuration dialogs

FIGURE 20.1

Netscape Messenger, the email program that's included in the Netscape Communicator suite.

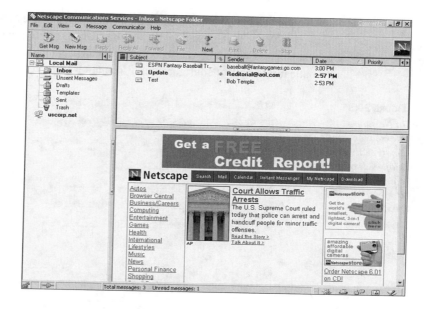

FIGURE 20.2

Outlook Express, the email program that's included with Microsoft Internet Explorer.

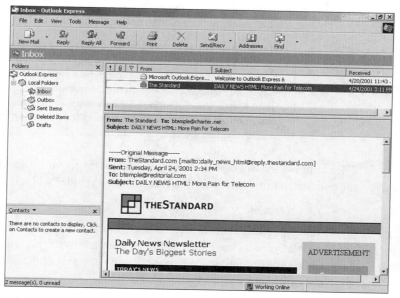

20

- In Netscape Messenger, by choosing Edit, Preferences to open the Preferences dialog box. In the list of Categories, choose Mail & Newsgroups. Complete the configuration settings in the Mail & Newsgroups category's Identity and Mail Servers subcategories (see Figure 20.3).

- For Outlook Express, by completing the Mail dialogs of the Windows Internet Connection Wizard (see Chapter 18, "Connecting to the Internet"). If you open Outlook Express without having configured it first, the Connection Wizard opens automatically to collect configuration information from you.

FIGURE 20.3

In Netscape Messenger, configure email settings in the Mail & Newsgroups category of the Preferences dialog box.

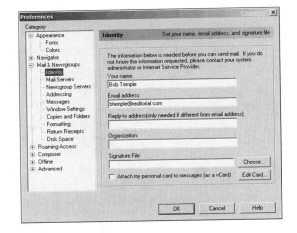

The automated setup routines supplied with programs such as Netscape Communicator and Internet Explorer not only set up your browser and Internet connection, but can optionally collect the information required to configure their email components (Messenger and Outlook Express). If you open Messenger or Outlook Express without first having configured them, a dialog opens automatically, prompting for the configuration information.

The configuration dialogs for most email programs require most or all of the following information, all of which your Internet Service Provider will tell you:

- Your full name.
- Your full email address. (Some configuration dialogs make you indicate the two parts of your address separately: the username—the part of the email address preceding the @ symbol—and your domain—the part of the email address following the @ symbol.)
- The address of your service provider's outgoing mail server, sometimes called the *SMTP server*.

- The address of your service provider's incoming mail server, sometimes called the *POP3 server* (some ISPs use another type of server called *IMAP4*). The POP3 address is sometimes (but not always) identical to the SMTP address.

Also, to ensure that no one but you gets your email, most ISPs require you to choose and use an email password. Some email programs let you enter that password in the configuration dialog so you needn't type a password each time you check your email.

Getting Around in Your Email Program

Before jumping right into sending and receiving messages, it's a good idea to learn how to get around in your email program, move among its folders (lists of messages), and display messages you select from a folder.

Choosing a Folder

Netscape Messenger and Outlook Express divide their messaging activities into a family of folders. In each folder, you see a list of messages you can display or work with in other ways. The folders are

- **Inbox.** The Inbox folder lists messages you have received.
- **Outbox (called *Unsent Messages* in Messenger).** The Outbox folder lists messages you have composed but saved to be sent later.
- **Sent.** The Sent folder lists copies of all messages you've sent, for your reference.
- **Deleted (called *Trash* in Messenger).** The Deleted folder lists messages you've deleted from any other folder.

To switch among folders in either Outlook Express or Messenger, click a folder name in the panel along the left side of the window (see Figure 20.4).

Displaying a Message

From the list displayed by each folder, you can display any message. You do this in either of two ways (the steps are the same in both Outlook Express and Messenger):

- Single-click the message in the list to display it in the Preview pane (see Figure 20.5) in the bottom of the window.
- Double-click the message in the list to display it in its own message window (see Figure 20.6).

In general, the Preview pane is best when you're simply scanning messages, and need to move quickly from one to the next. Use a full message window to read a long message, or to read a message you will reply to or forward (as described later in this chapter).

20

FIGURE 20.4

Select a folder to choose the messages you want to work with.

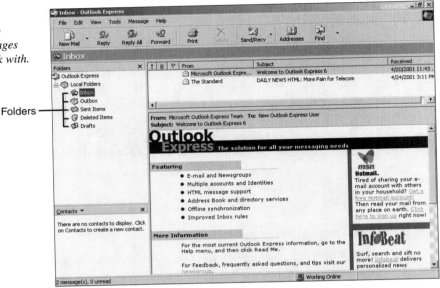

Folders

FIGURE 20.5

Single-click a message in a folder to display the message in the Preview pane.

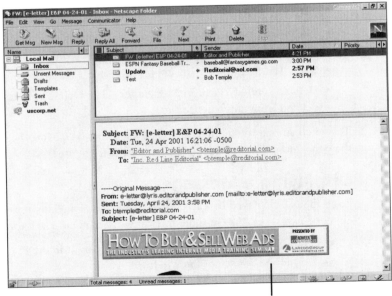

Preview Pane

Message window

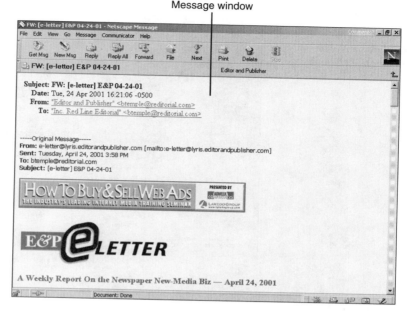

Message window

FIGURE 20.6
Double-click a message in a folder to display the message in a message window.

Composing and Sending a Message

When you have something to say, and the email address of someone to whom you want to say it, you're ready to go.

Writing Your Message

In most email programs, you compose your message in a window that's very much like a word processing program, with a special form at the top for filling in the address and subject information—the message's header. Below the form for the header, you type your message text in the large space provided for the message body.

The following steps show how to compose a simple email message.

Composing a New Message in Outlook Express

1. Click the New Mail button (see Figure 20.7).
2. In the To line (near the top of the window), type the email address of the person to whom you want to send a message (see Figure 20.8).
3. Click in the Subject line, and type a concise, meaningful subject for your message (see Figure 20.9). (The subject appears in the message list of the recipient, to explain the purpose of your message.)

20

New Mail button

FIGURE 20.7

Click the New Mail button in Outlook Express.

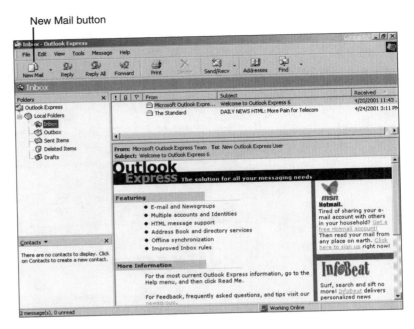

FIGURE 20.8

Type in the recipient's email address.

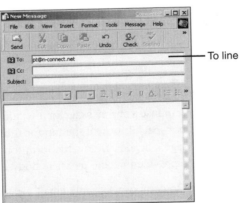

To line

4. Click in the large panel of the new message window and type your message, just as you would in a word processor (see Figure 20.10).

FIGURE 20.9

Type in a subject for the message.

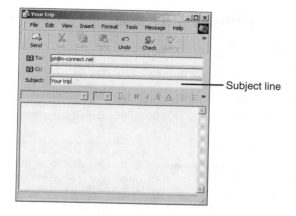

— Subject line

FIGURE 20.10

Type in your message.

It used to be that email programs automatically created text-only messages, because many email readers weren't configured to display HTML messages. The latest versions of both Outlook Express and Netscape Messenger allow you to create messages in HTML format.

What does this mean to you? Simply put, it allows you to format the text, using bold, italics, different fonts, and so on, so the message can have a personal touch. Be aware, however, that some of those who receive your messages might still be using email clients that don't allow them to display HTML messages.

20

Composing a New Message in Netscape Messenger

Follow these steps to compose a new email message:

1. Click the New Msg button (see Figure 20.11).
2. Follow Steps 2, 3, and 4 of the preceding steps for composing a message.

> You can send one message to multiple recipients in several different ways. For example, you can "cc" (carbon copy) your email to recipients other than your primary addressee(s). To do this, just enter their email addresses into the CC: field of the New Message window.

FIGURE 20.11
Click the New Msg button in Netscape Messenger.

New Message button

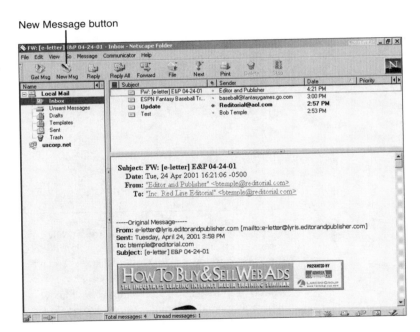

Sending a Message

After the header (To and Subject) and body (what you have to say) of the message are complete, you send your message on its way. In most programs, you do so simply by clicking a button labeled Send in the toolbar of the window in which you composed the message.

What happens immediately after you click Send depends upon a number of different factors:

- The email program you use
- Whether you're online or off
- How your program is configured

The message can be sent immediately out through the Internet to its intended recipient. If you're offline when you click Send, your email program can automatically connect you to the Internet to send the message. Otherwise, you must connect before sending.

However, instead of sending your message the instant you click Send, your email program can instead send the message to your Outbox (or Unsent Messages) folder, to wait. After clicking Send, you can open your Outbox or Unsent Messages folder to see whether the message is there (see Figure 20.12).

FIGURE 20.12

In some programs, messages are sent to wait in the Outbox or Unsent Messages folder, then finally go out to their recipients at a later time.

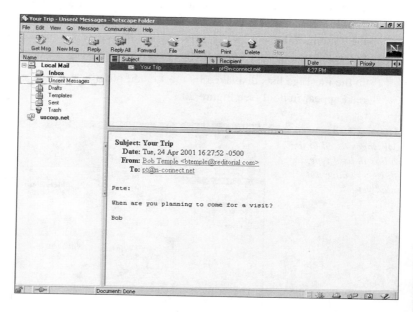

This Outbox scenario enables you to do all your email composing offline, saving as many messages as you want in your Outbox folder. Then, when you're all done, you can send all the messages in one step.

Here's how to send waiting messages:

- In Outlook Express, click the Send/Recv button (it might be labeled "Send/Receive" in your copy) to send all messages in the Outbox folder.

20

- In Netscape Messenger, click the Get Msg button (short for Get Messages) to send all messages in the Unsent Messages folder.

Receiving Messages

When others send messages to you, those messages go to your service provider's mail server, and wait there until you choose to receive messages. To receive messages

- In Messenger, click the Get Msg button on the toolbar.
- In Outlook Express, click the Send/Recv (or Send/Receive) button on the toolbar.

If you are offline when you click the Send/Recv or Get Msg button, Outlook Express and Messenger connect you to the Internet automatically (or prompt you to do so) to retrieve your new messages.

Your email program contacts your ISP, and checks for any new messages addressed to you. If there are none, the words "No new messages on server" appear in the status bar at the bottom of the window. If there are new messages, the messages are copied to your PC and stored in your Inbox folder, where you can read them any time, online or off.

In the message lists displayed by most email programs, the messages you have not yet read appear in bold (see Figure 20.13).

FIGURE 20.13

Messages listed in the Inbox in bold type are those you have not read yet.

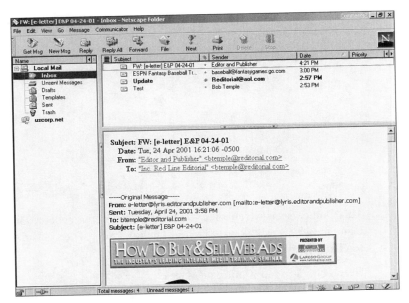

Messages you receive can contain computer viruses, particularly (but not exclusively) when those messages have files attached to them or they come to you from strangers. The best way to protect yourself from these files is to have a good antivirus protection program installed on your computer, keep it updated to protect against newer viruses, and never open an email or attachment from someone you don't know. Two of the top antivirus programs are Norton AntiVirus (http://www.norton.com) and McAfee VirusScan (http://www.mcafee.com).

Replying and Forwarding

Most email programs provide you with two easy ways to create new messages by using other messages you have received: *replying* (sending back an email message with additional notes to a person who has sent one to you) and *forwarding* (sending an email you receive to another person).

To reply or forward, you always begin by opening the original message. From the message window's toolbar, you then click a button or menu item with a label like one of the following (see Figure 20.14):

- **Reply**—Reply creates a reply to the person who sent you the message.
- **Reply All**—Reply All creates a reply to the person who sent you the message and to everyone else in the email's recipient list.
- **Forward**—Forward creates a new message containing the entire text of the original message, ready for you to forward.

Whichever button you click, a new message window opens. In the body of the message, a complete *quote* (part or all of the original message) appears (see Figure 20.15).

You can edit the quote, cutting out any parts that aren't relevant and inserting your own comments above, below, or within the quote.

In the message window of a reply, the To line is automatically filled in for you, with the address of the person from whom you received the message (or multiple addresses, if you chose Reply All). The Subject line is filled in with the original message's subject, preceded by Re:, to indicate that your message is a reply to a message using that subject. To complete the reply, all you have to do is type your comments above, below, or within the quote, and then click Send.

20

FIGURE 20.14

The Reply, Reply All, and Forward buttons offer different ways of responding to messages you've received.

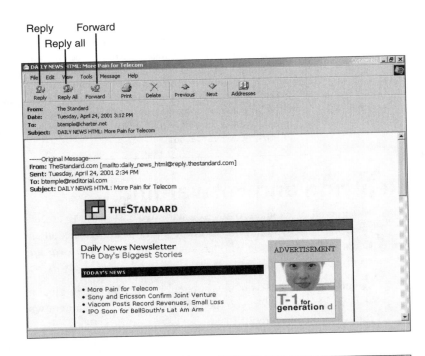

FIGURE 20.15

A reply or a forward includes a quote from the original message.

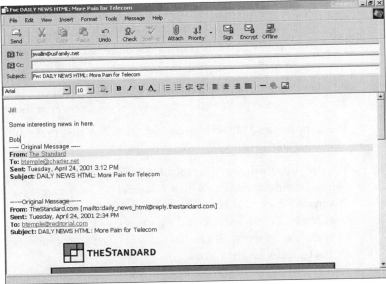

In the message window of a forward, the To line is empty, so you can enter the address of the person to whom you want to forward the message. (As with any message, you can enter multiple To recipients, and Cc recipients as well.) The Subject line is filled in with the original message's subject, preceded by FW: (forward). To complete the forward, address the message, type your comments above, below, or within the quote, and then click Send.

Using an Address Book

Most folks find that there's a steady list of others to whom they email often. Keeping track of those all-important names and addresses, and using them, is easier when you use your email program's *address book*.

When an addressee's information is in your address book, you needn't type—or even remember—his or her email address. Instead, you can simply choose the person's name from the address book, and your email program fills in the address for you. Some address books also support *nicknames*—short, easy-to-remember names you type in the To line of a message instead of the full email address.

Adding to Your Address Book

In both Outlook Express and Messenger, the easiest way to add to your address book is to copy information from messages you've received. For example, if you've received a message from Sue, you can use that message to quickly create an address card you can use to send messages to Sue.

To create a new address book entry from a message, begin by displaying the message in its own window.

- In Netscape Messenger, from the message window's menu bar, choose Message, Add Sender to Address Book. A New Card dialog box opens (see Figure 20.16). Make sure the name and email address boxes on the Name tab have been filled in, and complete any of the other, optional boxes you want. Click OK to save the new entry.

- In Outlook Express, from the message window's menu bar, choose Tools, Add Sender to Address Book. Make sure the name and email address boxes on the Name tab have been filled in, and complete any of the other, optional boxes and tabs you want. Click OK to save the new entry.

20

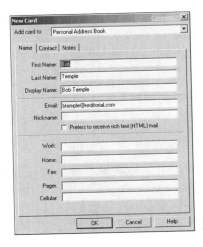

FIGURE 20.16

When you use a message you have received to add someone to your address book, that person's name and email address are entered for you, automatically.

To create an address book entry from scratch (without beginning from a message you've received)

- In Outlook Express, choose Tools, Address Book, click the New button; then choose New Contact from the menu that appears.
- In Netscape Messenger, choose Communicator, Address Book; then click the New Card button.

Addressing a Message from the Address Book

To use an address book entry to address a message (in Netscape Messenger or Outlook Express), begin by opening the New Message window as usual. Then open the address book list.

- In Netscape Messenger, choose Communicator, Address Book.
- In Outlook Express, click the little icon in the To line that looks like an open address book.

In the list, click the name of an addressee, and click the To button to add the addressee to the To line.

When done choosing recipients, click OK to close the address book, and complete the Subject line and body of your message.

Attaching Files to Email Messages

Once new Internet users get the hang of using their Web browsers and email programs, nothing causes more frustration than file *attachments,* which are external files—for example pictures or Word documents—that you send along with an email message.

The following steps show how to attach a file to an email message in Outlook Express. You'll send that message to yourself, so you can also learn how to detach and use a file attachment you receive. Note that the steps are similar in Netscape Messenger.

Do not open the file (by double-clicking its file icon or right-clicking it and choosing Open or Run) until after you have scanned it for viruses and determined that it's safe.

Attaching a File to an Email Message

The following steps show you how to attach a file to an email message that you want to send:

1. Compose and address your message (to yourself) as you normally would. Then click the Attach button (see Figure 20.17).

FIGURE 20.17

Click the Attach button in a new message.

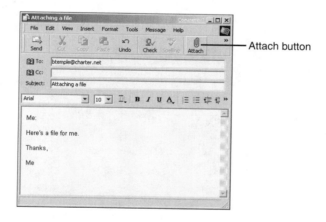

Attach button

2. Use the dialog to navigate to and select the file to attach, and then click the dialog's Attach button (see Figure 20.18).
3. Send the message (see Figure 20.19). If you do not immediately receive it, click Send/Recv again to receive the message.

20

FIGURE 20.18

Find the file, and then click the Attach button.

FIGURE 20.19

Send the message.

Step 4 shows how to open a file attachment directly from the message, which is okay because you know the source of the file (you). But as a rule, unless you're very confident about the source of a file attachment, you should skip Step 4, and instead do Step 5 to separate the file from the message. Then you can use your virus-scanning software to check the file for viruses before you open it.

4. In the header of the received message, you'll see an icon and a filename representing the attached file. To view the file, double-click the icon (see Figure 20.20).

FIGURE 20.20

To read the attachment in the received message, double-click the file's icon.

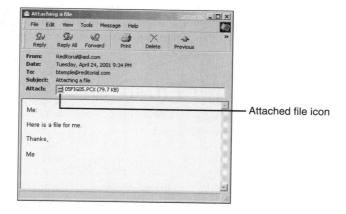

Attached file icon

5. If you want to save the file separately from the message (for use later), right-click the icon, and choose Save As (see Figure 20.21).

FIGURE 20.21

To save the file, right-click and choose Save As.

20

If you have your email program configured for formatting fancy, HTML-based messages, when you attach a picture file (such as a photo you've scanned) to a message, you might see the actual picture displayed in the message instead of an icon.

Don't worry if this happens; anyone you send to who has a similarly configured email program will see the picture the same way, and anyone who does not have such an email program will receive the picture as an attachment.

File attachments can dramatically increase the length of time it takes you to send a message, and the length of time it takes the recipient to receive messages. Avoid sending really large files (more than 300K), and before sending an attachment to someone you haven't sent to before, send a message describing the file and its size, asking if it's OK to send it.

Using the Web for Email

Increasingly, people are using Web-based email to communicate. Web-based email allows a user to send and receive messages directly from a Web page, rather than opening a separate email program.

The advantages of this type of email are twofold: You can access your email and send and receive messages from any computer connected to the Internet, so it's great for travelers; and typically, the email account is free. They are available all over the Web; Yahoo! and Hotmail, the Microsoft Network's Webmail offering, are the two biggest.

The primary drawback, however, is that these aren't full-featured email programs. Handling attachments to email is more difficult, if it's available at all. Saving emails is harder, too.

There is a combination of regular email and Web-based email that's a wonderful thing, however. Some ISPs offer a Web-based mail client to their regular members, so you can access your email if you're away from your regular computer.

America Online is one of these. AOL members can read their email from anywhere in the world, simply by logging on to the AOL site at www.aol.com. You simply sign in with your screen name and password, click the Check Your Mail! button, and you'll be able to read your messages. You can also reply, forward, or create new mail messages, right from the site (see Figure 20.22).

Each message appears as a highlighted and underlined link. Clicking on the link opens the message. It's pretty simple.

FIGURE 20.22
*America Online offers
a Web-based email
option so its members
can access their email
from anywhere in the
world.*

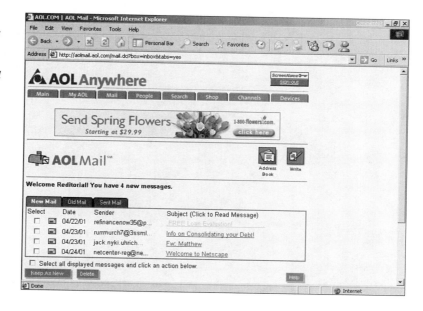

Summary

You learned a lot about email. As you saw here, the hardest part about email is getting
yourself set up for it. Composing, sending, and receiving messages is a breeze, and techniques that can make you even more productive—such as using an Outbox or Address
Book—are also pretty easy, and always optional.

20

CHAPTER 21

Chatting with Instant Messenging

Feel the need to reach out and touch someone, live and (almost) in person? Chat puts you online in a live conversation with other Internet users anywhere in the world. Chatting used to require a high degree of technical understanding; that's no longer the case. More and more people simply chat using their browser, through one of hundreds of sites that offer it.

Instant messaging is another way of reaching out and touching someone. What began as an America Online–only exercise is now available to anyone on the Web.

Understanding Internet Chatting

You may have heard people refer to chatting on the Internet as being in a *chat room*. Well, you don't have to go into a special room in your house that you designate only for these chats. Chats are divided by subject matter, and the term chat room really refers to the subject area you have entered on the Internet.

Room is an appropriate word to use, however, because it's very much like being in a room full of people, all talking about the same subject. Everything you "say" by typing it into your computer can be "heard" by everybody else in the room—they will see your words appear on their computer screen. That can be a very small group of people, or dozens.

Thousands of different chats are under way at once, each in its own chat room. When you join a chat, you enter a room, and from then on you see only the conversation that's taking place in that room.

In most chat rooms (often called *channels*), the conversation is focused on a given subject area. In a singles chat room, participants chat about stuff singles like to talk about. In a geology chat, people generally talk about rocks and earthquakes.

When you're in a chat room, everything that everyone else in the same room types appears on your screen. Each participant's statements are labeled with a *nickname* to identify who's talking. Those participating in a chat (known as members) choose their own nicknames and rarely share their real names. In a chat, you can be whoever you want to be, and so can everyone else.

Chatting Through Your Browser

Chatting through your browser is the simplest way to get involved in chatting online. For that reason, it's also the most commonly used type of chat online.

All kinds of sites offer chats for their users. Big portals like Yahoo! offer chats on a wide variety of topics. Specialized sites also offer chats for their users. Heck, even the Weather Channel (`http://www.weather.com`) offers chats.

There are really two different kinds of chats. There are open chats that can involve anyone and everyone from around the globe, all talking about a particular subject of interest. These are sometimes moderated by someone whose job it is to keep the discussion clean and on-topic. The other kind of chat is a celebrity chat, in which a particular person appears in a chat room at a specified time to answer questions. For example, a local TV news crew might have its anchorperson online in a chat room for an hour one night a week to talk with viewers.

Finding Sites with Chat Rooms

It's not very difficult to find sites that offer chats for their users. Simply go to any site that interests you, and look around for a chat button. Some sites will call it "interact" or "forums" or the like, but it's often there if you want to find it. The chances are pretty good that the site you've been visiting all along has a chat area, and you didn't even know it.

Chatting at Yahoo!

If you're really interested in chatting, however, a great place to start is at the Yahoo! site or that of another major portal. These sites will typically offer chat rooms on a wide variety of subjects, giving you the opportunity to get chatting and change "rooms" easily.

Take Yahoo! as an example of a portal with good chat capabilities. They make it pretty easy to get started, too. All you have to do is sign up, choose an ID and a password, provide some other basic information, and you're ready to go. To get started, go to the chat area at Yahoo! (chat.yahoo.com), and click on the Sign Up for Yahoo! Chat! link (see Figure 21.1).

FIGURE 21.1

Signing up for chatting on Yahoo! is quick and easy.

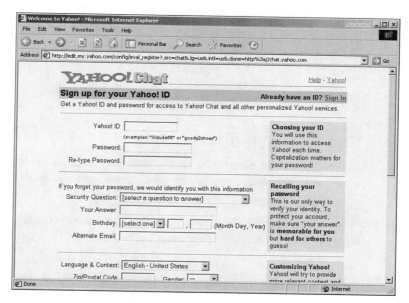

Signing up only takes a minute (after you've found an ID that's not already in use). Once your information has been accepted, click on the Complete Room List button to get an idea of what's out there in terms of chat.

Yahoo! chats are broken into categories, and each category contains several different rooms. For example, under the Music category, you'll find chats on subjects ranging from Britney Spears to jazz (see Figure 21.2).

After you've found a subject that interests you, just click its link to enter the room.

21

FIGURE 21.2

Yahoo! chat offers a wide variety of rooms from which to choose.

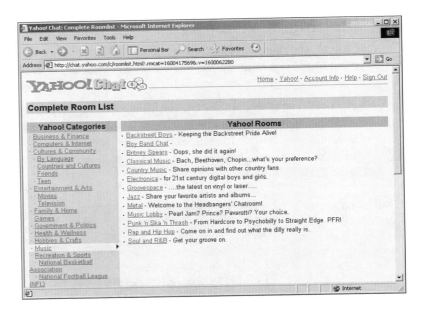

The Chat Window

Before you can be a successful chatter, you need to know the ins and outs of the chat room itself. Yahoo! is a good example, because its chat rooms appear much like those at many other sites.

After you've entered a chat, you'll see the chat window (see Figure 21.3). It's divided neatly into different frames, and each has its purpose.

The biggest pane in the window, in the upper left, is the viewing pane. This is where all the messages appear, including those that you write. Below that, you will see some formatting buttons that allow you to change the way your text appears, and the Chat: pane. This is where you will type any messages you write in the chat. Type it out, click the Send button, and they'll appear in the viewing pane, for you and all the others in the room to see.

Speaking of the others, they are listed in the member list pane, at the upper right. The list is by ID.

At the very bottom, you'll see some tools. There are also other special tricks you can do, as well:

- **Create Room**—You can create your own chat room if you wish. This is great if you want to have a private chat with a group of people, say for business purposes. Or, if you want to have the entire extended family all in one place to announce a baby on the way! You can set up your own chat room, make it password-protected so the ordinary Joes can't enter, then set a time for the chat and give the appropriate people the room name and password.

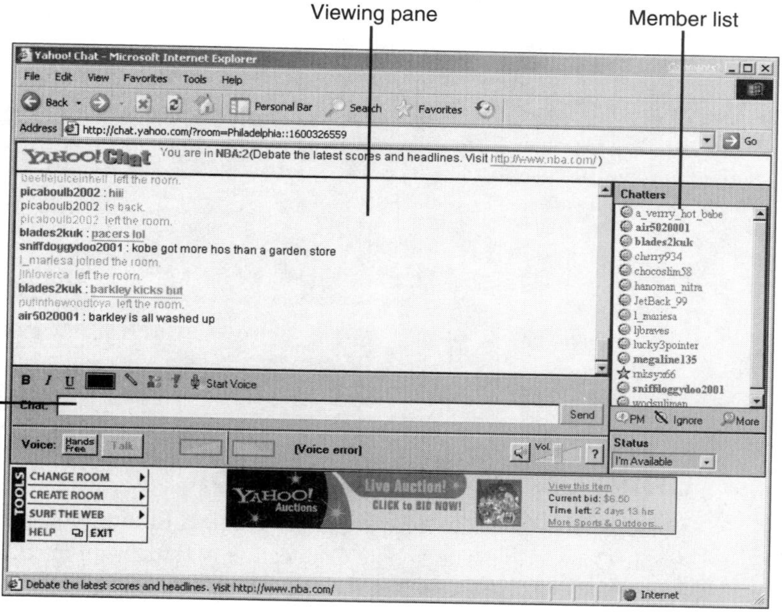

FIGURE 21.3

The Yahoo! chat window is similar to those of many other chats.

Viewing pane

Member list

Composing pane

- **PM**—Under the member list, you see the PM button. Use this to send a private message to someone in the chat room. Just highlight their name, click PM, and type your message to them.

- **Ignore**—If there's one person in the room who really bugs you, highlight their ID and click Ignore. You will no longer see any messages posted by that person.

- **Voice**—If your computer is properly equipped, you can participate in a voice chat by clicking the Start Voice button. You need a good sound card, speakers, and a microphone to participate.

Chatting in AOL

America Online's chats are one of the service's most popular features. Chat rooms are all over AOL. You'll find chat rooms in forums to discuss just about any topic the service offers.

21

Just choose a channel from the list on the left side of your AOL screen and you'll be able to find chats within that area of interest. For example, take the Parenting channel. If you click on the Parenting button, you'll find a special "Moms" area inside. Go there, and you'll find a Chat Now button. Click it, and you'll have a wide range of chatting options (see Figure 21.4—everything from a special chat for disabled moms to chats about dealing with teenagers, and so on.

FIGURE 21.4

AOL's chats are specialized by topic, so you can meet with people of similar interests.

Using the People Connection

As many chat rooms as there are in the Channel forums, you'll find many more in the People Connection. The People Connection is abuzz with chat 24 hours a day, 7 days a week. These are different than the chats in the various channels.

Chat rooms are so popular that there's a Chat button on the Welcome window that greets you when you sign on. You can click that or select People Connection from the People menu on the toolbar—either way, you'll go to the People Connection.

When you click the Chat button, you move into the People Connection screen. There are many options here; choose Chat Now, and you're dropped into a lobby chat room in Town Square (see Figure 21.5). Town Square is the generic chat category online—there are others (you'll see them in a moment). A lobby is just that: a waiting room where you can chat or move on to a room with a more defined topic of conversation.

At any given moment, there can be hundreds of lobbies in the People Connection. They are all given a number—the one shown in Figure 21.5 is Lobby 75.

On the right side of the chat window is a list of the people who are in the lobby with you (your screen name is there, too). You can find out a little something about the folks in your room by seeing if they have a Member Profile. To read a Member Profile, double-click a screen name from the room list and then click Get Profile on the dialog box that appears.

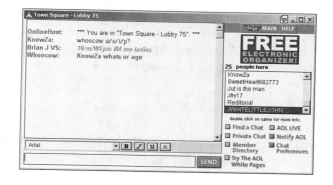

FIGURE 21.5

Your basic chat room—this one's a lobby.

When you first start out in a chat room, it's a good idea to sit and read the chat scrolling up your screen. It gives you a notion of what's being talked about, who's doing the talking, and whether you want to join in. If you want to participate in a lobby chat, simply type what you want to say in the text box at the bottom of the window and then press Enter (or click Send). Your chat appears in the chat window, and you can carry on a conversation.

If there isn't much going on in the lobby, you might want to move to a room with a more specific chat theme.

Moving to Another Room

To see a list of the currently active chat rooms in the People Connection, click the Find a Chat button at the bottom-right side of the chat window. A list of categories and chat rooms appears in the Find a Chat dialog box, as shown in Figure 21.6.

In the Find a Chat dialog box, you'll see a list of room categories in the box on the left side of the screen. When you highlight a category name and click the View Chats button in the middle of the window, the list box on the right of the screen shows all the rooms that are available for that specific category. At peak chatting hours, you might need to click the List More button a couple of times to see all the chat rooms in a given category.

FIGURE 21.6

Find a Chat helps you find rooms of interest.

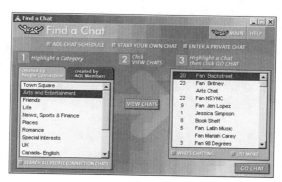

21

To enter a room, double-click its name in the list. You can also peek in and see who's chatting in a room. Click on the room's name in the list and then click the Who's Chatting button. A list of the members in the room appears, much like the room list in an actual chat room. You can use it to see who's around before you drop in for a chat.

You might notice that the categories list on the left side of the Find a Chat window has two tabs. The second tab reveals the same category list as the first tab, but the chat rooms listed in the right side are instead those that have been created by AOL members, not AOL staff. The list looks, and works, exactly the same as the one shown previously in Figure 21.6, but the rooms have all been created by AOL members.

You can create your own chat room from the list of Member Chats by clicking the Start Your Own Chat button (top middle of the Find a Chat window).

Using Microsoft Chat

Another type of chat involves downloading and using a chat client software program. These programs used Internet Relay Chat, or IRC, to conduct their chats. There are many such programs, but one of the best is Microsoft Chat—it's free, and it's a little bit unusual in that it makes the chat look like a comic strip.

If you don't have Microsoft Chat, you can download it free from the Tucows software directory at http://www.tucows.com or directly from Microsoft at http://www.microsoft.com.

Like any chat program, Microsoft Chat—henceforth to be known simply as Chat with a capital C—lets you communicate with chat servers. You can view the list of chat rooms, join a chat room, read what everyone says in the chat room, and make your own contributions to the discussion. What's different about Chat is the way it displays the conversation.

Most chat clients show the text of the conversation a line at a time and label each line with the speaker's nickname.

Chat, however, can display the conversation as text or as a comic strip, using little cartoon characters to represent members and showing their words in cartoon word balloons (see Figure 21.7). The folks at Microsoft think this approach makes chatting feel more human, more fun. In its first versions, Chat was actually named Microsoft Comic Chat.

A *balloon* is a little bubble you see in comics in which the words or thoughts of a character appears.

FIGURE 21.7

Microsoft Chat can make a chat session look like a comic strip, with a different cartoon character for each participant.

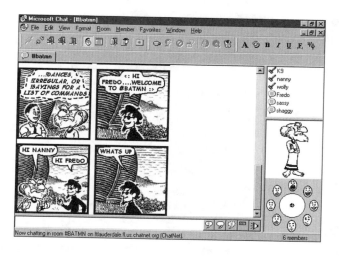

It's important to understand that most folks you'll end up chatting with probably won't use Microsoft Chat. Many will use ordinary text chat clients; they'll see your statements labeled with your nickname but won't see your comic character.

On your display, Chat converts all statements in a chat—even those made by users of text-only clients—into comics. Other Chat users in the same room appear as their chosen cartoon characters. For users of other chat clients, Chat automatically assigns and shows unused characters.

Joining a Chat Room

It's time to hit a server and see it for real. On the way, though, you'll perform some automatic configuration that Chat needs to operate properly.

1. Open Microsoft Chat by choosing Programs, Microsoft Chat.

2. Select the Show All Available Chat Rooms option, and then click OK to connect to the chat server listed in the dialog (see Figure 21.8).

3. A message appears. This message differs by server, but typically it contains any special rules or instructions for the server, plus any disclaimers in which the server operator reminds you that he's not responsible for what people say there.

4. A list of all chat rooms available on the server appears (see Figure 21.9). You are now connected to a chat server and are ready to chat—except that, as a new user, you have not yet selected a nickname and a comic character, as described next.

21

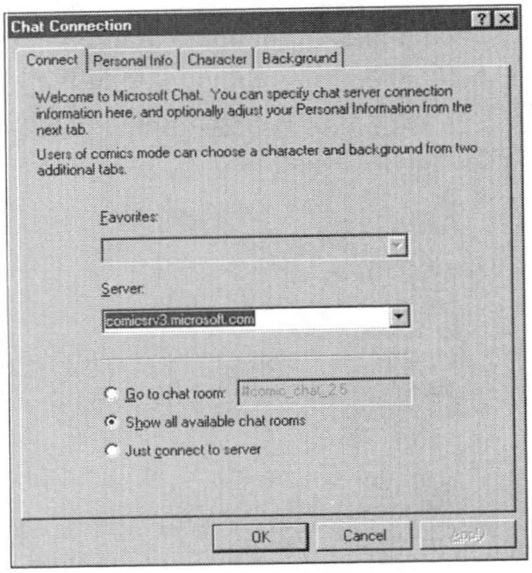

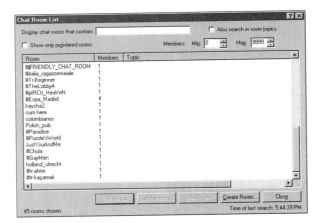

FIGURE 21.8

Select Show All Available Chat Rooms and then click OK.

FIGURE 21.9

A list of available chat rooms appears.

Choosing an Identity

Before you can join in a chat, you must create a nickname. And because of Chat's unique presentation style, you must choose a comic character, too. In addition, you can select a background that appears behind the characters in each panel of the comic, as you see it on your screen.

After you choose a nickname, character, and background, Chat remembers them for future sessions. You do not need to choose them again unless you want to change them.

Choose View, Options to open the Options dialog box, and choose the Personal Info tab if it is not already selected (see Figure 21.10).

FIGURE 21.10

The Personal Info tab allows you to set your preferences.

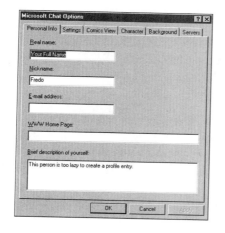

Click in the Nickname box and type a nickname for yourself. Your nickname should be one word with no spaces or punctuation, and it should also be unusual enough that another member hasn't chosen the same nickname. (If you attempt to enter a room where someone is already using the same nickname as you, Chat prompts you to change your nickname before entering.)

To choose the character you would like to use for your likeness, click the Character tab and click a name in the Character column. The Preview column shows what the selected character looks like—what you will look like to other Chat users if you stick with that character.

Entering a Room

To enter a chat room, you select a room from the chat room list. Figure 21.11 shows the list of chats available on the server. Each server has its own list, and the lists change often.

FIGURE 21.11

To enter any room in the list, double-click its name.

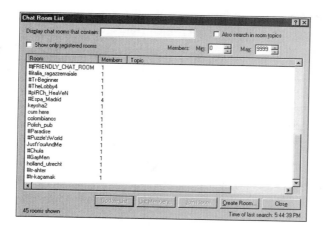

21

In the list, the name of each room begins with a pound sign (#). The name of the room is followed by the number of members currently in the room, and sometimes also by a description of the conversation that usually takes place there.

When you first arrive in a room, you might not see any comic panels right away. The server shows you only what's been said since you entered the room. After you enter, statements begin appearing one by one as members make them.

Now that you're in a room, you can just lurk or listen in on the conversation, or you can contribute to it by sending your statements for all the others to see. Note that you are not obligated to add anything to the conversation. In fact, just lurking in a chat room is a great way to learn more about chats before diving in.

When you're ready to contribute your comments to the chat, just type them in as you did in the browser-based chats we discussed earlier.

After you press Enter, those in the room who are using regular chat clients see your statement labeled with your nickname, so they know you said it. Those in the room who are using Microsoft Chat see your chosen comic character speaking the words in a *say balloon*, the type that surrounds words that comic characters say aloud.

You can format your words by picking a special balloon from the right side of the Compose pane. The balloons allow you to indicate you are thinking (bubbles) or whispering (dotted outline). You can also have your character express emotions by picking the appropriate face from the Emotion Wheel in the lower-right corner.

There are lots of other chat clients out there. If you want to look for others, you can always check the Tucows directory at http://www.tucows.com.

What Is Instant Messenger?

Instant messaging is a lot like chat, with a few key differences. One, most instant messages are sent to or received from people you know. Two, the conversations are just between you and one other person.

America Online members automatically get AOL's Instant Messenger and can use it within the service. If you know another person's screen name, you can use Instant Messenger to check to see if they are online. If they are, you can type them a quick message, and it automatically pops up on their screen.

Those who don't have AOL can still use Instant Messenger. You can download it from the Netscape Web site (http://www.netscape.com). It's a quick download, and it walks you through the steps of setting it up.

Sending "Instant" Messages

Instant Messenger lets you see, from among a list you set up yourself (a "Buddy List"), which of your friends are online at the same time you are (see Figure 21.12). You can exchange typed messages with those friends—but unlike email, those messages show up instantly. The moment you send a message to a friend who's online, he or she sees it, and vice versa. So you can carry on a live, interactive conversation, much like chat.

FIGURE 21.12

AOL Instant Messenger lets you exchange live messages with friends who are online at the same time you are—even if neither of you uses AOL.

The easiest way to sign up for Instant Messenger is to install Netscape Communicator. From Navigator's menu bar, choose Communicator, AOL Instant Messenger Service, and then follow the prompts to sign up.

Note that AOL Instant Messenger is not the only such service available. Another is Yahoo! Messenger, which you can learn about at http://messenger.yahoo.com. Internet Explorer offers a similar instant messaging system, called *MSN Messenger*. MSN Messenger provides a cleaner interface than AOL's Instant Messenger and is developing quite a following. MSN Messenger comes with Windows XP so you won't have to download software to begin using it.

Summary

Chat and instant messages are fun, as long as you stay among people whose reasons for chatting are the same as yours. Like a carnival or circus, chat is an entertaining place with a seedy underbelly and should be enjoyed with caution. But if you're careful, you can have safe, interactive fun with chat and instant messages.

21

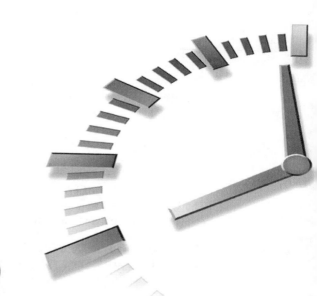

CHAPTER 22

Participating in Newsgroups

Now that you've gotten started with email and chat, it's time to look at a couple of other ways of communicating: newsgroups. Newsgroups share aspects of emailing and chatting, but they work in different ways by handling a larger volume of messages, sorted by topic.

Getting Started with Newsgroups

When you know how to use an email program, you know 90% of what you need to know to use newsgroups. Reading a message, composing a new message, and replying are all very similar in an email program and a newsreader.

Where a newsreader differs is that it retrieves messages from and *posts* (sends) messages to Internet newsgroups, sometimes known as discussion groups or, collectively, as Usenet. The newsgroups and their messages are stored on a family of servers called *news servers* or *NNTP servers*.

Your ISP or online service has a news server that you are authorized to use for reading and contributing to newsgroups. Access to one news server is all you need; the messages sent to any news server on the Internet are automatically copied—at regular intervals—to all news servers.

On any news server, you can open any newsgroup and read any current message posted to that newsgroup, no matter which news server the message was originally posted to. That's why a newsgroup on an ISP's server in New York has messages from folks in Canada, California, and the U.K.

Before you can open newsgroups and display their messages, you must configure your newsreader to contact your ISP's news server, and you must download the complete list of newsgroups from the server.

Configuring Your Newsreader

As with other types of Internet programs, there are many different newsreaders out there. In the Big Two Internet suites, the programs are the same ones you use for email: Netscape Messenger and Outlook Express. You just have to switch these programs from email mode to newsgroup mode.

To switch either program to newsgroup mode, you simply click your news server's name near the bottom of the folder list (see Figure 22.1). Observe that choosing the server changes the toolbar buttons and menu choices from those used for email to those you need for newsgroups.

FIGURE 22.1

To use Outlook Express (shown here) or Netscape Messenger for news-group activities, click your news server's name in the folder list.

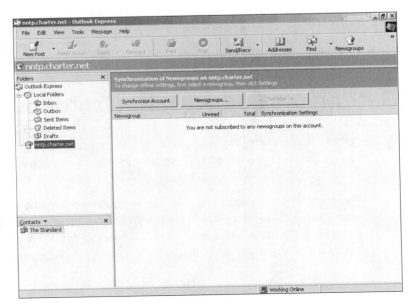

All newsreaders have a configuration dialog in which you enter the information required for communicating with your ISP's news server. That dialog always requires the address of your ISP's news server. If your newsreader is not part of a suite (and thus cannot copy configuration information from the email component), the configuration dialog also requires your email address and full name.

You'll find the configuration dialog

- For Netscape Messenger by choosing Edit, Preferences to open the Preferences dialog. In the list of Categories, choose Mail & Newsgroups. Complete the configuration settings in the Mail & Newsgroups category's Newsgroup Servers subcategory.

- For Outlook Express by completing the News dialogs of the Connection Wizard. If you choose your news server folder in Outlook Express without having configured first, the Internet Connection Wizard opens automatically.

Instead of using the Internet Connection Wizard, you can configure newsgroup access in Outlook Express by choosing Tools, Accounts, then clicking the Add button on the Internet Accounts dialog box.

Downloading the Newsgroups List

After your newsreader knows how to contact the server, you must download the complete list of newsgroups, which usually takes just a few minutes. If you open some newsreaders (including Netscape Messenger and Outlook Express) without first having downloaded the list, a prompt appears, asking whether you want to download the list.

If your newsreader does not prompt you, find a button or menu item for downloading the list by doing one of the following:

- In Netscape Messenger, make sure you are in newsgroup mode by clicking the name of your news server or choosing Communicator, Newsgroups. Choose File, Subscribe and, on the dialog that appears, click the Refresh List button.

- In Outlook Express, click the name of your news server, and then click the Newsgroups button. On the dialog that appears, click Reset List.

The list of newsgroups changes periodically, adding new groups and removing others. Netscape Messenger, Outlook Express, and some other newsreaders detect automatically when the list changes, and display a prompt asking whether you want to update your list.

Finding and Subscribing to Newsgroups

Once the list has been downloaded to your computer, you can find and subscribe to any newsgroups you want. While exploring Web pages devoted to topics that interest you,

you'll probably come across the names of related newsgroups. But newsgroups are easy to find, with or without a Web page's help.

> Unlike mailing lists, you are not required to subscribe to a newsgroup in order to use it. All subscribing really does is add the group to an easy-access list in your newsreader, to make visiting it convenient.
>
> Most people have a small list of groups they visit often, so subscribing makes sense. But in most newsreaders, you can pick a newsgroup out of the full list, or enter the group's name in a dialog box, to open the list without subscribing.

Newsgroups are perhaps the one Internet activity where names are a reliable indicator of content. Newsgroups are organized under a system of names and categories. The leftmost portion of the name shows the top-level category in which the group sits; each portion further to the right more narrowly determines the subject of the group.

For example, the top-level category `rec` contains recreational newsgroups, those dedicated to a recreational—rather than professional—discussion of their topics. So the hypothetical newsgroup name

`rec.sports.basketball.womens`

indicates that the discussion focuses on a recreational interest in women's basketball. There are thousands of `rec` groups, many `rec.sports` groups, several `rec.sports.basketball` groups, and just one `rec.sports.basketball.womens` newsgroup.

Some of the other major top-level categories include the following:

- `alt`—Alternative newsgroups, those in which the most freewheeling conversations are accepted
- `biz`—Business newsgroups and ads
- `comp`—Computer-related newsgroups
- `k12`—Education-related groups
- `misc`—Miscellaneous
- `sci`—Science-related groups

The following steps show you how to choose, subscribe to, and open groups in Outlook Express. If you are using Netscape as your newsreader, the steps are very similar. To get started, open the Communicator menu and select Newsgroups.

1. Connect to the Internet, open Outlook Express, and click the news server's name in the left-hand column (see Figure 22.2).

2. Click the Newsgroups button to open the list of newsgroups available to you (see Figure 22.3).

FIGURE 22.2

Click on the news server's name in the left-hand column of Outlook Express.

News server

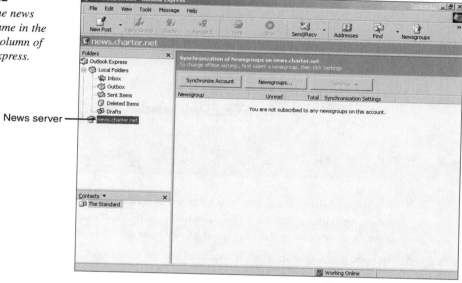

FIGURE 22.3

Click the Newsgroups button to open the list.

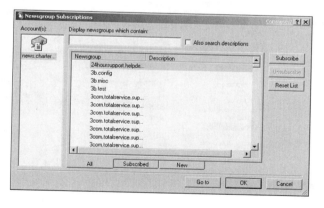

3. In the All tab, display the group's name in the Newsgroup box (see Figure 22.4). There are several ways to do this:

   - If you know the exact name of the group you want to subscribe to, type the name in the box.

   - Use the list to scroll to the group name, then click it. In the list, the groups are presented alphabetically.

- Enter a search word or phrase in the box and click OK to search for newsgroups of a particular topic.

FIGURE 22.4

Display the group's name in the Newsgroup box.

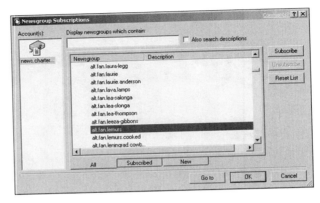

4. When the name of the group you want to subscribe to is highlighted, click the Subscribe button, then click OK. The newsgroup's name appears under your news server's name, and in the bigger list of newsgroups on your screen.

5. To open a newsgroup, click its name in the list (see Figure 22.5).

FIGURE 22.5

Click the newsgroup name to open a list of messages.

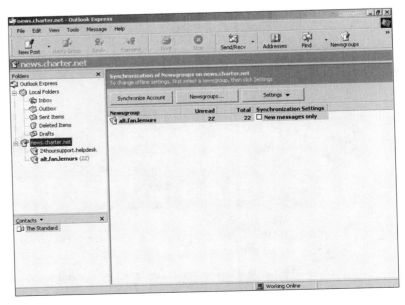

Reading Newsgroup Messages

Once you open and display a newsgroup's message list, reading messages is just like reading email messages in an email program. Single-click an item in the list to display it in the Preview pane (as shown in Figure 22.6), or double-click it to display the message in its own window.

> The message lists you see in an email program generally show messages that have been copied to your computer. But in most newsreaders, the messages in the list you see when you open a newsgroup are not on your computer; they're on the news server.
>
> All that's been copied to your computer are the message headers, to make up the list. When you display any particular message, that message is then copied to your computer. Because the messages aren't copied until you request them, you must stay online while working with newsgroups.

The tricky part about reading news messages is organizing the list in a way that works for you. Most newsreaders let you arrange the messages in myriad ways: Alphabetically by subject, by author, by date, and so on. (The options for sorting the message list in Netscape Messenger, Outlook Express, and most other Windows and Mac newsreaders appear on the View menu.) But the most useful sorting is by *thread* (a collection of related messages to a particular topic).

In effect, threads group messages by subject. Two messages can have the same subject but not the same thread, if neither is a reply to the other (or a reply to a reply to the other). If you sort messages by thread, and then by subject, you'll get all threads on a given subject grouped together.

When you sort messages by thread (see Figure 22.6), you can follow the flow of the conversation, click your way in order, through the messages to see how the discussion has progressed.

In most newsreaders, when messages are sorted by threads, the replies to a message do not appear automatically in the list; instead, a plus sign (+) appears next to the message's listing, to indicate that there are submessages—replies—to that message. To display the replies, click the plus sign.

FIGURE 22.6

You can organize your newsgroup message list by thread, to better follow the flow of individual conversations.

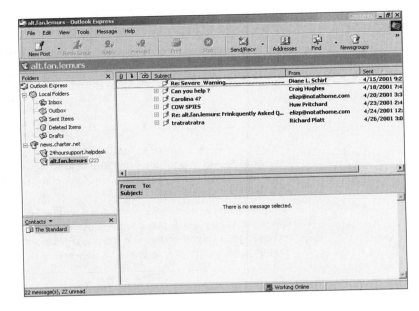

Composing and Replying to Messages

You compose and reply to messages in a newsreader exactly as you do in an email program. The only differences are in the message header, because instead of addressing a message to a person, you're addressing it to a newsgroup.

The only other important difference between sending email and newsgroup messages is the terminology you see applied on buttons and menu items:

- In email, you click Send to send a message; in a newsreader, it's either Send or Post.
- In email, you click Reply to reply to a message; in a newsreader, it's either Reply or Respond.

The easiest way to deal with that difference is to start in the right place. For example, when you want to compose a new message (not a reply) and post it to a newsgroup, begin by opening that newsgroup, then clicking your newsreader's button for composing a new message. (It's *New Msg* in Netscape Messenger, *New Post* in Outlook Express.) When the message window opens, you'll see that it's preaddressed to the currently open newsgroup.

When replying, open the message to which you want to reply, and then click the Reply (or Respond) button on the message window in which that message appears. In the message window that opens, the message is preaddressed to the appropriate newsgroup, the subject line is correctly phrased to add the reply to the same thread as the original message, and the original message is quoted in the message area (see Figure 22.7). Just add your comments, and edit the quote as necessary.

After completing a new message or reply, send the message by clicking the button or menu item labeled Send or Post.

FIGURE 22.7

Start a new message or reply while viewing the message list of a newsgroup, and that message is pread-dressed to the open newsgroup.

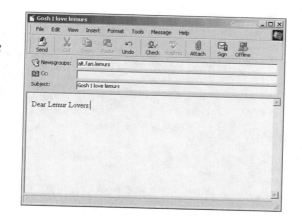

Summary

Newsgroups provide a simple way to keep up with a subject that's of interest to you. You can jump in and participate and, better yet, unsubscribe any time you want. Take some time to subscribe to one or two newsgroups, perhaps some related to your favorite hobbies or sports activities, and see what's available.

Part VIII

Enjoying the Internet

Chapter

CHAPTER 23

Searching for Information

There's just too much on the Web. It's like having a TV set with a billion channels; you could click the remote until your thumb fell off and still never find the *Seinfeld* reruns. Fortunately, a number of search sites on the Web help you find exactly what you're looking for, anywhere on the Web, and even beyond the Web in other Internet arenas. In this chapter, you'll discover what searching the Web is all about, and discover a simple but effective searching method: cruising categories. You'll also learn how to use search terms, and how to phrase them carefully to produce precisely the results you need.

What's a Search Site?

Put simply, a search site—which you may also see variously described as a search page, search tool, or search service—is a Web page where you can conduct a search of the Web. Such pages have been set up by a variety of companies that offer you free Web searching and support the service, at least in part, through the advertising you'll see prominently displayed there. Figure 23.1 shows a popular search site, Google.

The term *search engine* is sometimes used to describe a search site. But this term more accurately describes the program a search site uses, behind the scenes, to perform searches. When you hear someone refer casually to a "search engine," just remember that they probably mean "search site."

FIGURE 23.1

Google provides a simple interface and a powerful search engine.

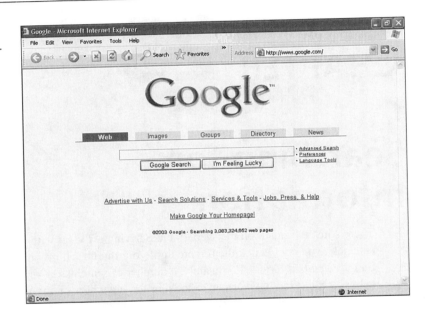

No matter which search site you use, and no matter how you use it, what you get from a search site is a page of links, each pointing to a page the search site thinks might match what you're looking for. When using a search site, your job is to provide that tool with enough information about what you're searching for so that the resulting "hit list" (see Figure 23.2) contains lots of good matches or you to explore.

FIGURE 23.2

*Search sites show you
lists of links—a "hit
list"—of Web pages
and other resources
that match what you
told the search site you
were looking for.*

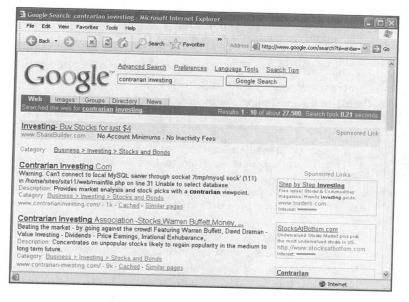

23

Can I Really Search the Whole Web?

Well, yes and no. Although using the various search sites works similarly, each has its
own unique search methods. But, more important, each has its own unique set of files—a
database—upon which all searches are based.

You see, no search site actually goes out and searches the entire Web when you ask it to.
A search site searches its own index of information about the Web—its database. The
more complete and accurate that database is, the more successful your searches are likely
to be.

The database for a search site is created in either (or both) of two ways:

- **Manually.** Folks who've created Web pages, or who've discovered pages they want
  the world to know about, fill in a form on the search site's Web site to add new
  pages (and their descriptions) to the database. If the search site's editors deem the
  site to be worthy of inclusion, it gets added.

- **Through a *crawler* (or *spider*).** All of these creepy-crawly names describe programs that systematically contact Web servers (at regular intervals), scan the contents of the server, and add information about the contents of the server to the
  database. (They "crawl" around the Web, like spiders—get it?) It takes the crawler
  a month or so to complete each of its information-gathering tours of the Web.

If a search site's database has been created by a crawler, the tool tends to deliver results that are more complete and up-to-date, whereas manually built databases tend to contain more meaningful categorization and more useful descriptive information. Also, most search sites with crawler-built databases do not offer you a way to search by browsing through categories—a valuable technique you'll pick up later in this chapter. All search sites, however, support the main search method: entering a *search term.*

Because search sites search a database and not the actual Web, they sometimes deliver results that are out of date. You might click a link that a search site delivered to you and find that the page to which it points no longer exists. That happens when a page has been moved or deleted since the last time the search site's database was updated.

How sites are ranked within their categories also varies from search site to search site. Some will simply list sites in alphabetical order. Some sell higher placement for a price, then list the rest in alphabetical order. Some display results based on the likelihood that the site matches your search term. For example, Google uses a unique page-ranking system that examines the Internet's elaborate system of links to determine a site's "value" based on the number of other sites that link to it.

Despite differences and strengths and weaknesses among the available tools, the bottom line is this: Any of the major search sites might locate a page or pages that meet your needs, or it might not. If you can't find what you want through one tool, try another. Because each tool has its own database, and each tool applies a different technical method for searching its database, no two search sites turn up exactly the same results for any given topic.

Where Are the Major Search Sites?

There are about a dozen, general-purpose search sites on the Net.

Table 23.1 lists the major players. You can visit any search site by entering its URL.

TABLE 23.1   The Top Search Sites

Tool	URL
Yahoo!	http://www.yahoo.com
Excite	http://www.excite.com
AltaVista	http://www.altavista.com

TABLE 23.1 continued

Tool	URL
Lycos	http://www.lycos.com
Google	http://www.google.com
WebCrawler	http://www.webcrawler.com
Ask Jeeves	http://www.askjeeves.com

23

Note that a few of the search sites listed in Table 23.1 are also *Web portals*, pages that are popular as home pages because they provide easy access to searching, news, and other popular services. Two other popular portals not only offer searches, but actually let you use several different popular search sites, all from the portal page. These are

- Netscape: http://home.netscape.com
- MSN: http://msn.com

For example, right from the Netscape portal, you can submit a search term to Netscape's own search engine, or to Infoseek, AltaVista, and other popular search sites (see Figure 23.3).

FIGURE 23.3

Some Web portals, such as the Netscape portal shown here, provide one-stop access to multiple searches.

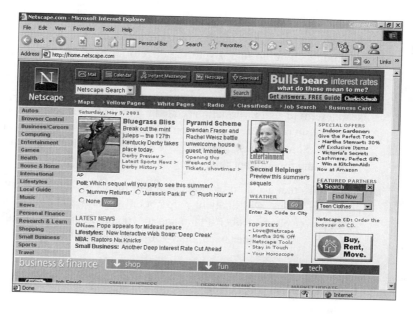

Before beginning to use search sites, take a peek at a few from the list in Table 23.1. While visiting these pages, watch for helpful links that point to

- Instructions for using the search site, often called Help.
- A text box near the top of the page, which is where you would type a search term
- Links to categories you can browse
- Reviews and ratings of recommended pages
- "Cool Sites"—a regularly updated, random list of links to especially fun or useful pages you may want to visit just for kicks
- Other search engines

Simple Searching by Clicking Categories

These days, all the major search sites accept search terms. But a few also supply a directory of categories, an index of sorts, that you can browse to locate links to pages related to a particular topic. Tools that feature such directories include Yahoo!, Excite, and Infoseek.

Why Use Categories Instead of a Search Term?

When you're first becoming familiar with the Web, forgoing the search engines and clicking through a directory's categories is not only an effective way to find stuff but also a great way to become more familiar with what's available on the Web. As you browse through categories, you inevitably discover detours to interesting topics and pages that you didn't set out to find. Exploring directories is an important part of learning how the Web works and what's on it.

Also, the broader your topic of interest, the more useful categories are. When you use a search term to find information related to a broad topic (cars, dogs, music, plants), the search site typically delivers to you a bewildering list containing hundreds or thousands of pages. Some of these pages will meet your needs, but many will be pages that merely mention the topic rather than being about the topic.

Some links that a search term delivers will match the term, but not your intentions; a search on "plant" will likely turn up not only botany and houseplant pages, but others about power plants, Robert Plant, and maybe the Plantagenet family of European lore. Categories, on the other hand, help you limit the results of your search to the right ballpark.

Using a Directory

Everything in a directory is a link; to find something in a directory, you follow those links in an organized way.

You begin by clicking a broad category heading to display a list of related subcategories (see Figure 23.4). Click a subcategory heading, and you display its list of sub-subcategories.

You continue in this fashion, drilling down through the directory structure (usually through only two to five levels), until you eventually arrive at a targeted list of links to pages related to a particular topic. You can explore those page links one by one, and after finishing with each, use your Back button to return to the search site's list and try another link.

23

FIGURE 23.4

A subcategory list in Yahoo!.

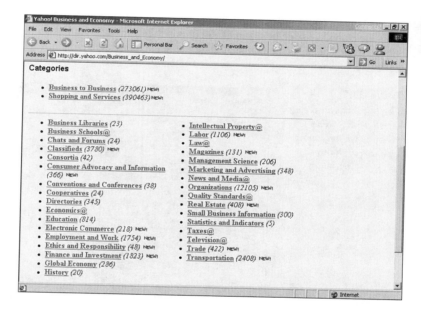

To try searching by categories, go to www.yahoo.com and enter a topic you want to search for in the text box next to the Search button. When you click Search, Yahoo! gathers all the categories related to your search term and you can then scan the topics for information you want to see.

Understanding Searches

Each of the search tools described thus far, and just about any other you might encounter on the Web, has a text box featured prominently near the top of its main page (see Figure 23.5). That text box is where you will type your search terms. Adjacent to the box, there's always a submit button, almost always labeled *Search*.

Typing a search term in a text box and then clicking the submit button to send the term to the search tool is known as submitting a search term. Such searches are sometimes also described as keyword searches, because the search term serves as a key to finding matching pages.

When you submit a search term, the search tool searches through its database of information about pages, locating any entries that contain the same combination of characters in your search term. Although the contents of the various search tool databases differ, the record for each page typically contains the page's URL, title, a brief description, and a group of keywords intended to describe the page's contents. If your search term matches anything in that record, the search tool considers the page a match.

After searching the whole database (which takes only a moment or two), the search tool displays a list of links to all the pages it determined were matches: a *hit list*.

Search term box

FIGURE 23.5

The text box you see on all search tool pages is where you type a search term.

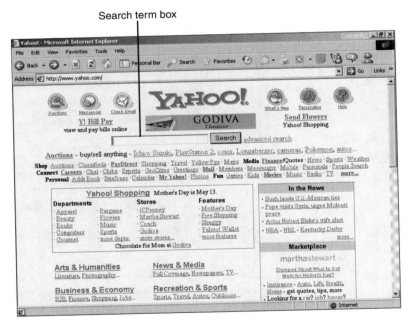

Each hit in the list is a link (see Figure 23.6). You can scroll through the hit list, reading the page titles and descriptions, to determine which page might best serve your needs, and then click the link to that page to go there. If the page turns out to be a near miss, you can use your Back button to return to the hit list and try a different page, or start over with a new search.

A hit list may show no hits at all, or it may have hundreds. Most search engines put the best hits at the top of the list, so even if your hit list has thousands of links, the links you want most likely will appear somewhere within the top 20 or so.

FIGURE 23.6

Excite organizes the hit list from best matches to worst.

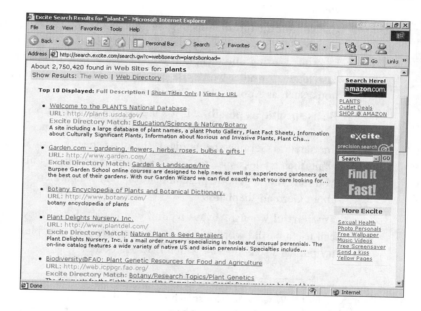

23

Some tools organize the hit list in smart ways, attempting to put the best matches at the top of the list so you see them first, and weaker matches lower in the list.

For example, suppose you use Godzilla as your search term. A particular search tool would tend to put at the top of the hit list all pages that use the word "Godzilla" in their titles or URLs because those are the pages most likely to be all about Godzilla. Matches to keywords or the page's description come lower in the list, because these might be pages that simply mention Godzilla, but aren't really about Godzilla. Even lower in the list, a tool might show links to "partial" matches, pages to which only part of the search term, such as those containing the word "God" or the partial word "zilla."

Phrasing a Simple Search

You can get artful and creative with search terms. But most of the time, you needn't get too fancy about searching. You go to the search site, type a simple word or phrase in the text box, click the submit button, and wait a few moments for the hit list to show up.

Here are a few basic tips for improving your search success:

- **Use the simplest form of a word.** The search term Terrier will match references to both "Terrier" and "Terriers." However, the term Terriers may fail to match pages using only "Terrier." Some search sites are smart enough to account for this, but some aren't. So try to use the simplest word form that's still specific to what you want.

- **Use common capitalization.** Some search sites don't care about capitalization, but some do. So it's always a good habit to capitalize words as they would most often be printed, using initial capitals on names and other proper nouns, and all lower-case letters for other words. Be careful to observe goofy computer-era capitalizations, such as AppleTalk or FrontPage.

- **Be as specific as possible.** If it's the German shepherd you want to know about, use that as your search term, not dog, which will produce too many hits, many unrelated to German shepherds. If the most specific term doesn't get what you want, then try less specific terms; if German shepherd fails, go ahead and try dog. You may find a generic page about dogs, on which there's a link to information about German shepherds.

- **Try partial words.** Always try full words first. But if they're not working out, you can use a partial word. If you want to match both "puppies" and "puppy," you can try pup as a search term, which matches both.

> When you use a search term in Yahoo! (http://www.yahoo.com), the hit list typically shows not only pages, but Yahoo! categories related to the search term. You can try one of the pages, or start exploring related category headings from the head start the search provides.

The following steps show you how to perform a simple search:

1. Go to AltaVista at http://www.altavista.com (see Figure 23.7).
2. Click the Search Term box, and type DaVinci for your search term.
3. Click the submit button, labeled Search, to reveal the hit list (see Figure 23.8).
4. Click any link in the hit list to see where it leads. You'll be taken to Web pages related to the search.
5. Click Back to return to the hit list. Scroll to the bottom of the page, and observe that there are links for moving ahead to more pages of the hit list.

Figure 23.7

Using AltaVista for your search engine.

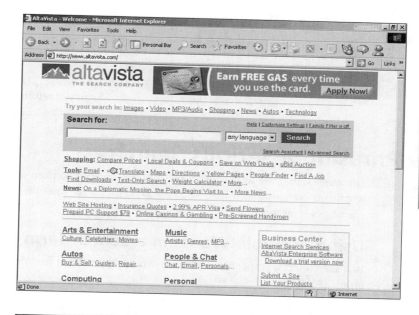

Figure 23.8

Click the Search button to reveal the hit list.

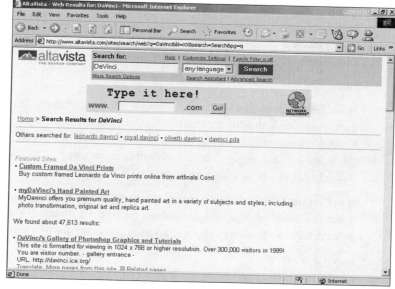

Observe that the Search Term box appears on every page of the hit list. You can start a new search at any time, from any page of the hit list, by entering a new search term.

Some search sites display the Search Term box only on the top page; to start a new search in those, just click Back until you return to the top page.

Phrasing a Serious Search

Sometimes, in order to phrase a very specific search, you need multiple words. And when you use multiple words, you may need to use *operators* to control the way a search site works with those words.

Using Multiple Words in a Search Term

In a search term, you can use as many words as you need in order to make the term specific.

For example, suppose you want to learn about boxer dogs. You could use the search term *boxer*. Although that term might turn up some hits about boxer dogs, those hits may be buried among hundreds of other links about prizefighters, China's Boxer rebellion, Tony Danza (actor and ex-boxer), and people named Boxer. So to make your search more specific, you could use two words:

boxer dog

Now the search engine will look for pages that contain both "boxer" and "dog," which greatly increases the chances that hits will be about boxer dogs, because most pages about all those other "boxers" mentioned earlier will not also be about "dogs." You still might see a link to a page about George Foreman's dog, if he has one. But the hit list will be a lot closer to what you want.

If my hit list is still cluttered with the wrong kind of pages, you might remember that a boxer is a breed of dog, so a page about boxer dogs probably also uses the term "breed" prominently. So you might try a third term to further narrow the hit list:

boxer dog breed

If you get too specific, you may accidentally omit a few pages you want—there may be boxer dog pages that don't use "breed" anywhere that would show up in a search database. So it's best to start off with a happy medium (a term that's specific but not overly restrictive), see what you get, and then try subsequent searches using more or less specific terms, depending on what's in the hit list.

Using Operators to Control Searches

Whenever you use multiple words, you're using operators, even if you don't know it. *Operators* are words you use between the words in a multi-word search term to further define exactly how the search site will handle your term. Using operators in this way is sometimes described as Boolean logic. There are three basic operators used in searching:

- **And**—When you use *and* between words in a search term, you tell the search engine to find only those pages that contain both of the words—pages that contain only one or the other are not included in the hit list.

- **Or**—When you use *or* between words in a search term, you tell the search engine to find all pages that contain either of the words—all pages that contain either word alone, or both words, are included in the hit list.

- **Not**—When you use *not* between words in a search term, you tell the search engine to find all pages that contain the word before *not*, then to remove from the hit list any that also contain the word following *not*.

Table 23.2 illustrates how and, or, and not affect a search site's use of a term.

TABLE 23.2   How Operators Work in Search Terms

Search Term	What a Search Tool Matches
Dodge and pickup	Only pages containing both "Dodge" and "pickup".
Dodge or pickup	All pages containing either "Dodge" or "pickup", or both words.
Dodge not pickup	All pages that contain "Dodge" but do not also contain "pickup". (This gets all the Dodge pages, and then eliminates any about pickups.)
Dodge and pickup and models	Pages that contain all three words.
Dodge or pickup or models	Pages that contain any of the three words.
Dodge not Chrysler	Pages that contain "Dodge" but do not also contain "Chrysler". (This gets all the Dodge pages, and then eliminates any that also mention Chrysler.)

Before using operators in search terms, check out the options or instructions area of the search site you intend to use (see Figure 23.9). Most search sites support and, or, and not, but some have their own little quirks about how you must go about it. For example, Excite and AltaVista prefer that you insert a plus sign (+) at the beginning of a word rather than precede it with and.

Another powerful way to use multiple words is to do an exact phrase match, which most search sites support. In an exact phrase match, you surround the multi-word term with quotes to instruct the search to match only pages that show the same words as the term, in the same order.

For example, suppose you want to know about the film *Roman Holiday*. A search on Roman Holiday will probably match any page that uses both of those words anywhere, in any order, together or separately. That'll still get you some good hits, but a lot of bad ones, too. A search on "Roman Holiday" (in quotes) matches only pages that use the exact phrase Roman Holiday, so the hit list will be much better targeted to what you want.

FIGURE 23.9
Click the Advanced Search link near Yahoo!'s Search Term box to learn how Yahoo! supports operators and other advanced search techniques.

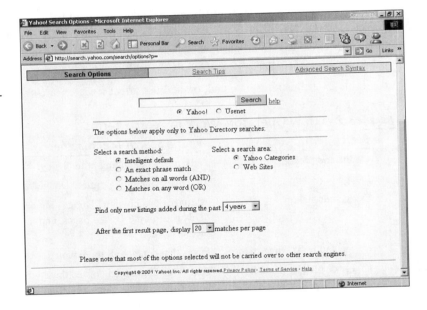

Conducting a Super Search

In high school, they warned you that you'd need algebra one day. If you ignored that warning (like I did), then you've forgotten all of that stuff about grouping parts of equations in parentheses.

If you remember algebra, then note that you can apply those techniques for super searches. For example, suppose you wanted to find pages about pro boxers (the kind that hit each other). You would need a hit list that matched all pages with boxer or prizefighter, but eliminated any that matched dog (to weed out the boxer dog pages). You could do that with either of the following algebraic terms:

(boxer or prizefighter) not dog

(boxer not dog) or prizefighter

If you can apply these techniques, drop your old math teacher a note of thanks for a job well done.

23

About Site Searches

The major search sites mentioned in this chapter are for finding information that may reside anywhere on the Web. Because they have that enormous job to do, they can't always find everything that's on a particular server.

However, large Web sites often provide their own search tools, just for finding stuff on that site alone. For example, Microsoft's Web site is huge, encompassing thousands of pages. So Microsoft supplies a search tool (you can open it from a Search link atop most pages) just for finding stuff at Microsoft. Even fairly small sites may have their own search tools; Figure 23.10 shows one for *Discover* magazine.

You use a site's search tool just as you would any search site, by entering a search term. Many such search tools even support multi-word searches and operators—but always check the instructions accompanying the search tool to find out whether it supports fancy searches.

FIGURE 23.10

Discover *magazine supplies its own search tool just for finding stuff on its site.*

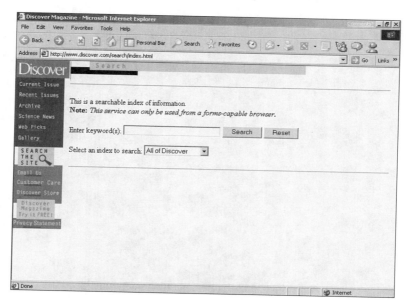

Summary

Most of the time, performing an Internet search is simple. Just type a likely sounding word in any search tool's text box, click the submit button, and wait for your hits. But the more you know about narrowing your searches by choosing just the right word, using multiple words, and using operators, the better your odds of always finding exactly what you're looking for.

CHAPTER 24

Downloading Programs and Files

People who use the Internet have one thing universally in common: They all use a computer. So it's no surprise that computer programs and files are the most common "things" you can acquire through the Internet. You can find online all kinds of Internet software, other kinds of programs (like games or word processors), documents (such as books or articles), and other useful files such as utilities and plug-ins. Once you locate the items you want using search engines, you'll be ready to download those files and prepare those files to use on your computer.

What's Downloading, Anyhow?

Downloading is the act of copying a computer file from a server, through the Net, to your computer so you can use it there, just as if you had installed it from a disk or CD-ROM.

Click a Link, Get a File

Whether you've thought about it or not, when you're on the Web, you're really downloading all the time. For example, every time you open a Web page, the files that make up that page are temporarily copied from the server to your computer.

But the downloading described here is deliberate downloading: You locate a link in a Web page that points to a file or program you want (see Figure 24.1). To download the file, click the link, and then follow any prompts that appear. It's really that simple.

> Observe that most of the file links in Figure 24.1 have the filename extension .zip. This extension indicates that these files are compressed archive files, also known as Zip files. You'll learn more about Zip files later in this chapter.

FIGURE 24.1

You can download files from the Web simply by clicking links that lead to files, such as those shown here.

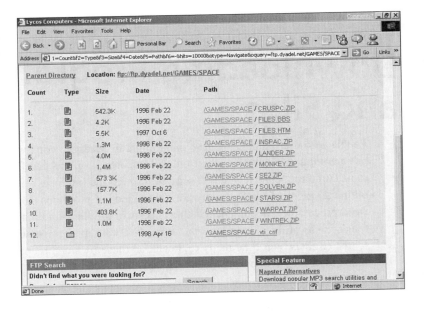

How Long Does Downloading Take?

The larger the file, the longer it will take to download. That's why the size of the file is usually shown somewhere in or near the link for downloading it (refer to Figure 24.1). The size is expressed in *kilobytes* (*K* or *KB*) for smaller files, or in *megabytes* (*M* or *MB*) for larger files. One K equals 1,024 *bytes*, or characters. One M equals 1,024K.

How long does it take to download a file of a given size? That depends on many factors, including the speed of your Internet connection, and how busy the server is. But over a connection of 28.8Kbps, a 1MB file typically downloads in around 10 minutes.

You'll find lots of great stuff to download that's less than 1MB. However, many programs or multimedia files can be much, much larger. A download of the entire Internet Explorer program from Microsoft's Web site can take several hours, even through a 56Kbps connection.

With experience, you'll develop a sense of how long downloading a file of a given size takes on your system. After you have that sense, always carefully consider the size of the file and whether you want to wait that long for it, before starting the download.

Just for practice, and to understand what to do when you locate a file you want, download the Adobe Acrobat reader, a program that enables you to display documents in the Adobe Acrobat (.pdf) file format, which are common online. If you already have an Adobe Acrobat reader, or just don't want one, you can cancel the download before it finishes.

1. Go to Adobe's Web site at http://www.adobe.com, scroll to the bottom of the page, and click the button labeled Get Acrobat Reader (see Figure 24.2).

24

Button

FIGURE 24.2
Click the Get Acrobat Reader icon.

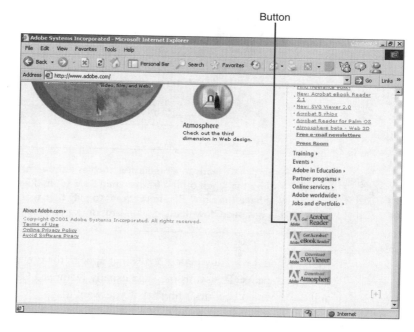

2. The first page you see will compare Acrobat Reader's functions with the full-featured Adobe Acrobat, which costs a couple hundred dollars retail. Because you're only downloading the free program for now, click Get Acrobat Reader at the bottom of the page.

3. Complete the choices on the form, and then click the Download button.

4. The exact dialog boxes you'll see differ by browser and computer type. Sometimes you may be asked whether you want to save it or run it from its current location. Usually it's smartest to choose the Save option, and then to open the file later. The next dialog box you might see prompts you to select the location (folder or desktop) and filename for the downloaded file (see Figure 24.3). Choosing a location is a good idea so that you can easily locate and use the file after downloading (you might even want to create a download folder to house all your downloaded files). Don't mess with the filename, though—if you don't supply a new filename, the file will be stored on your computer under its original name, which is usually best.

FIGURE 24.3

Choose a location for the file and save it to disk.

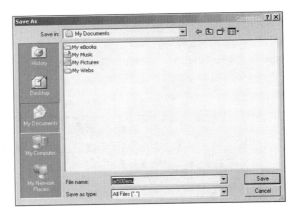

When a link leads to a media file, such as a sound or video clip, you can choose the Open option (rather than Save to disk) when downloading. If you have the right plug-in program to play that type of file, as soon as the file has been downloaded, your browser can play the file automatically.

5. After you deal with any dialog boxes that appear, the download begins, and a status message appears. The status message usually features a Cancel button, so you can quit the download before it finishes if you want to.

When the download is complete, the status message disappears. You can continue browsing or go use the file you just downloaded, which you can find in the folder you selected in the dialog box described in Step 4.

Choosing Files You Can Use

You can download any type of computer file. But not every file or program you find online works on every type of computer.

Web browsing enables different kinds of computers to all look at the same online content, so after a while people tend to forget that on the Web, PCs, Macs, and other types of computers each use different kinds of files and programs.

When you search for files and programs, you must make sure that the ones you choose are compatible with your computer type, and often also with your operating system (Windows 95/98/Me/NT/2000/XP; DOS; Mac OS9 or OS X; Unix flavor; and so on).

The Two File Types: Program and Data

Although there are dozens of different types of files, they all generally fall into either of two groups:

24

- **Program files**—A program file contains a program—a game, a word processor, a plug-in, a utility, and so on. Program files are almost always designed to run on only one type of computer and operating system. For example, a program file designed for a Mac typically will not run in Windows. However, many programs are available in similar but separate versions, one for each system type.

- **Data files**—A data file contains information that can be displayed, or used in some other way, by a program. For example, a word processing document is a data file, to be displayed by a word processing program. Like program files, some data files can be used only by a particular program running on a particular computer type. But most data file types can be used on a variety of systems.

Popular files are usually available from multiple servers, spread across the continent or globe. Often, a downloading page will refer to the servers as *mirror sites* because they all offer an identical copy of the file, a "mirror image."

Common Data File Types on the Net

When you encounter a link to a file, you'll usually have no trouble telling what system the file is made for.

Often, before arriving at the link, you will have navigated through a series of links or form selections in which you specified your system type, so when you finally see links to files, they all point to files that can run on your system. In other cases, the link itself—or text near the link—will tell you the system requirements for the file.

Even when the link doesn't fill you in, you can often tell a file's system requirements by its filename extension, the final part of the filename that follows the period. (For example, in the filename MONTY.DOC, the extension is DOC.) Table 24.1 shows many of the most common file types online.

TABLE 24.1   Common File Types You'll Find Online for Downloading

Extension	Type of File	Requirements
.exe, .com	Program file (a game, utility, application, and so on)	Runs on one (and only one) type of system. Always read any text near the link to be sure that a particular .exe or .com file will run on your computer.
.doc	Word document	Can be opened and edited in either the Windows or Mac version of Word, or Windows's WordPad program.
.pdf	Adobe Acrobat document	Can be opened in the Adobe Acrobat Reader program (available for a variety of systems) or in a browser equipped with an Adobe Acrobat plug-in. Can also be converted and displayed by some word processing programs.
.xls	Excel	Can be opened and edited in spreadsheet either the Windows or Mac version of Excel.
.txt, .asc	Plain text file	Can be opened in any word processor or text editor (such as Windows's Notepad) on any system, and displayed by any browser.
.wri	Windows Write	Can be displayed by Windows document Write (in Windows 3.1) or WordPad (in Windows 95/98/NT/XP).
.avi, .mp3, .mov, .qt, .mpg, .au, .mid, .snd	Various types of media files	Can be run by various player programs, or by your browser if it is equipped for them.
.zip	Archive, containing one or more compressed files	Must be decompressed (unzipped) before the files it contains can be used; see "Working with Zip Files" later in this chapter.

Finding Sites That Help You Find Files

Where you begin looking for a file depends on the manner in which that file is offered on the Web, or rather, in what way that file is licensed for use by those other than its creator. Most software falls into one of the following four groups:

- **Commercial**—The programs you can buy in a box at the software store. Many software companies have Web sites where you can learn about their products and often download them as well. Typically, you fill in an online form to pay for the software, and then download it.

- **Demo**—Demo software is commercial software that has some features disabled, or automatically stops working—expires—after you use it for a set number of days. Demo software is distributed free on commercial and shareware sites and provides a free preview of the real thing.

- **Shareware**—Shareware is software you're allowed to try out for free, but for which you are supposed to pay. After the trial period (usually 30 days), you either pay the programmer or stop using the program. Some shareware expires or has features disabled, like demo software, so you can't continue using it without paying.

- **Freeware**—Freeware is free software you can use all you want, as long as you want, for free.

24

All-Purpose Shareware Sites

Sites for downloading shareware appear all over the Web. Many popular shareware programs have their very own Web sites, and links to shareware products can be found on thousands of pages, such as Yahoo!'s shareware directory at `http://www.yahoo.com/Computers_and_Internet/Software/Shareware/`.

But when you're looking for a shareware, freeware, or demo program to do a particular job, you'll have better luck if you visit a Web site designed to provide access to a wide range of products, sites such as

- Shareware.com, whose easy-to-remember URL is `http://shareware.com` (see Figure 24.4).

- Download.com (Can you guess the URL?)

These sites provide search tools for finding files. But the hits they produce are always either links to files that match your search, or links to other Web pages from which those files can be downloaded.

The key to using Shareware.com, Download.com, and similar file-finders is to make sure that your search specifies both of the following:

- The kind of file or program you seek. Email, word processing, game, paint program—whatever you want.

- Your computer type and operating system. Windows 95/98/Me/XP, Mac OS8/OS9/OS X, and so on.

If you include this information in your search, the hit list will show only files and programs of the kind you want, and only those that run on your particular system.

FIGURE 24.4

Shareware.com, a directory for finding shareware, freeware, and demo software.

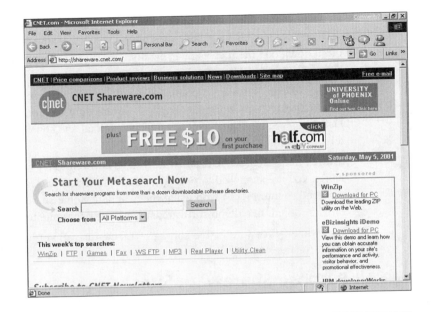

 If it's mainstream, commercial software you want to buy—you know, the stuff you buy in a box at the software store—check out one of the online software shops, such as Beyond.com (beyond.com) or MicroWarehouse (warehouse.com).

For practice, try finding a solitaire game for your system at Shareware.com by following these steps:

1. Go to Shareware.com at `http://www.shareware.com`, type `solitaire` in the box labeled Search For, choose your system type from the By Platform list, and then click the Search button (see Figure 24.5).

2. Read the descriptions of the solitaire programs for your system type, choose a program that you'd like to have, and click its filename.

3. A page appears with a description of the program. Click on the Download Now link, and a new list of links appears, each link pointing to the identical file stored on a different server. Click one to start the download (see Figure 24.6).

FIGURE 24.5
Type in **solitaire** *at Shareware.com and choose an operating system.*

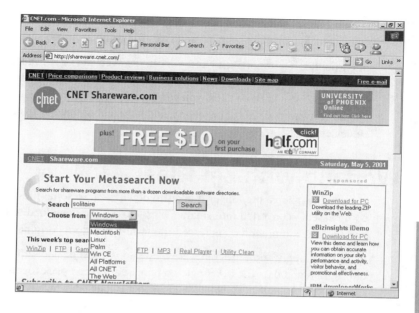

FIGURE 24.6
Choose a site from which to download the program.

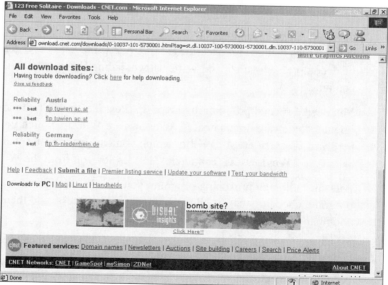

Commercial Software Sites

As a Web user, you have a lot to gain by frequenting the Web sites of any commercial software companies whose products you use regularly. There, you can not only learn about new and enhanced versions of products you use, but also pick up tips, free enhancements, product support, and fixes for common problems.

In particular, it's important to know about the Web site of the maker of the operating system you use on your computer: Microsoft's site (for Windows users) and Apple's (for Mac OS folks). On these sites, you can find all sorts of free updates and utilities for your operating system, fixes for problems, and news about upcoming new releases and enhancements.

Working with Zip Files

The larger a file is, the longer it takes to download. So some files online are compressed—converted into smaller files—to cut the download time. After downloading, you must decompress a compressed file to restore it to its original size and use it.

Also, most application programs are made up not just of one fat file, but of a collection of program and data files. A single compressed file can pack together many separate files, so they can all be downloaded together in one step. When you decompress a compressed file containing multiple files—which is sometimes called an *archive*—the files are separated.

Several forms of compression are used online, but most compression programs create archive files that use a format called *Zip*. A Zip file uses the extension .zip, and it must be decompressed—unzipped—after downloading before you can use the file or files it contains.

You need a special program to unzip Zip files. If you don't already have one, the most popular shareware unzippers for Windows are WinZip, which you can download from http://www.winzip.com, or PKZip, which you can get from PKWare at http://www.pkware.com. Windows XP can unzip Zip files for you from the Windows Explorer.

After installing an unzipping program, you can decompress any Zip file by opening the program, choosing the Zip file you want to decompress, and then choosing Extract from a toolbar or menu.

One special type of .exe program file is called a self-extracting archive, which is a compressed file or files, just like a Zip file.

Unlike a Zip file, however, a self-extracting archive file does not require an unzipping program. Instead, it decompresses itself automatically when you open it (usually by double-clicking). Most large applications offered online, such as Web browsers, download as self-extracting archives.

Watching Out for Viruses

A few years back, in the movie *Independence Day*, Jeff Goldblum stopped an intergalactic invasion by uploading a computer virus into the aliens' mothership and thereby scrambling the alien system.

Computer viruses are created by immature, sick people, who get a thrill out of cheap little tricks—viruses that display silly messages on your screen—or major attacks—viruses that crash whole computer systems.

If you saw *Independence Day*, you might have wondered, "If Jeff Goldblum puts a virus on the Internet, and I happen to download a file containing that virus, what might happen to my computer? Would I still be able to conquer Earth? Can I get Jeff to come over and fix it?"

Viruses are a significant threat to anyone who spends time online, uses email, and downloads files. It's just plain silly to work on the Internet and not arm yourself with some protection. You can catch a virus from files you download, and from email messages (and files attached to email messages). The key rule when it comes to email is to never open any message or open any file from someone you don't know.

To play it safe, try to limit your downloading choices to commercial sites or reliable shareware sources (such as Shareware.com). Big suppliers regularly scan files for viruses. In addition to exercising caution about where you download files from, you should also install and use a virus scanning program, such as Norton AntiVirus, which can find viruses in files and, in some cases, kill the virus while saving the file. And, make sure to keep your antivirus software current by regularly downloading the updates to it from the manufacturer.

> If you intend to scan for viruses, *do not* open or run a file you have downloaded until *after* you have used your antivirus software to check it for viruses.

Remember: A virus in a file does no harm until you open the file (or run the program, if the file is a program). So you can download anything safely, and then scan it with the virus program before you ever open or run it. If the virus program detects a bug it cannot remove, just delete the file to delete the virus.

Downloading Files in AOL

Members of America Online have a special advantage in the area of downloads: AOL's Download Center. After signing on to AOL, you can access it by opening the AOL Services menu and selecting Download Center (see Figure 24.7).

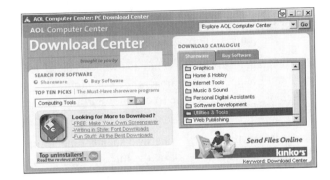

The right window offers two tabs: Shareware and Buy Software. The Buy Software tab connects you to commercial software, whereas the Shareware tab links to, well, shareware.

Both tabs are organized into catalogs that are full of software you can download. After you've chosen the type of file that you want, you'll find a list of files that will fit your needs.

America Online also offers a feature that's great for people who don't want to take the time to download a file during their online session. You can schedule a download for later by selecting the file(s) you want and clicking the Download Later button. Then, you can schedule the download for the middle of the night, when you're (perhaps) asleep.

Summary

Finding the files you need begins with starting at the right site: a commercial software site, a shareware search site, and so on. When you start in the right place, and understand the simple steps required to select, download, and (sometimes) unzip files, getting any files you want is a snap.

CHAPTER 25

Finding People

Using mainly the search techniques you've picked up in the preceding chapters, you can find people on the Internet—or rather, the email addresses, mailing addresses, or telephone numbers through which particular people can be reached.

This people-finding power is one of the Internet's most valuable and controversial capabilities. Applied properly, it can aid research, locate missing persons, track down deadbeats delinquent in their child support payments, reunite old friends, and even help adult adoptees find their birth parents, if they so desire. When abused, this capability aids stalkers and overaggressive direct marketers. Unfortunately, as is always the case with freedom of information, there's no practical way to preserve the benefit of this capability without also enabling its abuse.

Finding the People-Finding Sites

As with all types of search tools, every people-finder on the Web draws from a different database of names and contact information. Note that these tools don't find only people who have Internet accounts; they search public telephone directories, and thus can show you addresses and telephone numbers of people who don't even use the Internet.

In this chapter, you'll learn about people-finding methods and sites that are free on the Internet. There are a number of people finders that charge a fee. These can be useful for finding long-lost relatives or classmates, but they aren't necessarily better than the searching you do yourself. Do some research before paying for such a people-finding service.

For any particular name, a search using one tool may turn up no hits, while a search with a different tool may hit pay dirt. It's important to know where several different search tools are, so that if one tool fails, you can try another. Figure 25.1 shows a typical people-finder page.

If there's a possibility the person you seek has his or her own home page on the Web, using a special people-finding tool may not be necessary. It's usually a good idea to first perform an ordinary search with a tool like Google or AltaVista, using the person's name (plus maybe the city or town they live in, to help narrow the search) as your search term.

Such a search will likely turn up that person's home page, if they have one (along with any references to other folks who have the same name, of course). If you visit the home page, you'll likely find contact information on it.

You use these tools like any other search tool: Enter as much as you know about the person—name, city, and so on—and the tool finds matches in its database. But that database contains only contact information, so your search won't turn up all sorts of references that have nothing to do with contacting someone.

Some of the better people-finders include the following:

- Yahoo!'s People Search, at `http://people.yahoo.com`
- Excite's Email Lookup (for email addresses), at `http://www.excite.com/reference/email_lookup/email`
- Bigfoot, at `http://www.Bigfoot.com`
- InfoSpace, at `http://www.infospace.com`

FIGURE 25.1

InfoSpace is one of several handy people-finders on the Web.

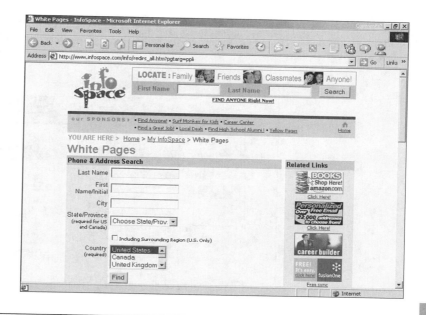

Depending on the people-finder you use and the options you choose, you may find a person's mailing address, phone number, or email address (or all three). There's also a chance, of course, that you'll find no matches.

25

Finding Yourself in Yahoo!'s People Search

Because you're probably already familiar with Yahoo!, Yahoo!'s People Search is a great first place to try finding someone.

1. Go to Yahoo!'s People Search at `http://people.yahoo.com` (see Figure 25.2).

2. Fill in the boxes in the Telephone Search form: First Name, Last Name, City, and so on, and then click the button labeled Search.

3. On the list of matching names (not shown), click Back to return to the People Search page.

4. Now fill in the boxes under Email Search, and click the Search button (see Figure 25.3).

FIGURE 25.2

Go to Yahoo!'s People Search site.

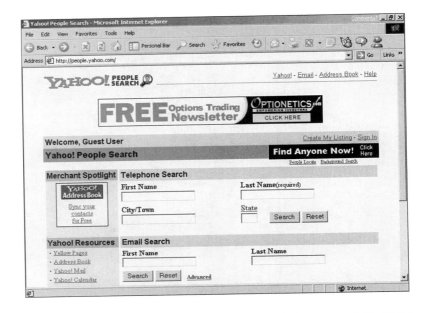

FIGURE 25.3

Fill in the Email Search form and click Search.

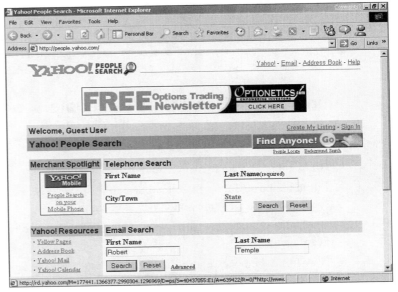

5. Just for fun, click Back to try another Email Search, but this time, leave some boxes empty, to see how these tools will show you more names to choose from when you don't have complete information about a person.

> **Your Privacy Is a Concern**
>
> If you found yourself in your Yahoo! searches, you may be wondering, "How did my phone number, email address, or other information get on the Web?"
>
> Most of the information in the search tool databases—including names, addresses, and phone numbers—comes from public telephone records. By agreeing to have your name, address, and phone number listed in the phone book, you've agreed to make it public, so there's nothing to prevent it from winding up in a Web database. Some databases may also obtain records from other online databases (such as your ISP's user directory), or even from online forms you've submitted from Web pages.
>
> So even if you have an unlisted telephone number (which phone companies call "unpublished"), a record about you may find its way into a database from another source. That's just one reason you must be careful about how and when you enter information about yourself in an online form.

Using People-Finders Through Your Email Program

25

There is a family of people-finding directories, known collectively as *LDAP directories*, that are specifically and solely for finding email addresses, both in North America and worldwide.

Some LDAP directories, such as the aforementioned Bigfoot (`http://www.Bigfoot.com`) are accessible through a Web page. But these and several other LDAPs may also be accessed from within some email programs. This enables you to search for an email address from within your email program—which is, after all, the place you need email addresses.

The two email programs included in the big two Internet suites both support LDAP searches, from within their address book, a utility that helps you keep track of email addresses.

Searching an LDAP directory from within your email program is just like using a people-finder on the Web: You fill in a name and other information in a form. The only difference is in getting to that form. Instead of opening a Web page, you go online, open your email program, and navigate to the LDAP search form.

For example, in Outlook Express, click the Find button and choose People (see Figure 25.4). A search dialog opens. Use the top list in the dialog to choose the LDAP directory to search, fill in the other boxes in the dialog, and then click Find Now.

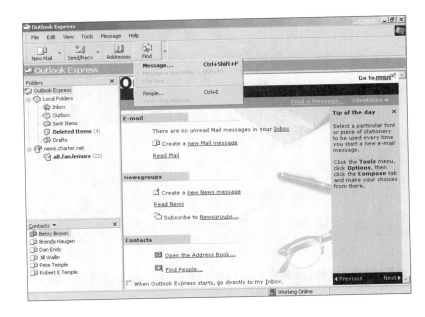

FIGURE 25.4

Searching an LDAP directory from within Outlook Express's Address Book.

Finding People in America Online

America Online members have an advantage when looking for others on the service—because America Online controls the database, it's easy to search.

However, the individual members are the ones who fill out their member profiles in AOL. So, the likelihood of your finding the person you're looking for depends directly on how well that particular member filled out their profile. Many people fill their profiles with jokes, making a serious attempt to find them unlikely to be successful (perhaps that's the point of the jokes!).

Another problem, of course, is the possibility that the person is not a member of AOL at all. If that's the case, you're just as well off to search using an LDAP directory over the Web.

There are several different ways to find people through (and on) America Online. In addition, there are ways you can learn about people if you know their screen name but nothing else. Here are the options:

- **People Directory**—This allows you to search the AOL member directory through either a Quick Search or an Advanced Search (see Figure 25.5). You can search for specific things in a person's profile, such as a city of residence, or you can search by name. To access this feature, open the People menu and select People Directory.

FIGURE 25.5

Searching AOL's Member Directory can help you find another AOL member.

- **White Pages**—Allows you to search for people through AOL. This is similar to a search over the Web. To access this feature, select White Pages from the People menu.

- **Get Directory Listing**—If you know a person's screen name and want to read their member profile, select Get Directory Listing from the People menu. Then, enter the screen name, click OK, and you'll see the person's directory listing.

- **Locate Member Online**—By selecting this option from the People menu, you can find out whether a given member is online at the present time. If you know the person's screen name, you enter it, and AOL will tell you what they are doing on the service at the moment.

Other Folk-Finding Tips

The all-around easiest ways to find people online are those I've already described. But if those don't pay off for you, try the following methods.

Try an Advanced Search

People-finders are designed first and foremost to be easy to use. For that reason, many do not display their most advanced tools at first. They present an easy-to-use, quick form for general-purpose people-searching, but also supply an optional, advanced form for more sophisticated searches. The advanced form comes in handy when the basic form doesn't dig up the person you want.

For example, on Yahoo!'s people-finder page, you'll see a link labeled Advanced, which brings up the Advanced search page shown in Figure 25.6.

Besides providing you with more options for more narrowly identifying the person you're looking for, the Advanced search provides a check box for *SmartNames*. When this check box is checked, Yahoo! searches not only for the exact name you supplied, but also for common variations of that name. If you entered "Edward," the search might match records for "Edward," "Ed," and "Eddy," too. This feature increases the chances of finding the right person when you're not sure which name form the person uses.

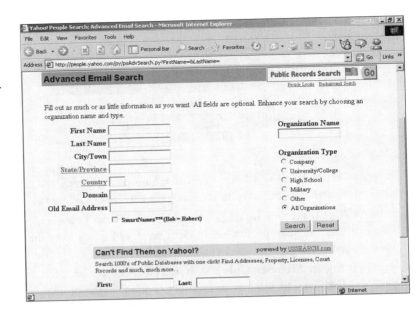

FIGURE 25.6

In addition to their basic, easy-to-use form, some people-finding tools also offer an advanced form for more sophisticated searches.

Use a Company or School Directory

Do you know the name of the company the person works for, or a school he or she attends? Many companies, colleges, and universities have their own Web sites, and those Web sites often contain employee and student directories you can browse or search (see Figure 25.7). Just search for and go to the Web site, then browse for a directory.

Try Name Variations

Might the person you're looking for sometimes use a different name than the one you've been using as a search term? Try alternative spellings (Sandy, Sandi) or nicknames. Try both the married name and birth name of people who may have married or divorced recently. You may even want to try a compound name made out of both the birth name and married name (for example, Jacqueline Bouvier Kennedy). I know both men and women who use compound or hyphenated married names.

Use Old Communications to Start the New Ones

Do you know either the mailing address or phone number of the person, and just want his or her email address? Don't be shy: Call or write, and just ask for the person's email address so you can conduct future communication online. Life's too short.

FIGURE 25.7

Like many companies and schools, the University of Minnesota offers on its Web site a searchable directory of students and faculty.

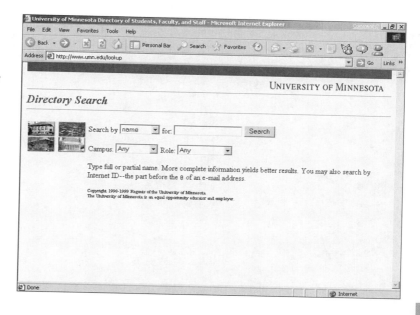

Summary

25

You know from earlier chapters that you can find all sorts of information and files online. But you may not have realized how easy it is to use the Internet to find an old friend or other contact you need. Most often, finding someone on the Web is a simple matter of opening a people-finding search tool and typing a name. And, if your search turns up an email address, you have a very powerful way of getting in touch with that person.

CHAPTER 26

Protecting Your Family's Online Experience

Is cyberspace a family place? If you have kids, you might be wondering. One day the media touts the Net as the greatest thing since the printing press, and the next it's the harbinger of the Apocalypse, an instrument of pornographers, pedophiles, and disgruntled loners.

Actually, it's neither (and both). It's a tool, and like any tool, it can be put to good uses or bad. A hammer can build shelter or bash a finger. I think an adult has a right to use the Internet any way he or she wants to—within the law and without bothering anybody. But if you have kids who will use the Net, you need to know how to insulate them from the Net's racier regions.

Choosing a Family Starting Point

A good first step for family Web surfing is to choose a good starting point, a "family home page" of sorts. A good general-purpose family page provides a jumping-off point in which all the links are family-friendly. Kids starting out should be taught to begin at that page, use only the links on that page, and use the Back button to return to that page after visiting any of its links. (If you make that page your home page, they can click the Home button to return to it anytime.) These habits corral a kid's surfing to a limited, appropriate range of sites.

One way to safeguard your Internet experience is to choose an Internet provider that censors content for you. These ISPs specialize in providing Internet service to families. Check out:

- `http://www.cleanfamily.com`
- `http://family.net`
- `http://ratedg.com`

For most folks who want their Internet service controlled for the kids but free for the adults, these services are an extreme. But if the principal surfers in your home are the kids, you might want to see whether one of these services has a local access number for you.

You'll probably want to browse and search for a family page that best fits your family. Here are a few good suggestions:

- Yahooligans! at `http://www.yahooligans.com`. A kid's offshoot of the Yahoo! search tool with links and a search engine that both lead only to good kid stuff (see Figure 26.1).
- 4Kids Treehouse at `http://www.4kids.com`. A colorful site with great links and activities for kids, plus resources for parents.
- Family.com at `http://www.family.com`. An online family magazine.
- Ask Jeeves for Kids at `http://www.ajkids.com`.
- The American Library Association's Cool Sites for Kids page at `http://www.ala.org/alsc/children_links.html`.

FIGURE 26.1

Yahooligans! makes a good starting point for family Web surfing.

Important Family Safety Steps

Everybody's different, and so is every family. It's not my place to say what's best for you or your kids, but if you want some guidance about keeping your kids safe online, permit me to offer a few suggestions here. Then follow your own judgment.

Supervise!

This one's so obvious, and yet so difficult. As a parent, I know that it simply isn't practical to supervise our kids every second of the day. And if you're a tired parent of a pre-teen, the idea of the kid going off to his room for an hour to surf the Net is appealing.

You must make your own choice about when to cut the cord, based not on what's convenient but on your kid. Some kids are mature enough to surf responsibly at seven, but others can't be trusted at 17. Only you know your kids well enough to decide.

If you're not sure whether your kid is ready to go solo but you don't have time to supervise, keep him offline until either you are sure that he's ready or you have the time. The Internet has lots to offer a kid, but your kid can live without it until the time is right for both of you.

26

Sure, some so-called experts say it's not good to spy on your kids. But if your kid surfs unsupervised and you want to know what she's been up to, open the browser's history file to see exactly where she's been. It's the cyber-equivalent of searching your kid's room for drugs or weapons.

If you, as a diligent parent, notice signals that your kid might be at risk, it's important for you to find a way to supervise or control that kid's online activities, *or* keep tabs on what she's been doing online, *or* pull the plug.

Don't Defeat Passwords

Your Internet connection, email account, and a few other activities require you to enter a username and password to prevent unauthorized access. Some software, particularly Internet connection software, enables you to enter the password in a dialog box once so that you never have to type it again. That's a convenient feature, but it enables anyone who can flip a switch to get online using your computer.

Good advice dictates that you leave your computer configured so that a password is required for both connecting to the Internet and retrieving email. Never tell your kids the passwords, and never log on or retrieve email in their sight.

This will ensure that you always know when your kids are online, and that they cannot receive email from anyone without your knowledge.

Be Extra Careful with Broadband

If you use a broadband Internet connection, your connection can be always online, always ready to go. This condition makes it awfully easy for a child to sit down at your computer and go where he or she maybe shouldn't.

Make sure you do not check any "remember password" boxes when setting up and using your broadband connection. This will help ensure that no one uses the Internet without your permission and supervision.

In Windows, you can set up a password-protected screen saver, so that when you leave your computer, after a few minutes of inactivity, a nifty animated picture or other display covers your screen. No one can clear that picture and do anything on your computer without entering the password. This is a great way to keep your computer—and your kids—safe, particularly if you use a broadband connection.

> To set up a screen saver, point to an empty area of your Windows desktop, right-click, choose Properties from the menu that appears, and then choose Screen Saver on the dialog box that appears. Be sure to check the check box marked "Password Protected."

Resist Chat

It's a shame to recommend resisting chat because there's plenty of good clean fun to be had in chat rooms. It must be said: Chat rooms are the most dangerous places on the Internet. This is not because of all the sex-related chat rooms, although it's related to those.

On the Web, the worst thing that can happen to a kid is that he or she will be exposed to *ideas*—words and pictures—that you don't approve of. In chat, your kids can easily meet up with people who may hurt them. People are much more dangerous than ideas.

It works like this: A pedophile or some other dangerous character—often posing as a kid—frequents chat rooms where kids hang out and establishes friendships, especially with lonely kids who are easy prey. As the friendship grows, the creep manipulates the kid into dropping the anonymous chat nicknames and exchanging email addresses for private correspondence. Eventually, a private, face-to-face meeting is arranged.

There already have been numerous cases of kids abused this way. And the initial contact is almost always made in a chat room.

> Most chat clients (including Microsoft Chat) include a dialog box in which you can not only create your chat nickname, but also enter personal information such as your name or email address.
>
> Because this information is accessible to others online with whom you chat, don't enter anything in such dialog boxes except your nickname.
>
> It's also a good idea to change your nickname from time to time, to keep chat friendships from getting too close.

In general, don't allow a child to use chat unsupervised, even if that child is trusted to surf the Web unsupervised. Even supervised chatting is risky—by teaching a child how to chat, you increase the chances that the child might sneak into a chat session unsupervised.

26

In fact, if you don't use chat yourself, perhaps it would be best not to install a chat client on your computer. Remember that many Web sites offer chat areas that anyone can access directly from his or her browser, without a chat to use the Net unsupervised, it's important that they know the rules for safe surfing. (Some folks suggest writing these rules up, having the kids sign them as a contract, and then posting the contract on the wall behind the computer.)

Tell your kids the following:

- Never reveal to anyone online your real name, email address, phone number, mailing address, school name, or username/password without a parent's involvement and consent. Any other personal information, such as birthday or Social Security number, is also best kept secret. And never, ever, ever send anyone a picture of yourself.

- Never reveal anything about your parents, siblings, teachers, or friends. Any such information can help a creep find you, and it exposes family and friends to risks, too.

- Never arrange to meet in person any online friend unless a parent consents before the meeting is arranged, the parent will be present at that meeting, and that meeting will take place in a public setting, such as a restaurant or mall.

- Anytime you come across anything online that makes you uneasy, go elsewhere or get offline. There's too much good stuff online to waste time looking at the bad.

- Never download or upload a file, or install any software on the computer, without a parent's consent.

Resources for Parents

Want to know more about protecting your kids online, teaching them to use the Net smartly, finding great family sites, or just plain old parenting advice? You'll find all of this and more at the following sites:

- Parent Soup at `http://www.parentsoup.com` (see Figure 26.2).
- The Parents Place at `http://www.parentsplace.com`.
- Kids Health at `http://www.kidshealth.org`.
- *All About Kids* magazine at `http://www.aak.com`.

FIGURE 26.2

Parent Soup is one of the best online resources for moms and dads.

Censoring Web Content

It's debatable how effective Internet-censoring and filtering programs are. First, most are really focused on the Web and aren't much protection elsewhere, such as in chat or email. And most censoring programs—erring properly on the cautious side—inevitably censor out totally benign stuff that you or your kids might find valuable.

Also, these programs might filter out sexual content, depictions of violence, and profanity, but what about ugly ideas? For example, these programs generally do not block out racist, sexist, or nationalist hate-mongering as long as those views are expressed without the use of profanity or epithets.

So even though these self-censoring tools are available, they're no replacement for adult supervision and safe-surfing practices. And if you really do supervise your kids, you probably don't need a censoring program. Still, you might find one or more of these programs useful, and they are getting better.

Getting a Safe-Surfing Program

Microsoft Internet Explorer has its own censoring program, which you'll learn about next. So does AOL, which you'll also learn about in a minute or two. But you might also want to check out the Web pages of other popular self-censoring utilities.

26

From these pages, you can learn more about each product and, in most cases, download a copy for your system:

- Net Nanny: `http://www.netnanny.com`
- SurfWatch: `http://www.surfwatch.com`
- Cybersitter: `http://www.cybersitter.com`
- The Internet Filter: `http://turnercom.com/if`
- Cyber Patrol: `http://www.cyberpatrol.com`

Using Internet Explorer's Built-In Content Advisor

Internet Explorer, in all versions starting with 3 and later, has its own built-in system called Content Advisor for controlling access to Web sites. Content Advisor works very much like the other safe-surfing programs, except it's a little harder to use than some, and it possesses many of the same strengths and drawbacks.

Understanding Content Advisor

Content Advisor relies on a rating system from the *Recreational Software Advisory Council* (*RSAC*), which also rates entertainment software and video games.

The RSAC ratings system assigns a score (0 to 4) to a Web site for each of four criteria: Language, Nudity, Sex, and Violence. The higher the score in each category, the more intense the content that page contains.

For example, if a site has a score of 0 in the Language category, it contains nothing worse than "inoffensive slang." A Language score of 4, however, indicates "explicit or crude language" on the site. After a Web site has been rated, the rating is built into the site so that Content Advisor can read the site's score before displaying anything.

Using the Content tab, you choose your own limit in each RSAC category. For example, suppose you are okay with violence up to level 3 but want to screen out all sexual content above a 2. After you set your limits and enable Content Advisor, Internet Explorer refuses to show you any page whose RSAC rating exceeds your limits in any category, unless you type in a password which you create. So, for example, if you screen out all nudity, then try to go to a pornographic Web site, you'll be blocked (see Figure 26.3).

There's one problem: Only a tiny portion of sites online have been rated. Enabling Content Advisor therefore blocks not only rated pages you might find offensive, but also all pages—offensive or not—that have not been rated, which includes most of the Web.

As you might guess, blocking unrated pages severely cramps your surfing and has little to do with protecting you from offensive content. As you'll see in the upcoming exercise, you can choose an optional setting to allow unrated pages, but doing so defeats the purpose of Content Advisor because those pages will be permitted regardless of their content. You can also create a special list of pages that are always accessible (or never accessible) regardless of the Content Advisor's settings, but obviously that list would be pretty short relative to the wealth of sites available online.

FIGURE 26.3

After you've enabled it, Content Advisor blocks Internet Explorer from displaying Web pages whose RSAC ratings exceed your limits.

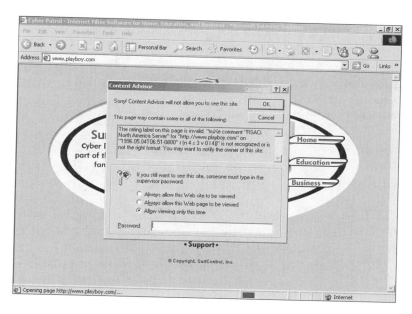

Content Advisor works for both Web browsing and Microsoft's Chat program, blocking entrance to unsavory or unrated chat rooms.

To use Content Advisor for Chat, replace Step 1 of the following exercise by opening Chat and choosing View, Options, and then choosing the Settings tab. Proceed with the remaining steps of the exercise.

However, note that although Content Advisor might keep kids out of X-rated chats, it does nothing to protect them from perverts who wander into G-rated chats. Good advice: No matter what censorship tools you might deploy, kids don't belong in chat. Period.

26

Enabling and Configuring Content Advisor

To enable and configure Internet Explorer's Content Advisor, follow these steps:

1. In Internet Explorer, open the Internet Options dialog box (choose Tools, Internet Options) and then choose the Content tab (see Figure 26.4).

2. Click the Enable button to display the Content Advisor (see Figure 26.5).

3. The Rating scale appears, showing the current setting for Language.

   Point to the slider control, click and hold, and drag the slider along the scale (see Figure 26.6). As the slider reaches each marker on the scale, a description appears below the scale with the type of language that setting permits. The farther to the right you pull the slider, the more lenient the setting. (Think of 0 as a G rating, 1 as PG, 2 as PG-13, 3 as R, and 4 as X.) After you've found the rating level you want, release the slider.

FIGURE 26.4

Open Internet Options and then choose the Content tab.

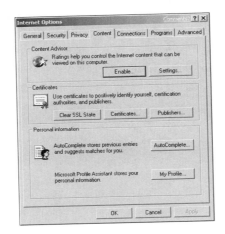

FIGURE 26.5

Click the Enable button to display Content Advisor.

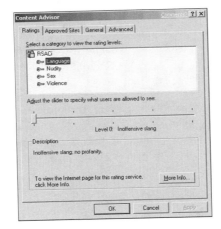

4. Click on Nudity and choose your rating for that category. Do Sex and Violence, too.

5. When you have finished choosing ratings, click the General tab and check either (or neither, or both) of the following options (see Figure 26.7).

Users can see sites that have no rating. Check this check box to allow the display of unrated pages. Content Advisor will continue to block rated pages that exceed your settings, but will permit unrated pages regardless of their content.

FIGURE 26.6

Adjust the slider to adjust the filtering level.

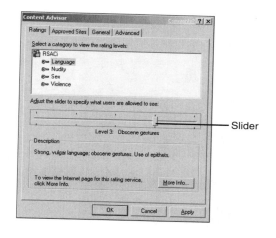

Depending on whether this is the first time you've accessed Content Advisor and the exact order of steps you follow, you will be asked at some point to choose the supervisor password. Once it's entered, no one can change any Content Advisor settings without entering it.

26

Supervisor can type a password to allow users to see restricted content. When this check box is checked, a dialog box pops up prompting for the Supervisor password whenever someone tries to open a page that Content Advisor would block. If the password is typed, the page appears. With this useful option, your kids can appeal to you for a temporary censorship waiver for a particular Web site.

6. Click the Approved Sites tab. Type the address of any Web site you want to be handled in a special way, and then click Always (to make this site always accessible, regardless of any other Content Advisor settings) or Never (to make this site inaccessible). Continue typing addresses and clicking Always or Never until the list shows all the sites for which you want special handling (see Figure 26.8). The approved sites show up with a green check mark next to them, while the disapproved sites have a red minus sign.

FIGURE 26.7

Click the General tab and then select User options.

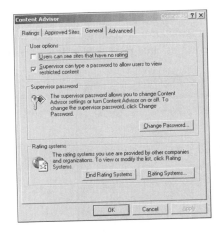

FIGURE 26.8

At the Approved Sites tab, enter lists of approved and disapproved Web sites.

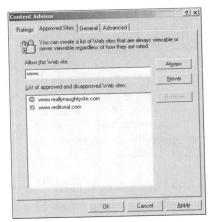

7. Click OK on any tab, and then click OK on the Internet Options dialog box. Your settings are now in effect, and they will stay in effect until you change them or click the Disable button on the Content tab. (The Supervisor password is required for disabling Content Advisor or changing the settings.)

Using AOL's Parental Controls

America Online has always touted itself as a family-friendly online service. As such, it's been at the forefront of developing technologies that allow parents to have control over what their children see and do online.

AOL's Parental Controls is a leader in this area, although it does suffer from some of the same drawbacks as some of the other Web-censoring programs. For example, if you choose the tightest security level ("Kids Only," which is designed for elementary-aged kids), it blocks such sites as the official sites of the Backstreet Boys, which your kids may want to see.

At the core of Parental Controls are the screen names. You can have up to seven screen names per AOL account. This allows families to pay one monthly fee, yet allow all of its members (unless it's a particularly large family) to have their own screen name.

Each screen name can also have its own settings, or level of access. Because of this, parents can let their teenagers see more content than their preschoolers are allowed access to. And, as long as you make sure each child only knows his or her own password, you can be relatively certain they're only seeing what you think is appropriate for them.

Parental Controls are available from the Settings tab within AOL. Click on Parental Controls, then click the Set Parental Controls link. You'll then be viewing the Parental Controls screen at which you can change settings (see Figure 26.9).

FIGURE 26.9

AOL's Parental Controls allows different settings for different family members.

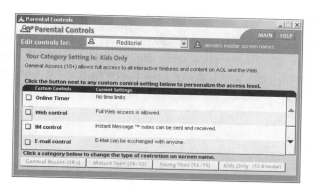

Each AOL account has a Master Screen Name; this is the only person who is allowed to change the Parental Controls settings for the others in the clan. You choose the screen name for which you would like to set Parental Controls in the box at the top of the window. Then, you're allowed to make the following choices for that person:

- **Online timer**—Allows you to set time limits for the user to be online.
- **Web control**—You can choose from four settings: Kids Only (12 and under), Young Teen (13-15), Mature Teen (16-17), and General Access (18 and older). Kids Only allows only access to AOL's Kids Only Channel, whereas General Access allows full, unrestricted movement on the Web.

26

- **IM control**—Allows you to set whether Instant Messages can be sent and retrieved.
- **Email control**—Allows you to customize whether email can be sent and retrieved, and from whom.
- **Chat control**—Allows you to block certain types of chat areas from access, or all chat within AOL.
- **Additional Master**—Allows you to make another screen name a Master, so you can have more than one person setting controls.
- **Download control**—You can determine what types of downloads (if any) you allow.
- **Newsgroup**—You can set the types of newsgroups you'll allow each screen name to access.
- **Premium Services**—Determine whether access to extra AOL services (for which you are charged extra) is allowed.

Summary

As you can see, there's no sure-fire way to protect unsupervised kids online. But there's no reason to worry, either. A few smart choices, along with your supervision and guidance, will enable your family to enjoy the Internet's benefits while steering clear of its troubles.

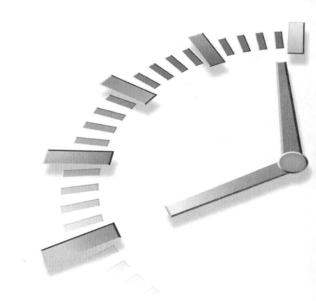

CHAPTER 27

Buying and Selling on the Internet

Today, you can buy or sell just about anything online. Companies are beginning to approach the Web not just as an intriguing place to experiment, but as a market they mustn't miss. In this chapter, you'll get a taste of *e-commerce* (electronic commerce) from both sides of the e-counter. First, you'll learn how to shop and invest online safely. Next, you'll learn the ways you can do business online, and learn how to get started.

Shopping 'Til You Drop

You can buy just about anything over the Internet from Web sites that sell products, also known as *virtual storefronts*. Figure 27.1 shows one such virtual storefront.

FIGURE **27.1**
Virtual storefronts are the hip way to buy online, 24 hours a day, without clerks standing over you to make sure you're not shoplifting.

Using only the Web-surfing skills you already possess, you can enjoy the benefits of online shopping:

- **24-hour, 365-day shopping.** Except for rare moments when the server is down for maintenance and repair, online stores are always open.

- **Access to product photos and specifications.** While you're browsing an online catalog, you often can click links to display product photos, lists of options, and even detailed measurements or other specifications. Such stuff can help you make an informed buying decision.

- **Search tools.** Pages with extensive product listings often include a search tool for finding any product available from the merchant.

- **Web specials.** Some merchants offer discounts or other deals that are available only to those ordering online and not to phone, mail order, or in-person customers.

- **Custom ordering.** Some stores feature forms that let you specify exactly what you want (see Figure 27.2). For example, PC sellers that are online, such as Dell or Gateway, let you choose your PC's specifications—processor, hard disk size, CD-ROM speed, and so on—from lists in a form. When you finish, the price for your system appears, along with a link for placing the order. At an online clothing shop, you can specify exact measurements, color, monogramming, and other custom specifications.

- **Mailing lists.** Many online merchants offer a form for subscribing to a mailing list with updates about new products and specials.

Making an online purchase usually requires typing your credit card number and other sensitive information in a form. That's something you should never do on a site that's not secure.

Explore virtual storefronts to your heart's content, comparing prices and other terms to make the best buy. But when you arrive at the actual page where you fill in your order form or open an account with the merchant, confirm that the page is secure. In most browsers, a secure site is indicated by either a locked golden padlock or a solid (unbroken) gold key near the bottom of the window. If you see a broken key, an unlocked padlock, or no icon at all, buy elsewhere.

You can find reviews of products and merchants all over the Web. One good way to find reviews is to use the product name along with the word "review" as a search term.

You might also want to check out the Web pages of consumer advocates who alert us to schemes, scams, and duds:

- Consumer's Union (publishers of *Consumer Reports* magazine): http://www.ConsumerReports.org
- Consumer World: http://www.consumerworld.org

FIGURE 27.2

Forms on virtual store-fronts can help you configure a custom order or get a price quote on one.

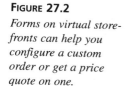

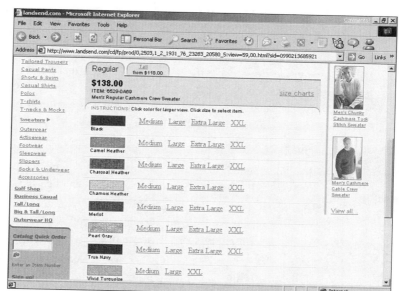

27

Using Accounts and Shopping Baskets

You already know how to fill out a form, and usually that's all there is to shopping. But many merchants equip their storefronts with either or both of the following to make shopping there more convenient:

- **Accounts.** When you set up an account with an online merchant, you give that merchant a record of your name and shipping address, and often your credit card information, too. After entering this information once, you can shop and buy there at any time without having to enter it again. All you have to do is enter an account username and password, and the site knows who you are, how you pay, and where to ship your stuff.

- **Shopping baskets (a.k.a.** *shopping carts*). A shopping basket lets you conveniently choose multiple products and then place the order for all of it, instead of having to order each item as you select it. Shopping baskets also provide you with a chance to look over your list of selections and the total price so you can change or delete items before committing to the order.

Often, accounts and shopping baskets require the use of *cookies* on your computer that store shopping cart information as you order items so you'll have a total when you're ready to pay for the items and complete the order. If you have configured your browser to reject cookies and you try to set up an account or make a purchase, you might get a message from the site informing you that you must accept cookies in order to shop there.

By following the steps that come next, you can get a feel for accounts, shopping baskets, and virtual storefronts by finding and ordering music CDs from CD Universe, a popular source for CDs, tapes, and videos. Note that you don't actually have to make a purchase; you may cancel before committing.

1. Go to CD Universe at http://www.cduniverse.com (see Figure 27.3).

2. In the Quick Search form at the top of the page, type the name of a recording artist in the box to the right of the Artist box, and then click Go.

3. After a few moments, a list appears with titles available from that artist (see Figure 27.4). If CD Universe isn't sure which artist you want, a list of artists matching your search term appears first. Choose one to display the list of titles.

4. Choose a CD or tape by clicking its price. If you're not sure which CD you want, click the title of the CD to learn more about it, including a list of songs.

FIGURE 27.3

Go to CD Universe to locate music you want.

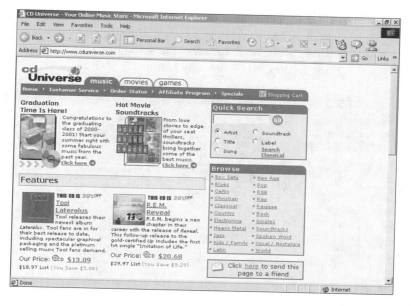

FIGURE 27.4

Review the list of albums before you finalize your purchase.

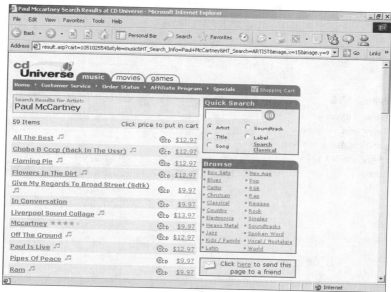

27

5. Review the info on the Shopping Cart screen, and then click Continue Shopping. Choose another title by clicking its price, and you will again see your Shopping Cart, now with two CDs listed (see Figure 27.5).

6. Click Complete Your Order to start the purchasing process. You will see the Account Entry screen (see Figure 27.6). To quit without purchasing anything, just leave the site now. To order your selections, click New Account, complete the form that appears, and follow any prompts.

FIGURE 27.5

You may choose another title to be added to your cart.

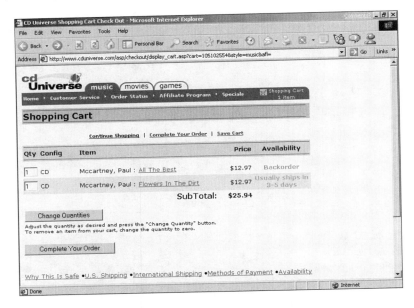

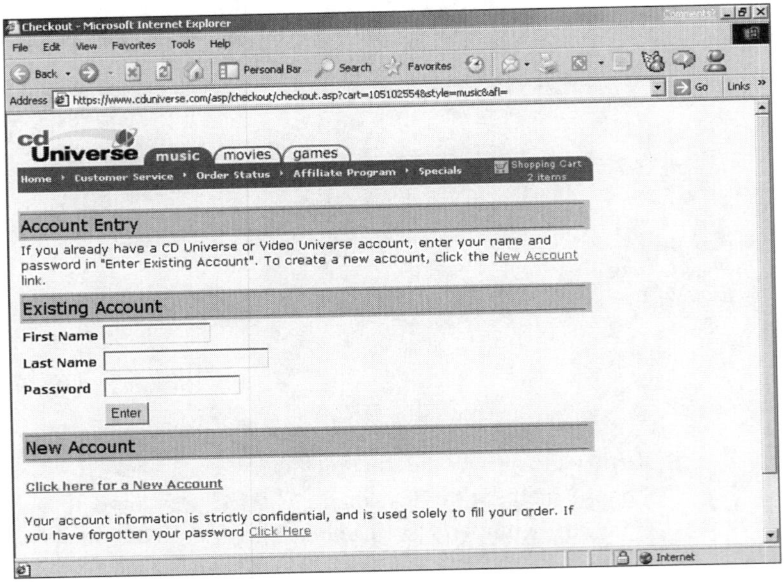

FIGURE 27.6

Either cancel your order now or fill out the New Account form to order your selections.

Immediately after you place an order from an online store, some sort of confirmation of your order should appear in your Web browser. Many stores also email you a confirmation of your order.

Print the Web page or a note of any information that appears in the confirmation—especially anything called an *order number*—and save any email message you receive. You'll need this information to query the merchant if your merchandise doesn't arrive within the time promised, or if it isn't what you ordered. If your order confirmation doesn't appear right away, find a shopping cart button to click to see your order.

Buying Stocks and Such

The Web is a great place to sell intangible goods, such as stocks or securities. After all, if the product is intangible, why shouldn't the transaction be?

Obviously, such purchases carry the greatest risk of all online shopping activities. They generally involve moving around large amounts of money and putting it at risk in investments. But if that's your thing, you should know that trading online can be substantially cheaper than using a traditional broker, and in many cases your transactions are executed much more quickly—usually within minutes or even seconds.

The steps for online investing are roughly the same as those for buying anything else online. Typically, you set up an account with an online brokerage, after which you may buy and sell at will.

However, note that opening an account with an online broker typically requires disclosing detailed information about yourself. You'll have to disclose your bank account numbers, Social Security number, and other private, sensitive information you don't have to reveal when making other kinds of purchases online.

Investment Starting Points

To learn more about investing online, or to take the plunge and buy those 1,000 shares of PepsiCo, consult the following sites.

27

For Financial Information and Advice

To learn more about online investing, read company profiles, and explore other money matters, check out the following sites:

- Microsoft MSN Money: moneycentral.com
- *Wall Street Journal*: http://www.wsj.com
- Dow Jones Business Information Services: http://bis.dowjones.com

- MoneyAdvisor: http://www.moneyadvisor.com
- Yahoo! Finance: http://quote.yahoo.com
- The Motley Fool: http://www.fool.com
- NASDAQ: http://www.nasdaq.com

For Making Investments

If you're ready to go ahead and put your money on the line (online!), visit these online brokers:

- American Express Financial Services Direct: http://www.americanexpress.com/direct
- E*Trade: http://www.etrade.com
- Charles Schwab: http://www.eschwab.com
- Ameritrade: http://www.ameritrade.com

Finding All the Sites Online That Sell What You Want

Instead of surfing blindly to various retailers and auction houses to find a particular item, you can call upon any of several services that search the shopping sites for a particular item and provide a list of links to sites that offer it. The price or current bid is included for each site (see Figure 27.7). These sites are sometimes called *shopping agents*.

Agents aren't foolproof—they can't find absolutely every site that might offer what you want. They'll only search the most popular shopping sites, or sites that have made a special business arrangement with them. But they might help you ensure that you get the best price (or best source) for that special item. And they often feature product information, reviews, and comparisons that can help you choose which product to buy. Check out:

- http://www.mysimon.com
- http://DealTime.com
- http://shop.Lycos.com
- http://ValueFind.com

FIGURE 27.7

Sites like MySimon search multiple shopping/auction sites to help you find out who has the product you want for the best price.

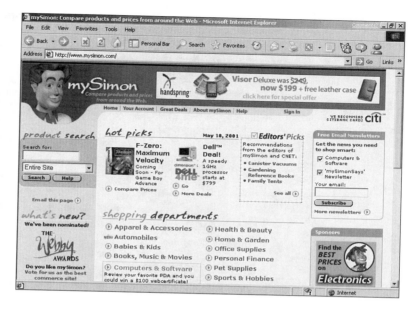

Buying and Selling Through Online Auctions

Lately, auction houses have joined the ranks of the hottest places to pick up bargains or unusual items on the Net. Not only are online auction houses great places to pick up new and used merchandise—and especially hard-to-find collectibles—but the bidding process can be a lot of fun, too. eBay, at www.ebay.com (see Figure 27.8), is the world's largest. Other auction sites exist also, including:

- Yahoo! Auctions: http://auctions.yahoo.com
- Amazon.com Auctions: http://auctions.amazon.com
- Auctions.com: http://auctions.com
- Butterfield & Butterfield: http://www.butterfields.com

In addition to buying and selling, you'll often see links to auctions on retail sites. You can bid on an item you might otherwise buy outright, and maybe save a bundle.

How Online Auction Houses Work

Although you can usually view the items up for auction without registering, you typically must register with the auction house—a quick process of filling in an online form—to bid on items or to sell an item. Once registered, you can use the search tools or categories on the auction house's page to browse for items to bid on. Note that most auctions go on for several days, and some go on for a week, so it's not necessary to sit in front of your computer for hours to join in the fun.

27

Figure 27.8

eBay, a popular online auction house.

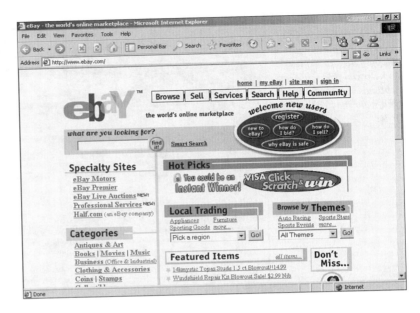

The auction house usually has no role in the actual financial transaction between seller and buyer, so a secure page is not really necessary. Typically, if you win an auction, the auction house emails both you and the seller to notify you about the win and to give you each other's contact info. After that, you and the seller have a set period of time in which to contact each other to arrange payment and shipping. Many sellers who use these auction houses are commercial merchants who can accept payment by credit card via email or telephone. Some individual sellers might require that you pay by money order or personal check.

eBay features a Feedback forum where buyers and sellers can post positive and negative comments about their experiences with each other. Before buying, you can always check out the comments others have made about the seller to determine whether that seller is a safe person to do business with.

To minimize the risk on bigger-ticket items, auction houses offer links to *escrow services* that make purchasing a little safer for buyer and seller (for a fee, of course).

The buyer pays the escrow service, not the seller. The seller does not ship anything until he knows that the escrow service has the buyer's money. When the buyer informs the escrow service that the item has arrived, the escrow service pays the seller.

Bidding Tips

If you want to try online auctions, here are a few important tips:

- Always check out the feedback about a seller before bidding to make sure the seller is reliable.

- Before you bid on an item, always search the Web or other sources to see whether the same item is for sale elsewhere and for how much. That way you can be sure not to bid more than you would pay for the same item elsewhere. (Try a shopping agent for this.)

- Check out any payment terms in the listing. If no terms are listed, use the links provided to email the seller and ask what forms of payment the seller accepts (check, money order, and so on). You might want to think twice (or use an escrow service) before dealing with a seller who accepts only money orders, which is the second riskiest way to pay by mail after cash.

- Don't get carried away. In the heat of the auction, it's easy to get caught in a bidding war and wind up paying way too much for that Elvis candleholder you think you simply must have. Decide the most you're willing to pay and stick to it. If you lose, there will be other auctions.

Selling Tips

If you're interested in trying to sell something online, here are a few quick tips:

- Be honest. Don't overstate the importance or worth of the item you're trying to sell. Don't call it an antique unless it is one. Don't call it one-of-a-kind and then sell another one next week. State as many details about your product as possible; *the more you tell the more you sell.* You want the buyer's trust and buyers trust sellers who give specific details, good and bad, about the condition of what's being sold.

- Be realistic. Everyone thinks his or her own stuff is worth more than it is. If you have something that's worth more to you than it would be to anyone else, that's a keepsake. Why sell it? Keep your minimum pricing reasonable.

- Provide a picture. Descriptions are great, but most people want to see the real piece. A high-resolution photo will help drive your price up.

- Send it quickly. As soon as you receive payment, send the item you sold. It'll ease anxiety for the buyer, and help drive up your rating on the auction service.

- Check other means of selling. Sometimes, the newspaper or online classifieds are still the best way to sell an item.

27

Using a Payment Service

Online payment services like PayPal (`http://www.paypal.com`) offer secure transactions that can allow you to send or receive a payment instantly. All you have to do is set up an account at one of the services, and you can start using it to buy and sell.

The payments are processed rapidly, and the security of the transaction allows the merchandise to change hands more quickly.

Summary

By now you're ready to begin spending money online, making money online, or both. You've seen that actually buying or selling on the Web is pretty easy, but doing either one well—taking into account all of the risks and issues surrounding these activities—takes preparation, care, and practice.

PART IX

Learning How to Network Computers

Chapter

CHAPTER 28

Understanding the Nature of Networks

Networks are ubiquitous. If you use a credit card or a debit card to make phone calls, or if you use a computer to access the Internet, you're directly relying on a computer network. Because networks control just about everything, and because networks are made up of computers (which people always seem to consider complex), it's easy to assume that networking is too complex for the average person. Here's a secret: Networking isn't really that complicated.

There's a lot of technical terminology in this book—what many would call *networking jargon*. Don't be put off by this. Networking is a specialized skill; like any other specialized skill, it has its own vernacular. You aren't expected to know everything about networking, but try to familiarize yourself with many of the concepts and terms presented here.

A network is first and foremost a system that enables communications among multiple locations and people. A network also creates synergy, where the sum of the whole is potentially greater than the sum of the parts.

What Is a Network?

If you've ever used a telephone, tracked a package with an overnight shipper, or purchased a new car from a dealership, you've used a network. Of course, they weren't computer networks—they were, respectively, the phone company's switching network, the overnight shipper's package-tracking network, and the car manufacturer's distribution network. And although these networks move phone calls, packages, and cars instead of computer data, they are examples that explain the fundamental purpose of a network. The single most important purpose of any network—computer or otherwise—is to link similar items together using a set of rules that ensures reliable service.

In the telephone network's case, the rules have to do with what happens when you dial a phone number based on how many digits you dial: If you dial seven digits, it's a local call; eleven digits is a long-distance call. For the overnight shipper's network, the rule is that your package is assigned a tracking number that must be recorded each time the package goes through a weigh station or transfer point. And for the car dealership, the rule is that there's only one reseller within a given geographical area; all new cars are delivered to that dealer, and that dealership has a direct link to the manufacturer.

Like other networks, computer networks have basic rules that ensure the safe delivery of information instead of telephone calls, overnight packages, or new cars. A basic set of rules for how a computer network should do its job might look something like this:

- Information must be delivered reliably without any corruption of data.
- Information must be delivered consistently—the network should be capable of determining where its information is going.
- Multiple computers must be able to identify each other across the network.
- There must be a standard way of naming and identifying the parts of the network.

These rules are simple, but they're the core of what a computer network does. Networks can be as simple as a file-transfer program that runs between two computers on a printer-port cable; networks can be as complex as the high-end banking systems that transfer data on pulses of light in fiber-optic cables. Despite this variety, all networks have the same basic goal: to ensure that data is shared quickly, reliably, and accurately.

How Networks Are Put Together

If you were to break a network down into its simplest components, you'd have two pieces. One is the *physical network*—the wiring, network cards, computers, and other equipment the network uses to transmit data. The other is the logical arrangement of these physical pieces—the rules that allow the physical pieces to work together.

Physical Networking—The Hardware

The physical network is easy to understand because it's easy to see—it's hardware! It's the wiring and network cards and computers and hubs and all the other stuff that allows the network to function. If you don't know what those things are, don't worry. It will be explained in the next few pages and throughout the rest of this book. The important thing to remember is that the physical part of networking is all hardware. It's tangible—you can hold it in your hands.

Physical Layout—What Are the Wires Like?

The physical side of the network is, at its simplest, made of wires strung between computers and other network devices. The wires connect to *network interface cards*, or *NICs*, installed in computers; NICs handle the computer's interaction with the rest of the network. With these two items, you can create a simple network.

For all practical purposes, there are only two types of physical layout that matter from a copper-wire "how do I wire it?" perspective: *bus* and *star*. Most of the equipment you'll find will be for a star *topology* (the pattern of the network's layout). You'll hear about *ring* and *mesh* topologies as well, but from a wiring perspective, a *ring topology* is essentially identical to a star topology. It's the way the network functions that differentiates star and ring.

Network Devices

To get this functionality from your network, you need a host of network devices to connect to each other in specific ways. Without getting into the specifics of how to hook these things together, let's take a look at the basic network devices you'll encounter throughout this book. The first devices are computers and printers, neither of which require a network to function.

- A *workstation* is the computer on which a user does his or her work—hence workstation.

- A *server* is a computer whose resources are shared with other computers.

- A *network printer* is a printer connected to the network so that more than one user can print to it.

Other devices that can be connected to a network were mentioned in the sections on physical topologies; these devices are specific to networks—without a network, these devices have no function. They're absolutely central to the process of networking:

- A *hub* or *MAU* is a device that provides the network with a single point of contact for all other devices.

28

- *Routers* and *bridges* are devices that move data between networks to create larger networks.

- Although *wiring* and *cabling* don't strictly sound like devices, they actually are—they are important to the process. Wire has to meet very stringent standards for networking to work, so it's included in the list of devices, although only peripherally.

The Logical Network

The physical network is the collection of wires, computers, and other hardware that can be picked up and held. It's the stuff that you can point to and say "that's the network." But all that hardware isn't a network by itself. There's another layer based on the function of that hardware, and that's what we call the *logical network*. The logical network is what users see and use when they're working at their computers on the network. Logical networks are collections of resources, such as hard drive space, printers, and applications, that workstations wouldn't have access to if they weren't connected to a network. Logical networks are not physical—they result from the organization of the physical network. In other words, the logical network is the organization of the hardware that results from networking software.

Examples of logical networks include things like *network protocols*. Network protocols (which we'll discuss in upcoming chapters) are special ways that computers have to communicate with each other—they're a lot like a language. If you speak only English and you're talking to someone who speaks only French, chances are you won't be able to communicate as well as if both of you were speaking the same language. For all their complexity, computer networks work the same way—they have to talk the same language, which in networking jargon is called a network protocol.

The logical network can include other things as well—in fact, it includes anything that isn't hardware. Novell's NetWare network software offers a logical network service called *NetWare Directory Services* (*NDS*) that organizes networked computers and printers; Microsoft's method for organizing the same things is called a *Domain* (or the *Active Directory* in Windows 2000). These services offer ways to organize your network so that the resources are neatly grouped according to their function—printers, servers, and so on.

If it's not part of the physical network, it's part of the logical network.

The Varieties of Networks

The basic organizational network concepts are *LAN* (*Local Area Network*) and *WAN* (*Wide Area Network*).

LANs

A *Local Area Network*, or *LAN*, is the least complex organizational distinction of computer networks. A LAN is nothing more than a group of computers linked through a network all located at a single site. LANs have the following parameters:

- They occupy one physical location, and one physical location only—hence the word local in the title.

- They have high-speed data transfer rates, typically 10 or 100 megabits per second.

- All data travels on the local network wiring.

Part of what makes a LAN a LAN is high-speed data transfer. Ethernet LANs usually transmit data at 10 to 100 megabits per second.

Although LANs are the simplest networks, that does not mean they are either necessarily small or simple. LANs can become quite large and complex; it is not uncommon in trade press magazines to read about LANs with hundreds or thousands of users.

WANs

When a series of LANs are too geographically scattered to make linking them at full LAN speeds impractical due to cost constraints, it's time to build a *Wide Area Network*, or *WAN*. Wide Area Networks are geographically scattered LANs joined together using high-speed phone lines and *routers*. A router is a device that manages data flows between networks.

Routers know the best ways for data to travel to get from point A to B—and they're always learning new routes.

Access to resources across a WAN is often limited by the speed of the phone line (some of the most popular digital phone lines have speeds of only 56 kilobits per second). Even full-blown phone company trunk lines, called *T-1*s, can carry only 1.5 megabits per second, and they're very expensive—it's not unusual to pay several thousand dollars a month to a phone company to use a T-1. When you contrast the speed of a 56-kilobits-per-second phone line or a 1.5-megabits-per-second T-1 with the speed of a local LAN or MAN running at 10 megabits per second, the slowness of digital phone lines is readily apparent. These speed restrictions are also called *bandwidth* issues. Of course, if you've got deep pockets, it's possible to run data over a *T-3* line, which provides 45 megabits per second...which is faster than many networks.

Bandwidth is a term used to describe the maximum speed at which a given device (such as a network card or modem) can transfer data. In other words, measuring bandwidth is like measuring how much air a fan can move: A fan that can move 100 cubic feet of air

28

per minute has a lower bandwidth than a fan that can move 1,000 cubic feet of air per minute. Bandwidth is measured in kilobits per second (kbps) or megabits per second. Comparing megabits per second with kilobits per second is a lot like comparing a running person and a fast car: The car (which compares to megabits-per-second data speeds) is much faster than the runner (who compares to kilobits-per-second speeds).

WANs are often built when it is important that all users have the ability to access a common pool of information such as product databases or Automatic Teller Machine bank records. As long as the purpose of the WAN is well defined and limited, the speed restrictions imposed by phone lines are not an issue for network designers. If the quantity of data to be transmitted is less than or equal to the capacity of the line, the WAN works fine.

Unlike LANs, WANs always require routers. Because most of the traffic in a WAN takes place inside the LANs that make up the WAN, routers provide an important function—traffic control. Routers must be set up with information called *routes* that tell the router how to send data between networks.

Figure 28.1 shows a WAN configuration. Note that the main difference between a LAN and a WAN is that a WAN is essentially a series of LANs connected by routers.

FIGURE 28.1
A typical WAN configuration.

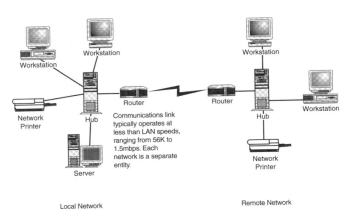

How the Internet Relates to Your Network

If you build a small network, you have a private network. If you connect a router to your network (and you're connected through an Internet Service Provider), some part of your network will wind up on the Internet.

Figure 28.2 shows how local networks connect to each other to make up the Internet.

FIGURE 28.2

The connections between local networks are what makes the Internet the Internet.

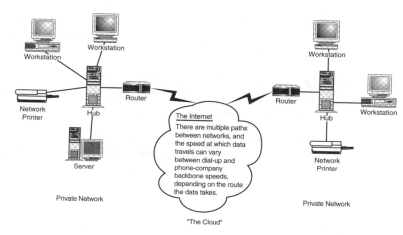

The Internet
There are multiple paths between networks, and the speed at which data travels can vary between dial-up and phone-company backbone speeds, depending on the route the data takes.

"The Cloud"

Understanding Bandwidth

As an astute reader, you're probably looking at Figure 28.2 and wondering what makes it different from the WAN in Figure 28.1. The two figures are almost the same. The important distinction is that, in Figure 28.1, the WAN is all part of a single network and is under one organization's control. By contrast, the only parts of the Internet that can be identified as strictly dedicated to the Internet are the extremely fast (also called *high-bandwidth*) phone lines that make up what's called the *backbone* of the Internet.

The backbone is a series of very high-speed phone lines (ranging from 155 to 622 megabits per second—really fast!) that phone companies use to transmit high volumes of traffic. Compare this speed to the speed of your LAN (where data moves at 10 megabits per second), and you begin to see why it's called the backbone. By contrast, the Internet is under no single organization's control. Even the high-speed phone lines that make up the backbone of the Internet aren't under one organization's control.

Understanding Different Kinds of Internet Connections

Here's an easier way to think of the various speeds of connection on the Internet. Because the Internet is always being compared to a highway, the following analogy is based on that metaphor.

28

The dial-up connection most users use to traverse the Internet is like a dirt trail. At best, it's a country road. It's still fun to travel, but you have to be prepared for the bumps. Dial-up connections aren't terribly expensive, but they're not something you're going to race your Lamborghini on, either. They're also not very reliable, so you've got to deal with regular interruptions in service.

The next step up in this metaphor are dedicated connections using 56kbps phone lines. They are faster than dial-up phone lines, but not by much. These are equivalent to two-lane state highways—better paved, more reliable, but you still can't go too fast on them.

Next in the lineup are trunk connections—T1s, E1s, and T3s (these lines may also be called OS1s, DS1s, DS3s, and other names, depending on which phone company you're dealing with). Using the road metaphor, these are the limited-access highways (interstate highways): They have two lanes in each direction, and you can travel as fast as you require.

Between 56k and T1 or faster access lies a new form of superhighway: high-speed data access provided over Digital Subscriber Lines (DSL) or cable modems. Typically, this access is at least as fast and sometimes faster than T1 access, but instead of being delivered to a place of business and costing huge amounts of money, it's delivered to your home and costs $50 a month or so. Essentially, if we continue to use the old, tired Infobahn metaphor, this is an exit at your house. DSL and cable modems represent the next generation of Internet access: digital dial tone. With DSL or cable modems, your Internet connection is up 24/7/365 (or as close as your service provider can come to that ideal), it's fast enough to do anything on the Internet that most users require, and it's part of your home. For those of us who have this access, giving it up just isn't a possibility; stories are legendary about homebuyers who rule out buying houses because DSL and cable modems aren't available.

Sometimes, however, traveling on the road just isn't fast enough. So we'll expand our highway metaphor into a travel metaphor. If you have to move a lot of people between New York and Los Angeles overnight, you don't drive them—you use a plane. The phone companies are like the airline companies because they have to move a high volume of something—in the airlines' case, it's people and cargo; in the phone companies' case, it's data. Both have to ensure that they have the hardware to move the volume of stuff they have to move. Another similarity between the phone companies and the airlines is that other forms of transportation (in the airlines' case, roads, trains, and buses; in the phone companies' case, lower-speed Internet connections) converge on a common location (an airport or a phone company's network center) and dump a bunch of their contents on the high-volume carrier.

To meet this challenge, the phone companies have created extremely high-speed networking lines—the *backbone* previously mentioned—based on optical fiber that can carry data at up to about 1,500 megabits per second (that's one and a half gigabytes per second). It's like the airline model in that it has a variety of locations at which you can get into the system (just as the airports are to the airline system), and it's redundant. (If your flight from New York to California isn't direct—and that's very expensive in both networking and flying—you may be routed through Atlanta, Dallas, Chicago, or some other large-volume hub.) The beauty of the Internet is that you generally don't have to worry how your data is routed; the backbone routers largely automate the process with help from ISPs who monitor traffic.

If you reconsider Figure 28.2, it's possible to see that the Internet is not all one network; it is a series of connected private LANs. Data travels among them and, depending on a given private network's degree of involvement in the Internet, each network can take responsibility for sending data on toward its intended destination.

Why Does the Internet Matter for Your Network?

As the Internet has increased in visibility, it's become a beacon for network designers everywhere. The Internet, unlike many smaller networks, is based on standards established by committee and common consent. These standards all exist in the public domain; none of the standards are proprietary, or the sole property of any single manufacturer. The result is that Internet-standard–based software is easy for software manufacturers to write because Internet standards are very well defined. (Their specifications are covered in exhaustive detail in a series of documents called *RFCs*, or *Requests for Comment*, which are readily available on the Internet.) Because these standards are in the public domain, software developed using these standards is also cheaper to manufacture—there's no need for software manufacturers to pay royalties on patented or copyrighted ideas.

The best thing about Internet standards, however, is just that—they are standards. If you use Internet-standard software on your network, it will be much easier to ensure that your computers and applications will be able to interact. In fact, many products from wholly different manufacturers can work with one another if they're standards-compliant. When software products adhere to Internet standards, the resulting application cooperation is called interoperability, which essentially means that Part A works with Part B without undue difficulty. And interoperability means a local network that functions more smoothly and less expensively than one whose parts don't interoperate.

28

Intranets, Extranets, and the Internet

Typically, if you build a LAN or WAN—that is, a private network—using Internet standards, you've created an internal Internet, or an *intranet*. Intranets offer a great deal of promise for simplifying the networking of different manufacturers' components; used properly, intranets can reduce costs and simplify life for your end users as well. An example might be a company Web site that distributes company news—it's much cheaper and environmentally responsible to put the newsletter on a company intranet than to create a separate paper copy for each reader.

If you connect your intranet to the Internet and make provisions for your customers and business partners to use pieces of your intranet to do business with you, you've gone a step beyond an intranet and created an *extranet*. Extranets, which fall under the current rubric *B2B* for *business-to-business*, are essentially intranets that use the Internet as a vehicle to interact with their customers, suppliers, and business partners. With the proper security precautions, extranets offer tremendous value; they reduce the costs of tying your computer systems to your various business partners' systems and potentially expose your products to a huge audience.

Networking's Breakthrough: Packet-Switched Data

Packet-switching is how all computer networks—from your network to the mighty Internet—move data around.

Packet-switched data is important for a variety of reasons:

- It allows more than one stream of data to travel over a wire at a time.
- It inherently ensures error-correction, meaning that data transmitted over a wire is free of errors.
- It allows data to be sent from one computer to another over multiple routes, depending on which routes are currently open.

It can be difficult to conceptualize packet-switching the first time around—but if you want to understand how networks work, packet-switching is something you have to understand. Here's a brief thought-experiment to help explain how packet-switching works.

Assume that you are an author writing a manuscript that must be delivered to an editor who lives a thousand miles away from you. Also assume (for the purposes of this thought-experiment) that the postal service limits the weight of packages it carries, and that your entire manuscript is heavier than the limit. Clearly, you're going to have to break up the manuscript in a way that ensures that your editor can reassemble it in the correct order without difficulty. How are you going to accomplish this?

First, you're going to break up the manuscript into standard sizes. Let's say that a 50-page section of manuscript plus an envelope is the maximum weight that the postal service will carry. After ensuring that your manuscript pages are numbered, you break the manuscript into 50-page chunks. It doesn't matter whether or not the chunks break on chapter lines, or even in the middle of a sentence—the pages are numbered, so they can be reassembled easily. If any pages are lost because of a torn envelope, the page numbers help determine what's missing.

Breaking up the manuscript into equal-sized chunks with a method of verifying the correctness of the data (through the use of the page numbers) is the first part of *packetizing data*. Packetizing is the process by which a computer breaks a single large chunk of data into smaller pieces so it can be transmitted over a network. The page numbers, which are a property of the data, are used to determine whether or not all the data has arrived; in networking terms, this is called a checksum. When data is packetized, the computer checks the values of the 1s and 0s in the data and comes up with a number that it includes in the packet of data.

Second, you put the 50-page manuscript chunks into envelopes numbered sequentially—the first 50 pages go into envelope number 1, the second 50 pages go into envelope number 2, and so forth until you've reached the end of the manuscript. The number of pages in each envelope is also written on the outside of the envelope; that is equivalent to a data packet's checksum. Finally, you write your editor's address as the destination and your address as the return address on the outsides of the envelopes and send them using the postal service. Figure 28.3 diagrams our hypothetical envelope and the relationship each element has to a data packet in a computer network situation.

FIGURE 28.3

The various parts of the envelope and how they correspond to the parts of a data packet.

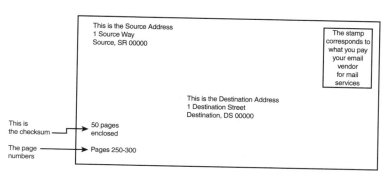

The route the envelopes take while in transit between your mailbox and your editor's desk is unimportant. Your editor gets mail from a different post office, but uses the same service, so the envelopes go through out-of-town mail. Some of the envelopes might be

28

routed through Chicago, others might be routed through Dallas—it's not important as long as all the envelopes get to the editor (see Figure 28.4). If the number of pages your editor receives does not match the number of pages written on the outside of the envelope, the editor knows something's wrong—the envelope came unsealed and pages fell out, or someone tampered with the contents. If you had sent your editor something over the Internet, the process would work the same way—the packets could have been routed through many different machines before arriving at your editor's computer.

FIGURE 28.4

Data packets can follow several paths across the Internet.

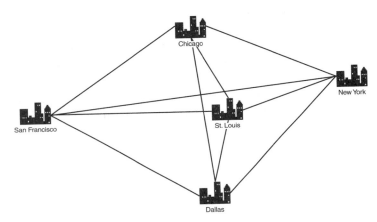

Mail can travel from New York to San Francisco across any combination of these routes.

In networking terms, each finished envelope is a packet of data. The order in which your editor—or a computer—receives them doesn't matter because the editor (or the computer) can reassemble the data from the envelope numbers (which were sequential), the *checksum* (the number on the outside of the envelope detailing how many pages to expect in this envelope), and the page numbers of the manuscript itself. If one envelope is lost in transit, after an agreed upon length of time, your editor can request that you send another copy of that specific envelope so that the editor has the entire manuscript.

Any data you send over a computer network is packetized—from the smallest email message to the largest files transferred across a wire. The beauty of packet-switching networks is that more than one computer can transmit data over one wire at a time. You can have lots of packets of data from multiple machines without confusion because each data packet (like each envelope in the preceding example) has the following elements:

- **A source address**—this is the return address, or where the packet came from.
- **A destination address**—this is where the packet is headed.

- **A sequence number**—this explains where this packet fits in with the remainder of the packets.
- **A checksum**—this ensures that the data is free of errors.

Because each computer has a different address (called a *MAC address*), transmitting data is essentially a process of sending mail from one piece of hardware to another electronically.

Sneakernet

Back when Ethernet networking was invented, computer users who were networked came up with a clever name for sharing files from files stored on computers that were not connected to the network. They called it *sneakernet*. What it meant was that if a user wanted to move files between nonconnected computers, he or she had to copy the file to a floppy disk, walk to the other machine (hence the *sneaker* in *sneakernet*), and copy the file to the other computer.

Needless to say, sneakernet is not an efficient way to move or manage files. It is time-consuming and unreliable to begin with, and it works easily only for files small enough to fit on a floppy disk. The worst thing about it is that data is decentralized, meaning that every user can conceivably have a different version of a particular file stored on their nonnetwork-connected computer. The chaos that ensues when users need the same version of a file and don't have it (usually because the file changes as users copy it to their machines and work with it before copying it to the next machine) can be truly horrific.

Benefits of Networking

Networking provides numerous benefits. Networks are easier to install than ever before. In spite of the technical nature of this in-depth network coverage, just using networks is easy and the benefits quickly become obvious.

Simplified Resource Sharing

Resource sharing is easier over a network; whether the network uses a peer or client/server configuration is immaterial.

Shared Disk Space

Networked computers can share their hard disk space with each other. At first glance, this doesn't seem momentous; after all, many computers have large hard drives. But it's not the file-storage capabilities that are important here—it's sharing applications and files. It is satisfying to be able to find a copy of a file you require, copy it to your desktop computer, and work on it without leaving your chair.

28

Shared Applications

Although sharing files is an important reason for networking, sharing applications is another, equally important reason. Shared applications can be as prosaic as using a copy of Microsoft Word stored on another user's drive or as elaborate as a groupware application that routes data from user to user according to complex preset rules.

A *groupware application* (also called *groupware* or *collaborative software*) is an application that enables multiple users to work together using the network to connect them. Such applications can work serially, where (for instance) a document is automatically routed from person A to person B when person A is finished with it, or it can be software to enable real-time collaboration. IBM's Lotus Notes software is an example of the former, and Microsoft's Office has some real-time collaborative features.

Shared Printers

A third aspect of resource sharing is shared printers. *Standalone printers*—that is, printers attached to computers that aren't networked—represent a significant capital expense. Printers typically also cost a lot to run—they consume ink or toner when they print, and inkjet and toner cartridges are typically expensive.

A visual example of resource sharing can be seen in Figure 28.5.

FIGURE 28.5
Resource sharing with a computer network.

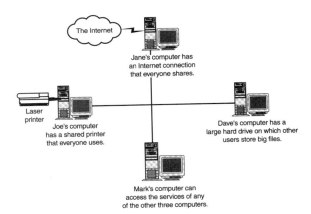

Networking Is Faster

Given everything else that has been said here, it seems obvious that networking is faster than not networking. And, in fact, it is faster. Just think about it:

- No more printing memos—use email!
- No more running from desk to desk to check everyone's availability for a meeting—use the group calendar!

- No more wondering whose Rolodex has the name of the person you need to call—you can get it from the contact database.

- No more racing around from computer to computer to get the file you need—just copy or open it from the network drive.

Centralized Management

If you were a preschool teacher with a bevy of three-year-olds, you wouldn't try to manage them all individually. Instead, you'd try to do activities in groups. Imagine trying to fill the needs of 25 three-year-olds, each engaged in a different activity—the mind boggles at the management strategies you'd need. Most reasonable people agree that this is the case; they also agree that managing children as a group works better.

Yet a great many of these same people, faced with a computer network, continue to treat network users' needs totally outside the context of the network. All too often, system administrators wind up running from desktop to desktop, installing, fixing, and managing idiosyncratic software installations. This is extremely inefficient—and it wears down the patience of the network users and the technical person whose job it is to support them.

A better solution to managing networks is to centralize management functions. Once computers are networked, there are a host of software utilities that enable the administrator to diagnose and fix problems and install and configure software.

Summary

In this chapter, you've learned what a network is, how a network works, the varieties of networks available, and how the Internet relates to your network. As you can already see, understanding networks in depth requires some technical background but using a network makes the setup worth the effort. Clearly, when computer resources are shared through a network, you reap a variety of benefits ranging from reduced costs to ease of use to simpler administration. The cost savings and per-worker productivity gains represented by networks will be appreciated by companies trying to economize; from the worker's viewpoint, he or she has received a bonus because he or she doesn't have to chase down information anymore. If applications such as email, calendaring, and contact management are added to the mix, the network begins to establish synergistic relationships (that is, relationships that produce more value than the sum of their parts would suggest) between users and data. A well-designed and functional network allows groups of people to interact in ways that extend their natural capabilities and enables them to accomplish a great deal more than they could without the network.

28

CHAPTER **29**

Getting Data from Here to There: How Computers Share Data

This chapter explains how networks pass data between computers. This process will be discussed from two separate vantage points: logical topologies, such as Ethernet, Token Ring, and ATM; and network protocols, which we have not yet discussed.

A Warning for the Technically Challenged

As you've seen throughout this book so far, computer hardware and software can be simple to understand and easy to use. So can network hardware and software. Nevertheless, all forms of data communications, at the network level, are rather technical by their very nature. So be forewarned that the rest of the material in this chapter is more technical than you've been used to so far. And although the rest of the networking chapters that follow depend on some of this chapter's material, this material is primarily aimed at readers who need to understand, manage, and set up a network that's larger than the typical two- or three-PC network in a household.

Without this in-depth discussion, this text could not possibly explain networks for the people who need to manage them in a nonpersonal setting and this applies to such networks that are rather simple. So if you just want to connect two PCs, consider skimming this chapter for some terms and moving to the next to gather more knowledge. If you need more information than that, you'll appreciate the level this chapter goes to.

Logical Topologies

In networking terms, a *topology* is nothing more than the arrangement of a network. The topology can refer to the physical layout of the network or the logical layout of the network.

Logical topologies lay out the rules of the road for data transmission. As you already know, in data networking, only one computer can transmit on one wire segment at any given time. Life would be wonderful if computers could take turns transmitting data, but unfortunately, life isn't that simple. As a result, there must be rules if the network is to avoid becoming completely anarchic.

In contrast to physical topologies, logical topologies are largely abstract. Physical topologies can be expressed through concrete pieces of equipment, such as network cards and wiring types; logical networks are essentially rules of the road.

Ethernet

When packet switching was young, it didn't work very efficiently. Computers didn't know how to avoid sending data over the wire at the same time other systems were sending data, making early networking a rather ineffective technology.

Ethernet was a way to circumvent the limitations of earlier networks. It was based on an *IEEE* (*Institute of Electronic and Electrical Engineers*) standard called *802.3 CSMA/CD*, and it provided ways to manage the crazy situation that occurred when many computers tried to transmit on one wire simultaneously.

CSMA/CD Explained

The foundation of Ethernet is *CSMA/CD*, or *Carrier Sense Multiple Access/Collision Detection*. Although this sounds complicated, it's actually quite simple. In an Ethernet network, all the computers share a single network segment, called a *collision domain*. A collision domain is the group of computers that communicate on a single network wire.

Each computer in a collision domain listens to every other computer in the collision domain; each computer can transmit data only when no other computer is currently transmitting. The segment is called a collision domain because if there's more than one computer in it, it's a cinch that at some point those computers are going to try to transmit data simultaneously, which is a big no-no. When two computers transmit packets at the same time, a condition called a collision occurs. In terms of networking, a collision is what happens when two computers attempt to transmit data on the same network wire at the same time. This creates a conflict; both computers sense the collision, stop transmitting, and wait a random amount of time before retransmitting. The larger the collision domain, the more likely it is that collisions will occur, which is why Ethernet designers try to keep the number of computers in a segment as low as possible.

In CSMA/CD, each computer listens for a quiet time on the wire. When the network wire is quiet (which is measured in nanoseconds—network quiet has no relationship to human quiet), a computer that has packets of data to transmit sends them out over the network wire. If no other computers are sending, the packet will be routed on its merry way.

Take a look at Figure 29.1 to see a diagram of an Ethernet topology.

FIGURE 29.1

An Ethernet topology: Only one computer can transmit data at a time.

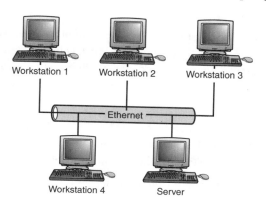

If a second computer tries to transmit data over the wire at the same time as the first computer, a condition called a *collision* occurs. Both then cease transmitting data, wait a random number of milliseconds for a quiet period, and transmit again; usually this solves the collision problem. It is really that simple.

Ethernet's Nuclear Family

Ethernet is broadly used to describe both the logical topology that uses CSMA/CD and the physical topologies on which CSMA/CD networks run. All the basic Ethernet topologies are described in IEEE standard 802.3. The members of the nuclear family are listed here:

- *10BASE-2*, or coaxial networking. The maximum segment length of 10BASE-2 is 185 meters. This is considered old technology even though it's still used in some home and small business networks, and is not used for larger installations.

- *10BASE-5*, or *thicknet*. Thicknet is also called *AUI*, short for *Attachment User Interface*. AUI networks are an intermediate step between 10BASE-2 and 10BASE-T. 10BASE-5 is a bus interface with slightly more redundancy than 10BASE-2. The maximum length of a 10BASE-5 segment is 500 meters. Like 10BASE-2, this is an old technology and is not typically used for new installations.

- *10BASE-T*, which runs over two of the four pairs of unshielded twisted-pair wire. In 10BASE-T, the maximum cable length from the hub to a workstation is 100 meters.

The Ethernet standard has grown to include faster networks including fiber-optic media as well as the more common media just described.

Token Ring and FDDI

Ethernet CSMA/CD networks provide a relatively simple way of passing data. However, many industry observers correctly note that CSMA/CD breaks down under the pressure exerted by many computers on a network segment that occurs in larger installations. The squabbling and contention for bandwidth that is part and parcel of Ethernet does not always scale efficiently.

In an attempt to circumvent this problem, IBM and the IEEE created another networking standard called *802.5*. IEEE 802.5 is more commonly identified with *Token Ring*, although FDDI also uses the 802.5 method of moving data around networks.

Token Ring works very differently from Ethernet. In Ethernet, any computer on a given network segment can transmit until it senses a collision with another computer. In Token Ring and FDDI networks, by contrast, a single special packet called a *token* is generated when the network starts and is passed around the network. When a computer has data to transmit, it waits until the token is available. The computer then takes control of the token and transmits a data packet. When it's done, it releases the token to the network. Then the next computer grabs the token if it has data to transmit (see Figure 29.2).

In comparison to the contentious nature of Ethernet, Token Ring and FDDI appear quite civilized. These two logical topologies do not have collisions in which multiple stations try to send data; instead, every computer waits its turn.

FIGURE 29.2

A Token Ring topology (FDDI works in the same fashion): The only computer that can transmit is the computer holding the token.

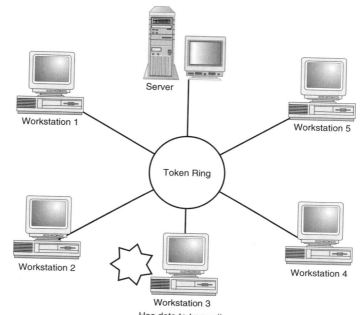

Server

Workstation 1

Workstation 5

Token Ring

Workstation 2

Workstation 4

Workstation 3
Has data to transmit.
It has taken the Token (an electronic message that's passed around the network)
and only it can transmit. When it's done transmitting data, it returns the Token to the ring,
where the next computer that needs to transmit will pick it up.
FDDI works basically the same as Token Ring.

Token Ring suffers slightly fewer bandwidth-contention issues than Ethernet; it holds up under load fairly well, although it too can be slowed down if too many computers need to transmit data at the same time. Ultimately, this situation results in network slowdowns.

Asynchronous Transfer Mode (ATM)

ATM networking is the newest topology available at this time. It is a wholly new topology; unlike Ethernet, Token Ring, or FDDI, it can carry both voice and data over network wire or fiber. ATM transmits all packets as 53-byte cells that have a variety of identifiers on them to determine such things as *Quality of Service.*

Quality of Service in packet data is very similar to quality of service in regular mail. In regular mail, you have a choice of services: first class, second class, third class, bulk mail, overnight, and so forth. When you send an overnight message, it receives priority over first-class mail, so it gets to its destination first.

ATM is fast. At its slowest, it runs at 25 megabits per second; at its fastest, it can run up to 1.5 gigabits per second (which is why phone companies use it for some of the huge trunk lines that carry data for long distances). In addition to its speed, ATM is exponentially more complex than either Ethernet or Token Ring. Most commonly, the 155 megabit per second speed of ATM is used for applications where quality of service and extraordinary speed are required. Currently, ATM equipment is both esoteric and expensive.

Network Protocols

At the base of a network system is the physical topology. On top of that is the logical topology. And on top of the logical topology are protocols. If the idea of "on top of" or "beneath" doesn't make sense, don't worry; it's based on a system for describing how networks work, called the OSI model, which is described in the following section.

Just as a logical topology is, a protocol is a set of rules for sending and receiving data across a physical network. Logical topologies instruct the hardware on how to packetize and transmit data across the physical topology; protocols handle the translation of data from applications (that is, software) to the logical topology.

If that all sounds confusing, don't worry. The next couple of pages discuss how protocols work, what some of the most popular protocols are, and how they're organized. Here is a list of the protocols you are most likely to run across:

- TCP/IP
- IPX
- NetBIOS/NetBEUI

To understand what network protocols are, you have to understand what they do and their function in relation to the rest of the network. To begin, let's examine the most popular theoretical model of networking: the OSI model.

The OSI Model (And Why You Should Be Familiar with It)

During the 1980s, a group called *Open Systems Interconnect*, or *OSI* for short, attempted to create a logical arrangement for the various parts that make up a network. In the long term, their efforts were futile (practically no one runs OSI protocols), but they did create a great model to explain how a network should work. The model is called the OSI seven-layer model, and it's a stalwart of networking theory (see Figure 29.3). The OSI model is useful to know, but it's not necessary to memorize—it simply provides a theoretical model you can use for network problems ranging from design issues to connection problems.

FIGURE 29.3

The OSI model shows how data is moved in a network.

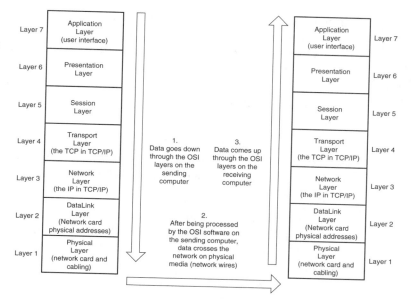

The OSI model is not particularly complicated. The trick is to remember that as the OSI layer numbers increase from 1 to 7, so does the level of abstraction. The lower the layer, the less abstract and more concrete it is. Each layer communicates only with the layer directly above or below it while moving data from electrical impulses on a wire into data on your screen.

Layer 7 (*Application*) deals with the software applications that you use on your screen. Layer 7 is concerned with file access and file transfer. If you have ever used applications such as FTP or Telnet, you have interacted with an example of Layer 7. In the postal model, the Application layer corresponds to writing a letter.

Layer 6 (*Presentation*) deals with the way different systems represent data. For example, Layer 6 defines what happens when it tries to display Unix-style data on an MS-DOS/Windows screen.

Assume that your letter is being sent to Mexico. A *translator* (equivalent to Presentation-layer software) can translate the data in your envelope into the local *lingua mexicana*.

Layer 5 (*Session*) handles the actual connections between systems. Layer 5 handles the order of data packets and *bidirectional* (two-way) communications. In a postal metaphor, the Session layer is similar to breaking a single large document into several smaller documents, packaging them, and labeling the order in which the packages should be opened. This is where streams of data get turned into packets.

Layer 4 (*Transport*) is like the registered-mail system. Layer 4 is concerned with ensuring that mail gets to its destination. If a packet fails to get to its destination, Layer 4 handles the process of notifying the sender and requesting that another packet be sent. In effect, Layer 4 ensures that the three layers below it (that is, Layers 1, 2, and 3) are doing their jobs properly. If they are not, Layer 4 software can step in and handle error correction. For what it's worth, this is where the TCP in TCP/IP does its work.

Layer 3 (*Network*) provides an addressing scheme. If you send someone a letter, you use a street address that contains a ZIP code because that's what the post office understands. When a computer sends a data packet, it sends the packet to a logical address, which is like a street address.

Layer 3 works with Layer 2 to translate data packets' logical network addresses (these are similar to *IP addresses*, about which you'll learn in a few pages) into hardware-based MAC addresses (which are similar to ZIP codes for networking hardware) and move the packets toward their destination. Layer 3 is similar to the mail-sorting clerks at the post office who aren't concerned with ensuring that mail gets to its destination, per se. Instead, the clerks' concern is to sort mail so that it keeps getting closer to its destination. Layer 3 is also the lowest layer that isn't concerned with the hardware. Layer 3 is where the term protocol really comes into play; the IP in TCP/IP stands for Internet Protocol.

Layer 2 (*Data-Link*), by contrast, isn't physical. In our postal model, this layer represents a set of rules governing the actual delivery of physical mail—pick up here, drop off there, and so forth. This is where the rules for Ethernet, Token Ring, FDDI, ATM, and so on are stored. It's concerned with finding a way for Layer-1 stuff (the cards and hubs and wire and so forth) to talk to Layer 3. Layer 2 is where network card addresses become important.

Layer 1 (*Physical*) could be compared in the real world as the trucks and trains and planes and rails and whatnot that move the mail. From a network perspective, this layer is concerned only with the physical aspects of the network—the cards, wire, and concentrators that move data packets. Layer 1 specifies what the physical aspects are, what they must be capable of doing, and (basically) how they accomplish those things.

If you refer back to the description of packet data in the previous chapter, you'll realize that if data packets are to pass over the network, the network (like the postal service) has to accomplish several tasks successfully:

- It has to be capable of transmitting data across a physical medium (copper wire, optical fiber, or—in the case of wireless networks—air).

- It must route data to the correct location by MAC address.
- It must be capable of recognizing the data when it arrives at the destination.
- It must be capable of checking the correctness of the transmitted data.
- It must be capable of sending messages to acknowledge that a particular packet has been received.
- It must be capable of interacting with users through an interface that displays the data.

As you can see, the various layers of the OSI model accomplish these goals admirably. OSI, however, was never actually implemented as a network protocol; instead, the existing protocols—mostly TCP/IP—were refined using the powerful OSI reference model.

TCP/IP

If you've read anything about the Internet that's deeper than a newsweekly's puff piece, you've probably heard of *TCP/IP*, or *Transmission Control Protocol/Internet Protocol*. TCP/IP is the protocol that carries data traffic over the Internet. Of all the network protocols in the marketplace, TCP/IP is far and away the most popular.

The reasons for TCP/IP's success, however, do not stem from the popularity of the Internet. Even before the current Internet boom, TCP/IP was gaining popularity among business networkers, college computer-science majors, and scientific organizations. The reason why TCP/IP has gained popularity is because it is an *open standard*—no single company controls it. Instead, TCP/IP is part of a set of standards created by a body called the *Internet Engineering Task Force (IETF)*. IETF standards are created by committees and are submitted to the networking community through a set of documents called *Requests for Comment (RFCs)*.

RFCs are draft documents freely available on the Internet that explain a standard to the networking community. All RFCs are considered "draft" documents because any document can be superseded by a newer RFC. The reason for this focus on RFCs is that they form a large part of the basis for the various standards that make up Internet networking today, including TCP/IP.

TCP/IP Defined

The name TCP/IP is a bit misleading—TCP/IP is just shorthand notation for a full protocol suite, or set of protocols that have standard ways of interacting with each other. TCP and IP share the name of the whole protocol suite because they form the bedrock of the whole protocol suite; they are respectively the transport (OSI Layer 4, which regulates traffic) and the network (OSI Layer 3, which handles addressing) layers of the TCP/IP protocol suite. The suite includes, but is by no means limited to, the ways of transmitting data across networks listed in Table 29.1.

TABLE 29.1   Some TCP/IP Suite Members and Their Functions

Name	Function
TCP	Transmission Control Protocol. Ensures that connections are made and maintained between computers.
IP	Internet Protocol. Handles software computer addresses.
ARP	Address Resolution Protocol. Relates IP addresses with hardware (MAC) addresses.
RIP	Routing Information Protocol. Finds the quickest route between two computers.
OSPF	Open Shortest Path First. A descendant of RIP that increases its speed and reliability.
ICMP	Internet Control Message Protocol. Handles errors and sends error messages for TCP/IP.
BGP/EGP	Border Gateway Protocol/Exterior Gateway Protocol. Handles how data is passed between networks.
SNMP	Simple Network Management Protocol. Allows network administrators to connect to and manage network devices.
PPP	Point-to-Point Protocol. Provides for dial-up networked connections to networks. PPP is commonly used by Internet Service Providers to allow customers to connect to their services.
SMTP	Simple Mail Transport Protocol. How email is passed between servers on a TCP/IP network.
POP3/IMAP4	Post Office Protocol version 3/Internet Message Advertising Protocol version 4. Both set up ways for clients to connect to servers and collect email.

As you can see, there are quite a few pieces in the TCP/IP protocol suite, and this is just the beginning—there are many more. All these pieces are necessary at some point or another to ensure that data gets where it's supposed to be going. The pieces listed in Table 29.1 are standards at this point, but the process of defining standards is far from over.

In contrast to the OSI reference model's seven layers, TCP/IP uses only four layers, some of which amalgamate several OSI layer functions into one TCP/IP layer. Table 29.2 compares OSI and TCP/IP layers.

TABLE 29.2   Contrast Between TCP/IP and the OSI Model

OSI Layer	TCP/IP Layer	TCP/IP Applications and Protocols Running at This Level
7 (Application)	TCP Layer 4 (Application)	FTP (File Transfer Program)
6 (Presentation) 5 (Session)		Telnet (terminal program), SMTP (mail transfer), POP3, and IMAP4 (mail clients)
4 (Transport)	TCP Layer 3 (also called Host-to-Host; a host is any system running TCP/IP)	TCP (Transmission Control Protocol), UDP (User Datagram Protocol)
3 (Network)	TCP Layer 2 (Internet)	IP (Internet Protocol)
2 (Data Link) 1 (Physical)	TCP Layer 1 (Network Interface)	Hardware (network cards, cables, concentrators, and so on)

From this table, you can see that TCP/IP accomplishes the functions required in the OSI reference model.

IP Addresses

TCP/IP got its start as part of the Unix operating system in the mid-1970s.

The original specification for TCP/IP was open ended—or so the designers thought. They created an address space, or standard way of writing addresses, which set up 2 to the 32nd power addresses (4,294,967,296 separate addresses). In the days when TCP/IP was still young, the thought that four billion computers could exist was a bit of a stretch, especially because computers—even cheap ones—cost $5,000 to $10,000 each. However, with the increased popularity of the Internet, these IP addresses have been disappearing at a tremendous clip. Every new Web site, for example, gets a new one and networks require more still.

The reason why IP addresses have disappeared so fast is because of the way the addressing scheme is designed. All IP addresses are written in dotted decimal notation, with 1 byte (8 bits) between each dot. A dotted decimal IP address looks like this:

```
192.168.100.25
```

Because each number is described by 1 byte, and because each byte is 8 bits (or binary 1s and 0s), each number can have a value of anything from 0 to 255. Because there are 4 numbers with 8 bits each, the total address space is said to be 32 bits long (4×8=32).

With a 32-bit address space that can handle four billion addresses, you might think that the Internet would never run out of IP addresses (or that it would take a while at any rate). Unfortunately, that's not the case. IP addresses are allocated to organizations that request them in what are called *address blocks*. Address blocks come in three sizes, based on the class of address. And once you've read about IP address allocation in the following sections, you'll agree that the present method of allocating IP addresses is inefficient given the way the Internet has grown.

Why IP Address Allocation Is Wasteful   Under the current 32-bit Internet address scheme, organizations must select a network class that will provide enough IP addresses for their needs.

The few remaining Class A addresses could potentially be assigned to organizations that need more than 65,536 (Class B-size) IP addresses, even if the organization doesn't require anywhere close to 16 million addresses.

Class B addresses are likewise assigned to organizations that require more than 256 IP addresses, whether or not they require anywhere near 65,536 addresses.

Class C addresses are, fortunately, available for small networks. However, keep in mind that if you take a full Class C, you have 256 addresses, even if you require only 20 addresses.

Fortunately, several solutions are on the horizon. The first is *CIDR*, or *Classless Inter Domain Routing*, which allows several Class C addresses to be combined. As an example, using CIDR, if you need a thousand network addresses, you can get four 256-address Class Cs and combine them for a total of 1,024 addresses (256×4=1,024), rather than tying up a whole Class B address of 65,536 addresses. CIDR, or *supernetting*, as it's been called, has become a means of efficiently allocating network addresses without wasting large chunks of Class B address space.

IPv4 is currently the world's most popular protocol. It's the backbone of the Internet, and most large networks rely on its standardization, interoperability, and reliability. If you elect to run your network on it, there will initially be an added dimension of complexity. However, once your network is set up to use IP, it will be capable of talking to any other computer of any type—from a personal computer to a mainframe—that can speak TCP/IP. It's the universal solvent of networking.

IPX

Internetworking Packet Exchange, or *IPX*, is Novell's answer to the complexity of IP. Novell designed IPX in the early 1980s before the current furor over IP and the Internet,

29

and it shows. IPX is a relatively efficient protocol that does several things for which network administrators are duly grateful:

- Unlike IP, IPX can configure its own address. This is very useful, particularly when there are a lot of systems to install.
- IPX is a "chatty" protocol. That is, it advertises its presence on the network. This characteristic is okay on networks with finite boundaries because the bandwidth it uses is not too bad. On a huge network (a WAN, for example), the chatty nature of IPX can become quite troublesome because it can overwhelm low-bandwidth WAN connections.

On the whole, IPX is easy to install and simple to use. Unfortunately, it's not an open standard; it's controlled by Novell. In spite of its ease of use, even Novell has acknowledged that IPX will eventually bow out in favor of IP.

NetBIOS and NetBEUI

Network Basic Input/Output System (*NetBIOS*) and *NetBIOS Extended User Interface* (*NetBEUI*) are single-site network protocols. NetBEUI is based on a way of passing data called *Server Message Block* (*SMB*), which relies on computer names to resolve destination addresses.

NetBIOS and NetBEUI are far and away the simplest to implement. Most often used for small *peer-to-peer LANs* (Local Area Networks without servers where computers might use files and printers connected to any other computer on the network), the NetBIOS and NetBEUI protocols are part of the networking suite that comes with every version of Windows (from Windows for Workgroups to the present), OS/2 Warp, and several third-party networking software packages such as Artisoft's Lantastic.

Summary

Congratulations! You covered a lot of ground in this chapter to ensure that you have a grasp of network topologies and protocols. You should have a good foundation for the next several chapters in which you'll learn the specifics of computer and network hardware and software. With the theory presented in this chapter and the knowledge of network hardware that's coming up, you'll have the basic knowledge to design a very powerful network.

CHAPTER 30

Mastering Computer and Network Concepts

Networks are made of computers in the same way a band is made of musicians. Each computer—and each band member—is unique, and in the right circumstances, they all work together. If they don't, then all you get is chaos.

Similarly, networks require that certain conventions be observed when computers are networked. Although each computer is unique, it nonetheless works in the same fashion as the other computers on the network. If you understand how a computer works, you'll be better prepared to understand how networks work. This chapter not only prepares you for the more challenging network chapters that follow, but also set you up to be ready for the hardware-upgrading and maintenance chapters that this book ends with.

This chapter introduces and explains basic network concepts in some depth. Some of the concepts covered in this hour have been mentioned earlier but are discussed here in greater depth. Some of this chapter may be review if you already understand computer hardware somewhat but the chapter's ultimate goal is designed to discuss hardware in light of networking.

Computer Hardware

Hardware comprises the physical components that make up a computer. It includes, but is not limited to, the following items:

- The CPU (Central Processing Unit)
- Memory
- Disks
- Add-in adapters
- Printer and communications ports

In the next few pages, you'll get a very high-level virtual tour of a PC. Although the descriptions will most correctly describe an IBM-compatible PC (the most common kind of personal computer), the concepts presented here also hold for just about any other computer designed with a modular, expandable architecture.

The CPU

A *CPU* (*Central Processing Unit*) is, in principle, nothing more than a chip of silicon that's had several layers of microscopic transistors etched and doped into it using extremely delicate and complex processes.

The CPU is the brain of computing—without it, there would be no computer. The CPU is the device that takes all of the data (represented internally by 1s and 0s) that make up the input from the keyboard and the mouse and the disks and whatever else you have in your system and processes it so that you can accomplish whatever it is you want to accomplish—see a display on a video screen, type a letter, create a spreadsheet...whatever.

Typically, CPUs are *microprocessors*, that is, they have multiple microscopic transistors in logical arrays. The earliest microprocessors had only a few hundred transistors per chip; modern microprocessors have millions of transistors on a square the size of your thumbnail.

Memory

A CPU is a microprocessor, but all circuit board chips are not microprocessors. Some chips are built as arrays that can hold the 1s and 0s that the CPU is processing; these are *memory chips*. When these chips are arranged into groups, the resulting memory devices are called *Single Inline Memory Modules* (*SIMMs*) or *Dual Inline Memory Modules* (*DIMMs*). SIMMs and DIMMs are the most common way to add memory to computers; when you buy memory from a retailer, you're buying memory modules instead of individual memory chips. You'll also hear about *DRAM* (*dynamic RAM*) and *SDRAM*. In spite of the difference in nomenclature, all memory works in essentially the same fashion. Just make certain that the memory you purchase is the same sort that your computer requires.

Disks

Memory makes a computer run faster. This is good. However, RAM is *volatile*, which means that it only works when the computer is turned on. Because RAM is made of chips that depend on an electrical power source to store data, when the power is cut, it can no longer store anything. And because you don't want to retype everything every time you turn on the computer—that was, after all, one of the reasons you bought a computer in the first place, to replace the typewriter that made you do that—there ought to be a way to store data so that it can be retrieved next time you turn on the computer.

That's why disks were invented. Hard disks fulfill two of the most common needs of the computer: Disks store data in a *nonvolatile* state (that is, the data stored on disks doesn't disappear when the power is cut), and they act as additional (very slow) memory when the computer needs more memory than is physically installed.

Modern disks for personal computers generally come in one of two varieties: *IDE* and *SCSI*. These are simply different methods by which hard drives connect to computers. Because devices of one type are not compatible with devices of the other type, it's important to know a bit about them.

Integrated Drive Electronics, or *IDE*, is a standard for hard drives that places the electronics that control the drive directly on the drive itself. *IDE* supports up to two drives connected to a single cable, and disk sizes up to 528 megabytes. The more recent version of the IDE standard, called *Extended IDE* (*EIDE*), can support larger disks; it's now common to see EIDE disks with capacities of up to 200 or more gigabytes. EIDE is now often called *Ultra DMA*.

Small Computer Serial Interface, or *SCSI*, is a standard for connecting all sorts of devices to a computer. SCSI allows from seven to fifteen devices to be connected to the computer in a chain.

Of the two standards, IDE is usually simpler to set up because it supports only hard drives and only two hard drives per cable. It's also generally less expensive than SCSI equipment, which is good to know if you're on a budget. On the other hand, SCSI is faster and more versatile; if you're setting up a server computer, SCSI drives are almost always a better choice than IDE drives.

30

Add-In Adapter Cards

The CPU fits into a socket on the motherboard. In addition to the socket for the CPU, the motherboard has sockets for aftermarket devices that handle several of the computer's functions. These devices, which fit into sockets called *expansion slots* on the motherboard, are called *adapter cards*. These cards are part of an electronic assembly that connects to a computer through a standard interface called a *card slot*. Adapter cards can provide a variety of services to the computer, including video, network, modem, and other functions as required.

Adapter cards handle a wide array of functions, including the following:

- Network adapters connect computers to the network.
- Video adapters provide a way for the computer to display images on a video monitor.
- Drive controllers connect floppy drives and hard drives to the system.
- SCSI controllers connect any devices that use the SCSI interface to the computer.
- Sound and video cards enable a variety of multimedia types—from CD to MP3—to be played on your system.

This list is not comprehensive; it does not include all the different types of adapter cards. Nonetheless, it does cover all the devices you are likely to encounter in a common computer.

Slot Interfaces

Although most motherboards have expansion slots, the expansion slots on all motherboards are not the same. Various computer manufacturers have devised different interfaces for cards used in their systems; in general, the interfaces are not compatible with each other.

For Intel-compatible computers, the most common slot designs are, in order of age from oldest to youngest, *ISA*, *EISA*, and *PCI*. ISA stands for *Industry Standard Architecture*, which was what IBM called this interface when it initially created it in the early 1980s. ISA has a 16-bit data path (which means that it can move only 16 bits of data simultaneously), and it runs at 8 megahertz, even if the rest of your computer is blazing along much faster. *EISA*, or *Extended ISA*, was an attempt to extend the ISA interface by increasing the data path to 32 bits and increasing the speed to 32 megahertz. One good side benefit of EISA is its *backward compatibility*, or its capability to be used with older equipment. ISA cards can be used in EISA slots (but not the other way around!)—they just don't get the speed and performance benefits of EISA.

PCI, or *Peripheral Component Interconnect*, was the result of an initiative by Intel, the microprocessor manufacturer, to allow add-in adapters to run almost as fast as the system in which they are installed. PCI is blazingly fast, offering data transfer rates of up to 128 megabits per second.

Most Pentium-level and newer Intel-compatible servers have a mixture of EISA and PCI slots to ensure good performance.

Network Adapter Cards

If you want to connect a computer to a printer, you use a printer port (if you don't count the USB ports discussed in Chapter 13, "Exploring Your Hardware Interface"). If you want to connect a computer to a network, you use a *Network Adapter Card* or *Network Interface Card* (the terms are synonymous), usually called either a *network card* or *NIC*, respectively.

Network cards are seldom difficult to install. Typically, you turn off the power to the computer, open the case, find a slot that matches the card's interface (it'll usually be ISA, EISA, or PCI), center the card above the slot, and press the card firmly into the slot to seat it. Once you have done that, turn the computer back on. When the computer is fully running, you can install the *device drivers*, or software that allows the computer to talk to the network card. Once the device driver software is installed, you usually have to reboot your computer one more time to load the driver and be able to connect to the network.

One important thing to remember about network adapters is that every card is assigned a unique 48-bit number (that is, a 6-byte number; remember that 8 bits equals 1 byte, so 48 bits equals 6 bytes) called a *MAC address*. MAC is an acronym for *Media Access Control*. The network wire and network cards and concentrators are also collectively called *network media*, which is where the media in Media Access Control comes from.

Video Adapter Cards

Because what we see on a video monitor screen is such an important part of how we interact with computers, the *Video Adapter Card*, or *video card*, is obviously an important part of the system. Video cards take the digital information the computer uses internally and converts it to an analog, or waveform, format that can be displayed on a computer monitor.

The minimum standard for video displays on modern Intel-compatible computers is called *VGA*, or *Video Graphics Array*. In order to meet the VGA standard, a video card must be able to display an image that is 640 *pixels* wide by 480 pixels tall, in at least 16 colors. (A pixel is a picture element; just picture one square in a grid and you've got the basic idea of a pixel.) VGA is a useful standard because so many manufacturers adhere to it as a baseline for their video adapters; almost all Intel-compatible video adapters have a VGA mode.

However, VGA is limited—640 by 480 with 16 colors does not provide particularly good screen resolution; it can't display images and colors very accurately. In an attempt to get around the limitations of VGA, video adapter manufacturers created several standards that extend VGA and make it more useful for computer users who actually have to spend time working at a screen: *Super VGA* (800 pixels wide by 600 pixels tall by 16 colors) and *Extended VGA* (usually 1,024 pixels wide by 768 pixels tall). Additional display settings for some adapters offer increased color depth, or the number of colors on the screen, that range from 256 colors up to 16.7 million colors, which is photograph quality.

Drive Controllers

Floppy drives, hard drives, and tape drives have to connect to the system to be useful. *Drive controllers* provide that connection. As noted earlier in this chapter, most common drive controllers operate in the IDE, EIDE, or SCSI standard. The rule of thumb is to use SCSI drive controllers for servers and IDE-related drive controllers for desktops because SCSI is fast and expandable and IDE is simple. Drive controllers are available in ISA, EISA, and PCI interfaces; if your motherboard has PCI slots, use a PCI controller no matter what kind of drive you use because the PCI interface will increase performance.

Client Operating System Software

Computer hardware is great, but it doesn't get you anywhere by itself. Hardware requires software, usually *operating system software*, to do anything useful. An *operating system*, or *OS*, is the software that enables users and applications to interact with the computer hardware. An OS is essentially a set of baseline functions for the computer. There's no reason why each program couldn't essentially contain an OS and boot the system, but an OS essentially frees application designers from having to redesign the world each time they write software. The OS also offers consistent user and programming interfaces and standard ways of doing simple tasks such as copying data between applications.

There are a variety of operating system types:

- **Single-tasking systems** such as MS-DOS—These can do only one task at a time.
- **Multitasking systems**—These can run several tasks simultaneously.
- **Single-user systems**—These are intended for use by one user at a time on one machine at a time.
- **Multiuser systems**—These are intended to support many simultaneous user sessions on one computer.

These distinctions are important when you select the various components of your network, so remember these terms.

Most readers of this book will use Windows (hence the title), and yet if you plan to work with networking in a small or large business environment, you will work with other operating systems in addition to Windows that will probably be running on most computers on your network. Therefore, as you learn more about networking in these networking-based chapters, you'll learn some about non-Windows operating systems.

30

Multitasking Versus Single-Tasking Systems

An MS-DOS system (which isn't common any longer) can, for all practical purposes, run one program at a time. DOS does not offer multiple sessions, so what you see on your screen is basically all that the computer can do.

DOS also doesn't have a windowing system. This means that each program in DOS fills up the whole screen. If you use DOS's task switcher, you can switch between different full-screen instances of programs, but when a program isn't in the foreground filling the screen, it's inactive.

Some operating systems are *multiuser*—which means that they can support multiple users, each user having a unique session. Unix is probably the best example of a multiuser system, although Digital's VMS and Linux also fit into this category. In a multiuser system, one computer runs one or more sessions simultaneously, and each user has a device called a terminal. Terminals are devices that look like a monitor but offer some additional connectivity services. ASCII terminals are generally connected via a serial port (a COM port, for PC users). ASCII terminals work at the command line—they don't have a graphical interface. X Terminals, by contrast, are usually network-connected devices that use Ethernet or Token Ring, and they offer a graphical user interface (*GUI*) called *X Windows* that appears in many forms (GNOME, KDE, CDE, OpenLook) and works in ways similar to Microsoft's Windows interface.

Multitasking systems are systems that can do more than one task at a time. Almost all multiuser systems are multitasking, but not all multitasking systems are multiuser. Unix supports terminals to its command-line interface and it can multitask. By contrast, Windows 98/Me/XP and Windows 2000 are multitasking but not multiuser.

If you're using a server, you almost certainly want to ensure that the server operating system *preemptively multitasks*. Preemptive multitasking is also desirable from a client applications perspective. It offers the user the ability to recover from a crashed application without being forced to restart the operating system.

In spite of the superiority of preemptive multitasking operating systems, there is still room for Microsoft's venerable single-tasking MS-DOS. Although MS-DOS has serious memory limitations, it is still a useful platform for terminal applications as well as for making use of older computers. Even if your company has standardized on Windows Me, Windows NT, or OS/2, it is useful to know a bit about the DOS (or Unix) command line because it's tremendously powerful.

What Networks Are Made Of

Although you were introduced to networking hardware in the previous two chapters, this chapter revisits both hardware and software from a network-specific perspective. The preceding discussion of computers looked at them as standalone devices, not connected to anything else. Now, you'll see how to take that hardware and software (and some other devices mentioned only in passing, such as hubs and MAUs) and discuss how they fit together to create a coherent whole.

Network-Specific Hardware

Network-specific hardware comes in two varieties. The first variety is computers that have been specifically built for networking but that could function without a network. The second variety is hardware such as network hubs, switches, cables, and routers that have no function outside a network context.

Servers

The term *server* is often used to describe a computer that shares its resources with other computers over a network. In the following sections, you learn more about servers—what they are, how they are different from regular computers, and what they're used for.

What Is a Server?   A server is a powerful computer that shares its resources with other computers on a network. In brief terms, that's what a server is and what it does. But a server is a great deal more—and, surprisingly, often a great deal less—than your desktop computer. Server hardware is usually built around two primary needs: moving data quickly and ensuring the safety and integrity of data.

For starters, a server is usually more powerful than your desktop computer. Even if your desktop computer has a ten-zillion-Hertz Perfectium processor, chances are that it lacks the *I/O*, or *throughput* (generally, a loose measure of the speed at which a particular piece of hardware can move data), to adequately service other computers' needs. No matter how fast your desktop computer is, if it can't move data off disks and onto a network wire quickly enough, it is not much use as a server.

A server usually provides some form of insurance against disaster. The network must remain up when disaster strikes.

No matter how fast a server operates, other computers on a network see only how fast it transmits data. A server that can't pass data to multiple clients efficiently is perceived as slow, even if it actually runs tremendously fast. As a result, server I/O is extremely important. Typically, servers have two potential I/O bottlenecks: limitations on the speed of a network card and limitations on the time it takes to read and write to the server's hard drive.

Network Card Speed The speed of the network card is determined by two things: the bus of the card and the speed of the card. For servers, PCI-bus network cards are the best choice right now because the PCI bus allows data to flow between the computer and adapter cards much faster than any alternative.

The speed at which the card transmits data is determined by the network type. If your network topology is 10BASE-T Ethernet, you can't transmit data faster than 10 megabits per second; if your topology is 100BASE-T or ATM, you may be capable of transmitting data at 100 or 155 megabits per second.

Redundancy If your data is on one disk, that's good. If your data can be copied across two disks, so that either disk can break and you don't lose data, that's better. If you can chain three or more drives together so that if you lose one drive, the remaining drives can reconstruct the data on the broken drive, that's better still. Remember that redundancy increases reliability. That's why it's used so often in servers, where no one can afford to lose data.

One popular redundant disk drive setup is called *RAID*, for *Redundant Arrays of Inexpensive Disks*; the special SCSI controllers that handle RAID are called *RAID controllers*. RAID operates in a variety of levels ranging from 0 to 5, but most people only need to know about levels 0, 1, and 5, since they're the ones that seem to get used the most.

RAID 0 is best described as several hard drives connected to a computer with no redundancy. The purpose of RAID 0 is simply to increase throughput—if data is spread over several drives, it can be read from and written to the drive more rapidly. But servers need redundancy, so RAID levels 1 through 5 are commonly used for that purpose.

RAID 1 is *disk mirroring* or *duplexing*. In disk mirroring, two SCSI drives of the same size connect to the RAID controller card, but the computer sees them as one drive. For example, in a RAID 1 configuration, if you connect two 4-gigabyte drives to the computer, the computer sees only 4 gigabytes of disk space rather than 8 gigabytes.

Despite its expense, mirroring is often the easiest means of providing redundant disk space. When a disk drive goes bad, replacing the blown disk and mirroring the good disk to the new disk will often suffice to put a computer system back on track.

30

RAID 5 addresses the shortcomings of RAID 1 admirably. RAID 5 typically requires three disks of equal capacity (compared to RAID 1, which requires two disks), but the net improvement is worth the cost. In a RAID 5 configuration, all data is spread across multiple disks in a process called *striping*, which is the process by which a RAID drive controller card writes data across multiple disks. Additionally, information about the file called *parity data* is also saved on all three disks. What this means is that any single drive in a RAID 5 set can fail, and the parity data on the other two drives can be used to reconstruct the data on the failed drive.

Hot swapping is not something you can do with your average desktop system. For critical networks, hot swapping allows you to swap a bad disk (perhaps one that has a mirrored backup) for the backup that still works, without taking down the network.

Concentrators: Hubs, Switches, and MAUs

As you may recall, one network topology didn't use hubs, switches, or MAUs: Ethernet 10BASE-2, also called *thinnet*, uses coaxial cable that runs from computer to computer. In spite of the fact that Ethernet 10BASE-2 doesn't use hubs, an explanation of how Ethernet 10BASE-2 works is helpful in understanding the role of hubs in topologies such as 10BASE-T, Token Ring, and FDDI.

Ethernet 10BASE-2   Ethernet 10BASE-2 runs on coaxial cable from computer to computer (see Figure 30.1). All data travels along this single wire whether its destination is the next computer on the wire or 20 computers down the wire. This wire is called a *segment*. Each segment functions for all practical purposes as though it were a single piece of wire. Here's a list of the conditions that must be met for 10BASE-2 to work:

- All the data must travel on this wire between all destinations.
- All computers must be attached to this wire so that they can "listen" to the network wire to see whether any other computers are transmitting data.
- Only one computer on a segment can transmit data at any given time. Computers can transmit data only when no other station is transmitting data.

In Figure 30.1, the wire that connects all the computers is called a *segment*. A segment is not one piece of wire; it's actually composed of a series of shorter wires that each begin and end at a computer. At each end of the segment is a device called a *terminator* that essentially marks the end of the network.

If any one of the pieces of wire that runs from computer to computer in an Ethernet 10BASE-2 segment breaks or (in some cases) if a computer crashes, the network crashes. Why?

FIGURE 30.1

An Ethernet 10BASE-2 network.

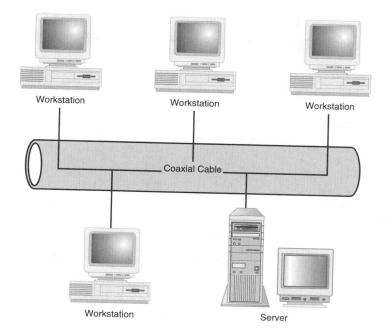

30

Well, because the termination on the segment will be missing. Because the termination will be gone, computers will lose the capability to determine whether any other computers are transmitting data on the wire. Because the computers can't communicate, they will drop any connections they have with other systems on the network.

Clearly, Ethernet 10BASE-2 is a fragile technology if it can crash when one wire breaks. Even though Ethernet 10BASE-2 is fragile, the three conditions listed earlier in this section must be met for effective networking. So the challenge is to figure out how to create a *logical segment*—that is, a network segment that mimics the effect of a single wire without being so fragile and temperamental that a single disconnection brings down the whole net.

10BASE-2 has been superseded by versions of Ethernet that use unshielded twisted-pair (UTP) wiring such as 10BASE-T and 100BASE-T. It's unusual to find 10BASE-2 networks anywhere any longer. At this point, you may be asking why we're discussing it at all, since it's an outdated technology. Here's why: The basic functions of Ethernet (a bus topology in which all computers listen on one wire properly terminated to kill off electrical bounce, CSMA/CD) is more easily pictured using a 10BASE-2 network than a 10BASE-T network. Fundamentally, both networks operate the same way, but 10BASE-2's physical layout makes it easier to associate with the characteristics of Ethernet than later networks. This is why in network diagrams, Ethernet is shown as a bus, whether or not it uses 10BASE-2, to remind us of the fundamentals of Ethernet.

In Search of a Logical Segment: Concentrators and Switches   Enter the *concentrator* or the *switch*, which, depending on the network topology, can be called a hub, a switch, or a MAU. All these devices share a single function—to create logical network segments. In networks that use concentrators, the individual pieces of wire that connect computers together no longer run from machine to machine. Instead, they run from the concentrator to the workstation in a star configuration. This point-to-point wiring is also called "home running" wire, since each wire goes from a central point (home base) to the field (offices, desks, cubes, and so on) (see Figure 30.2).

FIGURE 30.2

A star configuration with a hub (a.k.a. concentrator) at the center.

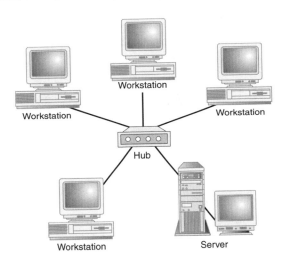

The presence of a concentrator ensures that no single network wire can break and bring down the network. A concentrator essentially is a complete segment in a box. If a wire from *Data Terminal Equipment*, or *DTE* (anything that can connect to the network—computers, printers, routers, and so on), is connected to a port on the concentrator, the concentrator can communicate with that port. If nothing is connected to a port, the concentrator bypasses that port and does not (unlike Ethernet 10BASE-2) see the lack of a connected port as a break in the network wire.

Given how complicated this arrangement is, a analogy is in order. Imagine a trucker whose truck is loaded in such a way that all the packages he carries must be unloaded in a particular order. He has to stop at John's house first, then Mary's, then Angela's, then Beth's, and then Mark's. If he gets to Mary's house and she's not there, he can't unload her package—and he's stuck. He can't go to the next station (Angela's) because he must deliver Mary's package first. He can't bypass this "break" in the system. The break in the system is equivalent to a break in the bus on a 10BASE-2 network.

Another (more sensible!) trucker has packed his truck so that he can get to any package at any time without difficulty. If he gets to Mary's house and she's not there, he just doesn't deliver the package and proceeds to the next delivery. He can bypass "breaks" in the system, which is what a concentrator helps a network do.

Concentrators increase the reliability of a network by ensuring that the segment is not interrupted or broken. In general, concentrators are "intelligent" enough to know when a device is connected and when it is not. In this way, concentrators have increased the reliability of networking adequately to make networking a mass-market technology.

The reliability of concentrators, however, is only the beginning of the story. The third condition we set forth—that only one computer on a segment can transmit data at any given time and computers can transmit data only when no other station is transmitting data—opens up several new issues.

Device Contention   If only one computer on any given segment can transmit data packets at any given time, the possibility that any single computer can grab hold of the network segment long enough to transmit data packets decreases as the number of computers on that network segment increases. When more than one computer or other network device has to transmit data packets at the same time, there are conflicts, and the network slows down. This process is called *device contention*, and it means that a single shared resource—in this case, the network segment—cannot service all the requests it receives in an efficient manner.

Most small-to-medium sized networks operate with a single logical segment, or only one wire, so that only one computer can transmit data at any time. At the same time, computers have become much faster and have developed ever-more-rapacious appetites for *network bandwidth*, or the time during which they can transmit data packets. As a result, many networks have excessive amounts of device contention and operate slower than users would like.

The solution to device contention demands that two additional conditions be met:

- Any equipment that can decrease device contention must be directly backward compatible with existing equipment.

- Any standard that can be applied to reduce device contention must work with current standards.

Network equipment manufacturers, faced with a steadily increasing demand for network bandwidth and the need to retain compatibility with the existing installed base of network adapters and concentrators, were in a conundrum. They had to reduce the number of stations contending for bandwidth on a given segment and at the same time increase connection speed.

To accomplish these goals, network manufacturers invented *switching technologies*. A network switch (which is available for all topologies, from Ethernet to Token Ring to FDDI to ATM) essentially creates a separate segment for each port on a switch (see Figure 30.3). Because only one computer per segment can transmit data at any given time, this clearly frees up computers to establish connections to other computers connected to the switch and transmit data with much less contention for bandwidth.

Another use for switches is to segment networks by connecting switch ports to older shared-media (single-segment) concentrators to create several smaller network segments, thereby increasing the per-computer bandwidth and increasing the response time of the network.

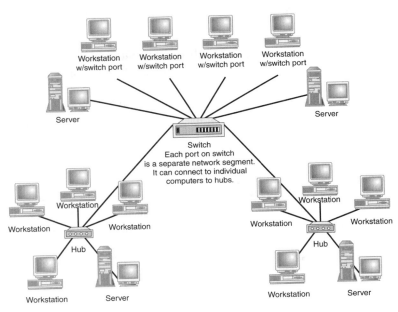

FIGURE 30.3

A network segmented through the use of a switch.

Premise Wiring: Cabling

No matter how well a network is designed, no matter the quality of its individual components, if the wire that joins the computers together isn't installed properly, the network will not work well. Network cabling is the invisible yeoman of the network. When it works well, it goes unnoticed; when it doesn't work, it can be very difficult to diagnose without very sophisticated tools.

In general, there are three types of network wiring: coaxial, twisted-pair, and fiber. Each type of cabling has different requirements if it is to meet network standards and work properly.

Coaxial Coaxial, used for Ethernet 10BASE-2 networking, has simplicity on its side. For internetworking two or three computers in a single space, Ethernet 10BASE-2 is hard to beat. Because no concentrator is needed, it is less expensive than Ethernet 10BASE-T, Token Ring, FDDI, or ATM. However, for reasons cited earlier in this hour, Ethernet 10BASE-2 is not advisable for networks in which reliability is a strong requirement.

With Ethernet 10BASE-2, up to 255 devices can be attached to a single segment, although once again, that maximum is not advisable. The maximum total length of a segment is 185 meters.

The wire used for coaxial networking is usually industry-standard RG-58 cable, which closely resembles the wire used to bring cable television into your home. RG-58 cable has a solid copper center conductor and a braided outer conductor. RG-58 is 50 ohm cable and requires termination at both ends of each segment using a 50 ohm *terminating resistor* (usually just called a *terminator*). Each computer attaches to the segment with a T-connector, which fits into the back of the network card in the computer.

Unshielded Twisted-Pair The next step up from coaxial cable is *Unshielded Twisted-Pair*, or *UTP*. UTP is far and away the most common wire used for networking.

The UTP wires used for networking are eight copper-conductor, four-pair wires very similar to the wire the phone company uses when it wires a home. The main difference between phone wire and UTP is that phone wiring generally has only two pairs of wire (four wires) and UTP has four pairs (eight wires). The wire must be terminated at each end of a point-to-point wire run according to very strict standards set forth in EIA 568B. EIA 568B specifies the order of the wires in the female jack (or the male patch cord) when viewed from above.

The maximum distance for Ethernet 10BASE-T using twisted-pair wires is 200 meters between the concentrator and the computer. For Ethernet 100BASE-T, the maximum distance is 20 meters between stations—quite a reduction in length!

Unshielded twisted-pair is currently the cable standard for most networks. It is relatively inexpensive, easy to install, very reliable, and easy to maintain and expand. If you elect to use twisted-pair cable for your network, find a professional cable installer if you must run wire through the walls and ceilings of your location. Fire regulations typically require that your installer follow building codes when installing cable. Cable run through open ceilings must be plenum rated, or capable of withstanding certain environmental and fire conditions without giving off toxic gases in a fire. Cable run through walls is often different than cable run through ceilings, and only your installer will know the local fire codes well enough to install the correct cable types in the correct locations.

Optical Fiber   The last type of network cabling is *optical fiber*. Optical fiber has taken on a mystique within the networking community over the last several years. Initially, the expense of fiber was such that it was used only for creating high-speed links between concentrators and other esoteric applications. However, the advent of Ethernet 100BASE-FX, which runs over fiber, as well as FDDI and ATM topologies, has brought fiber closer to the mainstream. The "fiber-to-the-desktop" mantra chanted by technology pundits at the beginning of this decade is finally beginning to see to fruition.

Rather than using electrical impulses transmitted over copper wire, optical fiber transmits network data using pulses of light. In spite of its increased acceptance, optical fiber remains extremely expensive to install and maintain. The average network administrator lacks the skills to run fiber and terminate it properly at each end.

Termination of optical fiber is both difficult and chancy. Unlike copper wire, the finished end of a piece of optical fiber must be polished and capped with a special tip that fits into special receptacles on network cards and concentrators. If the polishing and grinding of the end of the cable is off in any way, the cable will not work.

Ultimately, the cabling type you select depends on your needs. If you're just starting to network and you want to become familiar with basic software and hardware, try coaxial networking with two or three machines. If you're installing a network that must be reliable yet cost-effective, try twisted pair. And if you've got to provide your users with huge amounts of high-speed real-time data, install fiber.

Software: Network Operating Systems

In the following sections, you will learn about three network operating systems and one peer configuration. Because this book is devoted to beginning networkers, the network operating systems listed here are all primarily used on Intel-compatible systems.

Novell NetWare

Novell NetWare (now called *IntranetWare*) is the oldest PC-based product in the Network Operating System category.

NetWare is an intense and complex product. By contrast with other, newer network operating systems such as Microsoft Windows 2000, it is difficult and contentious. Its system console is a command line similar to DOS or Unix.

In the file, print, and directory services arena, NetWare is a formidable contender. For file and print services, it remains the standard at a great many companies. With the advent of NetWare Directory Services, or NDS, in NetWare version 4, it has cornered the directory services market.

As networks have grown more complex and require management of greater numbers of users, directory services have become a saving grace for network administrators trying to manage access across thousand-plus-user, multisite networks.

Unlike many newer PC-based network operating systems, NetWare was not designed with the Internet in mind due to its lack of native support for the TCP/IP protocol. A great many of the design choices Novell made appear to have been an attempt to simplify networking enough to make it palatable for PC users.

Microsoft Windows 2000 Advanced Server

Beginning in the late 1980s, Microsoft decided that it needed a high-end network operating system to compete with NetWare and Unix. After a ferocious three-to-four-year struggle (aptly described in Pascal Zachary's book, *Showstopper*), Microsoft had what it had set out to create: Windows NT. Initially, Windows NT version 3.1 (the first version, but renumbered to match the existing version of 16-bit Windows) was all one product—there was initially little if any differentiation between versions used for servers and versions used for workstations.

By the time Microsoft released Windows NT 3.5 in 1995, Microsoft had created two different versions of the operating system: Windows NT Workstation and Windows NT Server. To date, these have evolved into Windows 2000 Professional for the workstation market and Windows 2000 Advanced Server for the server market. For all intents and purposes, both OSs are built on the same basic platform, but Windows 2000 Server has a rich set of utilities and tools the Workstation product lacks. Although most Windows 2000 Server predates Windows XP, Microsoft continues to support Windows 2000 Server and is about to release Windows Server 2003 about the time of this book's publication.

The capability to connect to all sorts of networks was built in to Windows 2000 from the start. Additionally, it can handle the server portion of network application work, which makes it an ideal application server platform from the start. It uses the familiar Windows interface that simplifies administration—Windows 2000 is admirably well suited to small organizations because of its point-and-click administration (see Figure 30.4).

For the vast majority of beginning networkers, Windows 2000 Server is probably the easiest enterprise-class network OS to install and maintain. Do not construe that statement to mean that Windows 2000 is simple; it is not. But in comparison to other network operating systems, Windows 2000 has a certain amount of familiarity because it uses the ubiquitous Windows interface.

30

FIGURE 30.4

*A Microsoft Windows
2000 Server 4.0
screen.*

Unix

Unix is the result of Bell Labs' innovations some 30 years ago. It is a fully preemptive
network operating system with a rich interface unmatched by any other operating system.
Unfortunately, with Unix's richness comes a tremendous degree of complexity. Unix can
accomplish almost any task a computer can do, but the complexity of the interface has
unfortunately led to Unix being maligned as user-hostile. In spite of a much-undeserved
reputation for difficulty, Unix makes a fast file and print server and offers perhaps the
best application services of any network OS presented here.

Unix is best suited to networks in which an experienced system administrator is in
charge. Its complexity makes it unsuitable for the casual user or part-time system administrator, but in the hands of a truly knowledgeable system administrator, Unix can accomplish almost any task reliably and fast.

Client/Server Versus Peer Network Configurations: A Quick Guide

So far, you've seen the terms *client/server* and *peer networking* several times. In the following brief sections, you learn what client/server and peer really are, and what ramifica-
tions they have on you.

Client/server and peer are terms that describe the logical relationship between computers
on a network. Remember that a logical relationship is not the same thing as a physical

relationship—computers can operate in either client/server or peer on any network topology, from 10BASE-2 to FDDI.

Client/Server Networks In a client/server network, the computers are divided into servers and clients. The server is usually a dedicated, powerful machine bearing all the hallmarks of servers as described earlier in this hour; the clients are usually less powerful than the server and connect only to the server through the network. Figure 30.5 shows an example of a client/server network.

30

FIGURE 30.5

A client/server network.

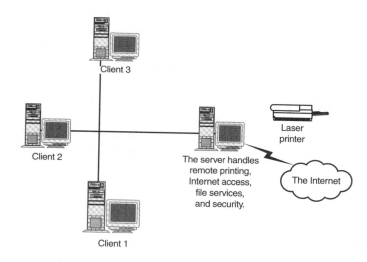

Client 3

Client 2

Client 1

Laser printer

The server handles remote printing, Internet access, file services, and security.

The Internet

The benefits of a client/server configuration (or *architecture*, as it is sometimes called) are mostly of interest to people who rely heavily on the network's reliability. They include the following:

- Centralized management of network resources
- The capability to set stringent and rigorous controls on security, file access, and other potentially sensitive material
- A significant reduction in management at the client
- The capability to secure and back up data from the server
- The capability to "scale"—that is, to increase in size gracefully

In the client/server relationship, clients can see only the server; they cannot see each other. This arrangement results in greater security and increased "replaceability"—if a client workstation fails, it is possible in a client/server architecture to simply replace the client workstation with a comparable machine. If the applications are run from the server's hard drive, once the new computer is connected to the network, the user will have access to most of what he or she had before the workstation failed.

The downsides of client/server are less apparent:

- Client/server networks cost more to implement than peer configurations because of the cost of the server—a dedicated machine that no one uses as a workstation.
- The server becomes a single point of failure. If it breaks, the network is down. Many servers have fault-tolerant features (as do RAID servers, described earlier in this chapter)—fault tolerance is truly necessary for client/server networks.

Client/server is almost always the architecture on which large enterprise networks are built. Reliability and scalability are almost always the stated reasons behind this choice, but make no mistake about it—data security and centralized management, which are big dollar-savers, are also a large factor in the choice of the client/server network.

Peer Networks   At the other end of the spectrum is the peer network (also called a *peer-to-peer* network). In a peer configuration, all user workstations also handle some server functions. For example, one machine with a large hard drive may be used to store some of the users' files. Another system, connected to a printer, may share that printer with other workstations. The chief fact about peer networking, though, is this: In a peer network, there is no server, and all computers can be used as user workstations (see Figure 30.6).

FIGURE 30.6

A peer network.

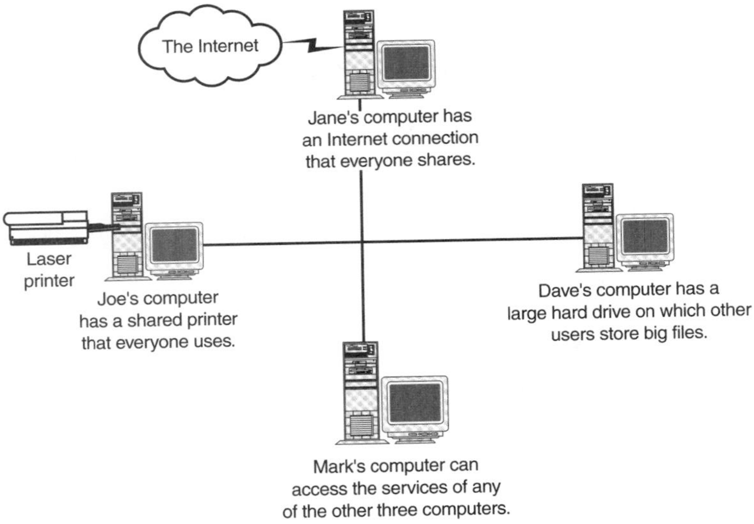

Jane's computer has an Internet connection that everyone shares.

Laser printer

Joe's computer has a shared printer that everyone uses.

Dave's computer has a large hard drive on which other users store big files.

Mark's computer can access the services of any of the other three computers.

A peer network has some distinct advantages:

- Ease of installation and configuration
- Inexpensive compared to client/server networks

However, peer networking has several downsides that (in the author's opinion) outweigh its benefits:

- It has a total lack of centralized control, which means that a peer network is basically unmanageable.
- It is tremendously insecure—security on a peer network is almost nonexistent.
- It is unreliable. Peer networking relies on the vicissitudes of user workstations, which means that the network can be seriously disturbed if (for example) the workstation to which the printer is connected is rebooted or locks up.

Peer networking is suitable only for the very smallest networks—those people who build to teach themselves networking or those in an office with no more than three or four computers. In the next chapter, you'll learn more about setting up the simple peer network.

Summary

By understanding more about computer hardware and network operating system software, you have hopefully gained a global understanding of how a computer works and what client operating systems are.

These are important, material concepts. If you don't know how a computer works, what the parts of a computer are, or what an operating system is, you really can't understand a network at the build-it-yourself level. So make certain that you've assimilated these concepts—not doing so can make networking more difficult than it needs to be.

CHAPTER 31

Networking for Simple Computer Setups

As stated throughout the last three chapters, by its very nature networking can be technical. To fully understand and administer an average network requires knowledge of terms and network technologies such as you've been learning. Having said that, hardware for simple peer-to-peer home and small business networks has gotten very inexpensive and simple to set up.

For those who do not need to understand networks but who only want to set up a simple one with over-the-counter hardware, and possibly take advantage of the new wireless technology that's so available, this chapter is written just for you. You learn just what you need to know to get your small network going so that you can share files, printers, and Internet access. If the surrounding networking chapters were slightly too advanced for your needs, fear not because any terms you need to understand will be re-examined here in light of your needs.

Why You Might Want to Install a Home Network

If you rummage through your basement or attic and dig out the old computer magazines and catalogs from the last few years, chances are you will find ads for several devices that allow you to share a printer between two or more PCs. Long before anyone gave any thought to setting up a home network, users were looking for ways to share peripherals, and the first peripheral they were likely to share was a printer.

Nowadays, printers may just be one item on a short list of shared peripheral devices and resources you want to make available to users on multiple PCs. in addition to printers, PC users are also inclined to share hard disks and other mass storage devices, modems or other communications devices, and files.

Users have found other novel reasons for networking two or more home PCs. For example, if you are really into gaming, networking your PCs is a great way to play head-to-head competitions.

If you've recently purchased a digital camera, you've undoubtedly run into a problem that can be solved by networking your PCs. Depending on the resolution of your digital camera and photos, you may have experienced the problem of creating files that don't fit on a floppy disk drive. You may have tried zipping (compressing) the files to move them from one PC to another; if this failed, you may have settled for using a lower resolution to make the files small enough to fit on a floppy disk. However, if your PCs were networked together, you'd have no trouble moving your files from one PC to another regardless of their resolution or file size.

Installing a Simple Home Network

In recent years, several companies have started offering home networking kits. Most of these are fairly simple starter kits consisting of a small network hub, two or more network cards, and some Ethernet cables (see Figure 31.1).

A *hub* is a device used to connect PCs together on a network. In large corporate networks, hubs may have several dozen or even several hundred connections, called ports, used to connect PCs to the network. In small home networks, hubs generally have from four to eight ports you can use to connect your PCs together. To connect a PC to a network using a hub, you plug one end of the Ethernet cable into the hub and the other end of the cable into the Ethernet card installed in your PC.

Many hardware-based firewall products have a built-in network hub called a *network switch*. If you already have or are planning to purchase a hardware-based firewall containing a network switch, there is no need to purchase a standalone hub. Use the firewall switch in place of the hub.

FIGURE 31.1

All needed components typically come with a home networking kit.

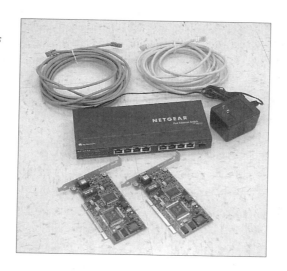

31

Before you rush right out and purchase one of these kits, which range from $75 to $150, you should know that you can sometimes purchase the same items separately for less. Check your local computer store or office supply superstore; you'll need a 10/100Mbps Ethernet card, a four or five port hub, and two 25-foot Ethernet Cat5 cables. You might also want to check eBay and other online sites for these materials.

Make sure that you purchase a hub designed for an Ethernet network (it's actually difficult to purchase a hub for a type of network other than Ethernet), with an advertised speed of 10/100Mbps for each of the ports. Make sure that each port is *auto-sensing*, meaning that the port can tell which speed it should send and receive data depending on its target device. You can purchase a hub with four, five, or as many ports as the manufacturer supplies. What all this means is this:

- Ethernet is the type of network you will be creating; the other type of network you could create is Token Ring, but most manufacturers don't make Token Ring components for home or small business use. As you saw in Chapter 29, "Getting Data from Here to There: How Computers Share Data," Token Ring offers advantages for larger businesses that won't advantage a small installation.

- 10/100Mbps is the minimum and maximum speed your network will use when communicating with the various devices on your network such as the PCs and possibly the communications device you probably will be attaching.

The network cards you purchase should be Ethernet cards designed to operate at speeds of 10/100Mbps. You will want to purchase Ethernet cards that fit into a PCI slot assuming your computer has a PCI slot (Chapter 30, "Mastering Computer Network Concepts," explained what a PCI slot is). Almost all PCI Ethernet cards are newer cards, which means they will almost definitely be plug-and-play cards, which ultimately means they will be easier for you to install. Some USB-based network adapters now exist and laptop users can get PC Card–based Ethernet adapters.

You can purchase network cables in many lengths. Just make sure that they are rated as *Category 5*, often just called *Cat5*, Ethernet cables.

Installing an Ethernet Card in Your PC

If you purchase an internal Ethernet card, you can install your Ethernet card by following these steps:

1. Turn off and unplug your PC, remove the cover, and install the Ethernet card into one of the vacant slots on your PC's motherboard (see Figure 31.2).

2. Replace the cover, plug in, and turn on your PC. If your operating system supports Plug and Play, it should detect the newly installed Ethernet card when it boots and begin the hardware installation of the new card (see Figure 31.3). Simply follow the instructions on the screen to install the driver for your Ethernet card.

FIGURE 31.2

Installing an Ethernet card into a PC slot.

FIGURE 31.3

Windows installing an Ethernet card using the Add Hardware Wizard.

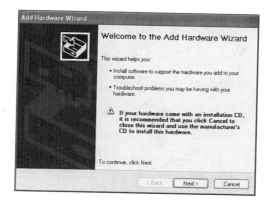

3. If the Add Hardware Wizard does not start automatically, follow the instructions that came with your Ethernet card to install the Ethernet driver.

> If your Ethernet card comes with an installation CD, the Windows XP Hardware Wizard will recommend that you cancel the wizard and proceed with the installation using the installation CD.

After you install the hardware driver for your Ethernet card, you must install the TCP/IP protocol. TCP/IP is the most common network protocol used today to allow devices on a network to communicate with each other. You will definitely need TCP/IP if you plan to share an Internet communications device on your network.

Installing TCP/IP on Your PC

To install TCP/IP on your PC, follow these steps:

1. In Windows XP, select Start, Control Panel, Network Connection; Windows should list the Ethernet card you just installed. Right-click the Ethernet card listed and select Properties from the shortcut menu to open the Properties dialog box for your Ethernet card (see Figure 31.4).

2. Click Install, select Protocol, and then click Add. When the choices for available protocols to add are listed, select Internet Protocol (TCP/IP) and click OK.

Finally, you must configure TCP/IP for use on your network. For a network with only two or three PCs, configuring TCP/IP settings is fairly simple. If you don't have a registered set of IP addresses, you will have to use what are called private network IP addresses (IP addresses that are not routed over the Internet and are reserved for use on private networks). The range of IP addresses you should use is from 192.168.0.1 through 192.168.0.254. For example, on your first PC, use the IP address 192.168.0.1. On the second PC, use 192.168.0.2. On the third PC, use 192.168.0.3, and so on.

FIGURE **31.4**

The Properties dialog box for your newly installed Ethernet card.

Configuring Your TCP/IP Settings

To install and configure TCP/IP on your PC for the card you just installed, follow these steps:

1. In Windows XP, select Start, Control Panel, Network Connection; Windows should list the Ethernet card you just installed. Right-click the Ethernet card listed and select Properties from the shortcut menu to open the Properties dialog box for your Ethernet card.

2. Scroll down the box labeled This Connection Uses the Following Item and select Internet Protocol (TCP/IP). Click Properties to open the Properties dialog box shown in Figure 31.5.

3. Select the Use the Following IP Address option and type the IP address **192.168.0.1** for your first PC, type **192.168.0.2** for the second PC, type **192.168.0.3** for the third PC, and so on for as many PCs as you have to network.

4. Leave the entry for default gateway blank because you don't have one.

The *default gateway* is typically the device used to connect your network to another network, such as the Internet. If or when you connect your network to a communications device such as a cable modem or DSL modem, you will enter the IP address you set for that device as your default gateway.

FIGURE 31.5
The Properties dialog box for TCP/IP settings.

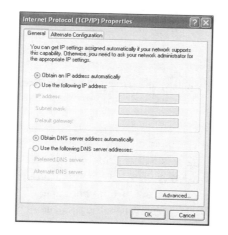

5. Windows should automatically fill in the appropriate subnet mask based on the IP address you enter.

6. Leave the entry for your DNS server blank, because you don't have one of these, either (yet!).

7. Click OK and continue closing all the dialog boxes and screens you previously opened.

Turning on File and Print Sharing

The last task you must perform to make your small network fully operational is to turn on File and Print Sharing. This feature allows you to share files and peripherals such as a printer.

To turn on File and Print Sharing, follow these steps:

1. In Windows XP, select Start, Control Panel, Network Connection; Windows should list the Ethernet card you just installed. Right-click the Ethernet card listed and select Properties from the shortcut menu to open the Properties dialog box for your Ethernet card.

2. Make sure that the File and Print Sharing for Microsoft Networks option is selected.

Sharing Your High-Speed Internet Connection

One of the main reasons for networking your PCs together is so that you can share a single communications line for the Internet. If you've upgraded to a cable or DSL modem

31

(if you want to, see Chapter 44, "Upgrading Your Modem," for details), either one is the ideal communications line to share across a small home network.

> Because of the complexity and variety of home network configurations, many cable and DSL broadband providers do not support access over a home network.

Your cable or DSL modem be attached with a Cat5 Ethernet cable plugged to the network card in your PC. You will use this same cable to connect your cable or DSL modem to your network. After you connect the cable from your cable or DSL modem to your network, you must also set the default gateway setting on each PC.

Connecting a Cable or DSL Modem to Your Network

To connect your cable or DSL modem to your network, follow these steps:

1. Locate the Cat5 Ethernet cable you used to connect your modem to your PC. Leave the cable connected to the modem and plug the other end of the cable into one of the ports in your hub.

2. At each PC, you must set the default gateway entry in your TCP/IP settings. In Windows XP, select Start, Control Panel, Network Connection; Windows should list the Ethernet card you installed in the PC. Right-click the Ethernet card listed and select Properties from the shortcut menu to open the Properties dialog box for your Ethernet card.

3. Scroll down the box labeled This Connection Uses the Following Item and select Internet Protocol (TCP/IP). Click Properties to open the Properties dialog box.

4. In the default gateway field (which you left blank when you previously configured TCP/IP on your PC), type the IP address you entered for your cable or DSL modem.

5. Turn on your cable or DSL modem.

6. To test your connection, start your Web browser (Internet Explorer, Netscape Navigator, or whichever Web browser you use) and see whether you can connect to a Web site. If you can't, make sure that all your cables are properly connected and that you followed all the previous instructions for installing and configuring your Ethernet card.

Network Security Concerns

You must be concerned with possible security violations on your PCs now that they are connected to a network—especially since you've turned on File and Print Sharing.

There are two ways to solve this problem on your network. You can install a software-based firewall program on each PC, such as ZoneAlarm, one you can download at http://www.zonelabs.com. Alternatively, you can install a hardware-based firewall product, which many users actually find a lot easier to configure.

Hardware-based firewall products, often called *cable/DSL firewall routers*, are not only simpler to set up and use than the software versions, but most also offer other advantages. Many hardware firewalls include a network hub or switch and router as part of the configuration, meaning that you don't have to purchase a separate hub to create your network.

31

Many hardware-based firewall products show what looks like a built-in network hub but refer to it as a network switch. A switch and a hub perform the same function on a network; the difference is that a switch performs it a little better. You could describe a switch as a "smarter" hub. A switch contains a few more electronics than a hub; these extra electronics are used to improve performance on your network. So don't be confused if you see a cable or DSL firewall advertised with a switch. Likewise, don't be alarmed when the manufacturer refers to the device as a router. The router function built-in to the device just allows you the ability to expand your home network later if you are so inclined.

One of the first manufacturers to offer cable and DSL users a combined firewall/hub/router product was Linksys (http://www.linksys.com/). Their product line continues to be one of the best sellers (see Figure 31.6).

FIGURE 31.6

A Linksys cable/DSL firewall router in operation.

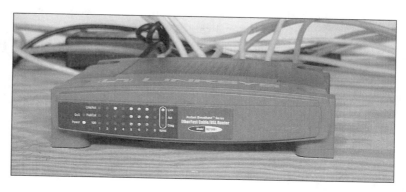

Linksys offers a combined firewall/hub/router device in configurations with one, four, and eight network ports for connecting PCs to your network. If you have already purchased a hub for your network, you can save money by selecting the 1-port Linksys model.

Other companies offering similar and comparably priced products are NetGear (`http://www.netgear.com`) and D-Link (`http://www.dlink.com`).

To connect your cable/DSL firewall/router to your network, you will need one more Cat5 cable. Make sure that you have one before you begin because many manufacturers don't always include one with the cable/DSL firewall router. Before you purchase the cable, check your hub to see whether it has a port designated as an *uplink* port. If your hub has an uplink port, you can purchase a standard Cat5 cable. If your hub does not have an uplink port, make sure that the Cat5 cable you purchased is a "crossover cable."

Connecting a Cable/DSL Firewall Router to Your Network

To connect your cable/DSL firewall router to your network, follow these steps:

1. Locate the Cat5 cable connecting your cable or DSL modem to your network hub. Unplug this cable from the hub and plug it instead into the network port on your cable/DSL firewall labeled *WAN*. WAN stands for Wide Area Network.

2. Take a second Cat5 cable and plug one end into one of the ports on your cable/DSL firewall router and the other end into the port on your hub labeled Uplink (see Figure 31.7). You may have to press the Uplink button on your hub to activate the port as an uplink port. If your hub does not include an uplink port, make sure that the cable connecting your hub and the cable/DSL firewall router is a Cat5 crossover cable.

3. Using one of the PCs on your network, follow the instructions included with your cable/DSL firewall router to configure the device. You will probably have to set IP addresses for both the WAN (Wide Area Network) side and LAN (Local Area Network) side of your cable/DSL firewall router. Many of these devices also allow you to run what is known as DHCP on your network so that you don't have to individually set IP addresses on each networked PC.

DHCP stands for *Dynamic Host Configuration Protocol*. This network service automatically provides IP addresses and other configuration information to each networked PC.

FIGURE 31.7

An uplink port on a network hub.

uplink port   uplink\normal button

Wireless Networking

Wireless networking components for home networks are fairly versatile, and manufacturers have designed them to function either as the heart of your network or as simply a part of it. The key to wireless networking is what is known as the Wireless Access Point such as the one shown in Figure 31.8.

FIGURE 31.8

A Wireless Access Point device from Linksys.

31

A typical configuration for which a user might employ one or more wireless components in a network is a standard Ethernet network set up in a basement or home office using a small Ethernet hub with one or more PCs connected and perhaps a cable modem or DSL modem providing high-speed Internet connectivity. A Wireless Access Point device such as the one shown in Figure 31.8 might be used to connect several other PCs located in other rooms in the house to this Ethernet network.

Installation is fairly straightforward. You simply plug the Wireless Access Point device into one of the ports on your Ethernet hub and then follow the manufacturer's instructions to configure the device. Typically, configuration amounts to little more than assigning the device an IP address.

The only other device that is needed to complete this configuration is a wireless network card for each PC connected to the network.

Wireless Ethernet cards typically are designed for laptop computers because just about all of them are manufactured as PCMCIA-type devices (see Figures 31.9 and 31.10). A few are also manufactured as USB devices.

> PCMCIA is a specification for devices manufactured to work with laptop computers. PCMCIA devices are designed to fit into the two small slots typically located on the sides of laptop computers.

FIGURE 31.9
A typical wireless PCMCIA network card.

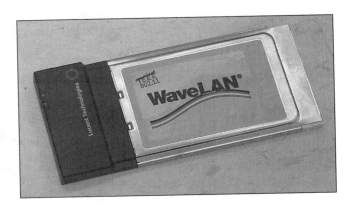

Many manufacturers have realized that even though wireless network cards were originally designed with laptop users in mind, there might also be a market for desktop users. Therefore, many manufacturers also offer a type of low-cost conversion card that enables you to use a laptop PCMCIA card in a desktop computer. As you can see in Figure 31.11, the conversion card is simply a PCI (or ISA) card with a built-in PCMCIA slot that allows you to insert the wireless laptop card into the slot, and then insert the entire card into a desktop computer.

FIGURE 31.10

A wireless PCMCIA network card being inserted into a laptop PCMCIA slot.

FIGURE 31.11

A conversion card for a wireless PCMCIA card with the card inserted.

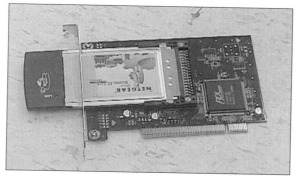

Using a conversion card/wireless card combo is no different than using any other type of Ethernet card in a PC in your network. You simply insert the card into a slot in your PC, install the hardware driver for the card, and then install and configure the TCP/IP protocol.

Installing a Conversion Card/Wireless Card Combo

To install a wireless Ethernet card in your PC, follow these steps:

1. Turn off and unplug your PC, remove the cover, and install the wireless Ethernet card in the conversion card into one of the vacant slots on your PC's motherboard.

2. Replace the cover, plug in, and turn on your PC. If your operating system supports Plug and Play, it should detect the newly installed Ethernet card when it boots and begin the hardware installation of the new card. Follow the instructions on the screen to install the driver for your Ethernet card.

3. If the New Hardware Wizard does not start automatically, follow the instructions that came with your Ethernet card to install the Ethernet driver.

 If your Ethernet card comes with an installation CD, the Windows XP New Hardware Wizard will recommend that you cancel the wizard and proceed with the installation using the installation CD.

After you install the hardware driver for your Ethernet card, you must install the TCP/IP protocol. TCP/IP is the most common network protocol used today to allow devices on a network to communicate with each other. You will definitely need TCP/IP if you plan to share an Internet communications device on your network. Also, you will need to turn on File and Print Sharing. You can do this by following the instructions in these earlier sections of this chapter: "Installing TCP/IP on Your PC," "Configuring Your TCP/IP Settings," and "Turning on File and Print Sharing."

Wireless Security Concerns

On wireless networks, you have a new set of security concerns. Wireless transmissions can be intercepted because they are essentially radio frequency transmissions. Most wireless devices allow you to turn on and use what is known as the *Wireless Encryption Protocol (WEP)*. WEP sets up an encrypted communications link between communicating wireless devices so that even if the transmissions are intercepted, they appear as gibberish so that anyone intercepting them will not be able to decrypt the transmissions. Don't worry about having to take any extra steps to use a wireless encryption device. The encryption-decryption is done automatically by the communicating devices after the devices are configured for the same network. Follow the manufacturer's instructions for configuring WEP on your wireless devices.

Summary

In this chapter, you learned how to connect your PCs together in a home or small business network so that you can share peripherals and resources. You also learned how to share one of the most important resources over your network: your Internet connection. You also learned about a hardware option for providing security on your network to protect against possible security violations and attacks over the Internet. Finally, you learned how to install a wireless network that does not require cables to connect your PCs to the network.

PART X

Diagnosing Problems and Planning Upgrades

Chapter

CHAPTER 32

Deciding to Upgrade

PC manufacturers sometimes appear to be releasing new models every quarter, if not more often. It's no wonder PC users are confused and more than a bit apprehensive each time they go shopping for a new PC. The intense competition of the hot PC market is both a blessing and a curse for users. If you've been watching PC prices nose-dive, you are already aware of the consumer blessing this competition has produced. Users appear to be cursed, however, by being forced to play the "wait-and-see" game: "If I wait just a little longer before I purchase, I can get a faster, more powerful PC and pay less for it."

You do have an alternative to the wait-and-see game. Despite the downward trend of PC prices, many users are opting instead to upgrade portions of their existing PC rather than purchase an entirely new PC. Although upgrading might not exactly match the performance of a new PC, selective upgrading of certain key components in your PC can substantially improve performance in the areas that matter most to you, depending on how you use your PC. In the previous part of this book, network users learned the special upgrade considerations they face; for the next few chapters, all computer users can utilize the upgrade information as these upgrades apply universally.

When to Consider Upgrading Your PC

The first decision you are faced with is whether to upgrade or purchase a new PC. If you are still using a PC with a Pentium 100 processor (or older) the decision has already been made for you. Your old PC should be considered nothing more than an obsolete boat anchor or doorstop, and you should be concerned only with deciding how much you will spend on a new PC.

If you are still using a PC with a second-generation Pentium processor, the decision may not seem so clear-cut (even though it really is). The second-generation Pentium processors (that is, Pentiums with a clock speed of 300MHz or less) are six or more years old and are not really capable of running the current batch of software at an acceptable performance level. But if you are content to perform some light word processing and spreadsheet tasks, and you occasionally want to browse a few Web sites on the Internet or play a few (older!) games, you may be able to squeeze another year or two out of that creaking old dinosaur.

Most major software manufacturers are now producing software optimized to run under these newer operating systems such as Windows XP. If you are running anything slower than 500MHz, it's time to upgrade.

> *16-bit* and *32-bit* are technical terms you will hear whenever the discussion turns to operating systems and programming, among other things. Quite simply, the terms refer to how computer instructions and data are processed by your computer, either in 16-bit units or in 32-bit units. Because a 32-bit unit is twice as large as a 16-bit unit, the assumption is that 32-bit programs and operating systems are twice as fast as their 16-bit counterparts. "Twice as fast" may be stretching it a bit, but the basic underlying assumption is generally true. Thirty-two-bit programs and operating systems are faster than their 16-bit counterparts.

What Components in My PC Are Upgradeable?

Almost every component in your PC—including the processor, memory, video card, disk drives, and more—is a candidate to be upgraded.

Which components you decide to upgrade is often determined by how you use your PC, but not always. Some upgrades make sense simply because the price of the particular component is too good to pass up. In the last few years, the price of hard disk drives has dropped dramatically. You can regularly see more than 50GB hard disk drives advertised for under $200.

If you're wondering where to start with your upgrading plans, Table 32.1 can give you some ideas on how to deal with some problems or issues you might already be facing.

TABLE 32.1   Quick Troubleshooting Table

Problem	Possible Upgrade Solution
PC locks up or can't load more than a few programs simultaneously	Add more memory
Programs or files load very slowly from CD-ROM drive	Upgrade to faster CD-ROM drive
32-bit software won't install	Upgrade to 32-bit OS
Can't format larger hard disk drive	Upgrade your BIOS
Can't increase video resolution or number of colors displayed	Upgrade your video card
Repeatedly seeing "out of disk space" error message	Upgrade/add new hard disk drive
All PC operations run slower than expected	Upgrade your CPU
System clock losing correct time or has wrong time	Upgrade your BIOS

32

Upgrading Your Memory (RAM)

Your PC's memory typically is one of the easiest and least expensive components to upgrade (see Figure 32.1). Upgrading your PC's memory has the added advantage of improving its performance. Sometimes the improvement in performance is large and other times it is small, but there is always an increase of some type.

The terms *RAM* and *memory* are often used interchangeably. RAM is short for Random Access Memory and is the electronic memory (chips) that your computer uses for running programs and storing temporary data. RAM is not the permanent storage area for files.

FIGURE 32.1
PC memory is proba-
bly the easiest of all
upgrades you can
make.

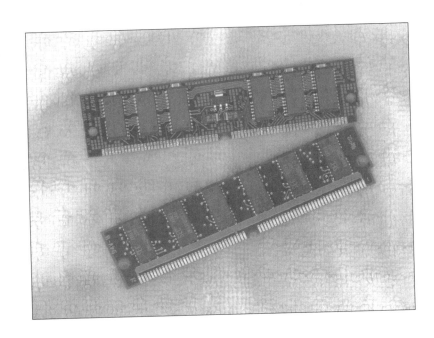

Upgrading Your Processor

Because your processor is largely responsible for how fast your PC and your programs run, upgrading your processor will generally make most things run faster. Bear in mind, if you replace the Pentium II 400MHz processor in your PC with a 500MHz Pentium II processor, your computer will not necessarily operate as fast as a PC built from the ground up, such as a 500MHz Pentium II computer. It is not just the processor that determines how fast your PC operates. Other technologies also come into play, and these differences contribute to the computer's speed and performance.

> *MHz* is the abbreviation for *megahertz* (millions of hertz per second) and is used as a measurement for the oscillating timing frequency used by processors. In simple terms, it is an indication of the relative speed of a processor.

Upgrading your processor generally yields some increase in performance.

Upgrading Your Hard Disk Drive

Upgrading your PC's hard disk drive (see Figure 32.2) is probably the second most common upgrade behind memory upgrades, largely because of the dramatic drop in hard disk pricing and the increase in available hard disk sizes.

FIGURE 32.2

You can never have too much hard disk storage space.

Upgrading a hard disk is also relatively easy. Although adding a larger hard disk drive might not seem like a significant performance improvement, consider your own habits in file creation and how often you acquire new programs you would like to try—especially if you regularly download shareware programs from the Internet.

If you once had or currently have a small hard disk (small being defined as any hard disk 10GB or smaller), and you regularly find yourself deleting files to make room for new files or programs, you can appreciate the performance improvement offered by the addition of a larger hard disk.

32

Upgrading Your Video System

The majority of the time you choose to upgrade your video system, it will be for a specific application. For example, you might need a larger or higher resolution monitor (see Figure 32.3) to work with a specific application, such as graphic artistry or CAD (computer-aided design). Many of the newer games also require better, faster video systems.

FIGURE 32.3

When purchasing a monitor, purchase one as large as you can afford.

Upgrading Other PC Components

The few components mentioned in this chapter are not the only items in your PC you can upgrade. In addition to memory, processors, hard disk drives, and video systems, you can also upgrade your floppy and CD-ROM drives, your PC's sound system, your modem (or whatever you use to communicate over the Internet), your computer's system board, chassis, power supply, and more.

You can get testing and performance monitoring software (see Figure 32.4), which provides before and after ratings on your components so that you can actually see the improvements your upgrades are producing.

FIGURE 32.4

The Benchmark component of Norton Utilities is one of several performance monitoring programs you'll be introduced to in the next few chapters.

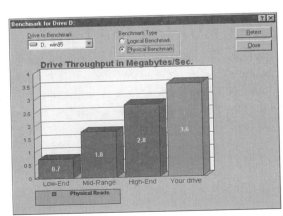

Summary

In this chapter, you learned what factors you need to consider when deciding whether to upgrade your PC. You also learned what components in your PC you can (or should) upgrade and the pros and cons of upgrading versus purchasing a new computer.

32

Chapter 33

Understanding System Components

Before you can begin upgrading the various components in your PC, it may help you to be able to identify each component and have a basic understanding of how each component functions. In Chapter 30, "Mastering Computer and Network Concepts," you saw an overview of your computer system from the hardware level but the perspective was from a network installer's perspective. Single computer owners and users on home-based or very small business networks, do not need the hardware depth that Chapter 30 provides. Here, you will learn what you need to know about your PC.

Eliminating Potential Hazards

Before you go tinkering around inside your PC, you must be aware of a few potential hazards that exist. Most of the potential problems you encounter can be far more damaging to your equipment than to you. Except for the power supply, the voltage inside your PC is far too low to be a serious hazard to you, but it can cause very serious damage to the sensitive electronic components.

This is one caution we cannot stress enough! The power supply in your PC is built using low release capacitors and contains more than enough wattage to kill you even after it is turned off and the plug is pulled. Absolutely, positively, do not open your power supply under any circumstances!

Although these precautions may seem obvious to anyone who works on any type of electrical equipment, they are nevertheless worth mentioning here:

- Unplug your PC before you begin any work on it that requires you to remove the cover. Too often, many users are content with merely pressing the on/off switch, but on/off switches have been known to malfunction or stick. To be absolutely certain that no power is running through your system, unplug the power cord either from the back of your PC or from the wall receptacle.

- Ground yourself to release any possible static electricity. This is especially important during the winter months when hot, dry air increases the potential for static electricity. All electronic components in your PC can be damaged or destroyed by one good jolt of static electricity. If you have a grounding wrist strap, attach it to your wrist. Otherwise, touch the metal case of your computer or the metal housing around the power supply to ground yourself. You can also touch a metal radiator pipe if you have one handy in your house or wherever you are working on your PC.

Static electricity is a bit hard to measure; however, to illustrate just how sensitive your PC's components are, the type of jolt you get from touching a doorknob after shuffling along a wool carpet in the winter is more than sufficient to destroy most components in your PC.

- Obviously, it should go without saying that you should not have water around, or any other liquids that can contribute to a possible electrical shock, when working with any type of electrical equipment.

- Be extremely cautious about working with any type of electrical equipment if you have a pacemaker or any type of heart condition.

- Make sure that you have an uncluttered workspace. A large kitchen table is an excellent place to work, and because many kitchens have tile or linoleum floors, you can also guard against static electricity at the same time. Consider spreading a large towel under or near your PC to catch any small screws that you might drop while working on your computer. White or light-colored towels make it easier to see small pieces.

Keep in mind, too, that some manufacturers will void your warranty if you open your case and go poking around inside your PC. Be sure that you check your warranty before you begin laying out your grand upgrade plans.

Differentiating Between Desktop and Tower PCs

PCs come in two standard configurations—*desktop models* and *towers*. Figure 33.1 shows a typical desktop model PC, and Figure 33.2 shows a basic tower configuration.

FIGURE 33.1

A typical desktop model PC.

33

Desktop models may come in several sizes, often with names such as full-size, baby-AT, or slim-sized to denote some difference in relative size, but they all follow the same basic design layout: a PC laid out horizontally or flat on the desktop.

Tower models also come in a variety of sizes with corresponding names such as mini-tower, midsize-tower, full tower, and so on. If you look closely, you can see that the design of a tower is basically just a desktop model turned vertically or on its side. Turning a desktop PC on its side to produce a tower model offers a few advantages. Towers generally take less real estate on your crowded desktop and larger tower models usually have additional space for more internal disk drives.

FIGURE 33.2
A typical tower model PC.

Even before tower models were developed, PC users got the idea that PCs can work just as well vertically as they do horizontally. Some innovative entrepreneurs even began marketing stands for PCs so that you could turn a desktop vertically. If you are still using a desktop model and you want to turn it on its side, go right ahead—just make sure that the PC is stable.

Regardless of whether you have a desktop or a tower PC, looking at it from the front you will likely notice several similarities. The first thing you will notice is one or more drives that use some type of removable media such as a floppy disk drive, a CD-ROM drive, a DVD drive, or perhaps a removable media type hard disk drive. On the front of some PCs you may also find a reset button. A reset button generally is used to reboot your PC much the same as if you powered off and then powered on your PC—what's known as a cold boot.

You may have heard the terms *warm boot* and *cold boot*. The terms describe two methods of rebooting or restarting your PC. As the names imply, a warm boot is a reboot with the power on; a cold boot is a reboot with the power off. The difference between the two booting methods is more than just the presence of electrical power. A cold boot is a more thorough or complete boot-up process because it also releases any data that might still be in several system caches or memory holding areas. A cold boot runs a more thorough *POST—Power On Self Test*. A warm boot is less stressful on your electrical components.

Some PC manufacturers also place the on/off switch on the front of the PC to make access to it more convenient. Although this placement is just as common as placing the on/off switch on the back or the side of the PC, many experts consider it a mistake because it opens the PC to the risk of losing data if you accidentally hit the power switch and turn off your PC.

Identifying Your PC's External Connectors

Before you start poking around inside your PC, you should become familiar with the external connectors typically found on a PC. Most of these connectors are usually found on the back of your PC. (Figure 33.3 shows the typical array of external connectors.)

The following is a list of connectors you typically find on the back of a PC:

- **Serial port.** Used for connecting serial communication devices such as modems, printers, plotters, and so on. Serial ports can be either 9- or 25-pin D-shaped male connections. Typically you find two serial ports labeled 1 and 2 or A and B.

- **Parallel port.** Used for connecting parallel printers and some types of external removable media drives and scanners. Parallel ports are 25-pin D-shaped female connections.

Male and *female connectors*? For those of you who are not sure how to identify a male or a female connector, a male connector is one that protrudes and a female connector is one that surrounds or receives. If you are still not sure which is which, ask your mother.

- **VGA video port.** This connector is what you plug your monitor into. It is a 15-pin D-shaped female connector.

- **Keyboard port.** Your keyboard is connected to this port by one of two types of keyboard connectors—the larger AT-style connector or the smaller PS/2-style DIN connector.

- **USB (Universal Serial Bus) port.** A 12Mbit/second interface that supports up to 127 devices. USB 2 transfer data at speeds up to 480Mbit/second and is backwards compatible to USB (also known as USB 1) so all your USB 1 hardware works in a USB 2 port.

- **Mouse port.** A standard port for plugging in a PS/2 mouse.

FIGURE 33.3

The rear view of a PC showing the external connectors typically found on a PC.

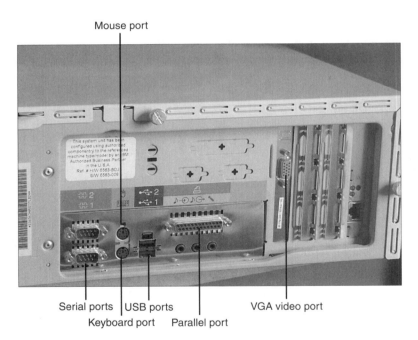

Mouse port

Serial ports | USB ports

Keyboard port   Parallel port

VGA video port

Identifying the Parts Inside Your PC

Before you begin working on your PC, it helps to be able to identify the basic components you might need or want to upgrade or repair. Think of it this way: Before you attempt to do any routine maintenance on your car, you should be able to identify items such as an oil filter, a spark plug, and a radiator. The same principle applies to your PC. Before you start pulling out your hard disk drives or your memory DIMMs, you have to be able to locate and identify them.

Identifying the Main System Board

After you remove the cover of your PC and look inside (remember to unplug your PC and ground yourself), you can see the main system board, also known as the *motherboard*—an affectionate term that supposedly originated in the days of Apple II computers (see Figure 33.4).

The terms *main system board* and *motherboard* are often used interchangeably and refer to the same component. Both are used in this book, so don't be confused.

FIGURE 33.4

A typical main system board.

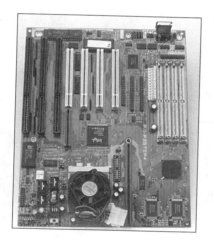

The main system board is usually mounted on the bottom of your PC if you have a desktop model, or on one side of your PC if you have a tower model. The main system board can be thought of as a connection or communication terminal. Most of the other devices in your PC connect to it, either directly through one of the many connectors built in to the main system board or through an interface card that plugs into the main system board.

Identifying the Microprocessor

The *microprocessor*, also referred to as the *CPU* or *chip*, is usually plugged into a socket or inserted into a slot on the main system board (see Figure 33.5) and is considered the brains of your PC. On some early model 486 computers, the CPU was soldered to the main system board, but CPUs haven't been soldered onto motherboards in more than a decade so don't worry that yours is permanently installed.

33

FIGURE 33.5

*A microprocessor
located on the main
system board.*

Most older microprocessors are roughly about 2 inches square, as you can see in Figure
33.5. Beginning with the Pentium II, Intel began housing their microprocessors in a container that is a little smaller than a VHS tape cassette (see Figure 33.6).

FIGURE 33.6

*A Pentium III micro-
processor.*

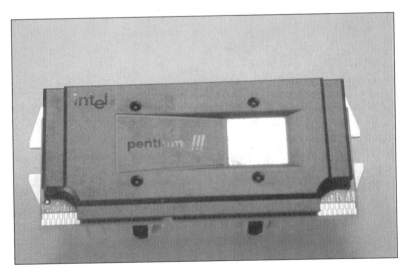

Another difference you'll notice about the Pentium II and the Pentium III model CPUs is
that the container that houses the CPU is not plugged into a socket as all previous models
of microprocessors were. Pentium IIs and later microprocessors manufactured by Intel
are plugged into the main system board using a slot designed especially for the Pentium
II. (In case you're interested, the slot is called slot 1.)

The microprocessor executes the instructions written into the programs that you run on your PC. Some examples of microprocessors are Pentium, Pentium Pro, Pentium II, Celeron, Pentium III, and Pentium IV CPUs.

> Sometimes you can't see your microprocessor because it is covered by a heat sink. A heat sink is used to help dissipate heat generated by your microprocessor and often looks like a black (or blue or silver) square or rectangle with a lot of small projections protruding from it.

When you hear a reference to the speed of a particular PC, such as 500MHz, 600MHz, 733MHz, 766MHz, 1GHz, and so on, the speed reference is actually to the speed of the CPU.

Identifying Memory (RAM)

The memory in your computer (also called RAM, or Random Access Memory) is built in to modules called DIMMs (Double Inline Memory Modules). DIMMs are electronic modules that sit in slots, usually located on your main system board (see Figure 33.7).

FIGURE 33.7
DIMMs in slots located on your main system board.

33

Even though memory (RAM) and hard disk space are both measured in megabytes (MB), don't confuse the two. Memory is used by your PC to run programs, and disk space is used to store files.

Identifying Disk Drives

Typically, PCs come equipped with three types of disk drives—floppy disk drives, hard disk drives, and some type of optical drive such as a CD-ROM, CD-RW, or DVD drive. All have changed considerably over the past few years.

> To cover some general terminology and measurements, a *bit* is a plus or minus electrical charge (more commonly understood as 1 or 0). Eight bits equal one byte. A *kilobyte* (*KB*) is 1024 bytes (2^{10} bytes). A *megabyte* (*MB*) is one million bytes, and a *gigabyte* (*GB*) is a thousand megabytes or approximately a billion bytes.

Originally, floppy disk drives were designed to accommodate 5 1/4-inch disks, and their capacity was only 160KB. Their capacity eventually grew to 1.2MB before they were gradually phased out and replaced by 3 1/2-inch drives. The 3 1/2-inch drive also went through its own evolutionary period, expanding from an original capacity of 720KB to its present storage capacity of 1.44MB.

Nowadays, virtually all PCs come equipped with a single 3 1/2-inch floppy disk drive (see Figure 33.8). However, a few manufacturers now offer you the option of including a Zip drive in addition to or even as a replacement for a 3 1/2-inch drive.

FIGURE 33.8

A 3 1/2-inch floppy drive in a PC.

PCs have had hard disk drives ever since IBM shipped its first PC/XT model back in 1984 with a 10MB hard disk drive. Since then, hard disk drives have become faster, and their capacities have expanded beyond what anyone could have imagined back in 1984. Now it is difficult to purchase a PC with a hard disk drive smaller than 20GB (gigabytes). Although floppy disk drives are easy to identify (just look for the device into which you insert a floppy disk), to the uninitiated, a hard disk may not have any identifying labels or obvious clues. Hard disk drives can be placed almost anywhere inside your PC. Typically they have a black or silver case, are usually less than 1 inch thick, and have a gray ribbon cable attached to one end. They may be mounted inside a chassis or cage and are not visible from the outside of the PC (see Figure 33.9).

FIGURE 33.9

A typical hard disk drive inside a PC.

Identifying Interface Cards

33

Interface cards are electronic circuit cards that enable your PC to connect to or interface with another device. There are dozens, if not actually hundreds, of different types of interface cards you can attach to your PC. To work with your PC, an interface card must be inserted into one of the slots located on your PC's main system board (see Figure 33.10).

Never remove or insert an interface card while the power to your PC is on. You can seriously damage both the card and your main system board.

The most common type of interface card is a video display card, which enables a monitor to work with your PC. If you follow the cord that runs from your monitor to your PC, you see that it is plugged into a connector on an interface card. This is your video card.

FIGURE 33.10

*An interface card
inserted into one of the
slots on your main sys-
tem board.*

On some PCs, the video card circuitry is built in to the main system board,
eliminating the need for a separate video interface card. You can, however,
upgrade these built-in cards by disabling them and then adding an actual
video card to your PC.

Here's a list of some other common types of interface cards you are likely to find inside
your PC:

- **Modem cards.** Used for communicating with other computers over telephone lines
- **SCSI (Small Computer System Interface) cards.** Used to attach SCSI devices
  such as scanners and external disk drives to your PC
- **Network interface cards.** Used to attach your PC to local area networks, or to
  cable modems or DSL modems

Identifying the PC Power Supply

The last device inside your PC that you have to be able to identify is your PC's power
supply. As the name implies, the power supply provides electrical power to the devices
inside your PC. *Transformer* might be a more appropriate name because the power supply
actually converts or transforms AC power into DC power and steps down the voltage
from 120 volts AC to 12.5 volts DC. The name *power supply* was tacked on originally,
however, and has stuck through the years.

The power supply is easy to identify because the power cord plugs into the power supply from the outside of the PC. On the inside of the PC, you should be able to see numerous cables running from the power supply to many of the devices in your PC, such as the main system board and the disk drives.

Summary

In this chapter, you learned about the major components found in most PCs and learned how to identify them in your own PC. You are now ready to learn more about monitoring your current system so you'll have an idea what you need for upgrading your system for better performance.

33

CHAPTER 34

Monitoring Computer Performance

After you make all of the changes and upgrades to your PC that you deem necessary, you will be curious to see how much improvement in performance your upgrades are making. To properly evaluate the upgrades you make, you need some type of hardware evaluation program, more commonly known as *performance monitoring* software.

Performance monitoring software enables you to take a set of base performance readings on your PC (before you begin making upgrades); as you make upgrades, you use the software to evaluate the (hopefully) improved performance in your PC.

Performance Monitoring Programs

In this chapter, you are introduced to a few additional utilities you can use to analyze your PC, monitor your computer system's performance to see how much improvement in performance you're gaining from the devices you upgrade, and possibly also diagnose problems with your system.

Some of the utilities shown here are commercial products, whereas others are available free (or for a minimal shareware registration fee).

Ziff-Davis Media Benchmarks

For years, the gold standard for benchmark testing performance in PCs was the Ziff-Davis testing suites consisting of the WinBench and WinStone testing programs. Ziff-Davis has greatly expanded its suite of testing and benchmarking software to what is now called the Ziff-Davis Media Benchmarks. In addition to benchmarking overall PC performance and PCs running standard business-related software, Ziff-Davis now offers testing programs for 3D graphics, CD-ROM subsystems, audio subsystems, laptop batteries, Web clients, and networking performance.

The testing programs offer no diagnostic functions but are some of the best performance testing programs you can acquire.

The suite of programs stress-tests your PC by simulating a series of real-world computational tasks, such as calculating a long and complex spreadsheet, reformatting and repaginating a long Word document, querying a large database, and performing a series of graphic-intensive display operations. You can select to run any one or all of the tests in the suite (see Figure 34.1).

In its first few incarnations, the original WinBench and WinStone utilities were available for download. It wasn't long, though, before the programs were expanded and the total size of the two performance testing suites had evolved to well over 130MB; Ziff-Davis started distributing the two programs only on CD. The cost for the CD plus shipping and handling was $6.

Recently, Ziff-Davis began distributing a scaled-down version, which you can once again download from their site at http://etestinglabs.com/benchmarks/winbench/winbench.asp.

You can still order the complete set of testing suites from the site at http://etestinglabs.com/benchmarks/reqfrm.asp (see Figure 34.2).

SiSoft Sandra

SiSoft Sandra (http://www.sisoftware.demon.co.uk/sandra/index.htm) is an excellent tool for identifying the components installed in your PC and identifying their configuration settings. The program is also one of the best benchmarking tools available on the Internet. It includes a wide array of benchmarking tools you can use to check your PC's performance (see Figure 34.3 through Figure 34.6).

FIGURE 34.1
WinBench performance-testing a PC.

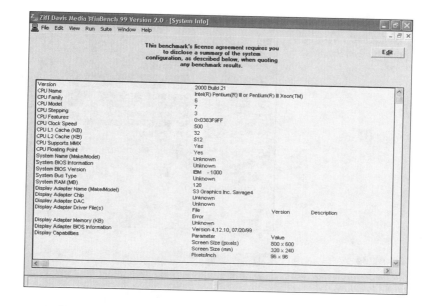

FIGURE 34.2
You can order your copy of the Ziff-Davis Media Benchmark testing suite from the Ziff-Davis Web site.

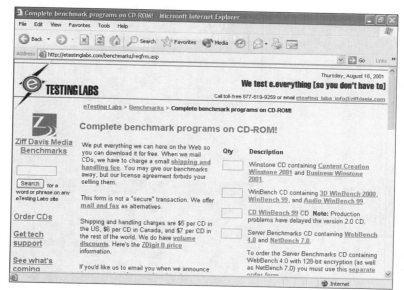

34

FIGURE 34.3

SiSoft Sandra reporting CPU benchmarks.

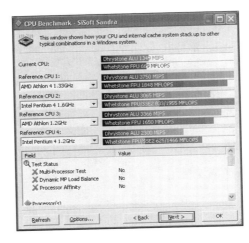

FIGURE 34.4

SiSoft Sandra reporting drive benchmarks.

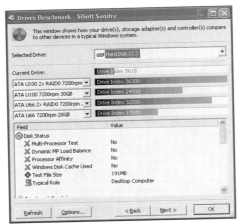

FIGURE 34.5

SiSoft Sandra reporting CD-ROM/DVD benchmarks.

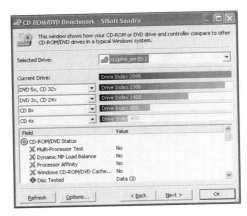

FIGURE 34.6

SiSoft Sandra reporting memory benchmarks.

Diagnostic Programs

Just as numerous performance and benchmarking utilities are available to give you an assessment of your PC's level of performance, you can also find an abundant supply of available diagnostic tools. Many diagnostic utilities are designed to inform you when a problem has developed, and there are also a few that periodically check your system for potential problems.

AMIDiag

If your computer is using AMI (*American Megatrends, Inc.*) BIOS, you can download and run a diagnostic program to perform some rudimentary diagnostics tests (see Figure 34.7).

FIGURE 34.7

The main menu of the AMIDiag diagnostics utility.

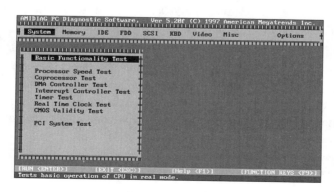

34

You can download a copy of AMIDiag at http://www.shareware.com (search for "diagnostics" or "amidiag"). If you want to purchase the full version, go to the AMI BIOS Web site at http://www.amibios.com.

The Norton Utilities

Besides including a performance monitor, the Norton Utilities also include a diagnostics application. Double-click the Norton System Doctor icon, and you will see an application screen similar to the one shown in Figure 34.8.

FIGURE 34.8

The diagnostics portion of the Norton Utilities, the Norton System Doctor.

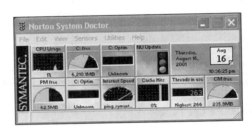

The Norton System Doctor is a collection of monitoring utilities that you can set to monitor your PC's memory, disk drives, general systems operations, and Internet and network connections. For example, under the disk drive sensor section, you can set the System Doctor to monitor general disk integrity, disk fragmentation, the physical disk surface, or just the amount of free space available. Under the general system section, you can set System Doctor to monitor CPU utilization or check whether your anti-virus definitions are up-to-date. Under the memory section, you can set System Doctor to monitor memory usage and alert you when you're running low on system memory, swap file space, or Windows system resources.

As you can see, the Norton System Doctor can be set to monitor much more than just the physical components in your PC. The aim of this diagnostics program is not just to monitor the health of your physical PC, but also the health of your overall system.

Norton Utilities makes versions of its utility suite for all versions of Windows. Because of the differences in how Windows XP handles hardware access from the way Windows 95/98 work, it is very important that you install the correct version for your system. Do not attempt to use the version designed for Windows 95/98 on a computer running Windows XP.

More Diagnostics Programs You Can Purchase

In addition to the programs already mentioned, here are a few other diagnostic programs you might want to consider trying or purchasing to help keep your system operating at peak performance levels:

- WinCheckIt/CheckIt—You can get more information about WinCheckIt/CheckIt at `http://www.checkit.com/products/products.htm`.

- PC Technician—You can get more information about PC Technician at `http://www.windsortech.com`.

- TuffTEST and TuffTEST-Pro—This is another PC diagnostic test worth kicking the tires on at `http://www.tufftest.com/` (see Figure 34.9).

FIGURE 34.9
TuffTEST and TuffTEST-Pro are another set of PC diagnostic tools you might want to try.

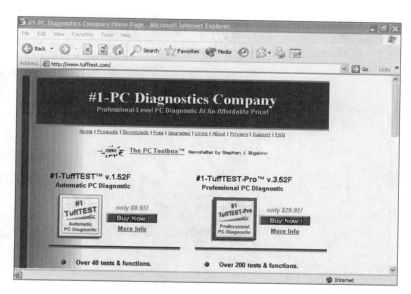

Hard Disk Diagnostics

One area of PC operations that many users seem to eventually have problems with is the PC's hard disk drive. Years ago, the saying was "It's not *if* you will have hard disk problems, but *when*." This seems almost passé now that hard disk technology has improved the reliability of hard disk drives to the point where most users never seem to experience a drive failure. Nevertheless, hard disk drives still do fail, and diagnostic programs are still designed to examine nothing but disk drives. One such program is Data Advisor from Ontrack Systems.

Ontrack Systems is primarily a data recovery company but produces Disk Advisor to help you avoid problems with your hard disk drive and hopefully avoid data loss. If you would like to download a copy of Data Advisor, go to the Ontrack Web site at `http://www.ontrack.com` (see Figure 34.10).

Remember, one of the best ways to avoid hard disk drive disaster is to perform regular backups.

34

Not all problems are hardware related. There are viruses that can destroy your files and/or operating system and make it appear as though the hardware has developed a problem. Make sure that you are running a good anti-virus program in addition to periodically checking your hardware. Make sure that you also update the virus definition files regularly.

FIGURE 34.10

Ontrack offers a variety of hard disk services.

As you become more familiar with using diagnostic tools, you will also learn which problems require corrective action and which don't. Most of the programs mentioned in this chapter also usually explain these so-called "gray areas." This is to prevent you from needlessly spending time and money trying to correct a problem that is actually within the tolerances of normal operating parameters. If you are not in the habit of reading manuals, you should develop this habit when it comes to diagnostic utilities.

Summary

In this chapter, you learned about a few programs you can use to help you assess the performance gains in your PC when you upgrade one or more components. You also learned about diagnostics tools you can use to help identify problems when they develop and a few diagnostic programs you can use to help spot small problems before they become more serious.

CHAPTER 35

Using the Tools of the Trade

In this chapter, you learn what tools you need to upgrade and repair your PC. This section on tools is divided into two parts. The first part describes a simple set of hardware tools you will need to do most upgrades, and the second part lists a more advanced set of tools you should consider obtaining if you are inclined to pursue more complicated upgrades and repairs.

A Simple Set of Tools

As you start to work on PCs, you'll quickly discover that you can perform about 90% of your upgrades and repairs with just a screwdriver. Make sure that you have both a medium-sized flat-head screwdriver and a Phillips screwdriver because some manufacturers favor one type of screw over the other. The exception here is Compaq. Since the first luggable Compaq was released in 1983, Compaq has used what are called *Torx* screws in all its systems (see Figure 35.1).

FIGURE 35.1

*A Torx screwdriver—
Compaq uses Torx
screws in all its PCs.*

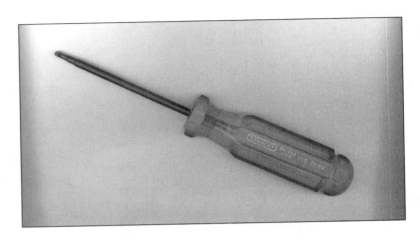

A Torx screw has a six-pointed, diamond-shaped (or some might say, an asterisk-shaped) slot. Most of the screws in Compaq PCs can be removed with a T-15 size Torx screwdriver, but a few need a smaller size T-12 Torx screwdriver. You can pick up a set of Torx screwdrivers for a few dollars in most good hardware or home supply stores.

Jeweler Screwdrivers

Although many users get by for years with nothing more than a screwdriver for making simple repairs and upgrades, you may find that a few more tools make working on your PC a bit easier. Another inexpensive set of tools that you will sooner or later find almost indispensable is a set of jeweler screwdrivers (see Figure 35.2).

Jeweler screwdrivers are usually sold as a set of six miniature screwdrivers (three Phillips and three flat-blade). You will find these screwdrivers extremely useful if you think you might be doing a lot of work on your PC.

Computer Toolkit

Many computer stores also sell small computer toolkits for $10–$20. These kits contain an assortment of PC-related tools (see Figure 35.3), some of which you may find useful and others of which you might not even be able to figure out what to use them for.

Three-Pronged Probe

One of the most useful tools you will run across in these types of toolkits is a device called a *three-pronged probe* (see Figure 35.4).

FIGURE 35.2
A set of jeweler screwdrivers.

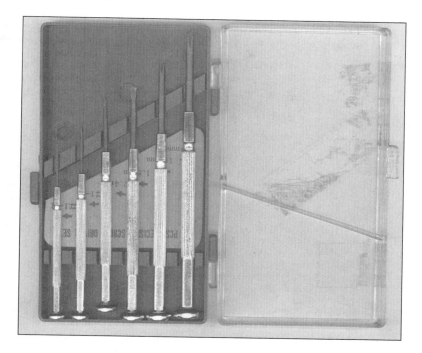

FIGURE 35.3
A typical PC toolkit.

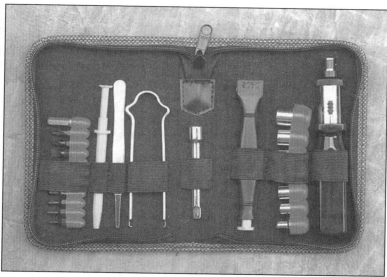

FIGURE 35.4

A three-pronged probe.

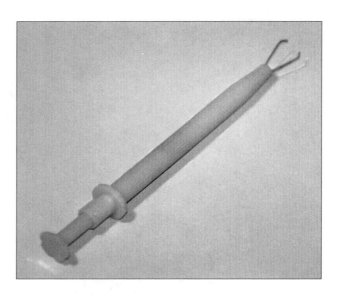

A three-pronged probe looks like a metal or plastic syringe with three moveable "fingers" where the syringe needle would normally be found. This is an invaluable tool for retrieving very small screws that you will invariably drop inside your PC. It's a lot easier and safer to retrieve the screw with a three-pronged probe than picking up your PC, turning it over, and shaking it until the lost screw comes tumbling out. A small pair of needle-nosed pliers or a small pair of surgical forceps, both sold in hobby and hardware stores, will work in place of the three-pronged probe, but you will likely find the probe easier to manipulate.

Don't attempt to substitute a magnetic probe for a three-pronged probe. Magnetic probes can damage components inside your PC.

Pencil and Paper

Two other tools you should make sure that you have in your toolbox are a pencil and paper. Whenever you attempt to replace any component in your PC, you should always draw a diagram first, listing exactly where in your PC the component is being removed from and any cables or attachments connected to that component.

Whenever you remove a cable from a component inside your PC, pay particular attention to the orientation of the cable. Several types of cables in your PC can be attached more than one way, which makes it extremely easy to accidentally install or replace a cable incorrectly.

While you have pencil and paper in hand, you should also get into the habit of keeping a log or journal of all the changes you make to your PC. This log should include all changes made to your system as well as components you add. Be sure to include the date the change was made plus any specifications on the component you add.

Labels

You will also find small self-sticking labels, such as Avery or Brady labels, extremely useful when working on your PC. You should attach a numbered label (numbered 1, 2, 3, and so on) to every wire or cable you remove, and mark on the diagram the corresponding numbered cable and its exact location inside your PC. This arrangement enables you to quickly and easily identify what each wire or cable is attached to.

Compressed Air

Finally, if you are like most PC users, you might open your PC once or twice a year, if that often. After 6–12 months or longer, you'll find a considerable amount of dust build-up in your system. A layer of dust in your PC causes more problems than merely one of aesthetics and a short bout of sneezing. A layer of dust can act as an unwanted layer of insulating material, trapping heat that otherwise would be dissipated through the normal fan-controlled air circulation system. In short, the more dust you let accumulate in your PC, the quicker it will overheat. Overheating damages the components in your PC and shortens their life spans.

One of the best solutions for preventing dust build-up is to periodically take the cover off your PC and "blow it out" using compressed air. Compressed air canisters (see Figure 35.5) can be purchased from virtually any office supply store for a few dollars and should be part of every PC user's repair and maintenance toolbox.

If at all possible, take your PC outdoors before you "blow it out." Otherwise you'll end up making a bigger mess by merely shifting the dust from the inside of your PC to the outside of your PC and all over your desk and room. If you can't take your PC outside, at least move it off your desk and to a place where you can later vacuum the dust you blow out.

35

FIGURE 35.5

FIGURE 35.5

A compressed air canister, which you can purchase in most office supply stores.

If you haven't already made your list of possible tools to purchase, here's a brief recap:

- PC toolkit (with Phillips, flat, and Torx screwdrivers)
- Jeweler screwdrivers (with mini-Phillips and flat screwdrivers)
- Three-pronged probe
- Pencil and paper
- Labels
- Compressed air

An Advanced Set of Tools

Unless you plan to become extremely involved in upgrading and repairing PCs, this section on advanced tools may seem overwhelming. But, read on. Although you may never get to apply this information to a hands-on situation, you may find it helpful the next time you have to take your PC in to a repair shop.

Soldering Iron

Very few computer experts recommend tinkering around inside your PC with a soldering iron—and with good reason. The individual components inside your PC, with very few exceptions, are meant to be replaced, not repaired. But keeping a soldering iron around in your toolbox can be quite handy if you know how and when to use it (see Figure 35.6). Almost always, the only time you'll use a soldering iron is if you need to re-wire a cable, changing where the cable's wires connect to a connector. Due to the wide assortment of cables available in most computer stores, and due to the standardization of computer equipment, a soldering iron certainly can be considered an optional tool in all but the rarest of cases.

FIGURE 35.6

A typical electrical soldering iron.

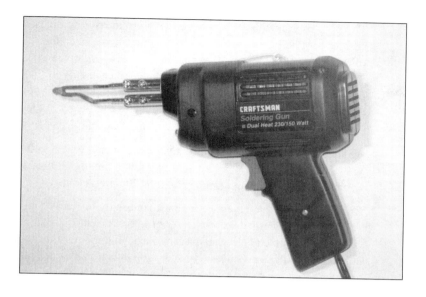

Voltage Meter

Another somewhat uncommon tool you may want to keep in your toolkit is a voltage meter (see Figure 35.7).

FIGURE 35.7

A voltage meter.

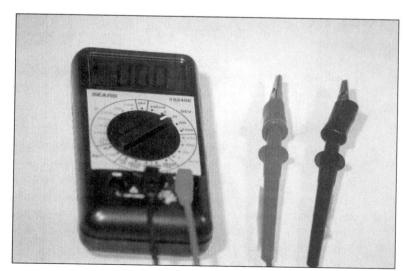

35

The primary functions of a voltage meter are measuring the flow of current and testing current continuity. Because most of the current you encounter inside your PC is DC (direct current), make sure that any voltage meter you pick up can measure both AC and DC voltage (most do). You'll use a voltage meter mainly to diagnose problems with your power supply. Each of the 4-pin connectors sprouting out of your power supply should deliver 5 volts of DC current. A voltage meter can help you quickly determine whether your power supply is failing or if one of the connectors has developed a short circuit.

Although the primary function of a voltage meter is to test voltage, if you buy one in the $30–$40 range, you'll wind up getting a few more useful functions that can be quite helpful in diagnosing and troubleshooting PC problems.

Another use for a voltage meter is as a continuity tester. When used as a continuity tester, you're more concerned with whether or not a current is passing through an electrical circuit than how much current is passing through the circuit. A good example here is in testing cables. Using the continuity tester, you attach one cable from your tester to each pin on your cable and test whether each pin (circuit) continues from one end of the cable to the other. It helps to know the configuration of the cable, but even if you don't you can still manage to test your cable using the trial-and-error method.

Safety Precautions When You Work on Your PC

Whenever you work on your PC, you must put a number of safety precautions into practice, not only to protect your PC from possible damage, but also to protect yourself from possible harm. Neither working on PCs nor PCs themselves is inherently dangerous, but you need to be aware of some hidden risks.

Unplugging Your PC

This is the number-one safety precaution you need to be aware of, and it cannot be repeated often enough. Either unplug your PC at the wall outlet or from the back of the PC. Don't merely rely on the on/off rocker switch because on/off rocker switches have been known to stick or malfunction. Besides risking a potentially lethal electrical shock, you can damage your PC and its internal components if you forget it is plugged in and try to remove an interface card or other electronic device while it is still receiving current. You could also accidentally drop a screwdriver or other metal tool on your main system board and cause a short, or worse.

The only time you should ever work on your PC with the power on is when you are troubleshooting your power supply, and then be sure to exercise extreme caution.

Grounding Yourself to Prevent Static Electricity

Although not properly grounding yourself against static electricity is much more of a potential hazard to your PC than to yourself, don't underestimate this risk, especially during the cold winter months when circulating air in homes and offices tends to be drier than normal. Most of the sensitive electronic components in your PC (for example, microprocessors, memory DIMMs, interface cards, and so on) can be seriously damaged or even destroyed by a few stray jolts of static electricity. Make sure that you touch a metal object such as a desk, a chair, or a filing cabinet before you begin working on your PC. Better yet, use a grounding strap around one of your wrists (see Figure 35.8) and clipped to a metal part of your PC, and make sure that you unplug your PC.

Also, if possible, move your PC to a room that does not have a carpeted floor because most carpeting used in homes and offices contains synthetic fibers, which can increase the potential for static electric discharges.

In addition, you might also consider investing $30–$50 dollars in a small room humidifier. Besides being healthier for your PC, it makes the environment a bit healthier for you as well.

There is considerable debate on whether you should leave your PC plugged in or unplug it when you use a grounding strap to reduce the risk of a static electric discharge damaging your PC or peripherals. I consulted an expert, George Crawford, PhD. in Electrical Engineering at Penn State University, on the "leave it plugged in versus unplug it" debate. Dr. Crawford says you definitely want to make sure that the grounding strap is clipped to a metal component in your PC, such as the frame or chassis, and that the PC is unplugged so that you are at the same electrical potential as the device you are working on.

Keeping Magnets Away from PCs

35

Static electricity is not the only type of electrical charge you want to keep away from your PC. Magnetic charges can also damage some PC components such as disk drives and monitors. Make sure that any tools you use are not magnetized (for example, screwdrivers and probes).

FIGURE 35.8

A wrist grounding strap used to prevent static electric discharges.

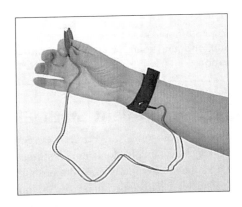

Summary

In this chapter, you learned what tools you need to perform upgrades and repairs on your PC. You were given a list of simple tools you should include in your toolkit plus a few advanced tools you might want to consider including if you decide you want to do more complex diagnostics on your PC.

PART XI

Upgrading Your Main System Components

Chapter

CHAPTER 36

Upgrading Your PC's Memory

Upgrading the memory in your PC actually amounts to adding more memory to your PC. Unlike upgrading other components, such as your processor or CD-ROM drive, you rarely, if ever, remove the memory in your PC and replace it with better or faster memory unless all your memory slots are already filled. In fact, when you upgrade the memory in your PC, you have to be careful that you add memory that is identical to the memory already installed.

The only exception to this general premise is that you may opt to remove a memory module of one size and replace it with a memory module containing more memory. For example, if your PC contains three 32MB-memory modules, you may replace them with three 128MB-memory modules. Although this practice might at first seem wasteful, considering the rapidly southward direction of memory prices in the last few years and the performance gains from increasing the amount of memory in your PC, replacing smaller-sized memory modules with larger modules can actually make sound economic sense and at the same time increase the performance in your PC.

Upgrading your PC's memory probably gives you the most bang for your buck in terms of a how much a single upgrade can positively impact your PC's performance. Although upgrading the processor can affect the speed of most operations, upgrading the memory can extend the capability of your PC by enabling you to perform more tasks simultaneously.

Memory Is Like Money—More Is Better

Adding more memory actually improves performance. Adding more memory enables you to run more programs faster, open more files, and perform more tasks simultaneously.

Your PC uses memory as a temporary storage area for your microprocessor to perform calculations, store data, and store programs you want to run. Anything stored in memory, or RAM as it is called, remains there only as long as the power to your PC remains on, which is why RAM is also referred to a *volatile memory*.

RAM, which is short for *Random Access Memory*, or simply called *memory*, is an electronic storage area used by your computer for data, information, and programs. RAM is where your computer moves information for rapid retrieval either before the information is saved to disk or as it retrieves previously saved information from disk. Your computer can access information in memory about 1,000 times faster than from disk. Even though memory and disk storage both use the same reference designators for size (for example, KB for kilobytes, MB for megabytes, and GB for gigabytes), when the term *memory* is used it always refers to the volatile electronic area where information is stored temporarily. It does not refer to your permanent disk storage area, which should correctly be called *disk space*, *disk storage space*, or *hard disk space*.

A lot of memory installed in PCs for about the last four years has been in the form of DIMMs (Dual Inline Memory Modules), shown in Figure 36.1. This is the type of memory module you should be looking at for your upgrades unless you failed to heed my earlier advice about dumping anything slower than a 500MHz PC.

FIGURE 36.1
A standard 168-pin DIMM.

Different Types of Memory

Memory modules that physically appear to be the same can differ dramatically in the actual speed of the memory and the type of memory used in the module. This is why it is very important to install only the exact type of memory designed for your PC. You can consult your PC's manufacturer or your user guide to determine the exact type of memory you can use in your system especially if you are upgrading a slightly older PC. Most of the newer memory being sold is with bus speeds of 133MHz. A lot of this memory won't work in older Pentium PCs, which usually have a maximum bus speed of only 100MHz. Check your memory speeds carefully.

Here is a brief overview of some of the types of memory you may encounter, both in older style SIMMs and newer style DIMMs:

- **DRAM (Dynamic RAM)**—The most common type of memory used in PCs. It is also the slowest and cheapest type of memory still used in memory modules.

- **FPM DRAM (Fast Page Mode DRAM)**—Another type of DRAM, which is slightly faster than standard DRAM.

- **EDO DRAM (Extended Data Out RAM)**—Another type of Dynamic RAM used in memory modules. It is faster and more expensive than standard DRAM.

- **ECC EDO RAM (Error Correcting Code EDO RAM)**—A very reliable and more expensive type of EDO RAM. Used primarily on network file servers and high-end workstations.

- **SDRAM (Synchronous DRAM)**—A faster and more expensive type of DRAM originally used in processor cache memory and also appearing in Pentium III–based and Pentium IV–based PCs.

- **DDR (Double Data Rate) SDRAM**—A newer designed SDRAM that allows RAM clock speeds up to (theoretically) 200MHz.

- **ESDRAM (Enhanced SDRAM)**—Another type of SDRAM that can (theoretically) support bus speeds up to 200MHz.

Another method you can use to check the type of RAM used in your PC is to check one of several Web sites specializing in selling memory. Two that immediately come to mind are Kingston (http://www.kingston.com/) and Crucial (http://www.crucial.com/).

Both of these well-known sites offer online databases you can access to find the exact type of memory used by your system (see Figure 36.2).

FIGURE 36.2

You can access the Kingston memory identification system to identify the type of memory for your PC.

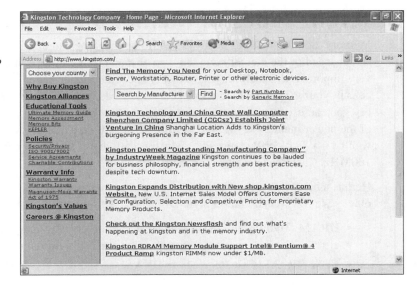

All you do is enter the manufacturer, system type, and model name, and the database will identify the exact type of memory installed in your PC by the manufacturer. It also will usually supply information on types of memory you can use for upgrading and the maximum amount of memory your PC can accommodate (see Figure 36.3).

If the PC you are currently using has standard DRAM installed, you might be tempted to spend a few extra dollars to upgrade to FPM or EDO DRAM. Don't waste your money. The slight difference in speed probably won't be significant without also upgrading your processor and perhaps your main system board. Although you won't see any significant performance boost in replacing standard DRAM with faster FPM DRAM or EDO DRAM, trying to cut costs and save a few dollars by replacing EDO DRAM with standard DRAM can have a dramatic effect on performance, albeit the wrong way. Using slower DRAM can noticeably degrade your PC's performance.

FIGURE 36.3

The Kingston memory type database displaying information on the type of memory used in an IBM PC.

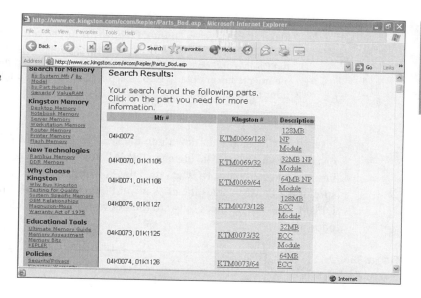

Installing Memory in Your PC

Before you can finalize your memory upgrade plan, you first must determine how much memory is currently installed in your PC.

Back in the days when you used SIMMs (Single Inline Memory Modules) in your PC, you had to be concerned with matching the SIMMs and installing them in pairs. That nonsense ended when PCs moved up to DIMMs. As long as you use the same type of DIMM in your PC, you can place a 16MB DIMM in the first slot, a 32MB DIMM in the second slot, and a 64MB DIMM in the third slot, and never give it a second thought.

Installing DIMMs

Before you begin to install additional DIMMs in your PC, take a minute and look closely at how the existing DIMMs are installed in your computer. The first DIMM in your PC should be installed in the first slot (labeled slot 0), the next DIMM into slot 1, and so on. Most PC motherboards will have three or four slots for DIMMs.

Installing DIMMs in Your PC

To install memory DIMMs in your computer, follow these steps:

1. Turn off the power to your PC and unplug the power cord. Remove the cover from the computer case.

Make absolutely certain that the power is turned off! If you attempt to install DIMMs in your PC with the power on, you are guaranteed to destroy the DIMMs and possibly also your motherboard! Also remember that all memory is susceptible to static electricity, so be sure to take proper precautions to reduce static.

2. Insert the DIMM straight down into the slot (unlike the older SIMMs, which installed at an angle). The clips for DIMMs fold inward when the DIMM is inserted and fold outward when the DIMM is removed (see Figure 36.4). The pressure of the DIMM forces the clips inward to hold the DIMM in place. To remove a DIMM, you simply press outward (and downward) on the clips and the DIMM pops up.

FIGURE 36.4
A DIMM inserted into a DIMM slot.

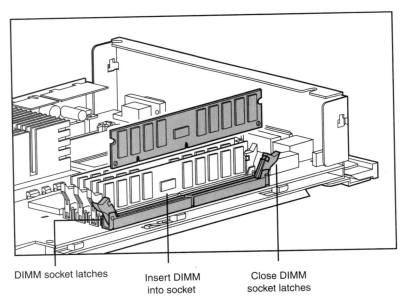

DIMM socket latches   Insert DIMM   Close DIMM
                           into socket   socket latches

Stretching Your Memory a Little Farther

Upgrading the memory in your PC is definitely one way to improve performance in your PC, but you also want to make sure that you are using the memory you have wisely.

Whatever version of Windows you are running, don't automatically start every program you think you might need. Even though Windows NT/2000/Me/XP do a much better job

36

of managing memory than Windows 95/98, opening unnecessary programs wastes systems resources and degrades performance. If there are programs starting that you did not set to start, check your Startup folder to remove the programs. To remove programs from your Startup folder, simply drag the icon out and place it into another folder.

If you are using any type of third-party disk compression software, turn it off. This software was advisable years ago before hard disk prices did a nosedive. Now these programs do little more than waste systems resources and degrade system performance. Windows XP has built-in file and folder compression that you can turn on as you need or want it.

If you are running Windows XP, make the following change in virtual memory (RAM paging memory) to improve performance: Make the initial value and maximum value of your paging file the same (see Figure 36.5). If you make the maximum size larger than initial size, Windows XP will waste resources adjusting the size up and down, and this continuous adjustment can affect performance. Select System from the Control Panel and then select Advanced, Performance Settings, Advanced (again), and then Change.

FIGURE 36.5

Making your initial and maximum page file settings the same in Windows XP.

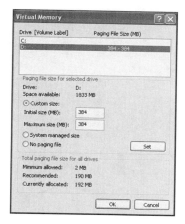

Summary

In this chapter, you learned about the various types of memory used in PCs, how to identify the memory installed in your PC, how to identify the type of memory needed for your upgrade, and how to upgrade the memory in or add memory to your PC. You also learned some tips on how to better manage your PC's memory depending on which operating system you are running on your PC.

CHAPTER 37

Upgrading Your CPU and BIOS

You learned in the last chapter that upgrading your PC's memory is the first part of the performance upgrade equation. Upgrading your computer's *CPU* (*central processing unit*, also called the *processor* or *microprocessor*) is the other half of the coin if you want to beef up your PC's performance. The CPU is the brain inside your PC. The CPU processes the instructions in your programs and operating system and is the single most important factor in improving your PC's raw computing speed.

And while many users exist who have given some thought to upgrading their CPU, most still don't give a second thought about upgrading their BIOS (Basic Input/Output System). Some PCs need a BIOS upgrade if they are to accept an upgraded processor. And some PCs need a BIOS upgrade to work with a removable media drive or some other new technology that will soon be coming down the pike. This chapter shows you how to upgrade both your CPU and your system BIOS.

Understanding Processors

In the last few years, PCs have come to be identified by the type and speed of the CPU installed. For example, most of you have heard someone describe their PC by saying they have a "Pentium III 850," or a "Celeron 733." What they're referring to is the type of CPU installed in their PC and the *clock speed* of the CPU.

Clock speed is a measurement of how fast—its maximum speed—a particular CPU is set to operate. The speed is the measurement in megahertz (abbreviated MHz) of an oscillating timing crystal used to control how fast the CPU can perform internal operations. Since the 486, the stated clock speed is the speed at which the CPU should be operating, according to the manufacturer. Later, you will see that is not always the case.

Intel Corporation (www.intel.com) makes most of the processors found in PCs today. The following sections discuss the processors Intel has made for PCs, starting with the Pentium.

The Pentium Series

Despite a succession of chips with numerical designations (for example, 286, 386, 486), Intel chose not to call its next-generation CPU the 586, but opted for the name Pentium because its legal department advised that numeric designations could not be copyrighted or trademarked. Intel released the first Pentium CPU in 1993. The original Pentium was developed to operate at a speed of 60MHz and delivered about twice the performance of a 486 operating at about the same speed (in megahertz).

The Pentium Pro Series

In 1995, Intel replaced the Pentium chip with the Pentium Pro, a processor optimized to run 32-bit applications. The Pentium Pro runs nearly twice as fast as the original Pentium when running 32-bit applications, but drops in performance when running 16-bit applications.

The Pentium Pro is physically larger than the original Pentium (see Figure 37.1), which necessitated that PC manufacturers redesign their main system boards to accommodate the larger-sized chip. This change in size also means that an upgrade to a Pentium Pro from either a Pentium or a 486 requires a motherboard upgrade.

FIGURE 37.1

A Pentium and Pentium Pro, showing the difference in size.

37

The Pentium II Series

The Pentium II processor is essentially a Pentium Pro with MMX. Intel developed MMX (Multi-Media eXtensions) as a series of instructions built in to the processor to enhance audio and video functions. The original Pentium II was released in May 1997 with a clock speed of 233MHz. Intel later released versions with clock speeds of 266MHz, 300MHz, and in 1998 speeds of 333MHz, 350MHz, 400MHz, and 450MHz.

Intel made another design change when it created the Pentium II processor. Intel designed the chip on a type of bus card that requires a special slot, termed *slot 1* on the main system board for the chip.

Because of this design change, there is no upgrade path to the Pentium II chip from any other Intel-designed CPU. The only upgrade options are from a slower clock speed Pentium II to a faster clock speed Pentium II. Intel also made a Pentium II Xeon CPU, but this chip was directed at use in file servers. Even these types of upgrades are limited because of changes in the other supporting chips used in the main system board. In preliminary tests, the difference in performance between a 300MHz Pentium II and a 400MHz Pentium II was only 17%. The difference in performance between a 350MHz and 400MHz Pentium II was only 7%.

The Pentium III Series

In February 1999, Intel released the Pentium III processor running at a speed of 450MHz. Within a few months, Intel released Pentium IIIs running at speeds up to 650MHz and hinted that it probably would not stop until the Pentium III hit 1000MHz, which it eventually did.

As you might expect in the Pentium III line of processors, if you were to upgrade from a 450MHz to a 1000MHz Pentium III processor, you would see more than a 100% increase in CPU performance, but not necessarily a 100% increase in PC performance. Other factors at work in your PC—such as the speed of your memory, the speed of the bus, and the speed of other peripherals—affect and retard the overall performance. It is also doubtful that a motherboard originally equipped with a 450MHz CPU can handle the vast jump in speed to 1000MHz.

As with the Pentium II, the Pentium III was released in a Xeon version, which was designed for the increased demands of a file server. Even though Intel later released the Pentium 4 line of processors, it continues to produce Pentium III processors.

The Pentium 4 Series

In November 2000, Intel released the Pentium 4 processor running at speeds of 1.4GHz and 1.5GHz (gigahertz), and then unexpectedly backfilled with a 1.3GHz model. It didn't take long for PC manufacturers to release workstations built on these new chips, and the race was on again. Intel has since released several additional Pentium 4 chips including a 3GHz chip and faster ones may be released by the time this text goes to press. With the Pentium 4, Intel made another radical design change, abandoning the processor-slot design and returning to the processor-socket design: The Pentium 4 CPU needs a 423-pin socket on the motherboard. If you want to upgrade from a Pentium III to a Pentium 4, you'll need a new motherboard.

The AMD Series of CPUs

Although Intel still controls the lion's share of the PC processor market, it is not the only game in town. One serious competitor that many PC users have turned to for CPU upgrades is Advanced Micro Devices, Inc., more simply known as AMD. AMD can be found on the Web at http://www.amd.com.

AMD was founded in 1969, and today is the largest competitor producing Intel-compatible processors. AMD is especially popular among the upgrade crowd because its CPUs perform as well as Intel's.

AMD's K5 series of processors directly competes against Intel's Pentium and Pentium Pro series; its K6 and K7 series are competitive with Intel's Pentium II and Pentium III series. Most recently, AMD's Athlon series is running neck and neck with Intel's Pentium 4 series. Keep in mind that the two CPUs are not interchangeable. You must have a motherboard designed specifically for the chip you plan to use.

37

In addition to being cheaper than comparable Intel CPUs, another factor that makes AMD's earlier model CPUs attractive is that they are pin-for-pin compatible with most main system board sockets used by Intel's 486 and Pentium series processors. This means that if you currently have a 486 or low-end Pentium, and you want to upgrade to a Pentium Pro or Pentium II level processor, AMD's K5 and K6 chips will more than likely fit into your existing main system board CPU socket. However, AMD made a dramatic design change when it introduced its K7 series of processors and lost its pin-for-pin compatibility claim. Despite the motherboard redesign, AMD garners a sizeable market share because its prices are almost always cheaper than an Intel CPU of comparable speed.

Even though the K7 looks very similar to Intel's Pentium II and Pentium III series processors, the K7 will not fit into a slot 1 motherboard. The AMD K7 requires a motherboard with a proprietary slot designed to accommodate the K7.

The Cyrix Series of CPUs

Still another alternative to Intel is Cyrix Corporation, formerly a division of National Semiconductor. Cyrix was bought in 1999 by Via Technologies and has pretty much lost most of its separate identity. You can find Via/Cyrix on the Web at `http://www.via.com.tw/jsp/en/products/C3/c3.jsp`.

Cyrix also makes socket-compatible processors that can replace or upgrade from Intel's Pentium and Pentium Pro series processors. Unfortunately, Cyrix has not kept pace in the neck-and-neck race between Intel and AMD; at last report, Cyrix produces processors with clock speeds only in the 500 to 700MHz range.

Identifying Your CPU

Before you can upgrade your CPU, you must correctly identify the CPU that is installed in your PC. In addition to identifying the CPU, you also have to know the clock speed of your CPU. After you identify the CPU in your PC, you can decide which CPUs lie along your upgrade path.

After you take the cover off your PC, look for what is probably the largest chip in your computer. On many older computers, the processor is in a plastic holder called a *ZIF socket* (see Figure 37.2).

ZIF stands for *Zero Insertion Force*. One common problem in inserting chips is the possibility of bending or breaking the pins when you push (or jam) the pins of the chip into very tight socket holes. In a ZIF socket, you don't have to push the pins of the chip into a socket. Instead, you merely place the pins into oversized socket holes and move a lever that grabs and locks the pins and holds the chip in the socket.

If you discover that your CPU is soldered to your main system board and that your motherboard does not include an empty upgrade socket, replace the cover and forget about upgrading. If you want a faster PC, you have to purchase a newer PC or replace the main system board.

FIGURE 37.2

An empty ZIF socket.

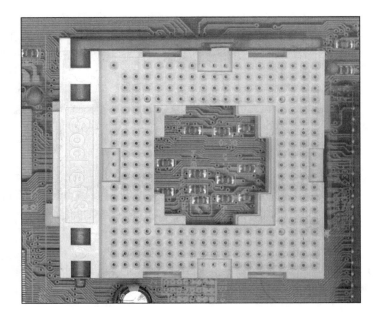

Don't be surprised if you remove the cover of your PC and don't see anything that looks like a CPU. On some smaller systems, it is common for disk drive housings to cover your CPU. If this is the case, you'll have to remove your disk drives to gain access to your CPU. Just pay careful attention to anything you remove (make a diagram if it helps you remember), and be sure to replace any components and cables exactly the same way you removed them.

After you've located your CPU, the first thing to look for is any writing on the CPU identifying what type it is. You are looking for information identifying the CPU as a Pentium, Pentium II, Pentium III, Pentium 4, or AMD (or Cyrix depending on the age) and information displaying its speed.

A *heat sink* and/or a fan covers many processors. A heat sink is nothing more than a metal attachment—often black, silver, or blue in color—that has several dozen fins or projectiles. Heat sinks are used to help dissipate the heat that processors give off.

You have to know exactly what type of processor is installed in your PC before you can purchase an upgrade. This information enables you to make sure that you purchase a faster upgrade processor as well as an upgrade CPU that is compatible with your computer system.

37

In choosing an upgrade processor, most experts recommend/suggest the 100% rule, which simply states that you should upgrade to a processor that is roughly 100% faster than what you currently own. For example, if you currently have a 300MHz Pentium, you should not consider upgrading to anything less than a 600MHz (or the next-highest speed chip) processor. The 100% rule should be your minimum upgrade.

In addition to speed, there are also slight voltage differences between some processors. If you know exactly what type of processor is currently installed in your PC, the company you purchased the upgrade from will be able to sell you an upgrade processor that is guaranteed to operate correctly in your PC. When ordering an upgrade processor, be sure to also get the make and model of the PC you are upgrading and the BIOS manufacturer and BIOS date. Note that you can obtain BIOS information by running the System Information utility on your System Tools Windows menu.

In addition to power consumption differences, Intel has also made changes in the socket design and number of pins in its processor chips—even in chips within the same family. For example, the earliest model Pentiums (the 60MHz and 66MHz models) could not be upgraded to the faster Pentiums in the 75 to 200MHz range because the pin design was changed from 273 pins to 320 pins (and later to 321 pins).

PC Bottlenecks

When you upgrade your CPU, the CPU may not provide as much performance improvement as you expect because of a bottleneck in your CPU. Your PC was designed around the original CPU. When you upgrade the CPU, you may have a faster processor, but you still have all the remaining equipment, which was designed to work with the original, slower CPU. In other words, even though the upgrade processor processes data faster than the original CPU in your PC, the upgrade processor is slowed down by the speed of your other components, which do not operate at the same speed as your new CPU.

Does this mean that it is a waste of money to upgrade your CPU? No, because a faster CPU results in faster performance. But just keep in mind that the new CPU is still working through a bottleneck—your older system.

Removing and Installing a CPU

If your main system board (your motherboard) is equipped with a ZIF socket—and almost all socket 7 are so equipped motherboards—removing the current processor is a snap.

If you are replacing a CPU in a plug-in card, skip to the section called, "Removing a CPU in a Plug-in Card from Slot 1."

Removing a CPU from a ZIF Socket

To remove a processor from a ZIF socket, follow these steps:

1. Make sure that you are grounded before you remove the upgrade processor from its container. Swing the lever out slightly to unlock it, and then swing back the ZIF socket lever to release tension on the pins.

2. Gently lift out the processor.

If your motherboard does not have a ZIF socket, you can still remove your processor with a minimal amount of effort. Many companies that sell upgrade processors include a processor extraction tool with the upgrade. Several types of processor extraction tools are available. Figure 37.3 shows you two types.

FIGURE 37.3

Two types of processor extraction tools.

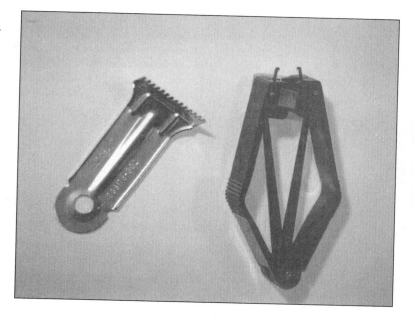

37

Removing a CPU Using a Processor Extraction Tool

To remove the processor using the extraction tool, follow these steps:

1. Follow the instructions that come with the processor extraction tool you purchase. If you purchase the large tweezer-like model, open its jaws wide enough to allow you to gently insert each of the two prongs under the sides of the CPU, and then gently squeeze the sides where the tool is its widest. This squeezing action gently lifts the CPU up and out of its socket. If you purchase the small pry-bar type of tool, gently insert it under each of the four sides of the processor and gently press down on the extraction tool. The tool is designed so that this downward pressure lifts up on the processor.

2. If your instructions call for you to repeat Step 1, do so as many times as is necessary until you can gently lift the processor out of the socket. Remember to take your time so that you don't accidentally bend the pins. You don't have to hurry to remove a processor.

Note that the notched corner of the processor is lined up with a similarly notched corner of the socket. When you insert the upgrade processor, you must make sure that the notched corners (or the dot) line up exactly as they do with the old processor.

> If the notch on the upgrade processor is not lined up exactly with the notch on the socket, your PC will not operate correctly and you could damage the upgrade processor and possibly also your motherboard.

Inserting the New Processor

To insert the upgrade processor in your PC, use these steps:

1. Make sure that you are grounded before you remove the upgrade processor from its container.

2. Locate the notch on your upgrade processor and on the processor socket.

3. Line up the notches and carefully insert the upgrade processor into the socket.

   If you have a ZIF socket, simply move the locking lever back to the lock position. If you do not have a ZIF socket, make sure that all the pins on the CPU are lined up with the holes in the socket, and then gently apply pressure to the center of the processor until it is firmly seated in the socket.

   Check to make sure that no pins are bent or sticking out the sides of the connectors. If you see any bent pins, use your processor extraction tool to remove the CPU. Then, using a pair of needle-nose pliers, very carefully straighten any bent pins and try again to insert the CPU into the socket.

Removing a CPU in a Plug-in Card from Slot 1

If you are upgrading an Intel-based CPU installed in a plug-in card, the task is almost as easy as replacing a CPU into a ZIF socket.

To remove a CPU in a plug-in card, follow these steps:

1. Make sure that you are grounded before you remove the upgrade processor from its container. The CPU plug-in card is held in place by two clips on either side of the card in a cardholder. The holder supports the card vertically into slot 1. Flip the clips outward, releasing the card.

2. Gently lift the card up and out of the slot.

Inserting a CPU Plug-in Card into Slot 1

To insert the replacement CPU card into slot 1, follow these steps:

1. Make sure that you are grounded before you remove the upgrade processor card from its container.

2. Read over the instructions accompanying your replacement CPU. The instructions will illustrate how to properly align the new CPU plug-in card into slot 1. Insert the CPU plug-in card into the holder and gently, but firmly, insert the plug-in card into the slot.

3. Flip the two clips on either side of the holder back to the upright position to hold the plug-in card securely in the slot.

> If you are currently using a PC with an Intel CPU in a plug-in card and are considering upgrading to AMD's new Athlon CPUs, *don't!*
>
> Although the Athlon CPU's plug-in card will fit into a motherboard designed with a slot-1 CPU slot, the Athlon CPU is electrically incompatible. The Athlon requires a different motherboard, which uses what is called a slot-A slot.

On many PCs, your new processor should be recognized and configured automatically to operate in your PC. If your PC displays an error message when you turn it back on, run your computer's hardware Setup program to configure the CMOS settings in your PC with your upgrade processor. Be sure to check your PC's instruction manual to see whether you need to set a jumper on the motherboard.

Overclocking Your CPU

In the last few years, some very industrious upgraders have discovered another way to get more bang for their bucks (or more precisely, more megahertz) out of their CPUs. The process is called overclocking.

Overclocking is simply running the CPU at a slightly faster speed than the speed certified by the manufacturer. When manufacturers test and certify their CPUs, many times they rate the CPU at a speed slower than the maximum the CPU is capable of running. In effect, they build in a little cushion to make sure that the CPU will perform at the stated speed. The key to overclocking is to adjust the CPU frequency/bus frequency ratio on your motherboard to a higher setting than is specified for your particular CPU. The CPU frequency/bus frequency ratio is often expressed as a timing setting such as 2x, 2.5x, 3x, 3.5x, 4x, and so on. To overclock your CPU, simply set the ratio to the next higher setting, if your CPU is not currently using the top setting.

> Overclock at your own risk! Even though many overclockers swear that this practice is perfectly safe, overclocking is not supported by any CPU manufacturer, and there is a potential for damaging or destroying your CPU and

motherboard by overclocking. If you are curious about overclocking your CPU, check out one of several Web sites that explain this practice in more detail, such as http://www.sysopt.com/overfaq.html.

Understanding What Your BIOS Is and What It Does

The next time you turn on your PC, pay close attention to the information displayed onscreen. The BIOS, which stands for Basic Input Output System, is software, or more correctly called *firmware*. It enables your computer to boot and your processor to access the hardware devices such as the hard disk drive, video card, system clock, and other peripherals. The BIOS also controls the POST (the Power On Self-Test), the diagnostic and initialization program that runs every time you turn on your computer.

Firmware is essentially software that has been embedded into certain chips in your computer and that runs automatically without intervention on your part. The distinction is usually made between programs that you can easily change, erase, and delete—software—and programs that you cannot easily alter—firmware.

Every BIOS is specific to a certain type of motherboard, so even if you notice that the BIOS in your computer is made by the same company that manufactures the BIOS in your neighbor's computer, it doesn't necessarily mean that the BIOS in one is identical to the other. If the two of you have different makes of PC, you can almost guarantee that the BIOSs are different in each.

The BIOS in various computers varies in size and functionality somewhat, but a core portion is about 64KB in size in every computer that claims to be IBM PC compatible.

Why You Need to Upgrade Your BIOS

Your BIOS was made about the same time as your computer, and although it may have served you well so far, many things have undoubtedly changed since your computer was manufactured. New types of peripherals have been invented, disk drives have gotten larger, and new types of video cards with higher resolutions have been created, among other things. In short, the BIOS in your computer has remained static while the rest of the computer industry has continued at its usual hectic, dynamic pace. For example, the

BIOS in some early model 486 computers was designed while most hard disk drives were still around 200 to 400MB in size. When users of these computers attempted to install larger hard disk drives—in the 2 to 4GB range—they discovered that their computers could not recognize more than the first 528MB of their new multi-gigabyte hard disk drives.

The reason behind this problem was that the BIOS in their computers was not able to understand *Logical Block Addressing* (*LBA*). In simpler terms, it means the BIOS cannot address all the storage space on the hard disk drive beyond the first 528MB because that is as high as it can count. The answer to this problem is simply to upgrade the BIOS. If you find that no BIOS upgrade is available for your PC (another hint that it's time to purchase a new PC instead of upgrading your current model), sometimes you can solve problems similar to the LBA problem by applying a software patch.

How Do I Upgrade My BIOS?

Early 486 model computers had chips on the motherboard that stored the BIOS routines and that had to be physically replaced in order to upgrade the BIOS (see Figure 37.4).

Later model 486 computers and all computers since the first Pentium models have what is called *flash BIOS*, which means that you can run a program on a floppy disk to upgrade your BIOS, which is then stored in *EEPROM* chips. No physical replacement of chips is necessary.

EEPROM stands for Electrically Erasable Programmable Read Only Memory and is a special type of chip used to store your BIOS programs. Under normal circumstances, the programs stored in EEPROM chips are stored permanently. You can, however, use special programs to update and replace the programs stored in EEPROMs. This is what happens when you upgrade flash BIOS.

Determining Whether You Need to Upgrade Your BIOS

If you install a new peripheral and it doesn't work and you have checked every part of the installation procedure and everything checks out okay, chances are you need to upgrade your BIOS. In most cases, this problem surfaces when you attempt to install not just a new peripheral but a new type of peripheral (for example, installing not just another hard drive but your first network card).

FIGURE 37.4
BIOS chips on an older 486 motherboard.

Also, if you receive notice from your computer dealer or from your PC's manufacturer that there is a defect in your current BIOS and they recommend that you upgrade, it is time to upgrade.

Establishing the Type of BIOS You Have

If you have a Pentium or later processor in your computer, you can rest assured that you have a flash BIOS. If you have a 486 processor, your chances are 50–50 that you have a flash BIOS (if you are still using a 486-based PC, forget the BIOS upgrade and just purchase a new PC; you're way overdue for one).

If you still have your original documentation, which lists the type of BIOS in your PC, the documentation also likely indicates whom to contact about upgrading your BIOS.

If you don't still have the original documentation that came with your PC, there is another method to determine the type of BIOS in your PC. Turn on your PC and write down all the BIOS information displayed when your computer boots. The BIOS information is usually displayed in the upper-left corner of your screen just after the PC completes the POST (Power On Self-Test). Look for the name of a company and a number that looks like some sort of serial number or version number. That number is the BIOS version (see Figure 37.5).

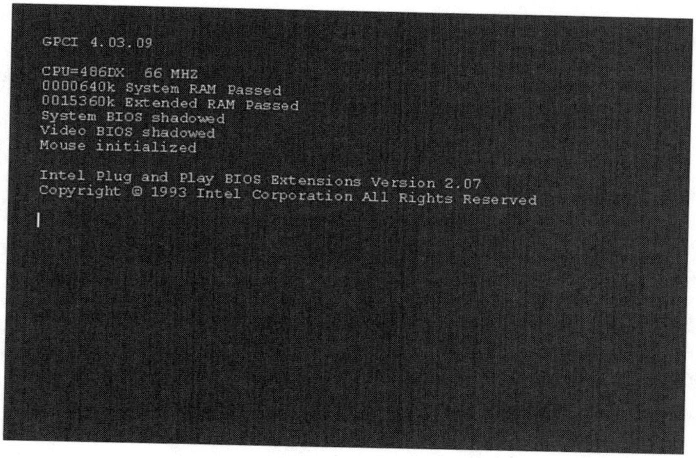

FIGURE 37.5

The BIOS version appears onscreen after the POST.

```
GPCI 4.03.09

CPU=486DX  66 MHZ
0000640k System RAM Passed
0015360k Extended RAM Passed
System BIOS shadowed
Video BIOS shadowed
Mouse initialized

Intel Plug and Play BIOS Extensions Version 2.07
Copyright © 1993 Intel Corporation All Rights Reserved
```

After you have the BIOS information about your PC, you can contact your PC's manufacturer to find out what type of BIOS you have. Be sure to also have the model of your computer when you contact the manufacturer or check the manufacturer's Web site.

Different Methods for Upgrading Your BIOS

If you do not have flash BIOS, and you insist on retaining and upgrading your old 486 (so you can experiment with Linux), you can contact your PC's manufacturer about ordering a new set of BIOS chips. You can also contact one of two BIOS upgrade companies, Micro Firmware, Inc. and Microid Research (Unicore Software). Micro Firmware can be reached at 800-767-5465 or 405-321-8333. You can also contact Micro Firmware at http://www.firmware.com. Microid Research can be reached at 800-800-BIOS and 508-686-6468. Microid's Web site is located at http://www.unicore.com; the company's MR. BIOS site is at http://www.mrbios.com, or you can try http://www.sysopt.com/ bios.html.

If you do have flash BIOS in your PC, and you have Internet access, you can most likely download the program to update your PC from a variety of sources. Look at the Web site run by your PC's manufacturer. Most computer manufacturers run a Web site and provide BIOS and other upgrades and updates for their customers. If your PC's manufacturer does not maintain a Web site, you can look on the Web sites run by several of the leading BIOS manufacturers. The following is a short list:

- Phoenix/Award—http://www.ptltd.com
- American Megatrends, Inc. (AMI)— http://www.megatrends.com

You can also check the company from whom you purchased your PC if you did not purchase directly from the manufacturer.

Installing Upgrade BIOS Chips

If you order BIOS upgrade chips for a computer that does not have flash BIOS, it's very easy to install the chips yourself.

To install BIOS upgrade chips onto your PC's motherboard, follow these steps:

1. Turn off and unplug your PC.

2. Discharge any static electricity by first touching the exterior of the PC's metal case, and then remove the cover from your PC.

3. Examine the new BIOS upgrade chips you ordered. Notice the size of the chips, their markings or labels, and most importantly, look for a notch or dot in one end of the chips (see Figure 37.6).

4. Now look on your motherboard and find chips that look similar to the chips you ordered. If you're not sure, check your PC's documentation for the exact location of your computer's BIOS chips. Record which direction the orientation notch is positioned.

5. Before you remove a chip, check your instructions for the order in which you must replace the chips. You want to make sure that you install the replacement chips (if there is more than one chip) in the correct socket.

6. The chips you ordered should have been shipped with a tool resembling a large set of tweezers with the tips turned inward. This tool is similar to the processor extraction tool shown in Figure 37.3. You also should have received instructions on how to use the chip extractor to remove your old BIOS chips. If the instructions are not included, simply place each of the turned-in tips under the long edges of the chips and gently lift upward, rocking back and forth, until the chip lifts out of its socket. Repeat this procedure for all your old BIOS chips. If a chip extractor did not come with your new BIOS chips, a trip to your local computer store can usually remedy this oversight.

7. As per your instructions, replace your old chips with the new chips you ordered. Make sure that you insert the new chips with the orientation notch facing in the same direction as the chips you just removed. Be very careful not to accidentally bend any of the pins on the chips as you insert them into their sockets. If the pins are spread too far apart, place the chip on its side on a hard surface such as a table-top and gently roll the pins until they are a little closer together. By placing the chip on its side and rolling it, you make sure that you bend all the pins together.

8. Double-check your work to make sure that the new chips are properly installed in the socket, that they are oriented properly, and that no pins are bent. When everything looks okay, turn on your PC. If the new BIOS chips are properly installed, your PC should boot as before.

FIGURE 37.6

A notch on one end of the BIOS chip indicates the chip's proper orientation.

Upgrading Flash BIOS

Upgrading a PC with flash BIOS is a snap. If you ordered the BIOS upgrade program from the manufacturer or your dealer, the program should come on a bootable disk. If you downloaded the BIOS upgrade program from the manufacturer's bulletin board or Web site, follow the instructions that came with the download to create a bootable upgrade disk.

To upgrade your flash BIOS with a bootable upgrade disk, follow these steps:

1. Turn off your PC.

2. Place your BIOS upgrade disk into your floppy disk drive and turn on your PC.

3. The bootable disk should automatically start the upgrade program and upgrade your flash BIOS. Watch your screen for any prompts asking you to enter any information about your PC. The entire upgrade procedure should take about 1 to 3 minutes.

4. When the upgrade is completed, remove the upgrade disk and reboot your PC.

> Make sure that you do not reboot or turn off your PC while you are upgrading your flash BIOS. You can permanently damage the BIOS—and your computer—if you do.

Summary

In this chapter, you learned the evolutionary history of the Intel line of processors beginning with the Pentium. You learned what upgrade paths exist for the various processors and that you do not have to stick solely with CPUs made by Intel. You also learned about some of the functions of your computer's BIOS, and some of the operations that can go wrong when your BIOS does not function with your computer or its devices. You learned what you have to do to identify the type of BIOS installed in your computer, and what you have to do to upgrade your PC's BIOS.

CHAPTER 38

Replacing Your Main System Board

Many computer experts believe that main system boards are better candidates for being replaced than upgraded. The reason for this belief is that any time you upgrade your main system board significantly, you most likely need to upgrade several other components in your PC as well. The CPU, memory, and possibly several of the interface cards in your PC will probably have to be upgraded to match the performance gains offered by the new system board. Rather than replace this much of your PC, it might be cheaper to forgo the main system board upgrade and just purchase a new PC.

For most users, the only financially justifiable reason for replacing a main system board is if the one currently in your PC is damaged. In that case, you'll replace the board with one identical or similar to your current board. You might also upgrade your motherboard if you are considering upgrading your CPU to the Athlon series in the AMD CPU line. These chips require a motherboard with a special slot/socket to accommodate them. Regardless of your reason for replacing your main system board, in this chapter you will learn all you need to know to accomplish this sometimes tricky procedure.

Are You Upgrading or Replacing?

Depending on how old your current PC is and what a new system board and components will cost, upgrading may or may not be a bargain.

 Main system boards are also referred to by the somewhat less technical name "motherboard." The two terms are used interchangeably in this chapter.

Although the price of a new system board may only set you back $150 to $250, after you add in the cost of the CPU, memory, and a new video card, your upgrade could be done for less than $400:

System board with 750MHz AMD series CPU	$220.00
128MB SDRAM	50.00
Video Card with 128MB VRAM	95.00
TOTAL	365.00

Check the advertising supplements in your Sunday newspaper and you'll see several companies willing to sell you a complete, new PC for around $800 to $1,000, and they'll probably toss in several hundred dollars worth of bundled software to sweeten the deal. Current system and peripheral prices make the upgrade fairly practical, or they will at least give you something to think about.

Another reason to upgrade your system board and CPU is if you decide to build your own custom-designed PC. If a custom-built PC is in your future, the information in this chapter will be instrumental in helping you do that.

How System Boards Have Changed

Main system boards have undergone dramatic changes since IBM released its first PC back in 1981. Most of the major changes and advances seen in system board design have resulted from changes or advancements in bus design, chipsets, and processors. Here is a brief overview of the six major bus designs that have been incorporated into PCs since 1981:

- **8-bit (or "original IBM PC") bus.** The original 8-bit bus design used in IBM PCs, XTs, and early PC-compatible computers.

- **16-bit ISA bus.** The first 16-bit bus was essentially a 16-bit upgrade of the original IBM PC bus; the ISA (Industry Standard Architecture) bus was used originally in the IBM AT computer and AT-compatible computers.

- **Micro Channel Architecture bus.** IBM's proprietary 32-bit bus; used in its PS/2 computer line. No manufacturer other than IBM ever used this bus design because other manufacturers did not want to pay license fees to IBM.

- **EISA bus.** The computer industry's response to IBM's proprietary MCA bus; used mainly in network file servers manufactured by Compaq; EISA stands for Extended Industry Standard Architecture. In addition to the EISA bus cards, you can also use ISA bus cards.

- **VESA local bus.** The first 32-bit bus design used in 486 computers that was fast enough to support graphical environments.

- **PCI bus.** Designed to overcome many of the speed limitations of the VESA local bus to support the higher bus speeds required by the Pentium processor line.

38

The 486-based PCs used both VESA local bus and PCI bus system boards. The first 486-based PCs were created using the VESA local bus design, but later were switched to the more advanced PCI bus. Pentium-based PCs have mainly used system boards with a PCI bus.

Bus design changes are not the only factors that have affected system board design changes. Main system boards have also undergone changes in their physical size and shape. Since the first 486-based PC rolled down the assembly line, system boards have come in one of seven basic sizes: standard AT, baby AT, LPX, ATX, and NLX are the older designs. In the last two to three years, some manufacturers have started shipping what is called a "baby ATX" motherboard and more recently a "micro ATX" motherboard. These diminutive ATX form-factor boards are scaled-down versions of the original ATX system board and usually have fewer PCI or memory slots.

Before you can select a replacement system board, you first must correctly identify the board currently installed in your PC. Because computer cases are often designed to accommodate a particular form-factor system board, if you purchase the wrong board, it may not fit your case.

The Standard AT System Board

This type of motherboard is so called because it roughly matches the size of the motherboard used in the original IBM AT computer—12 inches wide by 13.8 inches in depth. By today's standards, this is a very large board and fits only into full-sized desktop and tower computer cases. Most system board manufacturers have all but abandoned this size motherboard in favor of the smaller designs.

The Baby AT System Board

The baby AT system board, as you might guess, is a scaled-down version of the standard AT-sized motherboard. The miniaturization is caused by advancements in technology that enable many of the components on motherboards to be reduced in size. Figure 38.1 shows the basic layout of the baby AT motherboard.

FIGURE 38.1

Baby AT form-factor motherboard.

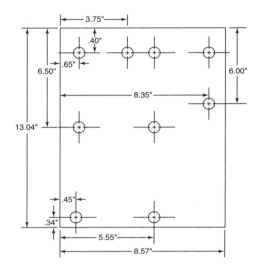

Figure 38.2 shows you the difference in size between the standard AT-sized motherboard on the left and the baby AT-sized motherboard on the right.

FIGURE 38.2

Standard AT motherboard and baby AT motherboard showing the difference in size.

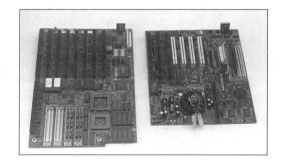

The LPX Motherboard

The LPX (and also the "mini-LPX") motherboard is easily identified by a unique design element not present in any other motherboard design. The LPX motherboard (see Figure 38.3) has a riser card inserted into a slot on the main portion of the board. The riser card contains slots into which your interface cards are inserted. The LPX design was developed by Western Digital and is still used in PCs manufactured by IBM, Compaq, and Gateway.

FIGURE 38.3

The LPX and mini-LPX motherboard form factors.

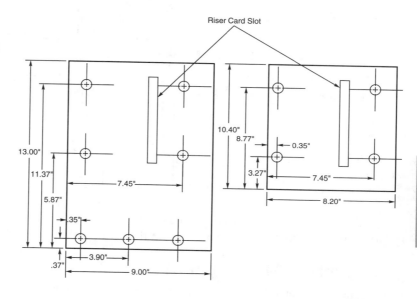

38

You may encounter two problems with an LPX motherboard: Because of the use of the riser card, these boards generally have less potential for expandability because they have fewer expansion slots. The other problem is that you may have difficulty finding a replacement motherboard except from the manufacturers who generally charge more for replacement boards than a third-party vendor.

The ATX Motherboards

The ATX motherboard, designed by Intel in 1995, is sort of a hybrid baby AT and LPX model, which at first appears to be turned sideways. This is the design used in many of the PCs manufactured in the last few years and is considered by some to be the *de facto* standard design. The design of the ATX enables PC manufacturers to produce fewer crowded and congested hardware configurations, making it easier to access components you might want to upgrade. Figure 38.4 shows the basic design of the ATX motherboard.

Because of the layout and positioning of components on the ATX motherboard—such as the location of the power connectors, mouse connectors, and keyboard—the ATX motherboard will not fit in cases designed for either the standard AT or baby AT motherboards.

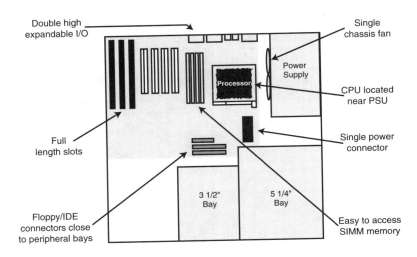

FIGURE 38.4

The ATX motherboard layout showing the location of PC features.

Double high expandable I/O

Single chassis fan

Power Supply

Processor

CPU located near PSU

Full length slots

Single power connector

3 1/2" Bay

5 1/4" Bay

Floppy/IDE connectors close to peripheral bays

Easy to access SIMM memory

The baby ATX and micro ATX motherboards are simply scaled-down versions of the standard ATX motherboard designed to fit into a case with a smaller footprint.

The NLX Motherboard

The NLX motherboard was designed specifically for computers using the Pentium II processor. The NLX design contains many of the best features of both the ATX and LPX boards (see Figure 38.5).

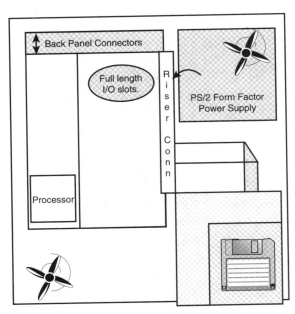

FIGURE 38.5

The basic layout of the NLX motherboard.

Back Panel Connectors

Full length I/O slots.

Riser Conn

PS/2 Form Factor Power Supply

Processor

Installing a New System Board

Regardless of which motherboard size or style you purchase, replacing your existing system board requires careful planning. Although replacing a motherboard may at first appear to be a major technological undertaking, in reality all you need is a little bit of planning and a bit more patience (and of course a screwdriver or two) to accomplish the job successfully.

Remember to unplug your PC and ground yourself before you remove the PC's cover. Make sure that you carefully remove each component from your existing motherboard and make sure that you place all the components on a safe surface, such as an uncluttered tabletop, where they cannot be damaged physically or by static electricity.

Removing Your Old Motherboard

Follow these steps to remove your old motherboard:

1. The very first task you must perform is to make a diagram of all the connections (ribbon cables, jumpers, thin-wire cables, interface cards, and so on). Pay particular attention to the orientation of each connector, especially those connectors that can be attached more than one way, as can ribbon cables. Notice that most ribbon cables have a red strip on one edge of the cable. This red strip is used to orient the first pin—called pin 1—to its correct position with the connecting plug. Be sure to label or identify each connecting device attached to your motherboard.

2. Read and reread any and all instructions that come with your new motherboard. There might be steps you need to take either before or after you install the new motherboard, such as moving jumpers.

3. Examine your existing motherboard in its case to see exactly how it is attached to the case. Notice the number and position of screws and nonmetallic connectors and supports.

4. Remove all interface cards from your motherboard by first removing the retaining screw and then gently lifting the card out of its slot. Sometimes, you may have to gently rock the cards to get them out. If any cables are attached to any of the interface cards, carefully remove and label each of the cables.

5. Carefully remove the memory DIMMs and the processor installed in your computer. If it is awkward to remove these now, you can wait until you have removed the motherboard from the case to remove the processor and memory DIMMs.

6. Remove any cables attached to your motherboard and label them one at a time. Note the orientation of the power cables connected to your motherboard. The power cables are the two multi-wire, multi-colored cables running from the power supply to the motherboard.

38

One way to easily remember how to reattach the power cables from your motherboard (on all but ATX motherboards) to the power supply is that the black wires are always on the inside edges of the two connectors next to each other.

7. When all components and connectors have been removed from your motherboard, remove the screws and standoff connectors (the small plastic supports) holding your motherboard in the case. Carefully remove the motherboard from the case. Note the orientation of your motherboard to its case. If you still have to remove the CPU and memory, do so and carefully put these chips in a safe place.

Now that you have your old motherboard out of the PC's case, half of your job is done. To install your replacement motherboard, you merely have to follow the same steps you took to remove your old motherboard, only in reverse order.

Replacing the Motherboard in Your PC

Here's what you have to do to replace the motherboard in your PC:

1. You might find it easier if you insert the CPU and memory into the new motherboard before you place the board back into your PC's case.

2. Place the new motherboard in your case, paying attention to any possible changes in the standoff connectors and connecting screws. Be sure to use all your screws to allow for proper grounding. Also, be careful not to damage the underside of the motherboard.

3. Replace the power connectors according to the diagram you made when you removed your old motherboard.

4. Replace your interface cards. On some older motherboards, users occasionally had problems with interface cards being placed over processors, but new motherboard designs, such as the ATX motherboard, rearranged the placement of CPUs and cards to avoid this problem. The biggest problem you can encounter with replacing all your cards is making sure that the new motherboard has the same number of expansion slots as your old motherboard. Be sure to reconnect any cables that were attached to the cards.

5. Perform any setup operations dictated by the instructions included with your new motherboard such as setting CPU speed and voltage.

When you have reattached everything to your new motherboard that was removed from your old motherboard, you are ready to turn on your PC and test your handiwork. If your

PC fails to start or displays any errors, note the error and check the instructions that came with your new motherboard. Recheck your work. When you have corrected the problem causing the error, retest your PC.

More Info on System Boards

If you're interested in getting more specific information on system boards, here are a few companies and Web sites you can check:

- **Abit**—http://www.abit.com/
- **ASUS**—http://www.asus.com/
- **DFI**—http://www.dfi.com/
- **EliteGroup**—http://www.ecs.com.tw/
- **FIC**—http://www.fic.com.tw/
- **Gigabyte**—http://www.gigabyte.de/
- **Intel**—http://www.intel.com/intel/product/components.htm
- **Iwil**—http://www.iwill.net/home/home.asp
- **Micro-Star**—http://www.msi.com.tw/about/main.htm
- **Soyo**—http://www.soyo.com.tw/
- **Supermicro**—http://www.supermicro.com/product.htm
- **Tyan**—http://www.tyan.com/products/html/systemboards.html

After you get all the information you're looking for on various system boards, you might want to check Tom's Hardware Guide (www.tomshardware.com/) for technical performance comparisons on various boards.

Summary

You have now learned about the various types of main system boards used in PCs, how to identify the various types of system boards, what criteria you use in deciding whether you want to upgrade your system board, and how to remove and install a system board.

38

CHAPTER 39

Upgrading Your PC's Case and Power Supply

Upgrading your PC's case and power supply may seem like a fairly inconsequential upgrade, but there is a method to this madness. As you begin to upgrade or, more specifically, add components to your PC such as additional hard disk drives, CD-RW or DVD drives, removable media drives, and so on, you are adding components that require both space and electrical power. Not too many PCs leave the factory with four or five empty drive bays. And if you have been giving some thought to adding a CD-RW drive, a Zip drive, and a second hard disk drive, you might be stopped dead in your tracks when you discover that you have only one empty drive bay left in your PC (if that).

As for electrical power, too many PC users have learned the hard way that as you continue to add components, you cannot just keep adding Y-connectors and expect everything to function properly. Upgrading your PC's case and power supply may seem like major surgery, but it is something the average PC user can easily accomplish with just a screwdriver, a little time, and a little patience.

Deciding to Upgrade Your Case and Power Supply

When you purchased your current PC, you probably thought it came in a perfectly adequate case. Everything was neatly arranged; the drives, motherboard, interface cards, and so on all fit together in a nice, neat, orderly package. So, why would you want to pull everything out and stuff all your components into a new box? Well stop for a moment, remove your PC's cover, and take a long, hard look inside your PC and see how much room there is for adding any extra drives or other components. Can you add one or two more hard disk drives? Can you add an internal Zip drive? Can you add a CD-RW drive? Can you add a DVD drive? Can you add a tape drive?

For whatever reason (most often to keep costs down), some manufacturers use a fairly small case when they design and manufacture their PCs. Whether the reason is to keep the package you place on your desk as small as possible or to keep the manufacturer's costs down by keeping their package (and packaging) smaller, the end result is that you have a PC that may not be as expandable as you'd like.

> Although most PCs can very easily be upgraded into a new case, some PCs, because of their proprietary design, cannot be upgraded simply because their manufacturers used a nonstandard motherboard and case design. If you open your PC and see a motherboard that does not seem to fit the designs mentioned in this chapter, the chances are good that your system cannot easily be upgraded, and you should not even attempt to upgrade to a new case unless you also consider upgrading your motherboard as well.

The obvious answer to the need for more room is simply to swap your existing case for a new one. To replace the case, you follow the same procedure, but reverse the process: Instead of placing a new motherboard in your existing case, you are placing your existing motherboard in a new case. To save yourself some time, remember that you probably don't have to remove the processor and memory DIMMs from your motherboard when removing it from one case and placing it in another.

What to Look for When Shopping for a New Case

Although the process is not exactly like buying a new car, when shopping for a new computer case, you want to look for certain features. Here are some of the features in a new case that definitely make your life easier and your upgrades smoother:

- **Multiple drive bays**—The main reason you are purchasing a new case is probably to add additional drives (hard disk drives, CD-RW drives, DVD drives, removable media drives, and so on), so make sure that your new case has more drive bays than you currently need so that you have room to expand (see Figure 39.1). Most cases have a mixture of 3 1/2-inch and 5 1/4-inch drive bays. The 3 1/2-inch drive bays are used to add additional hard disk drives (possibly also a second 3 1/2-inch floppy drive), and the 5 1/4-inch bays are used for CD-RW and removable media drives. If you run out of 3 1/2-inch bays with the proper mounting hardware, you can place a hard disk drive into a 5 1/2-inch drive bay. Keep in mind that some replacement cases may come with only one or two 3 1/2-inch drive bays.

> If you have SCSI hard disks, CD-RW drives, or removable media drives in your PC, it is possible to purchase a separate case that only houses your SCSI drives. These SCSI cases include their own power supply and fans and are a good way to remove some of the devices responsible for the heat buildup inside your PC. You will have to purchase a new cable for your SCSI chain because the cable you have now only works inside your PC. If you do decide to pursue this option, and you plan to retain some devices inside your PC as well, make sure that your SCSI card supports both external and internal devices simultaneously. Some SCSI cards don't.

39

FIGURE 39.1

A computer case with extra drive bays.

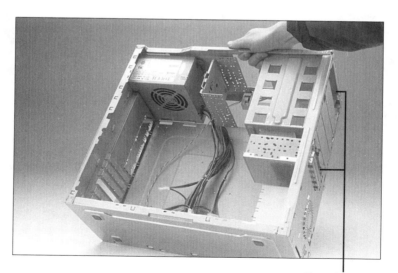

Extra drive bays

- **Multiple fans**—Keep in mind that as you add additional drives and other components into your PC, you also add more devices that produce heat. Look for cases with at least two fans to help disperse the extra heat buildup—in addition to the fan on the power supply. If possible, try to find a case with large fans or check the documentation to see whether you can add an extra fan.

- **Large power supply**—In this case, "large" means wattage, not physical girth. Try to get a power supply in the range of 250 to 400 watts. Keep in mind that those additional drives you plan to add all require extra power to operate.

- **Extra power connectors**—Although extra power connectors are not essential, having a few extra saves you a trip to the local computer store to purchase Y-connectors (see Figure 39.2).

- **Sturdy construction**—If you purchase locally, rather than through the mail, examine the case before you buy it (be sure to examine the actual case you purchase, not just a display model). Try to get a case that seems like it is constructed with heavier gauge steel rather than a flimsy type of sheet metal. Look to see whether the seams are even and that all seams meet with no gaps. Check to see that the cover or door fits securely and is easy to open or remove. If you purchase your case by mail order, try talking to several computer consultants in your area to see whether they can recommend one or more brands for you to purchase.

FIGURE 39.2

You can supplement extra power connectors with a few Y-connectors.

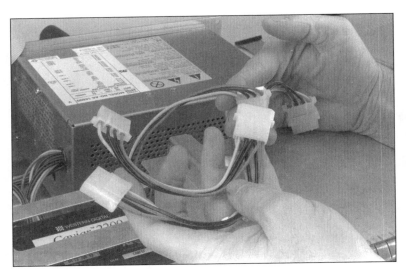

- **Front panel indicators and controls**—Many cases come equipped with several front panel indicators and controls. Although not all are essential, some can come in handy. The essential controls include a reset button, an on/off switch (which prevents you from having to reach around back to turn on your PC), and a drive activity indicator light. Make sure that instructions are included with your case to let you know how to connect the front panel controls and indicators to your motherboard. If your existing case has front panel indicators and controls, make note of how and where these controls are connected to your motherboard.

- **Removable mounting plate and drive bays**—A removable mounting plate (see Figure 39.3) makes it easier to install and access your motherboard. Removable drive bays, both internal and external, make it easier to install and access any drives that you install in your PC.

External drive bays hold drives that are physically accessible to you, such as floppy disk and CD-RW or DVD drives. Internal drive bays are bays holding drives that you don't need to physically access, such as hard disk drives.

FIGURE 39.3

A removable mounting plate makes it easy to access your motherboard.

39

- **Color choices**—While hardly essential to upgrading, a lot of manufacturers have caught on to the fact that many PC users are tired of staring at beige or dull gray cases and have started offering cases in virtually every color of the light spectrum, including clear or transparent.

Cases (which are also referred to as *chassis*), just like PCs, can be purchased as either desktop or tower models and come in a variety of sizes. Desktop case sizes are usually referred to as standard, baby AT, slimline, and micro. Desktop cases usually don't offer you as much expansion space as do tower cases. Just make sure that the case you purchase is designed for your type of motherboard.

Tower cases usually have a larger variety of available sizes, such as mini-tower, medium, large tower, server-size, super-sized, and mega-sized. Usually the difference in sizes is caused by the number of drive bays and the size (wattage) of the power supply.

Desktop units have the advantage of occupying a smaller piece of your office real estate and are generally less expensive than tower cases. Tower cases, on the other hand, offer more room for expansion and can be placed on the floor next to your desk so that they don't take up any valuable desktop space. When you place a tower on the floor next to your desk, you likely have to purchase expansion cables (that is, longer cables) for your monitor and keyboard.

Another option you might want to consider are rack-mount cases (see Figure 39.4).

Years ago, rack-mount cases were used only in large network server rooms, but with the proliferation of home networks and more users setting up their own Web servers, it's not impractical to think of upgrading to a rack-mount case.

FIGURE 39.4

A rack-mount case fits into a standard 19-inch relay rack.

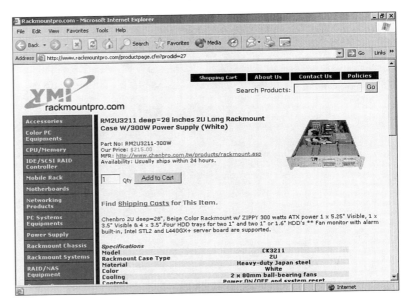

Rack-mount cases fit only into a standard 19-inch electrical relay rack (which you can purchase from over the Internet from companies such as Black Box or RP Electronics, or from your local electrical supply store), not something you typically find in the average home or basement office unless you have an extensive home network to go with it. The advantages of using rack-mounted cases is that they are typically a lot larger and offer a lot more expansion potential than most other larger cases. The downside however is the expense. Do a search on rack-mount cases and you'll see what I mean.

Upgrading Your Case

There are no hard and fast rules for upgrading your PC's case except that you should be patient, methodical, and make note of anything you remove or disconnect. However, here are a few suggestions you might want to follow after you unplug the power cord, ground yourself, and remove the cover from your existing PC case.

> Grounding yourself is extremely important to prevent damage from static electricity, but be sure to exercise the same caution with each component that you remove from your PC. Make sure to place your drives, system boards, DIMMs, and your CPU someplace where they are not subject to damage by static electricity.

The following is one method you can use to replace your existing case with a newer model:

1. Make sure that you diagram the location of every component before you move or remove anything. This diagram should include drives, cables, power connectors, and any miscellaneous items installed in your PC. Note also how any mounting hardware is installed. Make sure that you know how each component will fit into the new case.

2. Carefully remove your interface cards first. If cables are attached to any of the cards, remove the cables before you attempt to remove the cards. One card at a time, remove the screw securing the card in place and lift the card out of its slot. Place each card in a safe location so that it is not damaged.

3. Remove your disk drives and ribbon cables. Again, note how they are connected and which cables are connected to each drive. Also remove any mounting hardware used to support your disk drives. Carefully note how the mounting hardware is installed and where all mounting screws are installed.

4. Remove your memory SIMMs (or DIMMs) and CPU. When removing the SIMMs/DIMMs, be careful not to damage the SIMMs, DIMMs, or the clips holding them into each slot (see Figures 39.5 and 39.6). If your CPU is inserted into a ZIF socket (see Figure 39.7), remove the fan and/or heat sink if there is one, unclip the latch, lift it up to release tension on the pins of the CPU, and lift your CPU out of the socket. This step is often done by users as a means of making sure that the CPU and memory SIMMs are not accidentally damaged. If you feel comfortable leaving the CPU and SIMMs/DIMMs in place, do so.

FIGURE 39.5
Clips used to secure SIMMs in their slots.

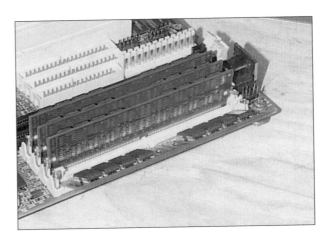

FIGURE 39.6
Clips used to secure DIMMs in their slots.

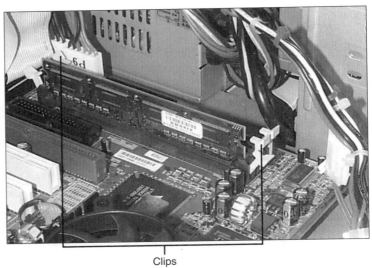

Clips

5. After every component has been removed from your case and motherboard, stop for a minute and note the remaining cables attached to your motherboard. Note in particular how the two power cables are attached to your motherboard's power connectors. In most cases, the two black wires on each power connector (if you have an AT-style motherboard) are next to each other (see Figure 39.8). Check to see whether your PC follows this convention. If it does not, make note of how the power cables are attached to the motherboard. Also note whether your disk drive ribbon cables are attached to connectors on your motherboard. If they are, note the direction and position of the red edge of the ribbon cable. Note, too, whether a

series of smaller cables and wires are attached to your motherboard from your case's front panel. These are for your front panel indicator connections and controls. Finally, note the placement of screws and standouts (plastic supports) for your motherboard. Remove all screws, making sure not to accidentally damage your motherboard with the tip of the screwdriver, and then remove your motherboard and put it in a safe place.

FIGURE 39.7

A ZIF socket securing a CPU on a motherboard.

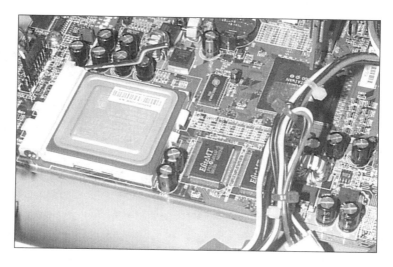

FIGURE 39.8

The two black wires on the power supply connectors (on an AT-style motherboard) are usually next to each other, as shown here.

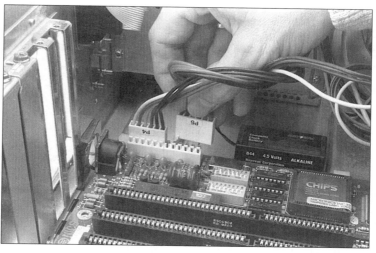

39

You don't normally remove the power supply because almost all new cases come with power supplies already installed.

To install your motherboard and components into the new case, simply follow the previous five steps in reverse order, making sure that you pay close attention to your diagrams and notes. Just be patient, take your time, and you should have no trouble installing the motherboard and components into your new case.

When you have double-checked every connection and diagram you've made, plug in your PC and press the power switch. Your PC should boot up just like before. If your PC does not boot, unplug the electrical cable. First check the power connectors to your motherboard to make sure that they are properly positioned. Then check to make sure that the SIMMs (or DIMMs), CPU, and the peripheral cards—especially the video card—are all properly seated. In most PCs, these are usually the components that, if not properly installed, keep your PC from booting.

Where You Can Purchase a New Case

Here are a few sites where you can purchase PC cases online:

- **Case Outlet**—http://www.caseoutlet.com/
- **Hansan Systems**—http://www.hansansystems.com/
- **Fum Da Electronics**—http://www.fumda.de/no_frames/pc_case.htm
- **Oak Computers**—http://www.oakcomputers.com/cases.html
- **Acme Technology**—http://www.acme-technology.co.uk/pc_cases.htm
- **Color Cases**—http://www.colorcases.com/

Power Supplies

When you purchase a new case, it usually comes equipped with a power supply, but you can also purchase power supplies separately. The two main reasons for purchasing a separate power supply are as follows:

- Your existing power supply fails.
- You want to add additional devices to your PC, and your existing power supply does not output sufficient wattage. Older PCs with only a few internal devices have been shipped with smaller wattage power supplies. If your power supply is in the 75 to 125W range, you should consider replacing it for this reason.

The most important factor to consider when purchasing a new power supply is whether it fits in your existing case. If you do not purchase a new power supply from the same company that supplied your original power supply, it probably is a good idea to remove the power supply you are replacing and take it with you to your local computer store.

This way you can compare the new power supply to the old one, check for size, and make sure that the power connection cables, mounting screws, and off/on switch are all in the same relative positions.

> One caution that cannot be repeated too often is the importance of making sure that you reconnect the power supply cables to your motherboard properly. Make sure that you note how the power supply cables (on an AT-style motherboard) are connected before you remove them. In most cases, the two black cables (on an AT-style motherboard) are next to each other when the two connectors are plugged into the motherboard. If you accidentally reverse these connectors, you can fry your motherboard. On an ATX-style motherboard, there is only one connector, which can fit only one way.

You can easily remove your existing power supply with just a screwdriver and a little patience. Remember to label each cable you remove and, most importantly, make sure that you unplug the power supply before you begin removing it from your case. Be careful that you remove only the screws holding the power supply in the case and do not accidentally remove the screws from the power supply itself.

> Don't even think about trying to open a failed power supply to attempt repairing it. First, they usually aren't worth repairing; a new power supply can be purchased for around $20 to $30. Second, power supplies are all manufactured with slow discharge capacitors, which can carry a considerable (and dangerous) charge even after they are unplugged.

Summary

In this chapter, you learned about upgrading your PC's case and power supply. You learned what criteria are important in selecting a new case and received a few tips on how and where to purchase one. You also learned step-by-step how to remove the components in your existing PC and how to reinstall them into your new case.

PART XII

Upgrading Your Storage Drives

Chapter

Chapter 40

Replacing, Upgrading, or Adding a Hard Disk Drive

Just as we've seen memory prices nose dive over the past few years, prices on hard disk drives have also dropped. In 1984, a Seagate 30MB hard disk drive cost around $350. Now you can easily pay less money for a drive 2,000 times larger and considerably faster.

Today, it's fairly common to see new PCs advertised with hard disk storage capacities in the 40GB to 80GB range. If the PC you are currently using has from 10GB to 30GB of disk storage (or less), you are long overdue for an upgrade. You will find that installing a hard disk drive in your PC is extremely easy.

Is Your Upgrade an Addition or a Replacement?

Like memory, when you upgrade your hard disk drive, in most cases you are actually adding a second disk drive to your system rather than replacing a smaller, slower hard disk with a larger, faster drive. In most PCs, accommodating a second hard disk drive is no problem. There are very few reasons why you should ever be forced to remove your existing hard disk and replace it with a new one. The following are the exceptions:

- Your PC physically does not have room (that is, there is no empty drive bay) for a second hard disk drive.
- You are switching from IDE drives to SCSI drives.
- Your hard disk drive fails and has to be replaced.

IDE Versus SCSI

The first major decision you have to make in upgrading your hard disk is choosing between the two types of drives—IDE and SCSI. In most cases, the decision is made for you by the type of disk controller installed in your PC. For the last five years, most PCs have been manufactured with an IDE controller built in to the system, but in the last year or two, some PC manufacturers have offered customers a choice between IDE and SCSI.

IDE stands for Integrated Drive Electronics, and *SCSI* (pronounced "scuzzy") stands for Small Computer System Interface. You might also see IDE listed as EIDE, for Enhanced Integrated Drive Electronics, which was a faster enhancement on the original IDE specification.

System Information, the Windows XP systems configuration program on your Windows menu, should have identified the type of disk controller and drive you have installed in your PC.

A *disk controller* is the interface that connects your disk drives to your motherboard. The controller can either be built in to the motherboard, as are most IDE controllers in most PCs built in the last few years, or they can come in the form of an interface card that is installed into one of the slots on your motherboard.

IDE is currently the more popular and widely used of the two disk types, primarily because IDE devices are cheaper to manufacture than SCSI devices. IDE also seems to have a slight edge in disk performance. Depending on how you have your PC configured and what operating system you are planning to use, a SCSI controller can actually give you better overall system performance. This is particularly true if you install two or more hard disk drives in your PC and use a true 32-bit operating system such as Windows XP.

Even though IDE drives are slightly faster than SCSI drives, SCSI drives do offer some significant advantages over IDE drives:

- SCSI drives put far less strain on your CPU than IDE drives. This can result in overall higher levels of system performance and reliability.

- SCSI drives perform better in 32-bit multitasking operating systems, such as Windows XP because SCSI controllers and drives can perform disk reading and writing tasks while other operations and programs are running.

- You can attach up to 15 SCSI drives or devices to a single SCSI controller; IDE drives are beginning to narrow the gap here, but using an IDE RAID controller you can attach at most only 6 IDE drives.

- A slower SCSI device, such as a CD-ROM drive, does not degrade the performance of a faster SCSI device (a hard disk, for example) if both are connected to the same controller. On older IDE controllers, a slower CD-ROM drive degrades the performance of a hard disk if both are on the same controller. That is why most PCs in the past were shipped with two IDE controllers on the motherboard—one for the hard disk drives and one for your CD-ROM drive. On newer systems with EIDE (Enhanced IDE drives), each device can operate at its optimal level of performance.

- A SCSI cable can be up to 10 feet long, enabling you to install multiple external (outside of your PC) SCSI devices; IDE cable can usually be no longer than about 15 inches, which limits most IDE devices to being installed inside your PC.

Although SCSI controllers and drives can be configured to produce a higher level of performance, SCSI drives are still mainly used in high-end workstations and network file servers rather than in standard desktop PCs.

Perhaps the biggest incentive for using IDE drives is their cost. A comparable IDE drive can easily cost half the price of a SCSI drive.

Also, because SCSI controllers are rarely built in to motherboards, you also need to purchase a SCSI controller (minimum of about $100) to install SCSI drives and devices.

Installing an IDE Drive in Your PC

As mentioned earlier, you can install only two IDE drives or devices on a single IDE controller. Most manufacturers now build two IDE controller connectors on their motherboards so that you can install two hard disk drives on one controller and a CD-ROM drive on the second controller. IDE controller connectors are easy to spot on your

40

motherboard. Just look for two 40-pin connectors side-by-side (see Figure 40.1). On newer systems that support the UltraATA/66 or UltraATA/100 specifications, these connectors will have 80 pins.

FIGURE 40.1

IDE controller connectors on a motherboard.

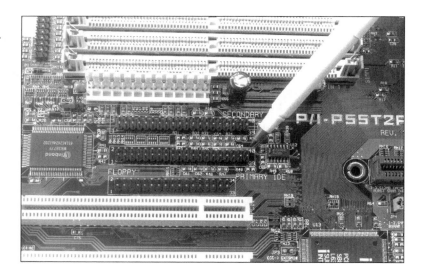

UltraATA/66 and UltraATA/100 are both IDE specifications that provide faster disk performance than the older UltraATA/33 or EIDE specifications.

Before you purchase a new IDE drive, make sure that your system can support the UltraATA/66 or UltraATA/100 specification (most new drives are made for these specifications). If your system cannot support these newer specifications, don't despair; you can simply purchase an IDE interface card that does support the newer specs.

IDE drives use a series of jumpers on the drives to designate whether a single drive is installed on one controller or whether multiple drives are installed on the same controller. The jumpers are installed on a 32 matrix of pins often found on the end of the drive near the power connector, but can also be found on the hard disk drive circuit card. When you purchase a hard disk drive, the instructions indicate where the jumper pins are located and how you are to designate the drives.

When multiple drives are installed on the same controller, one drive is designated the primary or "master," and the other drive is designated the secondary or "slave."

If two drives are installed on one controller, you must install the jumpers on one drive as you see in Figure 40.2 to designate it as the primary or master. You need to install the jumpers on the second drive to designate it as the secondary or slave (see Figure 40.3). If a single drive is installed on a controller, no jumpers are usually installed.

Replacing an Existing Hard Disk Drive

The easiest way to install a hard disk drive is by replacing an existing drive with a new drive because you can use the existing drive as your model for installing the new drive. All the mounting screws and connecting cables should be the same, eliminating any guesswork on your part.

When replacing an existing drive with a new drive, one of the first considerations is to determine how you are going to back up or transfer the files from the old drive to the new drive. If you have some sort of backup device (for example, a tape drive or a removable media drive, such as a CD-RW drive), this greatly simplifies the file transfer process. If you do not have a backup device, your only option is to back up your data files onto floppy disks and reinstall your operating system and programs onto the new drive after it is installed.

A number of disk image copying programs are available on the market—such as Norton Ghost and Drive Image—that can simplify this task by making an exact copy of your first drive to place on your new drive. Typically, however, these programs usually require some sort of large storage or backup device to temporarily store the disk image. If you have access to a network file server, these disk image copying programs can be a godsend.

FIGURE 40.2

Jumpers designating one drive as the primary or master.

40

FIGURE **40.3**

Jumpers designating one drive as the secondary or slave.

To replace an existing drive with a new drive, follow these steps:

1. Unplug your PC after unplugging the power and grounding yourself to prevent static electric discharges.

2. Locate the existing drive in your PC. Diagram how each cable is connected to the drive and how the drive is mounted in your PC. Note all connecting screws and mounting hardware and how the drive is physically installed in your PC.

3. Disconnect the 4-wire power cord from the hard disk drive.

4. Disconnect the ribbon cable from the hard disk drive. Note how the ribbon cable is attached to the drive (that is, the position and orientation of the red stripe, if there is one, on the ribbon cable).

5. Remove any screws used to mount the hard disk drive to your PC. Some PC manufacturers place the hard disk into a mounting bracket, and some manufacturers mount guide rails onto the sides of the drive. Most manufacturers try to install two mounting screws on each side of the drive for a total of four mounting screws to hold the drive securely in place.

6. Check to see whether any jumpers are installed on the existing drive. Follow the guidelines mentioned earlier for correctly installing jumpers on the new drive. Use the existing drive as your model, and make sure that you place the jumper (if there is one installed) on the new drive the same as the jumper is installed on the existing drive.

7. Attach the new drive to any mounting hardware or bracket, if one is used in your PC, and reinstall the drive into a drive bay or mounting position in your PC.

8. Reattach the ribbon cable and the 4-wire power cord to the drive.

When you turn on your PC for the first time, you will probably have to re-run your CMOS hardware Setup program to configure the new drive. This procedure varies from PC to PC—some newer PCs considerably automate this process, whereas some older PCs may require you to enter hardware values for the new drive, such as the number of drive heads, tracks, and sectors. This information is supplied with the drive, so make sure to hold onto your documentation. The only thing left to do is to format the drive (as explained in your documentation) and restore your files from whatever backup medium you used. Again, the documentation that came with your backup device will explain what you have to do.

> If your computer does not recognize your hard disk drive or reports a storage capacity far smaller than the reported size of the drive, it is possible you have an older BIOS in your PC that does not recognize large (larger than 550MB) drives. See Chapter 37, "Upgrading Your CPU and BIOS," for more information on replacing your existing BIOS.

Adding a Second Hard Disk Drive

Adding a second drive is usually just as easy as replacing an existing drive provided that you have an empty drive bay available. Again, you can use the existing drive as a template for how the second drive will be installed. When adding a second IDE drive, remember that one drive has to be designated the primary or master, and the other drive has to be designated the secondary or slave. In most cases, the existing drive is designated the master, and the drive you are adding is designated the slave. By designating the new drive as the secondary or slave, you do not have to concern yourself with backing up the files on the existing drive or installing an operating system on the new drive. The new drive (after it is formatted) will simply appear as the next drive letter after your existing drive (usually drive D:).

40

> If you have a CD-ROM drive installed in your PC and you are adding another hard disk drive, your CD-ROM drive will be bumped down a drive letter. For example, if your CD-ROM drive is designated drive D:, after you add another hard disk drive, the new hard disk drive becomes drive D: and your CD-ROM drive becomes drive E:. Usually, this is not a problem except when the software you install from a CD-ROM requires you to leave the CD-ROM in the drive while the program is running (as many games do). In this scenario, your program is looking for your CD-ROM files on drive D: instead of drive E:. If this happens to you, see whether there is a way to reconfigure your

> program to look on drive E: from the CD-ROM. If you can't reconfigure the software, you will have to reinstall it. If you do want to reorganize your drive designations, go into the Computer Management section of the Control Panel. But before you do that, make sure that none of your software expects to see programs or CDs on a specific drive.

You also must note how the ribbon cable is attached to the existing drive and attach the ribbon cable in the same position to the new drive you are adding. Note, too, that there are two connectors on the ribbon cable for attaching IDE devices. Because you are designating one drive the master and one drive the slave, it does not matter which connector you attach the new drive to (see Figure 40.4).

Before you begin, make sure that your PC has sufficient physical room for a second drive (that is, that you have an empty drive bay), and make sure that you have all the mounting hardware (for example, support frame, guide rails, and so on). Many hard disk drive kits now come with several sets of mounting hardware to cover all contingencies, but it never hurts to tell the sales representative what type of computer you have to ensure that the drive kit you purchase will work with your system. Most computer stores that sell hard disk drives also sell mounting kits (if the hard disk drive you purchase does not come with a mounting kit), and the kits usually identify most of the computers they are designed to work with.

Also, if you find that you are missing a 4-wire power cable, you can pick up a Y-connector (see Figure 40.5) at almost any computer store for around $5.

FIGURE 40.4

This figure shows two IDE drives and the positioning of jumpers and the ribbon cable.

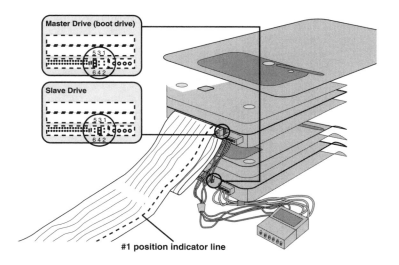

Master Drive (boot drive)

Slave Drive

#1 position indicator line

FIGURE 40.5

A Y-connector used to attach two devices to a single power connector.

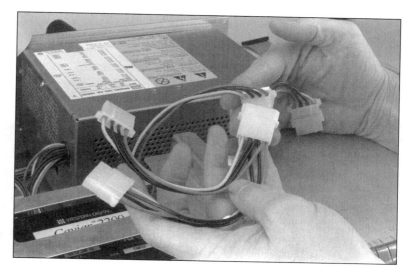

Installing a SCSI Drive in Your PC

Installing SCSI hard disk drives and devices is quite different from installing IDE drives. When you install SCSI hard disk drives and devices in your PC, you are creating what is called a "SCSI chain." The SCSI chain consists of a SCSI controller card, a SCSI cable, one or more SCSI devices, and a SCSI *terminator* at each end of the chain. It is important to remember that the terminators are always at both ends of the SCSI chain. I mention this because the end of a SCSI chain can be any of the following:

- A SCSI controller card with a built-in terminator
- A SCSI device, such as a hard disk drive, a CD-ROM drive, a tape backup drive, a scanner, and so on, also with a built-in terminator
- A physical SCSI terminator

Most newer SCSI controller cards are designed with both an internal and external connector for attaching SCSI devices (see Figure 40.6). Because of this design, a SCSI controller card can be in the middle of your SCSI chain or at either end, depending on whether you have internal or external SCSI devices or both. Most newer SCSI controller cards can also be self-terminating if they are at the end of the SCSI chain.

Another important difference in installing SCSI disk drives and devices is that every device on a SCSI chain has to have a unique ID number. SCSI ID numbers are simply a way of identifying one device from another on the SCSI chain. SCSI ID numbers are similar to designating one IDE drive the master and one the slave. For example, if you have three cats, you would not name them all "Max" because they would get confused when you called them. The same applies to SCSI devices. Unless they have unique ID numbers, confusion can occur when you have to access a particular drive or device.

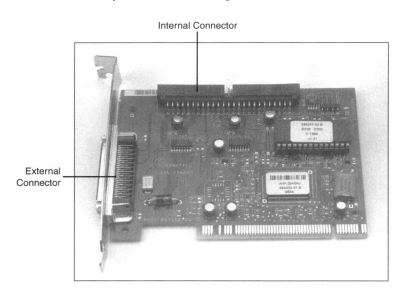

Internal Connector

FIGURE 40.6

A typical SCSI controller card showing both internal and external connectors.

External
Connector

In most instances, the SCSI controller is given the SCSI ID number 7, which means that you can use ID numbers 0–6 for your SCSI drives and devices; on newer SCSI controllers, you also can use the ID numbers 8–15. For hard disk drives, SCSI ID numbers are usually set using a series of jumpers, much the same way you use jumpers to designate IDE drives connected to the same controller. The instructions accompanying the drive explain how to install the jumpers for a specific ID number. You do not designate a SCSI drive as master or slave as you do with IDE drives. If you plan to boot your PC from the SCSI drive, its ID number must usually be 0. If you have both IDE and SCSI drives in your PC, you must boot your PC from the IDE drive, in which case the SCSI drive ID can be any number from 0–6.

Physically installing the SCSI drive into your PC is about the same as installing an IDE drive in regards to physical location and mounting hardware. You may have a bit more latitude and room to work because SCSI cables can be a lot longer than IDE cables.

To install an internal SCSI hard disk, follow these steps:

1. Unplug your PC and exercise safety precautions such as grounding yourself to prevent static electric discharges and unplugging your computer.

2. Install the SCSI controller card in an empty slot in the PC.

3. Set the SCSI ID on the drive according to how you plan to use it (that is, will you boot from the SCSI drive, will the SCSI drive exist in the PC with an IDE drive, and so on). In most cases, the ID number for the drive is set using jumpers.

4. Install the SCSI drive using the mounting hardware you have.

5. Attach the power cable to the SCSI drive.

6. Attach the SCSI cable to the drive. In every case I have seen, SCSI cables are notched or in some way designed so that the cable can be attached to the drive in only one way (see Figure 40.7).

7. If the internal SCSI drive is the only SCSI device you are installing, make sure that the SCSI cable (that is, the SCSI chain) is terminated after the drive. Make sure that the other end of the SCSI chain, which should be the SCSI controller, is also terminated. Many newer SCSI controllers will self-terminate if they detect that they are at the end of the SCSI chain.

FIGURE 40.7

A notched SCSI connector on a SCSI cable.

40

If you install an external SCSI device such as a scanner, termination is no longer at the controller card but at (or after) the last external device. Likewise, if you install an additional internal SCSI device such as a SCSI CD-ROM drive after the hard disk on the SCSI chain, the termination now falls after the last device on the chain. Just remember to terminate *both* ends of the SCSI chain. Be sure to remove any other terminators so that there are only two on the chain.

If the SCSI drive is the only drive in your PC, you do not have to make any changes in your CMOS settings unless you are removing an IDE drive and replacing it with a SCSI drive. In this case, you have to turn off or disable all *IDE parameters* (settings) in your CMOS hardware settings. You will have to run your hardware Setup (CMOS) program and in most cases set your IDE drive settings to "unused" or "disabled."

> IDE parameters are the settings you make in your hardware Setup (CMOS) program to identify the characteristics of your drive. These settings include the number of read/write heads on your drive, the number of physical platters (the metal disks that actually make up your hard disk), and the number of tracks and sectors defined on each platter surface. The surface of each hard disk platter is divided into a number of concentric rings called tracks. Each track in turn is divided into a number of wedge-shaped units called sectors.

Adding a Second SCSI Drive

If you ever decide to add a second SCSI drive, you need only to set the SCSI ID number to a number not being used before installing the drive into an empty drive bay. For example, if the first SCSI drive has the SCSI ID number 0, set the SCSI ID number of the second drive to 1. The next time you start up your PC, your SCSI controller will automatically detect the new SCSI device inserted in the SCSI chain.

Preparing Your Drives for Software

Before you can install files and software onto your new drive, you must create one or more disk partitions using FDISK or a similar utility and format the drive. A partition is nothing more than a defined area on your hard disk that you use to store files.

Using FDISK to Create a Disk Partition

If you use FDISK (which is stored on a DOS system disk that you can make by inserting a blank diskette in your drive, starting Windows Explorer, right-clicking over the disk drive, selecting the Format command, and selecting the System option before starting the format), you simply start up your computer using your DOS disk, and then start FDISK by typing **FDISK** at the DOS prompt.

> You have to set one, and only one, partition to be the active partition. The active partition is on the drive to which your computer boots. If you are adding a second drive, do not accidentally reset the active partition to the second hard disk drive, or your computer will not start.

To create a partition using FDISK, follow these steps:

1. Insert the DOS disk into the floppy drive and start up your computer. Start FDISK by typing **FDISK** at the DOS prompt.

2. From the menu of FDISK options, select option 1, Create DOS Partition. In most cases, you create a single partition on your entire hard disk drive.

> If you want to divide your hard disk into two or more logical drives, FDISK enables you to create more than one partition on a new hard disk drive that you install. (You might want to create totally separate [logical] disks [partitions] to store data on or to somehow separate other types of files. Creating logical drives is a matter of personal preference.) If you decide to create multiple partitions on a single physical drive, the usual configuration is to divide the drive 50/50—make 50% of the drive into the first partition and 50% of the drive into the second partition. But you can divide the drive in any configuration you want. Remember, too, that each partition you create exists as a drive with a separate drive letter (for example, C:, D:, and so on) on your PC.

3. Make one partition the active partition. This will be the partition (drive) to which you will start up your PC.

4. Press Esc twice to exit FDISK and restart your PC.

Using Partition Magic to Create Your Partitions

One problem with using FDISK to create your partitions is that FDISK is typically a DOS-based utility and limits your partition sizes to 2GB. If you are using Windows 98, you can create large partitions (larger than 2GB), but you must create them as *FAT32* partitions. If you are using Windows XP, you can also create partitions as *NTFS* partitions.

40

> *FAT32* is a partition type used in Windows 98, 2000, Me, and XP for supporting larger partitions and for more efficient file storage on large hard disk drives. *NTFS* is a secure partition type originally created under Windows NT 4.0, but now also available under Windows 2000 and XP.

Partition Magic is a disk partition creation utility that not only allows you to create partitions larger than 2GB, but also allows you to resize your partitions.

Formatting Your Drive

After you create your partition(s), you must format your hard disk. Formatting prepares the hard disk to accept and store files. Regardless of which operating system you eventually plan to install on your PC, you can first perform a simple DOS format, but only create a FAT16 disk partition up to 2GB. Then, if you need to change the formatting to a larger partition or to format the partition as FAT32 or NTFS, you can safely reformat the drive.

 On IDE drives, make sure that you don't perform what is called a "low-level" format. This is a procedure that is done at the factory and should not be performed by an end-user because you can ruin the drive if you do. You need a special utility to do a low-level format; typing FORMAT as instructed to do in the following steps performs a high-level format.

To format your hard disk, follow these steps:

1. Start your PC with your DOS disk.

2. If you are formatting the hard disk as your startup drive, type this command to format the drive and install DOS system files to make the drive bootable:

   `format c: /s`

3. If you are formatting a drive that will not be a bootable drive, type this command, where x: is the drive letter of the drive you are formatting. Make sure that you format each partition you create.

   `format x:`

Installing an Operating System on Your PC

After your hard disk drive is formatted, you can decide what operating system you want to install on your PC. Follow the instructions accompanying the operating system you plan to use to determine whether any additional preparation is necessary before you install the operating system.

Alternative to IDE and SCSI Drives

It used to be that your only choices for upgrading or adding a hard disk were IDE or SCSI devices. Now there is a third choice: FireWire. LaCie (at www.lacie.com) manufactures an external FireWire hard disk drive that is said to perform as well as most IDE and SCSI drives. The LaCie FireWire hard disk drive (see Figure 40.8) is sold as an external drive, which means that all you do to install it is plug in the cable from the hard disk to the FireWire card in your PC, the same way you would plug in an external SCSI drive to your PC.

FIGURE 40.8

The LaCie FireWire hard disk drive.

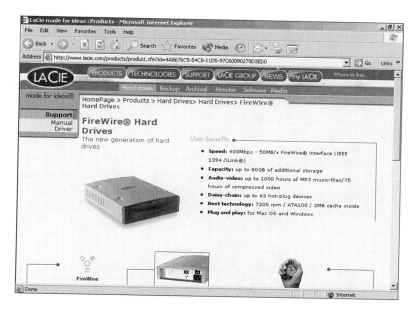

Although performance of the FireWire hard disk is said to be up to par with comparable-sized IDE and SCSI drives, the big drawback to FireWire hard disk drives is price. Early FireWire drives are roughly twice the price of their IDE cousins, and this does not include the cost of the FireWire interface card if your PC doesn't already have one. But like all innovations, as time goes on, expect the price to drop. Currently, there's no indication that a FireWire drive might fit a particular application better than either an IDE or SCSI hard disk drive (SCSI drives, for example, work better in file servers than do IDE drives).

40

Tips on Improving Your Hard Disk Performance

After you finish installing a hard disk drive in your PC and install the operating system, there are still a few things you can do to keep your drive operating in peak form.

Defrag Your Hard Disk Regularly

As you use your computer, you are continually creating and deleting files—even if you are not aware of it. Many software programs create temporary files that are deleted when you exit the program. When you format your hard disk, you are actually dividing it into small areas called sectors. Without going into a lot of technical detail, every time you create a file, your operating system saves a set number of bytes into every sector. When a sector is filled, your operating system uses the next available sector to save more of the file, and so on, until all the file is saved into however many sectors it needs. The sectors do not have to be next to each other to store parts of the same file. The operating system keeps track of which sectors are storing which files. So in a relatively short period of time, it's not only possible, but very likely, that your files are scattered all over your hard disk.

Although your operating system does a good job of keeping track of your files and find-ing all the sectors where a file is stored, locating files scattered all over your hard disk can take time and slow your PC's performance. To solve this problem and literally put your files back together (or at least move the files into adjacent sectors), you can use pro-grams called hard disk defrag (defrag being short for defragmentation) utilities.

You should regularly defrag your hard disk to keep the performance at peak levels. Figures 40.9 and 40.10 show before and after defrag shots of hard disk drive partitions. "Regularly" can vary depending on how you use your PC, but you should make a habit of checking your drives for fragmentations at least once a week.

FIGURE 40.9

A hard disk drive before it is defragged.

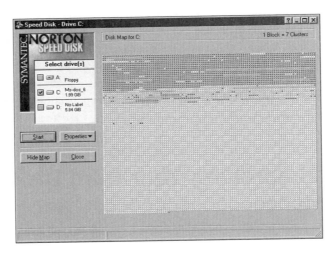

FIGURE 40.10

A hard disk drive after it is defragged.

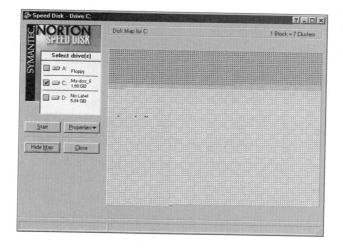

Never use a defrag utility unless it is specifically made for your operating system and its file storage system.

Delete Unneeded Files

As I said earlier, many programs create temporary files on your hard disk and are supposed to delete these files when you exit the program. But sometimes, for various reasons, these temporary files remain on your hard disk. Unneeded files take up valuable space on your hard disk and slow its performance.

All versions of Windows include a service or a utility you can use to locate and remove these unneeded files. Most of the time these files have the extension .TMP or .BAK.

One way to locate and remove these unneeded files is by using File Manager, which is included in every version of Windows.

To remove all files with the extension .TMP or .BAK, follow these steps:

1. Start the Windows Search utility. Select Start, Search, All Files and Folders to open the utility.

2. Choose the drive you want to check by selecting the drive letter icon in the Look In drop-down box.

3. Type *.TMP (or *.BAK) in the All or Part of the File Name text box and click Search. The Search utility performs a thorough search of the drive you select and locates every file with the extension .TMP or .BAK (see Figure 40.11).

40

FIGURE **40.11**

*The Windows Search
utility locates all files
with the extension
. TMP.*

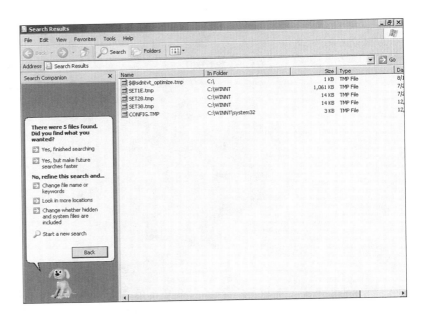

4. Highlight the files with the extension . TMP and press the Delete key to delete these unneeded files.

Some temporary files in Windows are files that Windows is using. While Windows is using these files, you cannot delete them.

Summary

In this chapter, you learned how to install a hard disk drive into your PC regardless of whether you are replacing your existing drive with a new, larger drive, or merely adding a second drive to your system. You learned the differences between IDE and SCSI hard disks, and hopefully learned enough to decide which to purchase. You also learned about the newer FireWire drives that one day might seriously compete with IDE and SCSI drives in the PC marketplace. You also learned a few tips on what you can do to keep your hard disk drives operating at peak levels of performance.

CHAPTER 41

Replacing or Adding a Floppy Disk Drive

In this chapter, the focus is on replacing rather than upgrading your floppy disk drive because floppy disk drives have not seen much in the way of advancements in about the last 8–10 years. Perhaps the last change in floppy disk drives occurred several years ago when most manufacturers standardized on the installation of a single 3 1/2-inch floppy disk drive, removing the 5 1/4-inch drive as a standard feature. Actually, there is no longer anything floppy about these diskettes but the name has stuck (they are also called diskette drives). It may not be long before the 3 1/2-inch floppy disk drive is relegated to being a museum piece because most software these days is shipped on CDs.

Whereas upgrading your floppy drive is not an issue, periodically these workhorses do go bad and you find yourself having to remove the old one and replace it with another 3 1/2-inch drive. Many of you may do this simply for nostalgia reasons because the average PC will continue to work without a functioning floppy disk drive and there isn't much use these days for floppy disks.

Replacing Not Repairing

In the past few years, many books on upgrading PCs have included chapters on repairing floppy disk drives. But floppy disk drives have been reduced to inexpensive commodity status and can be readily purchased at most weekend computer fairs for as little as $10–$15, so it makes little sense to worry about repairing what has literally become a "throw-away" computer component. There's also no concern with compatibility issues because all 3 1/2-inch floppy drives are virtually the same, nor do you have to be concerned with whether you have the correct mounting hardware because all the mounting hardware is already in place inside your PC.

> Even though floppy disk drives are not as essential to day-to-day computer operations as they once were, at roughly $10–$15 a pop, it makes good sense to keep a spare on hand as an emergency repair unit.

Diagnosing a Broken Floppy Disk Drive

Diagnosing a problem with a floppy disk drive is usually pretty simple and straightforward. In most cases, you discover the problem when you boot your PC (most POST operations will mention a nonfunctioning floppy disk) or when you attempt to use the drive, such as reading from or writing to a floppy disk (assuming that you even still have and use floppy disks). Following is a short list of symptoms that can appear when your floppy disk drive is malfunctioning. Check the drive using multiple disks to make sure that your problem is drive related and not disk related:

- Disk activity light does not come on when attempting to use the drive
- Cannot read a disk in the drive
- Cannot write to a disk in the drive
- Programs fail to recognize that a disk is in the drive
- Cannot format a disk in the drive

Keep in mind that any or all of these symptoms can also occur if the ribbon cable or power cord attached to the drive is loose or removed (see Figure 41.1).

So before you break out your toolkit and swap out the drive with your spare, make sure that you check the cables. You'd be surprised how easily and frequently cables come loose.

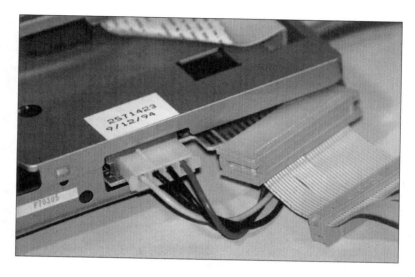

If you check the cables and they are securely in place, be sure to also check your CMOS settings by running the Windows XP System Information program. Make sure that they show a 3 1/2-inch, 1.44MB floppy disk drive as your A: drive. Also check to make sure that no other device you have installed is trying to use the same interrupt request (IRQ) setting that your floppy disk drive is using.

If your cables are secure and your CMOS and IRQ settings are correct and your drive still is not functioning correctly, it's a safe bet your disk drive is malfunctioning and you need to replace it.

Replacing a Broken Floppy Disk Drive

Replacing a broken floppy disk drive is as easy, if not easier, than installing a hard disk drive.

To replace a floppy disk drive, follow these steps:

1. Unplug your PC and ground yourself before removing the cover.

2. Examine your PC to see how the floppy disk drive is installed in your computer's case. Note how many screws are holding the drive in place and the locations of the cables attached to the drive. You may have to remove the front bezel (face plate) to slide the drive out.

3. Identify (and label, if necessary) where and how the cables are attached to the drive before you remove the cables. If you have to remove any other cables or chassis parts to gain access to your floppy disk drive, make note of these also. Notice that

41

the power connector for a 3 1/2-inch drive is smaller than the standard power connector (see Figure 41.2).

FIGURE 41.2

The power connector for a 3 1/2-inch floppy disk drive.

4. Remove all the screws holding the drive in place (see Figure 41.3), and carefully remove the drive from the drive bay.

5. Insert the new drive into the drive bay.

6. Replace all hardware mounting screws.

7. Reconnect the ribbon cable to the drive, making sure that you reattach the cable the same way it was attached to the original drive. Your ribbon cable might have two different connector types (see Figure 41.4). The second connector on the ribbon cable was previously used to connect drive B:, which on earlier model PCs was a 5 1/4-inch floppy disk drive (another carryover for PC nostalgia).

8. Reconnect the smaller power cord to the new drive.

When everything has been reattached and reconnected, turn on your PC to test your work. Notice whether the light on the drive comes on when you start up your PC. If the light comes on and stays on, it means that you have the ribbon cable on backward (reverse the cable). Place a floppy disk into the new drive and perform a few routine tests on the drive. Try issuing the DIR A: command to see whether you can read the contents of the disk. If there's no light, which usually indicates a setup problem, try DIR B:. You can use Windows Explorer to test your drive instead of DIR A:. Try formatting a disk in the drive and copying a few files to the disk. If all these tests work satisfactorily, you can be fairly certain that the disk drive you just installed is working okay.

FIGURE 41.3
*Removing the floppy
disk drive mounting
screws.*

FIGURE 41.4
*The ribbon cable
attached to your floppy
disk drive.*

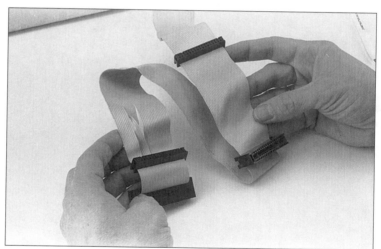

41

Alternatives to a Standard 1.44MB Floppy Disk Drive

If your floppy disk drive goes belly up, there are alternatives when selecting a replacement drive. You might want to consider one of several high capacity removable media drives (see Chapter 43, "Adding Removable Media") that will also read and write standard 3 1/2-inch, 1.44MB floppy disks. Most of these drives plug into one of your two

IDE ports—the same connectors to which you connect your hard disk drives. Although these high-capacity drives will read, write, and boot from standard 3 1/2-inch disks, they will set you back a few more bucks than a standard 3 1/2-inch drive. If you choose to use the high-capacity media they are designed for, expect to also pay a bit more than you will for formatted 3 1/2-inch high-density floppy disks.

Summary

In this chapter, you learned about the evolution of floppy disk drives, how to diagnose some problems that can occur with them, and how to replace a malfunctioning floppy disk drive.

CHAPTER 42

Replacing, Upgrading, or Adding a CD/DVD Drive

A CD-ROM drive is standard equipment in a PC, and some PC manufacturers have already started replacing them with CD-RW drives as standard equipment.

The main factor that has helped to push CD-ROM/CD-RW drives into the mainstream is their continuing drop in price. A top-of-the-line 56x (56-speed or faster) CD-ROM drive often sells for under $50, and average CD-RW drives can now be had for less than $80.

PC software vendors haven't embraced DVD technology as rapidly as the movie industry, but you can find a few software titles currently available on DVD, especially those that would still require a stack of CDs. For example, the first 110 years of the National Geographic (see http://www.nationalgeographic.com/cdrom/) comes on a single DVD—the CD edition of this title comes on 31 CDs!

Selecting a CD-ROM/CD-RW Drive

Despite all the hoopla you've read and heard about *DVD drives* replacing CD-ROM drives and making them obsolete, it hasn't happened yet. Considering the rate at which manufacturers are still cranking out new models of CD-ROM and CD-RW drives, this switch to DVD technology doesn't appear to be happening anytime soon.

 DVD stands for *Digital Video Disc* and is a rather new digital technology very similar to CD-ROM technology. DVDs differ from CD-ROMs in that DVDs can store several times the capacity of CD-ROM discs (CD-ROMs can store approximately 650MB).

The first thing you must understand about selecting a CD-ROM or CD-RW drive is its speed terminology. The first CD-ROM drives transferred data at a rate of 150Kbps (kilobytes per second). This initial speed came to be known as "single-speed" and was written as "1x." As CD-ROM drives progressively got faster, their speeds were measured in comparison to the initial single-speed drives. For example, a double-speed (2x) drive transferred data at a rate of 300Kbps (150Kbps×2=300Kbps). A quad-speed (4x) drive transferred data at a rate of 600Kbps (150Kbps×4=600Kbps). A six-speed (6x) drive transferred data at a rate of 900Kbps, and so on.

Several manufacturers have released 56-speed (56x) drives, and if history is any indicator, the advancement in CD-ROM technology won't stop there.

In selecting a drive, the data transfer speed is likely to be the first factor you consider, but it should not be the only factor. How fast a CD-ROM drive can transfer data is important, but how fast your CD-ROM drive can locate data (a parameter called its *seek time*) is also important.

Just as is true with your hard disk drive, the structure on a CD-ROM drive is composed of sectors and tracks. Seek time is defined as how fast the magnetic head (or in the case of a CD-ROM drive, the laser read head) that reads data can move from one track to another. Although CD-ROM drives cannot approach the seek time speeds of hard disk drives, about 8 to 10ms (milliseconds), a CD-ROM drive seek time of about 110ms is considered excellent.

Another factor to consider is the *cache* size on your CD-ROM. A cache is a holding area of memory built in to the drive to temporarily store data as it is being processed. Most drives have a cache of about 1 to 4MB; anything larger is a premium.

When you're considering a CD-RW drive, there are some additional factors you should consider. When you are describing the speed of CD-RW drives, you generally see three numbers written AAx/BBx/CCx where:

AAx is the speed when recording to standard blank recordable CDs

BBx is the speed when recording to re-writeable CDs

CCx is the speed when reading CDs

For example, if you have a CD-RW drive advertised as 6x/4x/24x, this means that it is a 6x-speed drive when recording standard blank CDs; it is a 4x-speed drive when writing to rewritable CDs; and it is a 24x-speed drive when reading CDs.

> Earlier recordable CD drives were designated CD-R; if you're wondering what the difference is between a CD-R drive and a CD-RW drive, both can record to blank CDs but only the CD-RW can record on rewritable (that is, reusable) CDs. Most CD-R drives have been replaced by CD-RW drives—another reason why CD-RW drives are slowly replacing other types of data backup devices.

Don't let speed be the absolute deciding factor in deciding on a CD-ROM or CD-RW drive. Just as you do with any other peripheral, you should check product reviews periodically in PC magazines and journals and on Web sites that specialize in reviewing new PC products, such as CNET's Computers.com at `http://computers.cnet.com/hardware/0-1091.html` (see Figure 42.1).

However, if speed is your number-one hang-up, don't despair. Go to the `www.cdspeed2000.com` site, download the CD-ROM speed comparison utility, take it in with you when you visit your local computer store, and test to your heart's content (see Figures 42.2 and 42.3), or use it to verify the speeds of the CD-RW you eventually purchase.

SCSI Versus IDE

Just as you had to decide between IDE and SCSI when you were selecting a hard disk drive in Chapter 40, "Replacing, Upgrading, or Adding a Hard Disk Drive," you also have to decide between IDE and SCSI when selecting a CD-ROM or CD-RW drive. The same factors concerning performance and cost apply when selecting a CD-ROM/RW type.

If you already have a SCSI controller installed in your PC, you are way ahead in terms of performance if you select a SCSI CD-ROM/RW drive. SCSI CD-ROM/RW drives, like SCSI hard disk drives, do not place as much strain on your CPU. If you already have a SCSI controller in your PC for your SCSI hard disk(s), you will most likely want to select a SCSI CD-ROM/RW drive. If your hard disk drive is IDE, you will most likely select an IDE CD-RW drive for your PC.

42

FIGURE 42.1

CNET's Computers.com Web site, one of the premiere product review sites.

FIGURE 42.2

The CD Speed 2000 site for testing CD-ROM, CD-RW, and DVD drive speeds.

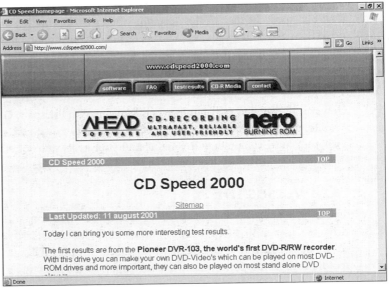

Figure 42.3

Running the CD Speed 2000 CD-ROM speed test.

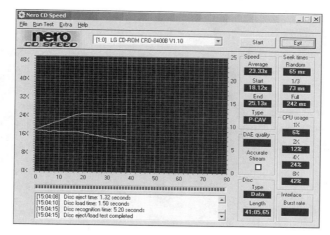

Installing the Drive in Your PC—Internal Versus External

As far as the physical installation is concerned, a CD-ROM drive is no different than a CD-RW drive. The difference between the two installations appears when you install the software for the drive. As you will see later in this chapter, after you perform the physical installation, you must install the hardware driver for your drive. With a CD-RW drive, you also must install some type of CD recording software. Once again, don't worry about which software product to buy; all CD-RW manufacturers include some type of recording software with the drives they sell.

If you plan to install a CD-ROM/RW drive with an IDE interface, the decision on internal versus external has already been made for you. All IDE CD-ROM/RW drives are internal because the IDE interface does not allow for a cable long enough to connect an external drive. Another major advantage an internal drive has over an external drive is its lower cost.

An internal CD-ROM/RW drive is generally about $40 to $50 cheaper than an external drive because an external drive requires a case and a separate power supply. The only real consideration you have for installing an internal drive is whether your PC has physical room for it. If you are out of drive bays, you have no choice but to install an external drive. Internal CD-ROM/RW drives are all a "standard" size and occupy what is called a "full-sized" drive bay slot (see Figure 42.4).

42

FIGURE 42.4

An internal CD-ROM drive in a drive bay slot.

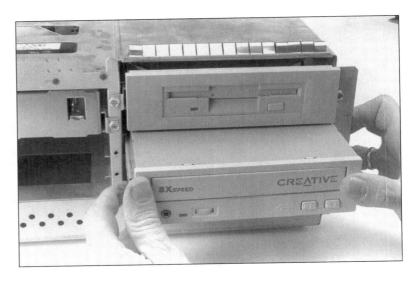

Installing an internal CD-RW drive is no more difficult than installing a hard disk drive.

> When handling any delicate electrical components inside your PC, make sure that you properly ground yourself to protect against static electricity and also make sure that you unplug your PC before working on it.

To install an internal drive, follow these steps:

1. Select a drive bay in your PC that you can use to install the drive. Make sure that you also remove the front panel on the case covering the empty bay. Make sure that you have an unused power connector you can plug in to the drive. If you don't have an unused power connector, go to your local computer store and pick up a Y-connector. Unplug one of your power connectors from another device and attach the Y-connector.

2. On most PCs built in the last three or four years, you find two IDE interfaces, usually labeled "primary" and "secondary" (see Figure 42.5). Your hard disk drive (if you have an IDE hard disk installed in your PC) should be attached by a cable to the interface labeled "primary." Make sure that you have a cable that will reach from the secondary interface to the bay where you are installing your new drive.

3. If you have to install any guide rails on the sides of your drive, install them according to the instructions accompanying the drive (see Figure 42.6). If drive rails are not included, but needed, be sure to pick up a set from your local computer store.

FIGURE 42.5
Primary and secondary IDE interfaces on the motherboard.

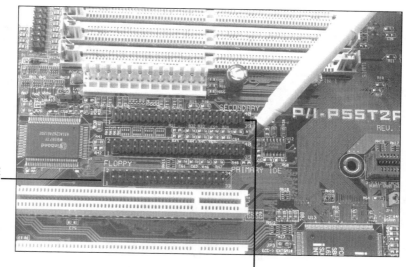

Primary IDE
interface

Secondary IDE
interface

FIGURE 42.6
Guide rails of various sizes used for installing CD-RW drives and other peripheral devices.

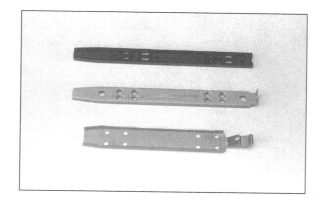

4. Insert the drive into the drive bay and attach the ribbon cable from the secondary (slave) IDE interface to the 40-pin IDE interface on the rear of the drive (see Figure 42.7).

Even though IDE interfaces can accommodate two IDE devices, do not connect the CD-RW drive to the same interface you connect your IDE hard disk drive to. The CD-RW drive, which is a much slower device than a hard disk drive, will degrade the performance of the hard disk drive if they're on the same interface.

42

If your PC has only one IDE interface connector, don't panic. Instead, just make a quick trip to your local computer store and purchase an IDE interface card. Such a card usually runs in the vicinity of $25 to $30. Don't worry about it conflicting with any of your existing IRQs or memory addresses. Most manufacturers realize that the IDE interface card is added as a secondary interface and usually assign it IRQs and addresses that are the same as a secondary interface. Just remember, when in doubt, ask the salesperson or the store's in-house technical guru.

FIGURE 42.7

The rear of a typical IDE CD-RW drive showing interface, power, and sound connections.

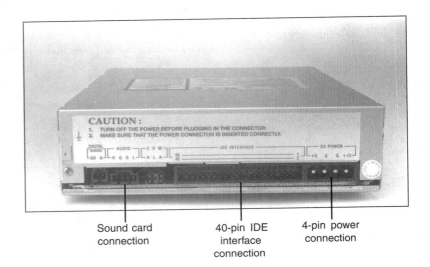

Sound card connection

40-pin IDE interface connection

4-pin power connection

5. If you also have a sound card in your PC, you can connect the audio cable to the audio connector on the rear of the CD-RW drive. Without the audio cable, you will not be able to play audio CDs through your sound system.

6. After everything is connected to your drive, adjust the drive so that it is even with the front opening of the drive bay. Tighten the screws to secure your drive in place.

7. Just as you did when you installed your hard disk drive, you will probably have to run your computer's hardware Setup program to complete the hardware installation. Also, you should have some type of software installation disk that you will need to run to install the appropriate driver, depending on the operating system you are running. If you are running Windows XP, when you restart your PC, Windows should automatically detect your newly installed CD-RW drive and install the proper driver (a feature known as *Plug and Play*).

In addition to a hardware driver for your drive, the disk that comes with your CD-RW drive also includes a number of utilities for your drive. One of the most enjoyable utilities is one that enables you to play music CDs on your new CD-RW drive. If you don't have a sound card in your PC, you can simply plug a set of headphones into the connector on the front of the drive next to the volume control.

Installing an Internal SCSI Drive

Installing an internal SCSI CD-ROM/RW drive is almost exactly the same as installing an internal IDE drive. The cable is a bit different, and just like with installing a SCSI hard disk drive, you have to set the SCSI ID on the CD-ROM/RW drive according to the instructions that came with your drive. Remember, too, that the SCSI ID number (0–6) you assign to the drive has to be unique.

All SCSI devices, such as hard disk drives and CD-RW drives, leave the factory with a preset SCSI ID, which in most cases you can leave as is. Just be sure to check that the ID set on the device isn't an ID you are already using on your SCSI chain. Two devices on a SCSI chain with the same ID will not operate.

Remember to check the termination on your SCSI chain. Some SCSI CD-ROM/RW drives come with a factory-installed terminator. If your CD-ROM/RW drive is not placed at the end of your SCSI chain, you have to remove the factory-installed terminator, or the devices on the chain after the CD-ROM/RW drive will not operate. Check your CD-ROM/RW documentation on how to remove the terminator. In many cases, you simply have to remove a jumper.

Installing an External Drive

Installing an external CD-ROM/RW drive is even easier than installing an internal drive. External CD-ROM drives used to be available only as SCSI drives, but now you can also find a few manufacturers producing external drives using either USB or Firewire interfaces. Regardless of which type you select, the manufacturer will almost always ship the drive with the appropriate cable needed to connect your drive to your interface.

42

If you are trying to decide between SCSI, USB, and Firewire, consider this:
SCSI will be the fastest but most expensive; Firewire should rank second in
both speed and cost, and USB will be the slowest and least expensive.

Many external SCSI CD-ROM/RW drives also ship with a SCSI interface card,
which saves you the trouble and expense of having to purchase a SCSI card
separately. If you find that you do have to purchase a SCSI interface card,
check with the manufacturer of the drive to see whether any types of SCSI
cards are recommended or whether any types of SCSI cards may not work
with your CD-ROM/RW drive.

After you have the drive, cable, and interface card, literally all you have to do is plug
them together. Insert the card into an empty slot (most likely SCSI, but also USB or
Firewire if your PC doesn't already have one) in your PC (see Figure 42.8). Next, connect one end of the cable to the connector on the end of the card (the connector protrud-
ing out of the back of your PC) and the other end of the cable to the connector on the
drive (see Figure 42.9).

FIGURE 42.8
*Inserting the SCSI
interface card into an
empty slot in your PC.*

With some SCSI CD-ROM/RW drives, you receive a SCSI terminator. The terminator
looks like the plug on the end of the SCSI cable without the cable attached (see

Figure 42.10). If you are installing a USB or Firewire drive, don't worry that you can't find a terminator—there isn't one.

There are two SCSI connectors on the back of your SCSI CD-ROM/RW drive. If you have to use the terminator to terminate your SCSI chain, plug the terminator into one connector and plug the SCSI cable into the other connector.

FIGURE 42.9

Plugging the SCSI cable into the interface card and into the CD-RW drive.

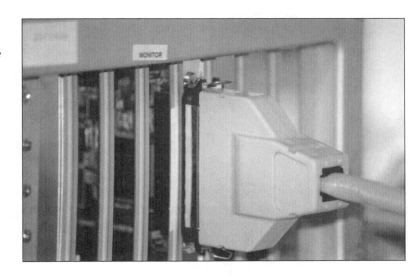

FIGURE 42.10

A typical SCSI terminator.

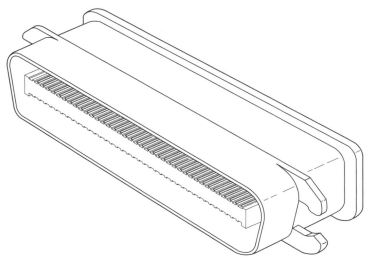

42

Remember that only the device at the end of the SCSI chain should be terminated. If the CD-ROM/RW drive is not at the end of the SCSI chain, you do
not have to terminate the chain at the CD-ROM/RW drive.

Don't panic if one or both of the SCSI connectors on the back of your
CD-ROM/RW drive looks different than the typical 50-pin Centronics connector
commonly found on many SCSI devices. Four types of SCSI connectors are
used on SCSI devices: the 50-pin Centronics connector, the 25-pin
D-connector, the 50-pin mini-SCSI connector, and the 63-pin SCSI connector.

Now, just plug in the electrical cord supplying power to the external drive, run the Setup
program for your PC, install the driver for the CD-ROM/RW drive from the disk
included with your drive, and you're done.

Your newly installed CD-ROM/RW drive should be detected when you restart your PC,
and Windows will attempt to automatically install the appropriate driver. Make sure that
you have your Windows disks handy.

What About DVD?

Undoubtedly, you've heard or read a lot of the recent press that DVD has been receiving
and may be wondering whether you want to upgrade to a DVD drive instead of a
CD-RW drive. If you do, consider the following:

- DVD drives (at least the second-generation DVD-2 drives) are compatible with
  commercial CD-ROM discs and CD-R (CD-Recordable) and CD-RW
  (CD-Writable) discs. The first generation of DVD drives did not read CD-R and
  CD-W discs. Make sure that you read the fine print and get a second-generation
  DVD-2 drive or upgrade kit.

- DVD drives are going through many of the same growing pains that early
  CD-ROM drives went through—namely, speed and cost. DVD drives read
  CD-ROM discs at 12x speeds.

- Upgrade kits for DVD drives can be a bit confusing and problematic for some
  users to install, especially because the upgrade kits include a "decoder" interface
  card that must be compatible with your existing video card. It is also possible to
  encounter IRQ conflicts when installing this new card in your PC.

- DVD upgrade kits are currently running in the neighborhood of $200 to $300. But just like the initial price of CD-ROM drives, DVD prices are expected to drop as they become more plentiful.

- Recordable DVD drives currently are available in three competing and incompatible formats, DVD-RAM, DVD-R, DVD+R, and DVD-RW. It is definitely worth waiting until this market has a shakeout and one format quashes the other (remember the competing Beta and VHS video formats?). Popular opinion is that DVD-R and DVD+R both will produce DVDs playable on the standard that eventually becomes set so either is probably safe to buy.

On the plus side, however, reports say that nothing currently on the market can match the quality of audio and video delivered by DVD. DVD was originally designed as a new distribution medium for home movies to compete with (or replace) analog VHS. The main requirement for the original DVD specification was the capability to store a typical two-hour movie on a single side of the discs. DVD discs currently store about 4.7GB of data (compared to only 650MB for CD-ROM discs) and include multiple audio tracks or vastly improved digital audio.

Many DVD upgrade kits include adapters for connecting the output from your PC to your TV to enable you to watch DVD movies either on your PC monitor or on your living room TV. Acceptance among the major Hollywood studios has been exceptionally good. Software manufacturers have not responded quite as fast. There are barely more than a handful of software titles, but vendors are still promising that titles will be forthcoming.

What Is a DVD?

DVDs look a lot like CDs, but there is a world of difference between the two media. Both are 120mm in diameter, but whereas CDs store a maximum of about 650MB of data, DVDs currently top out at around 4.75GB of data—about seven and a half times larger.

DVD originally stood for Digital Video Disc because the intended use for DVDs was as a new storage medium for full-length movies. But as the new storage medium began seeing usage as a repository for software and other mega-storage items, the name was officially switched to Digital Versatile Disc. Almost no one calls them by their official name, so just refer to them as DVDs.

Like CDs, DVDs store data as a series of pits etched on a reflective substrate layer of plastic, which is read by a laser. DVDs achieve their gargantuan storage capabilities by reducing the size of the data pit from 0.83 microns to 0.40 microns (a micron is 1,000[th]

42

of a millimeter) and by placing the ridges of the one concentric groove closer together—from 1.6 microns to just 0.74 microns. With a smaller target, you also need a tighter laser beam. Whereas the laser in CD-ROM drives uses a 780-nanometer wavelength, the laser beam in DVD drives uses only a 640-nanometer wavelength.

Enough with the rocket science. Just think of it as smaller data bits packed a lot closer together.

What You Will Find in a Standard DVD Upgrade Kit

When you purchase a CD-ROM drive, you get a drive and maybe a ribbon cable to attach the drive to your IDE or SCSI port. In a DVD upgrade kit, you will find a little bit more than just the DVD drive and a ribbon cable. In addition to the DVD drive, you will (should) also find what's called an *MPEG-2* decoder card.

MPEG-2 is an international graphics standard established by the Motion Picture Entertainment Group (MPEG) for audio and video compression and playback.

The decoder card (see Figure 42.11) is attached to your existing video card to allow DVD playback through your PC's video system.

FIGURE 42.11

A typical DVD decoder card that you will find in most DVD upgrade kits.

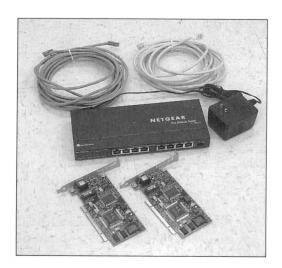

When you purchase a DVD kit, make sure that you choose one that includes an MPEG-2 decoder (hardware) card and not one that uses software for MPEG-2 playback. The hardware option is far superior to software emulations. Also, make sure that your decoder card supports resolutions at least up to 1,280×1,024.

For an internal drive you should also find an IDE ribbon cable in your upgrade kit. Most internal DVD drives for PCs are IDE (or more precisely, EIDE—Enhanced IDE). Most of the SCSI DVD drives you find are DVD-RAM drives.

> *DVD-RAM* drives are one of two competing writable DVD drive formats and most are SCSI instead of IDE (or EIDE).

You will also find a video cable for connecting your decoder card to your existing video card, and a cable to connect to your sound card.

Installing a DVD Drive in Your PC

Installing a DVD upgrade kit is no more difficult than installing a CD-ROM drive. Basically, what you will be doing is installing another device about the same size as a CD-ROM drive and another card similar to your video card.

> Make sure that you have unplugged your PC power supply and grounded yourself to prevent static electric discharges.

To install your DVD upgrade kit, follow these steps:

1. Make sure that you have an empty 5 1/4-inch drive bay in your PC and an empty slot on your motherboard. Also make sure that you have removed the front panel on the case covering the empty bay. Make sure that you have an unused power connector you can plug in to the drive. If you don't have an unused power connector, go to your local computer store and pick up a Y-connector. Unplug one of your power connectors from another device and attach the Y-connector. Make sure that the empty slot matches the type of decoder card in your kit (ISA versus PCI).

2. You should find two IDE interfaces, usually labeled "primary" and "secondary," on your motherboard. Your hard disk drive (if you have an IDE hard disk installed in your PC) should be attached with a cable to the interface labeled "primary." Make sure that you have a cable that will reach from the secondary interface to the bay where you are installing your new DVD drive. If you already have a CD-ROM

42

drive attached to the secondary IDE port, you can attach the DVD drive to this same cable. Just make sure that the cable will reach the connectors on both the CD-ROM and DVD drives. The best way to ensure an easy fit is to install one drive (CD-ROM or DVD) on top of the other in your drive bays (see Figure 42.12).

If you decide to install your DVD drive in a PC that already has a CD-ROM drive, make sure that you designate one of the devices the "master" and the other device the "slave." Your documentation will illustrate how you need to set the jumpers to make these configuration settings. You make the master/slave distinction only if you are placing two IDE devices on the same IDE port. If each device is connected to its own IDE port, you should be able to connect the device using the default setting configured by the manufacturer.

3. If you have to install any guide rails on the sides of your drive, install them according to the instructions accompanying the drive. If drive rails are not included, but needed, be sure to pick up a set from your local computer store.

FIGURE 42.12
A DVD drive and a CD-ROM drive installed together.

4. Insert the drive into the drive bay (see Figure 42.13) and attach the ribbon cable from the secondary IDE interface to the 40-pin IDE interface on the rear of the DVD drive (see Figure 42.14).

FIGURE 42.13

*Insert your DVD drive
into an empty drive
bay.*

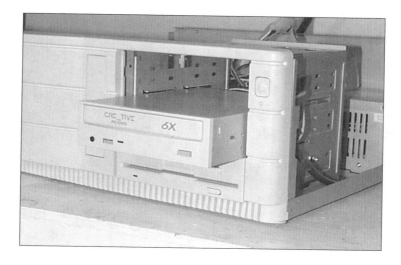

5. Connect the audio cable to the audio connector on the rear of the DVD drive and connect the other end of the cable to your sound card, following the instructions that accompanied your upgrade kit. Without the audio cable, you will not be able to hear audio when you watch DVD movies.

FIGURE 42.14

*Attach the IDE ribbon
cable to the DVD
drive.*

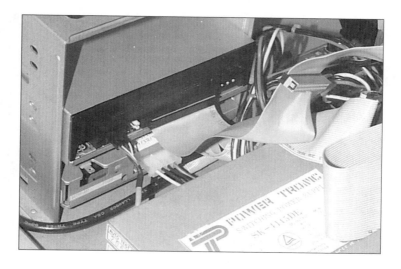

6. Attach the power cable to the power connector on the back of your DVD drive.

7. Insert the decoder card into the appropriate type of slot (ISA or PCI) on your motherboard (see Figure 42.15). Remove the cable connecting your monitor to your video card. Connect the video loopback cable in your upgrade kit from the decoder

42

card to your video card as shown in the instructions included in your upgrade kit (see Figure 42.16). Then connect the cable from your monitor to the video connector on your decoder card. You also must connect an audio cable (supplied with your kit) from your existing audio card to the decoder card if you want to hear audio from your DVD games and movies.

8. After you have everything connected to your DVD drive, adjust the drive even with the front opening of the drive bay and tighten the screws, securing your drive in place.

9. You should have some type of software installation disk or CD/DVD that you have to run to install the appropriate drivers, depending on the operating system you are running. When you restart your PC, Windows should automatically detect your newly installed DVD drive and install the proper drivers (a feature known as *Plug and Play*).

10. Replace your PC's cover. Plug in the PC and turn it on. If your kit comes with sample DVDs, pop one in and see how it looks. If your kit doesn't include one or more sample DVDs, it's time to make a trip to your local video rental store.

FIGURE 42.15

Insert the decoder card into an empty slot on your motherboard.

FIGURE 42.16
Connect the video loopback cable from the decoder card to your existing video card.

DVD Recordable/Rewritable Drives

So far, we've talked only about DVD drives that operate on a read-only format. But DVD drives are also available in recordable and rewritable formats. Do a little research on the Internet and you will discover that there are three competing formats that allow you to record your own DVDs: DVD-RAM, DVD-R, and DVD-RW. Table 42.1 shows the differences between these three formats.

TABLE 42.1   Comparison of DVD Formats

Format	Description	Capacity/Side	Possible Rewrites
DVD-RAM	Random access storage	2.6GB/side	100,000 to floppy disk or CD-RW.
DVD-R	Write-once	3.95GB/side	Provides 0 sequential write, similar to CD-R. No overwrite capability.
DVD+R	Write-once	3.95GB/side	Provides 0 sequential write, similar to CD-R. No overwrite capability. Slightly less compatible than DVD-R but the blank media is less expensive.
DVD-RW	Limited sequential	3.95GB/side	1,000 rewritability.

Needless to say, the four competing formats are not always compatible. For now, most experts believe that the DVD-R and DVD+R formats have the edge because of price and functionality, but you will note that these formats also offer the smallest storage capacity. For now, it is best to wait a little longer and let one of the three formats rise as the dominant format, much the same way that VHS beat out Beta in the VCR wars many years ago.

42

Summary

In this chapter, you learned about CD-ROM/CD-RW drives and how to select a drive as either an upgrade or a new component in your PC. You also learned about the differences between IDE and SCSI CD-ROM/RW drives and how to install each type. You learned about DVD drives as well and some of the information to help you decide whether you want to upgrade to a DVD drive.

You also learned about DVD drives, what features are important to look for when selecting a new DVD upgrade kit, and how to install the upgrade kit in your PC. You also learned the current status of recordable/rewritable DVD formats.

CHAPTER **43**

Adding Removable Media

Another category of devices that remain popular with PC users is read/write removable media drives. Excluding CD-RW, optical disk drives, and floppy disk drives, there are basically two types of mainstream removable media drives: tape backup drives and removable disk drives (removable disk drives that mimic floppy or hard disk drives).

Even though we are including tape drives in this category, when we mention removable media drives, most users think of the types of drives that mimic the functionality of floppy or hard disk drives and give users a source of cheap (or cheaper), unlimited file storage and backup.

Removable Hard Disk Drives

Removable hard disk drives have become extremely popular in the past several years. The price of these drives has dropped, and some models duplicate the performance of standard hard disk drives while giving the user the potential for unlimited disk storage and the ability to quickly back up data.

The biggest players in the removable hard disk market are Iomega, SyQuest, and Maxtor.

The Iomega Zip Drive

Maxtor (http://www.maxtor.com/) Iomega (http://www.iomega.com/) and SyQuest (http://www.syquest.com/) make the most popular removable hard disk drives. All three companies produce low-end and high-end models. Iomega produces the most popular low-end model—the *Zip* drive (see Figure 43.1).

These companies make several USB-2 and Firewire removable drives so they are often as simple to connect as plugging the drive into your computer. The rest of this chapter concentrates on other kinds of connections that you might face.

Zip drive cartridges are capable of storing 100 to +250MB of data, and the drives are available in both internal and external models. The external models use either a SCSI, USB, or parallel port interface. The internal models use either a SCSI or IDE interface. Zip drives are typically installed as a backup device because their performance (that is, their speed and capacity) is not quite up to par with standard hard disk drives, especially the models using an IDE or parallel port interface, which are somewhat slower than the SCSI models.

FIGURE 43.1
An external model of the Iomega USB Zip 250 drive.

You install the SCSI models using the same procedures as you would to install a SCSI CD-ROM drive. The IDE model Zip drive installs the same as an IDE model CD-ROM/CD-RW drive. To install a Zip drive with a parallel port interface (available only as an external model), you merely plug the drive into your parallel port and install the software.

Some computer manufacturers have started offering Zip drives as a replacement for a standard floppy disk drive. Although some users find this arrangement satisfactory, many experts think this option is still a bit premature because Zip drives still have not achieved universal status and they do not read or write existing 1.44MB 3 1/2-inch disks.

The SyQuest SyJet 1.5 Gigabyte Drive

The SyJet (see Figure 43.2) is one of SyQuest's high-end drives. It comes in SCSI (external), IDE (internal), and parallel port (external) versions.

FIGURE 43.2

The SyQuest SyJet removable media drive.

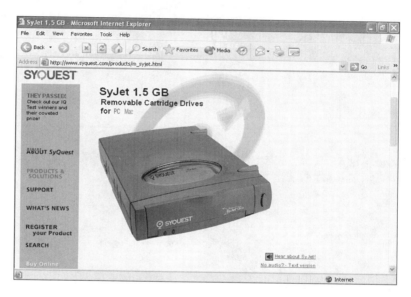

The SyQuest SparQ 1 Gigabyte Drive

The SparQ (see Figure 43.3) is SyQuest's middle-level drive. SyQuest manufactures the SparQ in only IDE and parallel port versions.

The SyQuest EZFlyer Drive

A third model in the SyQuest lineup of removable media drives is the EZFlyer (see Figure 43.4). The EZFlyer is SyQuest's low-end model targeted against the Iomega Zip drive. The EZFlyer comes in four different configurations:

- SCSI (internal and external)
- IDE (internal)
- parallel port (external)

FIGURE **43.3**
The SyQuest SparQ removable media drive.

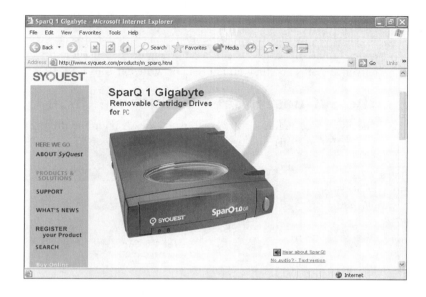

FIGURE **43.4**
The SyQuest EZFlyer removable media drive.

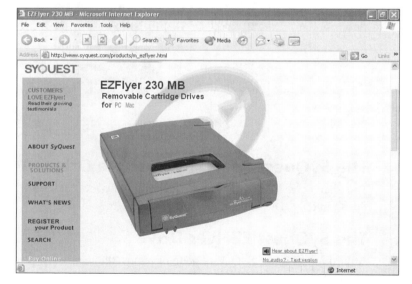

Other Removable Disk Options

Don't think for one second that if you want to add a removable disk to your PC that Iomega, Maxtor, and SyQuest are the only games in town. They aren't, even though they do command the lion's share of the removable disk market.

Other companies attempting to carve out their piece of this niche market include Sony, Castlewood Systems, and several manufacturers of the LS-120 drive.

Sony HiFD

Sony released a removable media drive positioned as a replacement for your 1.44MB floppy disk drive. Sony calls its 200MB drive HiFD (see Figure 43.5).

FIGURE 43.5

Sony's HiFD removable disk drive—a 200MB replacement for your floppy disk drive.

Sony is attempting to carve out a portion of the low-end removable disk market with its HiFD drive (http://www.ita.sel.sony.com/jump/hifd/index.html). In addition to providing 200MB of storage on each disk, the HiFD drives are also capable of reading and writing to standard 3 1/2-inch, 1.44MB floppy disk drives. So far, Sony has not made much of a dent in the Zip drive market because many analysts think the HiFD drive is overpriced despite its impressive performance.

Castlewood Systems

Castlewood Systems (http://www.castlewood.com/) produces the ORB, a 2.2GB removable disk drive (see Figure 43.6).

The LS-120 Drive

The LS-120 is another removable media drive you may have heard about. The LS-120 is made by several manufacturers and looks very similar to a standard 3 1/2-inch floppy disk drive. The LS-120, as the name implies, uses a disk with a capacity of 120MB in addition to being able to read and write to standard 3 1/2-inch 1.44MB floppy disks. The LS-120 is mostly sold as an internal model with an IDE interface but can also be purchased as an external model that connects to a parallel port.

The LS-120 is a good replacement option for the standard 3 1/2-inch drive, considering that it is bootable. Some PC manufacturers, such as Gateway and Compaq, also offer it as a replacement for the standard floppy drive.

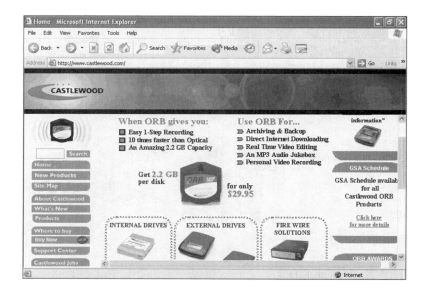

FIGURE 43.6

The Castlewood Systems' ORB removable disk drive.

Tape Backup Drives

Tape backup drives currently come in an assortment of sizes and capacities. At one time, tape backup drives were almost exclusively used to back up network file servers. Now tape backup drives are growing in popularity among individual computer users. Hard disk drives have grown in size to where it is inconceivable to think of backing them up using floppy disks; tape drives have been following the lead set by hard disk drives and are also dropping in price.

Choosing a tape backup drive is largely a matter of how much you want to spend. An expensive tape backup drive won't back up any better than a cheaper model, but an expensive drive will most likely back up your hard disk faster and use fewer tapes.

Tape drives come as both internal and external models and use both IDE and SCSI interfaces; a few tape drives are available with USB and Firewire interfaces, and some come with their own proprietary interface. There are even external tape drives that plug in to the parallel port on the back of your computer in the same way as Zip drives.

Here are some of the leading manufacturers of tape backup devices:

- OnStream—http://www.onstream.com
- Sony—http://www.ita.sel.sony.com/
- Compaq—http://www.compaq.com/
- Advance Digital Information Corp.—http://www.adic.com/

- Aiwa—http://www.aiwa.com/
- APS Technology—http://www.apstech.com/
- Artecon, Inc.—http://www.artecon.com/
- Exabyte, Inc.—http://www.exabyte.com/
- Hewlett-Packard—http://www.hp.com/
- IBM—http://www.ibm.com/
- MicroSolutions, Inc.—http://www.micro-solutions.com/

One of the best sources for finding up-to-date information on PC hardware components is the hardware section of CNET's Computers.com (http://computers.cnet.com/hardware/0-1016.html). In addition to listing just about every tape drive (and removable media drive) you could possibly think of, this site also does comparison reviews and allows you to compare prices on the products listed. Where applicable, this site also lists specifications on the products listed and points you to the manufacturer for more information.

If you're looking for more technical information, you should make a point to bookmark Tom's Hardware Guide (http://www.tomshardware.com/).

External Tape Backup Drives

The parallel port and USB-type drives are probably the easiest types of tape drives to install because all you do is plug the drive in to your parallel port and install the tape backup software. You don't have to worry about connecting cables, running your PC's Setup program, or even taking the cover off your PC. The drawback to these types of tape drives is speed —they are among the slowest tape drives on the market. Most users get around this limitation by performing their backups overnight or by dividing their backup procedure into sections that fit onto one tape.

Other external tape drives use a SCSI interface and install pretty much the same way as an external CD-ROM drive. All you need to do is set the tape drive to use an available SCSI ID number and insert it into your SCSI chain. If you place the drive at the end of the chain, remember to move your terminator.

Internal Tape Backup Drives

Internal tape drives use IDE, SCSI, and proprietary interfaces. Internal drives are installed pretty much the same as internal CD-ROM drives. You must take into account the same considerations, such as an available drive bay, the reach of the interface cable, and so on (see Figure 43.7).

Tape drive data cable

FIGURE 43.7

An internal tape backup drive being inserted into an empty drive bay.

Tape drive power cable

SCSI tape drives are typically faster and more expensive than IDE drives, so take this into consideration when deciding what type to purchase. Remember, too, that with a SCSI drive you need a SCSI interface card, if you don't already have one (see Figure 43.8).

FIGURE 43.8

A SCSI interface card.

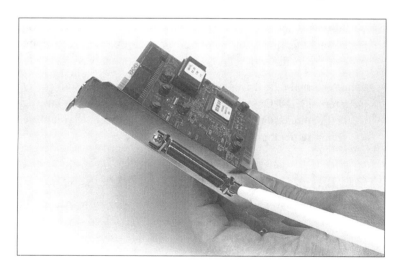

When deciding on what type of tape drive to get, pay attention to the storage capacity of the tapes each drive uses (see Figure 43.9).

FIGURE 43.9

A typical tape backup cartridge.

Although the general rule of thumb used to be that you should be able to back up each hard disk drive in your PC with one tape, the size of many of today's mammoth multi-gigabyte drives makes this rule a bit unreasonable. Fortunately, all tape backup software enables you to span a backup session across multiple tapes.

Be sure to pay attention to the cost of tape cartridges. Tape cartridge prices vary considerably from manufacturer to manufacturer, and capacity is not always an indicator of cost. Also purchase a tape head cleaner for your tape drive (and be sure to use it as recommended) to make sure that your tape backup unit is always performing in peak condition.

Installing a Removable Media Drive

Removable media drives come in two basic designs—internal models and external models. Internal models connect to either an IDE or SCSI interface inside your PC.

Installing an internal IDE removable media drive is no more difficult than installing an IDE hard disk drive.

When handling any delicate electrical components inside your PC, make sure that you have properly grounded yourself to protect against static electricity.

To install an internal IDE drive, follow these steps:

1. Select a drive bay in your PC that you can use to install the drive. Remove the front panel on the case covering the empty bay if there is one. Make sure that you have an unused power connector you can use to plug in to the drive. If you don't have an unused power connector, go to your local computer store and pick up a Y-connector. Unplug one of your power connectors from another device and attach the Y-connector.

2. On most PCs built in the last four or five years, you find two IDE interfaces, usually labeled primary and secondary (see Figure 43.10). Your hard disk drive (if you have an IDE hard disk installed in your PC) should be attached with a cable to the interface labeled primary. Make sure that you have a cable that will reach from the secondary interface to the bay in which you are installing your new drive.

3. If you have to install any guide rails on the sides of your drive, install them according to the instructions accompanying the drive (see Figure 43.11). If drive rails are not included with your device, but are needed, be sure to pick up a set from your local computer store.

FIGURE 43.10

Primary and secondary IDE interfaces on the motherboard.

Secondary IDE Interface

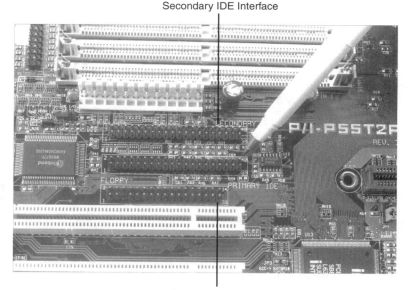

Primary IDE Interface

4. Insert the drive into the drive bay and attach the ribbon cable from the secondary (slave) IDE interface to the 40-pin IDE interface on the rear of the drive.

FIGURE 43.11

Guide rails of various sizes used for installing removable media drives and other peripheral devices.

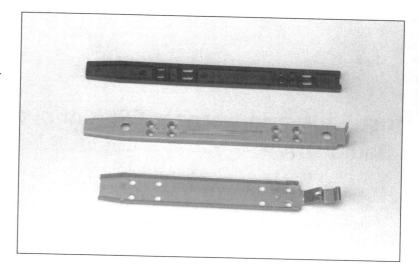

43

Even though IDE interfaces can accommodate two IDE devices, if you can avoid it, do not connect the removable media drive to the same interface you connect your IDE hard disk drive to. The removable media drive, which is a much slower device than a hard disk drive, will degrade the performance of the hard disk drive.

If your PC has only one IDE interface connector, don't panic. Instead, just make a quick trip to your local computer store and purchase an IDE interface card. It usually runs in the vicinity of $25 to $30. Don't worry about it conflicting with any of your existing IRQs or memory addresses. Most manufacturers realize that it is added as a secondary interface and usually assign it IRQs and addresses that would be the same as a secondary interface. Just remember, when in doubt, ask the salesperson or the store's in-house technical guru.

5. After you have everything connected to your drive, go ahead and adjust your drive so that it's even with the front opening of the drive bay. Tighten the screws to secure your drive in place.

6. You will probably have to run some type of software installation disk to install the appropriate driver, depending on the operating system you are running. When you restart your PC, Windows should automatically detect your newly installed removable media drive and install the proper driver (a feature known as Plug and Play).

In addition to a hardware driver for your drive, the disk that comes with your removable media drive also includes a number of utilities for your drive. These utilities will vary from manufacturer to manufacturer.

Installing an Internal SCSI Removable Media Drive

Installing an internal SCSI removable media drive is almost exactly the same as installing an internal IDE drive. The cable is a bit different, and just as you do when installing a SCSI hard disk drive, you must set the SCSI ID on the removable media drive according to the instructions that came with your drive. Remember, too, that the SCSI ID of the drive (0–6) has to be unique.

All SCSI devices, such as hard disk drives and removable media drives, leave the factory with a preset SCSI ID, which in most cases you can leave as is. Just be sure to check that the ID set on the device isn't an ID you are already using on your SCSI chain. Two devices on a SCSI chain with the same ID will not operate.

Remember to check the termination on your SCSI chain. Some SCSI removable media drives come with a factory-installed terminator. If your removable media drive is not placed at the end of your SCSI chain, you'll have to remove the factory-installed terminator or the devices on the chain after the removable media drive will not operate. Check your removable media drive documentation on how to remove the terminator. In many cases, you simply have to remove a jumper.

Installing an External Removable Media Drive

External removable media drives offer you a few more choices depending on what configuration each manufacturer decides to offer. External models can attach to a SCSI, parallel, USB, Firewire, or USB port on your PC.

To install your external removable media drive, simply plug it in to the appropriate connection port on your PC and then run the accompanying software to install the appropriate hardware driver. Remember, if you are installing a SCSI external removable media

43

drive, be sure to check the SCSI ID to make sure that it is not already being used by another device on your SCSI chain. If your drive is at the end of your SCSI chain, make sure that it is properly terminated. In most cases, the drive comes with a terminator, and your documentation will explain how to activate the terminator.

Tips for Getting the Most Out of Your Backup Drive

Whether you use a tape drive or a removable media drive as your backup unit, here are a few tips for getting the most out of your backup system:

- (Extremely Important) After you install your backup system, be sure to test it. Make sure that you fully understand how to back up the files on your hard disk drives. Be sure to test the restore procedure as well as the backup procedure. Try restoring a few files to a temporary directory.

- If you use a backup tape drive, make sure that you purchase top-quality tapes. Remember, the tapes you buy are your only insurance against disaster. Just as you wouldn't want to trust a cheap, cut-rate parachute, don't trust cheap, cut-rate backup tapes.

- Don't overuse your tapes. Tapes are a much more fragile medium than are hard disk drives. Tapes do wear out with extensive use. Extra tapes are a lot cheaper than the time it takes to replace unrecoverable data. Ten times is probably the maximum number of times you should use a tape.

- Create a backup schedule and stick to it. This way, you know which backup tape contains the data you are looking for.

- Tape backup drives require regular maintenance. Be sure to read the documentation and perform whatever routine maintenance the manufacturer prescribes, including regularly cleaning the read/write heads of your tape drive.

Summary

In this chapter, you learned about many of the options available to you if you decide to add a removable media drive to your PC. You learned about both high-end and low-end drives and about the selection of interfaces each model uses.

PART XIII

Upgrading Your Communications and Peripherals

Chapter

CHAPTER 44

Upgrading Your Modem

Modems are items formerly considered an extravagance but that have long since been seen as standard equipment. Originally brought to prominence by online services such as CompuServe and AOL, the modem became indispensable with the rise in popularity of the Internet.

With the development of 56K modems, this technology seems to have reached its technological limit over standard telephone lines. If you're considering upgrading your modem, this chapter should prove valuable to you in deciding whether to get a 56K modem or one of the other newer communications technologies.

Instead of puttering along the Internet at 40 to 50Kbps with your old analog modem, you can be warping through cyberspace at somewhere between 640 to 10,000Kbps! Pages that once took 10 to 20 seconds to load now appear almost instantly. Files that once took more than an hour to download now download in a few minutes. But quickly downloading pages and files is not the only reason to upgrade to a cable or DSL modem. The high speeds available with cable and DSL modems also make high-bandwidth Web site animation viewable and enjoyable and make it feasible to enjoy the higher resolutions required for streaming video and audio.

Understanding Modems

Modem is short for *MOdulate/DEModulate*, which is what a modem does to send and receive data from one computer to another. Your computer stores data in digital form. But standard telephone lines transmit information as sound, which is an analog signal. The modem in your computer system converts the digital information in your computer to an analog (sound) signal and transmits the analog signal over telephone lines to another computer. The modem there converts the analog signal that your computer transmitted back into a digital form (see Figure 44.1).

FIGURE 44.1

How modems modulate and then demodulate signals between PCs.

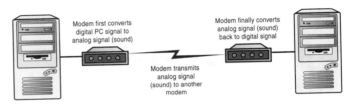

Modem first converts digital PC signal to analog signal (sound)

Modem finally converts analog signal (sound) back to digital signal

Modem transmits analog signal (sound) to another modem

Analog and *digital* are terms used quite freely and they have taken on several popular meanings. In the context of computer communications, analog refers to communicating by means of converting the signal in your computer to a measurable frequency and modulation, which happens to be sound waves. Digital refers to communicating by means of transmitting your message using a representation of the binary symbols 0 and 1 just as they are created in your PC.

Most standard modems today transmit data in the range of 28,800 to 56,000bps (bits per second). Don't be surprised (or disappointed) if you purchase a modem advertised to operate in this range but only get a maximum transmission speed of between 26,400bps and 50,000bps. Modem transmissions at higher speeds are largely governed by the quality of your telephone lines. Telephone lines for the most part are simply unshielded, twisted copper wire and are extremely vulnerable to interference from a variety of sources. Interference reduces the audio quality of the call you are making to your mother (whether you notice it or not), and reduces the transmission speed of your modem as well.

Selecting a Modem

Modems are available in both internal and external models. An internal modem is installed inside your PC (see Figure 44.2) and requires a slot on your motherboard. An external modem (see Figure 44.3) plugs in to one of your serial ports (using a serial cable).

Figure 44.2

An internal modem.

44

Figure 44.3

An external modem.

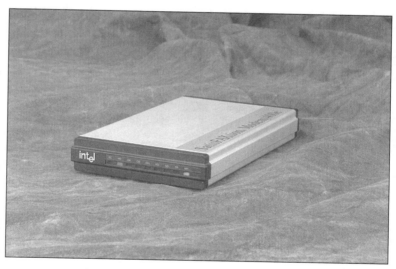

Functionally, you do not see any differences between an internal and an external modem; both operate exactly the same. When deciding which type to purchase, consider that an internal modem generally costs less than an external modem because it lacks a case and a power supply, but it takes up a slot in your PC. Both internal and external modems require an interrupt (IRQ) signal from your PC (the internal modem requires its own interrupt, whereas the external modem uses the interrupt signal assigned to the serial port the modem is connected to).

When you're in the market for a new modem, one of the best sources for finding up-to-date information on PC hardware components is the hardware section of CNET's computers.com (http://computers.cnet.com/hardware/0-1016.html). In addition to listing just about every modem you could possibly think of, this site also does comparison reviews and allows you to compare prices on the products listed. Where applicable, this site also lists specifications on the products listed and points you to the manufacturer for more information. If you're looking for more technical information, you should also make a point of bookmarking Tom's Hardware Guide (http://www.tomshardware.com/).

Installing Your Modem

The only difference between installing an internal modem and installing an external modem is what you do with the hardware. The software you install with your modem—the modem hardware driver and the communications software you plan to use with your modem—is exactly the same.

Installing an Internal Modem

Installing an internal modem is fairly simple because all you have to do is insert the modem into one of your available motherboard slots and then configure your PC or operating system to recognize the modem.

To install an internal modem, do the following:

1. Read the documentation that accompanies your modem thoroughly before you begin to install the modem. Check the documentation for your modem to determine whether there is a certain communications port (COM1, COM2, and so on) that your modem prefers to use. Check also to see whether there are any switches or jumpers you must set for the communications port you will be using. If you have jumpers on your modem, they are used to set your modem to use one of your two main serial ports, COM1 or COM2. Most modems are Plug and Play and if yours is also, you can skip this step. If you have to set your modem by setting a jumper, make sure that you are not setting your modem to use a serial port that is being used by another device, such as a serial mouse. This will create a device conflict and neither device will function properly. You can check for interrupt conflicts using the Windows XP System Information utility.

 Serial ports are used primarily for communicating with non-USB modems (and other serial devices) and are often referred to as COM (short for communications) ports. Your computer is designed to operate with two main serial ports, COM1 and COM2, but can be configured to have more COM ports.

2. Turn off your PC, unplug the cord from the wall or power supply, ground yourself to prevent static electricity discharges, remove the cover, and insert your modem into an empty slot (see Figure 44.4).

FIGURE 44.4

Inserting an internal modem in your PC.

44

3. Follow the instructions for installing any additional software that came with your modem. Make sure that you follow the instructions specifically for the operating system you are running.

4. Make a note of which communications port you use in installing your modem.

Installing an External Modem

External modems are even easier to install than internal modems. To install an external modem, follow these steps:

1. Turn off your PC.

2. Plug one end of your serial cable into an unused serial or USB port on the back of your PC; plug the other end into the serial or USB connector on your modem.

3. Turn on your modem and then turn on your PC.

4. Follow the instructions for installing any additional software driver that came with your modem for the operating system you are running.

5. Make a note of the communications port used by your modem when you install the modem driver.

Alternatives to Standard Modems

One of the problems mentioned earlier with modems is that they transmit an analog signal (sound) over standard phone lines and are subject to interference, which results in a degradation of signal and transmission speed. Alternatives to modems and analog signals do exist. For example, you can get fully digital communications lines, which are not subject to the same interference and signal degradation as analog modems. If you decide you want to investigate digital communications lines, start by checking with your local Baby Bell or your cable TV provider to see whether they are providing digital or broadband service.

ISDN

A technology that has been around for a lot longer than 56KB modems, but continues to receive far less press coverage, is *ISDN*.

ISDN stands for *Integrated Services Digital Network* and is a way of getting reliable communications speeds above 33.6KB using digital telephone lines, instead of the analog lines used for typical phone communication and standard modems. For connecting to the Internet at speeds of either 64KB or 128KB in both directions with the host computer, ISDN is almost universally available in the United States.

On the plus side, ISDN works over digital telephone lines instead of your standard analog, voice-grade lines, which means they are not susceptible to interference as are analog lines. Being digital means that, on an ISDN line, you will always get speeds of 64KB (or 128KB)—in both directions!

On the minus side, however, ISDN has a lot that has kept it from being widely embraced. For starters, you need to have a special ISDN communications line installed by your telephone company. The actual line is the same copper wire the phone company uses for standard telephone lines, but it is connected differently at your end and at the phone company's switching office. Prices for ISDN have been steadily coming down over the past few years, but prices still vary around the country and can be expensive for installation and monthly service. You can expect to pay in the range of $50 to $250 for installation of your line. Monthly charges also vary considerably. Some Baby Bells charge you a flat monthly rate; some offer you a tiered system of varying flat rate for a certain maximum number of hours; and some simply charge you by the minute for actual usage. ISDN is now almost exclusively available from the Baby Bells because most other ISPs that provide digital service are opting for DSL or cable modems; for this reason, ISDN has sort of fallen out of favor and may soon disappear except for some special or niche applications.

You also need a special ISDN interface—either an internal card or an external device—to access your ISDN line.

ISDN interface cards and devices have also been dropping in price and currently range between $100 and $300. If you have an empty slot in your case, it is best to get the internal interface card. The internal ISDN devices are cheaper because the external devices need a case or power supply. In addition, internal ISDN devices attain a slightly faster speed than do the external devices. The external ISDN device plugs into a serial port (the same way an external modem does), but standard serial ports can achieve speeds of only 115KB, which means that your ISDN device can achieve speeds of only 115KB rather than the advertised 128KB.

44

ADSL

ADSL is another digital service that continues to get a lot of press. ADSL stands for *Asymmetrical Digital Subscriber Line* and is a digital technology providing up to 7.1Mbps of transmission speed from the host computer to your computer and 64Kbps of speed from your computer to the host.

As is ISDN, ADSL is a digital signal that is not subject to line noise or interference, which means you always have a transmission signal operating at 7.1Mbps (downstream) and 64Kbps (upstream).

ADSL works over your existing phone lines but requires some additional hardware. The first device you need is called the *ADSL Terminal Unit-Remote (ATU-R)*—a unit often referred to as the "ADSL modem." You also need an Ethernet network interface card installed in your PC to connect to your ADSL modem. Note that there is a distance limitation to connecting ADSL to your home. You must live within about 12,000 feet (about 2 miles) of your local telephone switching office (the distance limitation for ISDN is about 3 miles).

Cable Modems

Cable modems are an attempt by the cable TV industry to cash in on the phenomenal popularity of the Internet. The cable modem system is a shared system operating at a reported 10Mbps.

If you work on a networked computer at work that is connected to the Internet, you are already familiar with the downside of a shared system. Regardless of how fast the transmission is, you are sharing it with other users, which means your communications begin to slow down as more people simultaneously log in to the system.

The "shared" nature of the cable modem communications line also means that additional security problems exist unless the provider takes some steps to eliminate or remove them.

Understanding a High-Speed Internet Connection

Cable and DSL modems and the high-speed connections they originate from are what we call *broadband communications*. Broadband is a type of data transmission in which a single transmission medium can carry multiple channels. Cable modems are attached to the same coaxial (coax) cable that brings cable TV into your living room; DSL modems are connected to the same copper wires that provide your basic telephone service.

> Just as you can watch cable TV at the same time you can surf the Web with a cable modem connection, you can likewise talk on the telephone at the same time you surf the Web using your DSL connection.

The diagram in Figure 44.5 shows the basic setup for both cable and DSL broadband services. As the diagram shows, broadband service is provided from either your cable TV provider or your local telephone company.

FIGURE 44.5

How cable and DSL broadband services connect to your PC.

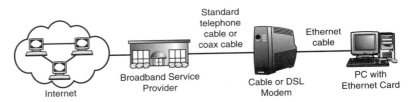

With both DSL and cable service, you must install an Ethernet card in your PC and connect it to either the cable modem or DSL modem using what is called an Ethernet or Cat5 (Category 5) cable.

> You can purchase a Cat5 cable for a few dollars at any computer store such as CompUSA, Best Buy, Circuit City, or Radio Shack.

Differences and Similarities in Cable and DSL Broadband

In addition to the faster communication speeds available with both broadband services, the major similarity between the two services is that both are always on. You do not have to dial in to your provider as you do with your older analog 56K modem—broadband connections are always connected to your Internet Service Provider.

There are major differences in the communications speeds available with each type of service. Cable modems offer the highest theoretical speed. Depending on your cable provider, speeds can range from 10 to 30 megabits per second downstream (what you receive) to 0.128 to 10 megabits per second upstream (what you send). I say the speed is "theoretical" because your transmission speeds largely depend on how many of your neighbors also have cable broadband service. Cable broadband has what is called shared bandwidth, meaning that the downstream and upstream speeds—or more precisely, the amount of data that can be transmitted each second—is shared by all the cable broadband subscribers. What this means is that as more cable broadband subscribers access the Internet simultaneously, your transmission speeds will slow down.

DSL broadband service is not shared, but it does have its own set of limitations. DSL has a distance limitation. Optimally, your home should be no more than 3.4 miles (5.4 kilometers) from the telephone company central switching office. Within this distance limitation, you can transmit at speeds of 1.5 to 8 megabits per second downstream (what you receive) to 0.090 to 1.544 megabits per second upstream (what you send). ADSL providers will often offer several different subscription packages that differ in the maximum transmission speeds available.

How to Obtain Cable or DSL Broadband Service

You can consult several Web sites to see whether DSL service is available in your area. All the Baby Bells allow you to check their sites to see whether DSL service is available for you, but they don't mention any competing companies that may be reselling DSL. Here is a short list of Web sites you can check for DSL and cable broadband availability and miscellaneous information:

- http://www.dslplus.com/
- http://compnetworking.about.com/cs/dslavailability/
- http://www.teamits.com/internet/?/internet/dsl/dslform.html
- http://www.catv.org/
- http://www.cable-modem.net/
- http://cable-dsl.home.att.net/
- http://www.cablemodeminfo.com/

There are numerous other sites you can check. Just go to your favorite search engine and enter **dsl availability**. You can also check the Web site of your Regional Bell Operating Company.

Providers of both types of service often include the actual cable or DSL modem (usually as a rented item) in their subscription packages along with the Ethernet card required to connect the modem to your PC. It is usually cheaper to purchase these items separately. Cable modems can range in price from $100 to $300. DSL modems are similarly priced. You will also need an Ethernet card to connect either device to your PC, which you can purchase for $10 to $20.

Installing a Cable or DSL Modem

As just stated, it is usually cheaper to purchase your cable or DSL modem rather than rent one from your provider (which isn't yours to keep after so many rental payments). You can usually purchase these devices online or from stores such as CompUSA, Best Buy, Circuit City, or Radio Shack. You don't have to purchase a modem with a lot of bells and whistles; just make sure that it conforms to the standards used by your provider—DOCSIS (Data Over Cable Service Interface Specifications) for cable broadband service or Discrete Multitone (DMT) for ADSL broadband service. Depending on your area, a DSL modem may not be for sale through anybody but your DSL provider.

Contact your broadband service provider and order the service you want. For ADSL broadband service, a visit to your home for installation is not required. DSL service can be turned on from the telephone company's central office. For cable broadband service, however, an installation visit is required because a splitter must be installed at the point where the actual coax cable enters your house to place your cable TV service and broadband service on separate cable lines inside your house. Don't worry; there is still only one cable coming to your house.

The first thing you have to do is to install the Ethernet card in your PC. You will need an Ethernet card for both cable and DSL broadband service. You can read about these cards in Chapter 31, "Networking for Simple Computer Setups."

After you install the hardware driver for your Ethernet card, you must install the TCP/IP protocol. For Windows XP, select Start, Control Panel, Network Connection; Windows should list the Ethernet card you just installed. Right-click the Ethernet card listed and select Properties to open the Properties dialog box for your Ethernet card (see Figure 44.6).

FIGURE 44.6

The Properties dialog box for your newly installed Ethernet card.

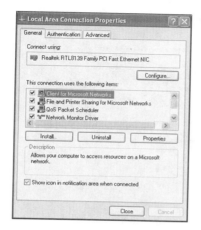

44

Click Install, select Protocol, and then select Add. When the choices for available protocols to add are listed, select Internet Protocol (TCP/IP) and click OK.

You must now configure TCP/IP for your broadband service. Your service provider should supply you with the following information:

- Your IP address, subnet mask, default gateway, and whether these configuration settings are static or dynamically assigned.

Many broadband service providers dynamically assign your IP address and other TCP/IP configuration parameters because dynamically assigned parameters are easier to manage (for them, not you).

- The IP address(es) of your provider's DNS (Domain Name Service) server(s).

To add and configure the TCP/IP protocol for your broadband connection, do the following:

1. For Windows XP, select Start, Control Panel, Network Connection; Windows should list the Ethernet card you just installed. Right-click the Ethernet card listed and select Properties to open the Properties dialog box for your Ethernet card.

2. Scroll down the This Connection Uses the Following Items box and select Internet Protocol (TCP/IP). Click the Properties button to open the Properties dialog box (see Figure 44.7).

FIGURE 44.7

The Properties dialog box for TCP/IP settings.

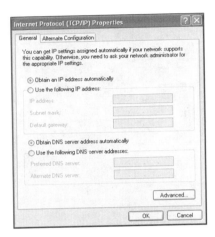

3. If your service provider provides you with a dynamically assigned IP address, select the Obtain an IP Address Automatically option. If your service provider gave you a static IP address, select the Use the Following IP Address option and enter the IP address, subnet mask, and default gateway IP addresses provided by your provider.

4. Repeat Step 3 for the DNS server address section of the dialog box.

5. Click OK, and continue closing all the dialog boxes and screens you previously opened.

Depending on how your broadband provider and service provider have configured their hardware and network, you may or may not have to install software provided by these service providers. If you do, insert the CD you received and install the software following the instructions provided.

Connecting Your PC to the Cable or DSL Modem

Now that you've finished configuring your PC, it's time to connect your PC to your cable or DSL modem. The procedure is the same regardless of which type of service you subscribe to.

To connect your PC to your broadband modem, follow these steps:

1. Plug one end of the Ethernet cable (the Cat5 cable) into the Ethernet card in your PC. Plug the other end of the cable into your cable or DSL modem. Look for a plug labeled "Ethernet."

2. If you are using a cable modem, connect the coax cable from the splitter (connected by your cable provider) to the cable modem. If you are using a DSL modem, connect a standard telephone cable to the modem and plug the other end into a phone jack. If you are using a DSL modem, make sure that you connect RF filters (see Figure 44.8) to all other phone lines connected to telephones in your home.

FIGURE 44.8
Two types of RF filters used with DSL connections.

3. Turn on your cable or DSL modem.

4. To test your connection, start your Web browser (Internet Explorer, Netscape Navigator, or whichever Web browser you use) and see whether you can connect to a Web site. If you can't, make sure that all your cables are properly connected and that you followed all the previous instructions for installing and configuring your Ethernet card.

Security Concerns

You may think that you're done with your broadband communications connection if you were able to successfully connect to a Web site using your Web browser. But there's one more important task you have to perform: You must secure your PC from hackers or attackers.

If you are not setting up a medium or large network, you don't need the depth covered there for your broadband experience. Nevertheless, you need to take security far more seriously than you have to if you only use a dial-up modem.

PCs connected to broadband services are frequently attacked and used to launch *Denial of Service* (*DoS*) attacks against large online organizations, companies, and universities. PCs on broadband service are targeted because the broadband service is always on and provides a high-bandwidth (high-speed) connection the attacker can use in an attack. The attack scenario works like this: The attacker scans known ranges of IP addresses used by broadband service providers for their customers, looking for vulnerable PCs. A "vulnerable PC" is a PC the attacker can easily access and install software that allows him to control that PC remotely. When the attacker has accessed several hundred PCs which he can control, he then uses them to launch a Denial of Service attack.

A Denial of Service attack is an attack in which the attacker commands the hundreds of PCs he now controls to send an unending stream of data to a single Internet site. Controlling several hundred PCs on broadband connections makes a Denial of Service attack easier because the high-speed connections allow each commandeered PC to send a tremendous volume of data to the site being attacked.

The site being attacked is overwhelmed with data, usually much more than the site is equipped to handle. The result is that legitimate users to the attacked site cannot access it because of the constant bombardment of useless data. Attacks like this have been known to continue for hours or days without end. The Internet Service Provider for the site being attacked can make adjustments in the hardware (network routers) to fend off the attack, but usually not before the attacked site has not been able to service its regular customers for hours or days.

To prevent your PC from being commandeered and used in a Denial of Service attack, you must install either software or hardware designed to prevent the attacker from accessing your PC. Such programs or devices are collectively known as *firewalls*. A firewall is a program or device used to prevent some type of intrusion or attack.

PC firewalls are by no means an absolute guarantee that your PC will not be attacked and commandeered, but they usually are enough of a deterrent to send the attacker off in search of easier prey.

Software firewall products are typically less expensive than hardware devices, and there are numerous ones to pick from. Here's a list of the best known:

- ZoneAlarm from Zone Labs (www.zonelabs.com)
- BlackICE Defender from Network ICE (www.networkice.com)

- Symantec Desktop Firewall (www.symantec.com)
- McAfee Personal Firewall (www.mcafee.com)

You can download and purchase all of these products online.

> Of the personal firewall products listed here, which is not by any means a total list of the products available, ZoneAlarm and Sygate are free for personal and home use.
>
> Windows XP users have a firewall option included in the new operating system. To activate this option, open the Properties dialog box for your Ethernet card (described previously) and click the Advanced button. In the Advanced dialog box, select the option to turn on your XP firewall.

44

Several companies have been marketing hardware firewall devices to cable and DSL broadband users. These multifunction devices contain small network hubs or switches and routers, as does the Linksys device shown in Figure 44.9. If you are connecting only a single PC to your broadband connection, then you obviously don't need a device designed for small networks, so save your money and don't buy hardware devices with functionality you don't need.

FIGURE 44.9

A cable/DSL firewall/router from Linksys.

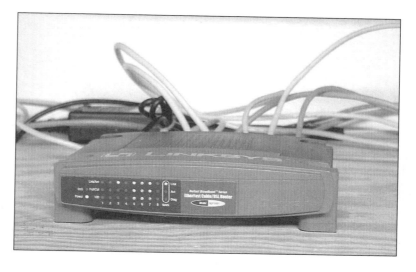

Summary

In this chapter, you learned how modems work, were presented with information you'll need to make a selection on an upgrade modem, and should have decided whether you want to upgrade to a 56KB modem. You also learned about some of the digital communications alternatives to analog modems, such as ISDN, ADSL, and cable modems.

The two primary types of broadband Internet services available in this country are cable modem service and ADSL. You also learned how these services work and some major advantages and disadvantages in each service. You learned how to select and install each service so that you can connect to the Internet. You now know more about the importance of security in an online world.

CHAPTER 45

Upgrading Your Keyboard, Mouse, and Other Input Devices

After reading the title of this chapter, you may start wondering what's wrong with your keyboard and mouse. Actually, the keyboard and mouse you are now using may be fine, but over the course of this chapter you will learn about some better alternatives for the common keyboards and mice usually shipped with PCs.

Is Anything Wrong with My Keyboard or Mouse?

The title of this chapter might prompt you to skip it because nothing is wrong with your keyboard or mouse. Well, the idea is not that anything is wrong with the keyboard and mouse that came with your PC, but that replacement keyboards and mice can make long hours of PC use easier and much more pleasant.

Keyboards and mice have improved considerably over the past few years—in design, functionality, and *ergonomics*.

> Ergonomics is the study of the relationship between people and their work environments. In simpler terms, it means producing tools in the workplace, such as chairs, desks, keyboards, and so on, that conform more to the way human bodies are designed and how they function rather than making human bodies conform to workplace tools. The idea is to increase comfort and reduce the possibility of injuries or stress.

Functionally, probably nothing is wrong with your keyboard, or at least we hope nothing is mechanically or electronically wrong with it. Like thousands of other PC keyboards, however, yours may be contributing to a physical problem that hundreds of orthopedic surgeons are seeing more and more of each year. You may have encountered the terms *repetitive stress injury* and *carpal tunnel syndrome*. These medical terms are used to describe an extremely painful and sometimes disabling condition brought on by continuously repeating a physical action that places your hands, arms, or legs in an unnatural position. Whether you are aware of it or not, most of us do this every time we use our keyboard.

Although we can absolutely in no way offer a diagnosis on whether you've suffered a repetitive stress injury or whether you've actually developed carpal tunnel syndrome, we can offer you some advice that may help you avoid problems down the road. Now that we've gotten the legal stuff out of the way (which should make the lawyers and suits happy), let's move right along.

The average flat keyboard forces you to bend your wrist outward so that your fingers are in position to reach all the keys. If you're a hunt-and-peck typist, this problem may not be so bad. If you are a touch typist, however, your wrists are probably angled outward at about 30 degrees. If you extend the legs on your keyboard to lift the back of your keyboard upward, you are putting more strain on your wrists because now you are also hyperextending them backward another 30 to 40 degrees.

This unnatural bending of your wrist for long periods of time, day in and day out, eventually can place stress on the nerves in your arms, hands, and wrists. You may have noticed after using your keyboard for several hours that you experience some tingling or numbness in your wrists or fingers. This could be the start of more serious problems.

After studying this problem for several years, designers have come up with what they call the ergonomic keyboard. Although several manufacturers have come up with various styles on the basic design of a keyboard split in the middle with the keys positioned in a more natural position, the Microsoft keyboard remains the most popular seller (see Figure 45.1).

FIGURE 45.1

A typical ergonomic keyboard.

45

The basic idea behind the ergonomic keyboard is that it places your wrists and hands into a more comfortable and natural position, with your palms facing more toward each other. This position places much less stress on the nerves and ligaments in your wrists and hands.

Ergonomics, however, is not the only direction keyboard makers are going. Added functionality is another. Keyboards are no longer just keyboards. You can now purchase keyboards with additional devices such as scanners (see Figure 45.2), trackballs, or touchpads built in.

Whether you purchase a keyboard for more comfort and functionality, or if you are just looking for a keyboard with a better feel than the one you are currently using, make sure that you get a keyboard with the correct type of plug for your PC. Most PCs today are manufactured with ports for the newer, smaller 6-pin PS/2-style keyboard plugs shown on the left in Figure 45.3.

This PS/2 type of plug is easy to identify because it is the same size as the plug used on mice. The other type of keyboard plug is the original AT-style plug, which is noticeably larger than the PS/2 plug.

Don't panic if, when you purchase a new keyboard and attempt to plug it in to your PC, you discover that your new keyboard has the wrong size plug. Most computer stores sell keyboard plug adapters for $5 to $10 that convert PS/2 to AT and vice versa (see Figure 45.4).

FIGURE 45.2

A keyboard with a built-in sheet-feed scanner.

AT Style Keyboard Plug

PS/2 Style Keyboard Plug

FIGURE 45.3

A 6-pin PS/2-style keyboard plug on the left and an older AT-style keyboard plug on the right.

FIGURE 45.4

Keyboard adapters for converting PS/2- to AT-style plugs.

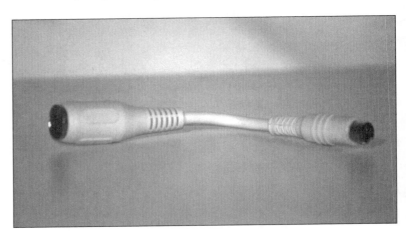

Another option to consider is a wireless keyboard. These are keyboards with a small built-in radio transmitter/receiver. Another small radio transmitter/receiver is plugged into the keyboard receptacle on your PC (see Figure 45.5). The radio transmitters in these devices are usually good for a distance of about 2 meters. Wireless keyboards are a good way to eliminate the bother of having another cord to deal with—especially if you like to recline in your easy chair while computing.

FIGURE 45.5

A typical wireless keyboard.

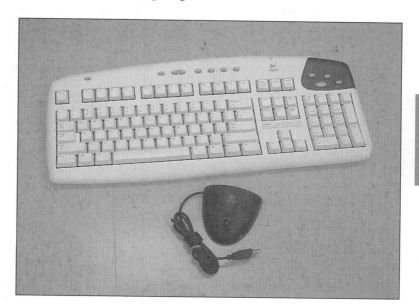

45

Fixing a Keyboard?

Even though some texts attempt to explain how to fix your keyboard, depending on the type of keyboard you have, you could start tearing it apart only to discover that it's about as difficult to put back together as grandpa's old pocket watch. If your keyboard goes bad, the trash bin is usually its fate. But this doesn't mean you can't occasionally perform some routine maintenance to help keep your keyboard clean.

Keyboards are great for attracting and collecting dust. Your keyboard is also quite good at attracting and collecting crumbs. Before this chapter ends, you'll see some fast ways to clean your keyboard and mouse.

Mice and Other Pointing Devices

For many users, the mouse is purely a functional device; either it is functioning, or it isn't! Mice and other types of pointing devices today, however, offer a lot more than mere functionality. Ergonomic mice have been designed to fit your hand. Cordless mice eliminate the cord's getting in your way. Some mice have two buttons; some have three; some are left-handed; and some mice even have built-in gyroscopic mechanisms that you can wave through the air instead of dragging across a pad. Another mouse innovation for people who surf the World Wide Web a lot is a mouse with a special scrolling wheel placed between the two buttons. The scrolling wheel enables you to scroll up and down long Web pages quickly and smoothly. A lot of applications now also support this scrolling action, including Microsoft's Office suite.

Several manufacturers are also producing optical mice. Instead of a ball, an optical mouse scans your desktop with a laser that produces a tracking precision much greater than a typical mouse with a roller ball (see Figure 45.6).

One main advantage optical mice have over other types of mice is that because there are no ball and rollers to attract dust and dirt, you don't have to clean them.

And if you don't like cords getting in your way, you can even get a cordless optical mouse (see Figure 45.7). The transmitter/receiver units on these devices have about the same distance limitations as with cordless keyboards—about 2 meters. One downside to using a cordless optical mouse is that the laser is quite a drain on the batteries. Expect battery life to be about 3 to 4 weeks with typical use.

FIGURE 45.6
A typical optical mouse.

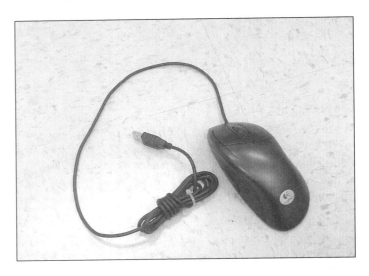

If you have limited desktop space and prefer to move your hand rather than move your pointing device, you should opt for a *trackball* rather than a mouse (see Figure 45.8).

FIGURE 45.7
A cordless optical mouse.

45

A trackball, simply stated, is a mouse turned upside down. The ball inside the pointing device is not moved across a pad, but instead your hand motions move the ball (which is usually much larger than the ball in a mouse).

FIGURE 45.8
A typical trackball pointing device.

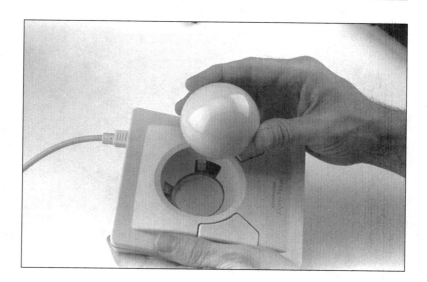

Another pointing device that can help you save desktop space is a touchpad. A touchpad is about the same size as a trackball, but instead of a large ball that you move to position the pointer, you touch a touch-sensitive pad with your finger to position the pointer. Just like a trackball, a touchpad can take a little getting used to, but it is another pointing device you may want to consider.

Just as you can purchase a keyboard with the wrong type of plug, mice also come out of the box with one of two types of connectors—a 6-pin DIN connector and a 9-pin serial connector. To give you the option of using either type connector, most manufacturers now include a mouse plug adapter with their mice (see Figure 45.9).

What's most important when selecting a new pointing device is comfort and ease of use. In other words, the mouse or trackball should move smoothly. Many large computer stores have a selection of mice on display that you can try to see how they feel and operate. Take this opportunity to try different sizes and styles of mice to see which type you prefer.

If you're in the market for a new keyboard or mouse, one of the best sources for finding up-to-date information on PC hardware components is the hardware section of CNET's computers.com Web site (`http://computers.cnet.com/hardware/01016.html`). In addition to listing just about every keyboard and mouse you could possibly think of, this site also does comparison reviews and allows you to compare prices on the products listed. Where applicable, this site also lists specifications on the products listed and points you to the manufacturer for more information.

FIGURE 45.9
A mouse plug adapter.

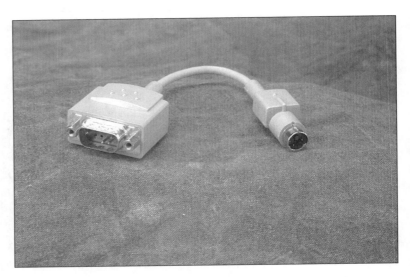

Tips on Cleaning Your Input Devices

Over time and with normal usage, your keyboard, mouse (provided you did not opt for an optical mouse), and other input devices attract dirt and dust on the ball and rollers. The best way to tell when your devices are dirty and need to be cleaned is when they start to behave erratically, such as your mouse pointer not moving in the direction you are trying to position it, or your keyboard keys becoming hard to press.

Cleaning Your Keyboard

Over time, your keyboard accumulates dust, crumbs (if you eat and work, as many computer users do), and other small bits of debris, which can cause keys to stick or make your keys slightly harder to press. The easiest method you can employ to clean your keyboard of these small bits of debris is simply to turn it over so that the keys are facing down toward your desktop and shake your keyboard firmly. Don't shake it hard enough to jar loose your keys, but give it a few good shakes to clear out the crumbs and other small particles.

If you have the misfortune of accidentally spilling a liquid on your keyboard, such as a soda or other soft drink, you may quickly discover that the sugar or other sweetener causes your keys to become sticky. If this happens, immediately stop what you're doing. Save any work you're doing and shut down your PC. Unplug your keyboard and take it to an empty sink. Soda and other liquids can be easily removed using rubbing alcohol. Take a bottle of alcohol out of your medicine cabinet and slowly pour it into the keyboard in about the same area where the spill occurred. The alcohol does not harm the electrical contacts in your keyboard and does a fairly good job of cleaning the spilled liquid. You may need to use more than one bottle of alcohol. You can usually tell when you have completely cleaned your keyboard by simply pressing the keys to check whether they still feel sticky. Just make sure that you allow sufficient time for the alcohol to dry (evaporate) before you plug your keyboard back in to your PC and begin using it again.

Don't use any cleaning products commonly used to clean your kitchen or bathroom because some can damage the plastics in your keyboard and others can leave residues, which can cause more damage. Isopropyl alcohol is about the safest (and often cheapest) cleaning product you can use.

Cleaning Your Mouse

Mice also get dirty. Usually the parts that get dirty are the rollers inside the mouse, which come in contact with the ball. Just as you did with your keyboard, reach for your

45

bottle of alcohol. This time, instead of pouring the alcohol over the ball and rollers, you want to remove the ball and, using a cotton swab soaked with alcohol, clean the rollers of any build-up of dirt and grease, which can accumulate over time. The instructions that came with your mouse can explain how to open it and remove the ball. Usually, it is just a matter of sliding or twisting a panel holding the ball in place. Just make sure that you understand how to replace the ball before you remove it.

Again, just as with your keyboard, don't use common household cleaning products that can damage your mouse.

Summary

In this chapter, you learned how to select a better and more comfortable keyboard and mouse and how important comfort and ergonomics can be when using them. You also learned how to overcome the problem of purchasing a mouse or keyboard with a plug that doesn't match your PC mouse and keyboard connections.

CHAPTER 46

Upgrading Your Video Card and Monitor

Most users make do with whatever video card came with the PC when it was purchased. There's actually nothing wrong with this video card philosophy. Chances are the video card installed in your PC by the manufacturer is more than adequate for 98% of the applications you run. So, why should anyone want to upgrade their video card? The answer is the same for any decision to upgrade a component in your PC—to get better performance!

Better performance in a video card can mean several things—higher video resolution, faster screen refreshes, better graphics, or more colors on your screen. For most users, the need for better performance in a video card is usually driven by a specific application: a high-end graphics art program, a CADD or engineering design program, or even a game using enhanced 3D graphics.

But if you are still using the same old 14- or 15-inch monitor, you're cheating yourself out of the very benefits you sought when you upgraded your old video card with a new one. The main reason most users upgrade their video cards is to gain higher resolution, which enables them to see more on their screen. But resolutions of 1,024×768 and 1,280×1,024 are nearly unreadable on 14- and 15-inch monitors unless you have a passion for squinting.

What's Currently Available in Video Cards

It's extremely difficult to purchase a bad video card. Video cards have been one of the fastest developing technologies in the computer industry in recent years, and surprisingly, this advancement has been driven largely by the computer gaming industry.

> *Video cards* are also referred to as *video adapters*, *graphic adapters*, and *graphic cards*. These terms all refer to the same device—the interface card installed in your computer that controls and produces video on your monitor. Although the term mostly applies to separate interface cards installed in your PC, the term video card can also refer to video display circuitry built in to the motherboard.

For years, computer gaming software has been pushing the display envelope for faster and more complex graphics and animation. Consequently, the entire computer industry has benefited from this small but demanding segment of the industry because these same video cards also deliver improved graphic performance for the more mainstream business application uses of computers.

Most of what's been happening with video cards for the last two to three years can be summed up in two words: speed and memory. Video cards have gotten faster and manufacturers are building them with more (and faster) video memory. On average, expect to see most if not all new video cards with 32MB or more of memory.

What to Look for in a Video Card

It's fairly easy to determine how much memory each video card has installed. The amount of memory installed on the card is usually printed in big, bold letters on the outside of the box. Video memory is usually referred to as *VRAM*.

> *VRAM*, short for *Video RAM (Random Access Memory)*, is a special type of high-speed memory designed for use in video cards. VRAM is typically not upgradeable because it is permanently installed in video cards.

How Important Is Video RAM?

Video RAM or video memory is important because it directly controls video resolution and the number of colors you can display on your monitor. Resolution is defined as the number of *pixels* (short for *picture elements*) displayed on your screen. A pixel is the smallest video display unit that can be displayed on your screen.

In standard VGA mode, there are 640 pixels displayed horizontally across your screen by 480 pixels displayed vertically, for a total of 307,200 pixels (640×480=307,200).

When you increase your resolution to 800×600, the number of pixels increases to 480,000 (800×600=480,000). The number of pixels displayed on your screen, however, is only half the story. Each pixel is made up of a color. In 16-color mode, the lowest number of colors for VGA, each pixel can be 1 of 16 possible colors. You need 4 bits of memory to support 16-color mode, and if you do the math, you'll see that you need 153,600 bytes of memory to support 16-color mode:

```
640_480=307,200
307,000_4=1,228,800(bits)
```

To convert bits to bytes, divide by 8:

```
1,228,800(bits)/8=153,600(bytes)
```

Unfortunately, 16-color mode does not produce very brilliant colors. A better color mode is 256 colors. To produce 256-color mode, however, you need to jump from 4 to 8 bits per pixel, or 307,200 bytes of memory. Your display is getting better but it is still not great. An improvement would be to increase your color or color depth to 65,536 colors. To jump to a color depth of 65,536 colors, however, you need 16 bits of memory for each pixel, for a total of 614,400 bytes of memory.

No video card manufacturer ever produced video cards with 614,400 bytes of memory. Instead, they rounded this number up to a more convenient 1MB of memory. So, to display VGA resolution at 65,536 (64KB) colors, you needed 1MB of memory on your video card. If you increased your resolution up to 1,024×768 at 64KB (65,536) colors, you needed 2MB of memory on your video card, and if you increased your resolution to 1,280×1,024 or the number of colors displayed to 16.8MB (16,777,216), then you needed 4MB of memory on your video card. Table 46.1 lists video memory requirements at various resolutions and color depths on cards you will typically see on the market these days.

TABLE 46.1   Video Memory Requirements

Resolution	Color Depth	Colors	Video RAM	Memory Required (bytes)
640×480	4-bit	16	256KB	153,600
640×480	8-bit	256	512KB	307,200
640×480	16-bit	65,536	1MB	614,400
640×480	24-bit	16,777,216	1MB	921,600
800×600	4-bit	16	256KB	240,000
800×600	8-bit	256	512KB	480,000
800×600	16-bit	65,536	1MB	960,000
800×600	24-bit	16,777,216	2MB	1,440,000
1,024×768	4-bit	16	512KB	393,216
1,024×768	8-bit	256	1MB	786,432
1,024×768	16-bit	65,536	2MB	1,572,864
1,024×768	24-bit	16,777,216	4MB	2,359,296
1,280×1,024	4-bit	16	1MB	655,360
1,280×1,024	8-bit	256	2MB	1,310,720
1,280×1,024	16-bit	65,536	4MB	2,621,440
1,280×1,024	24-bit	16,777,216	4MB	3,932,160
1,600×1,200	4-bit	16	512KB	960,000
1,600×1,200	8-bit	256	2MB	1,920,000
1,600×1,200	16-bit	65,536	4MB	3,840,000
1,600×1,200	24-bit	16,777,216	8MB	5,760,000

If all you're working on are spreadsheets and text documents, you're not going to see much difference between 16 colors and 65,536 colors displayed on your screen. If you are a graphic artist, however, the increase in color depth from 4-bit color to 24- or 32-bit color (16.8MB colors) is essential.

Demonstrating Video Resolution and Color Depth

To demonstrate video resolution and color depth using your existing video card, follow these steps:

1. Use the Windows XP System Information utility to determine how much video memory you have installed on your existing video card.

2. If your current video mode is not VGA (640×480 resolution) and 16 colors (color depth), change to this particular resolution and color depth: Right-click your desktop to open the display shortcut menu, select Properties, and then select Settings to open the Display Properties dialog box (see Figure 46.1). Make the appropriate change to Color Palette and Desktop Area.

> If your display adapter does not immediately give you the option of changing to VGA, 640×480 resolution, click the Advanced button on the Properties page, select Adapter, select List All Modes, and then select 640×480,16 Colors.

FIGURE 46.1

The Display Properties dialog box in Windows XP.

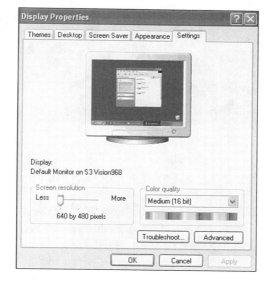

46

3. If you have Internet access, start your Web browser and proceed to the following Web page:

```
http://www.felixnet.com/wolfpark/wolftrip.htm
```

Select the second group of pictures and click the first picture to display it full-sized (see Figure 46.2). This picture has fairly vivid colors and good resolution when viewed at something better than 16-color VGA mode.

4. Repeat Step 2, staying in VGA mode (640×480 resolution), but select a better color depth (such as 256 colors or 65,536 colors). Go back and view the test picture

again and note the change in appearance. Take a few minutes to try various screen resolutions and color depths to see which combination produces the best results using your video card and monitor.

FIGURE 46.2

A test picture for comparing various video modes and color depths.

Video Speed

Video speed is often referred to as *refresh rate*, the speed at which the video card can redraw or refresh your display screen at certain resolutions. Most experts agree that your video card should have a minimum refresh rate of 72Hz at every resolution to avoid flicker, which can cause eye strain and fatigue. Although the type of memory installed on your video card can definitely affect refresh rate, the other factor controlling refresh rate is the speed of the *Digital Analog Converter (DAC)*. You should look for a video card with a DAC speed of at least 250MHz.

Ultimately, speed is important for a video card because a faster card can redraw or refresh your display screen and produce smoother animation when you are displaying moving objects on your screen. Again, this is a feature more important to graphic art programs, Web design applications, CADD engineering software, and video games than to a word processing program. But video speed is also important if you are working in any type of business graphic program or if you are viewing graphics or animation on the Internet. The bottom line is that any application benefits from a higher quality video card and eventually you will be faced with using some sort of graphical application.

Video card speed is a little hard to accurately test. Often it takes sophisticated testing programs to determine the relative speed of a particular video card. Most users lack the testing software and resources to test numerous video cards, so we must rely on the various computer industry journals to test and publish their results. These testing reviews can often be valuable sources of information that you as a consumer and computer user should regularly check before making any computer purchase.

So, what does all this mean when deciding whether you need a new video card? If you are an ardent game player and are trying to keep pace with the latest gaming technology, you most likely want the fastest video card you can get—one with 32MB of memory or more and one that can display ultra-fast 3D graphics.

If you are using any type of sophisticated graphics or animation software, you also want to consider upgrading to a video card that fits the same bill. However, an even less demanding reason technologically for upgrading your video card is purchasing a larger monitor. Although VGA mode (640×480 resolution) is perfectly acceptable on a 14- or 15-inch monitor, if you are looking at a 17-, 19-, or 21-inch monitor, you'll want to crank up the resolution to a higher level to take advantage of the larger display. For 17-inch monitors and larger, it is fairly common to use a resolution of 1,024×768 to 1,600×1,200 or higher. If you look back at the preceding section, you see that higher video resolution and higher color depth require a video card with more memory. Once again, use the Windows XP System Information utility to determine the specifics of your existing video card.

Although SysChk indicates the basics of your video card, if you are serious about expertly testing your video card and tuning your monitor, you should look into a professional testing utility such as DisplayMate from Sonera Technologies, located at http://www.displaymate.com (see Figure 46.3).

46

FIGURE 46.3

Sonera Technologies, the developer of DisplayMate, a profes- sional video-testing utility.

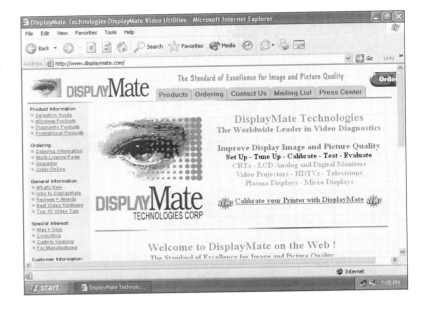

Installing a Video Card

There is very little setup involved when installing a new video card.

Regardless of which version of Windows you are using, before you remove your existing video card and install a new one, do this: Set your video mode to VGA and your colors to 16. This ensures that Windows, with the standard VGA driver installed, will definitely work with your new video card.

To install a new video card, follow these steps:

1. From the Start menu, select Control Panel and then select System to open the System Properties dialog box.

2. Select the Hardware tab and then choose Device Manager to access the Hardware Device Manager.

3. Click Display Adapters and then select the adapter in your PC. Right-click Uninstall to uninstall the driver for your display adapter (see Figure 46.4). Windows replaces the driver with the standard generic (and low resolution) VGA driver.

FIGURE 46.4

Uninstalling your video driver in Windows XP.

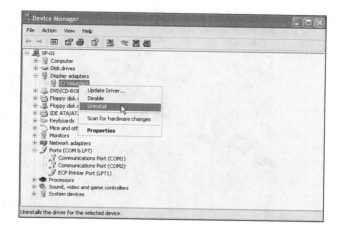

4. Click OK to reboot your PC.

> If you install a new video card that requires a video driver that is incompatible with the driver required by your previous video card, it is possible that your PC will not start Windows. To prevent this from happening, you can install the generic VGA video driver, which should work with just about every video card on the market.

46

5. Turn off and unplug your PC. Ground yourself and then remove the cover.

6. Unplug the cable from your monitor, which is connected to your current video card.

7. Remove your current video card and insert the new video card into the same slot on your motherboard (see Figure 46.5). If you are removing a card from an ISA bus slot and the new card requires a PCI bus slot, be sure to insert the new card into the proper slot. If you are removing a card from a PCI slot and the new card requires an AGP slot, be sure to insert the new card into the proper slot.

> *AGP (Accelerated Graphics Port)* refers to a special graphics slot designed by Intel, which began appearing about 4 years ago in PCs with Pentium II motherboards. Read the next section for more details on AGP.

FIGURE 46.5

Inserting a new video card into your PC.

Some motherboards have built-in video cards, which you must disable before adding an upgraded video card. To disable a built-in video card, consult the documentation that came with your PC. In many instances, you can disable a built-in video card by running the hardware Setup program used to configure your PC. To disable some built-in video cards, however, the manufacturer might have included a special video configuration utility.

8. Replace your PC's cover and attach the video cable to your new card. Plug your PC in and turn it on.

9. Install the video driver for your new card, following the instructions accompanying the new card. Because of Plug and Play, Windows should detect your new video card and begin the driver installation for you. Just follow the prompts to install the new video driver.

What About AGP?

If you regularly read the computer trade journals, another term you may have seen is *AGP (Accelerated Graphics Port)*. Strictly speaking, it is not an upgrade item. You cannot add AGP to your existing computer.

You need the 440LX motherboard *chipset*. You also need a video card that is AGP compliant and software that is written to use AGP's advanced capabilities.

A *chipset* is nothing more than a specialized processor or group of processors designed for a specific task. In references like this, it refers to a chipset installed in a particular series of motherboards.

So what does all this AGP hardware and software buy you? Amazing graphics texture and silky smooth animation, but surprisingly no additional display speed. In tests conducted on similar computer systems using an AGP video card and a PCI video card, the AGP card was not significantly faster, and in some tests, the AGP turned in the same or lower speed as the PCI.

Another drawback to AGP is that Intel set a rather relaxed standard. The only real qualification for AGP is that the AGP card fit into the proprietary AGP slot. In early models released by several manufacturers, some cards did not fully implement the full texturing features for enhanced 3D graphics. There are even different implementations of display speed on the so-called compliant video cards. Some cards operate at 66MHz and provide 264 megabytes per second of display video data, whereas other cards are able to effectively double these numbers. Reportedly, some manufacturers are working on cards that quadruple these figures.

Finally, little software has been written to take full advantage of AGP. The largest category, as you might guess, is games. Even the best AGP video cards do nothing to improve existing graphics software.

Upgrading Your Video Monitor

The main reason most users decide to upgrade their video cards is to gain higher resolution, which enables them to see more (often, a lot more) on their screen. But resolutions of 1,024×768 and 1,600×1,200 are nearly unreadable on 14- and 15-inch monitors unless you have a passion for squinting.

In the past, the biggest deterrent for most users interested in purchasing larger monitors was cost. As recently as a few years ago, most 21-inch and larger monitors were in the $2,000 to $2,500 range. Nowadays, these same monitors are advertised with prices in the $400 to $650 range, in part because of competition from the newly released 19-inch monitors in the $250 to $400 price range. For the average PC user, selecting an upgrade among this glut of lower priced, larger monitors can be confusing.

Why You Should Purchase a Larger Monitor

Plain and simple, the reason you want a new, larger monitor is that it enables you to see more of what is displayed on your screen. For example, if you are currently using a 15-inch monitor, upgrading to a 17-inch monitor may not seem like a big deal, but a 17-inch monitor gives you about 30% more onscreen viewing area. Upgrading from a 15-inch monitor to a 21-inch monitor gives you more than 50% more onscreen viewing area because you can comfortably set your display to a higher resolution. Table 46.2 shows the recommended resolution for 15-, 17-, 19-, and 21-inch monitors. Keep in mind that these are just recommendations, not chiseled-in-stone guidelines.

TABLE 46.2   Optimal and Acceptable Display Resolutions

15-inch	17-inch	19-inch	21-inch
640×480	640×480	640×480	640×480
800×600	800×600	800×600	800×600
1,024×768	1,024×768	1,024×768	1,024×768
	1,280×1,024	1,280×1,024	1,280×1,024
	1,600×1,200	1,600×1,200	1,800×1,440

To give you an idea how resolution can affect how much you can view onscreen, take a look at Figures 46.6 and 46.7. These three figures display the same information onscreen, but as you can see, as the resolution increases, so too does the amount of information visible onscreen.

Prices of larger monitors have continued to drop in the past year. A good 17-inch monitor can be purchased now in the range of $200 to $400. A good 21-inch monitor can be purchased now for between $400 and $600.

Purchasing a larger monitor has a downside. Larger monitors are just that—larger monitors! They take up more room on your desktop, and more importantly, larger monitors weigh a lot more. Some 21-inch models can tip the scales at 25 to 30 kilograms. You also shouldn't place a large monitor on top of your PC case since a mass weighing 25 to 30 kilos can bow or crack your PC's case. Fortunately, many *LCD (Liquid Crystal Display)* monitors are now sold in a more affordable price range and these monitors are much lighter than their heavier CRT counterparts. More about LCD monitors appears at the end of this chapter.

FIGURE 46.6

Resolution set at 640×480.

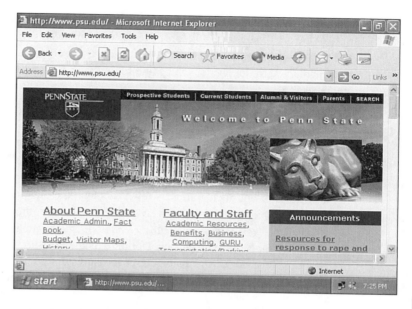

FIGURE 46.7

Resolution set at 1,024×768.

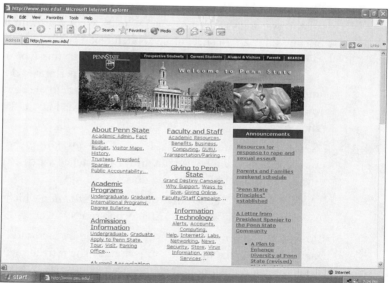

46

Another reason to upgrade to a newer monitor is that monitor technology has improved in the last few years. Monitors are not just bigger, they are also better. Monitors now produce clearer, sharper images with less distortion and flicker on the screen, which means if you regularly spend hours in front of your PC, you are less likely to suffer eye strain (or at least less eye strain than before). Newer monitors also generally are equipped with better controls (such as horizontal and vertical controls, contrast, brightness, and so on), which enable you to do a better job of fine-tuning your monitor to your own personal preferences.

Selecting Your New Monitor

Before you head out and plop down your hard-earned cash for a new monitor, there are a few guidelines you need to know about selecting a monitor:

- Be careful of dot pitch claims. A few years ago, the big buzzword for monitors was dot pitch. A computer monitor's screen is composed of thousands of very small dots called *pixels* (short for *picture elements*), which when set to the correct color, create the appearance of images. Dot pitch is the measurement between these dots. Unfortunately, not every manufacturer measures dot pitch the same way, so using dot pitch to compare one monitor to another quickly becomes a comparison of apples and oranges.

  Another problem with using dot pitch to compare monitors is that it only works on monitors using the dot-trio shadow-mask picture tube. In the dot-trio shadow-mask picture tube, a thin sheet of perforated metal coated with light-sensitive phosphor is what creates the actual dots. On monitors using this type of picture tube, you want to measure the shortest distance between the perforated dots. Some manufacturers measure the distance from the center of one dot to the center of an adjacent dot, but not every manufacturer uses the dot-trio shadow-mask picture tube in their monitors.

  Some manufacturers use what is called the *aperture-grille picture tube*. The aperture-grille picture tube uses an array of stretched wires coated with phosphor instead of a sheet of perforated dots.

  A third method is called the *slot-mask picture tube*, which combines portions of shadow-mask and aperture-grille technologies.

- Look for a high *refresh rate*. Another important factor to consider in selecting a new monitor is the monitor's refresh rate. The refresh rate is the speed at which the monitor can refresh or redraw the onscreen display. You want a monitor with a fast refresh rate because this tends to reduce onscreen flicker. Refresh rates are not determined by the type of picture tube the manufacturer uses, so refresh rate turns out to be a more legitimate gauge for comparing monitors. Refresh rates do vary according to the resolution used on the monitor. Select a monitor with a refresh rate of at least 72Hz (which means the screen is refreshed about 72 times a second) for the highest resolution you intend to use.

- How much control you have over your monitor. As strange as this may sound, many experts also suggest that you check to see the number of controls available on the monitor. A monitor with a lot of controls gives you greater latitude in fine-tuning your monitor.

 While we're on the subject of controls, if you can select a monitor with all the controls on the front rather than on the back, adjusting your monitor will be a lot easier.

- Check the actual size of the viewing area. The advertised size of the monitor is not the size of the display screen. Table 46.3 shows you approximately what you can expect for your display size (measured diagonally) when you purchase a certain size monitor. Keep in mind that, just like with your television set, the measurement is made diagonally.

- Is it a flat screen monitor? Having a flat screen as opposed to the slightly rounded screen will display images with less distortion. But be prepared to pay a little extra for a flat screen.

TABLE 46.3   Monitor Display Sizes

Monitor Size in Inches	Approximate Viewing Area
14	12.5
15	13.5
17	15.5 to 16
19	20.5 to 18
20	20.5 to 19
21	19.5 to 20

You really don't need a degree in electrical engineering to compare monitors and select the best one for your needs. If you really want to get down to a low-level technical comparison between monitors, a number of good software programs are available that you can use to test monitor performance. Two of the best are the WinBench series from ZD Labs (www.zdnet.com) and a program mentioned earlier in this chapter, DisplayMate by Sonera Technologies (www.displaymate.com).

For many users, however, the best way to choose one monitor over another is by performing a few simple tests in a local computer store.

When you're in the market for a new monitor, one of the best sources for finding up-to-date information on PC hardware components is the hardware section of CNET's Computers.com (http://computers.cnet.com/hardware/0-1016.html). In addition to listing just about every monitor you could possibly think of, this site also does comparison reviews and allows you to compare prices on the products listed. Where applicable, this site also lists specifications on the products listed and points you to the manufacturer for more information. If you're looking for more technical information, make a point of bookmarking Tom's Hardware Guide (http://www.tomshardware.com/).

LCD Monitors

Another type of monitor you might want to consider when deciding to purchase one is the *LCD monitor* (see Figure 46.8).

LCD stands for liquid crystal display, and is the type of monitor you see on laptop computers. You can also purchase freestanding LCD monitors to attach to your desktop PC. LCD monitors have low-glare screens and consume considerably less power than their CRT cousins (5 watts versus about 100 watts). LCD monitors excel when it comes to color quality and are actually better than many standard monitors.

FIGURE 46.8

A typical LCD monitor from Samsung, one of the leading manufacturers of LCD monitors.

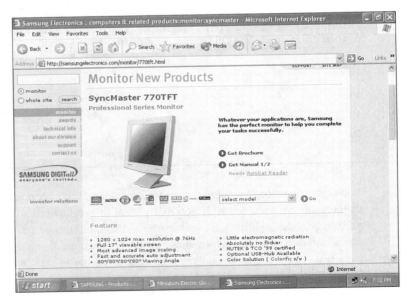

LCD monitors are still limited in size—you don't see many larger than 15 inches and they cost a bit more than CRT displays, even though their prices have been coming down in the last year or so. You can purchase a 15-inch LCD monitor for under $400.

Despite the slightly higher price tag, LCD monitors have one indisputable advantage over CRT displays—size. LCD monitors can easily be 1/10th the depth of CRT displays and weigh on average between 2 and 14 kilos.

If you've got a little extra cash in your monitor budget, then by all means go for an LCD monitor.

Setting Up Your New Monitor

As mentioned earlier, a larger monitor takes up more room on your desktop, so make sure that you have the available desktop real estate before you unbox your new monitor.

To set up your new monitor, follow these steps:

1. Turn off and unplug your old monitor. Turn off the power to your computer. Then disconnect your old monitor from your PC and remove it from your desktop.

2. Unbox your new monitor and carefully examine it for any signs of transit damage. Examine the video cable and connector that plugs into your PC.

3. Place your new monitor on your desktop. Do not place it on top of your PC. If a separate base accompanies your monitor, follow the instructions for assembling and placing your monitor on the base.

4. Adjust the height of the monitor so that the approximate center of the screen is at eye level.

5. Plug your monitor's video cable into your PC and connect the monitor's power cable.

6. Turn on your monitor and your PC.

7. Your new monitor should come with a disk containing drivers for Windows. These drivers enable your Windows operating system to properly adjust certain settings to those required by your monitor. Follow the instructions that come with your monitor for installing these drivers.

After your monitor is installed and correctly set up, be sure to adjust the resolution to the optimum setting, as recommended in Table 46.2. If you are installing a 17-inch monitor, adjust the resolution to at least 1,024×768. If you have a 19-inch monitor, set your resolution to 1,024×768 or 1,280×1,024. If you have a 21-inch monitor, adjust the resolution to either 1,280×1,024 or 1,600×1,200. Keep in mind that these are merely suggestions

46

for what many experts consider the optimum settings for certain size monitors. Your own preferences may dictate a higher or lower resolution. The best judge is what feels comfortable to you.

Summary

In the past chapter, you learned about selecting a new video adapter and a new, larger monitor. You learned about some of the factors to consider when selecting a new video subsystem.

CHAPTER 47

Selecting and Installing a Printer, Scanner, or Digital Camera

One of the basic peripherals for a PC used to be a difficult installation task for many users, but it is now a fairly simple procedure. Desktop printers have been around as long as PCs and still connect to PCs pretty much the same as they did back in 1981.

On the other hand, a new technology that seems to be making as big a splash with many computer users as printers originally did is digital imagery. In the past few years, many PC users have had the opportunity to dabble with digital imagery largely because of the availability of better quality and less expensive digital scanners and digital cameras. Scanners have never been less expensive, more available, or easier to set up and use. And digital cameras are slowly approaching the quality of film cameras while inching toward the price range considered affordable by most PC users.

Understanding the Types of Printers

All printers fall into one of two broad categories: *impact* or *nonimpact* printers. Impact printers employ some type of mechanical process to form characters or images by physically striking (or impacting) paper or some other printable medium. Some examples of impact printers are

- Dot-matrix printers
- Daisy-wheel printers

Nonimpact printers use a nonphysical (or nonimpact) process to transfer characters or an image to paper. Some examples of nonimpact printers are

- Laser printers
- Inkjet printers
- Thermal printers

Many years ago, dot-matrix printers reigned supreme primarily because of their speed and the fact that they were relatively inexpensive. Some of the better quality dot-matrix printers could also produce a relatively high-quality text, what was then called *near letter-quality text*.

Today, however, dot-matrix printers have declined significantly in popularity and have practically gone the way of the dodo now that laser and inkjet printers have dropped dramatically in price and have made true typeset-quality and color text affordable to the masses.

How to Select a Printer

For many users, price is ultimately the deciding factor in choosing between a laser and an inkjet printer. Laser printers (see Figure 47.1) are still slightly more expensive to purchase but cheaper to operate than their inkjet counterparts. The average per-page cost is lower. Keep in mind also that, among laser printers, the average cost per page can vary significantly because of the differences in laser printer toner cartridge prices.

Inkjet printers (see Figure 47.2) are less expensive but still command a higher per-page cost to operate because of the cost of ink cartridges. Laser printers still average about one-half cent per page, whereas inkjet printers can range anywhere from about 2 to 10 cents per page depending on whether you are printing in monochrome or color. It doesn't sound like much initially, until you begin to multiply these costs by several hundred or several thousand pages.

FIGURE 47.1
A typical desktop laser printer.

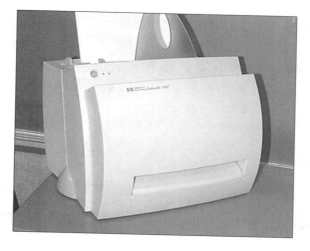

FIGURE 47.2
A typical desktop inkjet printer.

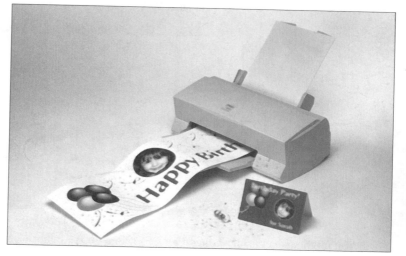

47

Price, however, should be only one of several factors you use in deciding what type of printer is best for your needs. In addition to price, other factors you should consider before purchasing a printer are

- Print speed
- Print quality
- Color versus monochrome
- The demand you plan to place on your printer—that is, the number of pages you think you will print each month

- The versatility of the printer; some manufacturers combine printers, scanners, copiers, and fax machines in one complete package

Comparing Various Printer Models

One of best places to begin looking when you want to start comparing printer features is the Computers.com site run by CNET at `http://computers.cnet.com/hardware/0-1016.html`. CNET maintains a fairly up-to-date listing of available printer models and will periodically review printers for you and make suggestions in various categories (see Figure 47.3).

FIGURE 47.3
CNET comparison categories for its reviewed printers.

You might also consider going directly to some of the major printer manufacturers' sites for more detailed information when you have narrowed down your choices. Here are a few sites to consider:

- Hewlett Packard—`http://www.pandi.hp.com/seg/printers.html`

- Epson—`http://www.epson.com/cgi-bin/Store/index.jsp`

- Brother—`http://www.brother.com/usa/printer/info/hl1240/hl1240_oth.html`

- Lexmark—`http://www.lexmark.com/`

- Kyocera—`http://www.kyocera.com/KEI/printers/index.htm`

- Tektronics—`http://www.tek.com/Color_Printers/`

- Okidata—`http://www.oki.com/english/Home.html`

Print Speed

Laser printers lead the race over inkjet printers when it comes to churning out a large number of pages per minute, but the inkjet is rapidly closing the speed gap. Most personal laser printers print in the 6 to 8 ppm (pages per minute) range, whereas many inkjet printers can print monochrome text (one color text, usually black) in the 4 to 6 ppm range.

Print Quality

Print quality is measured in resolution, similar to video resolution. Video resolution is measured by pixels (picture elements) on the entire screen measured horizontally and vertically (for example, 640×480 or 800×600). Printer resolution is also measured horizontally and vertically, but instead of the entire screen or page, the resolution is measured within a one-inch (1×1 inch) square. Instead of pixels, printer resolution is measured in dots per inch (abbreviated dpi—printers still have not adopted the metric system). For example, most laser printers now print at a resolution of 600×600 (or 1,200×1,200) dpi.

> The dots-per-inch resolution of a printer should be described using both the horizontal and vertical measurements (600×600 dpi), but often, if the measurements are the same, the description is shortened. For example, a resolution of 300×300 dpi is shortened to simply 300 dpi. Therefore, when you see the common resolution of 600 dpi, you know that the resolution is in fact 600×600 dpi.

47

Although most laser printers seem to have standardized on a resolution of 600×600 dpi, in contrast, inkjet printers run the gamut from about 600×300 dpi to 720×1,440 dpi. When printing text, laser printers seem to still have a slight quality edge over inkjet printers. However, when printing graphic images, many inkjet printers can produce much higher quality printouts than laser printers.

If you use dpi as one of your determining factors in choosing a printer, consider these suggestions:

- When printing text such as letters or manuscripts, 300 dpi is adequate. Most users cannot distinguish between text printed at 300 dpi and text printed at 600 dpi.

- When printing graphics, however, higher resolution almost always means higher quality output. Most users can distinguish between a graphic image printed at 300 dpi and the same image printed at 600 dpi.

Color Versus Monochrome

In deciding between color and monochrome, the decision is usually much simpler to make. If you need to print in color, you purchase an inkjet. If you are satisfied with printing only in black and white, get a laser printer.

> Color laser printers are available, but unfortunately, they are still in the $2,000 to $3,000 price range. Most users who require color still opt for inkjet printers, which can produce output at nearly the quality of color laser printers, and at a fraction of the cost.

Keep in mind that with an inkjet printer, you can also choose to print in just black and white. Many inkjet printer users produce draft copies of their output in black and white and print the final output in color. Doing so can save on color cartridge costs.

Installing a Printer to Work with Your PC

Printers are among the easiest peripherals to install, especially if you are running Windows XP. Windows will practically install the printer for you. Most printers today are designed to connect to your PC through the parallel port, so basically all you need to connect your PC and printer is a standard *Centronics parallel cable*.

> A Centronics parallel cable is a simple communications cable with a 36-pin Centronics male connector on one end and a 25-pin female connector on the other. You can purchase a Centronics parallel cable in most computer stores in lengths ranging from 6 to 15 feet. And don't believe that myth about parallel cables having to be less than 10 feet in length. If you need a 15-foot cable, go ahead and purchase one. Many stores now carry printer cables in lengths of 25 feet and longer.

Connecting the Hardware

Connecting your printer is a two-step process. The first step is connecting the hardware, and the second step is installing the correct printer driver.

Here's what you have to do to connect a printer to your PC:

1. Unpack and set up your printer according to the manufacturer's instructions. Be sure to carefully remove all the packing materials and restraints.

2. Plug the 36-pin male Centronics connector of your parallel cable into the parallel port on your printer (see Figure 47.4).

FIGURE 47.4

The Centronics parallel port on a printer.

3. Plug the other end of your printer cable (the end with the 25-pin female connector) into the parallel port on the back of your PC.

4. Turn on your PC and your printer.

Installing Your Printer Driver

The installation of your printer driver will typically begin as soon as you restart the operating system, provided that your printer is designed as a plug-and-play peripheral. Just about all printers made in the last few years are Plug and Play. Simply follow the onscreen prompts and insert the printer driver disk when instructed.

47

Before you can use your printer, you must install the appropriate printer *driver*. A printer driver is simply a small program that enables your PC to communicate with your printer.

Windows XP begins installing your printer driver as soon as the operating system restarts, but if it doesn't, follow these steps to start the driver installation:

1. Click the Start button to open the Start menu.

2. Select Printers and Faxes to open the Windows Printer Control section (see Figure 47.5).

FIGURE 47.5
The Printer Control section under Windows XP.

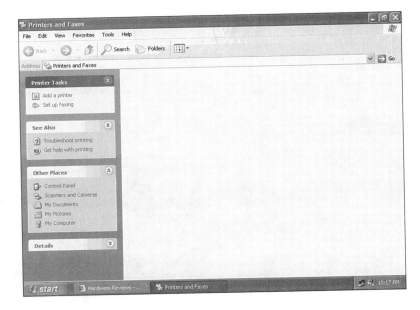

3. Click the Add Printer icon to start the Add Printer Wizard (see Figure 47.6) and follow the prompts to install your printer driver.

FIGURE 47.6
The Windows XP Add Printer Wizard used to install printer drivers.

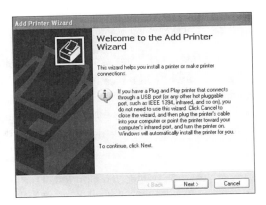

Installing a Second Printer to Work with Your PC

So far, we have discussed how to install only one printer to your PC. What if you have one PC but need to connect two printers? It's not uncommon for many users to have both a laser and an inkjet printer.

You can connect two printers to your PC in the following ways:

- You can set up the second printer next to the first printer and switch the printer cable from one printer to the other.

- You can purchase and install a second parallel port in your PC and connect the second printer to this second port using a second printer cable.

- You can purchase a hardware device called an A/B switch and use it to switch the communication signal from one printer to the other.

- If your second printer and your PC both have USB ports and you are using Windows XP, you can connect one printer to the parallel port and one printer to the USB port.

Method One: Switching the Cable

To connect two printers to one PC, switching the printer cable is the easiest but not necessarily the most convenient way to connect your two printers. You need to install printer drivers for both printers, and when you want to switch from one printer to the other, you simply unplug the cable from the back of one printer and plug the cable into the parallel port of the other printer. You don't have to turn the printers on and off and you don't even have to reboot your PC.

Regardless of which of the possible multiple-printer solutions you choose, remember that you need to select the appropriate driver in Windows for the printer you are attempting to use. In most Windows applications, you can select a different printer driver from the Print dialog box.

47

Method Two: Installing a Second Parallel Port

Installing a second parallel port in your PC for a second printer is perhaps the most convenient of your options. You can purchase a second parallel port on an interface card from most computer stores for $35 or less and install it in less than 10 minutes.

The interface card you purchase for your second parallel port might contain one or two serial ports as well. To prevent any possible conflicts with your existing serial ports, simply follow the instructions that come with the card to disable the two serial ports.

If you purchase a second parallel port, you must check a few settings on the interface card before you install it in your PC. First, make sure that the parallel port on the interface card is set to function as LPT2 and not set to function as LPT1. The parallel port in your PC is set to function as LPT1 by default. If both ports are set to LPT1, the two ports create a conflict and you will be unable to print to either port. Most add-on second parallel port cards are almost always set to LPT2 at the factory, so you shouldn't have a problem with conflicts. Most manufacturers seem to understand that you are adding an additional parallel port; however, make sure that you check the settings before you install the card.

Also check the memory address and the interrupt request (IRQ) that the parallel port on the interface card is set to use to make sure that they are not in conflict with the memory address and interrupt used by the parallel port (LPT1) in your PC.

Use Windows XP's System Information utility to check the memory address and interrupt in use by the parallel port in your PC. The interrupt is most likely 7 because this is usually the default interrupt used for LPT1. The memory address looks something like 3BC or 2BC. Just make sure that you check which settings your existing parallel port uses and set the new parallel port to use different settings.

To install a second parallel port in your PC, follow these steps:

1. Turn off and unplug your PC, ground yourself, and then remove the PC cover.
2. Insert the interface card in an empty slot in your PC.
3. Replace the cover, plug in your PC, and turn it on.
4. Run your PC's hardware Setup program and install or enable LPT2. If you have to include the interrupt and memory address in the setup process, enter the settings the same as they are on the card.

You now can connect the second printer just the same as you connected the first printer earlier in this chapter. When you install the driver for the second printer, remember to designate the output port as LPT2, the second parallel port in your PC.

Method Three: Installing an A/B Switch

An *A/B switch* is like a fork in the road—it enables you to travel in one of two directions. In this case, the A/B switch is a device that enables the signal from your PC to travel to one of two connected printers.

Essentially, the A/B switch is a device or electrical connector box with one cable attached to your PC and two cables attached to each of your two printers. The device is called an A/B switch because a physical switch enables you to select printer A or printer B.

The A/B switch is just a hardware device—meaning that you have no setup program to run. To install, just plug one cable from your PC into the input port on the switch. You then connect the remaining two cables from each output port to each of your printers. Now when you want to print to the printer connected to the first output port, you move the selector on the switchbox to the A position. When you want to print to the printer connected to the second output port, you move the selector on the switchbox to the B position. The biggest problem in using an A/B switch is making sure that you get the input and output cables installed correctly. But most A/B switches usually ship with more than enough documentation to walk you through the connections. An estimate of the price of an A/B switch is anywhere from about $35 to $75. You can purchase an A/B switch from most computer or office supply stores and from many electronics stores.

> Some laser printer manufacturers warn against using an A/B switch because of a possibility of damage to the printer with the sudden loss of signal (when you switch from one printer to the other). Check to make sure that your printer will safely work with an A/B switch before attempting to use one.

Method Four: Using Both Parallel and USB Ports

If your computer has both a parallel and a USB port, and you have printers that use both types of interfaces, it is a simple matter to plug each printer into its respective port. From the Print dialog box, select the printer to which you want to print.

Learning About Scanners

47

For basic home use, you can choose from three different types of scanners: flatbed, handheld, and sheet feed. Handheld scanners were designed basically for computer users with very limited funds to devote to a scanning device. A handheld scanner is a small device about the size of large TV remote control unit. You scan with it by slowly (and manually) sliding the scanner over the picture you are scanning. No one recommends purchasing a handheld scanner because the images they produce are almost always distorted—it is nearly impossible to move the scanner over the object you are scanning at a constant speed.

Because sheet-feed scanners were developed as a less expensive alternative to flatbed scanners, and because prices for flatbed scanners have been dropping steadily, it's likely that handheld scanners will all but disappear very soon. If you see one for sale, even at an unbelievably low price, don't waste your money.

For a home scanner, your selection should focus on two types—*flatbed* and *sheet-feed* models.

Sheet-Feed Scanners

Sheet-feed scanners are the less expensive of the two types recommended and have virtually replaced handheld scanners as the low-end model.

Besides being less expensive than flatbed scanners, one major advantage sheet-feed scanners have is that they occupy much less desktop space. The typical flatbed scanner takes up a desktop area approximately 14×20 inches, whereas the typical sheet-feed scanner only takes up an area approximately 12×4 inches (see Figure 47.7).

FIGURE 47.7
A typical sheet-feed scanner.

Although sheet-feed scanners are capable of scanning pictures and converting them to digital images the same as their flatbed cousins, most users who purchase sheet-feed scanners use them for *Optical Character Recognition (OCR)*.

Optical Character Recognition (OCR) is a way of using your scanner and special software to scan a page of text, such as a newspaper or magazine article, and convert what is being scanned into a text file. Some OCR programs can also convert the scanned document into several popular word-processing formats, such as Microsoft Word and Corel WordPerfect. Keep in mind that several good OCR programs are on the market, and even the best is not 100% perfect.

Sheet-feed scanners can scan pictures and photos and convert them to digital images, but most sheet-feed scanners have a lower optical resolution than their flatbed counterparts. Most sheet-feed scanners have a maximum optical resolution of around 300×600 dpi (dots per inch).

Flatbed Scanners

Of the two types of scanners recommended here, flatbed models (see Figure 47.8) are the more versatile because they allow you to scan single sheets, pages, or photos. You can also place larger, bulkier objects such as books and magazines on the flatbed for scanning. On many models of flatbed scanners, you can also attach optional sheet feeders for scanning multi-page documents (an excellent arrangement if you plan to do a lot of OCR scanning).

Flatbed scanners also tend to have a slightly higher optical scanning resolution than sheet-feed versions. Many home-use flatbed scanners have an optical resolution of 600×600 dpi and better.

FIGURE 47.8

A typical flatbed scanner.

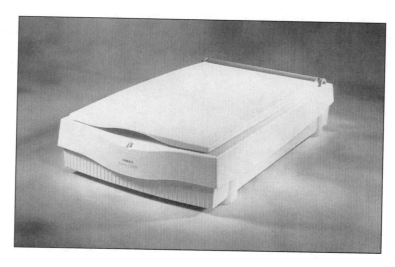

Selecting a Scanner

47

Now that you know about the types of scanners available, you're ready for a few helpful hints on how to select a scanner.

First, decide what you want to do with your scanner. If you just plan to scan a few documents and occasionally scan a few family photos, you can probably get by with a sheet-feed scanner. If you need a scanner for doing a lot of document OCR scanning, however, you probably will do better with a flatbed scanner with an optional sheet-feeder to save you the time and effort of lifting the flatbed cover and replacing documents.

If you need to scan pictures, photos, or artwork for direct transfer to a Web site, a sheet-feed scanner is probably satisfactory. Web artwork does not have to be of very high resolution. Currently, 72 dpi is good enough for Web work.

You should not attempt to scan antique or irreplaceable photographs through a sheet-feed scanner because these devices tend to curl or bend the photos during scanning.

However, if you want to scan pictures, photos, or artwork and plan to use some type of digital editing software on the scanned image—such as PhotoShop or Paint Shop Pro— you probably need the slightly higher optical resolution offered by a flatbed scanner.

Keep in mind how much scanning you plan to do. If you will be doing a lot of scanning, you probably will want to purchase a scanner with a SCSI or USB-2 interface for speed considerations. Most models are sold with one of those interfaces today.

As with most of the other PC peripherals covered in this book, when reviewing scanners or digital cameras, one of the best places to begin for product information and product comparisons is CNET's Computers.Com Web site at http://computers.cnet.com/hardware/0-1016.html. Some other sites worth considering for more detailed information include:

- Umax—http://www.umax.com/
- Hewlett-Packard—http://www.pandi.hp.com/seg/scanners_di_photo.html
- Agfa—http://www.agfa.com/
- Canon—http://www.usa.canon.com/
- Epson—http://www.epson.com/cgi-bin/Store/index.jsp

Installing Your Scanner

Just five years ago, it was next to impossible to purchase a scanner that did not use a SCSI interface. Now you can purchase scanners that connect to your PC using SCSI, parallel, serial, USB, or proprietary interfaces. Serial interfaces have all but disappeared on scanners, so for all intents and purposes, you only have to choose between SCSI, parallel, USB, and proprietary interfaces.

Because scanners are external devices, you connect them to your PC much the same as you would connect a printer, external CD-ROM drive, or an external tape backup drive. To install your scanner, follow these steps:

1. Unpack and set up your scanner, following the instructions supplied by the manufacturer. Make sure that you allow sufficient space on your desktop. Be sure to "unlock" the scanner arm in your scanner. The instructions will explain how to unlock the arm, which is shipped in a locked position to protect it from possible damage. The arm must be unlocked before you can use your scanner.

2. If you have to install an interface card (SCSI or proprietary) for your scanner, turn off and unplug your PC, ground yourself, remove the cover, locate an empty slot, and install the interface card into the empty slot.

Some scanner manufacturers include a SCSI interface card with their scanners, eliminating the need to purchase a separate SCSI card if you don't already have one. Sometimes, however, these supplied SCSI cards are designed to work only with the scanner they are shipped with and will not function with other SCSI devices. In effect, you are getting a proprietary interface card. If your scanner came with a card, use it instead of an existing SCSI card.

3. Connect your scanner to your PC using the cable shipped with the scanner. Follow the manufacturer's instructions. If you install the scanner into an existing SCSI chain, make sure that you maintain the integrity of the chain by ensuring that it is still terminated at both ends.

4. Insert the driver disk supplied with your scanner and follow the instructions to install the scanner software and hardware driver for your particular operating system. The scanner software consists of the hardware driver needed to allow your PC to communicate with your scanner and usually also several utility programs supplied by the manufacturer.

5. Start your scanning software so that you can test your scanner by scanning a document or a picture. If you get an error message or the scanner fails to scan, go back and check all your cable connections. Also check to make sure that the hardware driver is properly installed and configured and that your scanner is turned on.

Considering Digital Cameras

If you are interested in producing digital images for Web site composition or digital editing, a digital camera can save you a few steps and a lot of time over using a traditional film camera. You don't have to worry about getting your film developed and then scanning the photographs.

A digital camera is just what the name suggests—a photographic camera that produces digital images. A digital camera (see Figure 47.9) does not use film. Instead, it contains memory or some type of storage medium where images you take are stored until you download them to your PC.

A digital camera is highly convenient, especially when you consider that your images are almost immediately available for use and you don't have to stop to have your film developed. Nevertheless, digital cameras do have their drawbacks:

*   Digital cameras are still expensive. A good digital camera costs between $400 and $700. Lesser-quality digital cameras can be purchased for $200 to $400.

- Digital cameras still cannot produce images at the same quality of standard film cameras. Even a moderately priced 35mm film camera can produce photos superior to digital cameras. Film can produce images with a much higher resolution than the best digital cameras, even digital cameras costing several thousand dollars.

- The quality of printed photos taken by digital cameras still does not rival actual photographic prints; printed digital photos also tend to fade a lot faster than traditional photos.

FIGURE 47.9

A typical digital camera.

With all these negatives, you might wonder why anyone would ever bother using a digital camera. The primary reason is simple—convenience. The primary uses of digital cameras are in areas where the lower resolution produced by digital cameras is not a problem, namely Web-based graphics. Because Web-based graphics do not have to be any greater than 72 dpi, the convenience and lower resolutions offered by digital cameras make producing Web-based graphics a cinch.

Many users also purchase digital cameras because it is a lot easier to send photos as email attachments to friends and relatives than to reprint and mail photos in snail mail. It's also true that digital colors (while they are safely stored on your computer) never fade.

Selecting a Digital Camera

Digital cameras can range in price from a few hundred dollars to several thousand dollars. But don't get the impression that you can't get a useable digital camera without taking out a second mortgage. There are several dozen very good digital cameras priced in the $300 to $500 range (what most photographers would call "point-and-shoot" models), and several manufacturers are hard at work making more.

Just like every other product mentioned in this book, you need to check the popular PC journals for product reviews to get an idea how the various models of digital cameras in your price range compare. Just like scanners, the quality of digital cameras can vary considerably for models in the same price range. And just like scanners, because this is a hot market, manufacturers are constantly coming out with new and improved models, so it pays to check often.

You should begin your selection process by comparing current models at CNET's Computers.com at http://computers.cnet.com/hardware/0-1016.html. You might also want to look at the sites of some of the top manufacturers, such as:

- Kodak—http://www.kodak.com/US/en/nav/digital.shtml
- Canon—http://www.canon.com/
- Epson—http://www.epson.com/cgi-bin/Store/index.jsp
- Fuji—http://www.fujifilm.com/
- Olympus—http://www.olympusamerica.com/p.asp?s=12&p=16
- Nikon—http://www.nikonusa.com/usa_home/home.jsp
- Sony—http://www.sel.sony.com/SEL/consumer/ss5/generic/digitalstillcameras/

You also need to be aware of what add-on products are available for various digital cameras. Some cameras allow you to add additional memory to boost the number of photos you can take before you have to download images to your PC. Some cameras come equipped with the same type of peripheral slots found on laptop computers and allow you to use the same memory and hard disk peripherals available for laptop computers. There are also digital cameras that allow you to use floppy disks the same as you would use film in a traditional camera. When you take the maximum number of photos that will fit on a disk, you simply remove the disk, insert another, and continue shooting.

Most digital cameras come with a cable and software to allow you to connect to your PC and download the photos stored in your camera. The number of photos you can take with a digital camera varies considerably depending on the amount of memory or storage in the camera and the resolution of the photos you take.

If you are thinking of purchasing a digital camera, here are a few features to consider:

- At what resolutions can you take pictures? The minimum now for most entry-level digital cameras is 640×480. Many manufacturers are offering lower-cost models that take photos at resolutions of 1,024×768 and 1,152×864.

47

- Does the camera include a built-in flash? You need a flash of some type if you plan to take photos indoors. Does the camera have any type of flash mode? Backlight reduction? Red-eye reduction? Effective range?

- How much memory or storage capacity does the camera have? Is it expandable? The amount of memory determines how many pictures it can store at one time.

- Is the lens fixed focus, or can you zoom? What is the equivalent sized 35mm lens? Is it auto-focus or manual focus? Does it have a macro mode for taking close-up shots?

- What types of batteries does the camera use and (approximately) how long will they last (or how many photos can you take)?

- How long is the setup time between taking photos?

- Can you print directly from the camera? Does the manufacturer offer a companion printer?

- What is the color depth? 24-bit? 30-bit? More?

- Does the camera save images in the standard JPG format, or does it use a proprietary image format? If it uses a proprietary format, does it include a utility for converting that format to a standard format?

- Some cameras also allow you to include a few seconds of audio to help you catalog your photos. Do the cameras you are reviewing have this feature?

Although these aren't the only features that you should be concerned with in selecting a digital camera, this list will at least give you a start in making your selection.

Summary

In this chapter, you learned how to select and install a printer to your PC. You learned what criteria to use to judge printers and what steps you need to follow to connect your printer and install the appropriate printer driver. You also learned the various methods of connecting two printers to your PC.

You also learned about scanners and digital cameras, what features you need to be concerned about when selecting either a scanner or a digital camera, and how to install a scanner to work with your PC.

CHAPTER 48

Purchasing PC Components on the Internet

You have now learned a considerable amount about how to upgrade the various components in your PC. You also should have picked up a few tips about how to select the upgrade items. In this chapter, you will learn how to go about purchasing upgrading and replacement hardware items over the Internet. In a way, this chapter is a specific application of Chapter 27, "Buying and Selling on the Internet," in that this chapter focuses on buying computer components that you can use to replace and upgrade other components on your PC.

Purchasing Over the Internet

All the PC components mentioned throughout this book can very readily be purchased directly over the Internet and delivered right to your front door. Although many computer users continue to purchase items through mail order, not as many are purchasing over the Internet despite the fact that most of the companies selling mail order are also selling over the Internet. As expected, you have to make a few tradeoffs when purchasing over the Internet.

On the plus side:

- No sales reps will bother you by trying to sell you additional items you don't want or need.
- Most companies place their entire inventory on their Web sites, but place only a fraction of it in magazines and catalogs. This allows you to locate the exact model of whatever item you are looking to purchase.
- You have instant access to current pricing and inventory status. The key phrase here is "inventory status." If you are ready to purchase, you can instantly see who is ready to ship you the item you need.
- It's very easy to do comparison shopping (pricing) online and many, if not most, items can be purchased cheaper online as compared to purchasing in-store.

However, purchasing over the Internet also has a down side:

- You must know exactly what you want to purchase, which usually means manufacturer and model.
- You must purchase using a credit card. Because you are in effect purchasing from a computer system and not a person, you cannot pay with a check, a money order, or a company purchase order.
- You have to trust Internet security. This still seems to be the biggest turnoff for most potential online customers, but it doesn't have to be as you'll see throughout this chapter.

Locating Companies

Locating computer companies and computer supply companies who do business over the Internet is relatively easy. Look in any computer magazine, and you will see ads for dozens of companies—most will include a Web address of where you can find their online storefront.

You can also locate computer companies on the Internet by using the Internet. One of the best places to start looking is at Yahoo! (http://www.yahoo.com/). On the Yahoo! home page, you will see a link for Shopping. Click this link to enter the Yahoo! Shopping section (see Figure 48.1).

FIGURE 48.1
The Yahoo! Shopping section.

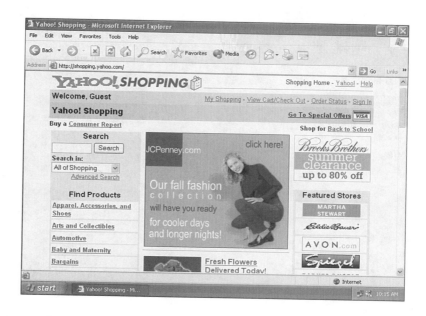

There are several other links you can try on this page. In this example, you'll see how to go shopping for a new active matrix LCD monitor. Select the Computer link, and then select the Monitor link. Finally, select the ViewSonic link to open the page listing ViewSonic monitors, both LCD and CRT varieties (see Figure 48.2).

FIGURE 48.2
ViewSonic monitors available on the Yahoo! Shopping page.

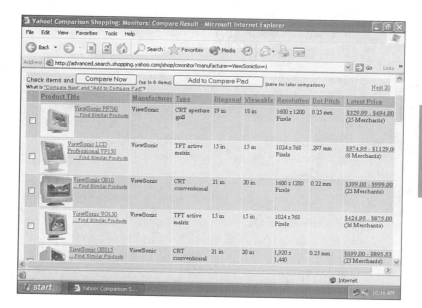

48

Select the price range to the right of the model you're interested in to see the prices offered by various online merchants (see Figure 48.3).

FIGURE 48.3

Various online merchants offering LCD monitors for sale on the Yahoo! Shopping site.

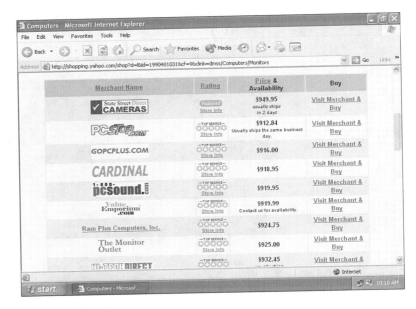

If you're in the market for something other than a new LCD monitor, here are a few other online shopping sites you might want to visit:

- Computer Discount Warehouse—http://www.cdw.com/
- PC Connection—http://www.pcconnection.com/
- Micro Center—http://www.microcenter.com/
- PC Mall—http://www.pcmall.com/
- Micro Warehouse—http://www.microwarehouse.com/
- The PC Zone—http://www.pczone.com/
- Insight—http://www.insight.com/
- Buy.Com—http://www.buy.com/
- TigerDirect—http://www.tigerdirect.com/

After you locate a few companies you think you might want to do business with, you should look at a few other things before you place your first order:

- How does the company ship the order and what does it charge? Some companies advertise what appear to be lower-than-competitive prices and then turn around and charge you exorbitant shipping and handling charges to make their profit. Find out what carriers the company ships with and find out whether it ships overnight delivery, 2nd day delivery, or 3 to 5 day ground delivery. For most computer components, shipping charges should be minimal considering that most computer components are rather small and lightweight. The exception, however, is computer monitors. If you opt for a 17-inch or larger monitor, bear in mind that the shipping weights can be 60 lbs. and up; and you will often see shipping charges in the neighborhood of $60 to $80 (see Figure 48.4). When comparison shopping on monitors, keep this shipping charge in mind and weigh it against possibly paying a state sales tax at a local computer store.

FIGURE 48.4

An example of shipping charges for a computer monitor.

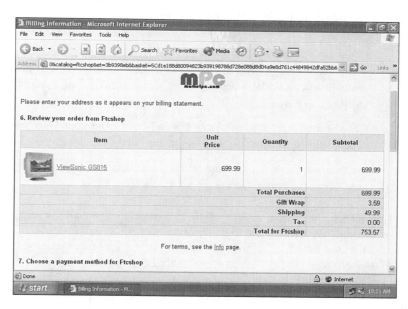

- What are the company's return policies? If you order the wrong part or if the item you order does not work with your computer, can you return it? Some companies will charge a 5% to 15% restocking fee for returned items.

- Will you be charged sales tax for the item? In most cases, you will not be charged sales tax for your state (assuming that your state has a tax) for the items you purchase unless the company has a physical presence in your state. If your state does have sales tax and you are not charged sales tax, in many states you are required (by your state) to pay what is often called a merchandise tax.

- Do any of the companies offer lowest price guarantees? Some companies will guarantee that theirs is the lowest price and will meet or beat a competitor's price. It never hurts to ask.

48

Internet Security

For online purchases, does the company use a secure Web site? A secure Web site is a way of conducting your transaction by establishing an encrypted connection between your computer and the Web site computer so that no one can tap into the communication session and see information you want to keep private, such as your credit card number. If the company is not using a secure site, make your transaction over the telephone using the company's 800 number.

The question of Internet security is probably the single most important factor still limiting online commerce. The main problem is not that the Internet commercial transactions are not secure. The main problem is that the Internet commercial transactions are not perceived as being secure.

You can very easily identify when you have a secure connection by two visible signs in your Web browser. The first sign is the address of the Web page you are viewing. A normal or unsecured Web page address begins `http://`, but a secure Web page address usually begins `https://`.

The second sign is some symbol or indicator from your Web browser that the Web site is secure. In Netscape, you will see an icon of a closed lock (see Figure 48.5).

In Internet Explorer, a secure Web site is illustrated by a Lock icon displayed on the status bar at the bottom of the screen (see Figure 48.6).

FIGURE 48.5

In Netscape, you see a Lock icon like this one, which indicates a connection with a secure Web site.

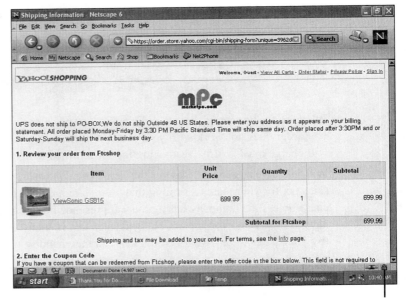

Netscape's secure site indicator

FIGURE 48.6

In Internet Explorer, you see this indicator informing you that you have established a connection with a secure Web site.

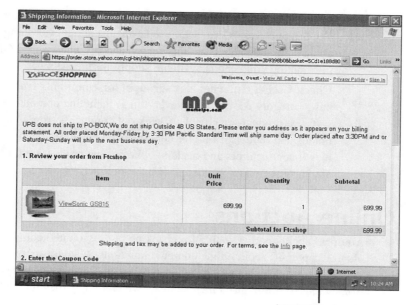

Internet Explorer's
secure site indicator

Tips on Buying PC Components

Finally, consider the following tips regarding your purchase of computer components over the Internet, by calling an 800 number, or simply by walking into a computer store.

- **Do your research first.** Before you buy any item for your PC, read a few product reviews comparing the item from several manufacturers. For example, if you are thinking about upgrading your CD-ROM to a CD-RW drive, look through some recent issues of some of the major computer industry journals and see what features are considered important and what type of comparison testing has been done. Some product reviews include either an "Editor's Choice" selection or a "Best Buy" recommendation. CNET has a hardware comparison Web site you can check at `http://www.computers.com`.

- **Get recent information.** Product reviews are an excellent way of getting information on products you want to purchase, but not if the information is two years old. Computer products change rapidly. Don't bother with reviews that are more than six to eight months old. If you can't find a recent review, wait a few weeks and there will be another one.

48

- **Make friends with the "computer guru" in your company.** Every company usually has one person who seems to know just about everything there is to know about computers. Seek out this person and become friends. Often, much of the information you need is available simply for the asking.

- **Check Usenet (Internet Newsgroups) for comments from other users.** Usenet has a category for just about everything, including computer hardware and every software product imaginable. Check out comments from other users on specific brands and models. Look for comments on customer relations with various companies (manufacturers and dealers), whether the product performed as advertised, and any information on problems with the product.

Online Auctions

You read about another source for checking out discounted computer parts and peripherals in Chapter 40 about online computer auctions. Many of these sites are selling merchandise from dealers or manufacturers who are disposing of excess or older inventories. Some are also selling used merchandise, which by law they must identify as used equipment.

Here are a few online auction sites where you can shop for computer equipment:

- DealDeal.Com—http://www.dealdeal.com/
- OnSale—http://www.onsale.com/atauction/computers/computers.htm
- CNET Auctions—http://auctions.cnet.com/
- eBay—http://www.ebay.com/

On some auction sites, you buy from the site and on other auction sites, you buy from a third-party seller. Check the rules of the site before you bid. Be sure to check all merchandise at the manufacturer's site before you bid to know exactly what you are bidding on, how old it is, and approximately how much it is worth.

Some sights will also list a history of the seller's previous auctions and whether there have been problems or complaints from other buyers. Be sure to check this information if it is available.

Is it safe to buy from online auctions? The vast majority of the time, it is. But when in doubt, use one of the many escrow services available for auction buyers.

An escrow service is a service that will hold your payment until you verify that you have received the item and that it is OK.

Summary

In this chapter, you learned about purchasing upgrade components for your PC over the Internet. You learned about some of the security precautions you should be aware of to maintain a secure connection with the company you are purchasing from. And finally, you learned a few tips on purchasing computer products whether you buy them online or in a computer store.

48

INDEX

disks, 441
memory, 440
interface cards, 495-496
memory, 440
   identifying, 493
   installing, 523-524
   stretching, 524-525
   types, 521-522
   upgrading, 479, 520
   volatile, 520
microprocessors. *See*
   CPUs
motherboards, 491
   advancements,
      546-547
   ATX, 549
   baby AT, 548
   LPX, 548
   NLX, 550
   standard AT, 547
   upgrading versus
      replacing, 546
operating systems,
   444-446
Pentium IIs/IIIs, 492
potential hazards,
   485-486
power supplies
   buying, 564
   identifying, 496
   installing, 565
   upgrading, 556
settings, transferring,
   203-205
shutting down, 15
toolkits, 508
towers, 487-489
transferring files
   between, 181-183

transformers, 496
troubleshooting, 479
   freezing, 38-39
   not turning on, 37
unplugging, 514
upgrading, 478, 482
   components, 478
   hard disk drives, 480
   memory, 479
   monitors, 481
   processors, 480
working on, 514
   advanced tools,
      512-514
   grounding yourself,
      515
   magnets, 515
   tools, 508, 511
   unplugging comput-
      ers, 514
concentrators, 450-451
configuring
   Content Advisor, 389,
      392
   data/time, 84
   email, 296, 299
   Internet accounts,
      266-267
      Connection Wizard,
         269-271
      signup programs,
         268-269
      supplied software,
         268
   monitors, 671-672
   mouse, 100-101
   My Pictures slideshows,
      225
   newsreaders, 332-333

screensavers, 131-133
TCP/IP, 466-467,
   639-640
**Connection Wizard
(Internet account config-
uration), 269-271**
connections
   broadband, 636-637
      cable versus DSL,
         636
      family Web surfing
         safety, 384
      resources, 637
      security, 641-643
      sharing, 467-468
      TCP/IP configuration,
         639-640
   cable/DSL firewall
      routers, 470
   cable modems, 468,
      640-641
   digital cameras, 215
   direct cable, 181
   DSL, 468, 640-641
   FireWire, 176
   Internet
      busy, 45
      dropped, 44-45
      high-speed. *See*
         broadband connec-
         tions
      networks, 415, 417
      slow, 43
   printers, 678-679
   USB, 176
connectors, 489-490
Consumer World, 397
Consumer's Union, 397

How can we make this index more useful? Email us at indexes@samspublishing.com

TV (Web), 249
Twins Web site, 276
.txt file extension, 364
Tyan Web site, 553
typefaces, 194
types
    BIOS, 540-541
    memory, 521-522

U

Ultra DMA, 441
Umax Web site, 686
uninstalling applications,
    154-155, 159-160
United Negro College
    Fund Web site, 276
Universal Serial Bus. *See*
    USB
Unix, 456
unplugging computers,
    514
unrecognizable CDs, 40
Unshielded Twisted-Pair
    (UTP) cabling, 453
unzippers, 368
Update application, 200
updating
    HSC, 144
    viewing, 202
    Windows, 199
        sources, 201
        yourself, 201-203
upgrade chips (BIOS), 542
upgrading
    applications, 59
    BIOS, 538-541
    cases, 561, 564

computers, 478, 482
    components, 478
    hard disk drives, 480
    memory, 479
    monitors, 481
    processors, 480
CPUs, 533
DVD upgrade kits,
    606-607
flash BIOS, 543
hard disk drives, 480,
    569
memory, 479, 520
monitors, 481, 665-668
motherboards, 546
power supplies, 556
processors, 480
US Internet, 263
USB (Universal Serial
    Bus), 176, 490
    connections, 176
    scanners, 211
utilities. *See* applications;
    software
UTP (Unshielded Twisted-
    Pair) cabling, 453

V

ValueFind, 402
VESA local bus, 547
VGA video ports, 489
video cards, 656
    adapter cards, 443-444
    AGP, 664-665
    color depth, 658-660
    installing, 662-664
    refresh rates, 660-661

    video resolution,
        658-660
    VRAM, 657-658
video clips
    arranging, 234
    importing, 231-232
    pasting together, 232-233
    trimming, 233-234
Video Random Access
    Memory (VRAM), 657
videos
    DVDs, 72-74
    finding, 165
    Web, 69
viewing
    Control Panel, 98
    email messages, 299
    Explorer, 108
    filmstrips, 227
    HSC, 138
    Media Library contents,
        68
    My Computer window,
        94, 107
    slideshows, 220
    updates, 202
    Windows Explorer, 107
virtual storefronts,
    395-397
viruses, 34
    antivirus programs,
        34-35
    downloading files, 369
    email messages, 307
VirusScan, 307
Visit Gallery button, 129
voice narratives, 236-237
volatile memory, 520
voltage meters, 513-514

Your Guide to Computer Technology

www.informit.com

SAMS Teach Yourself

One Book... All the Answer

John Ray and Robyn Ness
ISBN: 0-672-32532-2
$29.99 USA • $46.99 CAN

Ned Snell
ISBN: 0-672-32533-0
$29.99 USA • $46.99 CAN

Greg Perry
ISBN: 0-672-32534-9
$29.99 USA • $46.99 CAN

Greg Perry
ISBN: 0-672-32535-7
$29.99 USA • $46.99 CAN